The Blue Book on Information Age Inquiry, Instruction and Literacy

The Blue Book on Information Age Inquiry, Instruction and Literacy

Daniel Callison and Leslie Preddy

LIBRARIES
U N L I M I T E D

A Member of the Greenwood Publishing Group

Westport, Connecticut • London

To Patty, Britt, and Katherine for inspiration and patience.
—Danny

To my parents, Ron, and Rochelle Burton, for always believing in me.
—Leslie

Library of Congress Cataloging-in-Publication Data

Callison, Daniel, 1948-
    The blue book on information age inquiry, instruction and literacy / by Daniel Callison and Leslie Preddy.
        p. cm.
    Includes bibliographical references and index.
    ISBN 1-59158-325-X (pbk. : alk. paper)
    1. Information literacy—Study and teaching. 2. Media literacy—Study and teaching. 3. Inquiry-based learning.
4. Questioning. I. Preddy, Leslie. II. Title.
ZA3075.C34 2006
028.7071—dc22   2006023645

British Library Cataloguing in Publication Data is available.

Library of Congress Catalog Card Number: 2006023645
ISBN: 1-59158-325-X

First published in 2006

Libraries Unlimited, 88 Post Road West, Westport, CT 06881
A Member of the Greenwood Publishing Group, Inc.
www.lu.com

Printed in the United States of America

The paper used in this book complies with the
Permanent Paper Standard issued by the National
Information Standards Organization (Z39.48-1984).

10 9 8 7 6 5 4 3 2 1

Copyright Acknowledgments

The authors and publisher gratefully acknowledge permission for use of the following material:

Abstracts from H.W. Wilson for Key Word in Instruction articles from *School Library Media Activities Monthly*. Copyright ©
2006 by the H.W. Wilson Company. Material reproduced with permission of the publisher.

Figure 4.6 reprinted with permission from *Creating Classrooms for Authors and Inquirers* by Kathy G. Short and Jerome C.
Harste. Copyright © 1996 by Kathy G. Short and Jerome C. Harste. Published by Heinemann, a division of Reed Elsevier, Inc.,
Portsmouth, NH. All rights reserved.

Contents

**Part II: Introduction: Application of Inquiry
to the Student Research Process**

Part III: Key Words for Instruction in Information Inquiry

Preface

The purpose of this book is to provide definitions of key concepts relevant to inquiry teaching and learning and how they apply in K–college education within the emerging Information Age. Most of the concept applications for this book are set in the context of school library media programs as the center of educational experiences. Each of the writers for this book sees the opportunity to investigate questions as an interactive process supported by extensive access to resources and information advisors (librarians, teachers, professors, parents, and even peers).

This current collection of chapters and key word definitions comes from nearly a decade of columns written *for School Library Media Activities Monthly.* It is difficult to express enough thanks to Paula Montgomery for her encouragement and willingness to let those of use who have written for her explore initial ideas and experiment with educational concepts that school library media specialists need to know, appreciate, and apply. In short, thank you Paula. This book would not have become reality without you. Thanks to Sharon Coatney and Sharon DeJohn for their expertise in guiding many parts to make this new collective set of essays possible.

I also thank Leslie Preddy, a leader in school library media in Indiana, for her tenacity in taking abstract concepts and applying them to her school media student research program. Her application section in this text will bring reality to many readers and is likely to be the starting point for many who need concrete examples. Helping others think is what Leslie has often modeled in order to improve the student research process in her local school. Her practical ideas and organization have served to help many other school media specialists.

The core research for this publication comes from nearly twenty-five years of work by Carol Collier Kuhlthau at Rutgers, The State University of New Jersey. Her observations, insights, and scholarly publications have truly helped to give meaning to learning and discovery through the guided information search and information application processes.

The concepts and techniques presented in this book have been enhanced by the feedback from two valued colleagues in the Indiana University School of Library and Information Science program at Indianapolis: Carol Tilley and Annette Lamb. They continue to raise future possibilities for more to be written on the topics introduced in the following pages. If our Indiana group can continue to collaborate over the next few years, look for more publications on the levels of teaching inquiry: controlled, practiced, guided, and free (independent) inquiry. Also look for new aspects on inquiry:

Critical—using text and data for current local and national social action

Scientific—testing the value of information to solve problems

Graphic—extracting information from and presenting information in visual formats such as political cartoons, diagrams, maps, photos, charts, tables, and multimedia

Historical—using oral history to tell local stories and critical examination of primary sources.

Critical History—gaining a greater understanding of our true heritage; who are the real heroes and heroines, and what is real social history?

Personal—becoming aware of how we grow and mature as inquirers

Virtual—accelerating inquiry through modern communication technologies and defending arguments in an open forum

Media—how information pressed on us through popular mass communication must be understood and managed in our personal and professional lives

Social and Democratic—determining the value of information as evidence used in dialogue

The potential audience for this text is much wider than the school library media field. My own background, for example, is in instructional systems design, and I see the inquiry method as foundational to all teaching and learning situations—school, work, personal. I view the Socratic Method as an instructional technology. Perhaps Socrates was the original "techie"? For teachers at all levels and from all disciplines, inquiry can be the most powerful instructional technology to be employed, and it can be enhanced with the modern software and hardware that are advancing on educational settings worldwide.

The expanding Information Age offers challenges and opportunities for educators who can mentor learners to question intelligently, to test information and opinions, and to apply critical and creative thinking extended beyond the standard exams and typical reporting of facts. Authentic, observable investigation practice and products are possible if we and our co-educators, administrators, and communities provide the time and resources required.

This text, therefore, is an introduction to the elements of Information Inquiry as a function of information literacy and information fluency. It presents the challenge to think about information in the inquiry processes. Is the information we obtain, we live in, we manipulate, valid, truthful, relevant, recent, and best suited for the need at hand? How can we judge adequacy of information? How can we turn information into the evidence we need to make an argument, make a judgment, create a meaningful plan of action?

The school library media field has evolved greatly over the past fifty years. Much contained in this text will trace that evolution and attempt to make the case that professional development is still needed. National accreditation agencies often fail to see the school library media specialist as a valued teacher. Many who have entered the school library field do not understand or seem to have the ability to take the teaching role to the levels described in this text. Some do, however, and I believe that number is growing. It is from those exemplary applications of the student research process that this text draws to show models for success. But even exemplary examples at this point are only a beginning. We have a long road to follow if school media specialists and other teachers are to truly reach the level of master teacher of Information Inquiry. We have a steep spiral to climb in order to be masters of our own inquiry and discovery. See Figure A.

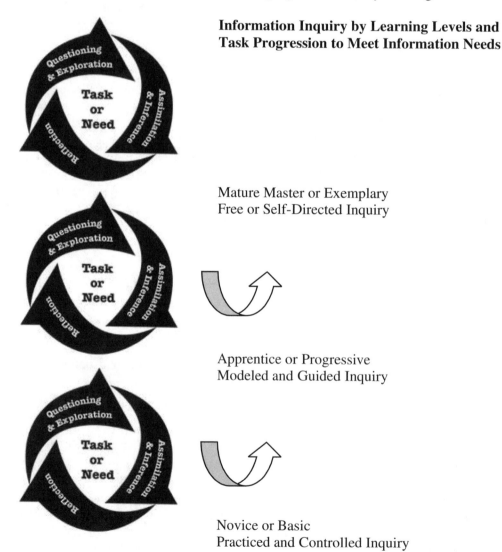

Information Inquiry by Learning Levels and Task Progression to Meet Information Needs

Mature Master or Exemplary
Free or Self-Directed Inquiry

Apprentice or Progressive
Modeled and Guided Inquiry

Novice or Basic
Practiced and Controlled Inquiry

Figure A. The *Information Inquiry Spiral* representing maturation of the learner © Daniel Callison 2006

Part I

Introduction to the Concepts of Information Inquiry: Teaching and Learning Methods for the Information Age

Chapter 1

Information Inquiry:
Concepts and Elements

Daniel Callison

This book contains a discussion of concepts, elements, and methods for the most exciting and natural form of learning and teaching—inquiry. Questions posed to oneself or by others drive the learning and teaching processes in school, on the job, and throughout life.

"The important thing is to never stop questioning."—Albert Einstein

"The fool wonders, the wise man asks." Benjamin Disraeli

"You can tell whether a man is clever by his answers. You can tell whether a man is wise by his questions."—Naguib Mahfouz

"Always question the 'why'; don't be satisfied with only knowing the 'how.' "—Catherine Pulsifer

"If you would have new knowledge, we must get a whole world of new questions."—Susanne K. Langer

"Judge a man by his questions rather than by his answers."—Voltaire

"We learn more by looking for the answer to a question and not finding it than we do from learning the answer itself." Lloyd Alexander

"Quality questions create a quality life. Successful people ask better questions, as they get better answers."—Anthony Robbins

"No man really becomes a fool until he stops asking questions."—Charles Steinmetz

"It is not the answer that enlightens, but the question."—Decouvertes

"It is better to ask some of the questions than to know all the answers."—James Thurber

"The real objective of education is to have a man in the condition of continually asking questions."—Bishop Creighton

"Animals are such agreeable friends, they ask no questions, they pass no criticisms."—George Eliot

Most animals learn by observation and by being trained. The human ability to ask meaningful questions sets us apart as creatures who wonder, doubt, devise, revise, challenge, and eventually change our environment to meet our needs. Higher-level thinking skills can move us not only to address initial questions, but to peel away bias and misinformation in order to identify the most critical questions and issues. We have the ability to identify problems and prioritize usefulness of resources to apply various possible solutions. Informed with the right data and information, human beings can be intelligent designers of their future (Burke 1995; Diamond 2005). Practice in Information Inquiry can help humans become mature consumers of information and wise investigators of endless questions.

Inquiry is part Socratic Method: a process of posing philosophical questions that guide the learner to eliminate potential hypotheses based on logical contradictions. Inquiry is part Scientific Method: posing a question and testing various hypothetical propositions until a seemingly reasonable conclusion can be found. Application of these methods to teaching dramatically reduces the use of lecture and expands greatly the freedom to question and explore under the guidance of an experienced mentor. Through inquiry, however, the teacher also is a learner. Both teacher and student are likely to find insights not held prior to the investigation of a series of questions. As a co-learner, the teacher serves as a model as well as a mentor.

Placing these methods within the context of the still emerging Information Age may result in a set of dynamics experienced more widely than during previous generations (Toffler 1980). Information access, possible today on a wide scale and available to an expanding proportion of the world's population, can result in a multitude of facts, documents, and opinions gathered or offered to address questions. The ability to search efficiently through such information, and the ability to effectively sort out that which is not relevant, that which is misleading, and that which is confusing, have become essential literacy skills in our modern electronic society—information literacy and media literacy (Breivik and Senn 1994; Doyle 1994; Tyner 1998).

The teaching and learning processes that combine inquiry strategies to seek answers to questions, raise new questions, and further question the content from the wide array of information accessed is presented in this text as *Information Inquiry*. Most of the terms and techniques in this book are drawn from constructivist and progressive educational theory.

Seeking one answer is never enough. Raising additional questions is always a goal. Learning that there are multiple answers or a spectrum of possibilities, although one or two seem to have the strongest potential to be "right," is mind-opening, humanistic, and at times euphoric. The roles of the teacher and student are expanded in this text to be interactive and cooperative. More specifically, the role of the school library media specialist is revised in this book to that of instructional media specialist. If those who serve in the professional school media field are to truly take the roles of teacher, learner, mentor, and model for inquiry, they need to understand and practice the concepts and techniques defined in these pages.

The challenge to educators is to harness this process and to bring inquiry into the learning environment in the form most clearly defined by John Dewey as practical problem solving to address real needs and interests. Although still stumbling, and at times regressing, in the provision of access to the freedom for learning that inquiry can provide, our education system should strive to move closer to providing what Walt Whitman called the great "bulk of our population" with the opportunity to investigate, invent, and become informed for themselves and for the greater good. These ideals must be applied more extensively to our public education system in order to create the informed electorate Thomas Jefferson envisioned. Inquiry in its broadest sense is, therefore, the process of learning how to learn.

Research and Information Inquiry

Although many of the models and techniques described in this text resemble research methods, and some of the activities may challenge students and teachers to think and act like researchers, there is no intent to pass off any of this as an approach for pure systematic research. The terms *student research, library research,* and *Information Inquiry* refer to the processes of engaging with text and other media to analyze, extract, synthesize, and infer information that will address student questions. These are difficult skills to apply, and even those who conduct applied or pure research for a profession find that rigor to meet high standards in application of these skills is challenging. Peer review and even the growing transparency of the Internet help to monitor the status of modern research across the sciences and the application of various research methods, qualitative and quantitative.

Knowledge gained by the student researcher may not be new knowledge to our pool of the shared human record, but through Information Inquiry and the processes described in this book, students can gain insight into knowledge that is new to them. They acquire knowledge in at least two tracks: first, an assimilation of knowledge in a discipline area or topic explored, and second, guided practice in information search, analysis, and management strategies necessary for problem solving in the Information Age.

The concepts and techniques outlined and applied over the coming chapters are related very strongly to research in today's scientific world, but they are purposefully designed to give a foundation that will help both students and teachers gain a working understanding of the inquiry processes. Many of the elements necessary to move into pure research are not possible, as students will not have access to nor understanding of the full refereed research knowledge base, methods to fully control treatments, access to large samples, analysis through application of complex statistical methods, and longevity leading to meta-analysis over time and among relevant studies. Such is probably obvious to most readers of this text, but it is surprising how freely many teachers, and librarians, misuse the term *research* and assume they are practicing such when in reality they are guiding a search for information—one part of the research process. Information Inquiry processes can take this search up several levels, to analysis of, assimilation of, inference from, and reflection about the information obtained. A passage from *e-Research: Methods, Strategies, and Issues* summarizes how humans can mature across research stages:

> Research is a natural human process that each of use engage in from earliest childhood to advanced age. As children, our research focuses on understanding and manipulating our environment, usually aided by toys and parents and later by friends and teachers. As adults, our research needs diverge to unique interests—often related to our occupation, but also covering our family concerns and leisure activities.
>
> . . . Discovering something new for an individual, even if it is knowledge or information known to others, is a valid research endeavor even if it does not warrant distribution in learned journals.
>
> As adults, the methods we employ in carrying out our research change over time as well. Through formal schooling we acquire the literacy skills that permit us to learn from the work of others. We also learn to conduct active tests by which our ideas are confirmed, refuted, and refined. We acquire the skills of reflection and intuition by which all parts of our mind and our experience are directed towards solutions to our research problems. We learn to apply our research in real-life situations to solve problems or further our practical understandings. Finally, and perhaps most importantly, we learn to communicate our ideas. Through communication our ideas are further developed and honed. From all of these processes we learn that good research, rather than providing simple answers, leads us to further questions and opportunities to increase our knowledge. (Anderson and Kanuka 2003, 2)

The Information Inquiry elements and techniques associated with the information literacy models in this text serve to take the student and teacher beyond the all too typical term paper assignment. From a topic assigned or selected from a narrow list of choices, students have been directed to access, extract, and cite information. Organization and neatness override decision processes and evidence of critical thinking. In the application of Information Inquiry to the student research process, the foundation is laid for mature research skills. Students, as information scientists, and teachers as instructional media specialists, engage in processes that can excite them to learn more. Through questions, exploration, assimilation, inference, and reflection teachers and learners grow in the expanding knowledge base of the Information Age. Together they can test information located, offered, and generated to determine valid and relevant evidence to meet their information needs and tasks.

Information Inquiry is a new term, first established in 1991 as part of a graduate education course at Indiana University, designed by Daniel Callison, Professor and Director of School Library Media Education. Information Inquiry includes the critical and creative skills found in information literacy and media literacy. It covers the range of inquiry, from posing personal questions to organized student research activities, to formal investigations and academic thesis experiences, to true research based on standard and rigorous methodologies. The Information Inquiry principles and elements gleaned from practice and tested models serve to define techniques for teaching and learning in the Information Age. These are methods not reserved for those in the school library media profession, but open for all educators who want to meet the learning demands all citizens face in our expanding digital world.

Specifically related to information literacy, Information Inquiry involves those processes to determine the adequacy of the information needed, located, and selected for use. Judgment of information adequacy will include reflection on the information in terms of age, authority, completeness, relevance to information need, task, argument, and audience. Through Socratic Methods applied to dialog, discussion, and debate, the ultimate task in Information Inquiry is to determine adequacy of information as convincing evidence from which justification can be made to present meaningful arguments, conclusions, and actions. Reflection includes considering the ethical methods in obtaining information, the limitations of the information acquired, and the adjustments that should be made to increase efficiency and effectiveness in information access and use to meet future needs and tasks.

The Five Elements of Information Inquiry

The five elements of information inquiry are commonly found in the many models and strategies that have been devised to teach the information search and use processes. They are also elements commonly found in description of how humans learn. These elements are illustrated in Figure 1.1 in a continuous cycle. Several of these elements interact, perhaps dozens of times, before the learner moves to the next element or experience. Sometimes the learner moves on purposefully and other times naturally, without consciously taking the next step. For those who apply inquiry to information literacy, the cycle will trigger each time a new piece of in-

formation is presented. Degree and depth of each element will depend on the information received or the stage of the investigation.

Figure 1.1. Cycle and interaction of Information Inquiry elements. Daniel Callison, copyright 1999, 2003, 2006. Reprinted from *Key Words, Concepts and Methods for Information Age Instruction*, Daniel Callison, LMS Associates, 2003, page 5.

Questioning

This element rests on the natural curiosity most humans have from birth. Depending on the level of intellectual nourishment before school and in school, curiosity can be destroyed, stymied, or greatly enhanced. Common questions are who? what? where? when? how? and the most difficult question, why?

This component, as it interacts with the other four, especially with exploration, becomes a more refined skill set. The result is the ability to ask more focused, relevant, and insightful questions. To become sophisticated in issue identification, clarity in defining critical problems for others to understand, and prioritizing the questions to be addressed based on what is known from the past and most likely needed for the future is the goal of the information inquirer as he or she matures in the questioning process.

Today, many questions are raised in an environment dominated by a flood of information that is often unorganized, misleading, and overpowering. Gaining meaning, understanding, and possible solution are the indicators of the successful end products of the Information Inquiry process. Conclusions are also the basis, however, for a beginning to another set of questions. Information Inquiry is based on a continuous questioning cycle, perhaps the essence of lifelong learning. Specifically, Information Inquiry deals with the questions posed from information accessed and critically evaluating that information as to its relevance, authority, and completeness.

Exploration

Closely tied to questioning, exploration is the initial action taken to seek answers to a question. There is therefore a continuous interaction between questioning and exploration as they drive and refine each other. In many cases, no specific questions are on the agenda, but the drive to satisfy curiosity moves the learner to read, view, listen to, and search through information. This preliminary examination of information often helps the inquirer to begin to focus on specific questions of interest and relevance (Kuhlthau 2000). Information sources may be very general and provide mostly background on the potential issues yet to be determined.

At a more informed level, questions become more focused. Exploration becomes a systematic search for and examination of resources and information to address specific questions. If available sources fall short, exploration may involve applying methods to access documents not readily available, or to gather original data in order to address the new, more focused and refined questions. How to search for, locate, obtain, analyze, synthesize, and apply this new information are the skills associated with information literacy.

The ability of the inquirer to be successful in applying information literacy skills is relative to age and information need. Guidance provided by mentors and experience gained through practice result in more efficient use of time to search, explore, and examine information and for further inquiry to be based on reflection and refined questions.

Assimilation

This component involves the actions to absorb and fit information to that which is already known, believed, or assumed by the learner. In some cases, assimilation means reinforcing or confirming what is known. In other cases, assimilation involves an altering of what has been accepted as knowledge by the individual learner or group of learners. In still other situations, new information may be rejected simply because it does not match held assumptions or beliefs of the information searcher. In such situations, the searcher's behavior may be to select only for those data or opinions that serve to "confirm" what the searcher believes to be true from the beginning of the inquiry process. These conflicts can lead to uncertainty, frustrations, and the searcher misleading himself or herself (Kuhlthau 1993).

Inquiry, properly applied, turns learning into more than a gathering of facts. Assimilation through inquiry leads to consideration of a wider range of perceptions and options than simply those assumed by the learner. As the inquirer matures, assimilation involves linking diverse new information to what is previously known. Inference is the attempt to apply that information to address questions or issues. Assimilation involves accumulation of knowledge, alteration of accepted knowledge, and constant consideration of alternatives.

New information assimilated with previously held information is accepted as knowledge by the learner. Such may be new knowledge on the part of the individual learner even if not new to others. Assimilated information can be accepted as knowledge whether the information is right or wrong. Thus, assimilation should involve not only the actions of reading and listening, but also the interactive processes of critical analysis, debate, as well as comparing and contrasting facts and ideas (Fitzgerald 1999). In Information Inquiry these processes help to test the validity of new information before it is fully assimilated.

Inference

This component involves the actions or processes for deriving a conclusion from facts and premises. Inference may involve personal choice and actions taken based on conclusions that seem most relevant and meaningful for the situation. On a personal basis, inference is usually an internal message to the self, and not one that is conveyed in a formal manner to others. Inference may or may not involve presentation of "findings" to another audience, although interpretation for presentation can be an excellent stimulant for clarifying inference and finding evidence that is meaningful for the audience who will receive the presentation. Inference to satisfy self, however, comes first. Assimilation and inference are constantly interacting as a decision process to accept or reject new information.

In most job or academic environments, inference may involve a wider communication of conclusions. The inference is either shared among members of a group working on the same tasks in a cooperative effort or is presented to those who might need a recommendation for action or need to evaluate the learner's ability to address a problem and communicate a solution. The degree of persuasion may be greater in real world situations, but most academic exercises can also carry the expectation that a major goal of Information Inquiry is to find evidence that supports inferences that seem reasonable, logical, and ultimately persuasive.

Information Inquiry involves learning environments in which the student may experiment with a variety of media to present a set of inferences. Formats include not only written papers and oral presentations, but use of multimedia. Teams are often encouraged to work together to present their findings and to represent varied options extracted from the information examination experience.

A sharing of the conclusions may lead to further assimilation of more information for both the presenter and the audience. Presentation of inferences often refines the meaning of the conclusions and may be delivered to an audience to both inform them and, often, to persuade them. In nearly all cases, inference will raise new questions for exploration.

Information within the inference component is most useful when it becomes evidence. The information may come from observation, literature review, expert or witness interview, or data from survey or experimental study, and may range in level from slight association to clear cause and effect. Evidence is necessary to support a claim, notion, plan for change, or hypothesis. Without evidence, inference leading to conclusions and recommendations cannot be justified. Evidence may be necessary to justify

the status quo or accepted norm. Evidence is always necessary to justify change.

Information Inquiry includes the processes for identifying evidence and the merits of that evidence. There are levels of evidence that are more or less convincing. Ability levels of the investigator will be a major factor in determining the level of evidence gathering that can be expected. Legal definitions of evidence for acceptable testimony, documentary evidence, physical evidence, scientific evidence, or exculpatory evidence may be beyond many K–12 inquirers, and yet novice researchers, even at young ages, should be aware that some evidence can be more convincing than others. Along with terms and steps that define the search for information, students need to be introduced to terms that help to form judgments on information—factual, authoritative, statistically valid, logical, emotional, anecdotal, hearsay, conventional wisdom, minority opinion, or dogma. The mature inquirer will find bias introduced at all levels of information inference, but at various degrees of influence.

The effectiveness of the evidence to justify actions or change may rest with the manner in which the evidence is presented as well as the audience or decision makers' ability to understand and assimilate the evidence. The quality of evidence can determine the strength of what is inferred. Therefore, Information Inquiry is not simply drawing information from multiple sources. It involves questioning the quality of the information and its source, testing the merits of potential conclusions, and understanding that credibility of the evidence may depend on the presenter's ability to make the evidence relevant to the experiences and beliefs of the audience. Analysis and synthesis are both critical and creative skills within the inference element.

Deanna Kuhn, professor of education at Columbia University, argues in her insightful text *Education for Thinking* (2005) that ultimately educators and learners should "regard learning as change in understanding" (60). "[W]e would like students to come to understand the world around them, so as to be able to function effectively in it and achieve their goals. . . . A critical set of cognitive skills, then, are the ones that enable us (learners and teachers) to extract information from the external world, allowing these mental models to be constructed, elaborated, revised, and updated" (61).

Kuhn concludes that inference is the culmination of inquiry. In order for this element to be constructive and meaningful, learners must be challenged to infer judgments not just from personal opinions or from random facts and figures gleaned from a convenient set of resources. Valid inference depends on the quality of the evidence gathered to fit the argument, proposal, or general information needs. Therefore, the ability to judge information, to validate it as relevant and meaningful evidence, is critical. Without students, along with teachers as learning mentors, engaged in testing and questioning information as valid evidence, the inquiry process will remain flat and nothing more than an exercise of locating, sorting, and arranging information in an appealing manner. To teach thinking is to teach how to challenge information and to establish information as evidence that best supports arguments, inferences, and conclusions in a logical, ethical, and convincing manner.

Reflection

This element raises the questions that bring the interactions of the other elements to a complete cycle. "Have I been successful in answering my question?" "Is this the best information to address this question?" "What new questions have come from the consideration of the evidence I have gathered?" Reflection involves evaluation and assessment, at formative and summative levels. Each time new information is encountered, reflection should be placed in the Information Inquiry cycle. Each time a project is completed, reflection by both teacher and student is needed.

As the learner matures in his or her ability, reflection will be used more and more within each Information Inquiry element as well as an overall action. Reflections to assess exploration, assimilation, and inference are formative in that the leaner is aware of the consequences of actions in one element on the limitations or opportunities in other elements. Reflection that is summative in nature allows the learner and teacher to consider decisions connected across a major assignment or large research unit.

The learner who masters self-reflection becomes more likely to be not only a true independent learner, but also one who can help others master the Information Inquiry interactions. The teacher who masters both formative and summative assessment processes will provide more clarity to guidance and feedback in judgment of learner actions. The teacher who understands and manages authentic learning environments will make assessment relevant to the student's cognitive framework and real life expectations. The teacher as a model of reflective behavior will serve as a mentor who learns from mistakes as well as successes. Modeling effective use of the Information Inquiry elements by teachers and school library media specialists, both taking the role of instructional media specialists, is essential for successful implementation of information literacy programs K–college.

The Demands of Inquiry

In many cases, the skill sets associated with Information Inquiry learning will seem demanding and beyond the norm. This is probably true. Wise use of information is not an easy task. The abilities, patience, and institutional support to make these skill sets and methods part of the normal curriculum are all likely to be less than sufficient in most corners of our public schools. The conclusion should not be that these more challenging skills and methods should not be adopted.

Teaching is the opportunity to provide meaningful situations for learners to experiment and deal with information problems. Teachers, whether classroom instructors, library media specialists, student peers, or parents, will best instill inquiry skills when they are seen as model users of the process. It is essential, therefore, that current and future teachers master the Information Inquiry process and information literacy skills outlined in this book.

Not every information problem requires the use of the inquiry method to derive a solution. Certainly we learn from observation, example, and directions. Often by trial and error we sift through solutions that seem to best fit the problem and often transfer the solution to similar problems. Many important skills and facts are mastered through routine practice. Memorization and meaningful application of these skills and facts can result in efficient learning in many situations.

Cornelia Brunner, Associate Director of the Center for Children and Technology, has mastered techniques for engaging children in inquiry-based projects that include multimedia as a presentation medium (Brunner and Tally 1999). The Education Development Center (http://www.youthlearn.org) provides an outline for her manageable Inquiry Processes. Guiding students through the first stage of the inquiry process—learning to pose real questions—will set the stage for manageable and successful projects.

Students should be guided to "Pose Real Questions": What do I want to know about this topic? What do I need to know? What do I know already, and how do I know it? What might a possible answer be? This process should not be a "bait and switch" that moves the student back to pursuing the teacher's interests, but should help the student stay on target to determine the true questions of interest to that student. Such questions, however, must ultimately be answerable, meaningful, and relevant to the curricular area being explored. Questions that have single, factual answers are not useful for inquiry exercises. Good inquiry questions have the following characteristics (Ciardello 1998):

- Age appropriate, but challenging enough that the inquirer will need to explore information new to him or her, and some resources will preferably be at a reading level that will be slightly higher than the student has experienced previously. Example: "When I am old enough to care for a horse myself, what are the most important things I should know?"

- Interpretative, having more than one answer, with evidence available from several perspectives. Relevant information is accessible within the school but will also involve access through other information bases as well as the Internet, local libraries, and subject experts. Examples: "What can be done to establish more recreational activities for young people in our community? What has been successful in other communities similar to ours? What are the costs? Who must be involved? What

role can we play as the young people of our community?"

- Evaluative, which can be workable if the purpose of the inquiry is to document opinions, beliefs, and various points of view gathered from literature and interviews. Here the student is charged with valuing, judging, defending, or justifying arguments and opinions. Examples: What are the issues related to gun control, and what are the opinions of various national and local groups? Other evaluative approaches can generate interesting inquiry projects. Examples: "Who are the five most influential spokespeople on gun control issues today? Why and how have they reached that level?" Ranking and rating judgments set the stage for not only documentation from media but gathering local impressions as well. Examples: "Who are the three most influential women political office holders in the United States today? Why and what is your projection on where each will be five years from now?"

- Controversial, which take older students into inquiry projects that can be structured around debates, argumentative essays, editorials, or persuasive presentations if the question is framed as a resolution, and claims to support or reject the resolution are supported with evidence. Example: "Resolved that the only firearms a private citizen should own are those that can be shown to be for small game hunting." Defining terms in such resolutions is as important as the quality of the evidence gathered.

- Testing a hypothesis following the scientific method, documenting the process and results. Example: "Driving a car at 50 miles per hour for one hour will consume less gasoline than driving the same car at 65 miles per hour for the same time over the same road. Will this be true across several vehicles of different style and weight? What other research should be conducted to see how automobiles can be more fuel efficient?" Students can be introduced to literature review processes to establish background from previous similar experiments and to answer the last question by locating examples of what many scientists already recommend.

- Divergent thinking from questions starting with predict, imagine. Examples: "What if you could create something totally different? What if we lived in a society where there were no guns? What would be different and similar to our society today?"

Zemelman, Daniels, and Hyde (2005), in their third edition of *Best Practice,* stated about the value of students being supported to raise their own questions, especially in practice of science inquiry:

In most U. S. science classrooms students rarely get an opportunity to ask and pursue their own questions. If students are to develop the ability to ask questions, they must practice doing so. Classroom inquiry will vary in the amount of direction from the teacher and the self-direction of the students. . . . Many teachers have found that the end of one inquiry can be the springboard for another based on authentic questions that have arisen. Students are highly motivated to pursue these new questions. However, teachers do not have to pursue every question students ask, nor are they prohibited from providing answers to questions [without entering into extensive inquiry]. How to respond to students' questions depends on the teacher's goal and context of the classroom. . . . not every question students might pose is suitable for investigation through inquiry. Some questions may be ill formed, others too costly, and some too far removed from the curriculum to be addressed. However, to avoid causing students to feel disenfranchised or crushing their zeal, the teacher can ask the student and the class to re-word or reformulate [the question, until it can be used] as a creative springboard to a more feasible inquiry. (149)

Best Instructional Practices and Inquiry

In many state curricular guides, especially in the science and social studies disciplines, inquiry has been formulated into principles of best practice based on years of educational research and observation (Zemelman, Daniels, and Hyde 2005). A few example statements in science follow:

- Teachers should build on students' curiosity about the natural forces of the world to stimulate scientific inquiry.

- For students to develop a deep knowledge of sciences, they must do more than merely cover topics. They must immerse themselves in doing science, conducting systematic inquiry.

- For true inquiry to occur, the teacher must ensure that students try to answer a scientific question with good evidence.

- Students can and should engage in systematic inquiry in a variety of ways; and

- Inquiry expects that students will learn specific concepts and develop the capability to carry out inquiries on their own. Inquiry differs from the process skills approach in that it tries to teach an overall method that incorporates process skills rather than addressing them separately. (144–150)

A few example statements in social studies follow:

- Students in social studies need regular opportunities to investigate topics in depth.

- Students need opportunities to exercise choice and responsibility by choosing their own topics for inquiry.

- Social studies teaching should involve exploration of open questions that challenge students' thinking.

- To make concepts real, social studies must involve active participation in the classroom and the wider community.

- Social studies should involve students in both independent inquiry and cooperative learning in order to build skills and habits needed for lifelong, responsible learning.

- Social studies reading should include engaging real-world documents and not just textbooks.

- Social studies should involve students in writing, observing, discussing, and debating to ensure their active participation in learning.

- Social studies learning should build on students' prior knowledge of their lives and communities, rather than assuming they know nothing about the subject. (177–181)

The reader will find many other ties between Information Inquiry and today's progressive curriculum in the chapters, concepts, key words, and practical examples that follow in this book.

Information Environments

Nearly everyone faces problems related to information, and nearly every problem faced is related to information (Wurman 1989). Often associated with the need to answer a question, information problems are as varied as the tasks we attempt to complete and needs we face every day. These problems are common in three environments most of us find ourselves in at some stage in life: academic, personal, and workplace.

The academic environment, involving tasks in typical school situations, is the main one used in this book to illustrate information problems and the techniques to address those problems. In some cases these techniques are steps the student can take on his or her own, while many others require interventions and guidance on the part of the teacher, either classroom or library media specialist.

In the academic setting problems can be real or contrived. Real information problems may be personal needs concerning how to enroll in a course or how to prepare for an exam. Other information problems may be simulations or exercises assigned as learning experiences. Typical are term papers and reports, which involve the use of multiple resources beyond the textbook.

Best practices would suggest that these resource-based information problems are stronger learning situations when they are as authentic as possible. Typical report assignments at any grade and across disciplines leave a lot to be desired in terms of challenging students and teachers to use multiple resources effectively and efficiently. Awareness of new resources and their location, and some practice in an exercise to extract and organize facts are often the only results.

A major purpose of this book is to provide descriptions of methods and activities through defining the key words in instruction that are most likely to illustrate effective means to raise the level of today's typical academic report projects.

As the student leaves the academic environment and enters the workplace, *authentic* takes on new meaning. While simulations and perhaps even field experiences in school took the student closer and closer to the "real world," on-the-job information problems soon convince most people that not everything necessary for job survival was taught in school.

At its best, however, Information Inquiry can establish a foundation for troubleshooting strategies that transfer from the academic to professional job and into personal information need environments. Although the details of the problems may differ, methods to address the information problems in real life are similar enough to support initial success in the real world. The former student soon finds information decisions may need to be made faster and may actually affect the personal lives of many others, and that repeated wrong decisions lead to termination of the job, not just a corrected paper.

Personal information needs are present throughout our lives. The elements of Information Inquiry are reflected in the constant questions raised by preschoolers. Information preferences are often displayed as well, as children may seek out information sources they find to be safe and reliable and that reinforce what they want to hear. These are habits learners carry with them as they explore the information world in more detail through academic situations. Learning to be critical and open-minded is a combination of skills often difficult for even the best students to master.

Information Problems

The student who demonstrates the ability to identify and summarize the information need and is a "problem identifier" as well as a "problem solver" may also be a student who has a broader perspective on assimilating new information with knowledge and beliefs held (Harada

2003). Information problems range from simple with quick answers to complex questions without any hope of answers. Building on experiences with locating and extracting information to address questions leads to a fundamental ability to match resources to information need. Harada has suggested that the following strategies are involved when an information literate student perceives or recognizes an information problem:

- Recall prior related experience.

- Define terms important for context [being] studied.

- Generate appropriate questions.

- Analyze alternatives.

- Devise solution plan.

- Plan experiment [analyze results of implemented solution].

- Validate concepts learned in terms of conclusions and solutions.

- Validate process [for solving problem] in terms of efficiency and effectiveness.

- Validate self-efficacy in terms of feelings and attitudes.

Starting in elementary grades, students can formulate questions that can be addressed through basic reference materials, simple Internet searches, further examination of the content of their textbooks, or even phone calls to local experts on the topic if necessary: question posed > resource located > acceptable response found. Such exercises can instill awareness of the value of different resources as well as confidence in information location if the student is successful. Such "quick solutions," however, are not authentic for most true information problems we encounter.

Most students will gain even more confidence by taking command of raising their own questions. Thus, beyond the worksheets and set reference questions for practice, students should be encouraged at an early age to branch out from the standard questions posed and begin to personalize what they seek to learn. These are the first steps in inquiry, stating one's own questions and exploring resources that lead to question and resource refinement, and discovery that reasonable, understandable answers do not exist for the vast majority of the questions students might raise.

While much of what will help introduce the novice to information resources will include practice with questions answered with a single resource, inquiry does not really blossom until multiple resources are used to check and verify facts or perspectives.

The range of information problems can be seen in the range of information literacy skills covered in the pages that follow. Each skill reflects how the average student at a given stage in intellectual development is expected to address a problem or set of problems.

As the novice encounters the more complex Information Inquiry tasks, he or she is likely to raise the following types of questions:

- What must I do? How much and how soon?

- What must I use? How many resources, and where are they?

- How will my answer be evaluated?

Other questions, such as those listed below, illustrate information problems expressed at higher levels of consideration. Although most students may not phrase their information need in the exact terms that follow, those who mature in the Information Inquiry process will explore ways to address not only these questions but many more. The mature inquirer expands questions to include the following:

- What is my need? What questions must be addressed? What do I know, and what do I want to find out?

- How do I locate the information I need? Where is the information most likely to be found, and who might help me locate it?

- What methods will help me search effectively so I can locate the most useful information? What methods will help me work efficiently so I can save time in searching and have more time to read, interpret the information, and fit it with what I already know?

- How much information do I need? How complete should my answer be? Who must I satisfy with the information: me, my teacher, my classmates, my parents, my boss?

- How much time do I have to determine an answer? To what extent might I seek additional resources if time is available? Does the information I have located give me any leads or links to additional information? When do I have enough information?

- What is the acceptable level of evidence? Is one document, Web site, or article enough? Should the information be current and from an accepted expert? Do I need a second source to confirm the first?

- How do I apply this information to solve my problem? Should I get opinions from others as to the usefulness and validity of the information?

- Is the information for me personally and to meet my own interests or needs, or must I also communicate the information to others? Who are these others? Teachers? Classmates? Employers? Do I present my interpretation of the information in different ways to different audiences? Do I know their understanding of the problem and their likely understanding, acceptance, or rejection of my conclusions?

- If an abundance of information is found, how do I decide what to select and what to exclude? If very little or no relevant information is found, and the questions are ones I must or want to address, how do I go about gathering original data?

- After finding information that seemingly supports my belief and information that seemingly counters what I believe, how do I determine which to accept and use? How do my own perceptions and biases fit against the perceptions and biases found in the information I have located?

- Based on all possible information, primary and secondary, it is not possible to come to a conclusion. What can be learned from this, and what might be done differently next time I try to answer these or similar questions?

These questions illustrate a wide range of information problems. They suggest challenging

tasks, all the more reason students should be introduced to efficient ways to search for information as early in their lives as possible.

Assessment of Inquiry

Various methods to assess student performance are ffered in this text. Such measurement should aim to give guidance to students as they move through inquiry projects, hopefully at each grade level, and grow more and more sophisticated in their ability to analyze the value of the information they read, view, and hear. The following outline is adapted from language arts curriculum (Callison 2004) and illustrates the potential areas to document student performance, perhaps in a grade-by-grade portfolio of student work containing examples of writing from inquiry experiences. Assessment rubrics relevant to the student's age level and the level of sophistication of the inquiry assignment can be constructed from the skills itemized under each question.

What do I need to do? Demonstrate your ability to

- analyze the information task;

- analyze the audience's information need or demand;

- describe a plan of operation;

- select important or useful questions and narrow or define the focus of the assignment; and

- describe possible issues to be investigated.

Where could I go? Demonstrate your ability to

- determine the best initial leads for relevant information;

- determine possible immediate access to background information (gaining the larger picture); and

- consider information sources within and beyond the library.

How do I get to the information? Demonstrate your ability to

- determine if information is pertinent to the topic;

- estimate the adequacy of the information;

- test the validity of the information;

- focus on specific issues within the boundaries of the information obtained;

- group data in categories according to appropriate criteria; and

- determine the advantages and disadvantages of different information formats and intellectual levels.

Of what should I make a record? Demonstrate your ability to

- extract significant ideas and summarize supporting, illustrative details;

- determine a systematic method to gather, sort, and retrieve data;

- combine critical concepts into a statement of conclusions;

- restate major ideas of a complex topic in concise form;

- separate a topic into major components according to appropriate criteria; and

- sequence information and data in order to emphasize specific arguments or issues.

Have I got the information I need? Demonstrate your ability to

- recognize instances in which more than one interpretation of material is valid and necessary;

- show that the information obtained is relevant to the issues of importance;

- if necessary, state a hypothesis or theme and match evidence to the focused goal of the paper or project; and

- reflect, edit, revise, and determine if previous information search and analysis steps should be repeated.

How should I present it? Demonstrate your ability to

- place data in tabular form using charts, graphs, or illustrations;

- match illustrations and verbal descriptions for best impact;

- note relationships between or among data, opinions, or other forms of information;

- propose a new plan, create a new system, interpret historical events, or predict likely future happenings;

- analyze the background and potential for reception of ideas and arguments of the intended audience; and

- communicate orally and in writing to teachers and peers.

What have I achieved? Demonstrate the ability to

- accept and give constructive criticism;

- reflect and revise again;

- describe the most valuable sources of information;

- estimate the adequacy of the information acquired and the need for additional resources;

- state future questions or themes for investigation that will continue your inquiry agenda; and

- seek feedback from a variety of audiences.

Literacy and Fluency

Information literacy, media literacy, and information fluency are defined and compared as key words later in this book. It is enough here to close this chapter with brief definitions of these terms in Information Inquiry.

Information literacy is a set of skills through which the student demonstrates the ability to recognize when information is needed and to take steps that lead to location and selection of information that can be used effectively to address the need (ACRL 2000). The resourcefulness to move through this process with confidence and the abilities to adjust to different databases and to deal with a variety of technology based information systems are signs of information fluency, or what Paul Glister (1997) calls "digital literacy."

While information literacy represents command over those skills needed at a given age level to function in academic settings of the Information Age, information fluency represents the ability to move beyond to levels of independent skill acquisition. Well versed in the use of information technologies, those who are information fluent are able to express themselves creatively, to reformulate knowledge, and to synthesize new information.

Jamie McKenzie describes students who have moved to the fluent stage as those who have the ability to "move across a menu of strategies until one works. [These students] do not allow themselves to get stuck in one place trying the same wrong tool or strategy over and over again, harder and harder. They are toolmakers and tool-shapers [(they can formulate their own strategies when necessary)] as well as tool users" (2000, 51).

The interactive processes that take place through Information Inquiry are the methods and techniques to help the student become information literate and to eventually strive for and achieve fluency.

References

Anderson, T., and H. Kanuka. (2003). *e-Research: Methods, strategies, and issues.* Person Education.

Association of College and Research Libraries (ACRL). (2000). *Information literacy competency standards for higher education.* http://www.ala.org/acrl/ilintro.html (accessed June 1, 2001).

Breivik, P., and J. A. Senn. (1994). *Information literacy: educating children for the 21st Century.* Scholastic.

Brunner, C., and W. Tally. (1999). *The new media literacy handbook.* Anchor.

Burke, J. (1995). *Connections.* Little, Brown.

Callison, D. (1993). The potential for portfolio assessment. In C. C. Kuhlthau (Ed.), *School library media annual, volume eleven* (30–39). Libraries Unlimited.

Ciardello, A. V. (1998). Did you ask a good question today? *Journal of Adolescent and Adult Literacy, 42* (3), 210–219.

Diamond, J. (2005). *Guns, germs, and steel: The fates of human societies.* W. W. Norton.

Doyle, C. S. (1994). *Information literacy in an information society: A concept for the information age.* ERIC Clearinghouse of Information and Technology. 82pp. (ED 372 763)

The Education Development Center. (2005). *YouthLearn.* http://www.youthlearn.ogr/ (accessed November 26, 2005).

Fitzgerald, M. A. (1999). Evaluating Information: An information literacy challenge. *School Library Media Research, 2.* http://www.ala.org/ala/aasl/SLMR (accessed November 26, 2005).

Glister, P. (1997). *Digital literacy.* Wiley.

Harada, V. H. (2003). Empowered learning: Fostering thinking across the curriculum. In B. K. Stripling and S. Hughes-Hassell (Eds.), *Curriculum connections through the library* (41–65). Libraries Unlimited.

Harada, V. H., and J. M. Yoshina. (2004). Moving from rote to inquiry. *Library Media Connections, 23* (2), 22–24.

Kuhlthau, C. C. (1993). A principle of uncertainty for information seeking. *Journal of Documentation, 49,* 339–355.

Kuhlthau, C. C. (2000). The information search process (ISP): A search for meaning rather than answers. *Library and Information Science, 43,* 35–42.

Kuhn, D. (2005). *Education for thinking.* Harvard University Press.

McKenzie, J. (2000). *Beyond technology: Questioning, research and the information literate school.* FNO Press.

Toffler, A. (1980). *The third wave.* Morrow.

Tyner, K. (1998). *Literacy in a digital world: Teaching and learning in the age of information.* Lawrence Erlbaum Associates.

Wurman, R. S. (1989). *Information anxiety.* Bantam Books.

Zemelman, S., H. Daniels, and A. Hyde. (2005). *Best practice: today's standards for teaching and learning in America's schools.* 3d ed. Heinemann.

Highly Recommended for Further Reading

Gross, M. (2006). *Studying children's questions: Imposed and self-generated information seeking at school.* Scarecrow Press.

Chapter 2

Key Foundational Documents for Information Literacy and Inquiry

Daniel Callison

Over the past five decades, many educators have attempted to define the key skills students should be taught, encouraged to demonstrate, and explore more fully on their own in order to survive in the Information Age (Thomas 2004). Many of these skills derive from curricula designed for practice of critical thinking, while others represent information skills associated closely with specific disciplines. Selected documents illustrate the evolution from a narrow library skill base to a more open and demanding critical inquiry process. These documents also call for a leadership role on the part of new instructional library media specialists.

1906: A Great Awakening

Kenneth Pray of the University of Wisconsin and W. F. Rocheleau of the Illinois Normal Academy wrote in their series Home Study of History in 1906, "within recent years a new element has been made prominent in history courses ... so prominent that wide-awake and progressive teachers find it necessary to recognize its utility and value. This is the use by teacher and pupil of other books and materials besides the text" (ii). In their introduction these two educators defined the textbook as a summary, an item of brevity, but containing an outline to provide a larger picture and relationships. Other resources, however, reproduce historical scenes, create personalities, explain motives, raise and suggest answers to the "why" questions, and instill reading habits if the teacher is also an appreciative user of literature. The up-to-date teacher, concluded Pray and Rocheleau, looks upon the library as an "essential" part of the school. That teacher realizes that the lifeblood of the subject flows through books (and other resources), while the text alone can furnish but the dry bones of information.

1955: A Learning Laboratory

Martin Rossoff served as the librarian for James Madison High School in Brooklyn. Rossoff authored several books decades prior to discussions on what the school media field now terms information literacy. His concept of the school library as a laboratory in which to debate issues and find evidence to support arguments was not new, but he is certainly one of the early practicing school librarians to place critical inquiry in the center of the school media program. A list of the questions from Rossoff that illustrate how his students were expected to explore their library and eventually debate positions illustrates his approach. Although his issues reflect a specific time period, the method for raising additional questions and proposing resolutions to these questions remains the same today:

- McCarthy—menace or savior of democracy?
- Are our civil rights in danger?
- Should Hawaii and Alaska be admitted to statehood?

- Is mercy killing justifiable?

- Should the government censor comic books?

- Should eighteen-year-olds be allowed to vote?

In the early 1970s, Rossoff wrote of his views concerning the need for educational change, "[T]eachers continue to require students to memorize large doses of information, extracted from inadequate textbooks, most of which is obsolete and most of which is forgotten once the test papers have been graded. This practice was inherited from an earlier stable period in history, when there were comparatively few facts to be learned. The question is now: Can this method succeed in an environment characterized by an unprecedented social and technological change, bursting accumulations of knowledge, and a disturbing uncertainty about the facts themselves?" (1971, 21).

Rossoff described the "new education" in terms of a curriculum based on broad concepts and development of the student's ability to reason. He saw application of new technological inventions to classroom instruction. A third consideration, he wrote, "in the readjustment of education was a theory of learning which holds that there was more to the process of education than mere stimulus and response or trial and error. While our knowledge of how people actually learn is still dim, there is general agreement that no learning took place unless motivation existed. Students have to be convinced that learning was worthwhile" (1971, 30).

Students can learn a great deal by themselves, with guidance, and they can learn a great deal from each other, with facilitation. Rossoff envisioned the school library as a center for exchange of ideas. This interaction among learners was the major purpose, and books, magazines, and equipment gathered in or near the library were all artifacts to support this process. The inquiry/discovery method, according to Rossoff, has merit but it is unquestionably impossible in schools that are without libraries as learning laboratories.

1960 and 1969: National Standards for School Library Programs

The 1960 *Standards for School Library Programs* was a milestone document, as twenty national educational associations collaborated with the American Association of School Librarians (AASL) to approve enhanced descriptions of the teaching role of the school librarian. In addition, the school library program was detailed as an important contributor to student education, support of teachers, and a center for print and nonprint resources.

Among other school library program services, the 1960 Standards stated, "Students use the school library as a laboratory for references and research in which they locate specific information and expand their knowledge by using a wide variety of materials" (18). As if predicting the skills for information literacy and inquiry, the 1969 Standards also included the following: "The pupil will not only need to learn skills of reading, but those of observation, listening, and social interaction. . . . Therefore, it is important that every media specialist participate actively in shaping the learning environment and the design of instruction" (1). "The media program is indispensable to the educational programs that now stress individualization, inquiry, and independent learning for students" (3).

Frances Henne, then professor at Columbia University, served as the chair for the 1969 Standards and was a member of the writing team in 1960. Her influence, along with that of dozens of other leaders from various national associations, stressed that, "In programs that provide systematically, through modular and flexible scheduling or in other ways, for the time the student spends in individual exploration and independent learning, the media specialist, the classroom teacher or teachers involved, and the student form a team that plans and guides the student's work. Throughout, the media specialist remains in close contact with the teachers. The move away from textbook-dominated teaching and from teacher-dominated teaching has made the school media center a primary instructional center that supports, complements, and expand the work of the classroom" (1960, 3).

AASL (2005) includes these statements in the opening of its policy on "Access to Resources and Services in the School Library Media Program":

> The school library media program plays a unique role in promoting intellectual freedom. It serves as a point of voluntary access to information and ideas and as a learning laboratory as they acquire critical thinking and problem-solving skills needed in a pluralistic society.

1985: Educating Students to Think

In the summer of 1985, a small group of educators were gathered in Chicago at the invitation of Tony Carbo Bearman, then executive director of the National Commission on Libraries and Information Science. Bearman's charge to the group was to explore alternative ways that school library media programs could move beyond just supporting simple skills for location of library resources to playing a stronger role in preparing young people for the demands of the Information Age.

Three individuals agreed to draft a position statement for the group: Jacqueline Mancall, then associate professor at Drexel University; Shirley Aaron, then professor at Florida State University, and Sue Walker, then program coordinator for library media services with the Lancaster, Pennsylvania, schools. This team combined years of professional experience, knowledge of the research record in school library media management, and most of all, knowledge of emerging educational theory on metacognition and national school performance review.

The final report from this group is one of the key foundational documents that define the shift away from teaching library skills based on tools and location toward instruction in critical thinking based on selection, use, analysis, and synthesis of information to meet the intellectual needs of individual students. The contribution Mancall, Aaron, and Walker made with this paper to moving the instructional role of the school library media specialist in a new direction was very influential on the 1988 and 1998 national guidelines for school library media programs,

both published under the title *Information Power.*

"Educating Students to Think" identified, among other current problems in public education, the following aspects with which school library media specialists as instructors as well as other educators must be concerned and change. Studies indicated that:

- Our educational system focuses primarily on teaching youth "what" to think rather than "how" to think.

- Failure to help students develop higher order skills has seriously limited their ability to cope adequately in an increasingly complex society.

- Students are often satisfied with their initial interpretations of what they had read and seemed satisfied with their initial efforts to explain or defend their points of view. Few students could provide more than superficial responses to [information comprehension and interpretation] tasks, and even the better responses showed little evidence of well-developed problem-solving critical thinking skills. (1986, 20)

Mancall, Aaron, and Walker called for the current school library media programs, which were library-centered, concentrating on physical objects collected and organized, to move toward programs that should be information-centered. These programs would be directed at greater understanding of student and teacher learning needs as well as the intellectual content of the resources held or accessed through the media center. Meeting the need for knowledge and learning should drive the program, not just what has been placed on the shelves. When the school librarian plans lessons, the target is meeting learning and teaching needs, not just the need of how to access what is on the shelf.

Among other new aspects for the school library media program, the position paper supported the information guidance service role proposed by James Liesener (1984), then professor of library media at the University of Maryland. He proposed that information guidance services be provided by knowledgeable intermediaries who would offer assistance to students as they attempt to find, interpret, and evaluate materials, information, and/or ideas. This is a key role for both teachers and school library media specialists who function as information advisors in an increasingly complex information world.

This information advising and teaching role should concentrate on establishing learning situations and interactions among teachers and learners on the following critical thinking skills:

- distinguishing between verifiable facts and value claims;

- determining the reliability of a source;

- determining the factual accuracy of a statement;

- distinguishing relevant from irrelevant information, claims, or reasons;

- detecting bias;

- identifying unstated assumptions;

- identifying ambiguous or equivocal claims or argument;

- recognizing logical inconsistencies or fallacies in a line of reasoning;

- distinguishing between warranted or unwarranted claims; and

- determining the strength of an argument.

New Guides to Teaching Library Research

Also in 1985, The Center for Applied Research in Education published the first edition of *Teaching the Library Research Process.* Based on her dissertation in education at Rutgers, Carol Kuhlthau introduced an analysis of the steps taken by successful high school students in the management of the typical research paper. Instead of looking at the process from the librarian's viewpoint (how to look up information and how to cite it), Kuhlthau examined the logical planning processes displayed as well as the doubts, frustrations, and anxieties of the students. The message was clear that school librarians had more to teach than location. They needed to also contend with the processes of thinking through the research assignment, the topic development, exploration of a wide number of resources in order to consider topic options and

foci, and helping students to learn how to make evaluative judgments about information.

Barbara Stripling and Judy Pitts, as high school librarians in Arkansas, followed in 1988 with their classic *Brainstorms and Blue Prints.* Their guide to the student research process gave a systematic approach matched to various learning styles and abilities. Their work helped many school media specialists increase their efforts to help students to think and plan rather than serving only as a guide to locating resources.

Initiatives for Curriculum Mapping

In 1984 Michael Eisenberg, then assistant professor at Syracuse, introduced his ideas on mapping the curriculum in support of the integration of library media skills across disciplines. This approach was intended to provide the school media specialist with a tangible role in curriculum development that might also ensure that library skills at the elementary school level would not be left in isolation and be seen to be without value. Eisenberg extended his ideas into practice with Bob Berkowitz, library media director in the Wayne Central School District of Ontario Center, New York (Eisenberg and Berkowitz 1988). Although this team introduced the information problem-solving strategy that was to become widely used by thousands of school librarians as a framework for teaching information skills, it is the philosophy for a change in the role of the school media specialist that is important to note here. Eisenberg and Berkowitz advocated the need for school library media specialists to initiate the analysis and revision in courses and lessons rather than wait to be called on for help by fellow teachers.

"Too often in the past," wrote Eisenberg and Berkowitz, "school library media specialists acted as minor partners in developing instructional materials and curriculum consultants only after the fact. However, in an educational climate calling for excellence and based on the use of information and developing critical thinking skills, library media specialists have both the opportunity and the responsibility to make a positive impact on the quality of learning, school-wide. . . . In addition to providing a full range of curriculum support services, the library media program has its own curriculum agenda: the library & information skills curriculum. . . . At the very highest level, there is more than an integrated curriculum; the overall school curriculum is actually information-based and the library media center becomes a setting for content learning as the classroom" (1988, 4–5). Mapping the curriculum could and should result in a concrete, visual outline of learning standards, associated with information skills K–12, and could be used as a guide for selection of the multiple resources necessary to launch such instruction.

Inquiry to Enhance Independent and Team Learning

In 1986 Daniel Callison, then assistant professor at Indiana University, outlined elements of free inquiry learning for the school library environment. He used principles from science education to illustrate how the discovery method also applies to teaching of library information skills. He recommended that students work in teams and explore and share their findings about information sources rather than simply listening to library tool orientations, and that the school media center environment needed to increase support of personal inquiry that would continue beyond assigned library research projects. The elements in this early inquiry model included the following:

- Lessons are planned and taught by librarians and teachers acting together.

- Objectives of the lesson are evolutionary and negotiated between student and teachers.

- Students document the processes of learning and share them with others.

- Content is driven by questions that students raise and answer by exploring resources in the library and beyond.

- The teacher provides direction for learning, but students are encouraged to take initiatives and work independently.

- Time for learning activities is flexible.

- Peer tutoring is encouraged.

- Peer interaction and teaming are supported.

- Projects are shared with peers and parents.

- Students may choose, and are encouraged, to extend their learning through additional independent inquiry projects. (Thomas 2004, 29)

A speech by Karen Sheingold to the American Library Association Annual Conference in New York in 1986 was printed in *School Library Media Quarterly* in 1987. Then director of the Center for Children and Technology at Bank Street College, Sheingold illustrated how inquiry is key to keeping children's knowledge active and vital. Her examples of critical inquiry associated with environmental education served to provide tangible activities for moving inquiry beyond just the books and walls of the library into social and political action learning.

Emerging Theory and Issues

In 1987 Carol Kuhlthau, then assistant professor at Rutgers, summarized an emerging theory of library instruction. She attempted to move beyond simple introduction of resources and tools for information location, to teaching skills, which help students seek meaning from the information they use. Information gains meaning when it becomes evidence. The task, therefore, is to build on the student's experiences and knowledge so that information encountered can be either discerned as useful evidence or discarded as quickly as possible if it has no relevance. Kulthau provided the first clear ties to Constructivist Theory for effective teaching of information skills.

Barbara Stripling (1989), who was later to become President of the American Association of School Librarians, summarized the impressions of one who has both practiced the techniques for inquiry instruction and managed the demanding operations of a school media program. While serving as editor of *School Library Media Quarterly* and as a library media specialist at the Fayetteville Public Schools in Arkansas, Stripling raised these questions and issues for future information literacy instruction:

Challenge 1: To provide intellectual and physical access to information and ideas for a diverse population whose needs are rapidly changing.

– How can we tell if students are understanding the information they find and are using it well?

– What thinking skills can we teach effectively in the library? How do they improve the students' abilities to understand, evaluate, and use information?

– How can we build a client/professional relationship with students that will enhance our credibility and encourage them to involve us while they search for and use information?

Challenge 2: To ensure equity and freedom of access to information and ideas, unimpeded by social, cultural, economic, geographical, or technological constraints.

– How does availability of computers at home affect students' online database searching skills?

– Do low-income students make less voluntary use of technology that is available in the school?

– Are there gender issues [that] pertain to extent of technology and information access and use?

Challenge 3: To promote literacy and enjoyment of reading, viewing, and listening for young people at all ages and stages of development.

– What programs have been most successful in engaging both students and teachers to read, for pleasure and for information?

– What can be done to foster reading interest among low-achieving students?

– What is the appropriate role of library media services in whole language education?

Challenge 4: To provide leadership and expertise in the use of information and instructional technologies.

– How can we shift the emphasis of library instruction from location to information use?

– What methods are successful in helping teachers to incorporate new technologies into their classrooms?

– How does the use of the new technologies improve teaching and learning?

Challenge 5: To participate in networks that enhance access to resources located outside of the school.

– What impact does electronic networking [telecommunications] have on the learning environment of the school; the community?

– When students are provided access to resources beyond the school, what effect does this have on their motivation and quality of learning?

1987: ALA and Information Literacy

In 1987 the president of the American Library Association, Margaret Chisholm, appointed a special committee to define information literacy, to identify models of information literacy development that seem appropriate for informal learning environments, and to determine implications of information literacy in education. Patricia Senn Breivik, long an advocate for information literacy standards in higher education, served as chair of the committee.

Ultimately, the committee stated, information literate people are those who have learned how to learn. They know how to learn because they know how knowledge is organized, how to find information, and how to use information in such a way that others can learn from them. They are people prepared for lifelong learning because they can always find the information needed for any task or decision at hand.

Information literacy, concluded the committee, is a means of personal empowerment. It allows people to verify or refute expert opinion and to become independent seekers of truth. It provides them with the ability to build their own arguments and to experience the excitement of the search for knowledge.

The ALA Presidential Committee on Information Literacy went on to describe situations in which people use information skills to address problems in business, citizenship, and personal needs as well as in school environments. From this report, one can conclude that information literacy, or Information Inquiry as a broader set of concepts presented in this book, has an impact on all areas of life, personal, professional, and academic. This can be illustrated by the intersections of information problems shown below.

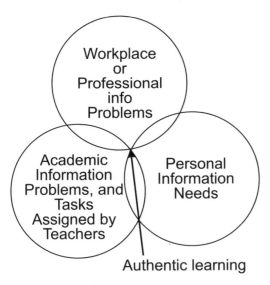

Figure 2.1. Relationship among workplace, personal, and academic information problem sets and authentic learning.

1989: Information Literacy and Higher Education

Two leaders in higher education in Colorado, one an administrator for library and information services and the other an administrator for faculty development and leadership, co-authored an extensive discussion of the role of the academic library in developing lifelong learners.

Patricia Senn Breivik, then director of Academic Libraries, and E. Gordon Gee, then president of the University of Colorado, jointly called information literacy the survival skills in the Information Age. They wrote: "Instead of drowning in the abundance of information that floods their lives, information-literate people know how to find, evaluate, and use information effectively to solve a particular problem or make a decision, whether the information they select comes from a computer, a book, a government agency, a film, or any of a number of other possible resources. Students have long relied on the knowledge of teachers and the information skills of librarians. In fact, when the volume of information was modest, they could often manage without becoming information literate themselves. What the information explosion has done is turn an old problem, functional literacy, into a new crisis. To address this crisis, we need a new educational philosophy based on a fuller understanding of the information explosion and a redefinition of literacy that includes information skills" (1989, 12).

Breivik and Gee also called for more collaborative communication between college librarians and secondary schools to help prepare high school graduates better for the complexities of the college library information search. They recommended having fewer lectures on "library instruction" and adoption of better teaching practices for the library-based curriculum. Academic experiences are better, they suggested, when the learning activity:

- imitates reality (is Authentic)

- is active and students have opportunities to learn by discovery

- is individualized

- is responsive to a variety of learning styles

- accommodates constantly changing information

- is provided in an environment that is least threatening.

The 1990s and the Information Literate Person

A school library supervisor and doctoral student in Arizona, Christina Doyle conducted a Delphi Study among dozens of educators versed in education for information and technology instruction. Her study was concluded in the early 1990s as the Information Age was beginning to burst on the world, with access to personal computerized communication never before experienced. Published in 1994 by the ERIC Clearinghouse on Information and Technology, the following characteristics of an information literate person have proven to be a benchmark in defining core information literacy skills. An information literate person

- recognizes that accurate and complete knowledge is the basis for intelligent decision making;

- recognizes the need for information;

- formulates questions based on information needs;

- identifies potential sources of information;

- develops successful search strategies;

- accesses sources of information, including computer-based and other technologies;

- evaluates information;

- organizes information for practical application;

- integrates new information into an existing body of knowledge; and

- uses information in critical thinking and problem solving.

1993: A Position on Information Literacy Standards

In 1993, The Wisconsin Educational Media Association printed an outline of the key skills for information literacy. Several other states developed similar information skill statements, which served as models to integrate these skills across their respective state curricula (Eisenberg, Lowe, and Spitzer 2d ed. 2004, 82–94). The Wisconsin paper has received the endorsement of the National Forum on Information Literacy, a group representing sixty educational associations. Selected portions of the outline are included here:

I. Defining the Need for Information

- recognize different [needs for and] uses of information (occupational, intellectual, recreational)

- [establish] a frame of reference for the information need (consider who, what, where, when, how, and why)

- relate the information need to prior knowledge

- [initiate a strategy] to solve the problem through consideration of a variety of questioning skills (yes and no questions for facts; open questions for working hypothesis)

Additional stages are defined for search strategy, resource location, interpreting the information, communicating information, and evaluation of the product and process:

IV. Assessing and Comprehending the Information

A. Skim and scan for major ideas and keywords to identify relevant information.

B. Differentiate between primary and secondary sources.

C. Determine the authoritativeness, currentness, and reliability of the information.

D. Differentiate among fact, opinion, propaganda, point of view, and bias.

E. Recognize errors in logic.

F. Recognize omissions, if any, in information.

G. Classify, group or label the information.

H. Recognize interrelationships among concepts.

I. Differentiate between cause and effect.

J. Identify points of agreement and disagreement among sources.

K. Select information in formats most appropriate to the student's individual learning style.

L. Revise and redefine the information problem if necessary.

1994: Model Information Literacy Guidelines

Sponsored by the Colorado State Library (Walster 1995), and often coordinated by Dian Walster and Linda Welborn (1996), a group of forward-thinking school library media specialists drafted an early version of learning standards for information literacy. Their model served as one of the key documents for later development of *Standards for Student Learning* by the American Association of School Librarians (1998). The philosophy, guidelines, and statements of student performance written by this Colorado group have helped to define the characteristics of the mature student information user for many public school curriculum guides. Selected portions are given here:

Philosophy: Information literate students are competent, independent learners. They know their information needs and actively engage in the world of ideas.

They display confidence in their ability to access information and to communicate. They operate comfortably in situations where there are multiple answers, as well as those with no answers. They hold high standards for their work and create quality products. Information literate students are flexible, can adapt to change, and are able to function independently and in groups.

Guidelines for Student Performance:

1. The Student as Knowledge Seeker. The student constructs meaning from information.

    • Determines information needs
        • states the purpose
        • explores options
        • defines a manageable focus
    • Develops information-seeking strategies and locates information
        • frames appropriate questions
        • identifies likely resources
        • uses a variety of strategies
        • builds a reasonable timeline
        • makes ethical decisions (see guideline 5)
        • records bibliographic information
    • Acquires information
        • questions others
        • listens actively
        • queries electronic resources
        • reads for significant details and concepts
        • views for significant details and concepts
        • extracts appropriate details and concepts

• Analyzes information relative to need
    • identifies criteria in terms of authoritativeness, completeness, format, point of view, reliability, and timeliness
    • applies criteria to information
    • retains only appropriate material
• Organizes information
    • creates outlines, storyboards or graphic organizers
    • assembles material to meet information need
    • credits appropriate sources
• Processes information
    • integrates information from a variety of sources
    • makes inferences
    • draws conclusions
    • constructs meaning
    • builds connections to prior
    • knowledge
• Acts on information
    • answers a questions
    • satisfies a curiosity
    • takes informed action
    • develops a product
    • solves a problem
    • presents information
• Evaluates process and product
    • determines level of product success (see guideline 2)
    • identifies process strengths and weaknesses
    • develops a plan to continuously improve the process

2. The Student as Quality Producer. The student creates a quality product.

    • Recognizes quality and craftsmanship
        • uses existing models and criteria as a guide
        • critically evaluates those models
        • develops personal criteria for quality product(s)
    • Plans the quality product
        • establishes a clear purpose
        • considers the audience
        • determines product content
        • chooses format
        • develops process
        • identifies necessary resources
    • Creates a quality product
        • uses resources and technology (see guideline 1)
        • reflects knowledge of learning styles

- integrates appropriate media (see guideline 5)
- Presents a quality product
  - communicates clearly
  - reflects established criteria
  - demonstrates effective presentation skills
- Evaluates quality product
  - evaluates the process and the product continuously
  - measures product against models and criteria
  - revises and refines as necessary
  - determines if product has achieved its purpose
  - decides if product has reached its desired audience
  - reflects on personal satisfaction with the product (see guideline 3)

3. The Student as Self-directed Learner. The student learns independently.

- Voluntarily establishes clear information goals and manages progress toward achieving them (see guidelines 1 & 2)
  - realizes that not all problems have a solution
  - makes choice to pursue or modify the search
- Voluntarily consults media sources [and media specialist]
  - reads for pleasure, to learn to solve problems
  - uses media sources for information and personal needs
  - seeks answers to questions
  - considers alternative perspectives
  - evaluates differing points of view
- Explores topics of interest
  - uses the library media center, public library and other information sources (e.g. electronic information, bookstores, directories, experts)
  - asks for help
  - recognizes organization and structure of information centers and resources
- Identifies and applies personal performance guidelines
  - engages in reflective analysis
  - internalizes the model and process of inquiry (see guidelines 1 & 2)
  - balances internal and external performance demands
  - reflects on personal satisfaction

4. Student as Group Contributor. The student participates effectively as a group member.

- Helps group determine information needs (see guideline 1)
  - works with group to define project or problem parameters
  - collaborates to determine: common definitions questions processes [for action] information access [strategies]
- Shares responsibility for planning and producing a quality group product (see guideline 2)
  - collaborates to define roles and divide responsibility
  - completes tasks in a timely manner
  - helps synthesize individual tasks into finished product
- Collaborates to determine relevant information
  - selects information using various resources and technologies
  - works with others to organize information helps integrate information from a variety of sources
- Acknowledge diverse ideas and incorporates them when appropriate
  - shows respect for others' ideas, backgrounds, and learning [and communication] styles
  - discusses opposing viewpoints constructively
  - helps create projects that reflect differences among individuals
- Offers useful information to the group, defends that information when appropriate, and seeks consensus to achieve a stronger product
  - offers well thought-out evidence justifying information presented
  - moderates ideas of group toward consensus, while allowing individuals to maintain their own opinions
  - demonstrates effective interpersonal communication skills
- Clearly communicates ideas in presenting the group product
  - assimilates ideas of others into group presentation
  - helps ensure that all participants' contributions are represented
  - uses a variety of media effectively to communicate ideas

- Evaluates the product, the group process, and individual roles continuously
  - works with the group to set criteria for the product
  - uses the criteria to determine the success of the product

5. Student as Responsible Information User. The student uses information [in a responsible and ethical manner]

  - Practices ethical usage of information and information technologies
    - applies copyright guidelines
    - cites references in proper format
    - does not plagiarize
    - recognizes copyright as protection from the copyright holder
  - Respects the principle of intellectual freedom
    - understands the concept of intellectual freedom
    - recognizes the importance of intellectual freedom
  - Follows guidelines and etiquette using electronic information sources
    - utilizes electronic resources to locate, retrieve, and transfer information
    - applies time and access constraints when using electronic resources
  - Maintains the physical integrity of information resources and facilities
    - follows policies and procedures
    - preserves integrity of print and nonprint materials
    - acknowledges and respects the rights of others
  - Recognizes the need for equal access to materials and resources

Also in 1994, Breivik and Senn published *Information Literacy: Educating Children for the 21st Century*. Based on many of the principles from Breivik and Gee's previous book on information literacy in the college and business environment (1989), this was an attempt to modify those skills for the K–12 environment. After the authors conducted interviews with leading school media specialists around the nation, many of the chapters were written to link teaching information literacy with the role of the school library media specialist. Specific examples were gathered from many schools.

The Breivik and Seen publication helped some administrators rethink the use of informa-

tion in educational settings based on what leading school media specialists were already doing, without waiting for the next century:

- From textbook to a variety of media resources
- From teacher as teller to teacher as guide and coach
- From facts as primary goal to questions as primary goal
- From information is prepackaged to information is discovered
- From rigid schedules for library skills to flexible planning for inquiry

1995: Redefining the School Librarian

The Library Instruction Round Table of the American Library Association published a collection of essays in 1995 that described the changing role of many librarians moving toward a much more involved educational responsibility, including more formalized teaching. This seemed to be true for librarians in all institutions, school, public, academic, and special. Callison (1995) took the instructional role further than simply presentation or even co-planning to the level that defines the educator in the critical-thinking curriculum as an evaluator of student performance.

In reviewing the recommendations from the Association for Supervision and Curriculum Development (Resnick, Klopfer, and Resnick 1989) as well as ideas from educators such as Kathleen Craver (1990) and Melvin Bowie (1990), Callison discussed the critical thinking curriculum and school media specialist roles in the evaluation of students. While many previous documents had shown a role for presenting information skills, few, if any, had clearly stated that in order for the school library media specialist to claim a full teaching role, he or she must also be involved in the evaluation and assessment of student performance.

The thinking curriculum is not a course to be added to a crowded program when time permits. It is not a program that begins after basics have been mastered. Skills in reasoning, problem solving, making judgments, and stating inferences need to spread from the top of Bloom's cognitive domain to all levels associated with learning. Each fact, each event, each concept presented should have a context and be questioned to the extent that relationships to the learner's personal abilities and individual needs are acknowledged.

This is not to say that learning is without steps or levels, or that there are no prerequisites. It is necessary, however, that students become aware of such increments themselves and that they construct their intellectual webbing based on as many informational items, thoughts, or conclusions as can be made relevant to their intellectual schema and to their own current and possible future social contexts.

ASCD recommendations suggest that construction of any thinking curriculum should employ the following practices in what they term "cognitive apprenticeship":

> Practice a real task. Writing an essay for an interested audience, not just the teacher who will give a grade; reading a text that takes some work (asking questions, discussion, comprehension, comparisons) to understand; exploring a physical phenomenon that is inadequately explained by a current concept.

> Contextualize the practice. Students would not do exercises on separating facts from opinions, but they would take on tasks of analyzing arguments (and statistics) on particular topics or participating in debates, both of which might engage them in a contextualized version of figuring out reliable information in a communication.

> Observe models. Students need plenty of opportunity to observe others doing the kind of work they are expected to learn or to do. This observation (reinforced with the challenge to evaluate or critique) gives them standards of effective performance against which they can judge their own efforts.

The "Thinking Curriculum" (Bowie 1990) is based on students practicing the process of raising questions; testing a variety of possible answers; and eventually voicing, writing, constructing, sculpting, drawing, and arguing the meaning of those answers. This information inquiry process is founded on gathering informa-

tion for the purpose of seeking various perspectives, not just a single conclusion. Most directly, it means that students must be engaged in a conversation of their own and with others.

Craver (1990) has given school library media specialists a superb summary of the implications from library and information science research related to new concepts in teaching critical thinking. Successful methods in placing students in the critical thinking mode include the expectation that the student generate his or her own analysis of a given text to identify, organize, and raise questions concerning issues presented.

Thoughtful discussion leaders and students reacting to peer opinions in groups tend to increase critical thinking. In a discussion situation, deliberate use of wait time conveys to students that they are expected to respond intelligently to posed questions. Open debate that results in capturing issues in written form followed by a cooling period in which students search for supportive or counter evidence may serve to raise the level of critical exchange.

Bowie (1990) listed very tangible activities that the school library media specialist and the classroom teacher can employ to challenge students in the reasoning process. Some of these are paraphrased here:

- Ask a class to gather and sort opposing viewpoints on a social issue; use all possible sources; analyze merits of each opinion including questioning of the qualifications of "authorities."

- Compile a file of popular advertisements (record television and radio spots as well) and lead students in a discussion of how information is manipulated (spoken and visual).

- Have students construct infinite bibliographies (pathfinders or webographies) to show location of information through a variety of formats both in and beyond the library, including human resources.

- Create activities that require comparison of maps, charts, and census data over time and in relation to major events.

Bowie termed her activities *intervention strategies*. This term is important to note because intervention is a concept that must be broadened in the evaluation role of the instructional library media specialist and the classroom teacher. Self-, peer, and mentor evaluations are considered at each stage of the inquiry process, not just at product conclusion. Intervention represents an opening created by either the teacher or the instructional media specialist to cue a point of instructional need (identification of the "teachable moment") . Intervention works best when collaboratively planned and implemented and classroom content–grounded.

Both the instructional media specialist and the classroom teacher need to be skilled, however, to handle interventions individually when necessary. The goal is to establish such critical thinking activities at the forefront of lesson planning to the extent that the word *intervention* can be dropped, and inquiry activities will become the curriculum. Using varied resources, raising questions, presenting results of the information search, and inference become the standard, not the exception. Inquiry and critical thinking become the curriculum, not simply a special process and set of skills added to lessons by a few teachers.

Above all, the teaching methods that work best to provide an environment for critical thinking should be used by the instructional library media specialist in teaching information use skills. Instead of always lecturing and saturating students with "how-to" methods and reference sources, actively involve them in learning. Let them raise problems and suggest solutions. Use cooperative learning teams whenever possible so peers teach, learn from, and motivate each other. Supplement the library resources with access to human expertise found in other teachers, parents, and community contacts. Interviews are conducted to gather more current information or to confirm facts found in often out-of-date print resources. To build activities within the limited confines of the school library is as undesirable as allowing a textbook to determine the parameters for learning.

In order to make inquiry units that are based on critical examination of information effective, Callison argued in his 1995 essay that students must have access to an extensive amount of material. This means that a variety of resources should be available in terms of format, date, reading level, and points of view. There is nothing new in the idea that school library media center collections should provide a variety of materials. What must be different in order to create an environment for critical examination of information is the depth of the school's library collection and the extent to which students truly have access to many information sources representing a wide spectrum of views. Three actions must be taken.

First, school library media collection development must take a sharp turn toward support of a few selected units. Build depth, not breadth. For these units, acquisition of items and agreements for electronic access should be extensive. Use of fiction, historical and scientific, may be necessary for some units to provide the student with a greater appreciation of the cultural context of the events being examined.

In some cases, collections of unique local resources may need to be gathered, boxed in special storage, added to over several years, and then controlled through a reserve system so that these difficult-to-obtain materials will be available to students when it comes time for the specific unit. Targeting a substantial portion of base collection funding, perhaps 25 percent or more, and seeking additional special funds will allow the resource pool to become rich with the various materials needed. Planning and mapping, as developed by David Loertscher (1985), creates more chances that the school media specialist will say "yes" to inquiry units. Depth of ownership and access is constructed so inquiry can have the resource base for the exploration component to become operational.

Second, the collection compiled in support of critical information units should not be sanitized and should come, as much as possible, in its "real world" packaging. For secondary school students this means that tabloids and other "supermarket checkout line materials" take a place beside the respected news magazines and newspapers usually recommended to students. It means that the extremes on both sides of an issue are easily accessible. Original documents are provided, not just some safe summary of opposing views. The spectrum of arguments should be full, with right to left opinions. Access to factual (and perhaps not so factual) data from government, private, and even personal records is pursued. Contacts with local public, academic, and historical libraries become part of the resource collection process.

Third, the long march to move materials to a centralized location called the school library media center will need to make an about-face. The school library becomes a clearinghouse, a dissemination center, and an often-used learning laboratory. It is a major access point for information, but widely disseminates to the classroom and to the students' homes. It is a center for discussions, documenting the discussions, and providing access electronically to these discussions for students and teachers.

Classrooms will need to house, and teachers will need to share, information materials as never before. In some cases, special collections of materials, realia, and artifacts for a given unit will need to be boxed and moved from one building to another as the inquiry unit is implemented at several schools over the academic semester. Some of these artifacts may be captured as digital library collections, to be accessed by anyone in the learning community.

District level acquisition services may find they serve a central role in development of these special traveling and digital collections to support projects at different buildings and different grade levels. Centralized distribution for telecommunication access to the distance learning program, digital archives, and communication with experts beyond the local community will become a collection of services managed by school library media professionals.

Until the mid-1990s, expanding the collection to give depth to selected areas was key to creating the resource base for teaching critical thinking curriculum and information literacy. While such resource depth and variety continues to be important today, broader access to resources through the Internet by 2000 placed nearly any topic before students as one to be explored with a rich information pool. It became increasingly clear that documents could be gathered from various viewpoints on nearly any controversial subject, primary documents could be viewed electronically, and subject experts could be contacted over new telecommunications. The need to give greater emphasis to skills that helped students determine the quality of information had risen to a much higher level than ever before.

1998: Library Power and Information Literacy Standards for Student Learning

The power of collaborative teaching, infusion of new dollars to build collections to give depth to the curriculum, and value of professional development of all educators in the meaning of information literacy was operational across several school districts in the DeWitt Wallace Reader's Digest Library Power Project. In cooperation with the American Association of School Librarians (AASL), this project involved dozens of school districts from 1988 to 1994. Documented by Doug Zweizig and Dianne McAfee-Hopkins (1999), both of Wisconsin University, the action research and evaluation evidence from the Library Power Project provided much of the context for the 1998 AASL national guidelines for school library programs.

Nine information literacy standards were identified through a national review process. The AASL standards committee, lead by chief author Delia Neuman, associate professor of library and information science at the University of Maryland, agreed on the following list as the key skills for student learning in association with school library media programs (AASL and AECT 1998):

Information Literacy
- accesses information efficiently and effectively
- evaluates information critically and competently
- uses information accurately and creatively

Independent Learning
- pursues information related to personal interests
- appreciates literature and other creative expressions of information
- strives for excellence in information seeking and knowledge generation

Social Responsibility
- recognizes the importance of information to a democratic society
- practices ethical behavior in regard to information and information technology
- participates effectively in groups to pursue and generate information

While these nine statements provide concrete definitions of information literacy skills, depth has been given to these standards for student learning through

- Indicators of student performance and levels of proficiency for each indicator,

- Standards in action to illustrate potential learning situations that require practice in information literacy skills, and

- Examples of content-area standards to show a relationship across all academic disciplines with information literacy.

An example of the depth behind each standard is illustrated below from Standard 2: "The student who is information literate evaluates information critically and competently."

Indicator 1. Determines accuracy, relevance, and comprehensiveness.

Levels of Proficiency:

Basic—Defines or gives examples of the terms "accuracy," "relevance," and "comprehensiveness."

Proficient—"Compares and contrasts sources related to a topic to determine

which are more accurate, relevant, and comprehensive.

Exemplary—Judges the accuracy, relevance, and completeness of sources of information in relation to a range of topics and information problems.

Standard in Action:

Students realize they will find conflicting facts in different sources, and they determine the accuracy and relevance of information before taking notes. They determine the adequacy of information gathered according to the complexity of the topic, the research questions, and the product that is expected.

Following is an example of a content-area standard:

Civics. Knows how to use criteria such as logical validity, factual accuracy, emotional appeal, distorted evidence, and appeals to bias or prejudice in order to evaluate various forms of historical and contemporary

political communication. (e.g., Lincoln's "House Divided," Sojourner Truth's "Ain't I a Woman?," Chief Joseph's "I Shall Fight No More Forever," Martin Luther King Jr.'s "I Have a Dream," as well as examples of campaign advertising and political cartoons.) (AASL and AECT 1998)

From just this one example it is clear that analysis and synthesis skills need to build from early learning environments up through school. Activities that place the student in information evaluation, problem-solving, and decision-making situations are necessary across all areas of the curriculum so students understand information literacy and inquiry as process skills relevant to all learning. The complexities of many of these skills also indicates that there will be various levels of success and failure, and the role of the instructional media specialist and other teachers as information intermediaries is much greater than simply helping with access and location. Interpretation must be at the center of the learning objectives so teachers and students experience high level challenges through analysis, synthesis, and evaluation.

Mary Ann Fitzgerald (1999), then assistant professor at the University of Georgia, published a key review of the literature on issues and methods for evaluating information. Her exhaustive review made light of the many biased behaviors, misguided interpretation, and naive assumptions information users of all ages display. Fitzgerald (2000) produced a guide to help students be critical thinkers when approaching new information. Among her recommendations for basic evaluation skills are to deeply consider and question documents that

- present personal attack or vindictiveness;

- fail to acknowledge leading writers associated with the field;

- claim to have no bias;

- provide overly broad definitions;

- are provincial, presenting a local perspective with little concern for the world at large;

- ignore practical issues; and

- are based on sarcasm.

Her reviews indicated a new group of documents on the horizon that would apply instructional strategies to teaching students how to critically analyze information.

Key Documents since 2000

In 2001, based on their experiences with the National Library Power Project, four leading thinkers and educators (Donham, Bishop, Kuhlthau, and Oberg) in school library media joined together to publish their findings on how inquiry-based learning was an apparent strength of the more successful programs observed in the late 1990s. Changes in teaching practices were described based on improved collections and flexible schedules to allow for co-planning and concentrated library resource use. Linear or step-by-step library research projects and single-skill worksheetd were replaced with inquiry-based projects that encouraged in-depth use of new resources and a variety of learning approaches that met the needs of different students at different learning levels.

Based on their work with thousands of practicing school librarians and fellow researchers around the world, David Loertscher and Blanche Woolls (2002) of San Jose State University published their revised review on information literacy. A nearly comprehensive guide to models and studies, this collection is likely to be expanded even more through future Treasure Mountain Research Conferences. Along with the revised compilation by Eisenberg, Lowe, and Spitzer (2004), nearly every early aspect of information literacy curriculum is touched. Loertscher draws on much from this publication to support his many workshops designed to discourage single-concept written reports from encyclopedias that are not much more than busy work. He illustrates how technology and multiple resources serve to make richer inquiry-based approaches affect and improve student achievement. Of note in relationship to the inquiry method promoted in this book are these conclusions from Loertscher and Woolls on theory and practice:

- Children come to school naturally curious but lose it if teachers don't encourage it.

- Encouraging students to form their own questions has a positive impact on learning.

- Students are likely to face the task of creating questions with uncertainty.

- The quality of the question [especially that from the student] is the best predictor of student performance.

- Questions requiring low-level thinking encourage copying and regurgitating answers.

- The best way to improve student projects is to reformulate the question.

- Good questions engage student interest.

In 2002, Pappas and Tepe, as a researcher team, tied inquiry to the appreciation and need for further discovery teachers and students experience from quality literature. Other teams, such as Small and Arnone (2000) in New York and Harada and Yoshina (2004) in Hawaii combined the theories of good instructional practice with field application to demonstrate the strengths of motivation and guided mentoring for successful student inquiry.

In 2003, Barbara Stripling and Sandra Hughes-Hassell edited the second essay collection in the Libraries Unlimited Principles and Practice series. This is an excellent addition to literature by many practicing school media specialists and educators. Of note is Stripling's outline of the inquiry process (Stripling 2003):

Connect
- Connect to self, previous knowledge
- Gain background knowledge to set context for new learning
- Observe, experience

Wonder
- Develop questions
- Make predictions, hypothesize

Investigate
- Find and evaluate information to answer questions, test hypotheses
- Think about the information to illuminate new questions and hypotheses

Construct
- Construct new understandings connected to previous knowledge

- Draw conclusions about questions and hypotheses

Express
- Express new ideas to share learning with others
- Apply understanding to a new context, new situation

Reflect
- Reflect on own process of learning and new understanding gained from inquiry
- Ask new questions

Also of note are indicators of student behavior that should help instructional media specialists evaluate the maturation level of student inquirers (Harada 2003). Some selected examples follow:

- Generates questions
- Poses problems
- Identifies central ideas and events
- Makes reasoned predictions
- Justifies views with sound evidence
- Explores knowledge in diverse contexts
- Applies knowledge in a novel way
- Explores alternative points of view
- Recognizes bias
- Critiques a situation or event from different points of view
- Demonstrates tolerance for other points of view
- Recognizes own prejudices
- Assesses and regulates own behavior
- Is open-minded about feedback and criticism

In 2005, eight presentations at the National Conference of the American Association for School Librarians were based on inquiry-based learning methods. Clearly, over the past thirty years methods that now center on student abilities to raise and explore meaningful questions have established themselves in the educational role of school library media programs. The methods are enriched by the resources and technologies collected and managed by professionals who act as both information and instructional specialists.

References

American Association of School Librarians. (2005). *Policy statement: Access to resources and services in the school library media program.* Adopted 1986, amended 1990, 2000, 2005. Available at http://www.ala.org/ala/aasl/aaslproftools/positionstatements/aaslposition.htm (accessed June 30, 2006).

American Association of School Librarians. (1960). *Standards for school library programs.* American Library Association.

American Association of School Librarians. (1969). *Standards for school library programs.* American Library Association and the National Education Association. ALA.

American Association of School Librarians. (1998). *Standards for student learning.* ALA.

American Association of School Librarians and the Association for Educational Communications and Technology. (1998). *Information power: Building partnerships for learning.* ALA.

Association for Supervision and Curriculum Development (ASCD). (1993). *Challenges and achievements of American education.* ASCD.

Beyer, B. K. (1985) Critical thinking: What is it? *Social Education, 49* (4), 270–276.

Bowie, Melvin M. (1990). The library media program and the social studies, mathematics, and science curricula: Intervention strategies for the library media specialist. In B. Woolls (Ed)., *The research of school library media centers* (21–48). Hi Willow Research and Publishing.

Breivik, P. S., and E. G. Gee. (1989). *Information literacy.* Macmillan.

Breivik, P. S., and J. A. Senn. (1994). *Information literacy: Educating children for the 21st century.* Scholastic.

Callison, D. (1986). School library media programs and free inquiry. *School Library Journal, 32* (6), 20–24. Also in L. N. Gerhardt (Ed.) and M. L. Miller (Comp.).,*School library journal's best* Neal Schuman, 1997.

Callison, D. (1995). Expanding the evaluation role in the critical-thinking curriculum. In *Information for a new age: Redefining the librarian* (153–169). Libraries Unlimited.

Colorado Department of Education and the Colorado State Library. (1996). Information literacy guidelines: Assessment for information literacy and assessment of school library media programs. *Indiana Media Journal, 18* (4), 39–71.

Craver, K. W. (1990). Critical thinking: Implications for library research. In B. Woolls (Ed.)., *The research of school library media centers* (121–134). Hi Willow Research and Publishing.

Donham, J., K. Bishop, C. C. Kuhlthau, and D. Oberg. (2001). *Inquiry-based learning: Lessons from* Library Power. Linworth Publishing.

Doyle, C. S. (1994). *Information literacy in an information society: A concept for the information age.* ERIC Clearinghouse on Information and Technology.

Eisenberg, M. B. (1984). Curriculum mapping and implementation of an elementary school library media skills curriculum. *School Library Media Quarterly, 12* (1), 411–418.

Eisenberg, M. B., and R. E. Berkowitz. (1988). *Curriculum Initiative: An agenda and strategy for library media programs.* Ablex Publishing.

Eisenberg, M. B., C. A. Lowe, and K. L. Spitzer. (2004*). Information literacy: Essential skills for the information age.* 2d ed. Libraries Unlimited.

Fitzgerald, M. A. (2000). Critical thinking 101: The basics of evaluating information. *Knowledge Quest, 29* (2), 13–20.

Fitzgerald, M. A. (1999). Evaluating information: An information literacy challenge. *School Library Media Research, 2.* http://www.ala.org/ala/aasl/SLMR/ (accessed November 29, 2005).

Harada, V. H. (2003). Empowered learning: Fostering thinking across the curriculum. In B. K. Stripling and S. Hughes-Hassell (Eds.), *Curriculum connections through the library* (41–65). Libraries Unlimited.

Harada, V. H., and J. M. Yoshina. (2004). *Inquiry learning through librarian-teacher partnerships.* Linworth.

Kuhlthau, C. C. (1985). *Teaching the library research process: A step-by-step program for secondary school students.* Center for Applied Research in Education.

Kuhlthau, C. C. (1987). An emerging theory of library instruction. *School Library Media Quarterly, 16* (1), 23–28.

Liesener, J. W. (1984). Learning at risk: School library media program in an information world. In *Libraries and the learning society* (69–75). ALA.

Loertscher, D. V. (1985). Collection mapping: An evaluation strategy for collection development. *Drexel Library Quarterly, 21*(2, Spring), 9–39.

Loertscher, D. V., and B. Woolls. (2002). *Information literacy: Review of the research.* 2d ed. Hi Willow Research and Publishing.

Mancall, J. C. (1991). (Un)changing factors in the searching environment: Collections, collectors, and users. *School Library Media Quarterly, 20* (2), 84–89.

Mancall, J. C., S. L. Aaron, and S. A. Walker. (1986). Educating students to think: The role of the school library media program. *School Library Media Quarterly, 15* (1), 18–27. Also available online at http://www.ala.org/aasl/SLMR/slmr_resources/select_mancall.html (accessed January 21, 2001).

National Forum on Information Literacy. P. S. Breivik, Chair. n.d. http://www.infolit.org (accessed March 15, 2002).

Newmann, F. M., W. G. Secada, and G. G. Wehlage. (1995). *A guide to authentic in-*

struction and assessment: Vision, standards and scoring. Wisconsin Center for Education Research.

Pappas, M. L., and A. E. Tepe. (2002). *Pathways to knowledge and inquiry learning.* Libraries Unlimited.

Resnick, L. B., L. E. Klopfer, and L. Resnick (Eds.). (1989). *Toward the thinking curriculum: Current cognitive research.* Association for Supervision and Curriculum Development.

Rossoff, M. (1955). *The library in high school teaching.* H. W. Wilson.

Rossoff, M. (1971). *The school library and educational change.* Libraries Unlimited.

Sheingold, K. (1987). Keeping children's knowledge alive through inquiry. *School Library Media Quarterly, 16* (2), 80–85.

Small, R. V., and M. P. Arnone. (2000). Turning Kids on to research: The power of motivation. Libraries Unlimited.

Stripling, B. (1989). Rethinking the school library: A practitioner's perspective. *School Library Media Quarterly, 18* (4),136–139.

Stripling, B., and J. Pitts. (1988). *Brainstorms and blueprints.* Libraries Unlimited.

Stripling, B. K. (2003). Inquiry-based learning. In B. K. Stripling and S. Hughes-Hassell (Eds)., *Curriculum connections through the library* (3–39). Libraries Unlimited.

Thomas, N. P. (2004). Information Literacy and Information Skills Instruction. 2d edition. Libraries Unlimited.

Thompson, H. M., and S. A. Henley. (2000). *Fostering information literacy: Connecting national standards, goals 2000, and the SCANS report.* Libraries Unlimited.

Tyner, K. R. (1998). *Literacy in a digital world: Teaching and learning in the age of information.* Erlbaum Associates.

Walker, H. T., and P. K. Montgomery. (1976). *Teaching media skills: An instructional program for elementary and middle school students.* Libraries Unlimited.

Walster, D. (1995). Student-centered information literacy programs: The Colorado vision. In B. J. Morris, J. L. McQuiston, and C. L. Saretsky (Eds.), *School Library Media Annual* (45–53). Libraries Unlimited.

Walster, D., and L. Welborn. (1996). Writing and implementing Colorado's information literacy guidelines. *School Library Media Activities Monthly, 12* (6), 25–28, 36.

Wisconsin Educational Media Association. (1993). *Information literacy: A position paper on information problem-solving.* WEMA. (ED 376 817).

Zweizig, D. L., and D. McAfee-Hopkins. (1999). *Lessons from* Library Power: *Enriching teaching and learning.* Libraries Unlimited and Teacher Ideas Press.

Chapter 3

Information Search and
Use Models

Daniel Callison

The information search and use models presented in this chapter are foundational to other models that have tended to give greater emphasis to the concepts of inquiry. Most of these models were created in the 1980s, when much of the thinking in the school library media field was just emerging from only how to teach basic library skills. Each model presented here was responsible for taking many school media specialists beyond simply teaching students information location skills. These models established much of the baseline for helping students and teachers address the dramatically increasing amount of information becoming available, even to those in elementary schools.

Elements of inquiry have been applied to some of these models based on recent field research and curriculum plans. The systematic approach to information problem solving is clearly present in these models. Each model provides an organization for information searching and use. Each model has taken into account the developmental abilities and emotions of the student researcher. Most have been developed and tested in a secondary school setting or an undergraduate academic institution. Most are derived from observation of students who have been successful in completion of academic assignments such as term papers, oral reports, and multimedia presentations.

The models presented here are the early building blocks to help learners manage the Information Age. Recent electronic tools, such as WebQuest (Dodge 2001) and NoodleTools (Abilock and Abilock 2005), are presented alongside to illustrate how these information search and use models can be translated to serve students and teachers well in searching and using the ever-expanding electronic information base.

Pathfinders

The Pathfinder model evolved in the 1970s from the use of annotated bibliographies (Borne 1996). The intention, however, was to give more than a list of selected resources organized by format, date, or author. Use of the Pathfinder outlined an approach to the library collection, a way to think about how to trace information on a given subject. The Pathfinder provided a visual connection of resources, working from general background resources to provide a beginning for understanding the topic before tracing the more specific resources. Not all possible resources are given, but rather key items along with key words for online searching and key classification numbers for browsing (Kapoun 1995).

The Pathfinder provides a map of key resources and access points on a given topic, across all formats, and, in some cases, to resources beyond the local library collection. The structure of the Pathfinder, or research guide, can give the student a sense of organization and a rich picture of potential resource options. An assumption, often false, is that the user will not only locate necessary information on the topic, but will grasp the layout of the Pathfinder as a search strategy that can be used for nearly any topic to be investigated. While some students make this leap, others require guidance and strong coaching in order to understand how to apply this search strategy to other situations.

While the Pathfinder may help the student explore the resource options, this method does little to aid the student in formulation of specific questions and seeking precise information. On the other hand, Pathfinders can, if they are easily available and cover a wide spectrum of topics relevant to the needs of the student, provide encouragement to the novice that these topics of interest are valid ones to explore.

Virtual Guides

With the growing number of school libraries providing research guides online, the Pathfinder approach has had a renewal in design and use. Similar to the WebQuest design discussed later in this chapter, electronic Pathfinders can be created by teachers and students as well as the school library media specialist to provide a tested path to useful resources and search strategies online. Joyce Kasman Valenza (2006), director of the high school (virtual) library at Springfield Township in Pennsylvania, describes her approach:

> Pathfinders are generally customized to meet the needs of a particular group of students for a particular assignment. Students click on a given topic [from selected titles contained in the school media center's website] and find a pathfinder laid out for them that includes potential keywords, definitions of key concepts, pertinent questions [perhaps based on questions found useful by previous students], call numbers for circulating and reference books, relevant print magazines and newspapers, subscription databases, quality subject-area portals, relevant Web sites, experts that will accept e-mail communication from students, streaming media resources, relevant blogs and wikis, and more.

> Take, for example, the high school junior faced with her first foray into library criticism. The research choices are vast. Without the benefit of an online pathfinder, in the best of all possible research worlds, the student might have some idea of research questions relating to her reading. She might understand what criticism is and what it is not. She might use the online catalog and go to the shelves to locate anthologies likely to contain the essays that

address the questions or references. Perhaps she would also visit major Web portals that gather free literary criticism, some as the one maintained by the Internet Public Library, or several substantial databases, including Gale's Literature Resource Center and Scribner Writers Series. The school librarian would want her to visit the collection of e-books available in the Net-Library and use specific strategies to find the most relevant essay. . . .

> Were a teacher to explain this complicated process of tracking down literary criticism, even the most serious student would probably be confused. When librarians scaffold that lecture—or replace it with an online pathfinder that links to resources and instructional tools [including style manuals] —the problem is magically resolved. (p. 58)

Use of Pathfinders, online or print, can also instill in students a systematic approach to nearly any topic, and an understanding that such paths tend to transfer from one library to the next. Examples of online Pathfinders and design steps are available at the following Web sites:

Designing Pathfinders for Children and Young Adults http://www.eduscapes.com/earth/path3.html

Springfield's Template for Creating Pathfinders http://mciu.org/~spjvweb/pathfinder.html

The Pathfinder Model

Background—Identify a few selected and key reference sources or Web sites, which will provide general overview on the topic, including definition of important terms, events, and people. The student should be encouraged to compile terms and names from these sources as potential subject tracings later. In addition, these background sources may contain bibliographies, which lead to other useful resources the student should obtain.

Browse—List the key classification numbers, either Dewey or Library of Congress, that will lead the user to groups of books to examine. An overview of several shelves may provide some idea of the range of related topics, while skimming the table of contents and indexes may lead to identification of some initial areas of interest and may also begin to give focus to a potential topic.

Subject Tracings—What are the specific subject headings that will lead to accessing information on this topic through the use of the online catalog and other databases? Are there key terms that may work best in Internet searching?

Ephemeral Items—Depending on the topic area, special vertical files may contain clippings that pertain to the topic, especially on a local basis. What topic headings should be considered?

Nonprint—Are there video programs relevant to this topic that provide an overview of the issues or illustrate specific related events?

Fiction—In some cases there may be young adult or classic fiction titles, which are important to read and gain a broader perspective while also refining questions to explore in more detail.

Associations—Some associations, national and local, will respond to requests for additional information and may even have an expert who can be interviewed. Web sites of associations and organizations relevant to the given topic should be listed here.

Suggested Questions—Questions that could help the student begin to focus on a problem area might be provided here and can trigger the more refined search for information.

The Presearch Process

Virginia Rankin (1999) has provided several useful techniques for improving the library research process, especially for middle school students. Perhaps her best contribution has been the advice she provides for the activities that lead up to searching for information, or "the presearch process." Although not a model as are others presented here, her techniques can be bundled into two strategy groups that include techniques and considerations to gain a more sure footing before entering the larger search for information on an assigned topic:

- Presearch Strategies

  - Learn to read for highlights, key words, and definitions.
  - Build a vocabulary of names and nouns that will likely take you to more information.
  - Relax, read, and reflect—read reference materials, popular materials, items that help to feed your curiosity and that you understand.
  - Brainstorm, take initial notes, categorize terms and ideas.

- Generate Workable Questions

  - Consider questions that interest you and will likely interest others.
  - Derive questions from presearch reading, but be prepared to revise questions as you explore more.
  - Find a balance between topics that are too broad and too narrow—consider time and resource limitations.
  - Consider options for presenting your findings—what format is assigned, best suited to your skills, most likely to convey a meaningful presentation? Will the format influence the illustrations, figures, and charts you might include?

Computerized Research Assistant

Ann Bevilacqua (1993), as a university reference librarian, was one of the first to use interactive computerized instruction to create a series of steps and functions that would assist the student researcher in either a high school or college library environment. Her software could be revised to match specific collections and local calendars. Heavy on planning, organization, and time management, Bevilacqua's Research Assistant helped students brainstorm topics, focus on emerging online databases, and prepare to write within a reasonable time frame. In many ways "ahead of their time," the software and process were especially useful to high school audiences, but many teachers and school media specialists were not ready for the computerized assistance.

Ten Steps of the Research Assistant

1. Understand the assignment.
2. Select a topic.
3. Do some general reading on the topic.
4. Formulate a thesis.
5. Do research in the library.
6. Make an outline.
7. Write a first draft.
8. Get supporting material for your argument.
9. Review and revise.
10. Put paper in final form.

Yucht's Flip It!

A creative educator and leader of workshops in student research method, Alice Yucht (1997) developed FLIP IT! in 1988 as a four-stage, nonlinear research process (McCarthy 2003; Taylor 2006). Refined over recent years to include use of electronic resource searching, Yucht's approach strives to instill in students IT—Intelligent Thinking:

Focus—keywords and search terms to be used

Links—locations and call numbers of resources

Input—kinds of information needed; note taking and bibliographic information

Proprieties—use a variety of sources, share materials, put materials away

The Information Search Process (ISP)

Applied in a wide variety of settings from elementary schools to colleges and professional work settings, and tested more extensively than any of the other models offered in this chapter, the Information Search Process (ISP) developed by Carol Kuhlthau (1994) of Rutgers University provides the framework that has changed how many librarian present the library research process. Kuhlthau's work has substantially changed the typical approach given in most grammar and composition texts prior to 1990. The standard

term paper outline, shown below, assumes the student has assimilated the necessary knowledge about the topic and has reached a comfort level with multiple resources to complete a rather complex set of tasks.

Typical Term Paper Steps

1. Select and limit the subject [often based on limits of time and resources without taking into account ideas, background and interests of the student].
2. Prepare a working bibliography—a list of available sources [often restricted to one library, without consideration of alternative ways to gather information such as interviews].
3. Prepare a preliminary outline [before potential research questions are raised].
4. Read and take notes [without exploring the texts for options that might help focus the project and support student interests and abilities].
5. Assemble notes; write the final outline [without reflection on quality of resources and validity of evidence gathered].
6. Write the first draft [with little if any peer review and interaction].
7. Write the revised draft [usually based on feedback from the teacher alone] and add footnotes and bibliography [without time to self-evaluate or to reflect on the process].

These steps clearly represent emphasis on the product, moving from one step to the next to efficiently complete the composition. Time, exercises, and instructor interventions were not provided to enrich and improve the student's ability to search for and to consider the merits of multiple resources prior to moving into the composition. More than any other feature, Kuhlthau's work has moved the exploration stage into the information search process. Understanding that there are phases of student adjustment, both in terms of feelings about the process and in assimilation of new information, new interactions between teacher and learner become critical.

Through the early stages of exploration, information search modeling and use on the part of the instructional media specialist and others teachers is very important. Time for the student to explore, raise questions, and gain a foundation on which to seek focus is extremely beneficial. But all too often, time is a resource that many teachers still do not provide.

Kuhlthau's process relies heavily on library resources and individual student actions to complete the composition. Her work reflects use of library resources prior to full emergence of modern electronic information resources and more extensive access to resources beyond the local library. Stronger emphasis on cooperative learning over the past decade by many educators has highlighted the possibilities for students to work effectively through collaboration in research and writing. Still, Kuhlthau's early ideas have provided one of the most important models in the information skill searching and use arenas. Her work has moved many instructional media specialists to increase the value placed on the processes of search and use, rather than concentrate on evaluation of student performance on the product alone (Kuhlthau 1987, 1991).

Kuhlthau's Prewriting Information Search Process (ISP)

INITIATION

- Task: prepare for the decision of selecting a topic.

- Thoughts: contemplate assignment, prior learning, consider options

- Feelings: apprehension and uncertainty

- Actions: converse with others, browse, write out questions

- Strategies: brainstorm, discuss, tolerate uncertainty

SELECTION

- Task: decide on topic

- Thoughts: compare topic criteria to personal interests, information available, time allotted; predict outcome of possible choices

- Feelings: confusion, anxiety, brief elation after selection, anticipation

- Actions: consult with others; read for overview

- Strategies: discuss options, read widely

EXPLORING INFORMATION

- Task: investigate information with intent to find focus

- Thoughts: unable to always express precise information needed; identify several focus possibilities

- Feelings: confusion, doubt, uncertainty

- Actions: locate relevant information; list interesting facts, ideas, names, and events; maintain bibliographic citations of useful sources and potential leads

- Strategies: tolerate inconsistency and incompatibility of information encountered both within the information and with own assumptions; intentionally seek and frame several focus possibilities; maintain list of descriptors; read to learn more about topic

FORMING FOCUS

- Task: formulate a focus based from information encountered

- Thoughts: predict outcome; consider again personal interest, requirements of the assignment, availability of materials and time

- Feelings: optimism, confidence in ability to complete task

- Actions: consider project themes

- Strategies: choose a particular focus and discard others or combine several themes to form one focus

COLLECTING INFORMATION

- Task: gather information that defines, extends, and supports the focus

- Thoughts: define, extend and elaborate on focus; select most pertinent information, organize information from notes

- Feelings: realize extensive work is completed and gain confidence that the project can be managed; with assimilated knowledge on focus, interest will increase

- Actions: seek out specific resources in libraries or other information collections; take detailed notes relevant to focus and research questions

- Strategies: use descriptors to refine search and locate most pertinent information; be comprehensive in search of all options regardless of format; seek guidance to meet specific information needs

PREPARE TO PRESENT OR WRITE

- Task: conclude search for information

- Thoughts: identify any additional information for specific gaps; also notice most of additional information is redundant and resources options are nearly exhausted

- Feelings: relief, satisfaction, but disappointment if some information needs are not met

- Actions: recheck sources for information overlooked in first review; confirm information and bibliographic citations; organize notes, write outline

- Strategy: return to library to make a summary search to assure all information leads have been exhausted

ASSESSING THE INFORMATION SEARCH PROCESS

- Task: to evaluate the library research process

- Thoughts: an increase in self-awareness; identify problems and successes; understand and plan research strategy for future assignments

- Feelings: sense of accomplishment; perhaps also some disappointment

- Actions: evaluate evidence of meeting focus, use of time, use of resources, use of library and librarian

- Strategies: visualize the process in time line or flow chart; write an evaluative summary statement; discuss process with teacher and librarian

ISP Applied to Inquiry-Based Learning

Kuhlthau's IPS Model was applied in a national series of projects funded in the 1990s under the title Library Power (Zweizig and Hopkins 1999). She and a collaborating team of researchers (Donham, Bishop, Kuhlthau, and Oberg 2001) documented how her strategies enhance student inquiry. Kuhlthau's ideas concerning the stages that encourage students to more fully explore resources prior to a search focus and to assimilate new information as their projects unfold are essential elements. These stages trigger a richer process than simply those topics assigned by teachers without consideration for student input.

In addition, it became clear that teachers and school library media specialists collaborating as instructional media specialists found an agenda for supporting inquiry through team teaching as well as cooperative selection and acquisition of quality resources (Hopkins 1999). If funded adequately, the information-rich collection provides the learning environment necessary to make inquiry methods successful. The end result is not only increased student learning, but an excitement about learning and teaching (Callison 1999).

WebQuest—The Internet Search Process

Bernie Dodge (2001) has defined WebQuest as an inquiry-oriented activity in which some or all of the information that learners interact with comes from resources on the Internet, optionally supplemented with videoconferencing (http://edweb.sdsu.edu/webquest/webquest.html) . He states that there are two levels of WebQuests, based on Marzano's dimensions of learning.

For short-term WebQuests the goal is knowledge acquisition and integration. At the end of the WebQuest, a learner will have grappled with a significant amount of new information and made sense of it. A short-term

WebQuest is designed to be completed in one to three class periods.

For a longer-term WebQuest, the goals include extending and refining knowledge. As a result of this learning experience, the student has analyzed a body of knowledge deeply, transformed it in some way, and demonstrated an understanding of the material by creating something that others can respond to. This experience will typically require a week to a month in a classroom setting.

The templates for development of a WebQuest have grown to be more complex over years of experimentation by thousands of students and teachers. The basic idea remains, however, that each WebQuest site provides

- A clear task description,

- Links to resources needed to address the problem,

- Examples of the process to accomplish the task,

- Guidance on how to sort and display information gathered, and

- A conclusion and summary of what the learner accomplished.

- Encouragement to move to higher learning domains

Dodge favors WebQuests, which draw on the following thinking skills defined by Marzano (1992; Marzano et al. 1988), to extend and refine knowledge:

Comparing—Identifying and articulating similarities and differences between or among things.

Classifying—Grouping things into definable categories on the basis of their attributes.

Inducing—Inferring unknown generalizations or principles from observations or analysis.

Deducing—Inferring unstated consequences and conditions from given principles and generalizations.

Analyzing errors—Identifying and articulating errors in one's own or others' thinking.

Constructing support—Constructing a system of support or proof for an assertion.

Abstraction—Identifying and articulating the underlying theme or general pattern of information.

Analyzing perspectives—Identifying and articulating personal perspectives about issues.

Manzano (1992) identifies two more dimensions of learning:

Using knowledge meaningfully—The application of knowledge to complete a meaningful and constructive task during which skills of decision making, problem solving, invention, investigation, and experimental inquiry are applied.

Productive habits of mind—According to Manzano, this is the highest dimension of learning according, as the learner has matured in development of habits that regulate his or her behavior and approach to new tasks.

He continues with the following outline:

Critical thinking:
- be accurate and seek accuracy
- be clear and seek clarity
- maintain an open mind
- restrain impulsivity
- take a position when the situation warrants it
- respond appropriately to others' feelings and level of knowledge

Creative thinking:
- persevere
- push the limits of your knowledge and abilities
- generate trust and maintain your own standards of evaluation
- generate new ways of viewing a situation

Self-regulated thinking:
- monitor your own thinking
- plan appropriately
- identify and use necessary resources
- respond appropriately to feedback
- evaluate the effectiveness of your actions

NoodleTools for Internet-Based Searching

Developed by a mother and son team, Debbie and Damon Abilock (2005), NoodleTools is an amazing collection of online tools designed and selected to help the student researcher at all levels, but especially in dealing with electronic documents (http://www.noodletools.com). A basic function is provision of an online framework for bibliography software, Noodlebib, and an inquiry-related research model is also provided. Debbie Abilock, editor of the American Association of School Librarians' professional journal *Knowledge Quest,* has formulated the model from years of experience as a school library media specialist and consultant. Her eight building blocks for research and selected description of student skills and strategies are:

- Engaging
  - Browses
  - Reads
  - Visualizes
  - Imagines
  - Questions
  - Discusses

- Defining
  - Self-questions
  - Activates prior knowledge

- Initiating
  - Brainstorms, clusters, webs through concept maps or outlines
  - Develops a search plan
  - Identifies potential search engines and sources
  - Develops criteria for evaluation sources

- Locating
  - Understands needs and search options
  - Preassesses the value of sources found

- Examining
  - Applies reading, listening, and viewing strategies
  - Applies questioning skills
  - Differentiates between primary and secondary sources, data, evidence

  - Determines authority, currency, objectivity

- Recording, Sorting, Organizing, Interpreting
  - Uses visual and linear notetaking
  - Highlighting and marginal notes; photocopy blackout; graphic organizers
  - Notes include data, evidence, paraphrased ideas

- Communicating and Synthesizing
  - Communicates effectively
  - Selects format to meet audience
  - Debates, defends, justifies
  - Multimedia presentations, visual enhancements
  - Clear conclusions, solutions, resolutions
  - Generates alternatives
  - Attributes sources

- Evaluating
  - Ongoing feedback on the process
  - Collaborative conferences
  - Self-critical
  - Applies evaluation tools including rubric and matrix formats
  - Addresses questions such as, "What does it mean?" and "Why does it matter?"
  - Proposes future modifications and strategies

Information Use Skills and Problem-Solving Models

An early advocate of a complete information skills process, Ann Irving (1987) gave detail to the skills needed to practice use of library resources. Key to her thinking, however, was the challenge to information users to apply higher order analysis and synthesis skills. Her outline laid the foundation for many that were to follow.

Irving's Study of Information Skills

1. Formulation and analysis of information need
2. Identification and appraisal of likely sources
3. Tracing and locating resources
4. Examining, selecting, and rejecting individual resources

5. Interrogating individual resources

6. Recording and storing information

7. Interpretation, analysis, synthesis, and evaluation of information

8. Organizing, shaping, presenting, or communicating information

9. Evaluation of the assignment

The REACTS Model

As secondary school library media specialists, Barbara Stripling and Judy Pitts (1988) were influenced by their close work with David Loertscher as school library media specialists in Arkansas in the 1980s. Based on Loertscher's Taxonomy for involvement of the media specialist in instruction and Bloom's Taxonomy for learning skills, Stripling and Pitts developed the REACTS model, which shows a progression of cognitive tasks for the student researcher. Lower level skills involve location and recall of facts or explaining the application of answers to who, what, and where questions. Higher level skills are more challenging and require the student to analyze and synthesize information.

REACTS—A Taxonomy for Thoughtful Research

Recalling—Fact finding: reporting on the information

Explaining—Asking and searching: posing who, what, where, and when questions and finding the answers

Analyzing—Examining and organizing: posing why and how problems and organizing information to fit the project

Challenging—Evaluating and deliberating: judging information on the basis of authority, significance, bias, and other factors

Transforming—Integrating and concluding: drawing conclusions and creating a personal perspective based on information obtained

Synthesizing—Conceptualizing: creating original solutions to problems posed

Information Problem Solving (The Big6)

The Big6 (Eisenberg and Berkowitz 1988) is one of the most popular models because of tremendous promotion of the process by the creators, and because in nearly any information problem situation, the model provides an effective way to think through what is needed to address it. The six steps in this model, as well as other similar models, provide a framework for a mental picture that helps the learner visualize the problem-solving process. Young learners gain confidence because they "see" the task can be managed. Applied across grade levels, this model defines terms for student research projects that allow for consistent scope and sequence curriculum (Wolf, Brush, and Saye 2003).

James Herring (2006), professor at Charles Sturt University, Australia, found that his PLUS Model, similar to the Big Six, also provides a useful scaffold for teachers and students to gain confidence in managing large information literacy assignments. Herring's model concentrates on four elements: (1) Purpose of Assignment and Existing Knowledge, (2) Location of Information, (3) Use of Information, and (4) Self- evaluation and Reflection.

Mike Eisenberg and Bob Berkowitz (1990) define the Big6 as an information literacy model, although others reference it as a metacognitive scaffold, and it is more widely classified as an information problem-solving strategy as originally developed by this team. The creators and thousands of practicing school library media specialists attest that the model is an essential framework to approach any information-based question.

Compact and efficient, the following six steps make for an understandable agenda leading to meaningful instructional collaboration between library media specialist and teacher. More important, their model can be understood quickly and therefore is more likely to be applied by learners in elementary as well as secondary school situations.

Information Problem Solving

1. Task Definition

    1.1 Define the problem

1.2 Identify information requirements

2. Information Seeking Strategies

   2.1 Determine range of sources
   2.2 Prioritize sources

3. Location and Access

   3.1 Locate sources
   3.2 Find information

4. Information Use

   4.1 Engage with information (read, view, listen)
   4.2 Extract information

5. Synthesis

   5.1 Organize information
   5.2 Present information

6. Evaluation

   6.1 Judge the product
   6.2 Judge the process

Minnesota's Inquiry Curriculum

Mary Dalbotten (1998), when serving as a consultant and media director at the Minnesota Department of Children, Families and Learning, applied inquiry concepts to information problem solving. Across all areas of the curriculum, the inquiry process was established as one of ten strands for student learning. The result was a dramatic increase in the use of library resources to support this statewide initiative (Kelsey 2006). These strands involved reading, writing, the arts, mathematics, science, cultures, decision making, managing resources, and languages. In all areas of the curriculum, Dalbotten found there were standards and learning activities for students to raise questions and apply data analysis that would imply possible answers. Data collection was broadly defined to include narrative or testimonial evidence as well as quantitative evidence.

Minnesota Inquiry Curriculum

1. Generate Questions: pose significant questions.

2. Determine Feasibility: identify strategy and method to address questions.

3. Collect Data: apply method to locate or generate new data.

4. Reduce and Organize Data: select data which is more relevant, organize to meet questions.

5. Display Data: present data in visual form to summarize and communicate findings.

6. Compile Conclusions and More Questions: What new questions come from this process?

Harada drew on the Minnesota Inquiry Curriculum to illustrate how inquiry can enrich the information problem-solving process based on the Big6 Model across the curriculum:

- **Language Arts**—Literacy appreciation and analysis requires strategic use of language, including being able to predict, validate, and synthesize. It also encourages analysis from multiple points of view and perspectives, and the ability to identify bias and stereotyping. Students are immersed in both literary and nonliterary modes of information. Active engagement is crucial.

- **Social Studies**—Historical analysis involves formulating questions, obtaining data from sources, testing these sources for their accuracy and authority, and detecting and evaluating propaganda and distortion. Students develop comparative and causal analyses and construct sound historical arguments. They use resources ranging from primary documents and artifacts to virtual field studies found on the Internet.

- **Mathematics**—Problem solving in mathematics challenges students to formulate problems, consider alternative strategies to solve them, and apply a strategy and verify results. To accomplish these aspects of problem solving, they must be able to collect, organize, and describe data; construct, read, and interpret displays of data; and formulate and solve problems that involve data collection and analysis. Mathematical inquiry provokes students to make sense of ideas in relation to one another and to the everyday world. The focus is on conceptual understanding, multiple representations, and connections.

- **Science**—Scientific inquiry necessitates that students understand key questions and concepts that guide scientific investigations. They must be able to formulate testable hypotheses, design and conduct the investigations, formulate and revise explanations and models using logic and evidence, and communicate and defend their findings. Students use a wide range of tools and make choices among alternatives. Carefully planned experiments can proceed in a predictable fashion or yield startling data that lead to new questions and investigations. The process is not random; it follows a purposeful sequence of testing, data collection and analysis, and drawing of conclusions.

- **Information Literacy**—Information seeking and use assumes that problems and issues investigated require student engagement with information in different formats and for different purposes. Students must be able to articulate the focus of their information search, generate questions that probe the problem, consider alternative strategies to locate and retrieve data, and evaluate their value and relevance. Students also need to explore organizational schemes to help them store and use their information and to hone their expertise with different communication formats. (2003, 45–46)

A Model for a Portfolio of Information Skills

Discussion has increased over the past two decades concerning the best ways to document student progress in the application of information skills. With the new emphasis on valuing the process as much as the product, many educators continue to seek ways to document student progress on specific inquiry skills. A series of questions associated with the process can serve as an outline or model for the contents of a student's information skill portfolio. The specific exercises that might address these skills would, of course, be modified to meet the grade level of the student.

Portfolios constructed over several years can provide evidence of a student's maturation in the information search, selection, and use processes. The following list of questions can provide the foundation for a student portfolio of Information Inquiry processes and products. It has been summarized by Callison (1993) based on the secondary school information curriculum outlined by Marland (1981).

Information Skill Portfolio Questions

What do I need to do?

The student should demonstrate the ability to:

- analyze the information task
- analyze the audience's information need or demand
- describe a plan of operation
- select important or useful questions and narrow or define the focus of the assignment
- describe possible issues to be investigated

Where could I go?

The student should demonstrate the ability to:

- determine the best initial leads to relevant information
- determine possible immediate access to background information (gaining the larger picture)
- consider information sources within and beyond the library

How do I get to the information?

The student should demonstrate the ability to:

- identify relevant materials
- sense relationships between information items (supporting or countering each other; one leading to others based on sources cited)
- determine which resources are most likely to be authoritative and reliable
- consider and state the advantages and disadvantages of bias
- present in resources

- consider discovered facts and search for counterfacts
- consider stated and personal opinions and search for counter opinions
- determine extent of need for historical perspective

How shall I use the resources?

The student should demonstrate the ability to:

- determine if the information is pertinent to the topic
- estimate the adequacy of the information
- test validity of the information
- focus on specific issues within the boundaries of the information obtained group data in categories according to appropriate criteria
- determine the advantages and disadvantages of different information formats and intellectual levels

Of what should I make a record?

The student should demonstrate the ability to:

- extract significant ideas and summarize supporting, illustrative details
- define a systematic method to gather, sort, and retrieve data
- combine critical concepts into a statement of conclusions
- restate major ideas of a complex topic in concise form
- separate a topic into major components according to appropriate criteria
- sequence information and data in order to emphasize specific arguments or issues

Have I got the information I need?

The student should demonstrate the ability to:

- recognize instances in which more than one interpretation of material is valid and necessary
- demonstrate that the information obtained is relevant to the issues of importance if necessary, state a hypothesis or theme and match evidence to the focused goal of the paper or project

- reflect, edit, revise, and determine if previous information search and analysis steps should be repeated

How should I present it?

The student should demonstrate the ability to:

- place data in tabular form using charts, graphs, or illustrations
- match illustrations and verbal descriptions for best impact
- note relationships between or among data, opinions, or other forms of information
- propose a new plan, create a new system, interpret historical events, and/or predict likely future happenings
- analyze the background and potential for reception of ideas and arguments by the intended audience
- communicate orally and in writing to teachers and peers

What have I achieved?

The student should demonstrate the ability to:

- accept and give constructive criticism
- reflect and revise again, and again if necessary
- describe the most valuable sources of information
- estimate the adequacy of the information acquired and judge the need for additional resources
- state future questions or themes for investigation
- seek feedback from a variety of audiences

References

Abilock, D., and D. Abilock. (2005). NoodleTools, Inc. http://www.noodletools. com (accessed December 27, 2005).

Bevilacqua, A. (1993). Research assistant. In L. Hardesty, J. Hastreiter, and D. Henderson. (Eds.). *Bibliographic instruction in practice: A tribute to the legacy of Evan Ira Farber* (77–90). Pierian Press. Research Assistant is copyright by Ann Bevilacqua.

Borne, B. W. (1996). *100 research topic guides for students.* Greenwood Press.

Callison, D. (1993). The potential for portfolio assessment. *School Library Media Annual, Volume 11* (30–39).Libraries Unlimited

Callison, D. (1999). A site-level Library Power case study of Lincoln, Nebraska: Educational excellence on the plains. *School Libraries Worldwide, 5* (2), 4562.

Dalbotten, M. S. (1998). Inquiry in the national content standards. In D. Callison, J. McGregor and R. Small (Eds.), *Instructional interventions for information use.* Hi Willow Research. Reprinted in M. B. Eisenberg, C. A. Lowe, and K. L. Spitzer (Eds.), *Information literacy.* Libraries Unlimited, 2004.

Dodge, B. (2001). The WebQuest Page at San Diego State University. http://edweb.sdsu. edu/webquest/webquest.html (accessed June 28, 2001).

Donham, J., K. Bishop, C. C. Kuhlthau, and D. Oberg. (2001). *Inquiry-based learning: Lessons from* Library Power. Linworth Publishing.

Eisenberg, M. B., and R. E. Berkowitz. (1988). *Curriculum initiative: An agenda and strategy for library media programs.* Norwood, NJ: Ablex.

Eisenberg, M. B., and R. E. Berkowitz. (1990). *Information problem-solving: The Big Six Skills approach to library and information skills instruction.* Ablex. The Big6 is copyright 1987 by Michael B. Eisenberg and Robert E. Berkowitz. http://www.big6.com (accessed December 27, 2005).

Harada, V. H. (2003). Empowered learning: Fostering thinking across the curriculum. In B. K. Stripling and S. Hughes-Hassell (Eds.), *Curriculum connections through the library* (41–65).Libraries Unlimited.

Herring, J. E. (2006) A critical investigation of students' and teachers' views on the use of information literacy skills in school assignments. *School Library Media Research, 9.* http://www.ala.org/SLMR (accessed July 1, 2006).

Hopkins, D. M. (1999). The school library collection: An essential building block to teaching and learning. *School Libraries Worldwide, 5* (2), 1–15.

Irving, A. (1985). *Study and information skills across the curriculum.* Heinemann Educational Books.

Kapoun, Jim M. (1995). Re-thinking the library pathfinder. *College and Undergraduate Libraries, 2* (1), 93–105.

Kelsey, M. E. (2006). Education reform in Minnesota: Profile of learning and the instructional role of the school library media specialist. *School Library Media Research, 9.* www.ala.org/aasl/SLMR/ (accessed June 30, 2006).

Kuhlthau, C. C. (1987). Emerging theory of library instruction. *School Library Media Quarterly, 16* (1), 23–27.

Kuhlthau, C. C. (1991). The process approach to bibliographic instruction. In L. Shirato (Eds.), *Judging the validity of information sources* (7–14)Pierian Press. .

Kuhlthau, C. C. (1994). *Teaching the library research process.* 2d ed. Scarecrow Press.

Marland, M. (1981). *Information skills in the secondary curriculum.* Methuen.

Marzano, R. J. (1992). *A different kind of classroom: Teaching with dimensions of learning.* Association for Supervision and Curriculum Development.

Marzano, R. J., et al. (1988). *Dimensions of thinking: A framework for curriculum and instruction.* Association for Supervision and Curriculum Development.

McCarthy, C. A. (2003). FLIP IT! An information literacy framework that really works for all ages! *School Library Media Activities Monthly, 19* (7), 22–23, 30.

Rankin, V. (1999). The thoughtful researcher. Libraries Unlimited.

Stripling, B. K., and J. M. Pitts. (1988). *Brainstorms and blueprints: Library research as a thinking process.* Libraries Unlimited.

Taylor, J. (2006). *Information literacy and the school library media center.* Libraries Unlimited.

Valenza, J. K. (2006). The virtual library. *Educational Leadership, 63* (4), 54–49.

Wolf, S., T. Brush, and J. Saye. (2003). The Big Six information skills as a metacognitive scaffold. *School Library Media Research, 6.* http://www.ala.org/SLMR (accessed December 27, 2005).

Yucht, A. (1997). *FLIP IT!: An information skills strategy for student researchers.* Linworth Publishing.

Zweizig, D. L., and D. M. Hopkins. (1999). *Lessons from Library Power: Final report on the evaluation of the national library power initiative of the DeWitt Wallace Reader's Digest Fund.* Libraries Unlimited.

Additional Web Sites for Pathfinders and WebQuests

Internet Public Library. Pathfinders. http://www.ipl.org/div/pf/entry/48496 (accessed August 13, 2006)

Ohio State University Libraries. Net Tutor. Resources Guides. http://liblearn.osu.edu/tutor/resources.html (accessed August 9, 2006)

Ralph, R. D. Ambergris: A pathfinder and annotated bibliography. http://www.netstrider.com/documents/ambergris/ (accessed August 9, 2006)

San Diego City Schools. Technology Challenge Grants. WebQuests. http://projects.edtech.sandi.net/projects/featured/featured.html (accessed August 1, 2006)

Saskatoon School Division Teacher Resources. Webquest! http://sesd.sk.ca/teacherresource/webquest.html (accessed August 10, 2006)

Spartanburg County School District Three. WebQuests. http://www.spa3.k12.sc.us/WebQuests.html (accessed August 10, 2006)

WebQuest Page. http://webquest.sdsu.edu/ (accessed August 1, 2006)

WebQuests.com. http://bestwebquests.com/ (accessed August 10, 2006)

WebQuest News. http://webquest.org/news/index.html (accessed August 13, 2006)

Chapter 4

Models for Information Inquiry, Composition, and Scientific Method

Daniel Callison

Models selected for this chapter will illustrate how the inquiry method has been summarized and applied to student academic activities supported by school library media programs and usually tied to writing and reporting in language arts, social science, and science curricula. Although Carol Kuhlthau's Information Search Process (ISP) is not included in this chapter (see Chapter 3), her research and development of the ISP Model and her many articles based on that model are essential to understanding and applying inquiry-based teaching and learning. No instructional media specialist should move into the field believing he or she is information literate without through study of Kuhlthau's work.

The models presented in this chapter are not the only models available, but they do serve to illustrate the evolution in how inquiry has been defined and validated as a powerful approach to both learning and teaching. Often very similar to the information search and use models described in the previous chapter, most of these models have their roots in the systematic outlines that have been proven to help students and teachers visualize the steps to effective and efficient information problem solving.

A model provides a visual example of the whole, although often it is not possible to represent the full dynamics of the process, or actions within a model. Therefore, in some cases the model may constitute a subset of the whole and illustrate the relationship among some specific tasks, skills, steps, or objectives. A common model is a taxonomy or a classification of abilities, attitudes, or actions according to some organized structure, usually working from the lowest and most simple to the highest and most complex.

The term *model* implies something or someone of exemplary status worthy of imitation. Factors from various situations, however, lead to modification of models in order for reasonable goals to be accomplished. The ability to comprehend and adjust for these factors is a key skill of the instructional media specialist, and that ability moves the specialist beyond the common expectations held of school librarians.

A process is a series of actions that lead toward a result or conclusion. The conclusion in the learning process is often the student's report or response to his or her questions or those questions assigned by others. This product is often the only item evaluated, when the processes involved may hold evidence of student performance, which are as valuable to evaluate. Thus, models may be presented as a way to identify the components of a process so that interventions to help students learn at point of need can be accomplished in an effective and efficient manner.

The models presented in this chapter are based on notions from individuals who have created them as ideal or best practice. Some are based on observation of student and teacher behavior in their search for and use of information. Others are based on practices of model teachers who design and present lessons. Other models illustrate specific learning processes the student experiences as he or she encounters new information and needs to assimilate it. In nearly all cases, these models are constructed from the basic components of Information Inquiry (Callison 1999, 2002, 2003):

Questioning > raising the information need, framing worthwhile wonderings

Interactions with >

Exploration > reading, viewing, listening, observing, considering, linking sources

Processes progress to next interactions >

Assimilation > accepting, incorporating or rejecting; linking to current knowledge

Interactions with >

Inference > application for solution, predicting and deriving meaning for self or sharing

Interactions considered by >

Reflection > evaluating process or product, adjustment for additional questioning

Recycles for new information, question, need, task, process or product >

Figure 4.1. Elements and interactions of Information Inquiry. Copyright 1999, 2002, 2003 Daniel Callison. Reprinted from *Key Words, Concepts and Methods for Information Age Instruction*, Daniel Callison, LMS Associates, 2003, page 5.

Models, although linear in presentation, assume interaction among the elements or steps described. The cycles are both internal or within the process as well as a representation of the external whole. The illustrations of the processes of learning are often similar, although each model will represent a slightly different application of these processes. Interactions among the information search stages, the learning stages, and among learners and mentors are difficult to illustrate in still linear stages and flat illustrations. The reader should consider in all models how the elements of inquiry cycle and recycle to form new questions and information assimilation.

An additional task of the instructional media specialist is to study these models and to consider situations in which a given model may best suit the needs of the teacher and learner. The result may be use of various models to better construct, organize, and manage the information environment so that adjustments can be made to search, access, and use information to meet the learner's abilities as well as information needs. Models provide illustration of search, learning, and teaching approaches that are likely to provide a high level of success if they are applied by thoughtful instructional media specialists.

The models are presented below under citations to key resources in which the model has been explained in more detail. Nancy Pickering Thomas of Emporia State University has provided an informative comparison of many of the library skills and information literacy models in *Information Literacy and Information Skills Instruction* (2004). Her insights are extremely valuable and should be examined along with the sketches of the models provided here.

Inquiry Models

Daniel Callison (1986) introduced several concepts from free inquiry methods in science education to the role of the school library media specialist. His argument was based on the premise that school librarians need to take a more active role in teaching and providing a facility that encouraged inquiry learning. Lessons and activities in the school library need to be more than an orientation to information tools housed in the library. Lecture presentations and worksheet activities fail to stimulate inquiry and hands-on learning that can result in more effective use of information resources. Collaboration among teachers and students as well as the school library media specialist should foster thematic units that raise student-generated questions and move access to information beyond the walls of the school.

Concepts from Callison's Free Inquiry Model for Teaching and Learning (1986)

- Cooperative learning is encouraged and honored.

- Objectives for the lesson are evolutionary and negotiated between student and teacher.

- Students document the processes of learning and share them with others.

- Content is driven by questions that students raise and answer (leading to more questions) by exploring resources in the library and beyond, and through interviews.

- The teacher provides direction for learning, but students are encouraged to take initiatives and work independently in small groups.

- Time for learning is flexible and may run over a full semester or year.

- Peer tutoring is encouraged.

- Peer interaction and teaming are supported and rewarded; students share discovery of information and evidence.

- Projects are shared with peers and parents in celebrations.

- Students may choose to extend their learning beyond the project and develop more expertise as they continue through their schooling.

Relationships Among Literacy and Inquiry (1998)

In 1998, Carol Tilley and Daniel Callison illustrated how the inquiry process includes learning skills associated with critical and creative thinking found in information literacy or media literacy. These components were illustrated as being overlapping and inclusive in inquiry instructional methods.

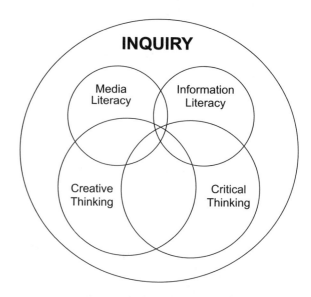

Figure 4.2. Relationships among media literacy, information literacy, creative thinking, and critical thinking within inquiry. Daniel Callison and Carol Tilley. Copyright 2000, 2003, 2006. Reprinted from *Key Words, Concepts and Methods for Information Age Instruction*, Daniel Callison, LMS Associates, 2003, page 39.

David Loertscher and Blanch Woolls (2002) included many examples of information use and inquiry models in their review of information literacy literature. Loertscher created the following model to illustrate the inquiry process, based on their review. The model shows interactions to be student-centered an in an evolving cycle for implementation.

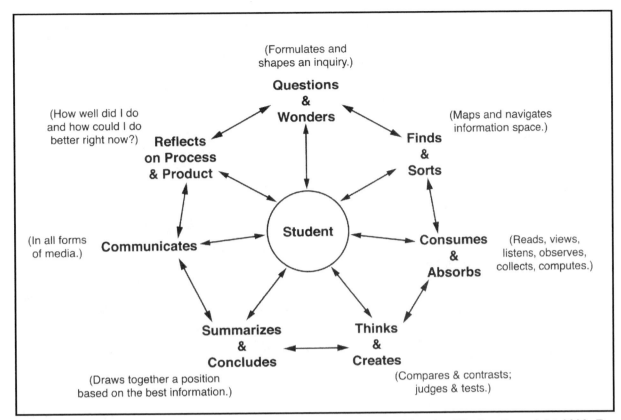

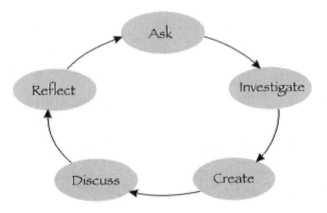

Figure 4.3. Student-centered inquiry cycle. David Loertscher and Blanche Woolls. Copyright 2002. Reprinted with permission from David Loertscher.

Designed in 1998, The Inquiry Page (Bruce, Bishop, and Bryan 2003) is a Web site (http://inquiry.uiuc.edu/) for a virtual community where inquiry-based education can be discussed and lesson plans shared. This group is centered at the University of Illinois. Their model features a continuous cycle, although inquiry is usually started with asking questions and followed by investigating solutions, creating new knowledge, discussing discoveries and experiences, and reflecting on new-found knowledge. Recognized as an award-winning model for teaching in academic settings by the Association for Library and Information Science Educators in 2006, this inquiry model has been the basis for many community learning projects as well.

Figure 4.4. Inquiry page model. Bertram C. Bruce and the Inquiry Project, University of Illinois at Urbana-Champaign. Copyright 1998. Reprinted with permission from Bertram Bruce.

8Ws Model for Information Literacy (2001)

Drawing from the basic 5Ws of newspaper reporting (who, what, where, when, and why), Annette Lamb (2001) expanded this alliterated structure based on influence from information use models (outlined later in this chapter). Her list is given in a cycle similar to other models, but she keeps the process open, allowing for entry at any point for the inquiry process to spark. Questions for inquiry come from personal issues more than from academic assignments.

- **Watching (Exploring)** asks students to explore and become observers of their environment. It asks students to become more in tune with the world around them, from family needs to global concerns.

- **Wondering (Questioning)** focuses on brainstorming options, discussing ideas, identifying problems, and developing questions.

- **Webbing (Searching)** directs students to locate, search for, and connect ideas and information. One piece of information may lead to new questions and areas of interest. Students select those resources that are relevant and organize them into meaningful clusters.

- **Wiggling (Evaluating)** is often the toughest phase for students. They're often uncertain about what they've found and where they're going with a project. Wiggling involves evaluating content, along with twisting and turning information to look for clues, ideas, and perspectives.

- **Weaving (Synthesizing)** consists of organizing ideas, creating models, and formulating plans. It focuses on the application, analysis, and synthesis of information.

- **Wrapping (Creating)** involves creating and packaging ideas and solutions. Why is it important? Who needs to know about this? How can I effectively convey my ideas to others? Many packages get wrapped and rewrapped before they are given away.

- **Waving (Communicating)** is communicating ideas to others through presenting, publishing, and sharing. Students share their ideas, try out new approaches, and ask for feedback.

- **Wishing (Assessing)** is assessing, evaluating, and reflecting on the process and the product. Students begin thinking about how the project went and consider possibilities for the future.

YouthLearn—2001

The YouthLearn Initiative (2001) is part of the Education Development Center in Massachusetts (http://www.youthlearn.org). Student projects are based on an inquiry process and enhanced with application of technology to present student findings. Questions are raised concerning the value of information located, and the inquiry process model condenses the key questions under four stages:

- Pose Real Questions

  - What do I want to know about this topic?
  - What do I know about my question?
  - How do I know it?
  - What do I need to know?
  - What could an answer be?

- Find Resources

  - What kinds of resources might help?
  - Where do I find them?
  - How do I know the information is valid?
  - Who is responsible for the information?
  - What other information is there?

- Interpret Information

  - How is this relevant to my question?
  - What parts support my answer?
  - How does it relate to what else I know?
  - What parts do not support my answer?
  - Does it raise new questions?

- Report Findings

  - What is my main point?
  - Who is my audience?
  - What else is important?
  - How does it connect?
  - How do I use media to express my message?

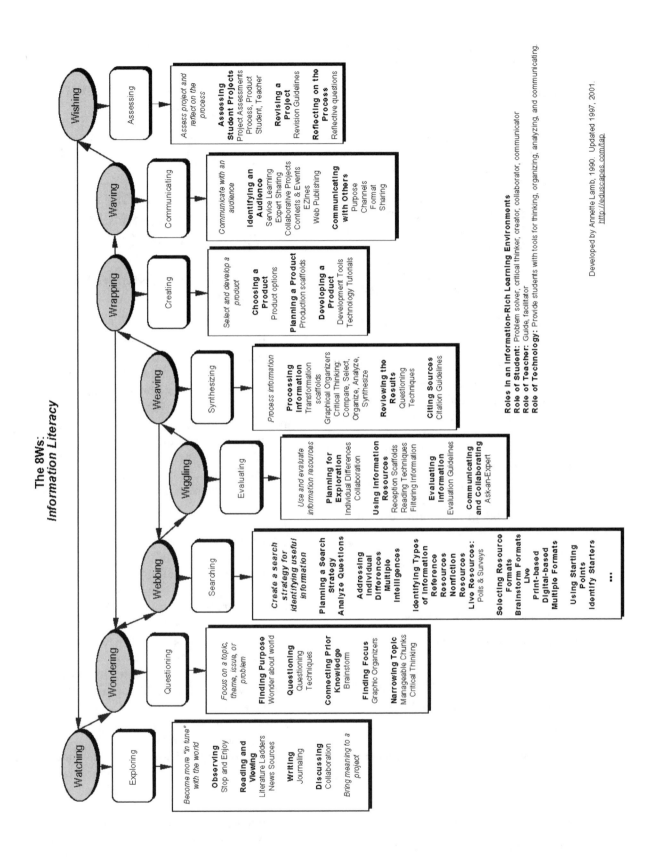

Figure 4.5. The 8Ws: Information literacy. Developed by Annette Lamb, 1990. Updated 1997, 2001.

Models for Information Inquiry, Composition, and Scientific Method

The McKenzie Questioning Research Cycle (2001)

McKenzie opens *Beyond Technology* with these statements:

> Questions and questioning may be the most powerful technologies of all. How might this be so? Questions allow us to make sense of the world. They are the most powerful tools we have for making decisions and solving problems, for inventing, changing and improving our lives as well as the lives of others. Questioning is central to learning and growing. An unquestioning mind is one condemned to "feeding" on the ideas and solutions of others. An unquestioning mind may have little defense against the data smog so typical of life in this Information Age. (2001, 1)

McKenzie's message is central to the inquiry process. Too often students are asked to use resources to "find out" or "cut and paste" without the challenge to raise and answer their own questions. Learning to formulate questions both as an individual and with groups is the most essential skill in the research cycle. McKenzie sees students in a more productive mode when they move through the Research Cycle several times before they begin to determine what they will report.

McKenzie's Research Cycle

Determine the essential questions.

Determine subsidiary questions.

Develop a research plan—what sources are needed?

Gather information—skim and select.

Synthesize and evaluate findings.

Revise questions.

Revise plan and [revisit or locate more sources].

Gather information again.

Sort and sift information again.

Synthesize [to envision, propose, or invent] and evaluate again.

Revise questions [and focus].

Revise plan [for access to most relevant sources].

Gather [more precise information].

Sort and sift [to show meaning].

Synthesize to [infer and evaluate].

Report findings.

Models That Apply Inquiry to Information Literacy (2002 to 2004)

Pathways to Knowledge and Inquiry

Majorie Pappas and Ann Tepe (2002) developed the Pathways to Knowledge model for Follette Software in 1997 as a framework to show how students and teachers can manage knowledge in the Information Age. Influenced by the information search models that preceded their work, this research team emphasized more inquiry concepts in their model in 2002.

Their model is constructed on the premise that the learning environment of today's student is no longer set within the walls of the school, but rather is everywhere—home, school, the community, libraries, and the Internet. The Follett Information Skills Model shows an expanding field of skills and options for the learner. Students gather information from many formats and are encouraged to use multiple presentation formats to share their discoveries. An interesting feature of this model is the assumption that students will best find interest and focus for their investigations as they gain appreciation for reading, viewing, and writing skills. Focus for inquiry ideas comes with discussing literature, current issues from mass media, and sharing ideas derived from both the established curriculum as well as additional personal interests.

According to Thomas (2004), "Pathways to Knowledge is bimodal in that in includes both an outline and process to guide student research and a plan for teachers and librarians to use in creating integrated information skills lessons. . . . Pathways to Knowledge actually comprises a variety of strategies, that students can employ heuristically as the [information] search proceeds" (53).

Pappas and Tepe (2002) have emphasized the following characteristics of inquiry learning in association with the Pathways Model:

- Students wrestle with big ideas through essential questions. All learning activities are anchored to a larger task or problem.

- Learning reflects a connection to the world we live in.

- Students and instructors assess accomplishment through student demonstration of new knowledge.

- Learners have choices. They must have ownership of the problem-solving process.

- Students interact with others to accomplish goals.

- Students test ideas against alternative views and alternative contexts.

- Students reflect on both the content learned and the process by which they learned it.

Pathways to Knowledge: Follett's Information Skills Model

APPRECIATION

Sensing, Viewing, Listening, Reading, Curiosity, Enjoyment

PRESEARCH

Establish a Focus

Develop an Overview: brainstorm, formulate initial questions, build background, identify key words, relate to prior knowledge, explore general sources

Explore Relationships: define questions, cluster, outline, webbing, listing, and narrowing and broadening

SEARCH

Planning and Implementing Search Strategy Identify Information Providers: home and computer resources, museums, zoos, historical sites, community agencies, libraries, etc.

Select Information Resources and Tools: indexes, people, Internet, media, reference resources, etc.

Seek Relevant Information: skim and scan, interview, confirm information and sources, record information, determine relevancy of information, explore and browse widely

INTERPRETATION

Assessing Usefulness of Information

Reflecting to Develop Personal Meaning

Interpret Information: compare and contrast, integrate concepts, determine patterns and themes, infer meaning, analyze, synthesize, classify, filter, organize, and classify

COMMUNICATION

Construct and Present New Knowledge

Apply Information: choose appropriate communication format, solve a problem, answer a question, and respect intellectual property

Share New Knowledge: compose, design, edit, revise, use most effective medium such as video, report, mural, portfolio, and animation

EVALUATION

Think about the Process and Product

Evaluate: end product, effective communication, redefining new questions, use of resources, meeting personal information needs

Applying Inquiry from British Models and a Focus from Canada

Jennifer Branch and Dianne Oberg, professors at the University of Alberta, teamed on a review of information skill use models that have their roots in the British educational system (2003). Their analysis of several models, including The Nine Step Plan from Marland (1981) and The PLUS Model from Herring (1996), provides these insights:

- From a constructivist viewpoint, it is very difficult for students to seriously engage in inquiry without having developed their knowledge of and interest in the inquiry topic. Time is needed to allow for background knowledge development. Without making those connections, it is often difficult for students to sustain their interest in the topic.

- Models should include a process for development of a topic focus or essential question to be addressed.

- Models often have a limited emphasis on planning. It is essential to help children understand the nature of the inquiry process. This understanding can help sustain students through the messiness of inquiry.

- Today's information search and use models should give more emphasis to critical evaluation of information. Early models tended to not include this process, as it was assumed that, in general, information retrieved from the library collection was valid and age appropriate. Wider information access and greater variations in information authority today make critical examination of information essential.

- Few early models include a variety of methods for students to share their findings beyond a written report. An inquiry model needs to address questions such as what the best way is to share their findings given the audience and the technology available. Sharing modes and media will differ based on factors that include audience, content, and presenter.

- Many models imply but don't explicitly acknowledge the importance of the part of the process that allows students the time and support to make their creation to share inquiry the best it can be. Models should acknowledge the need for reading, revising, rewriting, reworking, reviewing, and revisiting.

The Alberta Inquiry Model

Branch and Oberg facilitated the development of a teaching guide, *Focus on Inquiry* (Alberta Learning 2004). The Alberta Model is presented in detail in that guide, along with excellent examples for development of lessons.

The Alberta Inquiry Model

Phases	Inquiry Skills and Strategies
Planning	Establish Topic and Topic Focus
	Identify Information Sources
	Identify Audience and Presentation Format
	Establish Evaluation Criteria
Retrieving	Develop Information Retrieval Plan
	Locate Resources
	Collect Resources
	Select Relevant Information
Processing	Evaluate Information
	Choose Pertinent Information
	Record Information
	Make Connections and Inferences
Creating	Organize Information
	Create Product
	Think About the Audience
	Revise and Edit

Sharing	Understand the Audience
	Present Findings
	Demonstrate Appropriate Behavior
Evaluating	Evaluate Product
	Evaluate Inquiry Procedures
	Transfer Learning to New Situations, Including Beyond School

Process Assessment from the Alberta Experience

Branch (2003), as coordinator of the Teacher-Librarianship Distance Learning Program at the University of Alberta, collaborated with Diane Galloway Solowan, a practicing school media specialist at Beaumont Composite High School to test implementation of inquiry under the Alberta Model. Among the more useful findings of their work is the manner in which students and teachers were expected to take time to assess various segments of the inquiry process. Students were expected to journal their thoughts, voice their personal assessment in small group discussions, or participate in assessment discussions on major issues with the rest of the class. The time and attention given to reflection at various stages of the process enriched the total learning and teaching experience. Several of the activities and questions used to raise the process assessment are listed below. Many of these are similar to activities Kuhlthau (1985) developed as a result of observing high school students applying the information search process but have been updated to fit an inquiry-based learning context.

Assessing Planning

- Have students create an information pathfinder, step by step plan for gathering resources. [How does this compare to a summary by students at the end of the project showing how they actually located information and how one source may have led to others?]

- Have students write or talk about their perceived needs for their intended audience.

- Have students write or talk about their own inquiry process and compare it with the process of others in the class.

Assessing Retrieving

- Have students discuss strategies to fill gaps in their information retrieval.

- Have students write or talk about their retrieval strategy and what worked and didn't work.

- Have students write or talk about the sources they found most useful and why.

Assessing Processing

- Have students show and discuss graphic organizers they have created and discuss which have been most appropriate to their inquiry.

- Have students evaluate Internet sites for accuracy, objectivity, currency, authority, and content using a rubric or evaluation checklist [and have them discuss their findings].

- Have students write or talk about which resources were most useful for a deeper understanding of their topic and why.

- Have students write and talk about how they are creating ideas new to them and how they are linking those ideas to previous knowledge. [Is their knowledge changing or validated?]

- Have students write and talk about what new questions, problems, issues, and ideas have emerged.

- Have students write or talk about their reasons for sharing their new knowledge in a particular way.

- Have students write and talk about the ways they focused on the needs of their particular audience.

- Have students write and talk about what went well with their sharing and what things they need to improve on.

- Have students write or talk about the experiences of being in an audience—what things they responded to positively and negatively and why. [How will their observations influence how they may share information in the future?]

Applying Inquiry in Indiana and Hawaii

Leslie Preddy, school library media specialist at Perry Meridian Middle School and a leader in the Association for Indiana Media Educators, has developed a series of models and methods for student inquiry in the library research process. Her project was constructed on many of the early articles by Callison at Indiana University and was funded by the Indiana State Department of Public Instruction (http://pmms.msdpt.k12.in.us/imc/Inquiry/). Preddy's ideas and practices have been validated by dozens of other school media specialists in her state. A complete discussion of her model and activities are provided in this book.

Application of inquiry methods in school library settings by collaborative teams has validated many of the original concepts extracted from scientific inquiry education techniques. Violet Harada and Joan Yoshina (2004) from the University of Hawaii have summarized these concepts from their recent field studies in several Hawaiian public schools:

- Questioning is at the center of the learning experience. Real learning involves questions, more than simply the answers.

- Students help to negotiate the direction of the learning. While direct teaching is still valued, instructors spend more time listening to and observing what students do and ask questions that help students gain confidence in finding their own answers.

- Learning is social and interactive. By working cooperatively and collaboratively, people discover creative solutions to difficult situations and develop respect for diverse points of view on an issue.

- Solving problems is an integral part of the process. Students must challenge themselves with questions such as, "Why didn't this work?" and "What can we do next?" Applying systematic reasoning strengthens their abilities to distinguish causes from symptoms.

- Students learn by doing. Rather than learning solely through lectures and exercise sheets, students are engaged in hands-on and minds-on interaction. They perform tasks that require higher-order thinking.

- Products and performances reflect application and transfer of learning. Students not only demonstrate what they understand from their readings, discussions, and observations, but they also display how they might transfer that learning to different situations.

- Assessment is ongoing. It is done continuously, not just at the end of a project. Both students and teachers engage in the crucial aspect of learning as a process. Students assess to see what they are doing well and where they might improve in a specific phase of their work. Instructors assess to determine what's working and where they might modify their teaching.

- Learning is authentic. The learning experiences are linked to issues and situations about which students are genuinely curious and that they are likely to continue to apply the inquiry process to, beyond the academic project.

New Perspectives on Applying Inquiry from New York City

Barbara Stripling (2003), while director of Library Programs for New Visions for Public Schools in New York City, has offered an interpretation of the inquiry process in which she recognizes the need to build on previous knowledge based on Constructivist Theory. She adds skills and strategies to six stages of in inquiry process. The following outline shows Stripling's six stages and selected descriptors.

- Connect

  - Connect to one's own experience.
  - Connect to ideas of others.
  - Connect to previous knowledge and verify its accuracy.
  - Gain background and context.
  - Establish preliminary contact with idea through observation or experience.

- Wonder

  - Develop wonder questions that will lead to new understanding.
  - Frame and develop questions.
  - Make predictions or hypotheses based on prior knowledge, new information, and observations.

- Investigate

  - Plan investigation and develop search strategies.
  - Identify, evaluate, and use multiple sources of information.
  - Find and evaluate information to answer questions.
  - Formulate new questions or hypotheses.

- Construct

  - Organize information and detect relationships among ideas.
  - Draw inferences justified by evidence.
  - Test predictions.
  - Recognize points of view and bias and consider alternatives if necessary.

  - Construct clear and appropriate conclusions.
  - Connect new understanding to previous knowledge.

- Express

  - Select communication based on topic and audience.
  - Evaluate and revise one's own product based on self-assessment and feedback from others.
  - Express new ideas or take action to share learning with others.

- Reflect

  - Set high standards.
  - Reflect with others.
  - Ask new questions.
  - Set new goals for learning through future inquiry.

Virtualinquiry.com— Information Inquiry Online

Based on the book *Key Words, Concepts and Methods for Information Age Instruction: A Guide to Teaching Information Inquiry* (Callison 2003), its revision as this text, and the content of a graduate course in information inquiry that has evolved at Indiana University since 1992, a Web site has been established to illustrate and provide examples of inquiry activities. Virtualinquiry. com was created by Annette Lamb and Daniel Callison, professors at the Indianapolis-based graduate program in school media education. Lamb maintains the site content and teaches online courses related to inquiry, high technology learning, and electronic materials for children and young adults.

The site provides definitions and examples of various levels of inquiry: controlled, guided, modeled, and free. Inquiry is applied on a broad basis to include information problems encountered on a personal, professional, or academic basis. Up-to-date examples of tools and facilities are given along with examples of student work, ranging from typical school settings to personal inquiry exploration over a lifetime. The student as information scientist is an analogy emphasized on the site as well as in later chapters of this book.

Composition Models

The Authoring Cycle

The Authoring Cycle is a process developed by the whole language advocate team of Short, Harste, and Burke (1996) and has been applied in a variety of curricular areas, including introduction to writing and reading in elementary schools. Their cycle reflects the inquiry process and is based on heavy use of reading circles. Kids and teachers read for ideas, share ideas, inquire about more information, and use the process for learning through communication. Many projects are investigations in the local community tied to selected stories, biographies, and trade publications gathered in the classroom and in the school library.

Inquiry, to this team, is what education is about. Teaching reading as inquiry is quite different than teaching reading as comprehension. Writing as inquiry is quite different than writing

as transmission or even expression. Problems are not something to be avoided but opportunities to inquire. The very act of teaching itself becomes a process of inquiry. Both teachers and students are learners and often inquire together (Harste 1994). The elements for classroom inquiry are:

- **Voice**—all children bring language of their experiences and should be encouraged to recontextualize what they bring to the learning situation.

- **Connection**—students should be invited to make connections between what they bring to learning and what others bring. These connections provide a window for both error and expectations for the teacher.

- **Perspective**—knowledge is open rather than fixed. Knowledge changes over time as well as by how we look at it.

Figure 4.6. Underlying process of inquiry in the authoring cycle. Heinemann Publications, Kathy Short and Jerome Harste. Copyright 1996.

- **Tension**—difference, not consensus, propels the learning process. Learners have nothing to learn by concentrating on what they already know. Focusing on the new, the anomaly, the surprise is more efficient. When the surprise makes sense, according to Harste, learning has occurred.

- **Reflection**—learners take time to think about what they have learned as well as what implications it has for how they think and act in the world. The key to understanding reflection is thoughtfulness. Thoughtfulness means that new ideas force learners to adjust old ideas as well as how they act and interact with the world. Learners literally reposition themselves both mentally and physically in the world as a result of learning.

I-Search—Inquiry Finds the Writer in First Person

Marilyn Joyce and Julie Tallman, after field-testing the I-Search process as a research team in Georgia, concluded: "I-Search is an approach to research that uses the power of student interests, builds on personal understanding of the research process, and encourages stronger student writing. Originally developed by a college professor for his freshmen composition students, the I-Search is adaptable for use as a beginning research experience at the third grade or a sophisticated search at the graduate level" (1997, vii).

Frustrated with student papers that dealt with topics of little interest to the students or to him, Ken Macrorie (1988) moved the typical research paper into a personalized learning experience. He shifted many of the assignment parameters normally established by the instructor over to the responsibility of the student. The key task for the student became topic selection. More than thinking of a topic, the student had to think through a topic in an informed manner. This involves more time and effort by the student—to complete background reading, draft portions of a report, and share ideas with others, as well as seeking out experts to interview about the potential of a topic—than is normally provided in the all-too-typical high school term paper.

Through this process, the "topic chooses the student" in that eventually the students discover a set of questions that are personally interesting, so much so that they are motivated to give the time that is needed to explore the resources necessary to investigate the topic. When a student finds that he or she is asking friends, teachers, and parents a standard cycle of questions that the student continues to consider and reconsider, this is a strong indication that a topic for exploration is forming. Personal narrative is the writing style favored over dry third person or technical writing.

Moulton (1999) has labeled this personal approach "the multigenre paper" and encourages students to explore a wide variety of presentation formats (posters, poems, video and multimedia productions, drama, and more) in order to express themselves and their findings in a variety of ways. Some messages and some audiences simply do not fit the traditional approach of just words printed on paper. Students often collect personal artifacts to display with their multigenre papers, and current presentation technologies would provide visual software for multimedia support of these reports.

Students seem to express more personal perspectives under this open style (Duncan and Lockhart 2000). Journals seem to help them document personal observations concerning the issues related to the topic. Joyce and Tallman found value in students also making journal entries to discuss the value of the information sources used and for students to think through alternative ways to gain information. Journaling served to map a reflective pathway for the student as he or she faced the rather complex task of making many content and resource selections normally predetermined by the instructor. Most important, the I-Search Process takes topics out of the encyclopedic format that deals with just the facts and tempts plagiarism. To be personal and to express emotions, opinions, and ideas in-depth, I-Search students rely very much on originality.

The I-Search Steps

I. **Free-write**—give thirty to forty-five minutes to write freely and/or openly discuss what you know and find to be of interest about an issue or topic.

II. **Want to Know**—begin to classify what you know and what you really want to know about a set of issues or topic.

III. **Expert Knowledge**—extend your basic knowledge about the issues through wide reading of materials associated with the topic, but gain in-depth perspectives through interviewing an expert.

IV. **Tell a Story**—share what you know and what you would still like to learn with your classmates through a summary or story of what you have learned and how you gained the information.

V. **Refine**—make some choices about what are the most meaningful things learned for both yourself as well as audiences to whom you may report your findings.

VI. **Specific Research**—seek out the information to address remaining questions in a specific manner.

VII. **Composition Mechanics**—revise and edit the paper for clarity and correct spelling, and to acknowledge the sources of information.

Joyce and Tallman (1997) have summarized the application of the I-Search process with the following outline, which includes interventions on the part of the teacher to help provide guidance to learners as they work through information selection and use.

The I-Search Process

I. Topic Selection [Brainstorming]—Student input . . . topic selects you

A. Webbing

B. Skimming Resources

C. Intervening and Conferencing

D. Sharing

II. Finding Information

A. Generating Research Questions

B. Key Words and Names

C. Background Reading without Notetaking

D. Using Pre-notetaking Sheets and Preparing Bibliographies

E. Reading In-depth

F. Interviewing

III. Using Information

A. Highlighting Texts

B. Double-entry Drafting

C. Reflecting and Conferencing

D. Using Learning Logs

IV. Preparing the I-Search Product

A. Using First Person

B. Telling about Search

C. Using Learning Logs

D. Editing by Peers

V. Transferring the Research Process [to Future Tasks]

The Foxfire Model in Georgia and Cultural Celebration in Kansas

The local student reporting and journal writing approach developed by Eliot Wigginton (1991) in Georgia in the 1970s demonstrated that secondary school students could explore their own heritage through their local culture. The final product included a locally produced magazine with illustrations on a wide range of topics, from hog butchering to log cabin construction. Nationally, the result has included nearly a dozen best-selling books. The foxfire method was based on finding that one spark that would ignite student interest and then supporting that exploration through the basic journalistic model of discovering and reporting on "who, what, where, when, why and how."

Mike Printz, a national figure in young adult literature promotion and whose name is now carried on an annual award for young adult authors, was intrigued by Wigginton's methods and adapted them to his own projects in Topeka,

Kansas. He and his co-librarians and teaching staff guided hundreds of senior high school students through oral history products on local personalities. His philosophy for learning was based on first being a personal model for inquiry by reading extensively himself. Everything interested Mr. Printz. Each new book he read seemed to be the best one ever, and he promoted contemporary literature widely as a school librarian and friend of hundreds of teachers. His review and selection committees established national reading lists for secondary school curriculum for many professional associations, including the American Library Association.

Second, Printz wanted to guide the student researcher in exploring the local culture around the student and to find personal meaning in that heritage, while learning to understand the culture and heritage of others. In his last few years as a school librarian, Printz moved more into celebration of diverse cultures through art and literature. Lynda Miller, art teacher, and Theresa Steinlage, language arts teacher, helped to document these celebrations in *Cultural Cobblestones* (1994).

Celebration of student learning, based on the "Printz philosophy," was to establish through the school library an environment for the entire learning community to engage in a topic or theme. For a month to six weeks (at a few times across the entire school year), Printz would concentrate on the theme to the extent that everyone in the school, including principal, counselors, secretaries, and nearly all parents, would be engaged in the stories, films, books, and displays related to the topic at hand. Dozens of assignments around the school would be associated with the theme. Special student forums would run on numerous evenings in which students would make special presentations, guest speakers would respond to in-depth questions from students and parents, and student multimedia products were presented to inspire future use and future projects by other students.

Thus, student research became a means to provide documents for future learners. Similar to the foxfire projects, student research, writing, and artwork were valued as much as products from the professional ranks. Many of these student-produced programs became documents now housed with the local Kansas State Historical Society. Hundreds of Printz's students have testified how much these experiences influenced their thinking and their life after high school. Inquiry was sparked in school and carried on into life after school. Associating the name Mike Printz with quality contemporary literature that inspires young adults to question and explore issues pertaining to their personal maturation and local environment is much deserved.

A Model for Cultural Celebration

READ—For Enjoyment, Discovery, Ideas, and for Sharing Conversations

Identify Personal Interest Related to Local History and Culture

Explore Primary and Secondary Sources for Background

Seek and Record Interview for Oral History

Document through Photographs, Original Drawings, Original Poetry

Organize Student Products with Other Events for Celebration

Maintain Student Work in a Format for Future Use

Lab Report—Technical Writing and the Scientific Method

Nearly all models that have been designed to represent information literacy skills have come from social studies or the humanities. This is not surprising, as the creators come from those disciplines. Records of clear observation and precision of documentation actually have a stronger model in the sciences. Inquiry, after all, is basically the application of the scientific method to observe, document, and infer. The model for composition of the laboratory report reflects key elements that should be considered for any investigation.

The Lab Report Format Model

- **Purpose**—Statement of the reason for conducting the experiment. Purposes can be stated as questions.

- **Hypothesis**—The hypothesis is stated as an "if . . . then . . . " statement. The "if" part of the statement is based on related facts that one knows to be true. The "then" part of the statement is an educated guess about the outcome of the experiment.

- **Materials**—This is a list of all equipment and chemicals needed to do the experiment. Exact amounts are to be noted.

- **Procedure**—The procedure describes exactly what was done in terms of steps, time, amount, and method. The procedure may affect the results and should be detailed in narrative format. This documentation makes it possible for others to duplicate the experiment to validate or challenge results, or to move the experiment into a different setting with control of factors to help isolate causes and to transfer findings.

- **Observations**—The observation tells exactly what happened. An observation is measurable information and can include experimental data in the form of labeled tables, graphs, drawings, and other visuals.

- **Conclusions**—What conclusions are drawn and explained? Is the hypothesis supported or rejected, based on the data and observations? Part of the conclusion may be a new hypothesis and further questions for future experiments.

Support for inquiry-based learning in science has increased substantially over the past decade. An online "Inquiry Learning Forum" (http://ilf.crlt.indiana.edu), funded in part by the National Science Foundation and housed at Indiana University, provides a gathering point for current K–12 teaching practices in the application of inquiry to science education. The National Research Council has endorsed inquiry methods in its outline of the National Science Education Standards (*Inquiry and the National Science Education Standards* 2000). Research findings cited by the NRC are clearly in line with the elements of inquiry and models for application presented in this chapter:

- Understanding science is more than knowing facts.

- Students build new knowledge and understanding on what they already know and believe.

- Students formulate new knowledge by modifying and refining their current concepts and by adding new concepts to what they already know.

- Learning is mediated by the social environment in which learners interact with others.

- Effective learning requires that students take control of their own learning.

- The ability to apply knowledge to novel situations, that is, transfer of learning, is affected by the degree to which students learn with understanding.

Inquiry in Science Education—in All Education

According to the National Science Education Standards and the Division of Elementary, Secondary, and Informal Education (2001), inquiry is central to science learning. When engaging in inquiry, students describe objects and events, ask questions, construct explanations, test those explanations against current scientific knowledge, and communicate their ideas to others. They identify their assumptions, use critical and logical thinking, and consider alternative explanations. In this way, student actively develop their understanding of science by combining scientific knowledge with reasoning and thinking skills.

Inquiry-based learning has reemerged in recent years in key documents for best practices across grade levels and disciplines that include social studies and language arts as well as science education. Interactive discussions centered on what students have selected to read and question are found in elementary and secondary schools (Copeland 2005; Hill, Stremmel, and Fu 2005). Use of questions, application of advance organizers, and placing students in the position to clearly state and explain a hypothesis are skills advocated widely by administrative and teaching associations nationally (Marzano, Pickering, and Pollock 2001).

References

Alberta Learning. (2004). *Focus on inquiry: A teacher's guide to implementing inquiry-based learning.* Revised by J. Branch and D. Oberg. Alberta Learning and Education.

Branch, J. (2003). Inquiry-based learning: The key to student success. *School Libraries in Canada, 22* (4), 6–12.

Branch, J., and D. Oberg. (2003). The British models. *School Library Media Activities Monthly, 19* (10), 17–19.

Bruce, B. C., A. P. Bishop, and H. P. Bryan. (2003). The Inquiry Page. *Knowledge Quest, 31* (3), 15-17. The model and lesson units are online at http://inquiry.uiuc.edu/ (accessed December 28, 2005).

Callison, D. (1986). School library media programs and free inquiry learning. *School Library Journal, 32* (6), 20–24. Reprinted in L. N. Gerhardt (Ed.) and Marilyn Miller (Comp.), *School Library Journal's Best* (78–82). Neal-Schuman, 1997.

Callison, D. (1999). Inquiry. *School Library Media Activities Monthly, 15* (6), 38–42.

Callison, D. (2002). Information Inquiry. *School Library Media Activities Monthly, 18* (10), 35–39.

Callison, D. (2003). *Key words, concepts and methods for information age instruction: A guide to teaching information inquiry.* LMS Associates.

Copeland, M. (2005). *Socratic circles: Fostering critical and creative thinking in middle and high schools.* Stenhouse Publishers.

Division of Elementary, Secondary, and Informal Education. (2001). *Foundations: Inquiry—thoughts, views, and strategies for the K-5 classroom.* National Science Foundation. http://www.ehr.nsf.gov/EHR/ESIE/index.html (accessed March 14, 2001).

Duncan, D., and L. Lockhart. (2000). *I-Search, you search, we all learn to research.* Neal-Schuman.

Harada, V. H., and J. M. Yoshina. (2004). Moving from rote to inquiry: Creating learning that counts. *Library Media Connection, 23* (2), 22–24.

Harste, J. C. (1994). Visions of literacy. *Indiana Media Journal, 17* (1), 27–33.

Herring, J. (1996). *Teaching information skills in schools.* Library Association Publishing.

Hill, L. T., A. J. Stremmel, and V. R. Fu. (2005). *Teaching as inquiry: Rethinking curriculum in early childhood education.* Pearson.

Inquiry and the National Science Education Standards: A guide for teaching and learning. (2000). Center for Science, Mathematics, and Engineering Education, National Research Council.

Joyce, M. Z., and J. I. Tallman. (1997). *Making the writing and research connection with the I-Search process.* Neal-Schuman.

Kuhlthau, C. C. (1985). *Teaching the library research process: A step-by-step program for secondary school students.* Center for Applied Research in Education.

Lamb, A. (2001). *The 8Ws model for information literacy.* http://eduscapes.com/tap/topic71.htm (accessed December 26, 2006).

Loertscher, D. V., and B. Woolls. (2002). *Information literacy: A review of the research.* Hi Willow Research and Publishing.

Macrorie, K. (1988). *The I-Search paper.* Heinemann.

Marland, M., Editor. (1981). *Information skills in the secondary curriculum.* Methuen Educational.

Marzano, R. J., D. J. Pickering, and J. E. Pollock. (2001). *Classroom instruction that works.* Association for Supervision and Curriculum Development.

McKenzie, J. (2001). *Beyond technology: Questioning, research and the information literate school.* FNO Press. Related materials are online at http://fno.org and http://questioning.org (accessed December 28, 2005).

Miller, L., T. Steinlage, and M. Printz. (1994). *Cultural cobblestones: Teaching cultural diversity*. Scarecrow Press.

Moulton, M. R. (1999). The multigenre paper: Increasing interest, motivation, and functionality in research. *Journal of Adolescent & Adult Literacy, 42* (7), 528–539.

Pappas, M. L., and A. Tepe. (2002). *Pathways to knowledge and inquiry learning*. Libraries Unlimited. (Pathways to Knowledge: Follett's Information Skills Model is copyright 1997 by Follett Software Company. http://www.libsonline.com/product_follett_information.asp [accessed December 27, 2005].)

Short, K. G. (1996). *Learning together through inquiry*. Stenhouse Publishers.

Short, K. G., J. C. Harste, and C. Burke. (1996). *Creating classrooms for authors and inquirers*. 2d ed. Heinemann.

Stripling, B. K. (2003). Inquiry-based learning. In B. K. Stripling and S. Hughes-Hassel (Eds.), *Curriculum connections through the library* (3–39). Libraries Unlimited. .

Thomas, N. P. (2004). *Information literacy and information skills instruction*. Libraries Unlimited.

Tilley, C., and D. Callison. (1998). Information and media literacies: Towards a commoncore. In D. Callison, J. McGregor, and R. Small (Eds.), *Instructional interventions for information use*. Hi Willow Research and Publishing.

Wigginton, E., [and his students]. (1991). *Foxfire: 25 years*. Anchor Books.

YouthLearn. (2001). *The inquiry process*. Education Development Center. http://www.youthlearn.org (accessed December 26, 2005).

For Further Reading

Baden, M. S., and C. H. Major. (2004). *Foundations of problem based learning*. Open University Press.

Benjamin, A. (2002). *Differentiated instruction: A guide for middle and high school teachers*. Eye on Education, Incorporated.

Brandt, R. (1998). *Powerful learning*. Association for Supervision and Curriculum Development.

Callison, D. (1997). Anchored instruction. *School Library Media Activities Monthly, 13* (7): 39–43.

Callison, D. (2001). The brain. *School Library Media Activities Monthly, 17* (7): 35–38.

Caine, R. N., and G. Cain. (1994). Making Connection: Teaching and the Human Brain. Addison-Wesley.

Cognition and Technology Group at Vanderbilt. (1990). *Educational Researcher, 29* (6): 2–10.

Duch, B. J., and S. E. Groh. (2001). *The power of problem-based learning*. Stylus Publishing.

Fink, D. L. (2003). *Creating significant learning experiences*. Jossey-Bass.

Gardner, H. (1983). *Frames of mind*. Basic Books.

Goleman, D. (1995). *Emotional intelligence*. Bantam Books.

Harada, V. H., and J. M. Yoshina. (2004). *Inquiry learning through librarian–teacher Partnerships*. Linworth Publishing.

Healy, J. M. (1990). *Endangered minds*. Simon & Schuster.

Jensen, E. (1996). *Brain-based learning*. Turning Point.

Kovalik, S. (1994). *Integrated thematic instruction: The model*. Kovalik and Associates.

Small, R. V., and M. P. Arnone. (2000). *Turning kids on to research: The power of motivation*. Libraries Unlimited.

Welthousen, K., and I. Crowther. (2003). *Creating effective learning environments*. Thomas Delmar Learning.

Chapter 5

Information Literacy, Media Literacy, and Information Fluency

Daniel Callison and Carol L. Tilley

This book contains a section that provides definitions of educational concepts and instructional techniques related to information inquiry. Three terms, however, deserve special attention at this point as the reader progresses through the opening chapters, because each has become foundational to the inquiry process applied to Information Age instruction. Information literacy, media literacy, and information fluency are defined and discussed to show their relationships and their foundational influence on the emerging curriculum for critical and creative use of information from elementary school to college.

Levels of Literacy

When and under what circumstances does illiteracy become a social, indeed, a political, "problem?" Answers to such questions will surely depend upon what we take "literacy" to be. Is it simply being able to ritually sign your name (as it was throughout so many years of American voting history), or should we require that a literate person not only decipher but comprehend what a piece of written text is about, grasp not simply what is written (heard, or viewed), but what is meant? If we insist upon the latter criterion, then at what level of comprehension should we set the line? A common sense, pragmatic approach to all issues of this order must obviously start with, "It depends" (Bruner 1991).

In *Changing Our Minds,* Miles Myers (1996) describes the evolution of literacy in American society and education. For what he terms the new "translation/critical literacy," the primary literacy goal shifts from decontextualized parts (i.e., skills in isolation) to contextualized wholes (i.e., language experiences and communicative events). Within this framework, learners are actively aware of their own efforts to fashion themselves as thinkers. Because they influence how we think about and solve our problems, as well as communicate our answers, we must broaden our understanding of technologies and media.

Traditional print media, the news bite, the digital byte, and the pluralistic world of the Internet are all part of the communicative voice of this generation. Media merge to create multimedia, where written, spoken, and visualized images bring both improved clarity and new complexities to the communication process. Tables, charts, and icons appear more frequently to summarize data, express conclusions, and depict ideologies. Messages can be targeted at, tailored for, and delivered to a variety of audiences with increased ease, speed, and precision. While data are highly accessible and pressed on us constantly, the ability to identify, create, and convey meaningful information successfully becomes more challenging each day.

Various associations and societies, as well as individual educators, have attempted to create heuristics to help students meet these challenges. Often these come in the guise of literacy movements—media, information, computer, numeracy, visual—that seek both to address the perceived shortcomings of modern curricula and to create students who can negotiate the complex demands of the Information Age. By examining the two literacies, information literacy and media literacy, which seem to be most frequently prescribed, we hope to demonstrate that there is potential for dynamic interaction between them that can lead to a richer application of both approaches, and, ultimately, greater student success.

Media Literacy: Decoding for Reality

David Buckingham (2003), director of the London University Centre for the Study of Children, Youth and Media, offers the following definition of media:

> A medium is something we use when we want to communicate with people indirectly, rather than in person or by face-to-face contact. This . . . tells us something fundamental about the media, which forms the basis of the media education curriculum. The media do not offer a transparent window on the world. They provide channels through which representations and images of the world can be communicated indirectly. The media intervene: they provide us with selective versions of the world, rather than direct access to it. (p. 3)

While Buckingham's definition is useful for describing mass media, the "realities" of all communications, including face-to-face; how information is organized for retrieval; and how information is selected for assimilation are important events that impact the learner and his or her ability to gain knowledge. Understanding the agenda of the communicator, a process not always possible to conduct or comprehend, has tremendous implications for what is accepted and rejected as valid information. Knowledge and understanding, therefore, will move at different speeds and levels of meaning, and the best educators can offer is support as the learner and the teacher attempt to deal with the bias and spin placed on all information and communication.

A common assumption of media literacy is that people are confronted with a barrage of messages from mass media, including newspapers, magazines, movies, and television, whether they want the messages or not. Therefore, the lessons in media literacy often help the learner confront and live with these messages, not by turning them off, but by understanding the various intentions of the messages' producers. Through understanding the concepts and constructs of mass media, students are better able to determine what is real and what is important about the messages they receive. Ultimately, the power of the media over students may be lessened if they understand how to decode and evaluate these messages (Robinson 1994).

According to the Ontario Ministry of Education (1989), a media literate person understands that

- All media are constructs. Although media appear to be a natural reflection of reality, they are rather a carefully constructed presentation of reality that reflects an intended message or point of view.

- All media construct reality. Media offer a message or point of view that becomes real to the audience if firsthand information is not available. The audience accepts this mediated information as reality and uses it to judge the world.

Activity: Show students the video spaghetti harvest "documentary" that was first aired on the BBC show *Panorama* on April 1, 1957. What are the documentary conventions used to make this film believable? Discuss the implications of people accepting the content of this film as truthful.

- Audiences negotiate meaning in media. All people filter meaning from media through their own personal experiences, beliefs, and knowledge. Not everyone receives a mediated message in the same way; neither do all audiences receive the same message intended by the producer.

- Media have commercial implications. The audience is the commodity being bought and sold. Content and format depend on whom is paying for contact with the audience. The audience is defined by demographics. The message, point of view, format, and marketing are constructed to match the audience.

Activity: Have students collect advertising found on the main pages at Yahoo! (http://www.yahoo.com) or another popular World Wide Web directory. How do the advertisements seem to be targeted? For example, if the user looks at music listings, is there a banner advertisement for a music service on the page? Do the advertisers offer special deals to Internet users?

- Media contain ideological and value messages. Media sell a lifestyle, value, or belief to audiences in a palatable or subtle manner that often seeks to reinforce the dominant culture. Audiences tend to be aware of the messages with which they most disagree.

- Media have social and political implications. Most Americans get information about their world from the media. Family life, leisure activities, consumer patterns, politics, and government are all influenced by the media.

Activity: Have students work in groups to monitor at least one week's worth of national television news broadcasts and front page headlines from major local newspapers. Compare and contrast the amount and placement of coverage given to events across the different media. Discuss the implications this might have for people who get their news information from only one media outlet. The Television News Archive at Vanderbilt University (http://tvnews.vanderbilt. edu/) is a useful resource for this activity.

- Media have unique aesthetic forms that are closely related to content. The format both influences and limits the content. Information is tailored to the format and presented differently in different forms of media.

Activity: Compare descriptions and advertisements of movies as they appear in movie theater trailers, on television, on radio, in the newspaper, in magazines, and on the Internet. How does the depiction differ among formats? What are the predominant conventions of each medium?

The media literate person is in control of his or her media experiences because he or she understands the basic conventions of various media and enjoys their uses in a deliberately conscious manner. The media literate person understands the impact of music and special effects, for example, in heightening the drama of a television program or film. However, this recognition does not lessen the enjoyment of the action. Instead, it can prevent the viewer from being unduly credulous or becoming unnecessarily frightened.

Activity: Show a brief clip from a well-known movie such as *Jaws, Raiders of the Lost Ark, Lord of the Rings,* or *Titanic.* The first time through, show the clip with the original soundtrack. Then turn off the sound and use several different varieties of music for the soundtrack as you show the clip again. How do different soundtracks affect viewers' perceptions about what is happening on screen?

Provide opportunities for students to consider how popular movies have "rewritten" history. The *Pocahontas* interpretation by Walt Disney Company takes, some would say (Wineburg and Martin 2004), more than literary license to present an entertaining story. Modern animation can provide both a modern inspiration as well a cloud over history and original fairytales. Media literate students will investigate such interpretations to gain accurate historic information and to gain appreciation for original folklore.

Information Literacy: Problem Solving

"Information literacy" is the term being applied to the skills and attitudes required to master information problem solving. As in media literacy, the learner must understand how to decode messages. The information literate student is able to describe the need for more information and use it to counter bias and stereotypes and extend arguments. While the media literate student considers the same decoding tasks in relation to confronting the mass media, the information literate student seeks out and isolates the information problem regardless of setting—occupational, recreational, or intellectual (AASL 1993).

The information literate student has the ability to access and use information that is necessary to succeed in school, work, and personal life. Although similar to media literacy in skills of evaluating, comprehending, interpreting, and communicating information to convey a message with a purpose, the information literacy approach emphasizes problem identification and information search strategy skills. The information literate student successfully

- Defines the need for information. An information need is dependent on the person—his or her prior knowledge and experience—who has the need as well as the context in which it is placed. Information needs can be established and clarified through questioning.

- Initiates an information search strategy. Search strategies are most successful when the information seeker is able to identify and categorize concepts relevant to an information need. In addition, successful search strategies require the information seeker to understand the search system (e.g., indexes, online catalogs, Boolean logic) as well as to assess the potential value of retrieved information.

Activity: Before a formal search strategy is initiated, students should brainstorm individually to identify and cluster the relevant prior knowledge they have about the topic. A convenient way to do this is through webbing. This activity provides students with a basic map of the topic as well as potentially valuable search terms. The completed web also can serve as a useful conversation point between student and teacher to see where faulty understanding might lie or where students might need more direction.

- Knows a variety of access points for resources, data, and assistance in interpretation if necessary. The information seeker understands how to utilize a variety of information sources and agencies, as well as human resources, in order to gain useful information. In addition, he or she understands the value of consulting with resource specialists and critical peers to reframe and refine questions and inquiries if necessary.

Activity: At the beginning of a new unit or substantial project, work with students to identify potentially useful resources and contacts. These may be print or other media items as well as professionals, agencies, and businesses that can provide you and students with vital information about an area of interest. Build a database of resource and contact suggestions to use with classes or in the future.

Activity: When beginning research projects, assign students to pairs or small groups to act as critical friends in the information seeking and use process. Model for students how critical friends might be used to spot gaps in the information seeking process and to refine information needs. Allow students time each day in the research process to meet with their critical friends to discuss progress and pitfalls.

- Assesses and comprehends the information. The information seeker identifies information important to a need and assesses its reliability, bias, authority, and intent. He or she also organizes new information in meaningful ways to determine where gaps may exist and to formulate the central question or thesis that can be addressed (Doyle 1994).

The Critical Core

Central to both literacy movements is the set of intellectual abilities and skills students are expected to master. While the structure and discourse of this set may vary from one discipline to another, and even from one teacher's classroom to another, the key elements for student performance remain constant. Using Bloom's familiar *Taxonomy of Educational Objectives* (1956) as a framework, this set of skills and abilities can be described as follows:

Comprehension of messages, implicit and explicit

- Understanding the core message (hypothesis, argument, idea) being communicated
- Understanding nonliteral statements such as metaphor, symbolism, irony, and exaggeration
- Interpreting various types of social data
- Dealing with conclusions, including predicting continuation of trends

Activity: Present students with an editorial from a local newspaper or a mission statement from a national organization, such as the National Rifle Association (http://www.nra.org). Work with students to identify the core message as well as nonliteral statements that the writer uses. Is the message stated or implicit? The same mission statement or editorial can be used to discuss other pertinent elements such as biases, unstated assumptions, and persuasive devices.

Application of general ideas, rules of procedures, or generalized methods

- Applying established norms to phenomena described in written, oral, and visual communication, both personal and formal
- Identifying factors that cause change and predicting the probable effect of the change

Activity: Have students work in groups to stage videotaped mock news broadcasts. How did students organize and format their broadcasts? What conventions of televised news broadcasts did they incorporate? If students deviated from news broadcast norms, why did they choose to do this, and how did the audience (you and the other students) react? These conventions may range from the types of stories reported, the dress of the anchors and reporters, the sequencing of stories, or the broadcast sets. If staging broadcasts is too time-consuming, work with students to compare local or national news broadcasts to see what conventions can be identified.

Analysis of elements, relationships, and principles

- Recognizing unstated assumptions
- Distinguishing facts from hypotheses
- Examining the consistency of a hypothesis, argument, or line of reasoning with given information and assumptions
- Recognizing form and pattern in literacy or artistic works as a method to understand their meaning
- Recognizing the general techniques used in persuasive materials, such as advertising and propaganda, as well as social structures, such as peer pressure and authority status

Activity: The Opposing Viewpoints book series from Greenhaven Press often includes exercises for distinguishing fact from opinion. Make an overhead transparency from one of these exercises and work with students to determine relevant identifiers for factual and opinion or hypothesis statements. Demonstrate how to link facts and opinions that lead to establishing evidence to accept or reject a given proposal.

Synthesis of communication, action, or relationships.

- Selecting relevant parts and arranging or combining to form a meaningful whole conclusion or message
- Organizing ideas, statements, and evidence to create a written, spoken, or visual message
- Diagnosing actions that constitute a plan
- Formulating an appropriate hypothesis or argument based upon analysis of factors involved and modifying such in light of new evidence

Activity: Instead of having students present a group oral report for a project, ask them to create mock-ups (on posterboard) for, or, if you have capable students, actual World Wide Web pages, to present their findings. Stress the importance of proper page layout, good navigation, concise and coherent text, useful images, etc. Provide students with examples of both good and bad World Wide Web page design. Some examples and general guidance can be found at sites such as the Yale C/AIM Web Style Guide (http://info.med.yale.edu/caim/manual/) or Web Pages That Suck (http://www.webpagesthatsuck.com/).

Evaluation of internal evidence and external criteria

- Making judgments about the value of materials, methods, data, and various forms of evidence for given purposes
- Evaluating the accuracy of a communication from such evidence as logical reasoning, documented authority, and consistency
- Referencing established external criteria of excellence
- Posing revisions in evaluation criteria when warranted

Activity: Have students regularly evaluate their peers. Work together to create documents that can be used for evaluation purposes. Discuss why some criteria for evaluation may be more or less important than others. Count peer evaluation toward students' grades or give students credit for the evaluations they complete.

A worthwhile shorthand to condense these critical skills into more common language is as follows. Today's information and media literate citizen (student or teacher, in academic, social, or workforce situations) should be able to

- pose worthwhile questions;
- evaluate the adequacy of an argument;
- recognize facts, inferences, and opinions and use each appropriately;
- deal with quandaries and ill-formed problems that have no fixed or unique solutions;
- give and receive criticism constructively;
- agree or disagree in degrees measured against the merits of the issue and audience;
- extend a line of thought beyond the range of first impressions; and
- articulate a complex position without adding to its complexity.

The Two Literacies: Working Together in the Classroom

While there are many commonalities shared between media and information literacies, one difference is the selection of the communicative channel, that is, how to present or convey information. Media literacy promoters tend to give preference to the visual and audio modes associated with television and motion pictures. Many educators who promote media literacy argue that the best way to understand media is to produce media. However, information literacy is not void of the application of media production skills and activities. Basic composition abilities are essential for scripting, editing, and expression of commands that lead to the production of media programming. The usual communicative channel in information literacy has been the essay or written term paper, with video production gaining some application in recent years. New technologies that include advancements in group software and in multimedia authoring are changing communicative channels dramatically and moving the presentation mode of these two literacy sets closer.

More and more students are practicing information literacy presentation skills through collaborative efforts staged in electronic groupware composition exercises. Merits of evidence, for example, once shared can now be examined through electronic sharing of student essays while they are in the writing phases. Peer editing in these situations has started to reach new levels of critical analysis of evidence posed, sources quoted, and data extracted and displayed. Argument and counterargument can take place not only upon presentation of the final paper, video, or discussion panel, but also very effectively within the construction of the script, outline, persuasive paper, advertising plan, speech, or debate strategy formulation. Students can move forward in information analysis by demanding of themselves and their peers: Do you have a second source to substantiate? Do you have a series of documents over time that can be linked together to support your conclusion? Can you validate this source through reasonable credentials of the author or the institution the author represents?

In addition to electronic group composition processes, final products from the standpoint of information and media literacy are beginning to look very similar because of the greater ease of multimedia authoring through platforms such as HyperStudio and the World Wide Web. Text, animation, graphics, tables, icons, voice, and video blur the differences between media literacy and information literacy as verbal, visual, and audio manipulations have become increasingly necessary to deliver the final product. Multimedia presentation design and production involves the same dynamics of group composition as partici-

pants bring unique talents to the process and play different roles. But all students share in the process of critically selecting text, visuals, and sounds to construct the message. Audience analysis has recently gained some emphasis in both approaches as composition groups and media production groups struggle with conveying a message that will be received. Analysis of the intended audience's information need and level of information reception (understandings and assumptions the audience brings to the text or visual) are critical skills regardless of communication format.

Scenario: In the high school media center, students are preparing to produce a video news report set in a scene from the American Civil War. In order to solve the problems of set design, costumes, story content, language or dialect of the time, and frame of reference to events as chronologically correct as possible, these students have accessed a wide variety of resources. Some have searched the online catalog, including a database of historical materials available through their state's historical society. They have examined a Web site of visual resources from the U. S. Library of Congress. Some have interviewed Civil War experts using electronic mail. Others have gathered replicated Civil War songs and speeches from the local public library and from the nearby academic library through interlibrary loan. The students will be evaluated not only on the organization and presentation of the media event, but on how well they substantiate the authenticity of the information used for the production.

Information and Media Literacies Together: Creating Critical Classrooms

The most salient differences between media literacy and information literacy are found in the locus of intended influence. Media literacy involves the learner reacting to an external factor—learning how to decode messages sent to influence his or her thinking, feelings, and actions. Information literacy involves the learner reacting to an internal need to know more, to take systematic steps and to employ strategies in order to find meaningful evidence or information to solve a personal, academic, and workplace problem (see Table 5.1).

Table 5.1. Media Literacy Concepts and Information Literacy Standards

Media Literacy Education Key Concepts The Media Awareness Network http://www.media-awareness.ca	Information Literacy Standards American Association of School Librarians (AASL and AECT 1998)
1. All media are construction. The media do not present simple reflections of external reality. They present carefully crafted constructions that reflect many decisions and result from many determining factors. 2. The media construct reality. The media are responsible for the majority of the observations and experiences from which we build our personal understandings of the world. 3. Audiences negotiate meaning in the media. The media provide us with much of the material upon which we build our picture of reality, and we negotiate meaning according to individual factors. 4. Media have commercial implications. Media literacy aims to encourage an awareness of how the media are influenced by commercial considerations. 5. Media contain ideological and value messages. Explicitly or implicitly, the mainstream media convey ideological messages. 6. Media have social and political implications. Media have a great influence on politics and on forming social change. 7. Form and content are closely related in media. Each medium has its own grammar and codifies reality in its own particular way. 8. Each medium has a unique aesthetic form.	1. The student who is information literate accesses information efficiently and effectively. 2. The student who is information literate evaluates information critically and competently. 3. The student who is information literate uses information accurately and creatively. 4. The student who is an independent learner . . . pursues information related to personal interests. 5. The student who is an independent learner . . . appreciates literature and other creative expressions of information. 6. The student who is an independent learner . . . strives for excellence in information seeking and knowledge generation. 7. The student who contributes positively to the learning community and to society . . . recognizes the importance of information to a democratic society. 8. The student who contributes positively to the learning community . . . practices ethical behavior in regard to information and information technology. 9. The student who contributes positively to the learning community and to society . . . participates effectively in groups to pursue and generate information.

The *Standards for English Language Arts* (NCTE 1996) calls for instruction that makes productive use of the emerging literacy abilities that children bring to school. The combination of media and information literacies can drive the creation of new learning environments that demand the critical use of language in order to read, write, and communicate effectively to a variety of audiences. Within this framework, students can conduct research on issues and interests by generating ideas and questions and by posing problems. Students can also gather, evaluate, and synthesize data from a variety of sources to communicate their discoveries in ways that suit their purpose and audience. Based on these combined literacies, students also will have increased opportunities to use a variety of technological and informational resources to gather and synthesize information and to create and communicate knowledge.

New Media and Inquiry

Cornelia Brunner and William Tally (1999) are instructors at the Center for Children and Technology in New York City. Their work has involved application of inquiry teaching methods and technology production techniques to explore various activities to teach media literacy and critical thinking skills. This combination they call "New Media." Their vision of teaching and learning is based on the following principles:

- Learning is understood broadly, as the ability to use one's mind well in framing and solving open-ended problems in original ways, and in coordinating complex activities with others.

- Technology serves as a catalyst and support for an extended classroom inquiry that is open-ended and "messy," involving guessing, debate, and multiple materials.

- Technology serves limited roles and is integrated with other tools and media—students learn using many different resources, including books, libraries, museums, videos, and adult experts, in the school and beyond.

- Students work collaboratively (and competitively) in teams, helping each other to learn and sharing data in ways that model how real scientists collaborate.

Table 5.2. Six Questions to Ask About Any Media Message (Sperry 2006)

1. Who made, and who sponsored, this message, and what is their purpose?

2. Who is the target audience, and how is the message specifically tailored to that audience?

3. What are the different techniques used to inform, persuade, entertain, and attract attention?

4. What messages are communicated (and/or implied) about certain people, places, events, behaviors, lifestyles?

5. How current, accurate, and credible is the information in the message?

6. What is left out of this message that might be important to know?

Action Coalition for Media Education
www.acmecoalition.org

Alliance for Media Literate America
www.amlainfo.org

Center for Media Literacy
www.medialit.org

- Teachers play crucial roles in selecting goals and materials, and as guides and intellectual coaches to students. [School library media specialists can also collaborate in these roles and can enhance the environment by providing access to a greater spectrum of resources. Teachers do not wait for such collaboration, however, as the new media roles can be played by any teacher or team of teachers who understand and are able to enact them. The librarian is welcome, but is expected to engage in new media teaching under the inquiry philosophy and technology applications that are practiced by all other teachers. No one is simply a "resource helper" but all are model teachers and facilitators.]

- Broad subject matter decisions are made by teachers and more local ones by students, and teachers give students a role in determining performance criteria.

- The use of technology challenges the dominant mode of text-driven instruction in the school, making it more inquiry-based, collaborative, and varied in the use of resources. (27–28)

Adoption of methods to teach media and information literacy in core curriculum in America's public schools has been mixed. Recent national studies that reviewed new media literacy programs were summarized in 2006 by Nellie Gregorian, senior research director of the Michael Cohen Group. The following emerging trends were identified:

- Teachers do not view media literacy as an end in and of itself—rather, as a means for improving student's critical thinking skills, as well as [overall] academic performance.

- Teachers use media literacy as a hook to get kids more engaged with the core curriculum.

- Teachers' grasp of and commitment to media literacy is crucial for its successful integration into the middle school curriculum.

- Students learn media literacy concepts better through hands-on experiences.

Until media and information literacy are established as core elements of the curriculum, it remains unlikely that traditional curricular content and traditional instructional methods will be changed. A few more aggressive schools, often in an "alternative" setting, have pushed media and information literacy to the forefront of the curriculum, using the concepts to drive and create the curriculum rather than see these literacies as an add-on (Sperry 2006). The approach is usually based on the assumption that these literacies

- Are an expansion of traditional literacy that includes both analysis and production of all mediated forms of communication, from books to Web sites;

- Can and should be integrated across the K–12 curriculum at all grade levels and in multiple subject areas;

- Help teachers to more effectively address existing learning standards and engage students with varied learning styles;

- Stimulate teaching of critical thinking skills, such as understanding of bias and credibility through rigorous analysis and selection of appropriate media documents;

- Empower students to express and communicate their own ideas through multiple forms of media production; and

- Are essential for the development of informed, reflective, and active citizens in a democratic society, especially in the Information Age.

Information Fluency

Fluency normally is associated with the ability to speak and write easily, smoothly, and expressively. The levels of fluency change with communication challenges, audiences, and experiences. Practice in addressing information problems across different situations and with different techniques helps one become fluent and better able to address new information problem situations. Several definitions for information fluency have been suggested in recent literature associated with information literacy. A very broad definition is offered here to illustrate how information fluency involves a wide range of skills and abilities across several literacy areas.

Fluency should be considered as more than the ability to master one technique, strategy, or model for learning or teaching. Fluency should be considered on a much broader basis. A reasonable definition at this time is that information fluency is the ability to analyze information needs and to move confidently among media, information, and computer literacy skills, resulting in the effective application of a strategy or strategies that will best meet those needs.

Fluency is also the ability to move among several models for the information search and use processes. The mature, information literate student understands that elements of several models may be needed to deal adequately with the problem or project at hand (see Table 5.3). To base instruction on how to obtain and use information on one model is to restrict the potential of the learner for greater exploration through his or her own critical and creative thinking. Some models are best for introducing basic skills, and other models take students into more critical analyses of information. Ultimately, the person who is fluent in multiple literacy strands and strategies will be more successful in meeting the most complex information demands.

Table 5.3. Moving Among Information Literacy Models to Meet Need and Demonstrate Information Fluency

Information Need	Model Characteristics
Practice information problem solving	Specific, routine steps that organize and focus the approach; tasks often defined by teacher or authority not by student
Emphasis on entertainment over information	Concentrate on media literacy issues; consider multiple media options for presentation
Explore human opinion and personal feelings	Develop interview skills; enhance journaling abilities; give time to self-reflection
Explore extensive in-depth information	Move to advanced information search processes and student-centered learning techniques; develop critical analysis of information; link information to corroborate as evidence; read widely for scope and new ideas
Formulate new questions; explore new knowledge	Apply inquiry-based and student-directed approaches to information seeking and selection; new paths for inquiry based on a wide range of information leads; modify and validate conclusions based on authoritative evidence not preconceived notions

The mature information user understands and applies the guiding principles of scientific research methods. Most important, this mature information user seeks all evidence from as many legitimate sources as possible, analyzes the evidence gathered, is always open to new evidence, and makes decisions for actions based on the best evidence obtained. Those who have not matured in information fluency start with a conclusion and practice limited evidence gathering for the purpose of locating only the information that will support their initial conclusion.

Defining Information Fluency in the Wired World

In a paper presented to the Australian Library and Information Association in 1993, Homer Stavely identified several elements of information processing now greatly enhanced in the modern wired world: configuration, location, concentration, organization, representation, distribution, scale, and transformation. To move wired users toward information fluency, computer literary should involve not only teaching how to use a new communications tool, but also what can be done with application of this new tool to transform information across boundaries. Fluency is critical to exchanging information across cultural, gender, class, and ethnic boundaries. In 1999, the Committee on Information Technology Literacy (CITL) distinguished "fluency" as a term connoting a higher level skill set and ability than the terms "competency" or "literacy."

Some of the differences between fluency and competency are, first, that fluency entails a lifelong learning process; second, that fluency implies personalization of skills on levels of sophistication; and third, that fluency is composed of three kinds of knowledge: contemporary skills, foundational concepts, and intellectual abilities. An individual is computer literate when he or she is able to use the computer to satisfy personal needs. Skills leading to computer literacy usually include programming and operating skills, knowledge and awareness of computers, and a positive attitude toward computers. Some

definitions of "computer literacy" move close to "fluency" by defining it as a collection of skills, knowledge, understanding, values, and relationships that allow a person to function comfortably as a productive citizen in a computer-oriented society. Ulla Bunz from the University of Kansas and Howard Sypher from Virginia Tech reported in 2001 on their efforts to define a computer fluency scale. They worked from a general definition of information literacy as an ability to express oneself creatively, reformulate knowledge, and synthesize information regarding new information technology. Web editing, extensive e-mail management knowledge, and extensive Web navigation abilities tend to be current indicators of emerging fluency within the Internet culture.

Information Literacy and Fluency

Information literary is a set of abilities that allow an individual to recognize when information is needed and apply those abilities to locate, evaluate, and effectively use the needed information (see Table 5.4). An information literate person is able to

- determine the extent of information needed;

- access the needed information effectively and effectively;

- evaluate information and its sources critically;

- incorporate selected information into his or her knowledge base;

- use information to accomplish a specific purpose;

- understand the economic, legal, and social issues surrounding access and use of information; and

- access and use information ethically and legally.

Table 5.4. Information Exploration Hierarchy

Information Fluency	Highest levels of information evaluation and management for the mature information literate person relative to his or her age and ability levels. At the most sophisticated level, this person, often an information scientist, moves efficiently and effectively across a variety of information search strategies, information systems, databases, and communication technologies. This person has the accomplished background to assimilate, manage, and apply, or as an information scientist create, emerging technologies, databases, and information systems.
Information Inquiry	A teaching and learning process based on information and media literacy elements of questioning, exploration, assimilation, inference, and reflection. These elements are common to most linear models for information search and use, but represent the cyclical processes necessary to address new questions that arise in any investigation. Techniques involve a combination of ancient Socratic questioning methods and modern technologies to create exciting real and virtual learning environments for students and teachers to think and act critically and creatively. Learning is often based on authentic projects, issues, and reflections that are interwoven among personal, academic, and workplace information needs. Those who apply the philosophy, concepts, and techniques associated with Information Inquiry are Instructional Media Specialists, regardless of professional position as classroom teacher, library media specialist, computer specialist, or other role as educator or mentor. Specifically related to information literacy, Information Inquiry involves those processes to determine the adequacy of the information needed, located, and selected for use. Judgment of information adequacy will include reflection on the information in terms of age, authority, completeness, relevance to information need, task, argument, and audience.

Table 5.4. Information Exploration Hierarchy (*Cont.*)

Information Inquiry (continued)	Through Socratic Methods applied to dialog, discussion, and debate, the ultimate task in Information Inquiry is to determine adequacy of information as convincing evidence from which justification can be made to present meaningful arguments, conclusions, and actions. Reflection includes considering the ethical methods in obtaining information, the limitations of the information acquired, and the adjustments that should be made to increase efficiency and effectiveness in information access and use to meet future needs and tasks.
Information Literacy	The set of skills to find, retrieve, analyze, and use information. The Association of College and Research Libraries (ACRL, http://www.ala.org/ala/acrl) promotes information literacy as closely tied to course-integrated instruction. College students must demonstrate competencies in formulating research questions and in their ability to use information as well as an understanding of ethical and legal issues. This requires a campus culture of collaboration and focus on student learning. The American Association of School Librarians (AASL, http://www.ala.org/ala/aasl) promotes information literacy as the keystone to lifelong learning. The school library media specialist promotes information literacy as a teacher, an instructional partner, and an information specialist.
Media Literacy	Leading members of the Media Awareness Network (http://www.media-awareness.ca) define media literacy as the ability to sift through and analyze the messages that inform, entertain, and sell to us every day. It is the ability to bring critical thinking skills to bear on all media. It is the ability to question what lies behind media productions—the motives, the money, the values, and the ownership—and to be aware of how these factors influence content.
Information Skills	Understanding how to identity and extract information to address a basic information need; usually in an academic setting.
Library Skills	Learning how to locate and cite resources available in the local library.

Information fluency involves the abilities to

• transfer information and media literacy skills to address new information need situations;

• employ the use of modern computer technologies to obtain, select, analyze, and infer conclusions from information;

• employ critical thinking to derive evidence from information and creative thinking for the expression and application of that evidence to decision making; and

• move across multiple strategies and evaluation levels in order to address different information needs found in academic, workplace, and personal environments (see Figure 5.1).

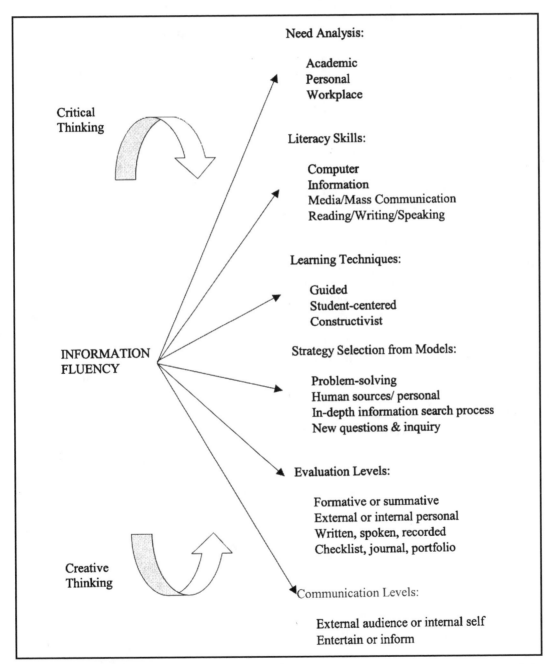

Figure 5.1: Selected interactions and relationships defining information fluency. Copyright 2004, 2006, Daniel Callison.

References

American Association of School Librarians (AASL). (1993). *Information literacy: A position paper on information problem solving.* AASL.

American Association of School Librarians and the Association for Educational Communications and Technology (AASL and AECT). (1998). *Information power: Building partnerships for learning.* American Library Association.

Bruner, J. (1991). *Introduction to literacy: An overview of fourteen experts,* (S. R. Graubard, Ed.). Hill and Wang Noonday Press.

Brunner, C., and W. Tally. (1999). *The new media literacy handbook.* Doubleday Anchor Books.

Buckingham, D. (2003). *Media education: Literacy, learning and contemporary culture.* Polity Press.

Bunz, U. K., and H. E. Sypher. (2001). *The computer-email-web fluency scale—development and validation.* Paper presented at the Annual Meeting of the National Communication Association. ED 458 657.

Committee on Information Technology Literacy. (1999). *Being fluent with information technology.* National Academy Press.

Doyle, C. S. (1994). *Information literacy in an information society: A concept for the information age.* ERIC Clearinghouse on Information & Technology, Syracuse University.

Gregorian, N. 2006. Media literacy and core curriculum. *Threshold,* (Winter 2006), 5–7. www.ciconline.org/threshold (accessed December 22, 2005).

Myers, M. 1996. *Changing our minds: Negotiating English literacy.* National Council of Teachers of English, 1996.

National Council of Teachers of English (NCTE). (1996). *Standards for English language arts.* NCTE.

Ontario Ministry of Education. (1989). *Media literacy resource guide: Intermediate and senior division.* Ontario Ministry of Education.

Robinson, J. (1994). Media literacy: The school library media center's new curriculum baby. *Indiana Media Journal, 16* (3), 66–72.

Sperry, C. (2006). The search for truth. *Threshold,* (Winter), 9–11. www.ciconline.org/threshold (accessed December 22, 2005).

Stavely, H. (1993). *Working in a wired world.* Paper presented at the Australian Library and Information Association Conference. ED 368 332.

Taxonomy of educational objectives: The classification of educational goals. (1956). Longmans, Green.

Wineburg, S., and D. Martin. (2004). Reading and rewriting history. *Educational Leadership, 62* (1), 42–45.

Chapter 6

Standards, Scope and Sequence, and Best Practices

Daniel Callison

Scope and *sequence* are instructional terms that carry both positive and negative connotations. Positive in that such written outlines provide an overview or full picture of the skills , activities, and potential levels of student performance across all grade levels. Such a complete plan allows educators from elementary and secondary programs to identify areas in which they may cooperate and reduce duplication of instructional activities. Educators also can gain some reasonable entry skill expectations so they can build activities based on the assumption that most of the students coming into certain later grade levels have been introduced to or have mastered key skills on which to build new experiences. As new teachers join the educational environment, scope and sequence plans can serve to provide an efficient map for novice instructors to identify where their lessons fit in the school district's plan.

If communication is maintained through professional development forums, curriculum can be coordinated. If not, scope and sequence plans become time-consuming and frustrating efforts for a few ambitious educators and the results are simply long lists of skills on paper that are of no practical use.

From a negative pedagogy, sequencing can result in lock-step instruction determined by the needs of the many and ignoring the learning problems of or advanced opportunities for the few. Each student is manufactured to come out the same, with the same training, at the same time. While sequential learning plans can serve as a guide to the important steps necessary to lead to more complex skills, effective application of sequenced sets requires the wise observation and evaluation of the master teacher. The objective should not be to program learners, but to match skills to abilities and experience levels so the learner gains understanding as soon as possible. Thus, many of the skill sets presented here can easily overlap from one grade level to another, with remediation necessary for some learners and opportunities for quick advancement necessary for others.

A combination of skills from library orientation, information literacy, technology use, and media literacy can be combined for a scope and sequence of skills for the Information Inquiry process.

Library Skills

As she has in many other areas of study and application of Information Inquiry, Carol Kuhlthau (1981) documented her early thoughts and experiences with teaching the use of the library and its resources. Kuhlthau's first experiences involved elementary school children and preceded her classic observations of high school student search behavior. Her application of educational theory provides a framework for scope and sequence of information and technology skills that are foundational to inquiry. She constructed her sequential library skills program on Piaget's stages of cognitive development (Opper, Ginsburg, and Brandt 1987):

Sensory Motor—Birth to Age 2

 – Learns through senses and movement.

Pre-operational—Ages 2–7

- Can use symbols to represent reality, such as language.
- Has an egocentric point of view.

Concrete Operational—Ages 7–11

- Can perform mental operations on a concrete level.
- Can categorize and use classification.
- Is not capable of abstract thinking.

Formal Operational—Ages 12–16

- Can use abstract thought.
- Can generalize.
- Can form a hypothesis.

A sequential structure matched to the normal skill development of the learner is assumed to increase the chances that the student will build his or her learning at the time of being able to understand meaning and application. Thus skill mastery builds from one level to the next and exercises are designed to introduce skills based on previously demonstrated mastery.

Kuhlthau is quick to emphasize that library and information skills are not separate school subjects. Like reading and writing, they are process skills—skills used to reach other learning goals. We read to derive meaning. We write to convey thoughts. We use library skills, according to Kuhlthau when she published many of her activities in 1981, to locate and interpret materials that expand our understanding and better enable us to make decisions and choices. When process skills are taught in isolation, learning problems, such as lack of motivation, retention, and transference, often result.

Kuhlthau built the elementary scope and sequence experiences toward skills involving inference. While location of information was a common part of her activities, the objectives involved information interpretation, appreciation, and application. These early exercises clearly were the basis for her later work with adults and young adults attempting to seek meaning and a deeper understanding of the library research process.

Levels of Learning

Few educators have made it through methods courses and graduate studies without a heavy dose of Bloom's Taxonomy for Educational Objectives. Written by a committee of distinguished educators in the mid-twentieth century, the classification of cognitive skills has had a strong influence on cognitive skill performance and measurement (Bloom 1956). These skill levels, building from knowledge, comprehension, application, analysis, synthesis, and evaluation, served as the framework for a scope and sequence information skills curriculum guide issued by the Washington Library Media Association in 1987.

The Washington sequence has been republished dozens of times over the past decade and contains a reasonable outline for identification of when to introduce certain skills. The guide also gives reasonable indication of when key skills are likely to be mastered because of student ability levels, and reminds us that all skills must continue to be reinforced in association with subject content and student need throughout the academic experience.

Constructed from a presearch set of skills for formulating questions as well as understanding how to search for resources, the Washington guide was one of the early scope and sequence plans to give emphasis to interpretation skills. These higher level skills include the following:

- Interpret, infer, analyze, and paraphrase

  - identify main ideas, opinions, and supporting facts
  - summarize important facts and details
  - relate to the central question
  - interpret graphic sources
  - derive valid inferences from information

- Organize information for applications

  - compare, summarize, and generalize
  - select appropriate organizational style (including chronological, argumentative, rank order of importance, problem solution, or topical)
  - determine most effective method of presentation
  - plan, practice, revise

- Apply information for intended audience
  - clear, well-supported presentation, relevant to the audience
  - draw conclusions based on obtained information
  - evaluate the project and search process

Technology Skills

In the Information Age, technology use skills have become essential for efficient means of search and retrieval. Technology tools can also play an important role in effective analysis, synthesis, and presentation of information. The International Society for Technology in Education (ISTE 2000) has issued national educational technology standards for students. Tied to subject content areas and constructed on new learning environments that require application of inquiry skills, these student behaviors are important to link to the library information skills scope and sequence.

Media Literacy Skills

Media literacy skills also have a place within the mix of library skills, information skills, and technology skills to make Information Inquiry complete. Several sources, especially those authored by David Considine (1995) and Kathleen Tyner (1998) provide ideas for both these skills and for student performance levels in a K–12 scope and sequence.

Scope and Sequence for Information Inquiry

Elementary School

Before completion of elementary school, the average student should have the following skills/be able to perform the following tasks through the Information Inquiry process:

1. Evaluation and selection techniques
   a. can select books and other resources of personal interest
   b. understands there are various forms of literature
   c. shows discrimination in selecting books

2. Search and reporting techniques
   a. can look up information in a general encyclopedia, print or nonprint
   b. can find nonfiction books on a specific topic
   c. is acquainted with bibliographies in books
   d. can focus on a specific question for which one may search for information to address the question
   e. can brainstorm ideas and information about the central question by recalling previous personal experiences
   f. can summarize the main ideas regarding the central question
   g. can recognize the use of library media center resources, including the consulting role of the library media specialist
   h. can recognize that library materials are indexed, and that this index may be in a variety of forms (card, computer)

3. Listening and viewing
   a. is able to attend to the sights and sounds of storytelling
   b. can participate in discussion following a story
   c. can recall, summarize, and paraphrase what is listened to and viewed

4. Literature appreciation
   a. can draw the point of the story into his or her own experience
   b. is familiar with many different types of literature

5. Technology application skills
   a. uses input devices (e.g., voice activation, mouse, keyboard, remote control) and output devices (e.g., monitor and printer) to successfully operate computers, VCRs, audiotapes, telephones, and other technologies
   b. uses developmentally appropriate multimedia resources (e.g., interactive books, educational software, and elementary multimedia encyclopedias) to support learning

c. works cooperatively and collaboratively with peers, family members, and others when using technology in the classroom or at home

d. practices responsible use of technology systems and software

e. creates developmentally appropriate multimedia products with support from teachers, family members, and student partners

f. uses technology resources (e.g., puzzles, logical thinking programs, writing tools, digital cameras, and drawing tools) for problem solving, communication, and illustration of thoughts, ideas, and stories

g. gathers information and communicates with others using telecommunications, with support from teachers, family members, or student partners

6. Media literacy

a. identifies media forms (e.g., news, drama, cartoon, advertising, entertainment)

b. can define terms and techniques involved in media production such as edit, pan, close-up

c. can discuss how stories occur in the media and compares these stories to types of stories he or she already knows

d. identifies and describes different stereotypes depicted in the media

e. identifies the difference between an event and the representation of that event in the media

f. discusses the ways in which media can affect the individual and the local environment

g. views media deliberately and critically

h. selects a medium and develops a simple theme for a story, and develops a story line

Middle School

Before entering high school, the average student should have the following skills/be able to perform the following tasks through the Information Inquiry process:

1. Evaluation and selection techniques

a. can use various parts of a book and other resources (Web site, video) to determine scope, format, and timeliness, and document the information found

b. is developing discrimination in selecting books and periodicals to read, films and television to view

c. knows the different types of biographical materials and can locate information in each

d. can distinguish the unique characteristics of various reference sources

e. understands the difference between fiction and nonfiction

f. is familiar with various magazines, newspapers, and other serials and understands they are a source of recent information

g. is familiar with various online databases and Web sites and is aware of selection criteria for acceptable electronic documents

h. uses information from the general resource materials to identify major/significant sources of information regarding the central question

i. recalls words, terms, methods. events, facts, and concepts by using broad, general information resources

j. understands the purpose of and applies selection techniques for compiling bits and pieces of information for later use; identifies key words and phrases and locates major headings, skims and scans for major ideas

k. locates and selects the most useful sources from among those available

l. evaluates the currency of information; can identify copyright date and understands the significance between dated and current information

m. distinguishes among fact, nonfact, opinion, and propaganda

2. Search and reporting techniques

   a. understands different classification systems, basic search techniques, and search engines

   b. can locate materials to discover what others have found out about a topic

   c. can use ideas gained through different materials

   d. can carry basic guided research through to a conclusion

   e. can present information in a written report, illustration, or oral presentation

   f. can make a bibliography of sources from various formats and understands the function of footnotes

   g. can use the nonfiction collection as a source of information

   h. understands how to extract information from television and film sources

   i. understands how to extract information from human resources

   j. understands the difference between primary and secondary resources

   k. uses a variety of questioning skills (yes/no, open-ended, follow-up, and probing)

   l. brainstorms ideas and information about the central question by recalling previous personal learning experiences

   m. understands that information can be used as evidence to support or reject a position

3. Listening and viewing

   a. interprets what is heard and seen

   b. can recall, summarize, paraphrase, and extend what is listened to and viewed

4. Literature appreciation

   a. can interpret meaning from many forms of literature

   b. understands use of resources to determine quality literature

5. Technology application

   a. applies strategies for identifying and solving routine hardware and software problems that occur during everyday use

   b. demonstrates knowledge of current changes in information technologies and the effect those changes have on common workplace environments and local society

   c. exhibits legal and ethical behaviors when using information and technology, and discuss consequences of misuse

   d. uses content-specific tools, software, and simulations, including Web-based tools, to support learning and basic information research

   e. designs, develops, and presents products, including Web-based pages and short video programs, based on using technology resources that allow for demonstration of curriculum-related concepts to audiences in school and beyond

   f. collaborates with peers, experts, and others using telecommunications and collaborative software to investigate curriculum-related problems, issues, and general information

   g. evaluates the accuracy, relevance, appropriateness, authoritativeness, comprehensiveness, and bias of electronic and print information sources pertaining to real world problems and issues

6. Media literacy

   a. identifies some major genres or categories (e.g. soap opera, sitcom, action adventure)

   b. identifies and uses media techniques such as camera angles, arrangement of people, different sound levels and mixing, and shot transitions such as fade, dissolve, cut

c. recognizes devices for controlling narrative, such as voice-over

d. follows multiple/parallel plots within a narrative

e. asks questions about the intended message and states opinions about the content concerning accuracy, relevance, bias

f. compares his or her own experiences with those attributed to that age group in the media

g. identifies some stereotypes in media depictions of various children in their age group and explains how they imply judgments of various social, racial, and cultural groups

h. identifies narrative patterns and how they are used in the presentation of fictional and nonfiction material in the media

i. considers how the same story can be adapted for different audiences and through the use of different media

j. identifies and discusses differences between an event and the representation of that event in the media

k. produces his or her own media to express an opinion or a viewpoint, promote an item or activity, or entertain

High School

Before graduation from high school, the average student should have the following skills/be able to perform the following tasks through the Information Inquiry process:

1. Evaluation and selection techniques

   a. understands and is familiar with documents (journals, newspapers, Web sites) that have different purpose, scope, perspective, bias

   b. is tolerant of review of information that does not immediately fit his or her personal perspective and seeks evidence from all perspectives before drawing a conclusion

   c. can discriminate between important and less important questions and resources

   d. explores information widely, and brings focus to the central problem based on background readings, personal experiences and interests, and identified need for further research

   e. can evaluate the process and projects of self, peers, and experts

2. Research and reporting techniques

   a. can conduct advanced and refined key word searches in online catalogs and multiple databases

   b. can conduct extensive searches through various search engines to compare and contrast electronic documents

   c. can develop and define the terms in a question regarding a problem, or otherwise limit a topic

   d. can carry basic research through independently and come to a conclusion

   e. can present information using multiple formats and styles that best fit the message and the audience

   f. formulates a working hypothesis and supports the central question or thesis statement with relevant evidence and original discussion and conclusion

   g. knows the value of a literature review to set the context for the research project and can summarize the main ideas regarding the central question

   h. understands advantages and disadvantages, and application of various methods to gather original data, including survey, interview, experiment, and case study

   i. understands a variety of modes to present findings and adjusts techniques and media to supply the best communication for a given audience or need

3. Listening and viewing
   a. can derive key information for evidence from interviews and critical examination of events and perspectives as depicted in educational and popular media
   b. interprets graphic sources for information from all media formats, including maps, charts, and other visuals or illustrations
   c. understands the potential for products to inform, persuade, and entertain

4. Literature appreciation
   a. values the information and literature products of the human record and gives credit to those items that have informed the inquiry process and product
   b. derives valid inferences from information and literature resources and understands potential for adding to and/or using these conclusions to solve problems and possibly add to the human record

5. Technology application
   a. identifies capabilities and limitations of contemporary and emerging technology resources and assesses the potential of these systems and services to address personal, lifelong learning, academic, and common workplace needs
   b. analyzes advantages and disadvantages of widespread use of and reliance on technology in the workplace and in society
   c. demonstrates and advocates legal and ethical behaviors among peers, family, and community regarding the use of technology and information
   d. uses technology tools and resources for managing and communicating personal and likely professional information
   e. selects and applies technology tools for research, information analysis, problem solving, and decision making for personal, academic, and likely workplace needs

   f. investigates and applies expert systems, intelligent agents, and simulations in real world situations
   g. collaborates with peers, experts, and others to contribute to a content-related knowledge base by using technology to compile, synthesize, produce, and disseminate information, ideas, models, conclusions and perceptions, and other creative works

6. Media literacy
   a. is widely knowledgeable of the terms that define the techniques and technologies of mass media
   b. recognizes that all forms of media contain messages
   c. has skills to decode and analyze media messages
   d. gains an informed understanding of media through critical analysis
   e. critically examines and interprets media messages in a historical, social, and cultural context; understands the relationship among audiences, media messages, and the world
   f. is able to access and articulate personal media use and speculate on the media use of others
   g. has knowledge of various media to solve problems, communicate, and produce self-selected and self-initiated projects as well as those assigned

Information Inquiry Across Disciplines

Over the past few years most new standards for various areas of the curriculum in schools K–12 have included statements that pertain directly to information literacy and inquiry. Examples from hundreds of such statements include the following:

Art: knows how visual, aural, oral, and kinetic elements are used in the various art forms.

Dance: improvises, creates, and performs dances based on personal ideas and concepts from other sources

Music: knows and appreciates songs representing genres and styles from diverse cultures

Theater: assumes roles that exhibit concentration and contribute to the action of dramatizations based on personal experience and heritage, imagination, literature, and history

Visual arts: uses visual structures and functions of art to communicate ideas

Math: uses models, known facts, properties, and relationships to explain thinking and justify answers or solutions

Science: uses data to construct a reasonable explanation, communicate investigations and explanations

History: draws conclusions about roles in life from data gathered through photos, documents, and primary sources

Civics: debates the issues pertaining to a proposed piece of legislation or plan to change the status quo

Comprehensive examples of current academic standards, K–12, across all fifty states can be found through these Web sites (each accessed January 9, 2006):

Mid-continent Research for Education and Learning—Content Knowledge, http://www.mcrel.org/standards-benchmarks/

Developing Education Standards, http://edstandards.org/Standards.html

StateStandards.com, http://www.statestandards.com/

Education World, http://www.educationworld.com/standards/

One can probably find the closest correlation to Information Inquiry skills in those required for scientific investigation: framing the question, testing the hypothesis, controlling experiments to isolate factors, comparing findings

to previous studies, providing the findings to others so conclusions can be validated, perhaps generalized, but always open for further discussion and often contested.

Examples from Language Arts

The modern language arts curriculum gives a very rich scope and sequence representation. A cadre of accomplished school media specialists in Indiana constructed a correlation between their state's new language arts standards (Correlation . . . Indiana Schools 2000) and those standards issued by the American Association of School Librarians (1998) for student learning. Selected student standards from the language arts illustrate the grade-level scope and sequence for these skills and how Information Inquiry is associated with this subject content area:

Kindergarten

- connect the information and events in texts to life experience
- distinguish fantasy from reality
- identify favorite books and stories
- share information and ideas, speaking in complete and coherent sentences

First Grade

- classify categories of words
- respond to who, what, when, where, and how questions and discuss the main idea
- confirm predictions about what will happen next in a text by identifying key words
- describe the roles of authors and illustrators
- discuss ideas and select a focus for stories or writing
- listen attentively
- ask questions for clarification and understanding
- use visual aids such as pictures and objects to present oral information

Second Grade

- use title, table of contents, and chapter headings to locate information

- recognize cause and effect relationships in a text

- organize related ideas together to maintain a consistent focus

- review, evaluate, and revise writing for meaning and clarity

- paraphrase information that is shared orally by others

- report on a topic with supportive or illustrative facts and details

- report on a topic with facts and details, drawing from several sources of information

Third Grade

- use glossary and index to locate information

- distinguish the main idea and supporting details in expository (informational) text

- discuss ideas for writing stories and use diagrams and charts to develop ideas

- use computers to draft, revise, and share writing

- write descriptive pieces about people, places, things, and experiences

- write for different purposes and to a specific audience or person

- organize ideas chronologically or around major points of information

- distinguish between the speaker's opinions and verifiable facts

Fourth Grade

- use organization of informational text to strengthen comprehension

- distinguish between cause and effect and between fact and opinion

- use multiple reference materials and on-line information sources

- understand the organization of information sources such as almanacs, newspapers, and periodicals

- ask thoughtful questions

- use examples and analogies to explain or clarify events and information

- evaluate the role of the mass media in focusing people's attention on events and issues

Fifth Grade

- use features of informational texts such as graphics and diagrams

- analyze text that is organized in sequential or chronological order

- recognize main ideas presented in texts, including the identification and assessment of evidence

- draw inferences, conclusions, or generalizations about content in text and support arguments

- discuss ideas for writing, keep a list or notebook of ideas, use graphic organizers

- use note-taking skills

- review, evaluate, and revise writing for meaning and clarity

- edit and revise writing to improve meaning and focus

- write basic research reports about important ideas, issues, people, or events

- ask questions that seek information not already discussed

- interpret a speaker's verbal and nonverbal messages, purposes, and perspectives

- select a focus, organizational structure, and point of view from an oral presentation

- clarify and support spoken ideas with evidence and examples

- analyze media as sources of information for entertainment, persuasion, and interpretation

Sixth Grade

- identify and interpret figurative language and words with multiple meanings

- identify the structure features of popular media and use those features to obtain messages and meaning

- connect and clarify main ideas by identifying their relationship to multiple sources

- note instances of persuasion, propaganda, and faulty reasoning in text

- explain the effects of common literary devices such as symbolism, imagery, analogy, and metaphor

- choose the form of writing that best suits the intended audience

- write informational pieces several paragraphs long

- use a variety of effective organizational patterns, including comparison and contrast

- use organizational features of electronic text, such as bulletin boards and databases

- use a computer to compose documents with appropriate formatting and citations

- edit and proofread one's own writing, as well as that of others, and share ideas on information needs

- support opinions and perspectives with documented evidence with use of visual media

- identify persuasive and propaganda techniques used in electronic media and mass media

- deliver meaningful narrative and informative presentations

- deliver persuasive presentations

- deliver presentations that offer potential solutions to problems

Seventh Grade

- locate information by using a variety of consumer and public documents

- analyze text that uses the cause and effect organizational pattern

- use strategies of note taking, outlining, and summarizing to improve writing structure

- identify topics; ask and evaluate questions; develop ideas leading to inquiry

- write biographical and autobiographical narratives

- write and present persuasive reports with supporting evidence and meaningful illustrations

- ask questions to elicit information from speakers, including evidence to support the speaker's claims

- arrange supporting details, reasons, descriptions, and examples effectively

- provide helpful feedback to speakers concerning the coherence and logic of the speaker's presentation

- analyze the effect on the viewer of images, text, and sound from educational and mass media

Eighth Grade

- compare and contrast features and elements of consumer materials

- compare the original text to a summary to determine if the summary is accurate; understand abstracting

- create compositions that have a clear message and coherent thesis

- support thesis or conclusion with analogies, paraphrases, quotations, opinions, and data and understand when information becomes evidence

- plan and conduct multiple-step information searches by using computer-based databases

- achieve an effective balance between researched information and original ideas, giving proper credit

- match the message, vocabulary, voice modulation, expression, and tone to the audience
- evaluate the credibility of a speaker, author, and other communicators of ideas, arguments, perspectives, and plans for change or support of status quo

Ninth Grade

- distinguish between what words mean literally and what they imply
- prepare an annotated bibliography of reference materials for a report
- synthesize the content from several sources or works by a single author
- critique the logic presented in functional documents
- evaluate an author's argument or defense of a claim
- discuss ideas for writing in collaboration with classmates, teachers, and other writers and develop drafts that are shared and revised
- use writing to formulate clear research questions and to compile information from multiple sources
- develop the main ideas within the body of the composition through supporting evidence
- integrate quotations and citations (footnotes) into a written text while maintaining the flow of ideas
- write documents related to career development
- write technical documents such as a manual or rules of behavior for conflict resolution
- choose and practice appropriate techniques for developing the introduction and conclusion in a speech
- produce concise notes for extemporaneous speeches

- compare and contrast the ways in which media genres cover the same event
- assess how language and delivery affect the mood and tone of oral communication

Tenth Grade to Twelfth Grade

- use clear research questions and suitable research methods
- develop the main ideas within the body of a composition through supporting evidence
- use appropriate conventions for documentation of text, notes, bibliographies, and references
- use a computer to integrate databases, visuals, graphics, and other resources
- use precise technical or scientific language when appropriate for specific forms and topics
- identify logical fallacies used in oral addresses, written documents, and mass media
- use multimedia for communications, including historical investigations, technical reports, and reflective and persuasive presentations
- critique the power, validity, and truthfulness of arguments set forth in public documents
- demonstrate an understanding of the elements of discourse and debate
- develop presentations by using clear research questions, based on creative and critical research methods
- use technology for all aspects of creating, revising, editing, and publishing (sharing and presenting)

Before Graduation from High School

This example from the 2001 Indiana Language Arts Standards illustrates a high degree of information literacy to be part of the student's proven skills before graduation:

- Students formulate thoughtful judgments about oral communication.

- They deliver focused and coherent presentations that convey clear and distinct perspectives and demonstrate solid reasoning.

- Students deliver polished formal and extemporaneous presentations that combine traditional speech strategies of narration, exposition, persuasion, and description.

- They use gestures, tone, and vocabulary appropriate to the audience and purpose.

- Students use the same Standard English conventions for oral speech that they use in their writing.

Comprehension

- Summarize a speaker's purpose and point of view, discuss, and ask questions to draw interpretations of the speaker's content and attitude toward the subject.

Organization and Delivery of Oral Communication

- Use rhetorical questions (questions asked for the effect without an expected answer), parallel structure, concrete images, figurative language, characterization, irony, and dialogue to achieve clarity, force, and artistic effect.

- Distinguish between and use various forms of logical arguments, including

  - inductive arguments

  - deductive arguments

  - syllogisms and analogies

- Use logical, ethical, and emotional appeals that enhance a specific tone and purpose

- Use appropriate rehearsal strategies to pay attention to performance details, achieve command of the text, and create skillful artistic staging.

- Use effective and interesting language, including information expressions for effect, Standard English for clarity, and technical language for specificity.

- Use research and analysis to justify strategies for gesture, movement, and vocalization, including dialect, pronunciation, and enunciation.

- Evaluate when to use different kinds of effects (including visuals, music, sound, and graphics) to create effective productions.

Analysis and Evaluation of Oral and Media Communications

- Analyze strategies used by the media to inform, persuade, entertain, and transmit culture (including advertisements; perpetuation of stereotypes; and the use of visual representations, special effects, and language).

- Analyze the impact of the media on the democratic process (including exerting influence on elections, creating images of leaders, and shaping attitudes) at the local, state, and national levels.

- Interpret and evaluate the various ways in which events are presented and information is communicated by visual image makers (such as graphic artists, documentary filmmakers, illustrators, and news photographers).

- Critique a speaker's use of words and language in relation to the purpose of an oral communication and the impact the words may have on the audience.

- Analyze the four basic types of persuasive speech (propositions of fact, value, problem, and policy) and understand the similarities and differences in their patterns of organization and the use of the persuasive language, reasoning, and proof.

- Analyze the techniques used in media messages for a particular audience to evaluate effectiveness and infer the speaker's character.

Speaking Applications

- Deliver reflective presentations that

  - explore the significance of personal experiences, events, conditions, or concerns, using appropriate speech strategies, including narration, description, exposition, and persuasion;

- draw comparisons between the specific incident and broader themes and to illustrate beliefs or generalizations about life; and

- maintain a balance between describing the incident and relating it to the more general, abstract ideas.

• Deliver oral reports on historical investigations that

- use exposition, narration, description, persuasion, or some combination of those to support the thesis;

- analyze several historical records of a single event, examining each perspective on the event;

- describe similarities and differences between research sources, using information derived from primary and secondary sources to support the presentation; and

- include information on all relevant perspectives and consider the validity (accuracy and truthfulness) and reliability (consistency) of sources.

• Deliver oral responses to literature that

- demonstrate a comprehensive understanding of the significant ideas of literary works and make assertions about the text that are reasonable and supportable;

- present an analysis of the imagery, language, universal themes, and unique aspects of the text through the use of speech strategies, including narration, description, persuasion, exposition, or a combination of those strategies;

- support important ideas and viewpoints through specific references to the text and other works;

- demonstrate an awareness of the author's style and an appreciation of the effects created; and

- identify and assess the impact of ambiguities, nuances, and complexities within the text.

• Deliver multimedia presentations that

- combine text, images, and sound by incorporating information from a wide range of media, including films, newspapers, magazines, CD ROMs, online information, television, videos, and electronic media-generated images;

- select an appropriate medium for each element of the presentation;

- use the selected media skillfully, editing appropriately, and monitoring for quality; and

- test the audience's response and revise the presentation accordingly.

Authentic Tasks Match Inquiry

The skills of Information Inquiry are most meaningful for teacher and student when placed in an authentic context. It may not always be possible to tie directly to the real world. Tasks mastered in near real world simulations have a better chance for transferring meaningful skills into the workplace. More important, learning experiences tied to local businesses, organizations, civic groups, and experts create a community of learners and teachers. Issues discussed and addressed in inquiry projects may be global in nature, but they will have the greatest benefit for the learner when applied locally.

Standards for authentic tasks were identified in 1995 by the Wisconsin Center for Educational Research (Newmann, Secada, and Wehlage 1995). In summary, the inquiry curriculum should be facilitated so that all learners have the opportunity to experience the following:

1. Organization of information: The task asks students to organize, synthesize, interpret, explain, or evaluate complex information in addressing a concept, problem, or issue.

2. Consideration of alternatives: The task asks students to consider alternative solutions, strategies, perspectives, points of view, experiences as concepts, problems, and issues.

3. Disciplinary content: The task asks students to show understanding and/or use of ideas, theories, or perspectives considered central to an academic or professional discipline.

4. Disciplinary process: The task asks students to use methods of inquiry, research, or communication characteristic of an academic or professional discipline.

5. Elaborated written communication: The task asks students to elaborate on their understanding, explanations, or conclusions through extended writing.

6. Problems connected to the world: The task asks students to address a concept, problem, or issue that is similar to one that they have encountered or are likely to encounter in life beyond the classroom.

7. Audience beyond the school: The task asks students to communicate their knowledge, present a product or performance, or take some action for an audience beyond the teacher, classroom, and school building.

Zemelman, Daniels, and Hyde (2005) recommend several best practices to make learning situations authentic. Among these are to

- Develop broad, interdisciplinary, thematic units based on student concerns and interests.

- Use tangible, tactile materials, artifacts, and live demonstrations [wherever] possible.

- Follow news and current events and issues, and connect them to the curriculum.

- Assign real, whole books, rather than synthetic basal texts created by publishers.

- Use primary source documents, not just textbooks, to teach history, science, and other subjects.

- Invite speakers [and] experts, and interview subjects from the community.

- Schedule time in flexible blocks that match the curriculum.

- Offer frequent performances, fairs, and exhibitions, inviting parent and community audiences.

- Launch family and community history projects.

- Join local service projects and involve students in community beautification or art projects.

- Support student service clubs and groups that reach out to the community.

- Take children on outdoor education, wilderness, ecology, and adventure programs.

- In conjunction with integrative units, have fact-finding tours on which students take notes, make observations, or conduct interviews—extracting information from human experts.

- Conduct survey or opinion research, by mail or in person, and follow correct social scientific methods; examine and understand application and limitation of the survey results.

- Develop volunteer relationships with local agencies, nursing homes, and hospitals.

- Display student artwork or research projects in off-campus settings—[especially in school and community libraries]. (250–251)

Developmental Stages Applied to Questioning and Inquiry

Based on experience, skills, and maturation, students move along a continuum for effective question development for inquiry. Maturation in such skills can be enriched by instructional media specialists, who include teachers from all subject areas as well as school library media specialists who model inquiry. Such modeling should include not only development of lessons that place students in the role of "question-raisers" but also place teachers and school library media specialists as people who wonder and question as well.

In addition, models do not have all of the answers, nor does any one institution (library or Internet) have all the answers. Model inquirers work with student inquirers to understand that some answers obtained are a beginning for more investigation and possible validation or rejection of data, information, or opinions. As a cognitive apprentice (Tilley 2001), the student inquirer grows in sophistication in the application of Information Inquiry skills across the levels of learning, until he or she can operate on a near independent basis. All inquirers, no matter how educated or experienced, turn to peers for feedback and assurance. The following characteristics of reasonable questions for students in Information Inquiry were presented by Daniel Callison and others at the 2004 National Conference of the American Library Association:

Controlled or Directed Inquiry—Meets Basic Standards and Manageable—a good place to start

- Assigned questions are drawn from academic standards that match a student's grade level.

- Questions can be addressed, for the most part, from information sources that are organized and accessible—from textbooks and other sources in the school or community library.

- The question may or may not be of general interest to the students, but is relevant to the academic standards at hand and therefore valued by teachers and most learners as important.

- The question is challenging and may be addressed with one source, but more likely requires several resources to address it.

- A final product leads to evaluation of student performance based on a consistent evaluation method across all students.

- Questions are clear and understood among students and teachers, and this allows for common conversations about information needs and information access with a general process that applies to all students.

Guided Inquiry—Challenging and Exciting—signs of maturing in application of inquiry

- The student, with guidance from the library media specialist and other teachers, selects inquiry questions based on personal interest and background knowledge of a topic—questions both reflect and drive the student's knowledge scaffolding.

- Interests and basic knowledge are enhanced through brainstorming exercises, such as presearch and concept mapping, along with information exploration and discussion, in order to raise and validate as many questions as possible that are challenging, meaningful, and researchable—question choices are based on student and teacher becoming more informed, not just questions assigned for a grade or by chance.

- Questions may be based on previous inquiry experiences—both students and teachers become better at implementing inquiry processes with practice, guidance, feedback, and personal reflection.

- There is a reasonable need to seek answers to the questions, and knowledge drawn from the inquiry exercise will be of reasonable value—there is a meaningful response to the question, "so what?"—a response that is more than, "I was required to do it."

- The questions are challenging enough that not only are multiple resources necessary, but also multiple inquiry techniques—a literature search, interviews, observations, surveys, and experiments.

- There are multiple answers or alternative responses to the questions so that the student must not only evaluate information sources, but also compare and contrast impressions from facts and data collected—the student considers the most plausible findings rather than one absolute solution, although one may seem to have more support than others.

- Results of the inquiry can be organized and visualized to share with others—it is possible to communicate findings in a meaningful and interesting way.

- Questions as well as findings have relevance to questions and findings by other students so that collaborative groups or teams can be formed to explore some questions together, and part of the reflection process includes a comparison of findings among all projects.

Carol Kuhlthau and Ross Todd have further elaborated on guided inquiry processes. Their foundation for guided inquiry can be found at the Web site for the Center for International Scholarship in School Libraries (http://www.cissl.scils. rutgers.edu/guidedInquiry/found.htm).

Free Inquiry—Extended Beyond the Classroom —personal, independent inquiry agenda

- Questions are drawn from the student's personal curiosity at the time of the assigned activity and are strong enough to continue beyond the academic experience—a lifelong learning mystery.

- The questions are so exciting to the student that he or she discusses them with friends, parents, teachers, community members, nearly anyone who will listen—questions may relate to what others are exploring or have interest in, but that really doesn't matter to the determined inquirer.

- New questions continue to emerge the more the student investigates and matures— becoming more sophisticated in the mystery and demanding higher level reasoning, higher level information, and more controlled methods to investigate for possible answers.

- The mature inquirer understands that misapplied methods will result in data that are misleading and useless.

- Initial questions were from a pool for "problem solvers," and new questions are for the inquirer as a "problem identifier" —the inquirer has matured to set his or her own research agenda.

- Depending on the set of questions, resources, and maturation of the inquirer, the inquiry becomes an independent process, with teachers and resource experts acting as advisors—colleagues may be sought out, but the focus for inquiry has become a personal exploration.

An Inquiry-Based Curriculum Applied

The inquiry-based curriculum developed by the International Baccalaureate Organization (IBO) (http://www.ibo.org) has been adapted by The Center for Inquiry magnet school in the Indianapolis Public School (IPS) system. In partnership with professors from Indiana University (Jerome Harste, Carolyn Burke, and Christine Leland), this school became an experiment under the leadership of principal Christine Collier. After nine years of growth and development, reading and writing initiatives across the curriculum are now driven by collaborative inquiry, extensive reading circle discussions, use of multiple resources for inquiry projects in all grades, and a strong tie with the community to investigate information issues of interest to students and parents. The result has been an expanding enrollment, plans for new inquiry-based schools, and clear improvement in student achievement at this IPS school while other schools fail to show gains in reading performance (http://www.302. ips.k12.in.us). A sample of the IBO curriculum is given below.

Inquiry is related to these strands across all grade levels:

- Who we are—nature of self, beliefs, and values, including friends, family, and community.

- Where we are in time and place—explore our orientation to history from local and global perspectives.

- How we express ourselves—expression through language and the arts.

- How the world works—natural and human-made phenomena; science and technology.

- How we organize ourselves—human systems and communities

- How we share the planet—responsibilities to share finite resources.

Typical inquiry projects may be designed to meet individual group needs and interests and evolve from a common set of planning questions and topics.

Sample Elementary Levels Inquiries into:

- Self—our similarities and differences
- Daily life in other cultures
- Ways people preserve and share their stories
- How motions is used to produce energy
- Making observations that help to sort and classify information
- Roles and responsibilities of leaders
- What living things need to grow in a healthy manner
- Making choices with money
- Recycling and conservation

Sample Middle School Inquiries into:

- What make someone a leader?
- Why people want to communicate and how it can be most effective?
- Early development of communities and regions compared to movement among people today.
- Oral and artistic presentation
- How lifestyle choices affect our body systems
- How one's culture impacts personal expression
- Local government and how it operates
- The effects of weather on a community
- Endangered and extinct organisms

Sample High School Inquiries into:

- How media influences cultural beliefs
- The power of persuasion
- Valuing the arts in society

- How new inventions, technologies and other discoveries impact society and our community
- Fossil fuels and their origins and alternative forms of energy
- Creating and running a business
- Rebuilding after a natural or man-made disaster
- How a government is shaped; roles of individual citizens in a government
- Independent inquiry projects through collaboration between student and teacher

Application of Technology to Information Problem Solving

The preceding standards lack the specific application of technology skills some favor in curriculum that addresses problem solving in the Information Age. Mike Eisenberg and Doug Johnson (2002), and Bob Berkowitz have teamed on several important presentations and documents that outline how technology skills should be addressed. Although not offered as a scaffolded scope and sequence, their outline plots technology skills as of 2001 against the Big6 information problem-solving model. Specific examples of some software and hardware would need to be revised to bring their list up-to-date, but such is the case with nearly any set of guidelines in which specific examples are given, especially involving emerging technologies. Their list, reprinted here for general educational use, remains valid today and is an important source for application of technology skills to information search and use processes as a part of inquiry learning and teaching.

TECHNOLOGY SKILLS FOR INFORMATION PROBLEM SOLVING

http://www.big6.com/showarticle.php?id=82
A Curriculum Based on the Big6 Skills Approach

(c) Michael B. Eisenberg, Doug Johnson and Robert E. Berkowitz Permission is granted for educational use or reprint of all or parts of this curriculum as long as the authors are properly and prominently credited.

---

1. TASK DEFINITION

The first part in the information problem-solving process involves recognizing that an information need exists, defining the problem, and identifying the types and amount of information needed. In terms of technology, students will be able to:

A. Communicate with teachers regarding assignments, tasks, and information problems using e-mail; online discussions (e.g., listservs, threaded Web-based discussions, newsgroups); real-time communications (e.g., instant messaging services, chat rooms, IP telephony); desktop teleconferencing; and groupware on the Internet, intranets, and local area networks.

B. Generate topics, define problems, and facilitate cooperative activities among groups of students locally and globally using e-mail, online discussions, real-time communications, desktop teleconferencing, and groupware on the Internet and local area networks.

C. Generate topics, define problems, and facilitate cooperative activities with subject area experts locally and globally using e-mail, online discussions, real-time communications, desktop teleconferencing, and groupware on the Internet and local area networks.

D. Define or refine the information problem using computerized graphic organization, brainstorming or idea generating software. This includes developing a research question or perspective on a topic.

2. INFORMATION SEEKING STRATEGIES

Once the information problem has been formulated, the student must consider all possible information sources and develop a plan for searching. Students will be able to:

A. Assess the value of various types of electronic resources for data gathering, including databases, CD-ROM resources, commercial and Internet online resources, electronic reference works, community and government information electronic resources.

B. Assess the need for and value of primary resources including interviews, surveys, experiments, and documents that are accessible through electronic means.

C. Identify and apply specific criteria for evaluating computerized electronic resources.

D. Identify and apply specific criteria for constructing meaningful original data gathering tools such as online surveys, electronic interviews, or scientific data gathering tools such as probes, meters, and timers.

E. Assess the value of e-mail, online discussions, real-time communications, desktop teleconferencing, and groupware on the Internet and local area networks as part of a search of the current literature or in relation to the information task.

F. Use a computer to generate modifiable flow charts, time lines, organizational charts, project plans (such as Gantt charts), and calendars which will help the student plan and organize complex or group information problem-solving tasks.

G. Use handheld devices such as personal digital assistants (PDAs), electronic slates or tablet PCs to track contacts and create to-do lists and schedules.

3. LOCATION AND ACCESS

After students determine their priorities for information seeking, they must locate information from a variety of resources and access specific information found within individual resources. Students will be able to:

A. Locate and use appropriate computer resources and technologies available within the school library media center, including those on the library media center's local area network (e.g., online catalogs, periodical indexes, full-text sources, multimedia computer stations, CD-ROM stations, online terminals, scanners, digital cameras).

B. Locate and use appropriate computer resources and technologies available throughout the school including those available through intranets or local area networks (e.g., full-text resources, CD-ROMs, productivity software, scanners, digital cameras).

C. Locate and use appropriate computer resources and technologies available beyond the school through the Internet (e.g., newsgroups, listservs, WWW sites, ftp sites, online public access library catalogs, commercial databases and online services, and other community, academic, and government resources).

D. Know the roles and computer expertise of the people working in the school library media center and elsewhere who might provide information or assistance.

E. Use electronic reference materials (e.g., electronic encyclopedias, dictionaries, biographical reference sources, atlases, geographic databanks, thesauri, almanacs, fact books) available through intranets or local area networks, stand-alone workstations, commercial online vendors, or the Internet.

F. Use the Internet or commercial computer networks to contact experts and help and referral services.

G. Conduct self-initiated electronic surveys through e-mail, listservs, newsgroups and online data collection tools.

H. Use organizational systems and tools specific to electronic information sources that assist in finding specific and general information (e.g., indexes, tables of contents, user's instructions and manuals, legends, boldface and italics, graphic clues and icons, cross-references, Boolean logic strategies, time lines, hypertext links, knowledge trees, URLs, etc.) including the use of:

   1. Search tools and commands for stand-alone, CD-ROM, networked or Web-based online databases and services;

   2. Search tools and commands for searching the Internet, such as search engines, meta search tools, bots, directories, jump pages, and specialized resources such as those that search the Invisible Web;

   3. Specialized sites and search tool commands that limit searches by date, location, format, collection of evaluated sites or other criteria.

4. USE OF INFORMATION

   After finding potentially useful resources, students must engage (read, view, listen) the information to determine its relevance and then extract the relevant information. Students will be able to:

A. Connect and operate the computer technology needed to access information, and read the guides and manuals associated with such tasks.

B. Know and be able to use the software and hardware needed to view, download, decompress and open documents, files, and programs from Internet sites and archives.

C. Copy and paste information from an electronic source into a personal document complete with proper citation.

D. Take notes and outline with a word processor, database, presentation or similar productivity program.

E. Record electronic sources of information and locations of those sources in order to properly cite and credit sources in footnotes, endnotes, and bibliographies.

F. Use electronic spreadsheets, databases, and statistical software to process and analyze statistical data.

G. Analyze and filter electronic information in relation to the task, rejecting information that is not relevant.

H. Save and backup data gathered to secure locations (floppy disk, personal hard drive space, RW-CD, online storage, flash memory, etc.)

5. SYNTHESIS

Students must organize and communicate the results of the information problem-solving effort. Students will be able to:

A. Classify and group information using a word processor, database or spreadsheet.

B. Use word processing and desktop publishing software to create printed documents, applying keyboard skills equivalent to at least twice the rate of handwriting speed.

C. Create and use computer-generated graphics and art in various print and electronic presentations.

D. Use electronic spreadsheet software to create original spreadsheets.

E. Generate charts, tables and graphs using electronic spreadsheets and other graphing programs.

F. Use database software to create original databases.

G. Use presentation software to create electronic slide shows and to generate overhead transparencies and slides.

H. Create and use projection devices to show hypermedia and multimedia productions with digital video, audio and links to HTML documents or other programs. Convert presentations for display as Web pages.

I. Create Web pages and sites using hypertext markup language (HTML) in a text document or using Web page creation tools and know the procedure for having these pages loaded to a Web server.

J. Use e-mail, ftp, groupware, and other telecommunications capabilities to publish the results of the information problem-solving activity.

K. Use specialized computer applications as appropriate for specific tasks, e.g., music composition software, computer-assisted drawing and drafting programs, mathematics modeling software, scientific measurement instruments, etc.

L. Properly cite and credit electronic sources (text, graphics, sound and video) of information within the product as well as in footnotes, endnotes, and bibliographies.

6. EVALUATION

Evaluation focuses on how well the final product meets the original task (effectiveness) and the process of how well students carried out the information problem-solving process (efficiency). Students may evaluate their own work and process or be evaluated by others (i.e., classmates, teachers, library media staff, parents). Students will be able to:

A. Evaluate electronic presentations in terms of the content and format and design self-assessment tools to help them evaluate their own work for both content and format.

B. Use spell and grammar checking capabilities of word processing and other software to edit and revise their work.

C. Apply legal principles and ethical conduct related to information technology related to copyright and plagiarism.

D. Understand and abide by telecomputing etiquette when using e-mail, newsgroups, listservs and other Internet functions.

E. Understand and abide by acceptable use policies and other school rules in relation to use of the Internet and other electronic technologies.

F. Use e-mail, real-time communications (e.g., listservs, newsgroups, instant messaging services, chat rooms, IP telephony) desktop teleconferencing, and groupware on the Internet and local area networks to communicate with teachers and others regarding their performance on assignments, tasks, and information problems.

G. Thoughtfully reflect on the use of electronic resources and tools throughout the process.

Michael Eisenberg, Doug Johnson, and Robert Berkowitz, 2002. Reprinted with permission from Michael Eisenberg.

Best Practices for Standards Related to Information Inquiry

Now in its third edition (Zemelman, Daniels, and Hyde 2005), *Best Practice: New Standards for Teaching and Learning in America's Schools* contains a review of progress teaching techniques that are successful in meeting the wide spectrum of learning standards found in most school districts. The authors, while presenting a comprehensive review of standards in reading, writing, mathematics, science, social studies, and the arts, have never acknowledged information literacy skills nor even the function of the school library media center. The authors do call for an increase in learning resources, especially trade book publications for the classroom and the use of a wide variety of reading materials normally acquired, maintained, and distributed through the school library. While the following list of inquiry-based techniques for best practices is useful, this guide has yet to reach "state-of-the-art" instruction as long as it fails to include the collaborative best practices that can be gained through interactions with the school library media program.

Among the best practices emphasized, several pertain directly to inquiry-based education and specifically Information Inquiry. A selected list of elements, attitudes and activities follows:

Common recommendations across all grades and disciplines include more attention to

- experiential, inductive, hands-on learning;

- active learning, with all the attendant noise and movement of students doing, talking, and collaborating;

- diverse roles for teachers, including coaching, demonstrating, and modeling;

- emphasis on higher-order thinking; learning a field's key concepts and principles;

- deep study of a smaller number of topics, so that students internalize the field's way of inquiry;

- reading of real texts: whole books, primary sources, and nonfiction materials;

- responsibility [for their work] transferred to students: goal setting, record keeping, monitoring, sharing, exhibiting, and evaluating;

- choice for students—choosing their own books, writing topics, team partners, and research projects;

- enacting and modeling of the principles of democracy in school;

- attention to affective needs and varying cognitive styles of individual students; and

- reliance on descriptive evaluations of student growth, including observation/anecdotal records, conference notes, and performance assessment rubrics. (2005, 8–9)

Among recommendations for teaching reading, increase

- teacher modeling and discussing his/her own reading processes;

- teaching reading as a process: activate prior knowledge; students make and test predictions; structure help during reading; provide after-reading applications; and

- writing before and after reading. (2005, 77)

Among recommendations for teaching writing (105), increase

- student ownership and responsibility; help students choose their own topics and goals for improvement; using brief teacher-student conferences; teaching students to review their own progress;

- writing for real audiences, publishing for the class and wider communities;

- teacher modeling writing; drafting, revising, sharing, and as a fellow author who demonstrates processes; and

- making the classroom a supportive setting by using active exchange and valuing of students' ideas, collaborative small-group work, conferences, and peer critiquing that give responsibility to authors.

Among recommendations for teaching mathematics (137), increase

- problem solving: everyday problems and applications, open-ended problems and extended problem solving projects, investigations and formulating questions from problem situations.

Among recommendations for teaching science (168–169), increase

- curriculum that includes natural phenomena and science-related social issues that students encounter in everyday life;

- understanding scientific concepts and developing abilities of inquiry;

- focusing on students' prior knowledge to foster conceptual change;

- providing opportunities for scientific discussion and debate among students;

- promotion of inquiry methods—implementing inquiry as instructional strategies, abilities, and ideas to be learned;

- activities that investigate and analyze science questions extended over periods of time;

- emphasizing multiple process skills (manipulation, cognitive, procedural) in context;

- using evidence and strategies for developing or revising an explanation;

- science as argument and explanation;

- communicating science explanations— student collaborative groups defending conclusions, analyzing and synthesizing data;

- doing more investigations in order to develop understanding, ability, values of inquiry, and knowledge of science content;

- applying the results of experiments to scientific arguments and explanations; and

- public communication of student ideas and work to classmates.

Among recommendations on teaching social studies (194), increase

- in-depth study of topics in each social studies field, in which students make

choices what to study (Saye and Brush 2006);

- activities that engage students in inquiry and problem solving about significant human issues (Wineburg 1991);

- richer content in elementary grades, using children's prior knowledge, from psychology, sociology, economics, and political science, as well as history and geography; younger students' experience can relate to social institutions and problems of everyday living;

- inquiry about students' cultural groups and others in their school and community, thus building ownership in the curriculum; and

- use of evaluation that involves further learning and that promotes responsible citizenship and open expression of ideas. (Laughlin, Hartoonian, and Sanders 1989)

Among recommendations on teaching in the arts (226), increase

- student originality, choice, and responsibility in art making;

- support every student's quest to find and develop personal media, style, and tastes; and

- using art as a tool of doing, learning, and thinking.

The AASL/AECT Standards for Student Learning

In 1998, the American Association of School Librarians and the Association for Educational Communications and Technology published milestone statements on information literacy standards for student learning. Over the past several years, these guidelines have changed the instructional approach in hundreds of school library media programs across the nation. Much still remains to be done to incorporate these standards at the state level and in national curricular guides as well as to integrate these standards across recommended best practices, but they have served the national school library audience well. Future national standards in school media are likely to build on these and to emphasize inquiry-based learning more than has been the case over the past thirty years. Students who combine knowledge of these AASL/AECT standards along with a wide understanding and ability to implement inquiry methods, student performance assessment, and technology management will be ready for positions of educational change and leadership.

Prepared by the American Association of School Librarians

Association for Educational Communications and Technology

INFORMATION LITERACY STANDARDS FOR STUDENT LEARNING AND INDICATORS

www.ala.org/.../ContentManagement/Content Display.cfm&ContentID=19937

Reprinted with permission.

Copyright © 1998 by the American Library Association and the Association for Educational Communications and Technology. Excerpt from *Information Literacy Standards for Student Learning,* published by the American Library Association. The full publication includes a chapter on the philosophy and the mission and goals of the information literacy standards, along with the following supporting material to illustrate how standards and indicators can be applied.

- Levels of Proficiency items for the indicators within each standard

- Standards in Action that provide examples of potential situations requiring information literacy for each standard

- Examples of Content-Area Standards for each standard

Information Power: Building Partnerships for Learning includes the full content of *Information Literacy Standards for Student Learning* with additional content designed to guide and support library media specialists' efforts in three major areas: learning and teaching, information access, and program administration. It also shows how skills and strategies in collaboration, leadership, and technology support these efforts.

This work is licensed under a Creative Commons License.

Introduction

Information Literacy Standards for Student Learning provides a conceptual framework and broad guidelines for describing the information-literate student. The standards consist of three categories, nine standards, and twenty-nine indicators. The core learning outcomes that are most directly related to the services provided by school library media programs are found in the three standards and thirteen indicators in the "information literacy" category. The other two categories—three standards and seven indicators for "independent learning" and three standards and nine indicators for "social responsibility"—are grounded in information literacy but describe more general aspects of student learning to which school library media programs also make important contributions. Taken together, the categories, standards, and indicators describe the content and processes related to information that students must master to be considered information literate. The standards and indicators are written at a general level so that library media specialists and others in individual states, districts, and sites can tailor the statements to meet local needs. These educators are the ones who know their student populations; their role is to apply these general statements in light of the developmental, cultural, and learning needs of all the students they serve. By offering broad guidelines for describing the information-literate student, Information Literacy Standards for Student Learning provides a conceptual framework and supporting material for local efforts.

Information Literacy Standards For Student Learning

INFORMATION LITERACY STANDARDS

Standard 1 The student who is information literate accesses information efficiently and effectively.

The student who is information literate recognizes that having good information is central to meeting the opportunities and challenges of day-to-day living. That student knows when to seek information beyond his or her personal knowledge, how to frame questions that will lead to the appropriate information, and where to seek that information. The student knows how to structure a search across a variety of sources and formats to locate the best information to meet a particular need.

Indicators

Indicator 1. Recognizes the need for information

Indicator 2. Recognizes that accurate and comprehensive information is the basis for intelligent decision making

Indicator 3. Formulates questions based on information needs

Indicator 4. Identifies a variety of potential sources of information

Indicator 5. Develops and uses successful strategies for locating information

Standard 2 The student who is information literate evaluates information critically and competently.

The student who is information literate weighs information carefully and wisely to determine its quality. That student understands traditional and emerging principles for assessing the accuracy, validity, relevance, completeness, and impartiality of information. The student applies these principles insightfully across information sources and formats and uses logic and informed judgment to accept, reject, or replace information to meet a particular need.

Indicators

Indicator 1. Determines accuracy, relevance, and comprehensiveness

Indicator 2. Distinguishes among fact, point of view, and opinion

Indicator 3. Identifies inaccurate and misleading information

Indicator 4. Selects information appropriate to the problem or question at hand

Standard 3 The student who is information literate uses information accurately and creatively.

The student who is information literate manages information skillfully and effectively in a variety of contexts. That student organizes and integrates information from a range of sources and formats in order to apply it to decision making, problem solving, critical thinking, and creative expression. The student communicates information and ideas for a variety of purposes, both scholarly and creative; to a range of audiences, both in school and beyond; and in print, nonprint, and electronic formats. This Standard promotes the design and execution of authentic products that involve critical and creative thinking and that reflect real world situations. The indicators under this Standard therefore deviate from the traditional definition of use. Rather than suggesting that students simply insert researched information into a perfunctory product, the indicators emphasize the thinking processes involved when students use information to draw conclusions and develop new understandings.

Indicators

Indicator 1. Organizes information for practical application

Indicator 2. Integrates new information into one's own knowledge

Indicator 3. Applies information in critical thinking and problem solving

Indicator 4. Produces and communicates information and ideas in appropriate formats

INDEPENDENT LEARNING STANDARDS

Standard 4 The student who is an independent learner is information literate and pursues information related to personal interests.

The student who is an independent learner applies the principles of information literacy to access, evaluate, and use information about issues and situations of personal interest. That student actively and independently seeks information to enrich understanding of career, community, health, leisure, and other personal situations. The student constructs meaningful personal knowledge based on that information and communicates that knowledge accurately and creatively across the range of information formats.

Indicators

Indicator 1. Seeks information related to various dimensions of personal well-being, such as career interests, community involvement, health matters, and recreational pursuits

Indicator 2. Designs, develops, and evaluates information products and solutions related to personal interests

Standard 5 The student who is an independent learner is information literate and appreciates literature and other creative expressions of information.

The student who is an independent learner applies the principles of information literacy to access, evaluate, enjoy, value, and create artistic products. That student actively and independently seeks to master the principles, conventions, and criteria of literature in print, nonprint, and electronic formats. The student is able both to understand and enjoy creative works presented in all formats and to create products that capitalize on each format's particular strengths.

Indicators

Indicator 1. Is a competent and self-motivated reader

Indicator 2. Derives meaning from information presented creatively in a variety of formats

Indicator 3. Develops creative products in a variety of formats

Standard 6 The student who is an independent learner is information literate and strives for excellence in information seeking and knowledge generation.

The student who is an independent learner applies the principles of information literacy to evaluate and use his or her own information processes and products as well as those developed by others. That student actively and independently reflects on and critiques personal thought processes and individually created information products.

The student recognizes when these efforts are successful and unsuccessful and develops strategies for revising and improving them in light of changing information.

Indicators

Indicator 1. Assesses the quality of the process and products of personal information seeking

Indicator 2. Devises strategies for revising, improving, and updating self-generated knowledge

SOCIAL RESPONSIBILITY STANDARDS

Standard 7 The student who contributes positively to the learning community and to society is information literate and recognizes the importance of information to a democratic society.

The student who is socially responsible with regard to information understands that access to information is basic to the functioning of a democracy. That student seeks out information from a diversity of viewpoints, scholarly traditions, and cultural perspectives in an attempt to arrive at a reasoned and informed understanding of issues. The student realizes that equitable access to information from a range of sources and in all formats is a fundamental right in a democracy.

Indicators

Indicator 1. Seeks information from diverse sources, contexts, disciplines, and cultures

Indicator 2. Respects the principle of equitable access to information

Standard 8 The student who contributes positively to the learning community and to society is information literate and practices ethical behavior in regard to information and information technology.

The student who is socially responsible with regard to information applies principles and practices that reflect high ethical standards for accessing, evaluating, and using information. That student recognizes the importance of equitable access to information in a democratic society and respects the principles of intellectual freedom and the rights of producers of intellectual property. The student applies these principles across the range of information formats—print, nonprint, and electronic.

Indicators

Indicator 1. Respects the principles of intellectual freedom

Indicator 2. Respects intellectual property rights

Indicator 3. Uses information technology responsibly

Standard 9 The student who contributes positively to the learning community and to society is information literate and participates effectively in groups to pursue and generate information.

The student who is socially responsible with regard to information works successfully—both locally and through the variety of technologies that link the learning community—to access, evaluate, and use information. That student seeks and shares information and ideas across a range of sources and perspectives and acknowledges the insights and contributions of a variety of cultures and disciplines.

The student collaborates with diverse individuals to identify information problems, to seek their solutions, and to communicate these solutions accurately and creatively.

Indicators

Indicator 1. Shares knowledge and information with others

Indicator 2. Respects others' ideas and backgrounds and acknowledges their contributions

Indicator 3. Collaborates with others, both in person and through technologies, to identify information problems and to seek their solutions

Indicator 4. Collaborates with others, both in person and through technologies, to design, develop, and evaluate information products and solutions

The College Student

Over the past three decades, the Association of College and Research Librarians (ACRL) has issued several outlines for standards of student performance and bibliographic instruction. In 2001, ACRL revised several statements and issued a new outline for the information literate student in higher education as well as collaborative roles between the academic librarian and college professor in ensuring that the practice of these skills will be integrated with disciplines of study. Although some of the skills overlap with previous statements found in scope and sequence for the educational experience prior to college, other items take information literacy to a higher level.

At the college level, inquiry becomes more discipline-focused. ACRL standards often refer to the need for the college student to begin to grasp the discourse and primary investigation methods of specific disciplines and to gain an understanding of how they differ. The ACRL competency standards for higher education are reprinted below, with permission, to illustrate the basic standard information use behaviors now expected of those who enter higher education, but increasing for the general information user in our society.

Information Literacy Competency Standards for Higher Education

http://www.ala.org/ala/acrl/acrlstandards/informationliteracycompetency.htm

Reprinted with permission

Standards, Performance Indicators, and Outcomes

Standard One

The information literate student determines the nature and extent of the information needed.

Performance Indicators:

1. The information literate student defines and articulates the need for information.

   Outcomes Include:

   a. Confers with instructors and participates in class discussions, peer workgroups, and electronic discussions to identify a research topic, or other information need

   b. Develops a thesis statement and formulates questions based on the information need

c. Explores general information sources to increase familiarity with the topic

d. Defines or modifies the information need to achieve a manageable focus

e. Identifies key concepts and terms that describe the information need

f. Recognizes that existing information can be combined with original thought, experimentation, and/or analysis to produce new information

2. The information literate student identifies a variety of types and formats of potential sources for information.

   Outcomes Include:

   a. Knows how information is formally and informally produced, organized, and disseminated

   b. Recognizes that knowledge can be organized into disciplines that influence the way information is accessed

   c. Identifies the value and differences of potential resources in a variety of formats (e.g., multimedia, database, website, data set, audio/visual, book)

   d. Identifies the purpose and audience of potential resources (e.g., popular vs. scholarly, current vs. historical)

   e. Differentiates between primary and secondary sources, recognizing how their use and importance vary with each discipline

   f. Realizes that information may need to be constructed with raw data from primary sources

3. The information literate student considers the costs and benefits of acquiring the needed information.

   Outcomes Include:

   a. Determines the availability of needed information and makes decisions on broadening the information seeking process beyond local resources (e.g., interlibrary loan; using resources at other locations; obtaining images, videos, text, or sound)

b. Considers the feasibility of acquiring a new languag or skill (e.g., foreign or discipline-based) in order to gather needed information and to understand its context

c. Defines a realistic overall plan and timeline to acquire the needed information

4. The information literate student reevaluates the nature and extent of the information need.

   Outcomes Include:

   a. Reviews the initial information need to clarify, revise, or refine the question

   b. Describes criteria used to make information decisions and choices

Standard Two

The information literate student accesses needed information effectively and efficiently.

Performance Indicators:

1. The information literate student selects the most appropriate investigative methods or information retrieval systems for accessing the needed information.

   Outcomes Include:

   a. Identifies appropriate investigative methods (e.g., laboratory experiment, simulation, fieldwork)

   b. Investigates benefits and applicability of various investigative methods

   c. Investigates the scope, content, and organization of information retrieval systems

   d. Selects efficient and effective approaches for accessing the information needed from the investigative method or information retrieval system

2. The information literate student constructs and implements effectively-designed search strategies.

   Outcomes Include:

   a. Develops a research plan appropriate to the investigative method

   b. Identifies keywords, synonyms and related terms for the information needed

---

c. Selects controlled vocabulary specific to the discipline or information retrieval source

d. Constructs a search strategy using appropriate commands for the information retrieval system selected (e.g., Boolean operators, truncation, and proximity for search engines; internal organizers such as indexes for books)

e. Implements the search strategy in various information retrieval systems using different user interfaces and search engines, with different command languages, protocols, and search parameters

f. Implements the search using investigative protocols appropriate to the discipline

3. The information literate student retrieves information online or in person using a variety of methods.

Outcomes Include:

a. Uses various search systems to retrieve information in a variety of formats

b. Uses various classification schemes and other systems (e.g., call number systems or indexes) to locate information resources within the library or to identify specific sites for physical exploration

c. Uses specialized online or in person services available at the institution to retrieve information needed (e.g., interlibrary loan/document delivery, professional associations, institutional research offices, community resources, experts and practitioners)

d. Uses surveys, letters, interviews, and other forms of inquiry to retrieve primary information

4. The information literate student refines the search strategy if necessary.

Outcomes Include:

a. Assesses the quantity, quality, and relevance of the search results to determine whether alternative information retrieval systems or investigative methods should be utilized

b. Identifies gaps in the information retrieved and determines if the search strategy should be revised

c. Repeats the search using the revised strategy as necessary

5. The information literate student extracts, records, and manages the information and its sources.

Outcomes Include:

a. Selects among various technologies the most appropriate one for the task of extracting the needed information (e.g., copy/paste software functions, photocopier, scanner, audio/visual equipment, or exploratory instruments)

b. Creates a system for organizing the information

c. Differentiates between the types of sources cited and understands the elements and correct syntax of a citation for a wide range of resources

d. Records all pertinent citation information for future reference

e. Uses various technologies to manage the information selected and organized

Standard Three

The information literate student evaluates information and its sources critically and incorporates selected information into his or her knowledge base and value system.

Performance Indicators:

1. The information literate student summarizes the main ideas to be extracted from the information gathered.

Outcomes Include:

a. Reads the text and selects main ideas

b. Restates textual concepts in his/her own words and selects data accurately

c. Identifies verbatim material that can be then appropriately quoted

2. The information literate student articulates and applies initial criteria for evaluating both the information and its sources.

Outcomes Include:

a. Examines and compares information from various sources in order to evaluate reliability, validity, accuracy, authority, timeliness, and point of view or bias

b. Analyzes the structure and logic of supporting arguments or methods

c. Recognizes prejudice, deception, or manipulation

d. Recognizes the cultural, physical, or other context within which the information was created and understands the impact of context on interpreting the information

3. The information literate student synthesizes main ideas to construct new concepts.

Outcomes Include:

a. Recognizes interrelationships among concepts and combines them into potentially useful primary statements with supporting evidence

b. Extends initial synthesis, when possible, at a higher level of abstraction to construct new hypotheses that may require additional information

c. Utilizes computer and other technologies (e.g. spreadsheets, databases, multimedia, and audio or visual equipment) for studying the interaction of ideas and other phenomena

4. The information literate student compares new knowledge with prior knowledge to determine the value added, contradictions, or other unique characteristics of the information.

Outcomes Include:

a. Determines whether information satisfies the research or other information need

b. Uses consciously selected criteria to determine whether the information contradicts or verifies information used from other sources

c. Draws conclusions based upon information gathered

d. Tests theories with discipline-appropriate techniques (e.g., simulators, experiments)

e. Determines probable accuracy by questioning the source of the data, the limitations of the information gathering tools or strategies, and the reasonableness of the conclusions

f. Integrates new information with previous information or knowledge

g. Selects information that provides evidence for the topic

5. The information literate student determines whether the new knowledge has an impact on the individual's value system and takes steps to reconcile differences.

Outcomes Include:

a. Investigates differing viewpoints encountered in the literature

b. Determines whether to incorporate or reject viewpoints encountered

6. The information literate student validates understanding and interpretation of the information through discourse with other individuals, subject-area experts, and/or practitioners.

Outcomes Include:

a. Participates in classroom and other discussions

b. Participates in class-sponsored electronic communication forums designed to encourage discourse on the topic (e.g., email, bulletin boards, chat rooms)

c. Seeks expert opinion through a variety of mechanisms (e.g., interviews, email, listservs)

7. The information literate student determines whether the initial query should be revised.

Outcomes Include:

a. Determines if original information need has been satisfied or if additional information is needed

b. Reviews search strategy and incorporates additional concepts as necessary

c. Reviews information retrieval sources used and expands to include others as needed

Standard Four

The information literate student, individually or as a member of a group, uses information effectively to accomplish a specific purpose.

Performance Indicators:

1. The information literate student applies new and prior information to the planning and creation of a particular product or performance.

   Outcomes Include:

   a. Organizes the content in a manner that supports the purposes and format of the product or performance (e.g. outlines, drafts, storyboards)

   b. Articulates knowledge and skills transferred from prior experiences to planning and creating the product or performance

   c. Integrates the new and prior information, including quotations and paraphrasings, in a manner that supports the purposes of the product or performance

   d. Manipulates digital text, images, and data, as needed, transferring them from their original locations and formats to a new context

2. The information literate student revises the development process for the product or performance.

   Outcomes Include:

   a. Maintains a journal or log of activities related to the information seeking, evaluating, and communicating process

   b. Reflects on past successes, failures, and alternative strategies

3. The information literate student communicates the product or performance effectively to others.

Outcomes Include:

a. Chooses a communication medium and format that best supports the purposes of the product or performance and the intended audience

b. Uses a range of information technology applications in creating the product or performance

c. Incorporates principles of design and communication

d. Communicates clearly and with a style that supports the purposes of the intended audience

Standard Five

The information literate student understands many of the economic, legal, and social issues surrounding the use of information and accesses and uses information ethically and legally.

Performance Indicators:

1. The information literate student understands many of the ethical, legal and socio-economic issues surrounding information and information technology.

   Outcomes Include:

   a. Identifies and discusses issues related to privacy and security in both the print and electronic environments

   b. Identifies and discusses issues related to free vs. fee-based access to information

   c. Identifies and discusses issues related to censorship and freedom of speech

   d. Demonstrates an understanding of intellectual property, copyright, and fair use of copyrighted material

2. The information literate student follows laws, regulations, institutional policies, and etiquette related to the access and use of information resources.

   Outcomes Include:

   a. Participates in electronic discussions following accepted practices (e.g. "Netiquette")

   b. Uses approved passwords and other forms of ID for access to information resources

c. Complies with institutional policies on access to information resources

d. Preserves the integrity of information resources, equipment, systems and facilities

e. Legally obtains, stores, and disseminates text, data, images, or sounds

f. Demonstrates an understanding of what constitutes plagiarism and does not represent work attributable to others as his/her own

g. Demonstrates an understanding of institutional policies related to human subjects research

3. The information literate student acknowledges the use of information sources in communicating the product or performance.

Outcomes Include:

a. Selects an appropriate documentation style and uses it consistently to cite sources

b. Posts permission granted notices, as needed, for copyrighted material

College Level Critical Thinking Skills

In 1995, the final report on an assessment of communication and critical thinking skills necessary for the successful college student was released by the U. S. Department of Education's Office of Educational Research and Improvement (Jones 1995). Ratings of skills were compared among groups of college educators, policy makers, and employers. Although there were some differences, commonly acceptable sets of these skills were identified as essential. They reflect many of the previously described skills of the information literate college student (Thompson and Henley 2000).

These skill sets also place analysis, synthesis, and evaluation on a higher level. The student becomes a critical thinker, based not so much on information location, but on abilities in analysis of arguments, meaningful communication, and cultivation of an inquiring mind. Accomplished skills in critical thinking take information literacy and inquiry to the higher levels toward which instruction should strive. We may not reach these levels in all Information Inquiry lessons nor at each grade, but these should be the standards toward which we construct any scope and sequence curriculum in the Information Age.

Critical Thinking in Communication and Inquiry Interpretation:

- categorize information
- classify data and make comparisons
- translate data from one medium to another
- clarify meaning of data
- recognize confusing, vague language
- ask relevant or penetrating questions
- identify and seek additional resources
- develop analogies or other forms of comparisons
- provide examples to explain ideas

Analysis:

- identify the explicit and implicit features of a communication
- examine ideas and purposes by assessing the constraints on the practical applications, as well as interests, attitudes, or views contained in those ideas
- identify stated, implied, or undeclared purposes of a communication
- identify the main conclusion of an argument
- determine whether a communication expresses a reason(s) in support of or in opposition to some conclusion or point of view
- assess the credibility of a communication and evaluate the strengths of claims and arguments
- determine if arguments rest on false, biased, or doubtful assumptions
- assess the importance of an argument and determine if it merits attention

- evaluate an argument in terms of reasonability and practicality

- assess statistical information

- determine how new data may lead to further confirmation or questioning of a conclusion

- determine if conclusions are derived from sufficiently large and representative samples

Evaluation:

- assess bias, narrowness, and contradictions

- judge consistency of supporting reasons and evidence

Inference:

- collect and question evidence

- formulate a plan for locating information

- determine if sufficient evidence is present to form a conclusion

- judge what background information is most useful

- seek evidence to confirm or disconfirm alternatives

- seek opinions of others

- assess the risks and benefits of each option

- develop new alternatives when appropriate

Present Arguments:

- clearly communicate and justify the results of one's reasoning

- present the crucial point of an issue

- evaluate key assumptions

- formulate accurately alternative positions

- illustrate central concepts with examples that apply to real situations

Reflection:

- monitor one's comprehension

- correct one's process of thinking

- make revisions in one's own arguments, when self-examination reveals inadequacies

- apply the skills of analysis to one's own arguments

Dispositions or Behaviors (signs of the mature critical thinker and inquirer):

- curious

- organized

- fair-minded

- open-minded

- flexible

- creative

- perseveres

- applies insight from other cultures

- willingly self-corrects

- learns from errors

In the practice and application of these critical thinking skills, college students should have the opportunity to find ways to collaborate with others to reach consensus, share testing of alternative approaches, and compare and contrast results in attempting to address problems and issues. The foundation for these skills, abilities, and behaviors can be established in the inquiry-based curriculum at the elementary school level if teachers and library media specialists collaborate as instructional media specialists to ensure information literacy and Information Inquiry.

References

American Association of School Librarians and Association for Educational Communications and Technology. (1998). *Information literacy standards for student learning.* American Library Association.

Association of College and Research Librarians (ACRL). (2001). *Information literacy competency standards for higher education.* http://www.ala.org/acrl/acrl/ilcomstan.html (accessed January 8, 2006).

Bloom, B. S. (Ed.). (1956). *Taxonomy of educational objectives: The classification of educational goals.* Longman, Green.

Callison, D., et al. (2004). *Information Inquiry: Key words, concepts, and assessments for* literacy K-college. National Conference of the American Library Association.

Center for Inquiry. (2006). *A magnet school in the Indianapolis Public School system.* http://www.302.ips.k12.in.us/ (accessed February 13, 2006).

Considine, D. 1995. An introduction to media literacy: The what, why, and how to's. *Telemedium, 41* (2), 1–8.

Correlation of the library information literacy standards and the language arts standards for Indiana schools. (2000). Indiana Department of Education School Library Media Specialist Leadership Cadre 2000. http://ideanet.doe.state.in.us/standards/welcome.html (accessed March 15, 2001).

Eisenberg, M. B., and D. Johnson. (2002). *Learning and teaching information technology—computer skills in context.* ERIC Clearinghouse on Information & Technology, Syracuse University. ED465377 http://www.ericit.org/digests/EDO-IR-2002.04.shtml or http://www.big6.com/showarticle.php?id=82 (accessed January 9, 2006).

Information skills curriculum guide: Process, scope, and, sequence. (1987). Washington Library Media Association.

International Baccalaureate Organization. http://www.ibo.org/ (accessed February 13, 2006).

International Society for Technology in Education (ISTE). (2000). *National educational technology standards for students: Connecting curriculum and technology.* . http://cnets.iste.org/students/s_profiles.html (accessed January 8, 2006).

Jones, E. A. (1995). *National assessment of college student learning: Identifying college graduates' essential skills in writing, speech and listening, and critical thinking.* U.S. Department of Education, Office of Educational Research and Improvement and the National Center for Education Statistics.

Kuhlthau, C. C. (1981). *School libarian's grade-by-grade activities program: A complete sequential skills plan for grades K-8.* The Center for Applied Research in Education.

Laughlin, M. A., H. M. Hartoonian, and N. M. Sanders (Eds.) (1989). *From information to decision making.* National Council for the Social Studies

Newmann, F. M., W. G. Secada, and G. G. Wehlage. (1995). *A guide to authentic instruction and assessment: Vision, standards and scoring.* Wisconsin Center for Education Research.

Opper, S., H. P. Ginsburg, and S.O. Brandt. (1987). *Piaget's theory of intellectual development.* Prentice-Hall.

Saye, J., and T. Brush. (2006). Comparing teachers' strategies for supporting student inquiry in a problem-solving multimedia-enhanced history unit. *Theory and Research in Social Education, 34* (2), 2–32.

Thompson, H. M., and S. A. Henley. (2000). *Fostering information literacy: Connecting national standards, goals 2000, and the SCANS report.* Libraries Unlimited.

Tilley, C. L. (2001). Cognitive apprenticeship. *School Library Media Activities Monthly, 18* (3), 37–38, 48.

Tyner, K. (1998). *Literacy in a digital world: Teaching and learning in the age of information.* Lawrence Erlbaum Associates.

Wineburg, S. S. (1991). Historical problem solving: A study of cognitive processes used in the evaluation of documentary and pictorial evidence. *Journal of Educational Psychology, 83* (1), 73–87.

Zemelman, S., H. Daniels, and A. Hyde. (2005). *Best practice: New standards for teaching and learning in America's schools.* 3d ed. Heinemann.

For Further Reading

Bruce, B. C. (Ed.). (2003). *Literacy in the information age: Inquiries into meaning making with new technologies.* International Reading Association.

Neely, T. Y. (Ed.). (2006). *Information literacy assessment: Standards-based tools and assignments.* American Library Association.

Chapter 7

Instructional Models Applied to Inquiry

Daniel Callison

Several prominent instructional models are offered here to illustrate that the instructional process has many elements similar to those illustrated in inquiry and information use models. The instructional media specialist and other teachers face similar task definition, information acquisition, and evaluation challenges as those confronted by the student researcher. More important, these models illustrate the additional considerations teachers face concerning levels of audience ability and interest, motivation, and multiple evaluation modes.

Careful planning will increase the effectiveness of instruction (Dick, Carey, and Carey 2004). The Indiana University professors Robert Heinich and Michael Molenda (Heinich, Molenda, Russell, and Smaldino 2001) describe their ASSURE model as a procedural guide for planning and conducting instruction that incorporates media. It serves as a basic, introductory guide to instructional planning and includes steps for design of original instructional materials when available resources do not fit the desired need.

Robert Gagné (1977), a major theorist in instructional design, revealed through his research that well-designed lessons begin with the arousal of the students' interests and then move to the presentation of new material. These stages or events of instruction involve students in practice, assessment of their understanding, and follow-up activities.

The ASSURE model also incorporates these instructional events:

Analyze Learners—analyze in terms of general characteristics, specific entry competencies, and learning styles.

State Objectives—a statement of what the student will be able to do as a result of the instruction.

Select Methods, Media, and Materials—select from available materials, modify existing materials, design new materials.

Utilize Media and Materials—preview materials, practice implementation, make final choices in order to conduct instruction.

Require Learner Participation—require active mental engagement of learners so that performance can be observed, evaluated, modified, or praised through feedback.

Evaluate and Revise—evaluate the impact of the instruction and to what degree learners met the objectives; revise for future lessons.

Classic Instructional Design

Philip Turner, professor and dean at North Texas University and an early advocate for the role of the school media specialist as an instructional player, emphasizes learner analysis in his model for instructional design. Recently revised with Ann Marlow Riedling, associate professor at Spalding University, *Helping Teachers Teach* (2003) is based on the classic instructional design model below. Needs assessment in terms of the teacher understanding the potential and limitations of the learning environment, resource availability, and learner ability all precede the development of activities and materials selection. New resources introduced by the school library media specialist, however, can greatly influence the revision and focus of instruction. The stages of this instructional design model are found in classic texts such as *Principles of Instructional Design* by Gagné, Briggs, and Wager (1992).

Stages of Classical Instructional Design

1. Define instructional goals—Develop statements of desired student accomplishments, perhaps linked to standards from local curriculum.

2. Conduct an instructional analysis—Identify what learning steps will be involved in reaching the goals.

3. Identify entry behaviors, learner characteristics—What does the learner bring to the situation in terms of skills demonstrated?

4. Develop performance objectives—What will students be expected to demonstrate in observable and measurable terms to show they have accomplished the desired skills?

5. Select an instructional method—The method will need to meet the limitations of location, space, number of students, and technology support: lecture, lab, simulation, small group discussion, debate, or other relevant methods.

6. Assemble instructional material—Materials available or that can be locally produced may influence the instructional method and vice versa. Often choices involve access to manageable tools, equipment, and print and nonprint resources that are age appropriate.

7. Plan and conduct formative evaluation—Obtain feedback through observation, interviews and exams at strategic points of the learning process.

8. Plan and conduct summative evaluation—Evaluate student performance and evaluate the effectiveness of the lesson and instruction. Were the objectives achieved?

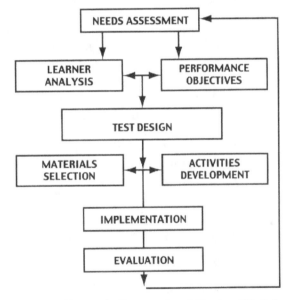

Figure 7.1. Turner's Instructional Design Model with school library media specialist as consultant. Philip Turner. Copyright 1993, 2003. Reprinted with permission from Philip Turner.

Turner and Riedling (2003) place needs assessment at the front of the instructional design process and make needs assessment a key portion of the evaluation process to repeat the cycle for future instructional planning based on reflection on the accomplished instructional event. Learner analysis and revision of instructional objectives never really cease, and they feed back into assessment of student performance, strategies for development of new activities, and new support materials.

Further, Turner and Riedling introduce various levels of instructional involvement for the school library media specialist:

- **Initial Level**—The school library media specialist selects and maintains materials, equipment, and facilities that assist the faculty in their teaching.

- **Moderate Level**—The library media specialist cooperates at a few stages of instructional design on a limited basis and the teacher remains the primary developer of the lessons and activities.

- **In-Depth Level**—The library media specialist, depending on the teacher's knowledge, experience, and expertise, may play a much stronger role as a consultant in needs assessment, materials selection, and evaluation for instruction. The extent of this consultation will also depend on the experience and expertise of the library media specialist. This level is close to the full role of the school librarian as instructional media specialist presented later in this text and nears the highest levels of curricular involvement illustrated later in this chapter by Loertscher's Taxonomy.

Cooperative Teaching Models for Library Skills and Literacy

Few library media specialists prior to the 1988 and 1998 AASL national guidelines for school library programs considered full integration of library information skills with the curriculum, and even fewer practiced any form of collaborative instruction. Publications written and edited by Thomas Walker and Paula Montgomery (1983) were among the first to illustrate the difference between library skills planned in relation to but separate from the classroom, and they illustrated a more integrated approach to library information skills instruction based on roles related in a cooperative basis between the school library media specialist and the classroom teacher.

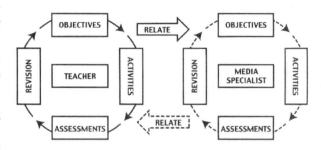

Figure 7.2. Related model of library media skills instruction. H. Thomas Walker and Paula Montgomery, 1983. Reprinted with permission from Paula Montgomery.

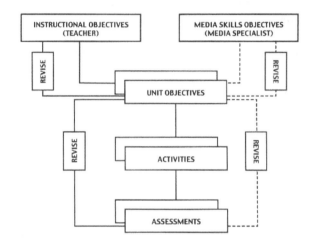

Figure 7.3. Integrated model of library media skills instruction. H. Thomas Walker and Paula Montgomery, 1983. Reprinted with permission from Paula Montgomery.

The Fully Integrated Collaborative Model

Patricia Montiel-Overall (2005), assistant professor at Arizona University, has introduced a series of models that illustrate a more collaborative approach in which there is little separation between the instructional responsibilities for information literacy between the library media specialist and classroom teacher. In addition, her model for Integrated Curriculum places the principal as the initiating force to establish expectations and provide rewards for collaboration. Ideally, all teachers share with the school library media specialist an instructional vision and planning across the integration of information literacy and subject content. Figure 7.4 demonstrates coordination. Coordination requires one person to manage events, activities, and schedules. In this model teachers and librarian work together to ensure efficiency and order. Either the teacher or the librarian can become the coordinator of events, activities, and schedules for students. Scheduling may help students feel a sense of order, but it is unlikely there is a relationship between coordinated events and student academic gains (see Figure 7.4). Teachers and the librarian work together but do not have to be involved in joint planning, thinking, or evaluation, although that would be a natural extension of cooperation. When teachers and the librarian engage in joint planning, thinking, and evaluation, it improves the learning experience for students. They may share objectives but do not necessarily have to create the learning opportunity jointly. Often cooperation involves dividing the work among participants (see Figure 7.5).

Integrated instruction involves teacher and librarian in shared thinking, planning, and evaluation. As collaborators they come together as colleagues to create a learning experience for the students that will facilitate their learning. They are aware of factors such as individual differences, developmental level, and prior knowledge that might affect the sequencing of material taught. Each collaborator brings to the process his or her expertise in the subject content, knowledge of standards to be included in instruction, methodology, research process, writing process, etc. The librarian and teacher are able to create a more powerful learning experience together than they could not create individually (see Figure 7.6).

Integrated curriculum involves all the elements of collaboration that occur in model C. However, collaboration affects the entire curriculum. Teachers and the librarian work to integrate subject content and information literacy at all grade levels. A key factor in ensuring collaboration throughout the school between librarian and teachers is the principal. The principal understands the impact collaboration can have on student academic achievement; encourages collaboration between classroom and library faculty; supports collaboration with resources and schedules designed to accommodate teacher and librarian time needs; provides professional development for faculty on collaboration and es-

tablishes norms for shared thinking, shared planning, and shared integrated instruction. To accomplish the enormous task of integrating instruction throughout the curriculum, the librarian and teachers are creative in their use of time and resources through such innovation as integrated lesson planning and cross-age instruction. Model D (see Figure 7.7) has the most potential for improving student learning because it supports conceptual development at al levels of the curriculum, creates a synergy among collaborators that transcends grade level and subject content, and provides multiple perspectives on designing and delivery of curriculum.

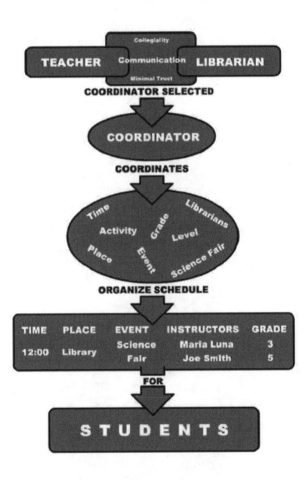

Figure 7.4. Integrated instruction, model A: Coordination. Patricia Montiel-Overall, 2005. Reprinted with permission from P. Montiel-Overall and ALA.

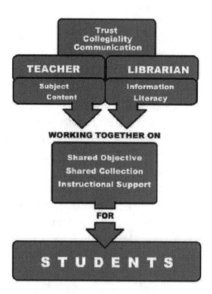

Figure 7.5. Integrated instruction, model B: Cooperation/partnerships. Patricia Montiel-Overall, 2005. Reprinted with permission from P. Montiel-Overall and ALA.

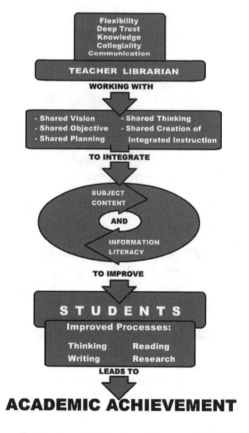

Figure 7.6. Integrated instruction, model C. Patricia Montiel-Overall, 2005. Reprinted with permission from P. Montiel-Overall and ALA.

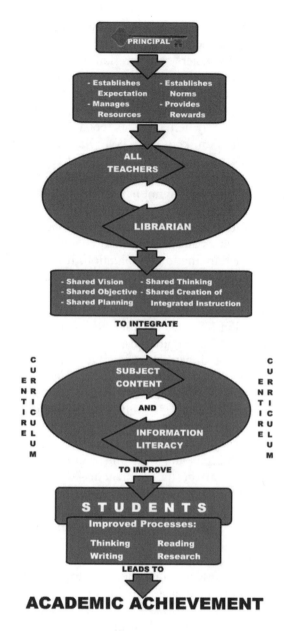

Figure 7.7. Integrated instruction, model DC. Patricia Montiel-Overall, 2005. Reprinted with permission from P. Montiel-Overall and ALA.

Constructivist Learning Environment Model

David Jonassen (1999), professor of instructional systems at Pennsylvania State University, is one of a growing number of instructional design theorists who believe that learning environments for effective advanced knowledge acquisition are best developed on the principles of constructivist learning theory. Although usually placed within higher education, his viewpoint has implications for secondary and elementary school settings as well.

A model that represents the attributes of meaningful learning under constructivist theory includes the following characteristics:

Active—manipulative, observant, interactive experiences and engagement in the activities to experience and learn by doing.

Constructive—articulative, reflective so learners try to deal with new experiences that present different ideas, information, or methods than those they have previously experienced.

Intentional—reflective and regulatory to meet a goal, and the learner articulates what goals are to be or have been reached.

Authentic—complex and contextual so that the learning tasks are challenging, and not overly simplified.

Cooperative—the learning tested, refined, and shaped through collaboration and conversation as the learner shares ideas with others in order to receive and give constructive feedback.

James O. Carey (1998), associate professor of library and information science at South Florida University, has applied the constructivist approach to instructional design for facilitating the education of students in information literacy. His dichotomy illustrates the differences between traditional teaching approaches and those needed to meet the new demands for meaningful learning in the Information Age. (See Figure 7.8.)

Carey's Comparison of Traditional Instructional Design with Constructivist Learning: A Dichotomy

1. Traditional:

   Teacher provides a motivational introduction.

   Constructivist:

   • Foster motivation through ownership by giving students choices in the content they explore and methods they use for exploration.

   • Situate the problem in a meaningful (authentic) context that is rich in content and interest.

2. Traditional:

   Teacher states what is expected, remind students of what students should know.

   Constructivist:

   • Problem scenarios should emphasize constructing process over finding answers.

   • Scenarios should require reflective thought, looking back to incorporate foundational knowledge into new knowledge.

3. Traditional:

   Teacher presents the new content with examples that will help the students recall for application.

   Constructivist:

   • Use cooperative learning so that students can negotiate the meaning of what they are learning.

   • Design problem scenarios of high complexity requiring use of multiple process strategies and knowledge skills.

   • Encourage multiple perspectives and interpretations of the same knowledge.

   • Situate the problem in authentic contexts.

4. Traditional:

   Provide students with opportunity to practice new skills.

   Constructivist:

   • Problem scenarios must be generative rather than prescriptive; that is, students construct their own investigation and knowledge acquisition rather than following steps of a prescribed process.

   • Encourage group participation for trying out and negotiating new knowledge and process

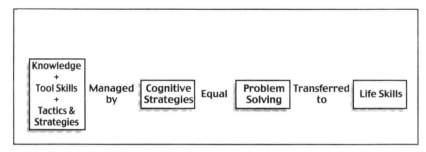

Figure 7.8. Carey's model for problem solving and life skills. James Carey, 1998. Reprinted with permission from James Carey.

5. Traditional:

Provide student with information about how well they are doing in their practice.

Constructivist:

- Balance the potential frustration of aimless exploration with just enough facilitation to ensure progress; facilitation techniques include modeling, scaffolding, coaching, collaborating, but fade as students become more skillful.

- Facilitate group interaction as needed to ensure peer review of knowledge and process.

6. Traditional:

Teacher provides a review and relates new skills to real-world applications and upcoming lessons.

Constructivist:

- Students should have opportunities to explore multiple, parallel problem scenarios where they will apply to a new scenario of information [need] processes they have previously constructed.

7. Traditional:

Teacher provides tests, performance checklists, rating scales, attitude scales, or some other means of measuring mastery of new skills.

Constructivist:

- Suggest tools that students can use to monitor their own construction of knowledge and processes; students should be reflective and critically review previous learning and newly constructed positions.

- Standards for evaluation cannot be absolute; but must be referenced to the student's unique goals, knowledge, and past achievement.

- The ultimate measure of success is transfer of learning to new, authentic environments.

Motivation and Instructional Design

Ruth V. Small (1998, 2004), professor of information science at Syracuse University, has written extensively on the application of effective instructional design associated with the teaching of information skills (Small and Arnone 2000). Her basic instructional model simplifies the planning process. (See Figure 7.9.)

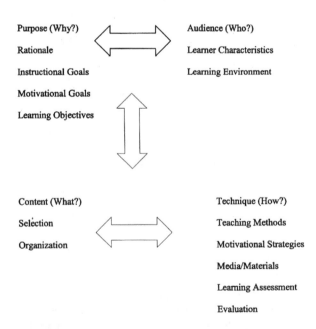

Figure 7.9. Small's Im-PACT model. Ruth V. Small, 1998. Reprinted with permission from Ruth Small.

Small (1998) draws on Keller's (1979) ARCS Model for the essential components to add motivation to instruction.

Keller's ARCS Motivation Model

Attention—The instructor uses strategies for arousing and sustaining curiosity and interest.

Relevance—The instructor links the instruction to important needs, interests, and motives.

Confidence—The instructor helps students develop a positive expectation for successful achievement of the learning tasks.

Satisfaction—The instructor manages extrinsic and intrinsic reinforcement.

Instructional Intervention

Instruction serves different purposes depending on the learners' needs and abilities. Those who must plan and deliver instruction in the search for and use of information are often limited to general presentations to a group of students, without the opportunity to meet individual needs. Kuhlthau (2003) and others (Callison, McGregor, and Small 1998) have explored effective methods for instruction that allow for instructional media specialists and others responsible for bibliographic instruction not only to introduce tools, skills, and search strategies, but also to intervene at point of need for more constructive and personalized guidance in the selection and use of information. The ability to identify information and learning needs is critical to the successful implementation of an information literacy program and requires active interaction between instructors and resource professionals who are willing to provide guidance at all levels.

Kuhlthau has defined the intervention role of the library media specialist or academic library instructor at five levels. Each level increases in focus on individual research needs, moving up from general organization of a collection and facility to counseling sessions that provide very specific feedback and a high level of expertise.

These levels of instruction have important implications for those who want to fulfill the role of instructional media specialist. Depending on the lesson or project and the abilities of the group, team, or individual student, different levels of instructional intervention will be necessary from those who attempt to teach information literacy and guide inquiry.

Kuhlathu's Levels of Intervention

ORGANIZER

The information skills instructor arranges, and manages resources; creates a user-friendly, self-service environment; and establishes policies that maximize opportunities for student access to information resources in anticipation or in advance of information needs.

LECTURER

The information skills instructor provides tours and orientation sessions focusing on location of collections and departments to acquaint students with organizational schemes and specific reference tools to increase student interest and use of the library and its resources.

INSTRUCTOR

The information skills instructor provides one or a series of cooperatively planned lessons on specific references and types of sources related to needs arising from classroom activities and tailored to the students' cognitive levels.

TUTOR

The information skills instructor presents informational resources in ways that show the relationships among different kinds of resources and recommends a sequence for their use.

Sessions are provided when student needs dictate and are based on collaborative planning and active teaching by both teachers and librarians.

COUNSELOR

The information skills instructor actively participates in the students' information search process, assists, and provides cognitive, behavioral, and emotional support for students related to their tasks at initiation, selection, exploration, formulation, collection, presentation and evaluation.

Kuhlthau and dozens who have replicated her research have shown an associated affective domain or maturation in attitudes and feelings toward the library research process. Over time and with experiencing success, the researcher gains self-confidence and learns to manage the anxieties associated with meeting a new learning experience. Feelings and attitudes of both the novice and experienced researcher will follow this cycle for each project:

> Uncertainty
>
> Confusion
>
> Brief elation upon initial topic selection
>
> Anticipation
>
> Doubt
>
> Optimism upon forming focus
>
> Confidence
>
> Increased interest
>
> Relief
>
> Sometimes satisfaction
>
> Sometimes disappointment
>
> Sense of accomplishment

Kuhlthau's research has changed the role of the school library media specialist and the academic librarian, as today they increasingly recognize student ability levels and information needs as they grow in their willingness to collaborate with instructors on a peer teaching level. Several principles come from Kuhlthau's work:

- Mastering tasks within a project is best learned by building from one to the next in scaffolded degrees of difficulty.

- The process is as important as (perhaps more important than, especially for the novice researcher) the product, and stages leading to completion of the product should be valued and evaluated.

- Student researchers need to learn how to deal with new information that creates uncertainties and be taught methods to assimilate new information in a constructive and unbiased manner.

- Much more time must be given to activities that lead to intelligent selection of research topics and search paths. As much thinking and general reading should go into presearch activities as into the analysis and synthesis of evidence for the final product.

Taxonomies for Instruction

The standard meaning of *taxonomy,* when applied to learning, is a systematic classification of what is to be learned, accomplished, and demonstrated. Classification sorts the kinds of capabilities that the individual acquires as a result of the events of learning. Various types of learning have been identified over the past sixty years of psychological research. These include classical conditioning, operant learning or simple habit formation, concept learning, problem solving, and discrimination or perceptual learning. Prominent names such as Benjamin S. Bloom and David R. Krathwohl in the 1950s and Robert Gagné and Jerome S. Bruner in the 1960s have been associated with different taxonomies for learning and student performance levels.

Such classifications have been useful to the practical teaching field, as they have often served to help identify and construct specific learning objectives and tasks. The taxonomy displays the range, level, and overall hierarchy of possible learning or demonstrations of student abilities through actual performance of tasks. Taxonomies serve to guide curriculum development through scope and sequence plans so educators can visualize the tasks and match learning activities to maturation levels.

Three domains are standard for most taxonomies in learning:

- **Cognitive**—range of intellectual capabilities from simple recall to creative and critical synthesis and evaluation.

- **Affective**—an emphasis on feelings and emotions that may be displayed and controlled as the learner matures.
- **Psychomotor**—physical tasks requiring practice and refinement through neuromuscular conditioning.

Different taxonomies in learning help us understand learning environments and expectations, and these may differ from one society to another. Much has been written, for example, about the changes in learning expectations placed on humans from the agricultural to the industrial to the current information revolutions. Three waves have caused dramatic changes in the priorities that society places on what students should be able to learn and perform in order to survive and succeed.

Evolution in learning theory has moved much of what educators think, plan, and do away form behaviorism and toward constructivism. More time is now invested in knowing the individual learner and providing means for the self-learner to mature as quickly as possible. Much of this is based on the assumption that we do not feel we can predict the stable tasks of the immediate future, and thus the students who are likely to be most successful in future societies are those who learn how to learn, adjust, and analyze problems for themselves. Scaffolding has an important role in development of meaningful learning activities. One experience builds on the next to advance the learner to the higher order skills that require the student to analyze tasks independent from guidance of teachers and mentors.

Other Instruction and Learning Classification Formats

A taxonomy provides one approach to classification and leads to a display of differences, relationships, progression, and hierarchy. Several other formats are useful as well:

- **Dichotomy**—a division of tasks or processes into two mutually exclusive or contradictory groups.

- **Rubric**—a set of scoring guidelines for evaluation of student work or job performance, usually given in progressive levels that represent stages to be mastered toward excellence.
- **Matrix**—a new structure that originates from a given framework, usually new dimensions of depth and complexity.
- **Discipline**—a recognized branch or segment of knowledge within a domain of rational learning; holds to some basic standards, but most grow and evolve within social contexts in order to be relevant and useful.
- **Scope and sequence**—a view, outline, or illustration of the range of skills, tasks, and performances, given in an order from basic to exemplary; often tied to specific grade levels and disciplines to show when the basic skill is to be introduced, reinforced, expanded, or mastered for the average student population. Exceptions for special students with exceptional talents or with learning disabilities will be so noted.

An Instructional Performance Taxonomy Applied to the Library Media Specialist as Instructor

The taxonomy that has influenced thinking more than any other concerning the role of the school library media specialist has been the classification offered by David V. Loertscher (2000), professor at San Jose State and national leader over the past thirty years in promotion of school library programs. Commonly referred to today as "Loertscher's Taxonomy," it has served to outline the progression toward higher level instructional involvement of the school library media specialist since its introduction in the late 1970s. His taxonomy has been used to measure school library media specialist instructional involvement in countless dissertations and field studies and state and national certification guidelines, and has been foundational to nearly every state and national school library program standard over the past thirty years.

Key to understanding the implications of Loertscher's School Library Media Specialist Taxonomy are the following concepts (Callison 1987):

- The professional strives to improve his or her role in instruction by engaging in activities at higher levels over time and experience. Success is scaffolded similar to a learning progression.

- Lower-level aspects are not completely discarded, and some may continue to be valid in certain situations. Over time, however, the accomplished library media specialist devotes a greater amount of time to the higher-order levels of the taxonomy.

- Positive attitude and vision may be the two most powerful elements in play to move both the library media specialist and other teachers up the taxonomy to higher collaborative efforts. Without a desire for progressive focus, the small, everyday tasks will smother the highest levels of this taxonomy.

- The school library media specialist must be willing and able to engage on a professional basis in the roles of educator and evaluator. More than simply calling oneself a "teacher-librarian," the library media specialist must take steps to be professionally active and earn respect as a valued team player and curriculum leader. Demonstrated performance will prove more than any certification credential.

- At the highest levels, the school library media specialist engages in curricular planning that not only enhances and helps teaching performance for all educators involved, but also leads to powerful changes in methods that can result in improved learning environments and greater student academic performance.

In the many studies that have applied Loertscher's Taxonomy to measure normal school media specialist performance, most practicing school librarians operate at Level 5 occa-

sionally, but most are often below (Callison 2002). Results from specially funded initiatives, such as the national Library Power Initiative (Zweizig and Hopkins 1999) have created the time and support to move many participating school media specialists to between Levels 6 and 8. Few examples can be found of school library media specialists engaged in the curriculum at Levels 9 and 10 on a consistent and effective basis.

Note that Loertscher's recently revised stages include access to technology at even the lowest stages. While technology has changed many aspects of information access over the past decade, what remain critical and most important for higher levels of operation are the actions of the school media specialist as an educator. The role of the Instructional Media Specialist, played by both the school media specialist and collaborating teachers as described in this text, is intended to bring educators who believe in promotion of information and media literacy based on inquiry teaching and learning methods to the highest levels of the taxonomy.

Loertscher's Taxonomy for Library Media Specialist Instructional Involvement (Revised 2000)

1. No involvement. The library media center is bypassed entirely.

2. Smoothly operating information infrastructure. Facilities, materials, networks, and information resources are available for the self-starter; delivered on request or self-identified need.

3. Individual reference assistance. The library media specialist serves as the human interface between information systems and the user.

4. Spontaneous interaction and gathering. Networks respond twenty-four hours a day and seven days a week to patron requests, and the library media center facilities can be used by individuals and small groups with no advance notice.

---

5. Cursory planning. There is informal and brief planning with teachers and students for library media center facilities or network usage, usually done through casual contact in the library media center, in the hall, in the teacher's lounge, in the lunch room, or by e-mail.

6. Planned gathering. Gathering of materials and access points to important digital resources is done in advance of a class project upon teacher or student request.

7. Evangelistic outreach/advocacy. A concerted effort is made to promote the philosophy of the school library media program.

8. Implementation of the four major programmatic elements: collaboration, reading literacy, and enhancing learning through technology and through information literacy. There is a concentrated effort made for the library media center to achieve its goal of contributing to academic achievement.

9. The mature library media center program. The library media center program reaches the needs of every student and teacher who is willing to accept its offerings.

10. Curriculum development. Along with other educators, the library media specialist contributes to the planning and organization of what will eventually be taught in the school or district.

Reprinted with permission from David V. Loertscher.

Loertscher (2005) warns against the use of rigidly defined scope and sequence activities that, if poorly implemented, lead back to isolated library skills exercises and have little relevance to the academic performance of students. Scope and sequence plans, however, can provide a range of levels to advance information literacy as long as skills reflect checkpoints for student performance and the processes of information literacy reflect constructivist methods of learning and teaching. Integration of information literacy skills can advance and even change curriculum to the extent that inquiry can drive what is taught and how it is taught. Constructivist methods must be understood and employed or educators will find what Benjamin Bloom (Anderson et al. 2000) discovered, that 95 percent of the demands for student performance in the typical school remain in the lowest levels of learning: recall of facts, not analysis, synthesis, evaluation, and presentation of information.

The AASL Program Assessment Rubric

In 1999 the American Association of School Librarians issued a *Planning Guide* to support the implementation of the association's revised national standards for school media programs. Tested and revised, especially among school media programs in Long Island, New York, the exemplary functions identified in the evaluation rubric of this guide challenge educators to reach for full implementation of inquiry methods. While the following statements from this taxonomy for instructional excellence are inspiring, few public school programs have reached such levels. These statements provide a summary of the instructional programs advocated in this text and that require the professional stewardship of school library media specialists and other teachers collaborating as instructional media teams.

- The library media program is a catalyst for intellectual inquiry. Students learn to incorporate information literacy skills into their work and become proactive users of information and resources.

- Teaching is facilitative, collaborative, and creative. Reflection and authentic assessment are built into all instructional units.

- Schoolwide programs enable and encourage students to use their own learning styles, abilities, and needs to solve complex information problems and present their solutions in different formats.

- Inquiry can take place by an individual or in a group. Students determine their own research needs and develop their own research strategies.

- Student learning is assessed through student presentations to peers and adults, by using student- and teacher-produced rubrics. Students may also present to professionals in the field of study.

References

American Association of School Librarians. (1999). *A planning guide for* Information Power*: Building partnerships for learning with school library media program assessment rubric for the 21st century.* AASL.

Anderson, L., et al. (2000). *Taxonomy for learning, teaching, and assessing: Revision of Bloom's taxonomy.* Allyn & Bacon.

Callison, D. (2002). The research record in school library media programs for the 20th Century. In A. Kent (Ed.), *The encyclopedia of library and information science* (Volume 71, 339–369). Marcel Dekker.

Callison, D. (1987). The media specialist as educator and evaluator. *Indiana Media Journal* (Summer), 13—19.

Callison, D., J. H. McGregor, and R. V. Small (Eds.). (1998). *Instructional interventions for information use.* Hi Willow Research.

Carey, J. O. (1998). Library skills, information skills, and information literacy: Implications for teaching and learning. *School Library Media Quarterly Online, 1.* http://www.ala.org/aasl/SLMQ/skills.html (accessed December 27, 2005)

Dick, W. O., L. Carey, and J. O. Carey. (2004). *Systematic design of instruction.* 6th ed. Allyn & Bacon.

Gagné, R. M. (1977). *The Conditions of learning.* 3d ed. Holt, Rinehart & Winston.

Gagné, R.M., L. J. Briggs, and W.W. Wager. (1992). *Principles of instructional design.* Harcourt Brace Jovanovich College Publishers.

Heinich, R., M. Molenda, J. D. Russell, and S. E. Smaldino. (2001). Instructional media and the technologies for learning. 7th edition. Prentice Hall.

Jonassen, D. H. (1999). *Computers as mindtools for schools: Engaging critical thinking.* Prentice Hall.

Keller, J. M. (1979). Motivation and instructional design: A theoretical perspective. *Journal of Instructional Development, 2* (4), 26-34.

Kuhlthau, C. C. (2003). *Seeking meaning.* 2d ed. Libraries Unlimited.

Loertscher, D. V. (2000). *Taxonomies of the school library media program.* Hi Willow Research and Linworth Publishing.

Loertscher, D. V. (2005). *Ban those bird units!* Libraries Unlimited.

Montiel-Overall, P. (2005). Toward a theory of collaboration for teachers and librarians. *School Library Media Research, 8.* http://www.ala.org/aasl/SLMR (accessed December 27, 2005).

Small, R. V. (1998). Designing motivation into library and information skills instruction. *School Library Media Research, 1* http://www.ala.org/aasl/SLMR (accessed December 27, 2005).

Small, R. V. (2004). *Designing digital literacy programs with Im-PACT.* Neal-Schuman.

Small, R. V., and M. P. Arnone. (2000). *Turning kids on to research: The power of motivation.* Libraries Unlimited.

Turner, P., and A. M. Riedling. (2003). *Helping teachers teach.* 3d ed. Libraries Unlimited.

Walker, H. T., and P. K. Montgomery. (1983). *Teaching library media skills.* 2d ed. Libraries Unlimited.

Zwiezig, D. L., and D. M. Hopkins. (1999). *Lessons from Library Power: Final report on the evaluation of the national library power initiative of the DeWitt Wallace Reader's Digest Fund.* Libraries Unlimited.

Chapter 8

Foundations of the Library Media Specialist's Instructional Role

Daniel Callison

Teacher-Librarian

The concept of "teacher-librarian" is not new. The position was introduced and defined within the pre-World War II educational environment by Mary Peacock Douglas (1941). As a national voice, but most specifically as a state leader for school library reform in North Carolina, Douglas extended the traditional definition of school librarian to include teaching credentials and responsibilities. Her rationale was based on the increasing number of instructional resources emerging for school teachers and the need for at least one professional teacher in each building to manage the resources and to promote their effective use.

Douglas envisioned, "Through the library, books are distributed to individuals, groups and classes. They are sent freely to classrooms, laboratories, shops and study centers—wherever they will be used. From all parts of the school, pupils, teachers, committees, classes, individuals go to the library to use books, magazines, pictures, and maps; to find facts and illustrative materials; to read" (1941, xvi). The school library Douglas described in her 1941 vision would been called "traditional" today, but her definition of the teacher-librarian as a professional who managed and extended a full library program as a service to quality education was an early indication of what hundreds who followed her would develop as effective resource laboratories for learning—the school library media center. To the list of required expertise for the school librarian she added professional training, knowledge of books and instructional resources, understanding of children, and "knowledge of teaching methods and knowledge of courses of study" (1941, 1). She placed high value on experience in teaching.

Perhaps no leader in school media education has done more to update and redefine "teacher-librarian" in modern terms than Ken Haycock. Professor, academic dean, award-winning educator, Haycock has established many forums to promote the concept of the modern teacher-librarian, including the founding and publication of the international magazine, *"Teacher-Librarian."* His work has influenced the professional preparation of thousands of teacher-librarians in Canada and Australia, and his ideas today influence many state and national school librarian certification programs in the United States as well (Haycock 1981). Although his definition of teacher-librarian can be found in many publications, Haycock (2003) summarized the characteristics of the teacher-librarian in a recent speech to an international forum on information literacy thus:

> . . . the teacher librarian is more likely to have an impact if he or she is certified, that is, qualified in teacher librarianship, trained in collaboration with classroom colleagues, actually collaborates as an equal teaching partner, and maintains active involvement in the instructional program.

According to Haycock, the professional competencies of the teacher librarian include that he or she

• places priority on staff relationships and leadership in the implementation of change;

- provides leadership in collaborative program planning and teaching to ensure both physical and intellectual access to information and commitment to voluntary reading;

- knows curriculum programs mandated by the province, district, and school;

- understands students and their social, emotional, and intellectual needs;

- has expert knowledge in evaluating learning resources in different formats and media, both onsite and remote, to support instructional activities;

- develops and promotes the effective use of informational and imaginative resources in all formats through cooperative professional activities;

- provides appropriate information, resources, or instruction to satisfy the needs of individuals and groups;

- uses appropriate information technology to acquire, organize, and disseminate information;

- manages library programs, services, and staff to support the stated educational goals of the school; and

- evaluates programs and services.

On a personal level, the teacher-librarian

- is committed to program excellence;

- seeks out challenges and sees new opportunities, both inside and outside the library;

- see the big picture;

- looks for partnerships and alliances;

- creates an environment of mutual respect and trust;

- has effective communication skills;

- works well with others in a team;

- provides leadership;

- plans, prioritizes, and focuses on what is critical;

- is committed to lifelong learning; and

- is flexible and positive in a time of continuing change.

The School Library Media Standards and Instruction

The American Association of School Librarians (AASL) and the Association for Educational Communications and Technology (AECT) have issued joint national standards/guidelines three times since 1975 in which the position of school library media specialist has been defined. With each revision, the role has moved closer to that of instructional media specialist. In 1975, with many school librarians resisting the change in their title to school library media specialist, responsibilities defined by the national guidelines included

- works as a member of curriculum committees;

- is involved with instructional groups; and

- provides staff development programs for teachers in the evaluation, selection, and use of instructional materials.

In 1988, the library media specialist was defined as information specialist, teacher, and instructional consultant. In 1998, the library media specialist was further defined as a leader of curriculum, with emphasis on information skills for student learning. To implement fully this leadership role, the national guidelines emphasized a collaborative role in association with as many other teachers as possible in the integration of information literacy across the curriculum.

In philosophy and in terms of best practice, AASL and AECT (1998) have progressed to descriptions that are very close to that of an educator who holds master level teaching experiences and skills, is committed to increasing the quality of teaching and challenges for learning, and invites fellow teachers to explore the best application of methods and technologies to the learning environment. Educators who hold these abilities and attitudes are instructional media specialists. They are potential members and leaders of instructional teams that can take the learning program to the high levels necessary for meaningful information inquiry.

From Teaching Library Skills to Facilitating Information Literacy

Kathleen Craver's (1986) exhaustive literature review on the changing instructional role of the high school library media specialist led her to conclude that from 1950 to 1984 there was a clear pattern of progressive development of the instructional role. The changes in the library media specialist's role from study hall monitor to curriculum designer can be termed substantive. Craver, however, also concluded that there is a time lag between the practiced instructional role and the one espoused in the professional literature and standards. Nearly two to three decades are likely to pass before national standard roles are widely adopted and practiced. Based on Craver's projection, wide implementation of the instructional roles defined in standards twenty years ago should be on the horizon.

Much of the adoption of innovation in roles has more to do with development of a new generation of educators as they enter the field than with a complete retooling of educators on the job. While one can find excellent examples of school media specialists who have given tremendous amounts of time and energy to retooling for the challenges of the Information Age, the full evolution to instructional media specialist over the next decade rests more with attitudes and skills held by those who are entering the schools as teachers of library media and information technologies now. Fresh ideas, combined with new technology skills and successful teaching experiences, seem to be the right mix, but the next decade is critical to the long-range future of those who want to expand the role of the school library media specialist as a teacher of information literacy.

A majority of practicing school library media specialists today see themselves in a supportive instructional role at most. Many at the elementary level find it difficult to engage in instructional development because of the lack of media staff support. Others cite limited instructional programming because of regimented schedules that either take them to too many schools or lock them into routine reading times for children and prevent meaningful contact with teachers. While time is often cited as the major barrier, often those practicing as school librarians do not have the desire or ability to take on the instructional roles described here. In too many cases, even when given the time and staff necessary, many in the role of school librarian would not move forward on instructional activities.

Positive Attitude + High Ability = Instructional Actions for Student Achievement

Attitudes and abilities are critical in implementing a new role, and those who are successful as instructional media specialists today move beyond the common barriers and bothersome problems that prevent engagement in instructional experiences. Many believe if you want to promote inquiry and you have the knowledge to do so, you can find a way. If you do not, the educational system unfortunately still allows for some to stay in the school library services as "keepers of the resources" rather than as educational leaders.

The role of the school library media specialist as instructor also seems to be influenced by the expectations of the principal as well as other teachers in the building. Most studies since 1975 (Callison 1998; Shannon 2002) have indicated higher expectations on the part of principals than school media specialists for participation in instructional activities. Neither group, however, has shown exceedingly high expectations for instructional leadership on the part of the school library media specialist.

There are indications of change, however. In recent years some studies have indicated that when the school library media specialist plays an instructional role in teaching and evaluating students in the use of strategies for information search and use, students seem to also show higher academic achievement. In addition, more and more new library media specialists are seeking out and demonstrating their instructional value (Library Research Service 2006; *School Libraries Work* 2006).

Defining the Instructional Role: An Evolution and Revolution

Margaret Chisholm, then at the University of Washington, and Donald Ely, from Syracuse University, proposed instructional design and teaching competencies for future school library media professionals in 1975. Chisholm and Ely visualized media programs organized under the guidance of a complete staff. Personnel would include several individuals, some with expertise in specific instructional design and production functions, others who would manage information access.

In the instructional role, the library media professional would conduct in-service media training for teachers and develop learning programs that would assist all individuals in access to and use of materials found in the school's collection. Instructional design tasks would involve clarification of learning objectives with teachers and analysis of learner characteristics in order to determine suitable teaching strategies, to provide alternative formats for presentation or use of information. Thus, more learners benefit from the resources regardless of learning abilities.

Chisholm and Ely placed the school media generalist in charge of all staff, including other professionals who held specializations in different information formats and services. The generalist would have department level chair status and coordinate overall planning for the media program. Specialists would provide support expertise in reference services, reading advisory, and media production. Such staffing is still held as ideal and remains out of reach in most school environments because of limited funds and lack of vision for such programs. The message from Chisholm and Ely nearly forty years ago is that the primary task role held by the leader of the media program is to initiate curriculum planning and to involve the media center staff in supporting new curricular initiatives as well as playing a major role in instructional design (Cleaver and Taylor 1983).

In 1980 Callison listed areas in which the school library media specialist can serve as a key instructional participant and recommended that as part of their annual review, school media specialists should document these actions in an annual report:

- serving on or chairing committees for course content and learning objectives review;
- designing and conducting workshops for professional development;
- facilitating the sharing of lesson plans;
- helping instructors not only plan, but also evaluate instruction; and
- providing supervision of independent study for students with advanced research needs.

In 1987 Callison categorized the instructional roles of the school library media specialists in stages reflective of those outlined by Loertscher in 1982. The taxonomy for instruction involvement for what Loertscher called the second revolution in the primary tasks of school librarians was based on a more proactive role in curricular development. Callison saw these roles as ranging from passive, to reactive, to active, to proactive, and at the highest as interactive in that school media specialists would be most effective as peer educators who engaged other teachers in interactive conversations for planning, presentation, and evaluation of student performance. Interactive approaches include modeling best practices, conducting instructional development workshops, and school media specialists and teachers sharing together in the overall implementation of an information skills curriculum. The instructional roles of the media specialist and the classroom teacher were not separate, nor parallel, but intertwined and dependent on each other for ideas and broad coverage of both subject discipline and information application. The new role of the school media specialist was more than providing location of resources; it was also to provide instruction in best use of resources. No longer was the offer from the school media specialist to be simply, "What may I help you find?"; it should become, "What may I help you learn?"

Margaret Hayes Grazier, then a professor in education at Wayne State University, provided one of the earliest and most clear models for the instructional role in 1976. Her model called for the media specialist to be involved at all stages of curriculum development, not just at the implementation stage. Grazier saw the role included in curriculum planning, implementation, and evaluation: the full cycle. Writing more than two decades before publication of the current national standards for school media programs, Grazier emphasized a new collaborative role for instruction as she illustrated the changes that must take place. Although many of her references to material formats are now out of date, she describes the collaborative instructional role in the following manner:

> The traditional media specialist offers storytelling, book talks, recreational reading, viewing, or listening. He teaches library skills. He supervises classes when teachers need planning periods or respite from classroom chores. His collections are resources for students engaging in independent study. Teachers envy the load of the traditional media specialist—no lessons to plan, no papers to correct. Whereas teachers must instill knowledge in immature minds, the media specialist appears to worry about maintaining order on the shelves and quiet in the room.

> In the new role the media specialist is an integral part of the teaching and learning functions. He collaborates in the selection of all learning resources—texts, workbooks, paperbacks, films, community people and agencies. He indexes all materials by curriculum objectives and level of difficulty. He disseminates information about new materials based on user need profiles. Using a variety of strategies he instructs about locating ' "and" ' evaluating resources, handling of equipment [for] production of materials [to support presentations]. He helps in the design of instructional strategies and content, adapting to the needs of teachers and working from task-centered orientation or from child-centered orientation [whichever is determined most suitable].

> He offers in-service programs to help teachers produce and use materials [effectively]. . . .

> Teachers perceive the new media specialist in the light of the many kinds of active collaboration in which they have engaged" (201)

Nearly three decades later, Grazier's scenario has come to life in countless national and state standards/guidelines for school media programs and has sparked to action across thousands of school library media centers. As Craver has suggested, the instructional role is evolving, and now moving into its third generation, the instructional media specialist is emerging.

Are we too late? When will it come?

In 1991, Carol-Ann Haycock, then president of the Human Resources Development Group, issued a statement concerning the changing role of and the emerging teacher-librarian. Her vision, shared by many others reflected in the readings listed for further study at the end of this chapter, places the responsibility for demonstrating the potential of the instructional media specialist on those who educate "teacher-librarians" as well as those who strive to practice the instructional role in public school throughout the United States and Canada:

> It does no good to blame or to complain. What we must do is provide information about and demonstrate that role. We must create the knowledge base and experiential base that will lead to understanding and support. And in doing so, we would do well to take note of some lessons from advertising and sales and from what we know about human learning. First, we must realize that we are involved in selling. What we are selling is potential; we must sell a vision of what could or should be. And that means we have to have a vision, preferably one that is commonly shared. Second, we must realize that people don't usually buy or learn on the basis of their first exposure. Think of how we are bombarded with advertising in our daily lives. Remember that it can take up to 35 repetitions for learning to occur. To present a case or say something once is not enough. It is necessary to create the vision, put the message out, and to keep it out there. Third, we must realize that information or talk alone is not enough. We also need to prove intent. We need to demonstrate, to the best of our ability, in the context of our own circumstances, the potential (i.e., the vision) of the role we want others to understand and support. (62)

More Recent Definitions of Instructional Roles

Kay Vandergrift, professor at Rutgers, The State University of New Jersey, has provided many insightful studies and comments on the school media specialist profession. Her 1994 list of library media specialist instructional responsibilities illustrates a more refined expectation nearly twenty years after Grazier, Chisholm, and Ely:

- Provides assistance in identifying, locating, and interpreting information housed in and outside of the library media center.

- Uses a variety of instructional methods to meet the needs of different user groups.

- Teaches the structure of various media and the distinctive uses of compositional elements in media such as film, video, and computer graphics.

- Demonstrates the effective use of newer media and technologies.

- Teaches the information curriculum as an integral part of the content and objectives of the school's curriculum.

- Includes instruction in accessing, evaluating, and communicating information.

- Integrates systematic learning activities with library media resources to emphasize higher-order cognitive strategies (critical thinking skills) for selecting, retrieving, analyzing, synthesizing, and evaluating information.

- Teaches the steps of research processes.

- Teaches students to articulate alternative responses to a particular work of art, literature, or social/political issue.

- Participates in school, district, and departmental curriculum design and assessment.

- Analyzes learner characteristics as a part of the instructional design process. (165)

These instructional tasks remain exemplary and progressive by today's standards. They take on an even more powerful mode when combined with understanding and application of the constructive process of learning outlined by Carol Kuhlthau (1993), also of Rutgers University. Although she cites constructivist methods from many education theorists, Kuhlthau draws on Jerome Bruner's (1977) ideas to outline the components that follow. These are essential for the instructional media specialist to understand so that instructional interventions become methods to facilitate student learning. Learning reaches near maximum when it is meaningful to both teacher and student.

> [Bruner] emphasized the individual's deep thinking, what he called interpretation, is central to the learning process. Bruner noted that it is not enough merely to gather information. If the individual is to understand it and learn from it, there is an essential, interpretative task. Interpretation is based on personal constructs built from past experience that enable students to go beyond the information they locate to create something uniquely their own. Bruner describes the interpretive task as occurring in five phases:
>
> - perception (encountering new information)
> - selection (recognizing patterns)
> - inference (joining clusters and categories)
> - prediction (going beyond the information given)
> - action (creating products of the mind)
>
> The concept of going beyond the information given to form a personal understanding is central to constructive theory. (Kuhlthau 1993, 12)

First and foremost in successful guiding of this learning process, the instructional media specialist initiates the process through open-ended problems, questions, or topics that need to be addressed by using a number of sources over a period of time. Kuhlthau informs us that these open-ended issues arise directly from the curriculum to initiate problem-directed research, rather than artificially imposed research assignments that only peripherally relate to the context, content, and objectives of the course of study.

Collaboration to Enable Content Integration Across the Curriculum

The instructional media specialist has a new role definition based on guiding students through challenging information selection and application tasks. These tasks are demanding, but also rewarding and motivating if they are personal and meaningful to the student.

Influence on learning styles, teaching methods, and student achievement is more likely when the instructional media specialist collaborates with other teachers in the integration of information skills and the curriculum. Kuhlthau (1993) has identified four basic enablers that must be in place for instructional media specialists (library media specialists and other teachers) to successfully implement a process approach for information skills instruction:

1. A team approach to teaching with administrators, teachers, and library media specialists playing essential [not just auxiliary] roles in the instructional team.

2. A mutually held constructivist view of learning compatible with the process approach that provides the foundation for actively engaging students in problem-driven inquiry.

3. A shared commitment to teaching skills for lifelong learning and for motivating students to take a responsibility for their own learning.

4. Competence in designing activities and strategies to improve learning. (16)

What the Research Says about the Instructional Role

Donna Shannon (2002), associate professor at the University of South Carolina, concluded an extensive review of the research concerning the competencies of the school library media specialist. Selected excerpts from her report highlight the issues related to the instructional role of the school library media specialist:

Teachers in successful schools are more likely to cooperate with the school library media specialists than teachers in unsuccessful schools (Bell and Totten 1992). But, other studies indicate that school library media specialists do not perceive the role as highly important (Johnson, 1993), that their involvement in the instructional program is marginal (Jones 1997; Kinder 1995; Lewis 1990; Pickard 1990), and that they engage in this role less often than they were trained or would like to do (Bishop 1996; Jones 1997; Kinard 1991; Stoddard 1991).

Factors that facilitate school library media specialist involvement in the school's instructional program have been identified in a number of studies. They include time for cooperative planning between classroom teachers and school library media specialists (Ervin 1989; Lumley 1994; Stoddard 1991), adequate staffing of school library media centers (Kinder 1995), personal characteristics of teachers or school library media specialists (Fedora 1993; Hughes 1998; Johnson 1993; Yetter 1994), and a school culture or organizational climate characteristic of effective schools (Bell and Totten 1992; Chapman 1990; Hughes 1998). Putnam (1996) found that while library media specialists may perceive their instructional role as an important one, a fixed-schedule program is a barrier to actual practice of that role in elementary schools.

Studies of exemplary school library media specialists indicate that they are considered important in their schools and they succeed in the roles outlined for school library media specialists found in national guidelines for library media programs including those related to curriculum and instruction (Alexander 1992; Gehlken 1994; Mosqueda 1999). The four exemplary school library media specialists studied by Alexander (1992) conformed to descriptions found in the professional literature and a list of desirable behaviors developed by library media professionals and school principals. These school library media specialists also possessed the characteristics of expert teachers as established by novice/expert studies on teaching.

Results of several research studies highlight the importance of the school library media specialist's interpersonal and communication skills. In their study of the personality and communication behaviors of exemplary school library media specialists, Herrin, Pointon, and Russell (1985) found them to be confident, open to change, and effective communicators. Based on their finding that these model school library media specialists spent three-quarters of their time in oral communication, the researchers recommend that library educators teach interpersonal communication skills as part of their curriculum.

The characteristics and interpersonal skills of school library media specialists are important factors in facilitating collaborative planning, innovative instructional approaches, and implementation of resource-based learning (Burks 1993; Farwell 1998; Hughes 1998; Johnson 1993). Johnson (1993) found that school library media specialists' confidence, initiative, communication skills, and leadership qualities were important factors for those who were active players in the total school curriculum and instructional program. Likewise, in her study of elementary school library media specialists participating in school-wide adoption of a whole-language approach to literacy instruction, Hughes (1998) found that librarians must be knowledgeable and possess interpersonal skills in order to function as catalysts for such reform.

There is overwhelming evidence of the importance for school library media specialists to possess effective communication and interpersonal skills. These competencies appear basic to all aspects of the work of school library media specialists and are judged essential by school administrators, teachers, and school library media specialists themselves.

[Shannon's References]

Alexander, K. G. 1992. Profiles of four exemplary elementary school media specialists. Ed.D. diss., University of Miami.

Bell, M. and H. Totten. 1992. Cooperation in instruction between classroom teachers and school library media specialists: A look at teacher characteristics in Texas elementary schools. School Library Media Quarterly 20, no. 2: 79–85.

Bishop, B. 1996. Design and development of an interactive, multimedia product that prepares preservice teachers to use the library media center program. Ed.D. diss., University of Houston.

Burks, F. 1993. Nature and extent of school library use in selected high schools in the greater Dallas-Fort Worth, Texas area. Ph.D. diss., Texas Woman's University.

Chapman, M. E. 1990. Library culture, library climate, and library productivity: An exploratory study (school library and media centers). Ed.D. diss., Peabody College for Teachers of Vanderbilt University.

Ervin, D. S. 1989. The effect of experience, educational level, and subject area on the philosophical acceptance, the perceived assumption, and the perceived barriers to implementation of the instructional and curricular role of the school library media specialist. Ed.D. diss., University of South Carolina.

Farwell, S. M. 1998. Profile of planning: A study of a three-year project on the implementation of collaborative library media programs. Ed.D. diss., Florida International University.

Fedora, A. P. 1993. An exploration of the scheduling patterns of two exemplary elementary school media centers. Ph.D. diss., University of North Carolina.

Gehlken, V. S. 1994. The role of the high school library media program in three nationally recognized South Carolina blue ribbon secondary schools. Ph.D. diss., University of South Carolina.

Herrin, B., L. R. Pointon, and S. Russell. 1985. Personality and communications behaviors of model school library media specialists. Drexel Library Quarterly 21, no. 2: 69–90.

Hughes, S. M. 1998. The impact of whole language on four elementary school libraries. Ph.D. diss., University of North Carolina at Chapel Hill.

Johnson, J. A. 1993. The school library media specialist as instructional consultant. Ph.D. diss., Southern Illinois University at Carbondale.

Jones, A. C. 1997. An analysis of the theoretical and actual development involvement of Georgia school library media specialists. Ph.D. diss., Georgia State University.

Kinard, B. 1991. An evaluation of the actual and preferred role of library media specialists in a major urban public school system. Ph.D. diss., University of Maryland.

Kinder, S. J. 1995. Teacher-librarians' perceptions and priorities in regard to elementary school library programs and services. Masters thesis, University of Regina, Canada.

Lewis, C. G. 1990. The school library media program and its role in the middle school: A study of the perceptions of North Carolina middle school principals and media coordinators. Ed.D. diss., University of North Carolina at Chapel Hill.

Lumley, A. M. 1994. The change process and the change outcomes in the development of an innovative elementary school library media program. Ph.D. diss., Kansas State University.

Mosqueda, B. R. 1999. The perceptions of the role of the library media program and the library media specialist in selected national blue ribbon schools in Florida. Ed.D. diss., University of Central Florida.

Pickard, P. 1990. The instructional consultant role of the school library media specialist. Ed.S. thesis, Georgia State University.

Putnam, E. 1996. The instructional consultant role of the elementary school library media specialist and the effects of program scheduling on its practice. School Library Media Quarterly 25, no. 1: 43–48.

Stoddard, C. G. 1991. School library media professionals in instructional development activities: Perceived time expectations and the identification of variables that enhance or limit instructional development practices. Ph.D. diss., Utah State University.

Yetter, C. 1994. Resource-based learning in the information age school: The intersection of roles and relationships of the school library media specialist, teachers, and principal. Ed.D. diss., Seattle University.

Shannon's review covers studies over the previous fifteen years. Most other studies prior to 1990 also indicate a lack of school media specialist understanding, high ranking, or ability to elaborate on the instructional role (Callison 1998; McCracken 2001). A national study completed after Shannon's review (Roys and Brown 2004) concluded that across all surveyed groups—principals, library science educators, and library science students—the most important characteristic for the ideal school media specialist was the ability to work well with other people. Attitude as well as ability are key elements that determine a successful instructional role. Consistently, exemplary instructional library media specialists have established their role and been successful because they see that role as the most important and prioritize their professional duties to enhance that role. Consistently, most principals tend to favor the instructional role over other roles, even those that involve management of resources.

There seems to be a lack of communicating the potential for the school media specialists' instructional role in the research and professional journals directed to administrators, but when asked if they would welcome instructional participation and even leadership from the library media specialists, school administrators tend to be positive. School library media specialists, as a group, have not been as positive.

Communication with the Chief Instructional Officer: The Principal as CIO

Gary Hartzell, professor at the University of Nebraska at Omaha and a former principal, has become a leading spokesperson urging school library media specialists to tell their stories of success to school administrators and to do so in the administrative professional literature and at conferences. According to Hartzell (2002), there's no question that principal support is vital to the establishment and maintenance of a quality library media program. The problem is that support flows from trust, and trust flows from understanding. Many principals do not understand what teacher-librarians really do, nor do they appreciate the potential the library media program has for contributing to student and faculty achievement.

Principals' perceptions of school libraries and teacher-librarians, according to Hartzell, have been shaped by four interactive forces. The first is their own experiences in school libraries as children, in which they perceived the library as peripheral to the classroom. The second is the effect of their professional training, in which the library's role in curriculum and instruction was conspicuously absent. The third is the nature of the teacher-librarian's work, which is to enable and empower others. The fourth is the low profile teacher-librarians and school libraries have in the professional literature read by teachers and administrators, which prevents them from updating their sense of what the library really is and can do. The cumulative result is that administrators have only a limited and inaccurate understanding of libraries and teacher-librarians. The only way to change principals' perceptions is to assault them directly, repeatedly, and from a multiplicity of directions. Reshaping perceptions takes time and effort and commitment. In the meantime, these erroneous perceptions will continue to guide most principals' relationships with school library media specialists.

While Hartzell's points are valid in many situations, in others there is more to the story. There should be an energized outreach to administrators that describes the potential for educators, including school library media specialists, who reach higher levels of collaborative team teaching and implement fully inquiry teaching and learning methods. Coupled with this should be a message to encourage superintendents and principals to seek out, recruit, and encourage teachers who have the abilities and positive attitudes to be successful in inquiry to take positions as school library media specialists. Research and the professional literature clearly show what is

possible and identify the characteristics of those educators who can take actions to make inquiry work. It is also apparent that there are many in professionals who do not live up to these expectations and should be encouraged to move out of their positions, regardless of certification credentials or degree earned.

Be Strategic

Michael Eisenberg, dean of the Information School at the University of Washington, has rightfully placed much of the burden on those currently in the school media field to take strategic steps themselves in order to enhance their field and themselves. Eisenberg wrote in *School Library Journal,* and has "preached" at many state school library media conferences in his keynote addresses (Eisenberg and Miller 2002):

Librarians seem to treat "strategic management" as a dirty phrase, something to be avoided or minimized at best. It should be just the opposite: strategic management turns vision into reality. As shown above, our vision is clear. But hard work alone isn't enough. Turning the vision of the school library program into reality requires two essential elements of good management: strategic thinking and strategic planning.

Strategic thinking is a way to approach problems and opportunities. Effective strategic thinking centers on attitude, insight, and political savvy, as well as flexibility. In many ways, attitude is everything. Success starts with attitude. A positive attitude breeds positive results, a negative one breeds failure. If you think you can't make something happen, chances are you won't. If you think you can, at least you have a fighting chance. Attributes of a positive attitude include passion, enthusiasm, optimism, and energy. Successful school librarians are often characterized by their positive can-do attitudes.

I'm not suggesting that school librarians be overly optimistic. Schools and libraries face changing demands, not to mention financial difficulties. But it's time to stop whining. Instead, start spreading the message that school library programs promote student achievement and well-being. (46)

A Practical Approach to the Principal

In order to convey the instructional potential for school media professionals, some practical steps in communication are very important. Although most studies on the perception of the role of school media specialists in instruction tend to show that principals as well as classroom teachers have held higher expectations than library media specialists, those who would try to move the instructional role to the forefront will find that further educating the school principal will lead to positive results.

Although such steps have been expressed by many previous practicing media specialists, Carol Kearney (2000), who has served as a media specialist at all levels in the Buffalo, New York, public schools, has generated the most current and comprehensive list (synthesized and paraphrased here from pages 24–31). The instructional media specialist should

- Bring to the principal's attention key concepts from national standards and association position statements, especially those issued by AASL and AECT.

- Share articles and ideas from professional journals that promote collaborative teaching and inquiry learning (often based on constructivist methods) and are centered on resource-based exploration through the media center.

- Lead in-service sessions that reflect the higher levels of Loertscher's Taxonomy for Library Media Specialists in Instruction and Turner's Model for Collaborative Instructional Design (see instructional models in previous chapters and see key word "Assignment") .

- Take field trips with the principal and key teachers to visit exemplary school library media programs in action.

- Schedule time to conference with the principal on the potential media center program goals and how they relate to student learning and standards across the curriculum, and may tie to local community library programs for school children.

- Compare notes on key issues with the principal: Do your agree or disagree that the instructional services of the school library program are understood and used effectively?

- Invite the principal to be a key player in several instructional activities as a speaker, one who responds to projects produced by students, one who attends to give praise to student presentations.

- Along with an advisory committee, discuss potential short-range and long-range goals for instructional services and evaluate using such instruments as *A Planning Guide for* Information Power.

- Present a semiannual report to the principal that is concise, easy to read, and relevant and highlights instructional engagements:
    1. curricular projects
    2. attempts at authentic learning activities
    3. lesson plans with new teachers
    4. resources selected in cooperation with teachers in direct support of a theme or unit
    5. statistics on frequency of instructional engagements such as booktalks, media production, information literacy instruction, introduction of new software, or evaluation of Web sites

- Take an active role on curriculum planning committees and seek out a leadership role during accreditation review cycles.

- Provide the most recent information on instructional trends through a professional collection; promote at faculty meetings and teacher workrooms.

- Demonstrate the value of team planning and the need for flexible scheduling to broaden access to resources and facilities, both in school and in the community, and show how such flexibility results in more challenging instructional units that are not limited by routine, fragmented class schedules.

- Plan in-service training for teachers on various instructional strategies or new technologies; seek collaboration with other teachers to plan and present in-service sessions.

- Compliment the principal on any signs of support for the school media program, especially when it is clear that the principal has provided additional time or resources in the investment for resource-based activities.

These same communication steps lead to greater instructional engagements among the instructional media specialist and other teachers. Beyond one-to-one media specialist and teacher collaboration, the instructional media specialist seeks to build teams for collaborative action. These teams function to take a long-range view of the methods involved in information inquiry. They consider multidisciplinary and multigrade approaches. Teams, based on successful steps in building units of study, will find that they grow stronger as they involve community educators, such as local public and academic librarians, as well as parents and other community members who have special expertise. Eventually inquiry methods become a way of thinking and doing and impact nearly all learning situations in both elementary and secondary schools.

Dianne Oberg, professor in teacher-librarianship at the University of Alberta, has monitored the research on communication and professional relations between school librarians and principals worldwide over the past two decades. Her latest summary (2006) indicates that there remains a gap that generally results in less respect between the two educator groups than is necessary for meaningful cooperation and support to take place:

- Principal support is critical to school library media program development.

- Principals need to serve as advocates for collaborative planning and information literacy instruction.

- Principals rarely recognize the instructional role of the school librarian.

- Many principals are hampered in their support for school libraries by lack of knowledge about the management and function of school libraries.

Teaching and Learning: What Works

It has grown increasingly clear over the past three decades that if school library media specialists are to play a meaningful role in the education of students K–12, they must do more than serve as managers of resources. They must initiate collaborative instructional roles with peer teachers, consult closely with the principal, and be seen as a model for reading promotion as well as effective application of technology for curricular enrichment at all grade levels. The stage is being set for school library media programs to become learning laboratories for students and teachers not only to seek information but to test and challenge information as it is explored to meet learning, teaching, and personal needs. Socratic teaching strategies have become more and more powerful in the Information Age as learners and teachers must understand how to form questions for discovery and move through the information maze in an efficient manner.

New research in the 1980s also helped to guide methods for teaching reading, writing, and meaningful use of information. A selected list of general conclusions from this research is given below from the U. S. Department of Education publication *What Works: Research About Teaching and Learning* (1986). These conclusions are also the basis for shifting the role of the school media specialist from an educator who reacts to the goals and actions of other teachers to that of instructional media specialist and a leader who understands teaching and learning methods.

- Parents are their children's first and most influential teachers. What parents do to help their children learn is more important to academic success than how well-off the family is.

- The best way for parents to help their children become better readers is to read to them—even when they are very young. Children benefit most from reading aloud when they discuss stories, learn to identify letters and words, and talk about the meaning of words.

- Children improve their reading ability by reading a lot. Reading achievement is directly related to the amount of reading children do in school and outside of school.

- Children who are encouraged to draw and scribble "stories" at an early age will later learn to compose more easily, more effectively, and with greater confidence than children who do not have this encouragement.

- A good foundation in speaking and listening helps children become better readers.

- Many highly successful individuals have above-average but not extraordinary intelligence. Accomplishment in a particular activity is often more dependent upon hard work and self-discipline than on innate ability.

- Belief in the value of hard work, the importance of personal responsibility, and the importance of education itself contributes to greater success in school.

- Parental involvement helps children learn more effectively. Teachers who are successful at involving parents in their children's schoolwork are successful because they work at it.

- Children get more out of a reading assignment when the teacher precedes the lesson with background information and follows it with discussion.

- Children learn science best when they are able to do experiments, so they can witness "science in action."

- Telling young children stories can motivate them to read. Storytelling also introduces them to cultural values and literacy traditions before they can read, write, and talk about stories by themselves.

- The most effective way to teach writing is to teach it as a process of brainstorming, composing, revising, and editing.

- Teachers who set and communicate high expectations to all their students obtain greater academic performance from those students than teachers who set low expectations.

- When teachers explain exactly what students are expected to learn, and demonstrate the steps needed to accomplish a particular academic task, students learn more.

- Students tutoring other students can lead to improved academic achievement for both student and tutor, and to positive attitudes toward coursework.

- Student achievement rises when teachers ask questions that require students to apply, analyze, synthesize, and evaluate information in addition to simply recalling facts.

- Students benefit academically when their teachers share ideas, cooperate in activities, and assist one another's intellectual growth.

Teaching and Learning Through School Library Media Centers: What Works

To conclude this chapter on the foundations for the emerging instructional role of the school librarian, it is useful to return to some of the work completed by Ken Haycock and the concept of the teacher-librarian. Haycock examined the contents of 586 dissertations, most of which were defended between 1960 and 1990. It is clear in some of the conclusions he draws from his meta-analysis that functions are defined and in place for the instructional role of the library media specialist. Collaborative actions, including close professional working relationships with the principal and the need for access to quality resources, are all evident as foundational elements. What seems to be missing is widespread understanding, acceptance, and even ability of most individuals in the role of library media specialist to accept and practice the role as an educator or as an instructional media specialist that Haycock terms the teacher-librarian. His conclusions include the following:

- Teachers with experience in cooperative program planning and teaching with a teacher-librarian have a more positive view of the role of the teacher-librarian and welcome closer collaboration.

- The development of student competence in research and study skills is most effective when integrated with classroom instruction through cooperative program planning and team teaching by two equal teaching partners—the classroom teacher and the teacher-librarian.

- Teacher-librarians in secondary schools are not involved in cooperative program planning and team teaching with classroom colleagues as equal teaching partners to the extent that principals, teachers, and teacher-librarians themselves believe they should be.

- An essential first step to improvement of resource center programs is clarification of the role of the teacher-librarian.

- Teacher-librarians who are less cautious and more extroverted than their colleagues tend to be more successful.

- Teacher-librarians need education and training in social interaction skills.

- Teacher-librarians require more extensive training in cooperative program planning and teaching, which builds on prior successful classroom teaching experiences.

- The role of the principal is the key factor in the development of an effective school resource center program.

- Elementary school principals generally have a broader conception of the role of the teacher-librarian than do the teacher-librarians themselves.

- The teacher-librarian and principal need to accept responsibility jointly for the development of teacher awareness and commitment to cooperative program planning and teaching.

- District level school media coordinators have high expectations for themselves but are not as involved in curriculum and public relations activities as they might be and as they should be.

Haycock has continued his review of research studies, especially dissertations, and reported these conclusions in 2006:

- Students and teachers are served best by teachers and teacher-librarians who collaborate to develop disciplined inquiry programs.

- Information literacy in its fullest form requires some classroom teachers to move from a behaviorist, skills-and-drills methodology to a constructivist, resource-based learning methodology.

- Teacher-librarians who feel confident in their ability to teach information literacy skills and strategies see them as being more important than do teacher-librarians who do not have this level of confidence and perceived competence.

- Students need to learn a framework or process to perform disciplined inquiry, guided by teachers and teacher-librarians who collaboratively follow students' processes with support and scaffolding through mentoring and social negotiation.

References

American Association of School Librarians and Association for Educational Communications and Technology. (1975). *Media programs: District and school.* American Library Association.

American Association of School Librarians and Association for Educational Communications and Technology. (1988). *Information power.* American Library Association.

American Association of School Librarians and Association for Educational Communications and Technology. (1998). *Information power: Building partnerships for learning.* American Library Association.

Bruner, J. S. (1977). *The process of education.* Harvard University Press.

Callison, D. (1980). You too are an important resource. *Instructional Innovator.* (October), 24–25.

Callison, D. (1987). Evaluator and educator: The school media specialist. *Tech Trends, 32* (5), 24–29.

Callison, D. (1998). History of the research on issues related to school library media programs and services 1925–1995. In Kathy Howard Latrobe (Ed.), *The emerging school library media center: Historical issues and perspectives* (91–136). Libraries Unlimited.

Chisholm, M. E., and D. P. Ely. (1976). *Media personnel in education: A competency approach.* Prentice-Hall.

Cleaver, B. P., and W. Taylor. (1983). *Involving the school library media specialist in curriculum development.* American Library Association.

Craver, K. W. (1986). *The changing instructional role of high school librarians.* University of Illinois.

Douglas, M. P. (1941). *Teacher-librarian's handbook.* American Library Association.

Eisenberg, M. B., and D. H. Miller. (2002). This man wants to change your job. *School Library Journal, 48* (9), 46–50.

Grazier, M. H. (1976). The role for media specialists in the curriculum development process." *School Media Quarterly* (Spring), 199–204.

Hartzell, G. (2002). The principal's perceptions of school libraries and teacher-librarians. *School Libraries Worldwide, 8* (1), 92–110.

Haycock, C. (1991). The changing role: From theory to reality. In Jane Bandy Smith and J. Gordon Coleman (Eds.), *School Library Media Annual Volume 9* (61–67).. Libraries Unlimited.

Haycock, K. (1981). Role of the school librarian as a professional teacher." *Emergency Librarian* (May/June), 4–11.

Haycock, K. (1992). *What works: Research about teaching and learning through the school's library resource center.* Rockland Press.

Haycock, K. (2003). *What all librarians can learn from teacher librarians.* Paper presented at the International Conference of Information Literacy Experts. International Alliance for Information Literacy and the National Forum on Information Literacy. http://www.infolit.org/documents/ Haycockspeech.html (accessed November 27, 2005).

Haycock, K. (2006). What works. *Teacher-Librarian, 33* (3), 38.

Kearney, C. A. (2000). *Curriculum partner: Redefining the role of the library media specialist.* Greenwood Press.

Kuhlthau, C. C. (1993). Implementing a process approach to information skills: A study identifying indicators of success in library media programs. *School Library Media Quarterly* (Fall), 11–18.

Library Research Service. (2006). *School library impact studies.* http://www.lrs.org/impact.asp (accessed January 3, 2006).

Loertscher, D. (1982). The second revolution: A taxonomy for the 1980s. *Wilson Library Bulletin, 56* (6), 417–421.

McCracken, A. (2001). School library media specialists' perceptions of practice and importance of roles as described in *Information Power. School Library Media Research, 4.* http://www.ala.org/aasl/SLMR (accessed November 10, 2003).

Oberg, D. (2006). Developing the respect and support of school administrators. *Teacher-Librarian, 33* (3), 13–15.

Roys, N. K., and M. E. Brown. (2004). The ideal candidate for school library media specialist: Views from school administrators, library school faculty, and MLS students. *School Library Media Research, 7.* www.ala.org/aasl/SLMR/ (accessed January 3, 2006).

School libraries work. (2006). Scholastic Publishing and Research. librarypublishing. scholastic.com/content/stores/LibraryStore/ pages/images/slw_06.pdf (accessed January 3, 2006).

Shannon, D. (2002). The education and competencies of school library media specialists: A review of the literature. *School Library Media Research, 5.* http://www.ala.org/ aasl/SLMR (accessed January 2, 2006).

Vandergrift, K. E. (1994). *Power teaching: A primary role of the school library media specialist.* American Library Association.

What works: Research about teaching and learning. (1986). United States Department of Education.

Chapter 9

The Instructional Media Specialist:
A Role for All Inquiry Educators

Daniel Callison

Who Is the Instructional Media Specialist?

The concept offered for consideration in this chapter is a description of a role that can be taken by educators from various certification levels, disciplines, and administration responsibilities. The term "instructional media specialist" is not offered as a title to replace "teacher," "school library media specialist," "resource specialist," or "teacher-librarian" but is a descriptor of the educator, any educator, who has the abilities and willingness to master and implement teaching and learning strategies that most effectively work in the Information Age learning environment. The prominent instructional method advanced and supported by the instructional specialist is inquiry, and this educator has the knowledge to analyze instructional needs and to deliver instruction in the appropriate mode.

What is proposed in this chapter is that all teachers become effective and efficient in information literacy skills and inquiry methods so that the school is filled with instructional media specialists. The role of the information literate and inquiry model teacher is not reserved just for the more progressive school media specialist, but is a role all educators (and administrators) should learn to play.

Needed: Leader and Master Teacher

The educator who is most likely to succeed in establishing Information Inquiry as a key method for teaching and learning is the instructional media specialist. Do such people exist in our schools today? Are they likely to increase in number in the future? From what teaching areas should they come and what training background should they have mastered? Is the instructional media specialist role one that can be played by several educators who come together as a collaborative team to change the learning and teaching environment within their school?

The potential role of the instructional media specialist has been described in a multitude of standards and models over the past few decades. There are practicing educators, usually found as library media, resource, or educational technology specialists, who practice several of the basic competencies of this role. A majority, however, do not, nor did many enter the school library media profession to accept or establish instructional leadership responsibilities.

The title "instructional media specialist" is used in this chapter and throughout this text to identify those educators who have the ability and the desire to engage in the higher levels of instructional collaboration for the successful implementation of inquiry methods to advance information and media literacy—to learn and teach Information Inquiry. These educators may be classroom teachers, library media specialists, or others who have an understanding of inquiry teaching and learning methods and know how these can be applied successfully to improving student performance in the Information Age. Many of these skills are derived, in part, from the school library media field, its history, instructional models, and standards. Many of these skills are derived from the basic characteristics of what we have come to know of exemplary teachers.

The school media specialist is not the only educator who can reach the level of instructional media specialist. Ultimately, it will be suggested in this text, all educators should strive for the level of instructional media specialist. All should model such skills for other educators to adopt and practice. Educators should include principals, parents, and even students as peer instructors in many situations. Teams involving various combinations of teachers with instructional media specialist characteristics should be encouraged, each with content and resource expertise to make inquiry projects successful. When the school library media specialist moves to the level of instructional media specialist and participates as a leader in instructional planning, implementation, evaluation, and management, then the ideals of the AASL national guidelines found in *Information Power* (AASL/AECT 1998) are most likely to lead to a community for "building partnerships for learning." (See Table 9.1 and Figure 9.1.)

Table 9.1. School Library and Instructional Media Hierarchy*

Instructional Media Specialist	Understands and applies correct educational theory and techniques for successful implementation of inquiry. Models and often participates in inquiry process. Uses reflection for summative and formative evaluation of self as well as students. May be certified in any subject of study, technology or media. Seeks a leading role in collaborative teaching, and welcomes the position as chair of curriculum planning. Is fluent in application of information search, use, and evaluation models as well as instructional design and communication technologies.
Teacher Librarian	Strives to promote and apply information literacy to all learning standards. Seeks collaborative teaching role with a wide variety of peers across the curriculum. Advises on instructional support and evaluation. Is the principal resource participant and promoter.
School Library Media Specialist	Knowledgeable in selection and proper use of a wide variety of resources to support instruction. Understands the merits of various forms of instructional media. Promotes reading through a variety of means that help to meet the needs of diverse learners. Knowledgeable searcher of online and print reference resources. A manager of a central resource center.
School Librarian	Understands how to support the local curriculum with selection and acquisition of specific resources to meet format, ability level and specific skill needs. Has a wide ranging knowledge of literature for children and young adults as well as instructional media in all formats, and provides readers' advisory. Manages access and use of local library resources within the school in print and electronic formats.

*Skills described show emphasis for that position, but each position is assumed to have knowledge and abilities of the skill sets below it.

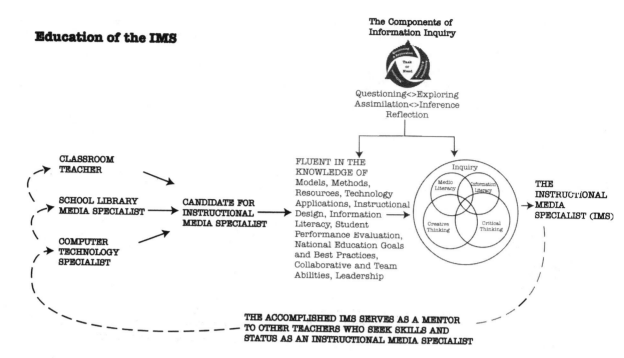

Figure 9.1. Education of the instructional media specialist. Daniel Callison, copyright 2003, 2006.

Searching for the Instructional Media Specialist

Is this instructional leader one who comes from the ranks of the computer technology specialists? Some would say yes, and yet others often find that these educators hold strong technical skills without the curriculum planning and instruction design skills. Too often individuals from this area, just as those from the library media area, stand to serve only as support staff who move to help when asked, but seldom take the initiative to create means to integrate technologies and move local educational programs forward.

There are important roles in technology management that the school library media specialist should play. Some of these tasks may be delegated to technical associate staff members, but as Jean Donham (2005), director of libraries at Cornell College, argues, the library media specialist has a leadership role in management of technology. In relationship to the services of the library, the media specialist may coordinate information search and retrieval training and on-line reference services, and advocate for integration of technology to support instruction across the curriculum.

Are classroom teachers from various subject areas good candidates? Do we limit our field to only those successful in the teaching of reading, or those who teach science, social studies, and language arts? Should we look for teachers with a wide subject background, including humanities as well as sciences? Should they have strong technical skills as well?

Perhaps effective communication or human interaction skills should be most important. Often teachers who enjoy complex projects and collaboration with others in a team situation will demonstrate the skills and attitudes needed to fill the role of instructional media specialist. They often possess creativity and a vision for meaningful instructional activities, and have practice in fair methods for evaluation and guidance of student work. They often lack the knowledge of a broad resource base and a wide understanding of many disciplines of study outside of their own, but these content areas can be understood quickly by those who have talents in collaborative teaching.

In nearly all cases, the educator who displays interest in and ability for the role of instructional media specialist tends to not relish the administrative responsibilities that go with management of a resource center. Skills in budgeting and resource acquisition, however, prove to be extremely beneficial to those who center their work on curriculum development. Knowing how to draw in funding as well as an understanding of how to deal with vendors so that the best resources can be acquired are management skills that will enhance the instructional media specialist's role. Organization of materials, bibliographic resource control, and inventory tasks, on the other hand, tend to take away from the instructional focus.

Renewing Preparation Programs for School Media

Most of the current higher education preparation programs for school library media specialists accredited by the American Library Association are at the graduate level. A common expectation is successful teaching experience as a core part of the expertise for the profession. This is a shift from just four decades earlier, when many school librarians were prepared for the field with "teaching credentials" but lacked evidence of teaching ability, innovation, and leadership. With credentials often granted at the undergraduate level, the school librarian from training programs in the 1970s was usually one with an undergraduate degree and no advanced graduate study in instructional design.

Carol Tilley and Daniel Callison (2001) of Indiana University have found a shift in the content emphasized in school librarianship education from 1990 to 1999:

- from audiovisual to multimedia and telecommunications;

- from library skills to information literacy;

- from resource acquisition to needs assessment;

- from isolation to collaborative teaching;

- from resource-centered to learner-centered programming; and

- from meeting general learning needs to diversified needs.

Delia Neuman (2001), professor at the University of Maryland and principal writer of the 1998 AASL/AECT national guidelines for school library programs, conducted a forum for leading educators in 2000. Based on analysis of comments gathered through decision support software, observations from these participants framed the following issues that must be addressed in current and future higher education programs if school librarians are to master the role of instructional media specialist:

- more emphasis on in-depth teaching and learning experiences;

- continued emphasis on information access and delivery, including ethical issues related to information use and understanding how to critically evaluate information;

- new emphasis on learning theory, information literacy, curriculum/instructional design, use of technology for instruction, teaching skills, reading/literacy, assessment of student performance, and attention to special needs/diversity.

- greater emphasis in the administrative roles for public relations, budget development, staff development; and

- much stronger emphasis on leadership skills, collaboration across disciplinary areas, provision of local professional development (including ability to work closely with preservice teachers), and application of technology for instructional purposes.

This is a very demanding skill set. These skills are relevant to many educators and reach beyond simply the school library media specialist to include many in the teaching ranks who also want to function as instructional media specialists in the Information Age.

In 2006, Nancy Everhart and Eliza Dresang, professors from Florida State University, introduced preliminary findings from their work to identify the characteristics of the twenty-first-century school library media specialist who will lead in educational change and make a true difference in student learning options. Their model curriculum for advanced school media professionals includes elements above and beyond the core library science education:

- Leadership in reading: promotion, advocacy, literacy, and literature appreciation

- Leadership in technology: assessment, curricular integration

- Information leadership: develop and demonstrate a philosophy for leadership

- Instructional role: grasp educational theory, collaborate for student learning across the curriculum

A Theory for Teacher and Librarian Collaboration

As an introduction to her elaboration on a very close instructional partnership for teachers and school librarians, Patricia Montiel-Overall (2005) supports her concepts with references to key educational theorists (see pages 121–122):

> Efforts to share responsibilities in education through collaborative practices represent an attempt to transform education into a community of learners where each member is considered capable of achieving academic success. The dynamic interaction among members of a community created through collaboration invites creativity and innovative thinking: two fundamental ingredients for academic success.

> In library and information science, collaboration between teacher and librarian is considered essential in preparing students for a complex society where vast amounts of information must be understood and managed. Professional guidelines encourage librarians to engage in collaboration with teachers to create a student-centered learning environment. . . .

> Collaboration is also extensively promoted in education as a way of improving teaching and learning. Most discussions of collaboration in education involve teachers, principals, special educators, parents, and other school communities. Noticeably absent from the literature in education are discussions involving collaboration between teachers and librarians. It could be argued that this is due to a lack of understanding about the changing roles of librarians. It might also be the result of a lack

of clarity about collaboration and the development of collaborative relationships between teachers and librarians. (24–25)

In 2006, Montiel-Overall presented preliminary findings for the basis of future studies on collaborative roles for school library media specialists. She predicted that, as with the Loertscher Taxonomy on the Instructional Role, different school media specialists would find more or less involvement depending on time, their duties in their building, and acceptance of fellow teachers, but ultimately, primarily the degree of support for collaboration from the school principal. She believed, however, that the full model for extensive collaboration was not likely to be found and is yet to be applied on a very wide basis in the field. The key to full development of meaningful collaboration may rest more with the school library media profession and active steps to demonstrate the possibilities than with any other educational group.

Collaborative Learning Communities for Teachers

It seems clear from the research that today's typical school library media specialists need to meet with teachers about instructional methods and situations, more frequently and in more depth than they do concerning resource provision. They need to learn how to improve their teaching and how to become engaged in a community of learning. A spirit of collaboration and peer support and a positive attitude to establish such is desperately lacking in the behavior of many of today's school library media specialists.

Even the best led instructional collaboration becomes nothing more than spur of the moment planning where cooperation is defined only by the classroom teacher rushing for support materials from the library that he or she has yet to examine and consider for full instructional impact. Inquiry method implementation takes time, practice, risk, and trust. It means being seen and valued as an instructional expert as well as a resource person, and the value has to be understood and respected by the school library media specialist first, and demonstrated, before other teachers will fully understand and accept the instructional media specialist as part of the community of educators.

The National School Reform Faculty is a movement of teachers who apply democratic governance principles to in-service professional development and in classroom management. Projects are student-centered and social service oriented, and contain a wide use of inquiry methods (http://www.nsrfharmony.org/faq.html). The NSRF Web site contains the following information that describes a professional community in Bloomington, Indiana, whose practices would benefit any group of teachers who seek more collaboration. The National School Reform Faculty (NSRF) is rooted in four beliefs:

- that school people, working together, can make real and lasting improvements in their own schools;

- that teachers and administrators must help each other turn theories into practice and standards into actual student learning;

- that the key to this effort is the development of a "learning community" based on public, collaborative examination of both adult and student work; and

- that to create this community, practitioners need high-quality training and sustained support.

What is a CFG?

A CFG is a professional learning community consisting of approximately 8-12 educators who come together voluntarily at least once a month for about 2 hours. Group members are committed to improving their practice through collaborative learning.

How did the idea of Critical Friends Groups develop?

In 1994, the Annenberg Institute for School Reform designed a different approach to professional development, one that would be focused on the practitioner and on defining what will improve student learning. Since the summer of 2000, Critical Friends Groups training is coordinated by the National School Reform Faculty (NSRF) at the Harmony Education Center in Bloomington, Indiana.

What are the purposes of a Critical Friends Group?

Critical Friends Groups are designed to

- Create a professional learning community

- Make teaching practice explicit and public by "talking about teaching".

- Help people involved in schools to work collaboratively in democratic, reflective communities (Bambino)

- Establish a foundation for sustained professional development based on a spirit of inquiry (Silva)

- Provide a context to understand our work with students, our relationships with peers, and our thoughts, assumptions, and beliefs about teaching and learning

- Help educators help each other turn theories into practice and standards into actual student learning

- Improve teaching and learning

What are the characteristics of a professional learning community?

Professional learning communities are strong when teachers demonstrate

- Shared norms and values

- Collaboration

- Reflective dialogue

- Deprivatization of practice

- Collective focus on student learning

- Spirit of shared responsibility for the learning of all students

Professional learning communities can develop when there is

- Time to meet and talk

- Physical proximity

- Interdependent teaching roles

- Active communication structures

- Teacher empowerment and autonomy

New Guidelines and New Position Statements

Over the past decade new position statements and refined national guidelines for building partnerships for learning have been issued by the American Association of School Librarians. AASL has supported development of the school library media program as not only integral to and supportive of the school curriculum, but also as a program that provides a mechanism for choice and exploration beyond the prescribed course of study.

The school library media center is a place where students may explore more fully classroom subjects that interest them; expand their imagination; delve into areas of personal interest; and develop the ability to think clearly, critically, and creatively about the resources they have chosen to read, hear, or view. Beyond this, many in the profession believe the school library media program to be not just a place, but a concept, a way of thinking and exploring. Thus, the student and teacher are not limited by walls or by a few information formats. The library media program, when guided by those with instructional expertise, is a pathway to the human conversations concerning historical, present, and future facts, events, people, issues, and ideas.

The AASL position statement on *The Value of Library Media Programs in Education* (AASL 2000) states, "School library media specialists are an integral part of the total educational team which prepares students to become responsible citizens in a changing global society. In today's information society, an individual's success, even existence, depends largely on the ability to access, evaluate and utilize information. Library media specialists are leaders in carrying out the school's instructional program through their separate but overlapping roles of information specialist, teacher and instructional consultant."

In the 1988 and 1998 national guidelines for school library media programs, as well as the AASL position statement on *The Role of the Library Media Specialist in Outcomes-Based Learning* (1994), the characteristics of the instructional role are defined. As information specialist, , working collaboratively with teachers, administrators, and parents

- provides knowledge of availability and suitability of information resources to support curriculum initiatives;
- engages in the developmental process with the planning team, using knowledge of the school curriculum and professional resources;
- facilitates the use of presentation tools in print, technology, and media for dissemination efforts; and
- serves as an expert in organizing, synthesizing, and communicating information.

As a teacher, the library media specialist

- determines learning outcomes, including those in information literacy, for all students in the school and/or system;
- plans, implements, and evaluates resource-based learning;
- integrates information literacy into all curriculum outcomes; and
- develops ongoing performance-based assessments for determining the achievement of outcomes.

As an instructional consultant, the library media specialist

- facilitates development of teachers' understanding and implementation of outcomes-based education;
- plans for learning environments supportive of curricular integration;
- previews and selects resources and technology to accommodate the learning styles and multiple intelligences of students; and
- designs and implements a variety of instructional strategies and experiences that engage each student in successful learning.

In order to fully implement resource-based education, along with enhancement of reading development as a key skill for learning, AASL takes the following position:

- The library media center is flexibly scheduled so that students and teachers have unlimited physical and intellectual access to a wide range of materials. Students are not limited to using only commercially prescribed or teacher selected materials.

- Students choose from a varied, nongraded collection of materials which reflect their personal interests.

- Students learn to identify, analyze, and synthesize information by using a variety of materials in a variety of formats.

- Multidisciplinary approaches to teaching and learning are encouraged.

- Teachers and library media specialists cooperatively select materials and collaboratively plan activities.

- Teachers and library media specialists share responsibility for reading and information literacy instruction. They plan and teach collaboratively based on the needs of the student.

- Continual staff development is critical to reading instruction.

AASL (2005) has also recently approved a *Position Statement* endorsing the principles of the National Certification Board (http://www.nbpts.org/). These statements can help to improve teacher certification options at the state level as well:

- Accomplished library media specialists have knowledge of learning styles and of human growth and development.

- Accomplished library media specialists know the principles of teaching and learning that contribute to an active learning environment.

- Accomplished library media specialists know the principles of library and information studies needed to create effective, integrated library media programs.

- Accomplished library media specialists integrate information literacy through collaboration, planning, implementation, and assessment of learning.

- Accomplished library media specialists lead in providing equitable access to and effective use of technologies and innovations.

- Accomplished library media specialists plan, develop, implement, manage, and evaluate library media programs to ensure that students and staff use ideas and information effectively.

- Accomplished library media specialists engage in reflective practice to increase their effectiveness.

- Accomplished library media specialists model a strong commitment to lifelong learning and to their profession.

- Accomplished library media specialists uphold professional ethics and promote equity and diversity.

- Accomplished library media specialists advocate for the library media program, involving the greater community.

New Research and New Models—Evolution Toward Instructional Media Specialist

Callison outlined the evolution of the school library of yesterday to the school media specialist of today and the instructional media specialist of tomorrow (see Table 9.2). Published in 1995, his outline remains valid today as the school library media specialist role continues to emerge in the Information Age with greater responsibilities for instruction and communication. The full instructional specialist role continues to elude many in the field, either by choice, situation, or lack of ability. Teacher education certification programs and professional associations must continue to seek educators who aspire to instructional leadership roles to enter the practicing school library media field.

Table 9.2. Evolution Toward Instructional Media Specialist as of 1995

Then	Now	Future
What may I help you find?	What may I help you learn and teach others?	
Library	**Information**	**Literacy and Inquiry**
Evolution from place and resources to professional guidance to concepts		
Librarian	**Media Specialist**	**Instructional Specialist**
Evolution from manager of resources to manager of ideas		
Items	**Networks**	**Ideas**
Place and organizational skills	Program and materials use skills	Personal interaction and communication skills
Skills in Materials Organization		
Gather resources locally In systematic manner for common access	Map collection to curriculum, enhance units through collaborative planning; guided access to resources beyond school and computerized format	Facilitate student-centered information needs and learning; collaborate in analysis of learner and evaluation of performance; access to resources based on meeting those needs in any format
Skills in Communication and Instruction		
Respond to requests, provide reading advisory	Teach information skills integrated with curriculum	Develop and model instructional techniques to best position information literacy and inquiry as a dominant teaching method in all areas of the curriculum.
Reactive	**Proactive**	**Interactive**

See rubric on professional, page 579.

Several recent studies (*School Libraries Work 2006*) have indicated a relationship between the instructional role of the school media specialist and higher performance by students in critical thinking and reading skills for information searching and use. In 2001, Smith found associations with higher student achievement at secondary school levels in Texas when school library media specialists

- collaborated to develop instructional units with teachers, and

- provided leadership in professional staff development for teachers.

Similar studies across sixteen states (Library Research Service 2006) have included various snapshots that tend to confirm that when the school library media specialist is engaged in the educational environment in an effective instructional role, there is also likely to be a higher than average number of students achieving at acceptable academic levels. The research team of Lance, Rodney, and Hamilton-Pennell (2001) found in Oregon that teacher-librarians from high schools with the best Oregon Statewide Assessment reading/language scores are twice as likely as their colleagues from the lowest scoring schools to plan collaboratively with classroom teachers, and their students are more than three times as likely to visit the library as part of a class or other group.

Quality of Instructional Actions Has an Impact

Callison (2004) reported that in Indiana elementary schools a library media specialist who has served full time at the same school for at least three years on an exemplary level in instruction, information access, and administrative services defined by the AASL evaluation rubric is a strong predictor of high student success on all of the language arts elements of the Indiana ISTEP standardized exam. These higher performing school library media specialists, the data show, are a function of a more enriching learning environment that includes a supportive administration, collaborative teachers, and an up-to-date resource collection and technology base. Dramatic improvement on student performance, however, may be seen most clearly in schools with high numbers of students on free lunch. Services of full-time school media specialists who work in collaboration with teachers to deliver reading promotion to meet diverse learning abilities seem to have more immediate impact in low-income schools than where students generally have the security of a steady financial environment. Further, the Indiana study documented that when a certified school media specialist serves the school on a full-time basis (without professional time divided among several schools), the library media center is more likely to have electronic connections to other school collections and the public library, secure more federal funding (nearly twice as much), provide more frequent instruction in the use of electronic resources, and maintain a local Web site linking to current and relevant professional resources.

The important aspect of the studies summarized above is that they demonstrated the value of actions rather than just items or an inventory of holdings. While the data from the state studies (*School Libraries Work* 2006) should not be held as evidence of cause and effect, several of the studies demonstrated that specific instructional actions taken by school media specialists, along with flexible schedules to enhance collaborative opportunities with many teachers, was a predictor of higher student achievement. Many of these studies reported strong relationships between large collections, large school media staff, and new facilities with student achievement. While there may be some impact, the overriding relationship among such factors is wealth. Modern schools with extensive collections and facilities and higher than average number of staff members are most often a function of a wealthier community. Students attending such schools are more likely to carry with them the wealth factor from home as well. This does not mean that they are all rich, but that they very likely come from a stable economic environment, can concentrate on academics because other life problems and security factors have been met, and are more likely to have support for their academic work at home with one or two parents dedicated to the child's well-being.

A few state studies have noted the value of a collection of materials that are up-to-date and supported with the latest understanding and use by teachers of instructional and informational software. Good resources put to good use in good hands can make a difference. In Pennsylvania (Lance, Rodney, and Hamilton-Pennell 2000) researchers reported that the mere presence of a large collection of books, magazines, and newspapers in the school library is not enough to generate high levels of academic achievement by students. Such collections only make a positive difference when they are part of schoolwide initiatives to integrate information literacy into the school's approach to standards and curricula.

More Time Devoted to Instruction Related to Student Achievement

A recent state study completed in Illinois (Lance, Rodney, and Hamilton-Pennell 2005) concluded, among other findings, that in Illinois high schools, eleventh grade ACT scores are highest when there is a high degree of true collaboration between library media specialists and classroom teachers in a wide spectrum of activities. Unfortunately, the research team ignored additional data that illustrate quality of time for instruction over merely the amount of instructional time available. Data on comparison of highest scoring schools compared to lowest scoring schools were reported, but the team chose not to make further analysis of the extreme measures. These data, however, clearly show, at all grade levels measured, that school library media specialists engaged in instructional and collaborative teaching activities much more frequently than school library media staff in the lowest achieving schools. The data from the Illinois study (Tables 90 to 95) are reviewed by this author to illustrate how important quality of instructional time can be over just the amount of time school library media staff may be available.

When the number of professional staff hours per 100 students was reported, the highest scoring schools were a little higher than the lowest scoring schools, but not by much more than 20 percent. Specific actions for instruction by school media specialists in the highest achieving schools were frequently more than three times those in the lowest achieving schools. A little more time was invested, and a lot more quality time was invested in the highest achieving schools.

The comparison at the high school level was actually reversed: more hours per 100 students were worked by school library staff in the lowest achieving schools than in the highest achieving schools. The highest achieving schools showed a greater portion of their hours of operation to be "after school," when high school students are likely to need greater access to resources and extended independent research assistance. In the Illinois high schools measured, the highest scoring high school library media staff gave

- 50 percent more time to "identifying materials for teachers,"
- 240 percent more time "planning with teachers,"
- 347 percent more time "teaching with teachers,"
- 42 percent more time "teaching information literacy to students,"
- 115 percent more time "providing in-service training to teachers,"
- 65 percent more time "motivating students to read,"
- 29 percent more time "managing the computer network,"
- 36 percent more time meeting with the principal, and
- 90 percent more time than the school library media staff in the lowest scoring schools in Illinois on student achievement tests "serving on school committees."

The point here is that while it is desirable to have more full-time, certified school library media specialists employed in schools across Illinois and the rest of the country, schools need to be very careful and selective in who they employ and how they support instructional actions and time allocations. It is not simply more school media specialists that are needed, it is current school media specialists improving on their instructional actions in terms of frequency and effectiveness. The need is recruitment of more school media specialists who will serve as instructional school media specialists in a collaborative educational environment.

Principals, Teachers, and Students Value the School Media Specialist's Instructional Role

Large studies conducted in individual states over the past decade have measured the impact on learning that can be linked to the school library media program (*School Libraries Work* 2006). This shift has been gradually moving away from simple measures of items related to single, standardized test snapshots that often result in positive, but not necessarily strong, relationships (Lance and Callison 2005). More and more, researchers are listening to administrators, teachers, and students about the valuable actions taken by the school media specialist to enhance learning and teaching opportunities. An effective school media specialist can have an especially strong influence on positive gains in student learning in schools that are considered disadvantaged. Usually this means a majority of the students are receiving lunch assistance. Quality school media programs in these low-income settings can compensate to some degree for the insecurities students face, especially in elementary schools. The positive impact on reading and other language arts performance is likely to be immediate and dramatic if resources are provided for new library materials, library assistants, and basic technology, but never strongly effective until all resources are coordinated and infused into the learning environment by a competent and progressive school media instructional specialist in collaboration with a supportive principal and teaching staff.

Some measures of quality performance on the part of certified, full-time school media specialists have been based on the professional criteria found in the AASL Rubric for 21st Century Assessment (AASL 1999). Farmer (2006), for example, found collaborative planning between teachers and professional full-time library staff to be a strong indicator of higher reading scores in California. Callison (2004) found that high or exemplary measures of full-time school media specialist performance over a three-year period to be a strong indicator of higher language arts scores in Indiana elementary schools. Overall, the impact studies conducted by Lance and others consistently indicate that when qualified school media specialists are willing and able to devote substantial time to engaging students and teachers in literature-based programs, one is likely to also find students who are performing at their potential for achievement in reading and writing. Productive and efficient school media specialists may be the strongest predictor of a quality learning environment in which educators strive to collaborate for the common educational good of all students, no matter how diversified in learning abilities and no matter the economic

level. Cause and effect, however, is not to be claimed in most of these studies. Already strong educational environments in affluent school districts tend to attract the best school library media specialists, and such high-performing environments may add as much to the performance of the media specialist as they add to the quality of the school.

The most recent state study completed just prior to publication of this book was conducted in Wisconsin by Ester Smith (2006). She found the same dramatic difference in the amount of time school media specialists in high academic performing schools spent on instructional actions compared to time on such activities by school library media specialists in low achieving schools. Extensive interviews were conducted at selected schools and a sample of the narrative reports from Smith's research team report provide an illustration of how highly regarded the school media specialist can be when he or she takes actions to be greatly involved in the curriculum.

Interviewers in Wisconsin found positive statements that supported a personality and ability level from school library media specialists to work productively with teachers and students, to relate to their learning and teaching needs, and to motive success. Selected paragraphs from the case studies include the following:

> "The library media specialist revived the program when she took the position about nine years ago. She made it a vital, fully integrated instructional program through collaboration with teachers. According to all those interviewed, the only weakness is that the facility is too small to meet demand for classes and limits the number of students that can be accommodated" (15).

> "The library media specialist collaborates with the public library in several ways. The public library holds twelve technology skills classes at the library media center each year [for community members]. The library media specialist informs the public library about projects students are doing and the public librarian in turn provides books through interlibrary loan. This benefits the students because the public library has a different collection. According to the principal, the leadership of the library media specialist provides is a key strength of the

program, 'It's people who make the difference.' In spite of the school's limited financial resources, the library media center holds a comprehensive, up-to-date nonfiction collection" (23).

"The teachers expressed great respect for the library media specialist and her accomplishments. They see her as an invaluable resource to themselves and their students. Her activities have both supported and enhanced their instruction and elevated student skills and competencies. Students consider the library media specialist an indispensable source of help academically as well as personally. They expressed great appreciation and admiration for her" (24).

"The library media specialist works closely with the principal; their offices are adjacent to each other. The principal and the library media specialist communicate daily. The principal walks through the library media center daily to observe student engagement in information skills instruction and literature activities. The library media specialist and the principal collaborate on the design of the school web page" (27).

"According to teachers, the library media specialist reaches areas of the curriculum that might otherwise not have been approached – she digs deep. The social studies teacher credits the library media specialist with 'revolutionizing her curriculum.' Previously, the teacher basically taught from the textbook. The library media specialist helped her change her instructional approach to using simulations (mock Supreme Court trails), research and integration of technology. The science teacher no longer teaches from the textbook, but by greater use of experimentation and technology" (39).

"According to the principal, the school is one of the top academically performing middle schools in the state. The library media center is central to students' academic performance. The current educational leadership wants students to learn how to learn, to self-reflect and be responsible for their own academic growth and development. The library media specialist is the moving force behind this philosophy. The

principal indicated that the middle school has created a culture of innovation. The principal encourages teachers to learn new things and to explore 'what's out there and then choose from it.' . . . the library media specialist joins in this process of modeling successful projects to others" (40).

"The library media specialist considers herself to be a teacher-librarian, a learning coordinator. Teachers come to her with their units and she identifies resources, web sites or other tools to support their lessons. During the first three years of the library media specialists' tenure in this school, she spent about 20 percent of her time planning units with teachers. Because so many units are now developed, she spends less time on that activity and more time in direct participation in instruction. The teachers consider the library media specialist very helpful across content areas because of her knowledge of the curriculum. Teachers recognize the expertise of the library media specialist and ask for her help. They have great respect for her. The library media specialist is very visible to teachers. With the objective of supporting all teachers, the library media specialist does not hesitate to go to those teachers who do not come to her" (47).

"The library media specialist indicated that she spends the majority of her time working with students and every time she is with students, she teaches them. Students interviewed reported that the library media specialist taught them how to evaluate web sites, and how to use keywords when doing searches. She also does an in-depth review of the research process. The students found her lessons very helpful and useful. She has also taught them how to problem solve and how to organize information. She 'never underestimates anybody.' In fact, she has confidence in their abilities and is very excited when students achieve" (48).

Smith also found in Wisconsin, as Lance found in Illinois, substantially greater time invested by library media specialists in actions related to instruction and promotion of information literacy and reading in the highest performing schools compared to the lowest performing schools. Greater time for such activities was often possible because of flexible schedules for time management and availability of adult clerical assistants to relieve the media specialist of many routine duties such as book circulation. These and the other recent state studies have provided a growing amount of evidence that instructional interventions or instructional influence, rather than economic affluence, should be the measures isolated and examined in more detail (Phye, Robinson, and Levin 2005). The power of interactive reading, writing. and library resource programs working together, for example, has yet to be measured (Oberg 2002).

The impact of such instructional programs may be more dramatic and meaningful for inquiry-based learning than measuring the multiple factors based on the number of books, video programs, and periodicals owned. Hopefully, future studies will also seek to examine the impact of the use of information searching technology for inquiry, rather than simply the ownership of such technology. Simply put: It is not so much a question of what you own, but how constructive you are with the resources you have.

The Added Power of Flexible Scheduling

In the hands of an experienced and progressive school library media specialist, the control of his or her schedule to work closely with fellow teachers and to establish inquiry projects across several days or weeks is an extremely important tool. Being able to serve the same building of teachers and students full time and to concentrate on a full year's schedule for programs, orientations, teamed presentations, and student evaluations can make the difference between inquiry-based learning that succeeds or fails. Such is not possible at any level, elementary through secondary, unless the professional library media specialist acts as an instructional specialist with command over a flexible schedule of his or her time. A portion of the schedule, if so determined by the specialist, may be devoted to frequent library visits from lower grade students in elementary schools, but benefits of inquiry learning will be much stronger based on collaborative teaching and management of time on a flexible basis. Joy McGregor (2006), a researcher who has monitored flexible scheduling studies over the past two decades, summarizes the research with these assertions:

- A particular educational need will drive the move to flexible scheduling.

- The principal's support is critical.

- When schools devised acceptable alternatives to providing teacher planning time (rather than simply using the school librarian to cover the class during planning time), the stress of implementing flexible scheduling was less.

- Personal qualities (teaching ability, energy, facilitating mindset) appeared to be very important to successful implementation.

- Certain teacher characteristics (trust children, team-player, innovators) promote successful use of flexible scheduling.

- Implementation can follow different paths and the approach depends on the situation.

- Support staff plays a critical role in successful implementation. Clerical duties expand and competent fulltime clerical assistance in the media center is critical to releasing the professional to conduct business as a professional.

- Both learning and the library become more relevant to students because they know they need the information and the skills.

- School library media specialists have a more integrated view of the library program and the outcomes possible through flexible scheduling than other educators.

- Acceptance is typically slow and should not be taken for granted.

- Full implementation of flexible scheduling is never truly complete.

Instruction for Inquiry

Over the past two decades of introducing online catalogs, electronic reference tools, and computerized databases to students and teachers, researchers have noted consistently the need for educated, tech savvy, and virtual gurus such as school media specialists to help the wider school population keep up with the Information Age (Marchionini 1989; Fidel 1991; Gross 1999). Intervention strategies learned from these studies have pointed to several recommendations for teaching skills in online searching in support of inquiry projects (Branch 2003):

- Explore and examine research process models, especially those pioneered by Kuhlthau as the Information Search Process.

- Focus equally on the affective learning domain along with the cognitive learning domain to support students in their emotional challenges as well as intellectual challenges.

- Provide time for students to gain background knowledge about the topic, especially if it was assigned and not student selected or selected with little knowledge beyond what has been stated in the student's textbook, before expecting focus. Guide students in constructing graphic organizers such as concept maps.

- Provide opportunities to reflect on the process throughout the research inquiry using journals and small group discussion and large group debriefing.

- Provide students with support and skills for dealing with large amounts of text; reading nonfiction; and use of strategies such as using key words, subtitles, skimming, and scanning.

In order to be successful in the instructional role, the library media specialist must demonstrate more than the skill to teach online search techniques. He or she must be knowledgeable about new national curriculum standards across all disciplines, be aware of new instructional materials in a variety of formats, understand instructional design and its application for teaching information literacy, and be welcoming to classroom teachers and students through the practice of clear, interactive communication skills.

Any inquiry project requires both emotional and cognitive support from peers and teachers and school library media specialists, ac-cording to Jennifer Branch (2003) of the University of Alberta. Her work with schools in Canada has demonstrated the challenges students face in inquiry projects that truly test their abilities to brainstorm, organize, synthesize, and maintain interest in a subject through the presentation stages. Basic instruction in the early planning stages can make the difference in student success or failure in the long run.

Recent professional development conducted in Canada to introduce inquiry-based instruction (Alberta Learning 2004) includes identification of the following factors to increase the chances that inquiry teaching methods will be successful:

- Administrators in the school or district have a clearly articulated vision for inquiry.

- The vision for inquiry is carried forward despite competing pressures.

- Two or more champions promote the vision for inquiry.

- Resources and space for inquiry are readily accessible.

- Teachers collaborate and support each other.

- Teachers, students and parents trust each other.

- Small, interdisciplinary teams of teachers work together.

- Problem-solving and investigative skills are valued throughout the school/school system.

The Ohio Study

A recent detailed study on the instructional impact of the school library media specialist has come again from the work of Carol Kuhlthau. This time teaming with Ross Todd, this multilevel investigation was funded by a collaborative coalition of OELMA, INFOhio (the state K–12 information network), the Ohio Department of Education, and the State Library of Ohio. Ann E. Tepe was the Project Director of the Student Learning through Ohio School Libraries, and Gayle Geitgey was assistant director for the project (see www.oelma.org/StudentLearning.htm).

Among other data gathered through observations, interviews, and surveys, the research team examined the instructional actions of school library media specialists in thirty-nine Ohio school libraries that had been identified as exemplary. A new model emerged (http://www.oelma.org/StudentLearning/documents/DynamicAgents.pdf) describing the exemplary school librarian as an information-learning specialist and a curriculum partner-leader. The library in support of the instructional role was described, in exemplary situations, as a knowledge space to transform information into knowledge. The study shows that an effective school library is not just informational, but transformational and formational, leading to knowledge creation, knowledge production, knowledge dissemination, and knowledge use, as well as the development of information values (see Figure 9.2). These characteristics are similar to the library as a learning laboratory (Callison 2000).

Model of the School Library as a Dynamic Agent of Learning

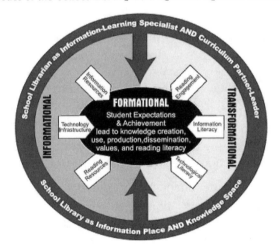

Figure 9.2. Model of the school library as a dynamic agent of learning. Ross J. Todd, Carol C. Kuhlthau and OELMA Copyright 2004. Reprinted with permission from Todd.

Based on their findings, Todd and Kuhlthau (2005a, 2005b) and the Ohio study research team concluded that students (Todd 2005) perceived the school library as a "dynamic agent of student learning and student achievement." The researchers also developed a more detailed profile of an effective school library. The following

eight characteristics can be used as a strategic roadmap for school librarians who want to place a stronger emphasis on instruction and learning in their programs (Whelan 2004):

Resource agents: The school library and librarian provide up-to-date, diverse resources to meet the curriculum's informational needs. The librarian provides instructional interventions by guiding students in their information choices through the effective use of these resources.

Literacy development agents: The school librarian engages students in an active and meaningful search process, enabling them to explore, formulate, and focus their searches, and providing a supportive environment (personal, physical, and instructional) for students to be successful in their research. Students understand that doing good research will lead to better knowledge of the curriculum content, as well as to academic success in their research projects.

Knowledge construction agents: The school librarian develops information literacy scaffolds for engaging students with information in meaningful ways, enabling them to construct and develop new knowledge and understanding.

Academic achievement agents: The school librarian is a dynamic agent of learning who helps students achieve better grades, particularly on research projects and assignments. An agent of academic achievement must be both a credentialed educator and a librarian.

Independent reading and personal development agents: The school library plays a role in fostering independent reading, particularly in lower grades. Reading materials that targets personal pursuits, pleasure reading, and reading for knowledge provide students with an important foundation. It is essential to promote and encourage reading literacy, academic achievement, and the development of independent, lifelong readers.

Technological literacy agents: The school library plays an important role in information technology by providing students with up-to-date software across multiple media. Lessons must go beyond teaching the effective use of software to include technical troubleshooting (disk, printing, Internet access) and problem-solving skills.

Rescue agents: Students face many information crises: they need last-minute resources, help with technology, solutions to technical problems, and help developing theses for projects. Indeed, even as a rescue agent, the library is opportunistic, responding to the multiple needs that arise from learning.

Individualized learning agents: The personal touch of a professional school librarian matters a great deal to students. Personal engagement with students is a critical component of an effective school library. School librarians who see themselves as information-learning specialists play a vital role in student learning.

Todd and Kuhlthau (2005b) identified many actions of the exemplary school library media specialists that demonstrated clearly their contributions to the learning environment and served as evidence to the research team of how school librarians can enable others to learn and succeed. These actions are based on the descriptions gained from teachers who indicated a collaborative teaching relationship with school media specialists. The most frequently described actions are paraphrased below:

Improving student process and product, content and delivery, as well as access to diversified materials to meet reader ability and needs:

- knowing research process linked to learning task
- identifying key ideas
- identifying ideas in conflict
- structuring ideas
- developing arguments
- developing organizational structures for ideas
- provision of staged feedback

Improving information seeking and use as well as improving learner attitudes:

- planned lesson, resources and evaluation together with other teachers
- schedule is open to be flexible in order to address learning and planning at point of need
- models determination of information selection, evaluation and quality, including websites
- models constructive use of online databases
- models stages of research process

Enhancing technology use and introducing new software and hardware:

- leads access to state-of-art technology
- teaches technical and evaluation skills

Use of library and associated information access skills and attitudes necessary:

- reduces anxiety in technology and library use
- guides to diversified resources to meet different levels of need
- engages in strategies to encourage and enjoy library services and sources—author visits, reading promotion, reading circles, sustained silent reading, special speakers, and writing workshops

Engaging in learning beyond formal classes and school:

- guide independent projects
- access to library databases, websites and other resources online at learner's home
- participates in ongoing review of learning and student achievement

Table 3

The Ohio School Library as a Dynamic Agent of Learning ESSENTIAL LEARNING FOUNDATIONS	
INFORMATIONAL The Resource Base	**TRANSFORMATIONAL** Learning-Teaching Intervention
Resources: Current, multi-perspective, multi-format resources with readability levels aligned with the local curriculum, and supporting Ohio's academic content standards.	**Information literacy:** Development of information literacy for engagement with information in all its forms in the context of curriculum needs, content strands and subject knowledge creation processes for effective engagement and utilization of information.
Technological infrastructure: State-of-art technology to acquire, organize, produce, and disseminate information, and function as a gateway to information.	**Technological literacies:** Development of media and technological skills, which include critical thinking skills and communication competencies; as well as the appropriate and ethical use of technology for information access, retrieval, production, and dissemination via electronic resources, networks, and the Internet.
Reading resources: Reading materials targeted beyond informational curriculum needs – personal pursuits, pleasure/leisure reading.	**Reading engagement:** Development of approaches to promote and encourage reading for academic achievement and life-long learning through participation in national and state reading celebrations and initiatives; reading to students, promoting literature, reinforcing reading skills, and encouraging independent reading for personal enjoyment; engaging in a range of activities to foster sustained love of reading.

FORMATIONAL
Student Expectations and Achievement

Knowledge creation: Students achieve through being able to define problems, frame questions, explore ideas, formulate focus, investigate, analyze and synthesize ideas to create own views, evaluate solutions and reflect on new understandings.

Knowledge use: Students develop transferable skills for sustaining knowledge creation beyond the classroom.

Knowledge production: Students can use technology and information tools to produce new knowledge and demonstrate achievement. They create information products that accurately represent their newly developed understanding.

Knowledge dissemination: Students can communicate ideas using oral, written, visual and technological modes of expression – individually or in teams.

Knowledge values: Students are ethical, responsible users of information who accept responsibility for personal decisions and information actions. They demonstrate concern for quality information and value different modes of thought.

Reading literacy: Students have high levels of reading literacy. They become independent, life-long sustained readers.

Figure 9.3. The Ohio School Library as a dynamic agent of learning: Essential learning foundations. Ross J. Todd, Carol C. Kuhlthau, and OELMA http://www.oelma.org/StudentLearning/SLFindings.asp. © 2004. Reprinted with permission from Todd.

Collaboration for an Integrated Curriculum

The attributes of a collaborative teaching and learning environment, in which the school librarian engages in curricular issues on a par with other teachers and actually leads in many aspects in addition to providing expertise in resource access and use, include (Montiel-Overall 2005) deep trust, collegiality, respect, equality, expertise recognized and valued, and communication that is constructive and frequent. Members of this educational community make the effort to work well with others (see pages 121–22):

> Integrated curriculum involves [teacher librarian collaboration] TLC across the curriculum. Teachers meet regularly with the librarian to integrate information literacy and content through joint efforts that involve co-thinking, co-planning, co-implementation, and co-evaluation across the curriculum at the invitation of the principal or through involvement in curriculum planning committees.

At such high levels of collaboration, the principal is critical to implementation and maintenance. Without the principal providing time, resources, encouragement, and rewards, the full collaborative community in most school settings will not survive (Oberg 1996).

Instructional Collaboration at the College Level

Information literacy models and skill sets presented in this book are highly relevant to the issues for information literacy diffusion at the college level (Dewey 2001). Collaboration is also a vital issue. Instructional words, methods, and concepts are defined within the elementary and secondary school settings, but in nearly all cases these will transfer to the college setting as well. The library is a learning laboratory, tied closely to the academic lessons of the college, and serving as the learning environment that increasingly includes a variety of collaborative workspaces.

Collaboration between the academic librarian and professor is also part of a similar instructional role sharing on the college campus that has been described above for the lower school setting. Patricia Knapp's application of the library college concept at Monteith College in the early 1960s was an experiment to fully integrate library instruction with the local liberal arts college curriculum. The project failed, in large part because faculty members were unwilling to or did not understand how to cooperate with librarians in the instructional process. In general, teaching modes based mostly on lecture and textbook did not match the inquiry process that immersed the student in multiple resources. Knapp concluded:

> Our original notion that the ineffectiveness of traditional library instruction is due to its isolation from content courses was reinforced by our experience with the pilot project. But we are no longer content with the simple goal of getting the library somehow or other built into such courses. The relationship is more complicated than we thought. If it is to be effective, the library program must be not merely presented in the context of content courses, but truly consistent in goals and methods, in tone and style, with the overall education program in which it occurs. (51)

Evan Ira Farber, famed advocate for library instruction and innovator of many techniques in bibliographic instruction at Earlham College in Richmond, Indiana, has always argued that the role of the library on the college campus is to enhance the teaching/learning process. College librarians are agents of this process and design facilities, organize collections, provide information access, and collaborate in teaching the use of information sources in order to deliver on this role. Farber, as many others in the academic library field do today, advocated decades ago that the following elements must be in place:

- Library and information use instruction is best presented at point of need and is more likely to be effective when integrated with specific course content.

- Both the professor and the librarian have educational goals and should share and build from both in development of library-based projects so that students learn both subject content as well as information process skills.

- Library and information instruction should be constructed on analysis of student need and ability to determine what the student knows and brings to the situation, along with the expectations of the professor, before formal instruction begins.

- In the emerging Information Age, technologies will increasingly both cover and create basic instructional needs, while more and more students will benefit from computer-assisted tutorials, keeping up-to-date with the vastly expanding information options and search engines will still require guidance from the librarian.

- The Information Age moves the librarian into the role of information advisor or information counselor, more demanding than the role of reading advisor; as readers' advisor one informs the reader of the classic titles and sources, but as information advisor the librarian models and provides guidance in the selection, analysis, and application of the most relevant information possible for the student to access. (Kuhlthau 2004)

A growing number of college reference and instructional librarians are finding constructive ways to collaborate with high school library media specialists in order to share information literacy teaching strategies and to prepare students for the information demands they will face as they enter college. Inquiry activities that place college resources, often accessed electronically by students at their local school, in the hands of student researchers before they enter college help to provide a rich and expansive application of information literacy (Dennis 2001).

Collaboration and the Information Commons

Collaboration is also viewed by some academic librarians as a process that should be used to enhance peer learning. Students should experience a "community of inquirers" and through interaction learn to help each other. Janice Sauer, of the University of Alabama Library, wrote in her 1995 award-winning essay, "Librarians cannot expect to encourage any sense of complexity and multiplicity by using library assignments that expect single right answers. Nor can they encourage critical thinking by expecting students to learn tools without a larger view of context and diversity. No one can expect undergraduates to understand that they are to learn to participate in the construction of understanding and knowledge unless we actually encourage the practice of construction" (135).

What better way is there to teach how knowledge is constructed than by using the same collaborative method used to construct knowledge? As Barbara Fister (1990) states, "Group inquiry gives the students a working model of a scholarly community in the microcosm of the classroom. Before a person is able to think, they must first experience direct social exchanges with others. . . . Collaborative learning requires the establishment of an environment in which the teacher does not have the answer. The questions asked must be so complex [for the given learner] as to require analysis, debate, negotiation, and consensus before an answer can be suggested" (147).

As the instructional words, concepts, and methods defined in this book demonstrate, Information Inquiry lays the foundation for both critical and creative thinking through strategies, modeled by instructional media specialists and other teachers beginning in the very early grades and continuing through higher education environments. A typical floor plan for "Information Commons" workspaces appearing in a growing number of college libraries is shown in Figure 9.4. Technology is combined with print resources and group workspaces for collaborative learning enterprises. Similar Information Media Commons environments are beginning to emerge in secondary schools, where students may work together to seek, select, test, and present their Information Inquiry projects. (See Figures 9.4 and 9.5.)

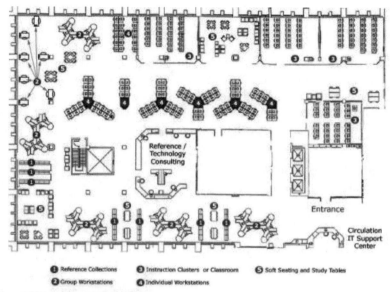

Figure 9.4. Information commons floor plan and group work at the Indiana University Main Library Commons.

Figure 9.5. Team projects, group debate, and discussion at the IUPUI University library Commons, 2005. What similar environments are possible K–12?

References

Alberta Learning. (2004). *Focus on inquiry: A teacher's guide to implementing inquiry-based learning.* Alberta Learning and Education.

American Association of School Librarians. (1994). *The role of the school library media specialist in outcomes-based learning.* AASL Position Statements. http://www.ala.org/ala/aasl/aaslproftools/positionstatements/aaslpositionstatementrolelibrary.htm (accessed June 6, 2001).

American Association of School Librarians (AASL). (1999). *A planning guide for* Information Power: *Building partnerships for learning with school library media program assessment rubric for the 21st century.* AASL.

American Association of School Librarians. (2000). *The value of library media programs in education.* http://www.ala.org/ala/aasl/aaslproftools/positionstatements/aaslpositionstatementvalue.htm (accessed January 7, 2006).

American Association of School Librarians. (2005). *Position statement on support for National Board of Professional Teaching Standards certification.* http://www.ala.org/ala/aasl/aaslproftools/positionstatements/teachingstandardsps.htm (accessed January 3, 2006).

American Association of School Librarians and Association for Educational Communications and Technology. (1988). *Information power.* American Library Association.

American Association of School Librarians and Association for Educational Communications and Technology. (1998). *Information power: Building partnerships for learning.* American Library Association.

Branch, J. L. (2003). Instructional intervention is the key: Supporting adolescent information seeking personal. *School Libraries Worldwide, 9* (2), 47–61.

Callison, D. (1995). Restructuring pre-service education. In Betty J. Morris (Ed.), *School library media annual 1995.* (100–112). Libraries Unlimited.

Callison, D. (2000). Learning laboratory. *School Library Media Activities Monthly, 17* (4): 37–39, 45.

Callison, D. (2004). *Survey of Indiana school library media programs.* AIME Conference, Indianapolis, Indiana. http://www.ilfonline.org/AIME/Survey.htm (accessed January 30, 2006).

Dennis, N. (2001). Using inquiry methods to foster information literacy partnerships. *Reference Services Review, 29* (2), 122–132.

Dewey, B. I. (2001). *Library user education: Powerful learning, powerful partnerships.* Scarecrow Press.

Donham, J. (2005). *Enhancing teaching and learning.* 2d ed. Neal-Schuman.

Everhart, N., and E. T. Dresang. (2006). *School library media specialists for the 21st century: Leaders in education to make a difference.* The ALISE National Conference, San Antonio, January.

Farber, E. I. (1993). Bibliographic instruction at Earlham College. In Larry Hardesty, Jamie Hastreiter, and David Henderson (Eds.), *Bibliographic instruction in practice* (1–14). Pierian Press.

Farmer, L. S .J. (2006). Library media program implementation and student achievement. *Journal of Librarianship and Information Science, 38* (1): 21–32.

Fidel, R. (1991). Searchers' selection of search keys. *Journal of the American Society for Information Science, 42*, 490–527.

Fister, B. (1990). Teaching research as a social act: Collaborative learning and the library. *RQ* (Summer), 506–509.

Gross, M. (1999). Imposed queries in the school library media center. *Library and Information Science Research, 21* (4), 501–521.

Knapp, P. (1966). *The Monteith College library experiment.* Scarecrow Press.

Kuhlthau, C. C. (1993). Implementing a process approach to information skills: A study identifying indicators of success in library media programs. *School Library Media Quarterly* (Fall), 11–18.

Kuhlthau, C. C. (2004). *Seeking meaning.* 2d ed. Libraries Unlimited.

Lance, K., and D. Callison. (2005). Enough already?: Blazing new trails for school library media research. *School Library Media Research, 8.* www.ala.org/aasl/SLMR (accessed July 1, 2006).

Lance, K. C., M. J. Rodney, and C. H. Hamilton-Pennell. (2000). *Measuring up to standards: The impact of school library programs & information literacy in Pennsylvania schools.* Pennsylvania Citizens for Better Libraries.

Lance, K. C., M. J. Rodney and C. Hamilton-Pennell. (2001). *Good schools have school librarians: Oregon school librarians collaborate to improve academic achievement.* Oregon Educational Media Association.

Lance, K. C., M. J. Rodney, and C. Hamilton-Pennell. (2005). *Powerful libraries make powerful learners: The Illinois study.* Illinois School Library Media Association.

Library Research Service. (2006). *School library impact studies.* http://www.lrs.org/impact.asp (accessed January 3, 2006).

Marchionini, G. (1989). Making the transition from print to electronic encyclopedias. *International Journal of Man-Machine Studies 30,* 591–618.

McGregor, J. (2006) Flexible scheduling: Implementing an innovation. *School Library Media Research, 9.* www.ala.org/aasl/SLMR/ (accessed July 3, 2006).

Montiel-Overall, P. (2005). A theoretical understanding of teacher and librarian collaboration (TLC). *School Libraries Worldwide, 11* (2), 24–48.

Montiel-Overall, P. (2006). *Toward a theory for teacher and librarian collaboration* The ALISE National Conference, San Antonio, Texas, January.

National School Reform Faculty. (2006). http://www.nsrfharmony.org/default.html (accessed January 3, 2006).

National Standards Board. (2006). http://www.nbpts.org/ (accessed January 3, 2006).

Neuman, Delia. (2001). Re-visioning school library media programs for the future. *Journal of Education for Library and Information Science, 42* (2), 96–115.

Oberg. D. (1996). Principal support: What does it mean to teacher-librarians? In L. A. Clyde (Ed.), *Sustaining the vision: A collection of articles and papers on research in school librarianship in honor of Jean E. Lowrie.* (221–230). Hi Willow Research.

Oberg, D. (2002). Looking for the evidence: do school libraries improve student achievement? *School Libraries in Canada, 22* (2): 10–13, 44.

Phye, G. D., D. H. Robinson, and J. R. Levin (eds.). (2005). *Empirical methods for evaluating educational interventions.* Educational psychology series. Academic Press.

Sauer, J. A. (1995). Conversation 101: Process, development and collaboration. In *Information for a new age* (135–170). Libraries Unlimited.

School libraries work. (2006). Scholastic Publishing and Research. librarypublishing.scholastic.com/content/stores/LibraryStore/pages/images/slw_06.pdf (accessed January 3, 2006).

Smith, E. G. (2001). *Texas school libraries: Standards, resources, services, and students' performance.* Texas State Library and Archives Commission. http://www.tsl.state.tx.us/ld/pubs/schlibsurvey/index.html (accessed January 3, 2006).

Smith, E. G. (2006). *Student learning through Wisconsin school library media centers: Case study report.* Division for Libraries, Technology and Community Learning: Wisconsin Department of Public Instruction. http://www.dpi.wi.gov/imt/ (accessed July 1, 2006).

Tilley, C. L., and D. Callison. (2001). Preparing school library media specialists for the new century: Results of a survey. (based on The KALIPER Project for the University of Michigan, 1999–2001.) *Journal of Education for Library and Information Science, 42* (3), 220–227.

Todd, R. J. (2005). Listen to the voices: Ohio students tell their stories of school libraries. *Knowledge Quest, 33* (4), 8–13.

Todd, R. J., and C. C. Kuhlthau. (2005a). Student learning through Ohio school libraries, part I: How effective school libraries help students. *School Libraries Worldwide, 11* (1), 63–88.

Todd, R. J., and C.C. Kuhlthau. (2005b). Student learning through Ohio school libraries, part II: How effective school libraries help students. *School Libraries Worldwide, 11* (1), 89–110.

Whelan, D. L. (2004). 13,000 kids can't be wrong. *School Library Journal, 50* (2), 46—50. http://www.schoollibraryjournal.com/article/CA377858.html (accessed January 3, 2006).

Recommended Tools to Document Time and Accountability

Everhart, N. (2000). School library media specialists' use of time: A review of the research. *School Libraries Worldwide, 6* (1): 53–65.

Miller, N. A. S. (2003). *Impact: Documenting the LMC program for accountability.* Hi Willow Research.

Miller, N. A. S. (2005). *Oklahoma Association of School Library Media Specialists Time Task Study.* AASL Judy Pitts Research Forum. http://www.oklibs.org/~oaslms/OKTimeTaskReport.pdf.

Miller, N. A. S. (2005). *Time & task tracker for school library media personnel.* Hi Willow Research.

Chapter 10

The Student as Information Scientist

Daniel Callison

This chapter is based on an analogy presented by Daniel Callison and Annette Lamb at the 2005 National Conference of the American Association of School Librarians in Pittsburgh. Elaborations on this analogy related to levels of Information Inquiry and field experiences can be located on the Internet at http://www.virtualinquiry.com.

Information literacy standards for student learning, indicators for student performance, and hundreds of collaborative lesson plans around the country give us some indication of the skills students are expected to master as effective and efficient users of information. Hopefully the goal is that all involved in information literacy education become wiser consumers of information. In mastering the elements of Information Inquiry, teachers and school librarians acting as instructional specialists model, teach, and learn with their students the best ways to test and select information that is valid and relevant to solve information problems (Callison 2000).

The Scientific Method and Inquiry

The basic definition of the scientific method includes these steps:

- observation and description of a phenomenon

- formulation of a hypothesis to explain the phenomenon

- use of the hypothesis to predict existence of other phenomena

- performance of experimental tests of the prediction and inferring a conclusion

- (sometimes) presenting, debating, and/or application of findings (see Table 10.1).

Table 10.1. What Scientists Do

Observe	Watching carefully, taking notes, comparing and contrasting
Question	Asking questions about observations, asking questions that can lead to manageable investigations, evaluating and prioritizing questions
Hypothesize	Suggesting possible explanations consistent with available observations
Predict	Suggest an event or result in the future based on analysis of observations
Investigate	Testing through gathering data and use of methods relevant to the questions
Communicate	Informing others through means of communication relevant to the conclusions and the audience addressed

The inquiry process gives heavy emphasis to development of questions at each step. What questions come from observation? What questions are relevant to the hypothesis? What questions formulate the prediction? What questions are answered from the test of the prediction, and what questions, new and old, remain unanswered in part or in full?

The process of Information Inquiry involves application of the ancient Socratic Method of teaching through self-posed and mentor-posed questions in order to gain meaning in today's overwhelming Information Age. Application of the scientific method gives a systematic structure to inquiry, a scaffold for levels of thinking and doing (Callison 2001). It places students and teachers in the role of "information scientists." This analogy will be explored as one that may open new paths for students and teachers not only to investigate phenomena identified from typical subjects of study, but also to test and predict the value, relevance, and meaning of information itself. As "information scientists," should learners be expected to journal, debate, compare, and present their observations on the value of the information encountered and the need for information that may not be available or possible to obtain?

The Professional Information Scientist

A case is not being made here to equate specific tasks of the professional information scientist with skills expected of the student information scientist. There are, however, some potential practices for the student that can be drawn from the business of adult information scientists. Gary Marchionini (1999), a professor of information science at North Carolina University, has grouped his field of investigation into classification, use behavior, knowledge dissemination, social informatics, and human/computer interaction. These are defined in Table 10.2 and Figure 10.1.

Table 10.2. What Professional Information Scientists Do

Classification Theory	In what manner can knowledge or information be represented so effective and efficient information retrieval can take place? In what manner should such representation change to meet different discourse, various disciplines, and changes in information format?
Information Use Behavior	In what manner do humans seek or not seek, and use or not use, information? What information do they find useful and not useful, and why? How do diverse cultures and media formats affect these behaviors?
Knowledge Creation & Dissemination	In what manner can information be best communicated or transferred to meet the needs of different groups? How is knowledge communicated, validated, valued, and assimilated, and what patterns in these processes can be documented? What do these patterns tell us?
Social Informatics	What is the role(s) of information in the social and cultural milieu? Issues studied may involve information equity, information security, political or economic values of information, and intellectual property rights.
Interaction Studies	Also termed *information architecture* or *information design*, this area draws from studies related to human-computer interaction. Software and Web site usability studies are common. Scientists seek to determine the processes that influence and are influenced by human use of information systems. Scientists strive to determine ways that interactive experiences can be well structured and properly positioned within the wider or global electronic information infrastructure.

Student Information Scientist and Instructional Specialist in the Learning Laboratory—Visit virtualinquiry.com

The student information scientist is at the center of the inquiry environment. They are supported by a cadre of caring, supportive, instructional specialists that each have an important role in nurturing the young information scientist. These student scientists and instructional specialists conduct their inquiries within an engaging learning laboratory filled with information resources needed to support the maturing student information scientist.

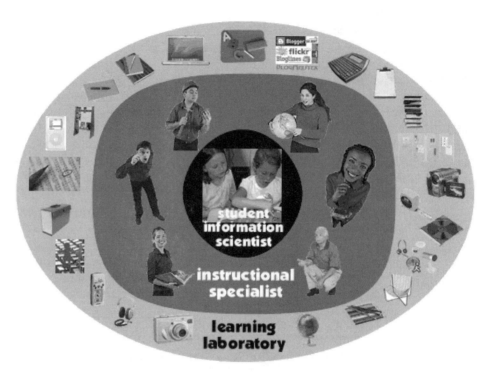

Instructional Specialist

The school library media specialist, classroom teacher, and other building educators all play an important role as instructional specialists facilitating the work of the student information scientist. As professional educators, they are able to apply effective teaching strategies to assist young learners.

Learning Laboratory

Today's learning laboratory is much more than a traditional school library. The laboratory reaches beyond the walls of the school library media center into all areas of the school and outside the walls of the school into the local community and world of the Internet. This engaging learning environment includes a wide range of information resources, tools, spaces, and opportunities.

Figure 10.1. Student information scientist and instructional specialist in the learning laboratory.

What Student Information Scientists Might Investigate

Information science is an emerging and complex discipline. Is application to K–12 school settings meaningful? Yes, although student activities, processes, and products will need to be scaled to meet student abilities, needs, and interests. Consider the value of the following experiences (Callison 2000):

- **Key terms and strategies:** Build a search strategy based on the concept map of your topic (Gordon 2002). What have been the most effective search terms used to locate information on your topic? Answers might involve several combinations across different databases and different aspects of the information need. Illustrate or discuss these with other members of your class so that through comparison you may identify the best search strategies for various databases on various topics. What information would not have been available to you if you did not have access to online databases? The World Wide Web? Your school library? How would lack of access in each case have changed your report? How might you test this?

- **Journal your research experience:** As you encounter each new piece of information, describe how it helps or hinders your investigation. Write about how new information either confirms or counters what you have believed or have hypothesized. What information are you willing to accept that actually changes your mind, and why? What information do you reject, and why? In summary, along with your final report, do you believe you gave a fair and open mind to consider new information you encountered along the way? How might you involve others in judging your ability to fairly accept or reject new information?

- **Question evolution:** How did your research questions evolve over the information search process? Document what you learned in each new source that may have influenced your questions and illustrate this inquiry evolution. How did your questions change after conversations with your teacher? Presenting your idea to your classmates? Illustrate how the questions clustered into groups for various investigations. Show how the questions became more detailed, specific, or interesting as you explored more background information. At what point did you know you had the question you wanted to focus on for your inquiry project? Given your experience, what criteria are most important in determining a constructive inquiry project for you? Figures 10.2 and 10.3 provide a generic framework for students to illustrate question evolution through exploration of print, nonprint, and human resources.

Similar to concept maps, students can illustrate how an initial question expands and evolves as a new information source (book, Web site, human, video, etc.) is introduced. Each new ring represents a new set of questions derived from a new source and linked back to the initial question.

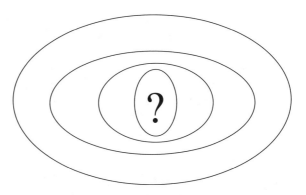

Figure 10.2. Question exploration ring.

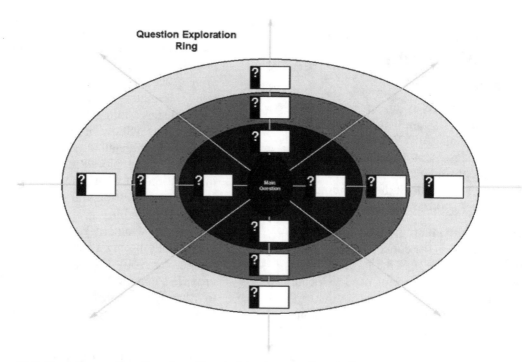

Figure 10.3. Question exploration ring. Created by Annette Lamb 2005. From virtualinquiry.com Copyright Annette Lamb and Daniel Callison 2005.

- **Rating resources:** What specific resources from various general formats (print, electronic, human) did you find most useful for your investigation, and why? What were the limitations? What are examples of leads to other relevant information you received from these formats? Consider "citations and references" in books, "links" from one authoritative Web site to another, and "recommendations" from people you interviewed for additional names, events, or resources to search. Illustrate how you have linked these information leads together.

- **Useful patterns:** After each class member describes several of his or her best information resources and where these were accessed, what predictions can you make about the best locations for finding useful information on future questions similar to those addressed by members of your class? Do you see any patterns in specific indexes, online databases, or library resources beyond your school?

- **Authority:** Test for degrees of bias–chart such and compare objectivity in resources (Callison 2005). Of the Web sites ex-

plored by members of your class, which were considered the most authoritative, and why? Do these observations provide any clues or give you any notions as to how to judge future Web sites? What criteria would you establish to help you determine the value of future Web sites? How do these criteria apply to other information sources?

- **Classics:** If your inquiry topic deals with a major historical event, biography, or controversial issue, consider what justifies a few of your sources as "classic" or the most respected sources on your topic. What evidence would you site to make the case that a source is so important that you would not have been able to complete your investigation without it? Is it a source that was referenced by many other sources? Is it a source that gave you a great deal of information that was relevant and meaningful to you? How might the most important resources on a given topic be determined, organized, and disseminated for others to use?

- **Experts:** Is there an author who seems to be the most authoritative on your topic?

What convinces you of that high authoritative status? In what future situations might you seek out this author again? Why is it important to learn the experts and key sources in a given field on a critical social issue?

- **Audience analysis** (Callison and Lamb 2004): In what manner can your report or your group's report be best presented to the rest of the class? To parents? To students older than you? To students younger than you? To a local group of decision makers who could take steps to make changes based on your report? What needs to be considered in terms of presentation format and content for each group who will hear your presentation? How can you determine if you have communicated the message you intend and that your audience has understood the conclusions you have drawn? How will you modify your presentation based on the feedback you get from your audience? How can you test and rehearse your various presentation approaches?

- **Linking evidence:** In what manner can various pieces of relevant information be linked to provide evidence for a logical argument and the establishment of a reasonable conclusion? What information is lacking that would make the argument more convincing? How would you go about finding information or gathering data that will help you fill that information gap? Can you make predictions of places to seek information or steps to obtain information based on your previous experience? (See Figure 10.4.)

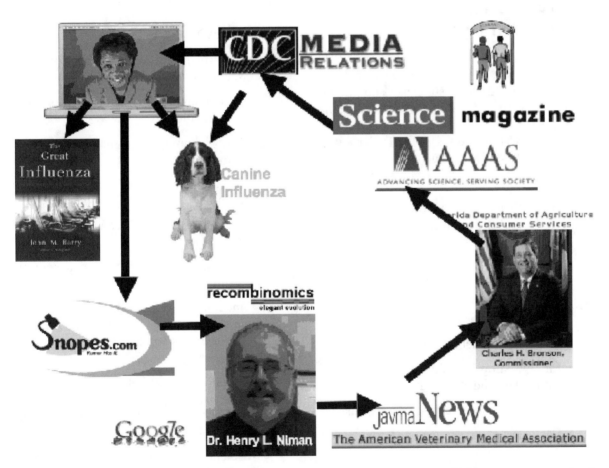

Figure 10.4. Visualizing the student information scientist's information search: links to resources and evidence. Annette Lamb. Copyright 2005.

- **Original Data:** How do you determine whether you need to gather original data through personal observations, interviews, or experiments? What specific questions will you try to answer? How will you select a method to gather these data? How will you go about a systematic and controlled way to guard against your own biases as you gather these data?

- **Future applications:** You have completed your project and have received your evaluation. In what ways will you change your approach to a future similar project? In what ways would you keep your approach the same? What have proven to be your most valuable paths to information and gaining an understanding of the relevance and meaning of that information?

Ability Levels for Science and Inquiry

According to the National Academy of Sciences (*Inquiry and the National Science Education Standards* 2000), students should be supported at very early grades to raise questions and discuss methods to address those questions. These abilities should transfer to similar situations in which students deal with information search and use problems and test methods to address those problems. The Academy recognizes the following progression of abilities, Set within the framework of the scientific method,, to deal with activities related to scientific inquiry:

By Grade 4

- Ask a question about objects, organisms, and events in the environment
- Plan and conduct a simple investigation
- Employ simple equipment and tools to gather data and extend the senses
- Use data to construct a reasonable explanation
- Communicate investigations and explanations

By Grades 5 to 8

- Identify questions that can be answered through scientific investigation
- Design and conduct a scientific investigation
- Use appropriate tools and techniques to gather, analyze, and interpret data
- Develop descriptions, explanations, predictions, and models using evidence
- Think critically and logically to make the relationships between evidence and explanations
- Recognize and analyze alternative explanations and predictions
- Communicate scientific procedures and explanations
- Use mathematics in all aspects of scientific inquiry

By Grades 9 to 12

- Identify questions and concepts that guide scientific investigations
- Design and conduct a series of scientific investigations
- Use technology and mathematics to improve investigations and communications
- Formulate and revise scientific explanations and models using logic and evidence
- Recognize and analyze alternative explanations and models
- Communicate and defend a scientific argument

Fundamental to these abilities are some basic understandings that students should be engaged in for discussion and application as early as grade school:

- Scientific investigations involve asking and answering a question and comparing the answer with what scientists already know about the world.
- Scientists use different kinds of investigations depending on the questions they are trying to answer.

- Scientists develop explanations using observations (evidence) and what they already know about the world (scientific knowledge).

- Scientists make the results of their investigation public; they describe the investigation in ways that enable others to repeat the investigations.

- Scientists review and ask questions about the results of other scientists' work.

Similar Standards in Social Sciences and Humanities

Similar standards for student performance are common in documents from state education agencies, local school corporations, and national associations. Application of the scientific method and Information Inquiry as a student of information science is also found in the social science portions of curriculum outlines. Such is never an "add on" to the curriculum, but always a clear, basic expectation that enriches the learning experience and takes both teaching and learning to levels that are beyond simply memorizing facts, names, and events. Mary Dalbotten's (1997) organization of student performance skills across the curriculum is a valuable tool to relate national learning standards to critical and creative thinking for inquiry. Examples that illustrate this follow:

History and Social Sciences

- Historical thinking skills enable students to differentiate past, present, and future times; raise questions; seek and evaluate evidence; compare and analyze historical stories, illustrations, and records from the past; interpret the historical record; and construct historical narratives of their own.

- Real historical understanding requires that students have the opportunity to create historical narratives and arguments of their own. Such narratives and arguments may take many forms—essays, debates, and editorials, for instance. They can be initiated in a variety of ways. None, however, more powerfully initiates historical thinking than those issues, past and pres-

ent, that challenge students to enter knowledgeably into the historical record and to bring sound historical perspectives to bear in the analysis of a problem.

- On contemporary issues across the full range of social science studies, students should practice skills that focus on relevant local and global issues in which they use information to identify, describe, explain, explain a position, take a position, and defend a position. An example is for the student to evaluate historical and contemporary political communications using such criteria as logical validity, factual accuracy, emotional appeal, distorted evidence, appeals to bias or prejudice, and establishing criteria for judging information sources in light of such manipulation of communication. Another common example, this time relevant to simulating what political scientists do, is evaluate, take, and defend positions on the influence of the media on American political life.

Language Arts and Humanities

- Students present information, concepts, and ideas to an audience of listeners or readers on a variety of topics. Students adjust their use of spoken, written, and visual language to communicate effectively with a variety of audiences and for different purposes.

- Students read a wide range of print and nonprint texts to build an understanding of texts, of themselves, and of the cultures of the United States and the world; to acquire new information; to respond to the needs and demands of society and the workplace; and for personal fulfillment.

- Students apply a wide range of strategies to comprehend, interpret, evaluate, and appreciate texts. They draw on their prior experience, their interactions with other readers and writers, their knowledge of word meaning and of other texts, their word identification strategies, and their understanding of textual features, including graphics.

- Students conduct research on issues and interests by generating ideas and questions, and by posing problems. They gather, evaluate, and synthesize data from a variety of sources (print, nonprint, artifacts, people) to communicate their discoveries in ways that suit their purpose and audience.

- Students use a variety of technological and information resources (libraries, databases, computer networks, video, mass media, human experts) to gather and synthesize information and to create and communicate knowledge.

- Students participate as knowledgeable, reflective, creative, and critical members of a variety of literacy communities.

Scaffolds for Inquiry Skills

Barbara Stripling has written one of the most comprehensive and convincing essays on the relationships among inquiry-based learning, information literacy, and K–12 curriculum. Among a rich list of curricular ties, she offers the following examples that illustrate how teaching inquiry involves applications at different grade levels with the instructional media specialists working collaboratively to facilitate a progressive scaffolding of investigative experiences from elementary to secondary school:

- Evaluation of sources is critical to inquiry in social studies because of the interpretative nature of the discipline. Students should assess the value of a source before they even look at the specific information within the source. If teachers and librarians have selected the source, then they should share their thinking process with students. The criteria that need to be emphasized (at age-appropriate times) are authoritativeness of the author/publisher; comprehensiveness of the information (students are seeking in-depth information, not collections of superficial facts); organization and clarity of the text (students need to be able to find and comprehend relevant information without getting lost in extraneous links or subtopics); and quality of the references (the sources of the cited evidence) [and further understand our quality citations can lead to additional relevant evidence]. Obviously, in the age of the Internet, responsibility for evaluation of sources has largely shifted from librarians to students. Careful instruction and guidance must accompany that shift.

- Use of primary sources is an important component of inquiry in social studies. Students must be taught to observe and draw valid interpretations from artifacts, ephemera, images, maps, and personal accounts. Student must be taught to interpret the primary sources in light of its context (e.g., a soldier writing a letter about a recent skirmish may think it the bloodiest battle of the war because he was injured; a photographer shooting a peace march from a low angle may convey a huge crowd, while an overhead shot might show a small crowd with empty streets behind it). Because so many sources are being digitized, students have more access to primary sources than they have ever had before [and the amount available online will grow tremendously over the coming years]. Primary sources may be particularly exciting to elementary students who have limited background knowledge. They, therefore, need scaffolding to foster the validity of their interpretations. [Frances Jacobson Harris (2002) has demonstrated how challenging it is to manage visual and artifact interpretation skills of middle grade students.]

- Evaluation of specific information and evidence is also a key thinking strategy for inquiry in social studies. Librarians and classroom teachers probably want to emphasize discernment of fact versus opinion and help students understand how each can be used effectively. Students, particularly as the secondary level, must learn how to identify point of view and recognize its effect on the evidence. Their responsibility is to find enough evidence from different points of view that they [may consider] . . . a balanced perspective. Sources that present opposing viewpoints are helpful to provide that [attempted] balance of evidence. Secondary students must also be taught to detect degrees of bias (from slightly slanted point of view to heavily slanted propaganda). (2003, 26)

Modeling Inquiry with Early Nonfiction

Stephanie Harvey and Anne Goudvis (2000, 2003) have established themselves as purveyors of reading strategies that work in elementary school settings. They promote modeling by all teachers (and, we will add, all library instructional media specialists) of the processes for engaging themselves and their students in the understanding and use of nonfiction text. A few of their exercises for early readers of nonfiction are summarized below. Each of these will lead to early practice to help guide and model inquiry and scientific mindedness. Children are naturally curious, but as humans they need help in organizing, making selections, prioritizing, and eventually gaining focus on what is meaningful to both themselves and their likely audiences. Students are invited to make initial choices and are guided by teachers who model and present options so that students are enabled to make logical revisions and extensions to what they bring to the nonfiction text.

For each of the examples from Harvey and Goudvis below, copies of text pages are made for students to feel free to mark and highlight. If original pages are used, teachers and students use postem-notes. Sometimes different colors allow several students to contribute their ideas together to the same text pages and clearly show personal contributions. Notes can be moved from the text pages to large sheets of paper on which the postem-notes can be organized to show patterns of observations. Charts and tables of combined ideas can be generated. These same methods can be used to produce individual or group thinking for concept maps through the use of software such as Inspiration.

- Asking Questions Throughout the Reading Process: Readers ask questions before, during and after reading. Look at the cover [of the book] and read the title. Record any questions you might have before you start to read. While reading, highlight or mark a part of the text or picture where you have a question. When you finish reading, write down any remaining questions. Suggest possible answers to your questions.

- Predicting: While reading, highlight or mark a sentence or picture with P when you find yourself making a prediction. Write a sentence that had helped you think of the prediction. After you finish reading the complete text, note if your prediction was confirmed or contradicted.

- Synthesizing Information: While reading, highlight or mark a picture or part of the text with SZ for synthesize when you have a new idea. After completing the text, review your SZ notations and combine them into one or two major ideas you got from the entire text.

- Determining Important Information: Look for the any of the following text cues to important information:

  – Cause/Effect: since, because, due to, for this reason, therefore

  – Comparison/Contrast: likewise, as opposed to, however, but, nevertheless

  – Problem/Solution: one reason for that, a possible solution

  – Question/Answer: how, what, when, why, the best estimate, in could be that

  – Sequence: until, before, after, finally (2000, Appendix F)

Problem Identifiers

In recent years, Violet Harada (2003) and Joan Yoshina (2004), at the University of Hawaii, have implemented several collaborative inquiry-based projects across K–12 learning environments. Harada (2003) has approached each project with problem-solving strategies modeled by the teacher and library media specialist team, but with the twist that before students can understand solutions they must be engaged to act as "problem identifiers." A typical sequence to foster problem awareness and solution options at the secondary school level follows:

- **Brainstorming:** Students work in small groups to brainstorm ideas generated by the driving question posed. Example: What does it mean to live healthier?

- **Webbing:** Each group creates a web with questions linked from the issue-driving question and each group shares their ideas with the rest of the class. Under teacher and library media specialist guidance, students create a total class web that reflects all key ideas. This can be the first of many information products from the students to be displayed for other teachers, students, and administrators to see the development of a critical thinking, problem-solving project.

- **Exploration of sources:** Students focus on general information sources and gather ideas from each source to share with the class. Such background reading and viewing helps to formulate questions that make sense and help students see which questions are also of greatest interest among classmates.

- **Individual journaling:** Students begin to generate their own questions in a personal journal and expand this list as they engage in more reading, viewing, and small group discussions. Students apply guidance from the teacher and media specialist to select good questions.

- **Choosing a research focus:** Based on personal interest, relevance to the inquiry theme for the class, and availability of resources likely to support the investigation, students select questions for their extended investigation.

- **The research process:** Students step through the standard process of seeking information, selecting evidence, and discussing what can be inferred from the evidence, need for additional sources, a summary of conclusions to address their questions, and methods of presenting results.

Along the way, many instructional problems arise. A brief list of these and how they are addressed illustrates collaborative roles that need to be played by the teachers and media specialist:

- Journal accounts revealed that students knew less about the general topic of nutrition than the teacher anticipated. The teacher added two more sessions for students to explore information resources, including more time to browse and report on resources in the library.

- Observations showed that students were fuzzy about key word searching. The library media specialist spent another session on key word search strategies.

- Observation revealed that students had limited prior knowledge about conducting surveys. The teacher added two sessions in which she presented models for surveys.

- Students were able to gather survey data more quickly than anticipated. Time for the survey was reduced from two weeks to one.

- Observations indicated that students had different interpretations of data. The teacher used another session to guide students in consensus of interpretations.

Sandy Guild (2003), a high school librarian in Pennsylvania, conducts research conferences with students as they work through the inquiry process. Two of her conversation guides are outlined below, with the standard questions she raises:

Background Reading

- What best describes the kind of relationship you are investigating?

  - Cause and effect
  - Application of a concept
  - Influence
  - Comparison
  - Other

- What is the most exciting discovery you have made so far?

- On the back of this paper, draw a simple concept map using the results of your background reading. Include major people, places, concepts, and relationships that you have been able to identify.

- Using the concept map as a guide, briefly state what your thesis question is currently.

- What is confusing in the research you have conducted so far?

- [Adding to her list] What is reassuring in the research you have conducted so far?

Conferencing about Questions, Arguments, and Sources

- State the focus of your paper and list the topic areas that relate to it.

- On the back of this sheet, draw a simple concept map of your developing thesis. Be clear what kind of relationship(s) organize(s) your thesis.

- What new questions have you developed as a result of your research in supporting your thesis?

- What part of your argument is weakest?

- What resource so far has been the best for information? Why?

- What information are you looking for that you have not been able to find?

Barbara Stripling (2003), director of Library Programs at New Visions for Public Schools and former president of the American Association of School Librarians, has summarized the mentoring roles for instructional media specialists that are most likely to encourage inquiry-based learning. These roles are paraphrased as follows:

- **Catalyst**—when convinced of the power of inquiry and other investigative strategies based on the scientific method, take steps to change traditional curriculum so that student learning is centered on inquiry; take leadership.

- **Connector**—see the total curriculum, recognize the best teachers, support the best learning projects, acquire access to the most useful instructional materials, and connect these whenever there is an opportunity; demonstrate the potential.

- **Coach**—model and reward the inquiry process by practicing it as a value process before students and other teachers; encourage and praise successful inquiry projects; assess practice and reward team efforts.

- **Caregiver**—independent learning is also encouraged and guided to meet special needs and interests supported by resources that meet specific levels; motivate each learner to achieve at his or her highest ability.

Added to this list is:

- **Communicator**—demonstrate results of the process as well as products so that learners and teachers can visualize possibilities; display student efforts in critical and creative thinking.

The Information Learning Laboratory

In the Information Inquiry learning laboratory, elementary and secondary, artifacts of the process as well as the products are displayed. Inquiry is illustrated on the wall as well as online for sharing, feedback, and modeling (Callison and Lamb 2004). Space is available for devising and testing information value, logic of arguments, and acceptance or rejection of evidence (Callison 2000, 2005). The laboratory may include the library and classrooms—multiple spaces where student work can take place. Some of the tangible aspects of the laboratory are that

- Student journals have double entries with space devoted to reflections on the quality or limitations of information located and information still needed.

- Final reports include a section in which the student describes the value of the sources located; predicts best information for similar future projects; and describes the value of peers, parents, teachers, and librarians who may have helped to guide the inquiry.

- Large sections of wall space or bulletin boards are available for students to display the progress in their investigation by showing evolution of questions, expansion of concept maps, resources linked to generating new ideas, linkages from general information sources to more specific data and evidence, and rating of the quality of resources used. (See Figures 10.4, 10.5, and 10.6, pages 175 and 182.)

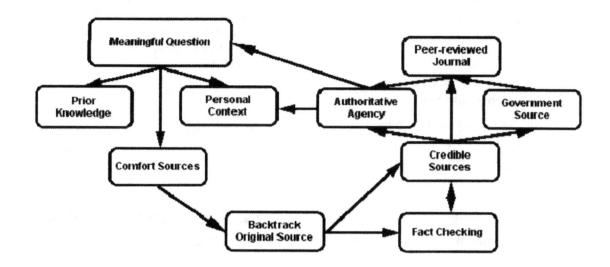

Figure 10.5. A visual map of linking resources and processes.

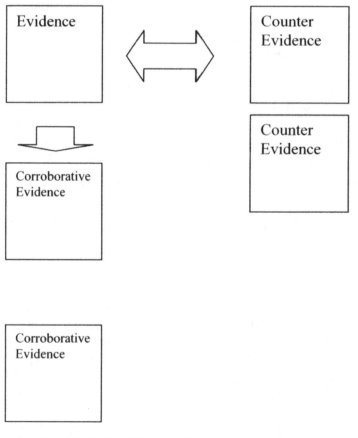

Figure 10.6. A beginning visual map to link evidence and arguments.

- Space is provided for students to lay out evidence on large table tops and work in groups to assimilate the evidence, argue the merits of evidence, and link evidence together to support and reject arguments. Instructional media specialists mentor and model the processes.

- Video recording areas are provided for students to practice and critique oral presentation of arguments, practice debating issues, and organize multimedia presentations.

- Electronic discussion groups are maintained for the purpose of sharing ideas, arguments, and evidence. Software is used to support linking these items together to formulate a variety of ways to present findings and to express needs yet to be met before other conclusions can be determined.

- Portals are created so students may view and critique peer work at various draft stages.

- Connections are provided for access to databases and human resources beyond the school.

- A collection of previous student work is maintained, artifacts of both process and product, for future students to access and consider as they enter a level of inquiry new to them.

- Parents, students, teachers, and administrators may view examples of student inquiry work at special events sponsored through the library media center. Information Inquiry Fairs, similar to Science Fairs, may be based on themes and are advertised as celebrations of learning accomplishment. In addition to student poster presentations, illustrations are provided of the thought processes to focus on the most critical questions and the most valuable resources. Teacher process and product work is displayed also.

- The laboratory is always available for student information scientists who wish to return, often on an individual basis, to further their reading on and investigations of problems that continue to interest them long after the academic assignment has been completed.

References

Callison, D. (2000). Inquiry, literacy and the learning laboratory. In Lyn Hay, Kylie Hanson, and James Henri (Eds.), *New millennium, new horizons* (55–64). Centre for Studies in Teacher Librarianship, Charles Sturt University.

Callison, D. (2001). Scaffolding. *School Library Media Activities Monthly, 17* (6), 37–39.

Callison, D. (2005). Bias. *School Library Media Activities Monthly, 21* (5), 34–36.

Callison, D., and A. Lamb. (2004). Audience analysis. *School Library Media Activities Monthly, 21* (1), 34–39.

Dalbotten, M. S. (1997). Inquiry in the National Content Standards. In Daniel Callison, Joy H. McGregor, and Ruth Small (Eds.), *Instructional interventions for information use: Papers of Treasure Mountain VI* (246-304). Hi Willow Research. . Reprinted in Michael B. Eisenberg, Carrie A. Lowe, and Kathleen L. Spitzer (Eds.)., *Information literacy: Essential skills for the information age* (221–231). Libraries Unlimited, 2004.

Gordon, C. A. (2002). Methods for measuring the influence of concept mapping on student information literacy. *School Library Media Research, 5.* www.ala.org/aasl/SLMR (accessed November 1, 2005).

Guild, S. L. (2003). Modeling recursion in research process instruction. In Barbara K. Stripling and Sandra Hughes-Hassell (Eds.), *Curriculum connections through the library* (141–155). Libraries Unlimited.

Harada, V. H. (2003). Empowered learning: Fostering thinking across the curriculum. In Barbara Stripling and Sandra Hughes-Hassell (Eds.), Curriculum connections through the library (41–64). Libraries Unlimited.

Harada, V. H., and J. M. Yoshina. (2004). *Inquiry learning through librarian-teacher partnerships*. Linworth Publishing.

Harris, Frances Jacobson. (2002). There was a great collision in the stock market: Middle school students, online primary sources, and historical sense making. *School Library Media Research, 5*. www.ala.org/aasl/SLMR (accessed November 11, 2005).

Harvey, S., and A. Goudvis. (2000). *Strategies that work: Teaching comprehension to enhance understanding*. Stenhouse Publishers.

Harvey, S., and A. Goudvis. (2003). *Think nonfiction*. 30-minute video tape with study guide. Stenhouse Publishers.

Inquiry and the national science education standards: A guide for teaching and learning. (2000). National Academy of Sciences, National Research Council, and the Center for Science, Mathematics, and Engineering Education.

Marchionini, G. (1999). Educating responsible citizens in the information society. *Educational Technology, 39* (2), 17–26.

Stripling, B. (2003). Inquiry-based learning. In Barbara Stripling and Sandra Hughes-Hassell (Eds.), *Curriculum connections through the library* (3–40). Libraries Unlimited.

Chapter 11

Online Inquiry Learning, Virtual Schools, and the Digital Divide

Annette Lamb and Daniel Callison

Online learning and virtual schools allow students to take classes anytime and anywhere. These emerging learning environments require school library media specialists to expand their thinking about their resources and services. Creation of a virtual library can provide access to remote materials that enhance the experience of online learners. However, even more important is ensuring that students possess the information skills needed to be successful in this virtual learning environment.

Online learning involves information, instruction, and/or interaction through the Internet or an Intranet using instructional materials and tools such as Web-based resources, e-mail, discussion boards, blogs, chats, and video. Schools are increasingly offering structured online learning programs as primary or supplementary learning opportunities. Students may select from individual courses or enroll in a virtual school. These cyberschools offer a complete range of courses for graduation. Some virtual schools are part of a traditional school system, while others are statewide programs.

Students are able to take online courses while sitting in a traditional classroom, the school library, at home, or in any other location. One of the benefits of online learning is the potential for distance learning, where students are able to take courses anytime from anywhere. For instance, distance learning allows students in rural areas to do much of their work at home rather than riding the bus to school every day (Mason and Rennie 2006).

Status of the States in Online Learning and Virtual Schools

In their 2004 report, *Keeping Pace with K–12 Online Learning: A Snapshot of State-Level Policy and Practice,* John F. Watson from Evergreen Consulting Associates, Kathy Winograd from the University of Denver, and Stevan Kalmon from the Colorado Department of Education surveyed the online programs and approaches in twenty-two states and conducted in-depth studies of eleven states to gain insights into the current state of online learning.

Many states have well-established online education, programs including California, Colorado, Florida, Idaho, Illinois, Michigan, Minnesota, Ohio, Pennsylvania, Texas, and Wisconsin. While some states have developed statewide programs, others are relying on district-level initiatives. Most states focus on Web-based online learning; however, Alaska and South Dakota make extensive use of videoconferencing.

While most programs supplement traditional schools, virtual schools are increasingly popular. For example, cyber charter schools can be found throughout the United States. Florida's Virtual School has a large and well-established statewide presence, including an online curriculum that partners with local school districts.

The opportunities for online learning are diverse and growing. Although most programs serve high school students, there are a small number of middle school offerings. Many schools offer hybrid courses that combine face-to-face with online learning.

Some virtual schools offer synchronous courses, in which students participate in live interactions through chat or videoconferencing. However, most online learning is asynchronous, meaning that students and teachers interact using e-mail, discussion boards, and other Web-based resources.

While some school districts build their online curriculum and technology from scratch, most use existing software tools such as Blackboard or entire virtual high school systems such as eClassroom.

The Purpose and Goals of Online Education

Although the majority of students still attend traditional K–12 schools, an increasing number of students are exploring online learning options. From online Advanced Placement (AP) courses to entire school curriculums, a wide range of distance learning opportunities is available to today's students.

Online education programs are being developed for a number of reasons, including to

- Accommodate more students in less space;

- Address individual learning styles and needs;

- Offer wider course offerings, particularly advanced courses;

- Provide opportunities for students at risk for dropping out because of pregnancy, high mobility, disciplinary problems, or other reasons;

- Reduce long bus rides for rural students;

- Address scheduling conflicts;

- Accommodate the needs of accelerated learners; and/or

- Extend local offerings with outside experts and resources.

Most virtual high schools share some of the following goals:

- Provide high-quality online courses aligned to standards.

- Use qualified teachers and e-mentors to facilitate learning.

- Expand the boundaries of space and time.

- Extend course offerings.

- Accommodate individuals with special needs.

- Use technology for content delivery and interaction.

Online learning and virtual schools face many issues, including the following:

- Quality assurance

- Competition between cyber schools and physical school districts

- Adequate access to technology, resources, and support for remote students

- Involving online students in traditional school activities

According to Annette Lamb (2005), professor in the School of Library and Information Science at Indiana University—Indianapolis, virtual schools can provide a diverse environment that reflects a range of cultures, opinions, and ideas promoting cultural understanding, global awareness, and international perspectives. Although most students attend virtual schools in their local area, many online classes are using technology to provide virtual experiences beyond their local geographic base.

Building an Online Social and Learning Community

It is often cited as a shortcoming of online learning that students may not have the array of social communication activities normally available in traditional learning situations. Many virtual schools have been founded on basic drill tutorials that may help students practice routines in spelling, math, and grammar, but do little to challenge students to develop group learning abilities. Practicing communication skills through discussion, team projects, and oral presentation all seem at first to be difficult to establish in virtual school settings.

While not identical to face-to-face interactions, online learning can create new modes for social performance, often more precisely monitored for feedback and assessment than what can be done by one teacher in a classroom where he or she must observe many conversations at once. Online communication provides a concrete interactive trail.

Social communication skills are essential for the student to mature in his or her role to select and use information effectively. Inquiry-based learning becomes most effective when the student matures in information selection and communication skills to the levels that involve less interaction with the teacher and more interaction with other students. The student becomes a collaborative colleague with other students to determine the value of questions, argument, evidence, and problem-solving strategy options.

Online postings, for example, can include pieces of evidence with proper citation that serve to link to previous evidence posted by other students in order to illustrate, argue, or confirm an event, issue, opinion, question, or thesis statement. In such online posting strands, students clearly have their names associated with meaningful contributions in terms of both frequency and quality.

Rena Palloff and Keith Pratt (2003), online educators from the School of Education at Capella University, believe that online learning reaches high levels of social learning and reflective practice when most of the students are engaged in:

- Active interaction involving both course content and personal communication.

- Collaborative learning evidenced by comments directed primarily student to student rather than student to instructor.

- Socially constructed meaning evidenced by agreement or questioning, with intent to achieve agreement on issues of meaning.

- Sharing of resources among students.

- Expressions of support and encouragement exchanged between students, as well as willingness to critically evaluate the work of others.

- Highest levels of online contribution, including inference, judgment, and strategy: conclusions—solutions—ideas for implementation—evaluation of success or failure.

Of course, this level of mature interaction may not emerge until students are young adults and adults, but teachers of Information Inquiry, in either the traditional or online learning mode, should seek to establish opportunities for each student to practice social communication as a contribution to the learning of others as well as the student's own learning.

To this end, Palloff and Pratt have identified and recommended many instructional techniques to facilitate an online learning community. Among their more effective techniques, the online instructor should:

- Post introductions and bios.

- Create a social space in the course (for more informal conversations so that students can "get acquainted") .

- Encourage judicious use of chat for socializing.

- Model openness, honesty and humor.

- Involve learners in co-creating some learning opportunities.

- Orient students to the realities (opportunities and limitations) of online learning.

- Be willing to allow learners to take charge of the learning process as much as possible.

- Rotate leadership in small group activities.

- Establish minimum posting requirements and monitor compliance. (2003, 27)

Depending on the online age group and expected performance, online participation can be evaluated based on rubrics that identify high performance in terms of frequent and meaningful contributions that are relevant to the issues and contributed opinion, insight, facts, observations, or other levels of evidence that moved the discussion along. Ultimately, regardless of the online audience level, participants who tend to draw useful conclusions from the discussion and who participate in offering reflections that evaluate both the process and the group product are most likely to receive the highest grades for online discussion.

Netiquette

Online instructors often share stories about managing student behavior, which are often similar to situations found in traditional classrooms but usually involve a slightly different twist .

Online students can be noisy and rude. Online environments provide a little more room and time to address such students through personal e-mail and to show specifically where the student may be preventing e-classmates for learning.

Quiet students can be guided individually as to how to contribute more and to build their contributions into a meaningful chain that reflects their learning pattern. This individualized assistance is often accomplished through personal chats and e-mails rather than through public forums that can be embarrassing for some students.

Other typical "problem students" can include the "know-it-all," the procrastinator, and the "must-have-an-A" student. In each case, as long as the student will engage in online conversations with the instructor, there can be time for personalized communication.

Plagiarism and cheating can be issues in online courses just as in the traditional classroom. The key to reducing plagiarism is the development of quality assignments. Palloff and Pratt give useful advice again, suggesting that the instructor:

- Be alert to changes in student online behavior, differences in writing styles used for posting in chat areas, and completion of longer written assignments.

- Modify and revise assignments from one online course offering to the next.

- Grade for evidence of process participation and self-reflection as well as the product.

- Require the use of and consideration of recent sources of information. Very recent data and opinions have not found their way into most of the online papers that can be purchased or electronically cut and pasted from the Internet. (2003, 34)

Use of an acceptable online communication mode can be a sign of a student being on his or her best online behavior. Introduction to and modeling of proper "netiquette" by the instructor may serve to reduce some online behavior difficulties. Netiquette for online communications and more effective learning includes the following practices:

- Focus on one subject per message and use pertinent and understandable subject titles.

- When posting a long message, inform readers at the beginning that there is more content than normal, or divide the posting into two or more messages.

- Check in to the discussion frequently. Online participation means that the student "attends" online class on a regular and frequent basis and does not wait to unload contributions at the end of the discussion period or end of the course. Making up for "lost time" only costs all other class members additional time to read such late comments.

- Give proper credit to quotations, references, and other sources of information, not only because such is proper but because this will provide guidance to fellow students to get more information relevant to the data or opinion presented. Links to relevant Web sites from which the information was taken or summarized are expected.

- Capitalize words to highlight a point, or perhaps to show the title of a resource. Otherwise a message in all-caps is considered SHOUTING!

- Get permission to forward or use a classmate's message to further discussion.

- Humor is helpful, but there is sometimes a fine line between humor and criticism that is considered an insult. Emoticons such as ☺ and :) help to signal agreement, approval, and lighthearted contributions.

Orientation

The success of online learning, for both the instructor and the student, may depend on the quality of the orientation to the online environment and the collegiality among the participants.

Key elements of orientation to an online course have been detailed by Susan Ko and Steven Rossen (2004) in their very practical guide to teaching online. Supported with practical examples from other online instructors, they offer these important suggestions:

- Provide an introduction, including your expectations for online students. Online courses require extreme self-discipline. A great deal of time will be spent visiting and reading relevant Web sites and print resources. Technology has its frustrations, and the cyberdog may "eat your homework." Student success is often tied to flexibility, patience, determination, motivation, and self-confidence on the part of the instructor as well as the student.

- Provide requirements for computer equipment and software. Basic expectations for modem speed, hard drive capacity, optional freeware, and software are typical "need to know and understand" items.

- Describe the basic computer skills needed. Basic expectations may involve electronic cut and paste, sending attachments, use of a browser, and how to download from the Internet.

- Provide an introduction to the course management software used to deliver the course. This can include a growing number of areas as the software has grown more sophisticated. Access points to assignments, class rosters, chat areas for different purposes, evaluation, and feedback sections are all common. Links to resources such as libraries and local area experts are being added to these management tools and can provide students with portals to a fast array of resources that will demand their time to contact and to make wise selection of the most relevant resource. Online reference librarian services, grade school to college or through the public library, are being added as well.

- Provide either a first assignment or a preliminary practice exercise that will require the student to use as many of the online software options as possible. This may provide demonstration of strengths and weaknesses that need to be addressed early, both to help the deficient student and for the instructor to consider higher level interactions should the online group prove to have online learning experience and sophisticated online abilities.

- Provide a site for typical responses to "frequently asked questions" (FAQs). A "student services Web site" should provide links to institutional contacts that contain such information as names with e-mail addresses for resource and administrative staff, institutional policies, and a virtual library system that is maintained for the school.

- The best virtual school library Web sites act as a portal to relevant state or national virtual information sites, thus providing access to the growing electronic information base, often free to the online user enrolled in online education. Virtual school library media Web sites also provide links to WebQuests (online links to collections selected for relevance to specific academic topics), online public and academic catalogs, reading lists, study guides, homework help, and most of all—how to ask a librarian either online or in person! More details are provided below.

School Library Media Services Supporting Online Learning

Like virtual schools, today's school library media center is not bound by place or time. Increasingly school libraries are offering online services to support both traditional and distance learning courses. Teachers offering online courses expect the library to provide the same services that are available in the place-based library in a virtual environment, such as journal articles and videos. According to Kathleen Craver (2002), cyber libraries naturally complement online learning. Without a well-organized, readily available virtual library, online students will resort to poor quality materials often found using search engines on the Internet.

Students taking online courses need access to quality information and resources. Many school library media specialists have designed virtual libraries to meet these needs. Beyond links to Web resources, many of these virtual libraries include reference assistance, tutorials, and access to subscription-based educational resources. Many virtual schools integrate online educational subscription services such as BrainPop, World Book, and NetTrekker.

According to the National Association of State Boards of Education (2001), to enrich the online curriculum, resources should be grade-level appropriate. Students should deeply explore content from online libraries, museum holdings, primary documents, real data, and experts in the field.

The following list highlights some of the services provided for online students through a virtual school library:

- Instructional resources such as online tutorials, WebQuests, practice/testing environments, instructional modules, virtual labs, and simulations

- Informational materials such as pathfinders, electronic databases, reference resources, streaming video, and digitized primary resources

- Virtual adventures such as Web-based tours and virtual field trips (i.e., museums, zoos, historical places, science expeditions)

- Live interactions using video-conferencing, such as special events, expert interactions

- Collaborative online learning such as e-mail, blogs, discussions, project sharing, collaborative science experiments, collaborative writing, online books discussions, online author visits, and expert discussions

- Online assistance such as technical support, reference questions, mentoring, and peer tutoring

- Sharing space such as virtual galleries of student work, online newspapers, and collaborative writing areas

- Online requests such as interlibrary loans and multimedia ordering of items that can be sent through the mail to students

Many states are providing resources that support these endeavors. For example, Indiana's INSPIRE provides pathfinders, electronic databases, and other subscription services free to schools. The Kentucky Virtual Library was designed as a statewide online library to support online learning. The Kentucky Virtual Library offers selected links to electronic databases, library catalogs, self-paced tutorials, digital collections, a virtual reference desk, and access to government information.

Many schools use virtual reference assistance from outside resources. For instance, AskColorado is a service provided by the Colorado libraries and used by many of the Colorado cyberschools.

Noeleen Fleming, Liz Blumson, and Deborah Turnbull (2002) work with the University of Queensland Cybrary, which is used to provide a virtual connection between high school and university online collections. In addition to online electronic information materials, they also coordinate AskaCybrarian, an online reference service from the University of Queensland, Australia, that is available to high school students.

Gary Hartzell (2001), professor of Educational Administration and Supervision at University of Nebraska at Omaha, explored implications of school reforms such as distance learning on school library media services. He notes that online learning challenges the idea that going to school means interacting with an instructor in a specific building and classroom. This offers new opportunities and challenges for school library media services in three areas. First, cooperation and networking are essential in distance education program development. The function of the library media center broadens to include contacts and resources beyond the school. Second, teacher librarians become instructional consultants matching resources to learning needs. Third, because online learning is technology intensive, the media specialist must be ready to deal with hardware and software issues.

Media Center Web Sites Support Online Learning

Laurel Anne Clyde, professor of Social Sciences, Reykjavik, Iceland, has identified the following purposes of Web sites developed and maintained for the school library media center:

- To provide direct access to the Internet for students.

- To help students save time in locating valid and current information through the Internet.

- To provide a guide for teachers to locate Internet sites relevant to their curriculum.

- To provide information to parents and to increase involvement of parents in the school and the school library.

- To create a library without walls and access to information 24/7.

- To serve as an electronic brochure in describing activities of the school and the media center.

- To encourage positive public relations between the school and the community.

- To provide links to the school's online catalogue as well as access to the online catalogues of other schools, the public library and even a local academic or government library.

- To support the curriculum with links to homework help, standards, and typical remedial assignments.

- To showcase student work—the best in student achievement from essays, to book reviews, to student website design, to student produced multimedia. (2000, 242)

Clyde noted the following features for school library media center websites to be increasing in frequency as a portion of the site and growing in importance in the support of online learning. School library media specialists who provide a website are adding these features:

- Links to Internet engines and online resources for teachers.

- Photograph of the school and facilities, especially labs and library.

- Book reviews by students and recommended reading lists tied to the curriculum and for reading pleasure.

- A guide to how to select the best information from the Internet.

- Basic Internet tutorials concerning how to combine terms and search at more advanced levels. (2000, 243)

Joyce Kasman Valenza is the librarian at Springfield Township High School in Erdenheim, Pennsylvania. She and a growing number of other tech-savvy school media specialists are creating the online framework for a modern virtual school library, complete with research guides, pathfinders, and access to resources beyond the school building. What are school virtual libraries? Valenza (2006) answers that with this description:

> Designed and maintained by school librarians, virtual libraries are multipage online resources devoted to the needs of their specific learning communities. From a home page, users access search engines, databases, references, and general library and school information. Like signage in a physical library, the virtual library home page creates signage for the Web, providing a picture of online information environments. Students see various topics listed there, such as general library information, databases and catalogs, links for students and teachers, and college and career information. (2006, 54)

Valenza extrapolates what she is creating through her virtual library to the role of the school librarian in the twenty-first century:

> As bandwidth improves and as more K-12 schools connect with Internet2 (the cleaner, faster Internet formerly used only by universities and other research institutions) it will be the job of the teacher-librarian, as collaborator and information technologyspecialist, to connect to external classrooms, museums, and subject-matter experts. Last year [2005], the Springfield Township Middle School Library hosted a virtual reading group that

brought together a group of its students with out-of-state peers. The high school gifted class met online with a postdoctoral University of Pennsylvania fellow for a lively discussion following a unit on the brain. The advanced French class joined classes from six other schools in the region for an online bilingual seminar with graduates students from French West Africa. As more schools connect to Internet2, libraries can connect students and teachers to new archives of high-bandwidth resources, such as those just emerging from San Francisco's Exploratorium and the Library of Congress.

Librarians will be responsible for making sense of the new media jungle. As collections of media shift from VHS to DVD to streaming [and online interactive video], teachers will need to access a new expanded wealth of audio and video resources and facilitate student use of this rich information [pool]. (59)

Virtual Information Inquiry

Successful online students are self-directed, disciplined, and willing to ask questions. They are organized, good readers, and able to work independently. Because online courses generally attract students from the low and high ends of academic achievement, a wide variety of online resources and materials is essential. However, even more important is the preparation of students for this learning environment.

Patricia Deubel (2004), an educational consultant, found that effective cognitive-based learning models for online learning include apprenticeship, incidental, inductive, deductive, and inquiry-based.

Mary Ann Fitzgerald and Chad Galloway (2002), both from the University of Georgia, observed high school students using virtual library resources and identified ways to help them use these materials more effectively. They emphasized the importance of collaborating with teachers to integrate Information Inquiry into resource-based projects. Students need opportunities to use an information search process within the context of online resources. In addition, teachers need to become dedicated virtual library users so they feel comfortable integrating resources into the curriculum.

In their report *Keeping Pace,* Watson, Winograd, and Kalmon (2004) have expressed concern that strategies be identified for meeting the needs of students with disabilities, highly mobile students, at-risk students, and other students not in the mainstream of education.

Many teachers are not aware of the electronic resources available for use in online courses. The school library media specialist must work collaboratively in planning online courses to ensure that adequate online resources are available, including digitizing materials, acquiring permissions, purchasing subscriptions, and organizing Web resources. In addition, the teacher-librarian can work with the teacher to ensure that students have the information skills needed to be successful in using these materials.

Holly Gunn (2002), a teacher-librarian in Halifax, Nova Scotia, Canada emphasized the importance of designing a virtual library to support student learning by considering how users access and use the information in the virtual space. Consider how students interact with the teacher librarian in the face-to-face environment and how online resources can be constructed to facilitate online collaboration. For example, many virtual school libraries provide tutorials and reference services online. Fitzgerald and Galloway (2002) also noted the importance of configuring the virtual library to facilitate effective use and providing online mini-lessons, job aids, or tutorials to address common problems.

Delia Neuman (1997), professor of Library and Information Science at the University of Maryland, studied the potential of digital libraries as an environment for higher-level learning in schools. She found that electronic information resources provide a critical venue for helping students learn to access, evaluate, and use information to solve problems. However, to maximize the learning benefits, educators must draw on research from a variety of fields, including reading comprehension, interface design, and problem solving, to build the types of online learning environments that will promote information fluency.

Carol Kuhlthau (1997), professor of Communication, Information, and Library Studies at Rutgers University, recommends a theory for creating learning environments in digital libraries based on the concepts of acting and reflecting, feeling and formulating, predicting and choosing, and interpreting and creating. She suggests that by taking a constructivist learning approach in the digital library environment, students are able to develop skills and strategies that transfer to situations in the real world.

Data on the Digital Divide: Computer and Internet Use by Children and Adolescents

Key findings of a national survey released in 2003 by the U. S. Department of Education include the following:

- Most children and adolescents use computers and access the Internet. About 90% of children and adolescents ages five to seventeen (47 million persons) use computers, and about 59% (31 million persons) use the Internet.

- Use begins at an early age. About three-quarters of five-year-olds use the Internet, and over 90% of teens (ages thirteen to seventeen) do so. At least 75% of teens now use the Internet.

- There is a "digital divide." Computer and Internet use are divided along demographic and socioeconomic lines. Use of both technologies is higher among Whites than among

- Blacks and Hispanics and higher among Asians and American Indians than among Hispanics. Five- through seventeen-year-olds living with more highly educated parents are more likely to use these technologies than those living with less well-educated parents, and those living in households with higher family incomes are more likely to use the Internet than those living in lower income households.

- Disability, urbanicity, and household type are factors in the digital divide. Five-through seventeen-year-olds without a disability are more likely to use computers and the Internet than their disabled peers, and children and adolescents living outside of central cities are more

likely to use computers than those living in central cities.

- There are no differences between the sexes in overall computer or Internet use rates. In contrast to the 1990s when boys were more likely to use computers and the Internet than girls were, overall computer and Internet use rates for boys and girls are now about the same (Cooper and Weaver 2003; Agosto 2001).

- More children and adolescents use computers at school (81%) than at home (65%). Computer use at school exceeds use at home by thirty percentage points or more for Blacks and Hispanics. However, home use is slightly more prevalent than school use for two groups: (1) children and adolescents whose parents have at least some graduate school education, and (2) children and adolescents who live in families with incomes of $75,000 or more per year.

- Home is the most common location for Internet access, followed by school. Although nearly all schools have Internet access, children and adolescents are more likely to access the Internet from their homes. Of those children and adolescents who use the Internet, 78% access it at home, compared to 68% who access it at school.

- Many disadvantaged children and adolescents use the Internet only at school. Among the group of children and adolescents who access the Internet at only one location, 52% of those from families in poverty and 59% of those whose parents have not earned at least a high school credential do so at school (DeBell and Chapman 2003, iv–vii).

These findings raise some important questions for educators. In what ways does the growing use of the Internet at home by adolescents in more affluent families change the role of the information and technology educator? About three-fourths of Internet users ages five to seventeen use the Internet to complete some form of school assignments. Are there new roles that information technology educators should play in assisting learners at home? Do home users find more freedom and support for Internet use in

---

their home environment than they do in their school environment?

What should be done to reduce the Internet access gap between young users in affluent environments and their peers in economically disadvantaged setting? The school setting continues to be key to providing some equity across student groups in learning computer skills, that is, digital search strategies as well as electronic information selection, management, and presentation.

However, are there powerful "out of school" or "beyond school" Internet uses that must be provided to the disadvantaged student in order to reduce this portion of the digital divide over the coming decade? Which environment is more powerful for student Internet access and critical thinking, the school or the home? How can these environments be more closely aligned so that best practices can be implemented in both on a year-round basis?

Internet Access in Public Schools

A second survey from the U. S. Department of Education in 2003 updated data on access to the Internet in public schools across the nation and has provided some indications of the shifts in the digital divide since 1994. Selected findings include the following:

- In 2002, 99% of public schools in the United States had access to the Internet compared to 35% in 1994.

- Only 3% of instructional classrooms had access to the Internet in 1994 and this has increased to 92% in 2002, increasing the opportunity for immediate teacher or student access and perhaps leading to greater integration of Internet use with instruction (i.e., information at point-of-need and locating information relevant to a "teachable moment," although the government report did not present data or comment on such).

- In 2002, the ratio of students to instructional computers with Internet access in public schools was 4.8 to 1, an improvement from the 12.1 to 1 ratio in 1998 when this was first measured.

- The gap between the ratio of students to instructional computers in highest poverty schools compared to lowest poverty schools has nearly disappeared; 5.5 to 1 in high poverty schools compared to 4.6 to 1 in low poverty schools.

- Making the Internet accessible outside of regular school hours allows students who do not have access to the Internet at home to use this resource for school-related activities.

- In 2002, 53% of public schools with Internet access reported that they made computers with Internet access available to students outside of regular school hours; 73% of secondary schools provided access outside of regular school hours. Of all the schools providing access outside of regular school hours, 96% provided access after school, 74% before school, and 6% on weekends. There were not data gathered on access through the school library media center nor on evening access to media center resources or the Internet stations in the schools.

- Since 99% of public schools were connected to the Internet in 2002, most schools had the capability to make information available to parents and students directly via e-mail or through a website. Nationwide, 86% of public schools with access to the Internet had a website or webpage in 2002, up from 75% in 2001.

- Nationwide, 87% of public schools with Internet access reported professional development was provided for teachers during the year prior to the survey concerning how to integrate use of the Internet into the curriculum. However, 42% of the reporting schools indicated that under one-fourth of their teachers attended such professional development, while 41% reported a majority of their teachers participated. Previous national surveys conducted in 2000 indicated only about one-third of the teachers responding felt well or very well prepared to use the Internet for instructional purposes. (Kleiner and Lewis 2003, 1–14)

Tech-Savvy Teens and Tech-Shy Teachers

Perhaps the most challenging digital divide is a generational one—found in nearly all public schools. Over just the past two years, the gap between teen and teacher has widened. And the gap is growing, not just between the tech-savvy teen and the tech-shy teacher over forty, but also between tech-savvy teens and young teachers, even pre-service teachers. The speed of technology access and increase of use has accelerated to the point that some believe many teens not only lead in the learning curve, but are now defining it.

The Pew Internet Project (http://www.pewinternet.org) has sponsored studies that document the growing gap between student and teacher. Senior research analysts Douglas Levin and Sousan Arafeh authored a study in 2002 in which they reported the following about the widening gap between Internet-savvy students and their schools:

- More than three-fourths of the nation's teenagers go online, often in connection with schoolwork. But for the most part, the students surveyed said their educational use of the Internet occurs outside of the school day, with little direction from their teachers.

- Most online teens (87%) say they go online from multiple locations. The vast majority (83%) report their primary access is from home. Another 11% say they go online most often at school and 3% say they go online most from a friend's house. Two percent say their primary connection is from someplace else, like the library, work, or an Internet café.

- Over 40% of teens go online everyday.

- Forty percent of teens report they have taught themselves how to use e-mail and the Internet; often these teens are the primary teachers of Internet use to other members of their family.

- Of the online teens responding, 94% say they use the Internet for school "research" with over 70% of these teens saying they used the Internet as the major source for their most recent school project or report. About a fourth of those responding reported using mostly library sources and about 4% said they used both the Internet and the library equally. For many teens, the Internet has replaced the library as the primary tool for completing the information search process on major school projects.

- The more "Internet-savvy" teens say their teachers are not inclined to use the Internet during class time, often because the teacher lacks proper training, believes there is too much risk in student access to controversial sites, follows strict administrative policies that limit the use of the Internet, and has a general lack of understanding of how to relate use of the Internet to academic needs.

Because not every student has Internet access at home, the vast majority of students say their teachers will not assign projects that require use of the Internet. Time also is mentioned as a barrier, as regimented class schedules tend to prevent time to explore freely and analyze Internet content. In a recent study conducted in Indiana, high school teachers tended to encourage use of the Internet over use of online databases because such searching was quick and assignments could be completed faster. Teachers believed more authoritative information could be found through more complex searching of online databases selected by the school librarians, but teachers admitted they personally did not understand how to conduct advanced searches and did not believe additional time should be invested by their students in such searching (Williams, Grimble, and Irwin 2004).

Other studies sponsored by Pew have illustrated how a growing number of teens have found the time, freedom, and parental support to engage fully with the Internet at home, more so than they often find at school. Nearly 70 percent of the parents of teens who use the Internet report that they sit down with their son or daughter and search together frequently.

Teens often complain that not enough is invested in current nonfiction, print reference resources at school, as they do not have access to such at home. Teens do experience wide access to data that can be acquired through the Internet at home but are in need of guidance through more in-depth print tools for the purpose of validating or expanding findings located through electronic sources. All too often such comparisons do not take place and are seldom required in the compilation of evidence for reports at school.

The Pew Internet Project has listed the following typical Internet-based homework helpers used by tech-savvy teens—sites more teachers need to access and reference themselves:

- Aggregate or portal sites such as About.com

- Article and information sites such as Academic Assistance Access and Inspire

- Essay sites such as AcaDemon and NoCheaters.com

- Ask-an-Expert sites such as Ask KidsConnect

- Book notes and summary sites such as Sparksnotes

- Online encyclopedia and library sites such as Questia

- Tutoring service sites such as Herzog Interactive

Tech-savvy teens see the Internet not only as an information access tool, but also a quick and dependable "24/7" communication connection for counseling; a source for virtual study groups; and a virtual locker, backpack, or notebook for storage and manipulation of information gathered. Teachers of Information Inquiry who understand these technology-use modes will be important leaders in changing the current educational structures to allow for seamless learning among school, home, and workplace. Perhaps one approach at this time is to identify those teens who can serve as constructive models for their peers and their teachers and actually involve them in training sessions and even professional development retreats.

Much of what is reported in these surveys should give current school library media specialists cause for reflection, discussion with administrators, and future planning. The following elements are now critical to development of the near-future successful information delivery program in the public schools, especially at the secondary school level:

- Provision of virtual reference services, with controlled online chat areas for group discussions and homework advising, "24/7" communications, and interactive links to college and public library reference stations.

- Development of online tutorials for introduction to or review in different search strategies, awareness of online databases, and methods for identification of valid and relevant information from the Internet. Such services do not replace face-to-face orientations nor reduce the need for individual information advisory from the professional instructional media specialist, but these online services must be available for the growing student population that will use the Internet more and more on an independent basis.

- Shifting the library media center to a learning laboratory as a center for group work; discussion and debate leading to the testing of ideas, evidence, and presentations; and a clearinghouse of multimedia delivery to classrooms and homes.

Information inquiry is a critical component for creation of engaging virtual experiences. As most schools consider providing online learning opportunities, it will be increasingly important for school library media specialists as instructional specialists to work collaboratively with teachers to provide quality virtual library services that are accessible regardless of time or location of inquiry projects. As Marc Prensky suggests in his latest book, *Don't Bother Me, Mom, I'm Learning* (2006): "Our young people generally have a much greater idea of what the future is brining than we do. They're already busy adopting new systems for communicating (instant messaging), sharing (blogs), buying and selling (eBay), exchanging (peer-to-peer technology), creating (Flash), meeting (3D worlds), connecting (downloads), coordinating (wikis), evaluating (reputation systems), searching (Google), analyzing (SETI), reporting (camera phones), programming (modding), socializing (chat rooms), and even learning (Web surfing)" (10).

Prensky (2001) has divided the Information Age population into today's students, who are the digital natives—born to swim in the electronic, multimedia world—and the digital immigrants: adults (including nearly every educator: administrator, teacher, technology coordinator, and school library media specialist). In such a world, teachers turning to students for mentorship (K–college) may become more useful and common than many have envisioned (Chuang and Thompson 2006).

References

Agosto, D. E. 2001. Propelling young women into the cyber age, volume 4. www.ala.org/aasl/SLMR (accessed January 8, 2006).

DeBell, M., and C. Chapman. (2003). *Computer and internet use by children and adolescents in 2001.* U.S. Department of Education, National Center for Education Statistics. NCES 2004-014. http://nces.ed.gov (accessed March 20, 2004).

Chuang, H., and A. Thompson. (2006). Students teaching teachers. *Educational Leadership, 63* (4), 70—71.

Clyde, Laurel A. (2000). School library websites: The state of the art. In Lyn Hay, Kylie Hanson, and James Henri (Eds.), New millennium and new horizons (242–255). Centre for Studies in Teacher Librarianship. Charles Sturt University. .

Cooper, J., and K. D. Weaver. (2003). *Gender and computers.* Lawrence Erlbaum Associates.

Craver, Kathleen W. (2002). *Creating cyber libraries.* Libraries Unlimited.

Deubel, Patricia. 2004. Guidelines for selecting quality K-12 online courses. *T.H.E. Journal* (November). http://www.thejournal.com/magazine/vault/A5135.cfm (accessed March 15, 2005).

Fitzgerald, Mary Ann, and Chad Galloway. (2002). Helping students use virtual libraries effectively. *Teacher Librarian 29,* (1) (October), 8–14.

Fleming, Noeleen, Liz Blumson, and Deborah Turnbull. (2002). UQL Cyberschool. http://www.slaq.org.au/Highlights/slaq2002/uql_cyberschool.htm (accessed March 15, 2005).

Gunn, Holly. (2002). Virtual libraries supporting student learning." *School Libraries Worldwide, 8* (2) (July). http://www.accesswave.ca/~hgunn/special/papers/virlib/ (accessed March 15, 2005)

Hartzell, Gary N. (2001). The implications of selected school reform approaches for school library media services. *School Library Media Research, 4.* http://www.ala.org/ala/aasl/aaslpubsandjournals/slmrb/slmrcontents/volume42001/hartzell.htm (accessed March 15, 2005).

Kleiner, A., and L. Lewis. (2003). *Internet access in U.S. public schools and classrooms: 1994–2002.* U.S. Department of Education, National Center for Education Statistics, and Westat. NCES 2004-011. http://nces.ed.gov (accessed March 20, 2004).

Ko, Susan, and Steven Rossen. (2004). *Teaching online: A practical guide.* 2d ed. Houghton Mifflin.

Kuhlthau, Carol Collier. (1997). Learning in digital libraries: An information search process approach. *Library Trends, 45* (4) (Spring), 708–724.

Lamb, Annette. (2005). From potential to prosperity: Twenty years of online learning environments." In G. Kearsley (Ed.), *Online learning: Personal reflections on the transformation of education.* Educational Technology Publications.

Levin, D. and S. Arafeh. (2002). *The digital disconnect: The widening gap between Internet-savvy students and their schools.* Pew Internet Project. http://www.pewinternet.org (accessed March 20, 2004).

Mason R., and F. Rennie. (2006). *Elearning: The key concepts.* Routledge.

National Association of State Boards of Education (NASBE). (2001). *Any time, any place, any path, any pace: Taking the lead on e-learning policy*. NASBE. www.nasbe. org/Educational_Issues/Reports/e_learning.pdf (accessed March 15, 2005).

Neuman, Delia. (1997). Learning and the digital library. *Library Trends 45* (4) (Spring), 687–707.

Palloff, R. M., and P. Keith. (2003). *The virtual student: A profile and guide to working with online students.* Jossey-Bass Books.

Prensky, M. (2001). *Digital game-based learning.* McGraw-Hill.

Prensky, M. (2005). Listen to the natives. *Educational Leadership, 63* (4), 8–13.

Prensky, M. (2006). *Don't bother me mom—I'm learning!* Paragon House Publishing.

Valenza, J. K. (2006). The virtual library. *Educational Leadership, 63* (4), 54–59.

Watson, J. F., K. Winograd, and S. Kalmon. (2004). *Keeping pace with K-12 online learning: A snapshot of state-level policy and practice.* Learning Point Associates. http://www.imsa.edu/programs/ivhs/pdfs/Keeping_Pace.pdf (accessed March 15, 2005)

Williams, T. D., B. J. Grimble, and M. Irwin. (2004). *Teachers link to electronic resources in the library media center,* volume 7. www.als.org/aasl/SLMR (Accessed January 8, 2006).

Selected Relevant Web Sites

Copyright and Plagiarism Check Web Sites
(each accessed July 1, 2005)

Copyright Clearance Center http://www.copyright.com/

Copyright Management Center http://www.copyright.iupui.edu/index.htm

Plagiarism.com http://plagiarism.com/

TurnItIn.com http://turnitin.com/

Virtual Reference Web Sites

AskaCybrarian http://www.library.uq.edu.au/askcyb/

AskColorado http://www.askcolorado.org/

Virtual Platform and Training Resource Web Sites

ALN Web http://www.aln.org/

APEX Learning Systems http://www.apexlearning.com/

Blackboard http://www.blackboard.com/k12/index.htm

eClassroom http://www.eclassroom.com/

Illinois Online Network http://www.mvcr.org

MERLOT (Multimedia Educational Resource for Learning and Online Teaching) http://www.merlot.org

OnlineLearning.net http://www.onlinelearning.net/

Rubrics for WebLessons http://webquest.sdsu.edu/rubrics/weblessons.htm

Tapped In http://www.tappedin.org/

WebBoard http://www.akiva.com

WebCT.com http://www.webct.com/

Sample Virtual School Web Sites

Alaska, Delta Cyberschool http://www.dcs.k12.ak.us/

Arkansas Virtual High School http://arkansashigh.k12.ar.us/avhs_main.htm

Colorado Online Learning http://www.col.k12.co.us/

Connections Academy http://www.connectionsacademy.com/

Florida Virtual School http://www.flvs.net/

Hawaii, E-School http://www.eschool.k12.hi.us

Idaho Digital Learning Academy http://www.idla.k12.id.us/

Illinois Virtual High School http://www.ivhs.org/

Kansas, Basehor-Linwood Virtual Charter School http://vcs.usd458.k12.ks.us/public/ and http://www.ksde.org/outcomes/virtualcurrent.html

K12 Virtual Academy http://www.k12.com/virtual_academy/

Maryland, Virtual High School http://mvhs1.mbhs.edu/

Michigan Virtual High School http://www.mivhs.org/

Minnesota Department of Education—Online Learning http://education.state.mn.us/html/intro_online_learning.htm

Oklahoma, Advanced Academics http://www1.advancedacademics.com/

Texas Education Agency—Web-based Learning http://www.tea.state.tx.us/technology/wbl/index.html

University of California College Preparatory Initiative (UCCP) http://www.uccp.org/

Utah, Electronic High School http://www.ehs.uen.org/

Wisconsin Virtual School http://www.wisconsinvirtualschool.org/

Sample Virtual Library Media Center Web Sites

Arkansas, Fayetteville High School http://fayar.net/east/library/

Arizona, Arcadia High School http://www.susd.org/schools/high/arcadia/library.htm

California, Chico High School http://dewey.chs.chico.k12.ca.us/

California, Redwood High School http://rhsweb.org/library

Georgia, Lovett School of Atlanta http://www.lovett.org/libraryweb/library.htm

Georgia, Paideia School of Atlanta http://www.paideiaschool.org/library/default.htm

Greece Athena Media Center http://www.greece.k12.ny.us/ath/library

Hunterdon Central Library http://central.hcrhs.k12.nj.us/imc

Illinois, Bartlett High School http://www.u46.k12.il.us/bhs/library/

Illinois University Laboratory High School http://www.uni.uiuc.edu/library

Indiana, Goshen High School http://www.goshenhs.org/media/index.html

Maryland, Springbrook High School http://www.mcps.k12.md.us/schools/springbrookhs/media.html

Pennsylvania, Springfield Township High School http://mciu.org/~spjvweb/

School Libraries on the Web http://www.sldirectory.com/index.html

School Library Websites http://www.eduscapes.com/arch/archschool.html

Texas, Mesquite High School http://www.mesquiteisd.org/mhs/library/

Washington, Erie Elementary School http://mte.asd103.org/library/library.htm

Washington, D. C., National Cathedral School http://207.238.25.30/library/upperlowerlib.htm

Whippany Park High School Media Center http://www.whippanypark.org/library

Wisconsin, Jefferson Middle School http://www.madison.k12.wi.us/jefferson/lmc/

Selected Virtual State Library Web Sites

Alaska http://sled.alaska.edu/kids.html

California http://www.clrn.org/home/

Connecticut http://www.iconn.org/

Delaware http://www.state.lib.de.us/

Florida http://www.firn.edu/

Indiana http://www.inspire.net/inskid.html

Kentucky http://www.kyvl.org/

Maryland http://www.sailor.lib.md.us/

Minnesota http://www.pals.msus.edu/webpals/

North Carolina http://www.nclive.org/

Ohio http://www.infohio.org/

Oklahoma http://www.odl.state.ok.us/kids

Pennsylvania http://www.powerlibrary.net/

Washington http://www.librarysmart.com/

Wisconsin http://www.wiscat.lib.wi.us/

Wyoming http://gowyld.net/wyoming/wykids.html

Additional Web Sites on the Digital Divide

Digital Divide Network. http://www.digitaldividenetwork.org

Falling Through the Net. http://www.ntia.doc.gov

GirlTech. http://www.girltech.com

Pew Internet Project. http://www.pewinternet.org

For Further Reading

Barron, A. E., et al. (2006). *Technologies for education: A practical guide.* 5th ed. Libraries Unlimited.

Curtis, M., et al. (2004). *Palm OS handhelds in the elementary classroom.* International Society for Technology in Education.

Warlick, D. F. (2005). *Raw materials for the mind: A teacher's guide to digital literacy.* 4th ed. The Landmark Project.

Chapter 12

Learning Resources Management to Support Inquiry Learning

Daniel Callison

Collection development has ranked among the most important tasks of the school library media specialist since the creation of the position (Callison 1990; Zweizig and Hopkins 1999). Selecting, acquiring, organizing, and providing access to resources remain common skills of the professional trained in library and information science for school service. There are levels beyond these basic functions. These higher levels involve placing the development and management of learning resources at the center of the instructional communications role leading to creation of curriculum.

Note that this is not just support of teaching or enhancement of a given curriculum. It is taking the power of learning resource development and access to levels of establishing new areas of curriculum. As instructional specialists, the school librarian and other teachers determine learning needs through analysis of learners, analysis of the learning environment, and the mixture of access to and ownership of learning resources that will make meaningful learning objectives a reality.

Collection development and resource management have certainly expanded in the past decade to include greater investment in access to information through databases and other electronic systems. Increasingly, this has meant acquiring information through subscribed access, not physical ownership. Collection, however, still implies written, print, audio, or visual information items. Although some school media centers have included for years collections of other useful instruction realia such as statues, globes, puppets, and games, efforts to broaden the scope of instructional learning resources have remained fairly narrow over the past two decades. There remain, for example, inventories of what is owned by the library and what is owned by the classroom; territories of resource ownership within the school and no initiatives to share.

Learning resources include those technologies, materials, environments, and people who can be orchestrated in such a manner that diverse learning needs can be met, and can, at times, take educators beyond the common standards now defined for individual content areas and grade levels. The actions that lead to access or ownership of needed learning resources and the management and application of those learning resources form the basis for decision-making conversations among collaborating educators.

Outcome Measures for Collections and Policies

Early national and state guidelines for school library media collections, from 1900 to 1980, tended to provide lists of input items necessary to establish a school library. By the 1975 guidelines, a large portion of the national publication was devoted to a list of specific number of projectors, record players, books, and other input resources per teacher or per pupil recommended for the school library program. These standards also tended to describe materials and equipment to be housed in a central location, seldom recognizing the need for integrating collection and equipment with the classrooms across the school. Certainly books and equipment were loaned out to teachers in classrooms, but the resources were expected to funnel back to the central clearinghouse, the school media center, for inventory and repair.

Such input measures made sense in a time when many were still attempting to construct school library programs and gather collections to demonstrate how they should appear and operate. The 1980s saw a change in approaches to program evaluation and educational management. With the decision-making processes moved more and more to the building level and with greater control of the budget, and faculty selection and evaluation delegated to principals, output measures came into fashion. Management by objectives included instruction by objectives. What specifically was expected as a result of the items collected and the actions of those involved in the teaching and management?

In 1984, Callison published a systematic approach to school library program and collection planning based on an attempt to defuse these dangers:

- The local library media program has no direction as it attempts to spread funds to meet each of the items adopted by state and national standards.

- The school administration views the library media program as just one more element that slices into a budget developed from strict formulas based on declining enrollment and a stagnant tax base.

- Funds are spent to expand the library media collection mainly on what the commercial market has to offer at the time [and tends to be promoted to school librarians through slick trade publications] without any firm and defined direction for support of developing current areas of the instructional program. (205)

Ten years later, Callison (1995) reported, from data gathered on Indiana school library media programs, a strong positive correlation between the dollar amount per student for the school library media fund and the frequency of budget and planning conversations between the principal and the library media specialist. In elementary school programs, for example, those reporting weekly conversations averaged $9.45 per student, and those reporting no specific meetings on planning or budgets averaged $5.53 per student in 1993—over 40 percent higher in the schools with frequent conversations. More frequent conversations also seemed to lead to more frequent grant applications and greater access to state and federal funding (See Table 12.1).

The relationship between frequent conversations and higher budgets may include many factors that impact the outcome. Wealthier schools may also be more likely to have media specialist positions with support staff so that time for such additional conversations can take place. However, the value in communicating the needs of the school library media program in terms of dollars needed to purchase specific materials in support of student learning should not be underestimated.

Responding to the Needs of Learners

Several national associations for public school accreditation, North Central (http://www.ncacasi.org) and the Southern Association of Colleges and Schools (http://www.sacs.org/), as examples, now expect justification of school re-

Table 12.1. Frequency of Conversations Between Principal and SLMS and Average Per Pupil Media Funding in Indiana Public Schools, 1993

Grade Level	State	None	Annual	Monthly	Weekly
	Average				
Elementary	$5.91	$5.53	$5.92	$6.79	$9.45
Jr. High	$5.85	$5.60	$5.94	$6.21	$6.75
Sr. High	$5.43	$4.65	$6.03	$6.57	$6.51

sources and staff to match the determined learning needs of the students. Specific formulas or numbers per student are no longer mandated. Making the tie between school library resources and student achievement can be challenging but can also place the school library media specialist in a stronger collaborative role if the correct steps are taken (Coatney 2004).

Sandra Hughes-Hassell and Jacqueline Mancall (2005), professors at Drexel University, have published a new guide for collection development in public and school settings based on "responding to the needs of learners." Analysis of collection needs is driven by analysis of local learner needs and is based on communication and collaboration with key educators. The library media specialist is a team leader in the effort in order to make informed selection choices based on input from teachers, local public librarians, and the students themselves. In this new model, the school library media specialist becomes the Learner-Centered Collection Manager, who acts as an informed change agent, leader, and resource guide. In order to create meaningful policies, make quality selections, and negotiate the necessary budget, Hughs-Hassel and Mancall expect school library media specialists to have at their very core of behavior and ability an understanding of educational theory and collaborative interactions in a community of best practice.

Hughes-Hassel and Mancall move the collection process away from inputs and outputs to higher levels of outcomes of higher student achievement. The key questions for determining the strengths and weaknesses of the collection are (2005, 40):

- How well do the items support the learning styles of my learners (visual, auditory, bodily-kinesthetic)?

- How well do the items support the learning differences of my learners?

- How well do the items support the ethnic diversity of my community?

- How well do the items support the reading levels of my learners?

- How well do the items support attainment of curricular standards or benchmarks?

- How well do the items support large-group, small-group, and individual work?

- How well do the items help students create the expected student product?

Budgeting under this process becomes a combination of program and zero-based factors. The Learner-Centered Collection Manager documents need, states objectives, relates the need to the curriculum, and, most of all, makes the budgetary case to the stakeholders who determine money flow. These stakeholders can include the principal, parents, superintendent, school board, grant agencies, and more. Various funding sources may be used to support different areas of the collection, as some funds may come to the school media center with fewer regulations than money granted in the local school budget. Money gained from book fairs, local parent groups, or grants, for example, may be funds that are very flexible to spend on such information sources as special speakers, field trips, distance education, cutting edge equipment, or other items not generally allowed by some accounts in some school districts.

The budget should include a list of priorities, those items likely to be most needed and that have the most impact on the widest audience or for special need audiences. Projections of needs over the next two to three years may also be shown so that long-range plans for possible alternative funding sources can be considered. Professional relationships with other local libraries may help to influence acquisition decisions at those institutions. Resources provided by the local public library, for example, can be enhanced to support the learning plan of the school as well (Callison 1997). Data gathering, analysis, communication, justification, and demonstration of the impact of the resources all become important elements of collection develop rather than simply accepting whatever the district funding system has determined to be the allocation increase or decrease for school library materials. John Eye (2003), for example, concluded in his dissertation that there is a very strong relationship (+.902) between the age of the nonfiction collection in elementary and middle school libraries and student reading scores. After controlling for socioeconomic status, the more recent and relevant the nonfiction collection, it seems, the higher the reading scores are for students through the eighth grade. His finding substantiates common observations in practice, that current appealing books will attract more readers, especially males, and serve to engage students in more reading practice and information application. Keeping the collection current, especially in nonfiction, can pay educational dividends.

Mapping and Targeting for Profile and Depth

David Loertscher's (1996) collection mapping techniques help to facilitate learning resource plans and application to learning standards. Central to his approach is visualization of the collection's strengths and weaknesses for communication to several audiences. This may involve budget plans tied to learning standards for communication to administrators. Bulletin board displays that show targeted subjects of the learning resource collection for growth and relationship to the curriculum communicate to teachers a vision for curriculum enrichment. Newsletters that illustrate for teachers and parents the results of new learning activities brought about by collaborative investments in a wider range and more depth of learning resources help to communicate to adult audiences how student learning needs are being met.

Loertscher's ideas for collection mapping are important concepts to guide local schools to determine and promote their own special profile of resources tied to their curriculum needs. Some of his concepts are paraphrased below (1996, 13):

- Move from balanced collections, which offer a little of nearly everything, to focused collections, which provide depth.

- Consider not only what the critics prefer, but also what kids and teachers need to meet learning standards valued locally.

- Combine librarian selection and knowledge in selection with more collaborative selection respecting the instructional resource expertise of fellow teachers.

- Move from a budget set by information formats to seeking additional dollars justified by information need and learning standard categories or projects.

- Move toward clearer understanding among all educators involved as to how the curriculum can be supported, enhanced, and even changed because of the depth of learning resources made accessible.

Loertscher recommends a visual map to illustrate the future path for collection development:

Show where the collection currently provides a springboard to further development. Have administrators and teachers assist in deciding what collection targets to pursue. What new emphasis areas should be created? Which areas are already good, but will require regular updating? Given the current funding, which collection segments should receive priority? If teachers do not buy into collection development, the collection will remain the property of the library media specialist and will be of little or no consequence in unit planning. (55)

Sample Target Areas for Learning Resource In-depth Collections

The following set of very selective knowledge content areas, organized by school levels, is intended to illustrate possibilities. The subject areas, including learning objectives, information literacy standards, and proficiencies, should be determined by the professional educators within the school and school district. Targeted areas may evolve over several years, but eventually they serve to create a profile for the learning resource collection. They establish the thematic or project units in which students are immersed for applying the demands of the inquiry process and use of multiple information resources.

Each of the areas suggested below, as well as many other areas, can be greatly enriched through the use of human, print and nonprint, and fiction and nonfiction resources creating an information-rich learning environment. A majority of the planning, lesson presentation, resources access, and budget for learning resources may be directed toward these few selected areas. The following profiles address specific student performance objectives from the content knowledge areas recommended by the Mid-continent Research for Education and Learning and the Association for Supervision and Curriculum Development (Kendall and Marzano 2000). Key terms, given in all capital letters, can provide a shorthand for bulletin boards and charts to illustrate the profile. Potential questions and themes students will be able to explore because of these new resources could be added as well.

An Elementary School Learning Resource Profile

History—FAMILY, COMMUNITY, STATE

Understands and knows how to analyze chronological relationships and patterns.

Knows how to identify the beginning, middle, and end of historical stories, myths and other fiction, and narratives.

Knows how to develop picture time lines of their own lives or their family's history.

Understands family life now and in the past, and family life in various places and cultures.

Understands family life in a community of the past and life in a community of the present (e.g., roles, jobs, communication, technology, style of homes, transportation, schools, religious observations, cultural traditions).

Understands personal family or cultural heritage through stories, songs, and celebrations.

Knows ways in which people share family beliefs and values (e.g., oral traditions, literature, songs, art, religion, community celebrations, food, language).

Understands the history of a local community and how communities in North America varied long ago and to some degree today.

Understands the challenges and difficulties encountered by people in pioneer farming communities.

Understands daily life in ethnically diverse urban communities, past and present.

Knows the history of the local community since its founding, the people who came, the changes they brought, and significant events over time.

Knows how different groups of people in the community have taken responsibility for the common good (police and fire departments, senior citizen home, hospitals, soup kitchens, churches, city government, etc.).

Language Arts—COMPOSITION, INFORMATION USE, READING, MEDIA

Understands how to use strategies in prewriting, drafting, revising, editing and publishing.

Writes autobiographical compositions, expressive compositions, responses to literature, and personal letters.

Gathers and uses information for research purposes.

Generates questions about topics of personal interest.

Uses a variety of sources to gather information

Uses a variety of strategies to plan research.

Uses electronic media to gather information.

Uses reading skills and strategies to understand a variety of familiar literary passages and texts including classic and new titles from fairy tales, folktales, fiction, nonfiction, legends, fables, myths, poems, nursery rhymes, picture books, predictable books.

Uses reading skills and strategies to understand a variety of informational texts (e.g., textbooks, biographical sketches, letters, diaries, directions, procedures, magazines, encyclopedias).

Uses text organizers.

Uses the various parts of a book.

Summarizes and paraphrases information in texts.

Uses prior knowledge and experience to understand and respond to new information.

Uses viewing skills and strategies to understand and interpret visual media.

Understands the main idea or message in visual media (e.g., pictures, cartoons, television reports, newspaper photographs).

Understands techniques used to convey messages in visual media (e.g., animation, different tones of voice in audio production, adjusting messages for different audiences).

Understands the different ways in which people are stereotyped in visual media.

Mathematics—REAL WORLD APPLICATIONS

Understands the general nature and uses of mathematics.

Understands that numbers and the operations performed on them can be used to describe things in the real world and predict what might occur.

Understands that mathematical ideas and concepts can be represented concretely, graphically, and symbolically.

Science—LIFE CYCLE

Understands the structure and function of cells and organisms

Knows that plants and animals progress through life cycles of birth, growth and development, reproduction, and death; the details of these life cycles are different for different organisms.

Understands relationships among organisms and their physical environment.

Knows the organization of simple food chains and food webs.

Knows that transfer of energy is essential to all living organisms.

Knows that an organism's patterns of behavior are related to the nature of that organism's environment.

A Middle School Learning Resource Profile

The Arts: Music—MUSIC HISTORY AND CULTURE

Understands the relationship among music, history, and culture.

Understands characteristics that cause various musical works to be considered exemplary.

Understands the functions music serves, roles of musicians, and conditions under which music is typically performed in various cultures of the world.

The Arts: Theatre—COMPOSITION AND PERFORMANCE

Demonstrates competence in writing scripts.

Creates characters, environments and actions that create tension and suspense.

Creates improvisations and scripted scenes based on personal experience and heritage, imagination, literature, and/or history.

Civics—DIVERSITY AND COMMUNITY

Understands the role of diversity in American life and the importance of shared values, political beliefs, and civic beliefs in an increasingly diverse American society.

Knows how diversity encourages cultural creativity.

Knows major conflicts in American society that have arisen from diversity.

Knows ways in which conflicts about diversity can be resolved in a peaceful manner that respects individual rights and promotes the common good.

Knows how an American's identity stems from belief in and allegiance to shared political values and principles, and how this identity differs from that of most other nations which often base their identity on such things as ethnicity, race, religion, class, language, gender, or national origin.

Geography—ECOSYSTEMS

Understands the characteristics of ecosystems on earth's surface.

Understands the distribution of ecosystems from local to global scales.

Understands the functions and dynamics of ecosystems.

Knows the potential impact of human activities within a given ecosystem on the carbon, nitrogen, and oxygen cycles.

History—NATIVE AMERICANS, INDUSTRY, DEPRESSION, CIVIL RIGHTS, WORLD LEADERSHIP

Understands the United States territorial expansion between 1801 and 1861, and how it affected relations with external powers and Native Americans.

Understands the short-term political and long-term cultural impacts of the Louisiana Purchase.

Understands how early state and federal policy influenced various Native American tribes.

Understands the social and political impact of the idea of Manifest Destiny.

Understands how the industrial revolution, increasing immigration, the rapid expansion of slavery, and the westward movement changes American lives and led to regional tensions.

Understands the major technological developments that influenced land and water transportation, the economy, international markets, and environmental issues.

Understands social and economic elements of urban and rural life in the early and mid-19th century.

Understands the elements of early western migration.

Understands the causes of the Great Depression and how it affected American society.

Understands economic aspects of the Great Depression.

Understands the environmental and social impact of the Great Depression.

Understands various political influences on the Great Depression.

Understands how the Great Depression was experienced locally.

Understands the causes and course of World War II, the character of the war at home and abroad, and its reshaping of the U. S. role in world affairs.

Understands military strategies used during World War II.

Understands the dimensions of Hitler's "final solution" and the Allies' responses to the Holocaust and war crimes.

Understand the legacy of World War II (e.g., the decision to use the atomic bomb, purpose and organization of the United Nations).

Understand how World War II influenced American society.

Understands the struggle for racial and gender equality and for the extension of civil liberties.

Understands the development of the civil rights movement.

Understands the involvement of diverse groups in the civil rights movement.

Understand the development of the post-World War II women's movement.

Language Arts—COMPOSITION, RESEARCH, READING & INQUIRY, MEDIA

Uses a variety of strategies for prewriting, drafting and revising, editing and publishing.

Evaluates own and peers' writing.

Writes compositions that address problems and solutions.

Writes in response to literature.

Gathers and uses information for research purposes.

Gathers data for research topics from interviews (e.g., prepares and asks relevant questions, makes notes of response, compiles responses).

Uses a wide variety of resource materials to gather information.

Uses reading skills and strategies to understand and interpret a variety of literary texts (e.g., fiction, nonfiction, myths, poems, fantasies, biographies, autobiographies, science fiction, tall tales, supernatural tales).

Knows the defining characteristics of a variety of informational texts (e.g., textbooks, biographical sketches, letters, diaries, directions, procedures, magazines, essays, primary source historical documents, editorials, news stories, catalogs, technical directions, consumer documents).

Summarizes and paraphrases information in texts (e.g., arranges information in chronological, logical, or sequential order, conveys main ideas, critical details, and underlying meaning; uses own words; preserves author's perspective and voice).

Uses viewing skills and strategies to understand and interpret visual media.

Uses a variety of criteria to evaluate and form viewpoints of visual media including news programs (popular and serious), web sites, and documentaries.

Science—PLANETS, SCIENTIFIC METHOD

Understands the composition and structure of the universe and the earth's place in it.

Knows the characteristics and movement patterns of the planets in our solar system including how planets differ in size, surface, orbits, and satellites.

Understands the nature of scientific inquiry.

Knows there is no fixed procedure called "the scientific method" but that investigations involve systematic observations, carefully collected and relevant evidence, logical reasoning, and some imagination in developing hypotheses and explanations.

Understands that questioning, response to criticism, and open communication are integral to the process of science.

A High School Learning Resource Profile

The Arts: Visual Arts—CLASSICS AND CULTURE

Understands the visual arts in relation to history and cultures.

Knows a variety of historical and cultural contexts regarding characteristics and purposes of works of art.

Knows the function and meaning of specific art objects within varied cultures, times, and places.

Economics—HISTORICAL AND MODERN INTERNATIONAL ROLE

Understands the patterns and networks of economic interdependence on earth's surface.

Knows the spatial distribution of major economic systems and their relative merits in terms of productivity and social welfare of workers.

Understands the historical movement patterns of people and goods and their relationships to economic activities.

Understands the advantages and disadvantages of international economic patterns.

Health—PERSONAL FITNESS

Understands how to monitor and maintain a health-enhancing level of physical fitness.

Knows the effects of physical activity and nutrition on body composition.

Knows how to monitor intensity of exercise.

Knows the characteristics of a healthy lifestyle.

Designs a personal fitness program that is based on the basic principles of training and encompasses all components of fitness.

History—IDEAS, FREEDOMS, COLONIES, CIVIL WAR CONFLICT, PROGRESSIVE POLITICS, AGRICULTURAL HERITAGE

Understands the historical perspective.

Analyzes the values held by specific people who influenced history and the role their values played in influencing history.

Analyzes the influences specific ideas and beliefs had on a period of history and specifies how events might have been different in the absence of those ideas and beliefs.

United States History

Understands how political, religious, and social institutions emerged in the English Colonies.

Understands influences on the development of representative government in colonial America.

Understands how gender, property ownership, religion, and legal status affected political rights.

Understands characteristics of religious development, diverse religious groups and religious freedom in North America.

Understands characteristics of the social structure of different regions of colonial America.

Understands the course and character of the Civil War and its effects on the American people.

Understands the influence of Abraham Lincoln's ideas on the Civil War.

Understands the impact of the Civil War on Native Americans.

Understands how the Civil War influenced Northern and Southern societies, rich and poor, and various ethnic groups.

Understands how the Civil War influenced both military personnel and civilians.

Understands how Progressives and others addressed problems of industrial capitalism, urbanization, and political corruption.

Understands the origins and impact of the Progressive movement.

Understands major social and political issues of the Progressive era.

Understands how the Progressive movement influenced different groups in American society.

World History

Understands the processes that contributed to the emergence of agricultural societies around the world.

Understands how agricultural communities maintained their produce and livestock.

Understands what archaeological evidence has revealed about the cultural beliefs of early agricultural societies.

Understands social and cultural factors that define agricultural communities.

Language Arts—COMPOSITION, INFORMATION ANALYSIS, MEDIA LITERACY

Uses a variety of strategies for prewriting, drafting and revising, editing and publishing.

Writes persuasive compositions that address problems/solutions or causes/effects.

Writes descriptive compositions and reflective compositions.

Gathers and uses information for research purposes.

Uses appropriate research methodology (e.g., interview, survey, experiment, field study, other).

Uses a variety of primary sources if relevant.

Uses a variety of criteria to evaluate validity and reliability of primary and secondary source information.

Synthesize information from multiple research studies to draw conclusions and to go beyond those found in any of the individual studies.

Uses reading skills and strategies to understand a variety of literary texts (e.g., fiction, nonfiction, myths, poems, biographies, autobiographies, science fiction, supernatural tales, satires, parodies, plays, American literature, British literature, world and ancient literature).

Uses reading skills and strategies to understand a variety of informational texts (e.g., textbooks, biographical sketches, letters, diaries, directions, procedures, primary historical documents, editorials, news stories, periodicals, career or job-related materials, speeches, memoranda, government documents, maps).

Uses discussions with peers as a way of understanding information.

Uses a variety of criteria to evaluate the clarity and accuracy of information (e.g., bias, use of persuasive strategies, consistency, clarity of purpose, logic of arguments, expertise of author, propaganda techniques, authenticity, faulty modes of persuasion).

Uses viewing skills and strategies to understand and interpret visual media.

Uses a range of strategies to interpret visual media.

Understands the conventions of visual media genres.

Understands that the rules and expectations about genres can be manipulated for particular effects or purposes.

Mathematics—REAL WORLD APPLICATIONS, COMPUTERS

Understands the general nature and uses of mathematics.

Understands that development of computers has opened many new doors to mathematics just as other advances in technology can open up new areas to mathematics.

Understands that mathematics often stimulates innovations in science and technology.

Science—GENETICS, EVOLUTION, SCIENTIFIC INQUIRY METHODS

Understands the principles of heredity and related concepts.

Knows the chemical and structural properties of DNA and its role in specifying the characteristics of an organism.

Knows ways in which genes may be altered and combined to create genetic variation within a species and is aware of the ethical issues pertaining to current and possible future applications of these processes.

Understands biological evolution and the diversity of life.

Understands the concept of natural selection.

Knows how variation of organisms within a species increases the chance of survival of the species, and how the

great diversity of species on earth increases the chance of survival of life in the event of major global changes.

Understands the nature of scientific inquiry.

Understands the use of hypotheses in science.

Designs and conducts scientific investigations.

Knows that investigations and public communication among scientists must meet certain criteria in order to result in new knowledge and methods.

Technology—INVENTIONS, SOCIAL AND ECONOMIC ISSUES, CAREERS

Understands the relationships among science, technology, society, and the individual.

Knows that science and technology are pursued for different purposes.

Knows ways in which social and economic forces influence which technologies will be developed and used.

Knows that alternatives, risks, costs, and benefits must be considered when deciding on proposals to introduce new technologies or to curtail existing ones.

Knows the role of technology in a variety of careers.

Collaborative Conversation for Collections and Curriculum

At the current time, collaboration is probably the most overused and least fulfilled concept in discussions on the roles of library media specialist and classroom teacher. Definitions of the key terms for instruction in this book have been constructed on the principle that all educators involved understand and promote the elements of Information Inquiry and the methods for effective instruction in information and media literacy.

Thus, classroom teachers and teachers of school library media possess the abilities of the instructional media specialist. All parties bring to the planning table the ability and willingness to share ideas, resources, teaching and evaluation roles, and an understanding of how to implement best practices to meet content knowledge

Table 12.2. Initial Roles in Collaborative Planning for Inquiry
(Donham, Bishop, Kuhlthau, and Oberg 2001, 80)

Planning for Inquiry	
Unit Topic or Theme:	
Student Expectations:	
Teacher	**Library Media Specialist**
Experiences for generating inquiry	Resources for background/exploration
Criteria for acceptable topics	Availability of resources
Reading to become informed	Locating relevant information
Reading for themes	Researchable questions and gaining focus
Reading for meaning	Selecting information resources
Taking and organizing notes	Search strategies for focused topic
	Generating a bibliography
Plan and organize final product	Using variety of presentation tools
Assess student learning about the topic:	Assess student learning about research:
Content Knowledge	Process

Reprinted with permission from Donham.

standards. Planning, design, and learning resource selection conversations at this level can become very powerful and actually result in a dynamic exchange that not only enhances standard curricula, but actually begins to change it to meet local needs and to capitalize on local human resources within the community.

Donham, Bishop, Kuhlthau, and Oberg (2001) describe roles of the teacher and library media specialist that initiate planning for inquiry. They display these roles as separate, with the teacher providing criteria for topics and the library media specialist providing expertise in resources (see Table 2.2).

If one stays at the initiating level, the "division of labor and expertise" given in Table 12.2. is reasonable. However, as collaboration matures, the classroom teacher and the teacher of library media should begin to cross over these boundaries. This is especially true for the role of the classroom teacher who gains expertise in resource selection, information searching, and understanding of the processes involved in inquiry. Collaboration brings both closer to the roles of

instructional media specialist an educator who selects and applies learning resources to help meet learner needs (Montiel-Overall 2005).

The most important reason for building a library media collection in the school is to support the curriculum. (Promotion of reading for pleasure is also an important reason. Reading for pleasure should also be part of a progressive curriculum that promotes inquiry.) Teachers collaborating as instructional media specialists and who are creative and critical thinkers ARE the curriculum. Without engaging as an equal partner with other instructional media specialists, the school librarian can probably feel safe in examination of standard textbooks, review of curricular guides, and frequent visits to curriculum planning or department meetings to gain basic information about what areas of the curriculum will most likely use multiple resources in support of classroom projects.

Working together with creative and critical players, however, the real curriculum is often waiting to be written as ideas spin from the general standards provided by state or national groups.

This team becomes a curricular think tank. The collection of learning resources that supports these planning activities may be purely experimental in that some resources are gathered for preview to help germinate ideas and methods. Internet locations are explored to see what is available and what resources might need to be created locally. In an information-, text-, and technology-rich environment, such exploration and experimentation with learning resources to create curriculum should by now be THE reason for a school library media (learning resource) center.

Knowledge of students is more than knowing the subject matter a given teacher teaches; it also includes the reading ability of a given student, the entry level abilities and experiences of the student group, and the expectations of current standard curriculum guides. The collaborative planning process becomes even more constructive when the teacher team members learn from each other their own expectations for student performance.

Diane Hopkins (1999) has reported the impact of collaboration between school librarians and other teachers on the decisions to renew or update school library collections at the national Library Power sites. This nationwide project involved eighteen school districts across America between 1994 and 1998. Loertscher's collection mapping approach was a prominent technique used to provide a visual plan and guide for general strengths and weaknesses of each school's collection.

But it was the specific lesson planning conversations, coupled with the challenge of encouraging school librarians to play a more active role in curriculum development, that led to additional funds being invested in learning resources, based on mutual agreements reached by teachers, librarians, and administrators as a collaborative team. Hopkins reported:

> Over the years, although school librarians sought to involve teaching in library collection development, teachers were seldom continually involved in evaluating the collection or in selecting materials for the collection. The result was that even when current library materials were available and appropriate for instruction, the materials were less likely to be used by either teachers or students in conjunction with teach-

ing and learning. Thus, too often, there was a lack of connection between the collection development process and instruction. Library Power sought to connect teachers and librarians through the selection and use of library materials. These practices lead to more relevant collections that were more likely to be used in instruction. (8–9)

When input from teachers is more than a quick oral or written request to purchase a book or a video, or an indication that more materials in some general subject area are needed, the opportunity for more collaborative interaction may evolve. The dynamics of planning are then not limited to just what is available, but are extended to how access can be provided to obtain what is really needed, desired, or can be locally produced. Options for immediate access or for off-site availability can be determined and managed.

Critical and systematic planning leads to more competent use of the collection and eventual construction of new collection areas supporting emerging curricular themes. This process gives depth and texture to collection mapping.

Rethinking Access Over Ownership

Deb Kachel (1997), a district media supervisor in Pennsylvania experienced in collection analysis, writes:

> School library media specialists traditionally have viewed building collections as resources under their jurisdiction. Today, however, all school collections should be made available to the entire student body and faculty to make the most efficient and cost-effective use of resources. This is especially true as education moves toward more inter-disciplinary teaching and student-selected, project-oriented learning. School library media specialists should assume some responsibility, along with fellow teachers and administrators, for making these collections more [widely] known and available [in the learning community]. Adding such collections to an online catalog and noting in the location field where they can be found [classroom, departments, local

public library] is a satisfactory way of offering [knowledge of] availability. (2)

Another goal of instructional resource development should be to establish resource accessibility with other libraries, especially local school and public libraries, to the point that the school librarian is less and less likely to respond to new curricular initiatives by saying "not enough resources are available." Rather, the school librarian responds with a menu of options that, together with other teachers, can be played out over time to establish a rich pool of learning resources based on specific learning objectives. Mancall (1994) provides the following example:

> Consider what happens when we work with a teacher who is planning a major unit and has requested materials on a specific subject for which we hold very few, if any, materials in-house. Take the example of an elementary science teacher who wants her students to investigate garden insects and their relationship to the environment. If we are truly part of the curriculum planning and unit development process, we work with the teacher to clarify the basic instructional purpose of the unit. Is she really interested in the life cycle of specific insects, or is the lesson's intent environmental issues? If her objectives are knowledge of particular insects, we are in the position to suggest which ones should be studied with in-house materials and which one could not. We may have extensive holdings on specific insect species but very limited materials on current research about the environmental effects of using pesticides. For this information her students will require access to current magazines and government studies [through guided searches of the Internet, and contacts with the local public librarian and senior high school librarian]. (11–12)

Rethinking Resource Budgets

Budgets for school library collections are usually constructed on one of the following: format, services, circulation, or curriculum. Traditionally budgets have been categorized by information format: books, periodicals, nonprint, computer software, computer hardware. Such account divisions lead to dollars wasted to purchase resources by format, say for video programs, when the real need might be in periodicals but dollars cannot be shifted.

A materials budget based on services has account divisions that support curriculum resources, recreational reading, general reference, management costs, and special projects. This places several important output measures at competition with each other for future dollars.

Some advocate that shifts in school media collection budgets be based on evidence of use. Therefore circulation data would be gathered to determine shifts in distribution of dollars, with those areas showing more use or demand receiving a growing portion of the budget. For a resource center that expects to demonstrate its value by supporting the curriculum, "popularity" may not be the most important factor to measure. Rather, resource need as determined by review of the collection compared to instructional plans by the educators involved may be more reasonable. Measures for popular or recreational reading may depend on circulation numbers (Bertland 1991; Doll and Barron 1991), but dramatic shifts in dollars should be justified by planned instructional units very likely to repeat in the future and that are tied to learning standards.

Other budget distributions may be based on curriculum or grade levels. Under this budgeting process, areas of the curriculum are defined in terms of expected resource need and dollars are budgeted for history, language arts, science, and so forth. Enrollment levels for different grades may also influence where dollars are placed. Number of students does not equal the potential for a unit. Certainly the number of students who may become involved in projects related is a factor to consider, but high enrollment numbers in history classes should not automatically outweigh low numbers in science classes when more projects, and therefore more resource need, may come from the science teachers.

In general, outside of the growth in investments in technology, school library media funding remains stagnant and has declined in many states compared to funding increases for other areas of education (Miller and Shontz 2003). The per pupil investment has nearly doubled in most states over the past twenty-five years because of increased expenses for transportation, facilities, and salaries. Some library media specialists wonder if there are enough dollars available to them to even give the time to considering how or why to construct a budget (Miller 2003).

A learning resources budget process is based on two important principles. First, the needs of the learner are identified and drive the content description for the budget. Second, dollar resources are shared or combined from as many sources as possible (grants, departmental funds, principal resource accounts, district media director accounts, parent organization funds, shared collections with the public library and other schools) so that these learning needs can be met. These principles, in turn, not only drive the account descriptions, but also are the basis for conversations leading to lesson plans and responsibilities for resource identification.

Figure 12.1. Sample budget plan for learning resources and inquiry theme.

Target Learning Resource Area: Diversity
Inquiry Project Title: Valuing Diversity in Our Community
Grade Level: Eighth Number of Students: 60
Collaborating Teachers: Social Studies—Mr. Williams and Ms. Feller
Teacher of Library Media, Inquiry and Information Literacy: Ms. Kelly
All three collaborating as experienced instructional media specialists
Duration of Project: 4 weeks, spring term, 2004
Learning Objectives: Students will investigate and report on the
     diversity of ethnic, religious, social and political groups
     within their local community compared and contrasted to
     their country.
Knowledge Content Standards: Upon completion of this inquiry unit the student will:
- know a variety of forms of diversity in America and his/her local community
- describe how diversity encourages cultural creativity and elaborate on specific examples found locally
- list major conflicts in American society and the local community that have arisen from diversity issues
- understand constructive ways in which conflicts can be resolved in a peaceful manner that respects individual rights and promotes the common good; provide examples from local history if possible
- understand how an American Identity stems from belief in and allegiance to shared political values and principles and contrast this to other countries in which identity is based on narrow allegiance to a specific ethnicity, religion, national origin, and/or political structure.

Information Literacy Standards: The student will practice skills in Information Inquiry to become more proficient in the following:
- compare and contrast sources to determine which are most accurate, relevant, and comprehensive
- identify bias in a variety of resources
- summarize and communicate findings in a meaningful way for peers

Resources Budgeted	**Funding Source**	**Dollar Amount**
Update print materials	Library	$ 3500

- expand biographies on diverse political, religious and social leaders; add multiple copies of those the most prominent personalities; expand by two titles per student or 120 new titles at a variety of reading levels grades 4–10. Invest in paperback editions when possible. Some popular names should be viewed as likely consumable items to be replaced or updated within three years.

Figure 12.1. (*Cont.*)

- expand documents describing conflicts based on diversity, including conflicts in the last thirty years around the world as well as in the United States; expand by one title per student or 60 new titles at a variety of reading levels grades 4–10.
- collect newspaper articles, booklets, and other resources that depict local diversity issues over the past three decades; duplicate those items which seem most useful, not available for purchase, are copyright free, and which are most likely to deteriorate with student handling
- collect selected documents which serve as concrete examples of extreme bias to compare to resources containing a more balanced and tolerant content; a half dozen items
- collect examples of documents which serve to illustrate misleading and inaccurate interpretation of facts to compare to those which provide a more reasonable interpretation; a half dozen items

Update nonprint materials   Library $ 1500

- add recordings or video programs which serve to illustrate diversity, conflicts resulting from diversity, and resolution of conflicts; seek one title for every three students or about two dozen new titles

Computer software   Department $ 550

- a simulation game designed to place students in decision-making roles to meet issues and conflicts which result from different opinions and beliefs; to be added to the library media center's collection

Supplies and duplication   Principal $ 300

- additional dollars are promised by the administration to support use of more paper and duplication of resources than is normally expected in a typical project

Guest speakers   PTA $ 300

- sponsored by the parent/teacher association, transportation costs will be covered to bring in up to ten local resource people for presentations and individual interviews on diversity in the community and conflict resolution

Field trip   PTA $ 900

- expenses for transportation, substitute teachers (including the instructional library media specialist), funded by the parent/teacher association for a one day trip to the Museum of Civil Rights located 70 miles from the school

Interlibrary loan   Library $100

- gather titles from public library and other schools which are needed for the four week duration; some postage may be needed or other loan costs involved

Writing journals   Department $ 210

- blank notebooks to serve as research journals, interview records, for note gathering, and to document student reflections on the research process; student keep the notebooks following the completion of the project

Poster resources   Library $280

- free-standing, two-fold blank posters which will provide the normal means for students to display their findings; depending on abilities, students will have other presentation options

Figure 12.1. (*Cont.*)

Resources Owned	Location	ApproximateValue
Digital cameras	Library	$ 700

   • document interviews and field trip

Video recorders	Library	$ 700

   • record interviews of local personalities

Online resources	Library & Classroom	$ N/A

   • documents through the Internet; compose webquest for the most relevant examples to get students started

Print resources	Library	$ 1200

   • identify the titles owned which will serve as a core to help students do their exploratory reading as a basis for further in-depth research

   • value of print resources local public library places on reserve to support the project ($2400)

Best Practices of Those Who Manage Learning Resource Collections

Those who budget time and dollars to support curriculum through building relevant instructional learning resource collections tend to (Callison 2003)

- analyze local student and teacher needs through observations, conversations, and keeping current with learning behavior research;

- develop a collection policy and public relations that profile those areas of the collection that will help to improve and advance selected portions of the curriculum;

- broaden their review of and sharing of selection aids beyond just those directed toward school librarians; they read reviews from teacher magazines and call for personal preview of materials when necessary;

- weed out old, misleading materials and resources;

- retain a few selected misleading items and access other examples so that teachers and students can be shown the comparison to accurate information sources;

- seek ways to expand the budget by sharing plans with others and requesting a "buy-in" so that the project will become reality; they have a nose for grant funding;

- realize that full curriculum support is expensive and risky and takes time, and there they have patience and seek commitment to the process from collaborative teachers who they know will carry through with instruction based on their time and dollar investments;

- think in terms of resources as more than print or nonprint information items, but realize there is a great deal of information to be gained through expert human resources;

- collect unique realia that will help to give fun and excitement to projects—including art pieces, displays, models, and games; and

- share collection items and collection access across classrooms (including multiple copies and classroom sets), subject areas, and libraries; they share in the success of information-rich instructional units.

Collecting Student Work Gives Ownership and Rewards Creativity

Lesley Farmer (2001) has described an excellent process to reward successful information literacy projects in which students have produced information. Through an established selection process, "original student products can be an exciting addition to the library, providing interesting resources for other students to consult and enjoy" (10). Often, student products that have met final criteria of the classroom teacher and library media specialist become some of the most popular items in the school library. In elementary collections, student-written story books often have the highest circulation. Documentaries produced by students in secondary schools, some winning awards in local and state media fair competition, become primary sources of student interviews and local perspectives.

Farmer recommends adding to local collections the anthologies of student prose and poetry compiled by the language arts department. She also notes that selection of student products will bring a closer review of issues regarding copyright and plagiarism. Maintaining the collection of student work may offer special challenges for cataloging and shelving, but the end result is often new pride shown by students as their work is presented in library-quality format for sharing with their friends and parents. As Farmer concludes, "Student work deserves an authentic audience. It also deserves to be used to enhance the school as a learning community" (14).

Teachers of Information Inquiry may find that maintaining collections of previous student projects on themes of inquiry that are repeated from year to year will provide a foundation for students to gain a faster exploration of background information as they read or view previous student products. This also provides students with a tangible idea of product options. Teachers and library media specialists who use access to previous student work wisely will find that it will accelerate the inquiry process and allow new student groups to move through initial brainstorming and question development faster. There is no harm in this, as students will also move to more in-depth inquiry than was experienced by groups who preceded them. True inquiry never stops and has many layers of investigation that can come from the knowledge learned from those who have explored similar questions before. Real inquiry is the product of many investigators over time, and access to previous work will only serve to multiply the questions.

New, Welcoming Collections Needed: Weed Out the Old and Attract More Inquiry

Four of the factors that stand in the way of exciting inquiry projects are, first, old book collections that tell students and teachers just by sitting on the shelf that they are out-of-date and uninviting to explore. Second is the continued practice in too many schools that libraries are the central and only "keeper of the books." School classrooms, especially in elementary schools, should be extensions of the library, each housing growing, robust collections that are refreshed from new library holdings and rotated among classrooms. The school library media specialist should manage instructional resources across the school. Third is failure to encourage frequent traffic between the classroom and the library media center on a flexible basis. Groups of students, individual students, and entire classes need frequent access to resources if reading, writing, and inquiry are to flourish. In elementary schools, this is time to explore and discuss resources, including nonfiction materials—print and electronic. And fourth, too many practicing school librarians refuse to do anything to change the first three factors. A major first step toward inquiry-based activities is to weed and update the collection.

Current: occurring in or belonging to present time; most recent. Why is this an important learning resource and collection development term? Key to becoming effective users of information is learning the importance and relevance associated with the copyright date of a book or other resource, deciphering the true date of a Web site, and determining data that are the most recent. Although teachers of information literacy have always alluded to the currency of information as one strand in the test for authoritativeness, practice in the selection and use of truly current data has become an extremely critical Information Age skill.

School library media collections that have become out-of-date because of lack of weeding and limited expenditures for new materials confound the selection of current and timely information. Often such situations only reinforce the false notion that the only place to find really up-to-date information is through the computer or television. While we know that such electronic telecommunication systems are essential for tracking current events, they also may be misleading at times. Teachers of information literacy strive to establish current collections so that situations can be created in which students learn the value of recent information as well as gain a level of trust that current information can be found through the school library media center (Dickinson 2005).

Aging Collections

If you have served as a school library media specialist for over twenty years in the same building and have been the only one to evaluate the age of your collection, there is a good chance that nearly half of your nonfiction collection is out-of-date and of little use in the modern school information laboratory (McGriff 2004; Basinger 2005). There is also a good chance that the nonfiction books in the school library are, on average, seven to ten years older than the nonfiction books in the same subject areas in the local public library. If this is hard to believe, take a sample of the copyright dates of ten books in each of several areas such as space exploration, computers, civil rights, health, or ecology. Compare what you find to the holdings at the local public library (Davis 1999; Clancy 2004). You will soon discover why many students prefer to get their print resources at the public library rather than their school library: much more to select from and newer—unless the school library media specialist is heavily involved in inquiry projects and has given sufficient attention to updating the school's collection.

Extensive weeding, which includes collaboration with selected teachers who want and know updated resources, is essential. New library media specialists entering a school that has been under the direction of the same person for twenty or more years will likely find that a top priority for the first years of their service will be to manage a systematic revitalization of the collection through extensive weeding.

Numbers gathered for the 1994 survey for the U. S. National Commission on Libraries and Information Science illustrate some aspects of the currency problem, and more recent state surveys continue to confirm these numbers (Lynch, Weeks, and Kramer 1994; Callison and Knuth 1994):

- One in four elementary school library media centers did not have a world atlas with a copyright of 1990 or more recent.

- In most elementary and secondary school library media centers, the average copyright date for books dealing with health and medicine was between 1970 and 1984.

- In over a third of the elementary and secondary school library media centers, the average copyright date of books dealing with space exploration was between 1960 and 1979.

- A third of the school library media specialists rated their collections in science and technology as "poor"; 44 percent rated their collections in health as "poor"; 70 percent rated their collections in mathematics as "poor"; and nearly 75 percent rated their collections in careers, foreign language, and English as a second language as "poor."

In several individual state surveys taken between 1990 and 2000, the following trends seemed to be consistent from one area of the country to another:

- One-third of the nonfiction books on the shelves of school library media centers are over twenty-five years old.

- One-fourth of the audiovisual materials (mostly filmstrips) held in school library media centers are over twenty-five years old.

- Over half of the nonfiction books in the areas of physics, chemistry, geography, and travel are over twenty-five years old.

- Over a third of the nonfiction books in the areas of civil rights, space travel, health education, evolution, and astronomy are over twenty-five years of age.

What's Missing in the Old Stuff

Think of the descriptions of the Soviet Union or China in filmstrips, atlases, and travel books published twenty-five to thirty years ago. Go to your school library media center shelves in areas such as world politics, space exploration, medicine, or environmental studies, and the following will be evident in most of the books that deal in general with any of those topic areas:

- Very little pressure on South Africa to end apartheid.

- Modern Strategic Arms Limitation Talks have yet to begin.

- Scientists have yet to build the first continuous-wave laser.

- Scientists have yet to discover the process by which RNA code is transcribed on DNA.

- First black hole discovery has not been made.

- First transplants of human eye, heart, or lung have yet to be performed.

- First pocket calculator has yet to be sold.

Common content provided in older publications includes:

- You have to be twenty-one to vote.

- Asbestos and DDT are recommended as safe.

- Benefits of smoking cigarettes include healthy relaxation.

The concern may not be so much that children accept the information as fact in such dated books, but we must be concerned by the poor impression made on those students who want the most recent and relevant information possible. For those students who can discriminate in the selection of current information, their out-of-date school library media center is an embarrassment. For those who can't or don't discriminate, an out-of-date collection is fundamentally harmful to their intellectual health.

Students May Lack Age Sensitivity

Issues related to student misuse of dated resources were flagged over twenty years ago in studies conducted by Jacqueline C. Mancall and M. Carl Drott (1983) at Drexel University. They examined papers written by several thousand secondary school students and concluded that students show relatively little sensitivity to age when selecting materials. They observed that insensitivity to age seems to be more of an oversight rather than a conscious selection strategy. The average age of the books cited by students who wrote science reports was several years older than the average age of books used for papers in the humanities or social sciences.

One conclusion from the researchers was that some use of the older material may reflect what was available in the collections to which students had access. Clearly, even then, school collections in the science areas were dated. It may be that science book collections do not receive the attention necessary to update them because few library media specialists have expertise in the science field. Most have academic backgrounds in humanities and history. However, it may also be the case that science book collections age with little attention given to evaluation because science teachers and students will tend to seek out current information from periodicals, newspapers, journals, and, most recently, the Internet.

The Mancall and Drott study raised the need for more education of students so that they might demonstrate a greater sensitivity to the age of materials used. Practice in critical analysis of the content of science texts and trade books may help students form a sense for demanding and expecting the most timely information possible. Practice in critical comparison of the content found in various formats and in similar publications that are revised and updated over time would help to acquaint the student with how dramatically the world has changed, especially in such areas as environmental studies, health education, medical practices, and applied technologies.

Take Any Old Science Book

A reasonable recommendation often made in cases where there has been extensive weeding of the science collection is that these books be removed from the educational environment. They should be destroyed and classrooms should not become salvage yards for old science texts and trade books. That recommendation probably has a great deal of merit, though it may be difficult for some to even consider that out-of-date books be eliminated completely and removed from the reach of teachers and students.

However, some useful instructional exercises may be developed from a few selected titles held from those weeded. Consider students role-playing as "textbook publishers" or "editors for revised editions" and determining what needs to be done to bring a given "oldie" up-to-date. Depending on the content of the old titles and the subject matter of the class, students might be directed to work in teams to revise a chapter or a set of titles. With access to a wide range of current science materials, including an array of science journals and open use of the Internet, their task might include at least some of the following Information Inquiry challenges:

- **Terms:** Identify and define important key terms essential to this field of science today, but not included in the vocabulary when the older text was written.

- **Illustrations:** Not only correct illustrations for content, but also experiment with more current means of generating illustrations, such as animation, time-lapse photography, or computer graphics.

- **Names:** Are the people who were named as prominent in the field during the writing of the older text still prominent today? What new names have come on the scene, and why should they be added or take the place of some previous personalities?

- **Events:** What have been the key events in this field over the past two or three decades that influence the tone or overall message to be conveyed in a revised text as compared to the older text?

- **Diagrams, charts, and tables:** Update statistical information, but show a progression over time whenever possible. Display such numbers so that the reader can see change and evolution or constant patterns.

- **Research:** Find key research conclusions over the past decade and relate them to findings reported in the old text so you can discuss findings that are no longer considered valid and earlier findings that have been substantiated by current investigations.

Establish a context for current information applied to successful projects. The results of student Information Inquiry should be displayed—on bulletin boards in the school media center, in school hallways and classrooms, on the school's Web site, and in newsletters to parents. A concluding activity might be for students to participate in selection of new science books to be acquired for the library media center collection. The knowledge from their Information Inquiry experience can be useful in making such selections.

References

Basinger, C. (2005). Collection inventory for a high school library. *PNLA Quarterly, 69* (4), 8–11.

Bertland, L. H. (1991). Circulation analysis as a tool for collection development. *School Library Media Quarterly, 19* (2), 90–97.

Callison, D. (1984). Justification for action in future school library media programs. *School Library Media Quarterly, 12* (3), 205–211.

Callison, D. (1990) A review of the research related to school library media centers. In Blanche Woolls (Ed.), *The research of school library media centers* (231–258). Hi Willow.

Callison, D. (1995). Restructuring pre-service education. In B. J. Morris (Ed.), *School Library Media Annual 1995* (100–112).. Libraries Unlimited.

Callison, D. (1997). Expanding collaboration for literacy promotion in public and school libraries. *Journal of Youth Services in Libraries, 11* (1), 37–48.

Callison, D. (2003). The historical context: An evolution toward knowledge management." In Joy McGregor (Ed.), *Collection management for school libraries* (33–70). Scarecrow Press.

Callison, D., and R. Knuth. (1994), *The AIME statewide survey of school library media centers: Expenditures and collections.* ERIC Clearinghouse. ED 374 824.

Clancy, C. M. (2004). *Collection development in school and public libraries: An analysis.* MSLS Thesis, University of North Carolina, Chapel Hill.

Coatney, S. (2004). What about the collection? *Teacher-Librarian, 32* (2), 47.

Davis, J. (1999). *Sex education books for young adults: An evaluation and comparison of materials in a public and school library.* MSLS Thesis, University of North Carolina, Chapel Hill.

Dickinson, G. (2005). Crying over spilled milk. *Library Media Connection, 23* (7): 24–26.

Doll, C. A., and P. P. Barron. (1991). *Collection analysis for the school library media center: A practical approach.* American Library Association.

Donham, Jean, Kay Bishop, Carol Collier Kuhlthau, and Dianne Oberg. (2001). *Inquiry-based learning: Lessons from* Library Power. Linworth Publishing.

Eye, J. G. (2003). *The relationship between school library media programs and student achievement on standardized reading tests in Utah.* Ed.D. dissertation. University of South Dakota.

Farmer, L. S. J. (2001). Collecting and using original student work. *The Book Report, 19* (5): 10–14.

Hopkins, D. M. (1999). The school library collection: An essential building block to teaching and learning. *School Libraries Worldwide, 5* (2), 1–15.

Hughes-Hassell, S., and J. C. Mancall. (2005). *Collection management for youth: Responding to the needs of learners.* American Library Association.

Kachel, D. E. (1997). *Collection assessment and management for school libraries: Preparing for cooperative collection development.* Greenwood.

Kendall, J. S., and R. J. Marzano. (2000). *Content knowledge: A compendium of standards and benchmarks for K–12 education.* 3d ed. Mid-continent Research for Education and Learning and the Association for Supervison and Curriculum Development. McREL.

Loertscher, D. V. (1996). *Collection mapping in the LMC: Building access in a world of technology.* Hi Willow.

Lynch, M. J., A. C. Weeks, and P. Kramer. (1994). *Public school media centers in 12 states.* National Commission on Libraries and Information Science.

Mancall, J. C. (1994). Refocusing the collection development process: Collecting, cooperating, consulting. *Taproot, 3* (1), 8–12.

Mancall, J. C., and M. C. Drott. (1983). *Measuring student information use.* Libraries Unlimited.

McGriff, N. (2004). Collecting data: Collection development. *School Library Media Activities Monthly, 20* (9), 27–29.

Miller, M. and M. Shontz. (2003). The SLJ spending survey. *School Library Journal* 49 (10): 52–59.

Miller, P. (2003). Establishing a budget. *School Library Media Activities Monthly, 19* (5), 37–38.

Montiel-Overall, P. (2005). Towards a theory of collaboration for teachers and librarians. *School Library Media Research, 8.* http://www.ala.org/aasl/SLMR (accessed January 9, 2006).

Zweizig, D., and D. M. Hopkins. (1999). *Lessons from* Library Power: *Enriching teaching and learning.* Libraries Unlimited.

Highly Recommended Guides for Weeding School Library Collections and Developing Budgets

Baumbach, D. J., and L. L. Miller. (2006). *Less is more: A practical guide to weeding school library collections.* American Library Association.

Dickinson, G. K. (2003). *Empty pockets and full plates: Effective budget administration for library media specialists.* Linworth Publishing.

Morris, B. J. (2004). *Administrating the school library media center.* 4th ed. Libraries Unlimited.

Part II

Introduction: Application of Inquiry to the Student Research Process

Leslie Preddy

I was not born an effective library media specialist. I worked very hard and tried to do whatever I attempted with intense passion and thoroughness. By 2000, hard work and love for what I did weren't enough. I felt I was a floundering library media specialist and was searching for the reason why my collaboration efforts seemed to have reached peak interest, which was moderate, at best. It was at this time that the Indiana Department of Education Office of Learning Resources awarded me a grant "to foster awareness of information literacy standards and how the library media specialist and classroom teacher develop a partnership to incorporate them into lessons." Through the grant I met Dr. Daniel Callison, who generously shared his time, much of it with the only compensation being my gratitude, and the elements of Information Inquiry. We worked with and learned from five collaborative teams of library media specialists and classroom teachers from throughout the state to pilot implementing inquiry into their collaborations: Lauralee Foerster and Julie Sumrall at Jefferson High School (Lafayette), Janella Knierim and Kelly Dumas at Sugar Grove Elementary (Terre Haute), Kym Kramer and Jenny Stapp at Fishback Creek Elementary (Indianapolis), Beth Slightom and Betsy Wheatley at Fall Creek Valley Middle School (Indianapolis), and Jenny Moore at Perry Meridian Middle School (Indianapolis) teamed with me. I firmly believe that it is due to Dr. Callison's guidance and resources, developed through the grant (http://pmms.msdpt.k12.in.us/imc/Inquiry/index.htm), that collaborative lessons in my school nearly doubled from 2002 to 2004 and collaboration moved from cooperation to co-planning, co-teaching, and co-evaluating.

By 2003 I firmly believed that inquiry worked, but our experience with inquiry was teaching us that we needed to do our own research, collect our own data, and find out whether that belief was true. Indications from data collected during the 2003–2004 school year on 140 Perry Meridian Middle School eighth-grade students were that:

- Reflecting and journaling leads to focus on critical problems and better management of communication between student and educators;

- The value students placed on research abilities increased with each consecutive inquiry project; and

- While using inquiry, there was a positive correlation between student achievement and effective teacher–library media specialist collaboration.

The use of information inquiry in my school library changed my professional life for the better, and I think it will positively affect the practice of all school library professionals.

Chapter 13
Middle School Inquiry Research Basics

Leslie Preddy

Information Inquiry is an effective theory when applied to building students' awareness of how our world revolves around questioning and problem solving. Information Inquiry is defined by Dr. Daniel Callison as "an application of the ancient Socratic Method of teaching through self-posed and mentor-posed questions in order to gain meaning in today's overwhelming Information Age." Within that context, the educator incorporates information processing skills throughout the journey. The meaning behind Information Inquiry in relation to student research has far-reaching potential. When trying to make sense of the world around us and helping students make sense of that world as well, inquiry is a powerful tool. Inquiry allows students, teachers, and library media specialists to work together toward becoming independent thinkers, doers, and creators. As Yogi Berra said, "The future ain't what it used to be."

Inquiry is a component of school curriculum, national goals and standards, and many states' standards. It is not something to teach in addition to everything else, but rather a method to gain perspective and focus energy while meeting those standards. Students applying Information Inquiry become better researchers and better able to adapt the process learned to real-life strategies. With modifications for students' cognitive ability levels, it is an effective and natural technique for the inquisitive of all ages. According to Dr. Patricia Wolfe, a leading interpreter of brain research, "We need to teach content within a context that is meaningful to students, and that connects to their own lives and experiences . . . Too often, the curriculum is taught in isolation, with little effort put into helping students see how the information is, or could be used in their lives. Too many students never comprehend . . . how the content they are learning fits in the larger scheme of things" (2001).

A Planning Guide for Information Power: Building Partnerships for Learning defines inquiry as "the process for formulating appropriate research questions, organizing the search for data, analyzing and evaluating the data found, and communicating the results in a coherent presentation" (1999). It gets to the heart of what educators are concerned about: valuing the process a researcher goes through as much, if not more, than the final product. Inquiry is a method for recognizing the need to teach ourselves and others to think things through as we question, read, analyze, investigate, reflect, internalize, hypothesize, and present our findings and theories in a way that is audience appropriate. It is a way to move away from simply reporting the facts and to move toward developing the recursive questioning skills (See Figure 13.1) necessary for students to become independent thinkers with a self-awareness and ability to problem solve throughout life.

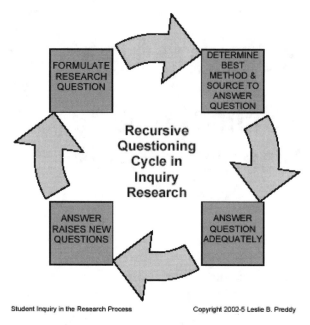

Figure 13.1. Recursive questioning cycle in inquiry research. Leslie Preddy. Copyright 2002, 2006.

Planning for Inquiry

Planning for an inquiry research project is a collective effort between the library media specialist and classroom teacher. A teacher's passion for a particular subject, the curriculum, and standards initiate the inquiry topic and are often used as a basis for guided inquiry research.

Collaboration between the classroom teacher and library media specialist should include sharing roles and responsibilities, with a clear understanding of the division and sharing of tasks. Spend time planning, designing, implementing, and assessing. Just as students will be expected to do during the inquiry project, keep a collaboration log, journal, notebook, or folder and put all notes, collaboration expectations, guidelines, and requirements in it. It doesn't have to be fancy, typed, or formally structured; it should just be kept together so that it is easily accessible. The library media specialist is willing to make modifications as necessary to suit the needs of the collaborative teacher's teaching styles. All participating educators adapt to the students' learning styles. Recognize that collaborative planning for inquiry is a fulfilling, challenging, and creative process, not traditional and mechanical. Share a willingness to jointly evaluate and revise before, during, and after the inquiry unit or task. Enjoy being collaborative

partners and benefit from the opportunity to learn from one another and grow as educators. Learn each other's strengths and use those strengths to the collaboration's advantage.

The library media specialist should be willing to set aside or postpone other administrative responsibilities and routine activities to devote attention to the inquiry unit, students, and classroom teacher. This requires focusing on the role of teacher-librarian instead of administrator-librarian. To be approachable, useful, and needed, appear available, interested, and focused on the inquiry unit and people.

Educator (Classroom Teacher and Library Media Specialist) Roles for Inquiry

Using inquiry requires educators to break out of the traditional teaching role and wear a variety of professional hats: Appraiser, Coach, Guide, Instructor, Motivational Speaker, and Role Model, just to name a few:

- **Appraiser:** As an appraiser, continually observe and evaluate student efforts, abilities, and learning throughout the process. Assessments can be made through a variety of means: rubrics, observations, checklists, interviews, surveys, self-evaluations, and peer evaluations.

- **Coach:** As a coach, use methods similar to those employed by an athletic coach, to help students practice and progress toward research autonomy. A coach demonstrates for the student how to succeed with techniques and strategies, and then allows for "warm up," "practice," and "cool down" for consistent, long-term improvement. Act as the students' coach as they move through the research inquiry process. Continue verbal encouragement and inspiration along the way. Be observant and go to the aid of students in need.

- **Guide:** As a guide, observe student activity and help lead students through difficult spots. Ideally, guide in a way that requires the students to solve their own problems. A guide does not have to give all of the answers, but may help with the route a student should travel to reach a desired destination.

- **Instructor:** As an instructor, lead discussions that establish a basic knowledge about the subject from which to build. Work collaboratively to develop students' reading and study skills, their capacity to distinguish differences between report writing and research, and their ability to generate age-appropriate, researchable questions. Give students opportunities to practice using supporting evidence, analytical thinking, and drawing conclusions. Develop mini-lessons to be taught as the need arises in relation to research methods instead of teaching in an artificial environment.

- **Motivational Speaker:** As a motivational speaker, take on the role of empowering and inspiring students as individuals, in small groups, or as whole classes to succeed. Motivate students to continue even when things get rough. Give students the encouragement that elicits personal desire and the will to excel. Instill in students the self-esteem that is sometimes crucial for having the drive necessary to proceed on the quest for knowledge. Encourage students to believe in themselves enough to make it through the more difficult situations that arise when researching.

- **Role Model:** Be a role model. Demonstrate throughout the inquiry process information literacy and inquiry skills and methods. Lead by example through modeling methods, techniques, and expected behavior. Go through the inquiry research process alongside the students.

Symbiotic Relationships: Student and Educator Responsibility

Topic Selection and Questioning

Generate the inquiry from the students' foundational knowledge by building on what they know instead of what they don't know. Provide the classroom time necessary for students to have the opportunity to learn enough about the subject. This creates groundwork for interest within which students generate personal interests and inquiry research questions. Many state and national standards are written in the context of students' generating their own questions to investigate. For example, Indiana's English/Language Arts academic standard 7.4.5 states: "Research and Technology . . . Identify topics; ask and evaluate questions; and develop ideas leading to inquiry, investigation, and research." Allow students the intellectual opportunity to select and specify a topic or category within a curricular topic to investigate that is not only related to what they have been learning in class but is also of interest to them. With ownership of what is being researched comes the unexpected responsibility for what and how the student is learning.

Interpret, Analyze, and Evaluate

Help students understand how to interpret what information is important and should be held and what should be disregarded throughout the inquiry research process. Give students the training and tools necessary to acquire the skills that allow for age-appropriate interpretation, analysis, and evaluation of information. Cultivate in students the skills required to develop, implement, analyze, and interpret interviews, surveys, and questionnaires. Help students learn how to use a variety of traditional and nontraditional resources. Allow students the opportunity to learn about the resources available in the community: home, school, local, state, national, international, and virtual.

Students as Learners and Teachers

Be observant and encourage peer mentoring and tutoring. A person learns and retains more from teaching and sharing. Allow students opportunities to bounce thoughts, ideas, and new knowledge off fellow students. Provide students with experience and the freedom to take a teachable moment and show a peer how to do something they've already learned. Students surprise me every year with what they can teach

each other. I often see what I had just taken a moment to show an individual applied the next day by that student to help his or her peers. I see students who would not normally be considered by the classroom teacher as positive role models or classroom leaders actively helping other students, even if it's something as small as sharing a book they've come across that they think will help a peer. Give students an opportunity to demonstrate expertise with peers. If a student has a gift for navigating the Web, editing video, locating key information in a book, translating instruction, or some other talent, allow him or her to relate that information to peers in need. Learn not to underestimate the value of peer information sharing. Include a formal situation for peer counseling, in which students are paired to share research findings and how they anticipate presenting or reporting personal thoughts and findings. This can be done as frequently as an end of day informal conversation with a peer or as infrequently as a formal peer conference scheduled toward the end of research. As a component of the project conclusion, allow for peer evaluation and self-evaluation. Students will consider peers' comments as sincere and often as more legitimate than those of an adult. Obligating students to evaluate themselves requires them to internalize and self-analyze, which is vital for self-awareness and future research success.

Evaluating Inquiry Research

Evaluate the inquiry process separately from the students' final products. For inquiry to be most effective and fulfilling, educators should devote the time and effort necessary to jointly evaluate students.

Evaluate and give value to the research process as much as the final product. Evaluate the process through an observation log, students' ability to meet deadlines throughout the project, on-task behavior, completing pre-research activities, selecting and locating a variety of traditional and nontraditional sources, daily reflections, asking for help when appropriate, keeping a research notebook or journal, peer assessments, and self-assessment.

Create an observation log that includes a list of the students and observable behaviors deemed important by collaborating teachers. In the course of inquiry, monitor through observations and informal conversations with students. Note when a listed skill is observed and demonstrated. (See Figure 13.2.)

Offer a variety of product options for reporting and presenting inquiry research findings that meet the needs of the auditory, visual, and kinesthetic learner. Allow for a limited or total student choice of what and how students will share their inquiry experience and knowledge. The product should be evaluated for its written and oral aspects, aesthetics, accuracy, and coherence. Evaluation can be done by the students, educators, administrators, community leaders, field experts, and peers.

Students	Inquiry Observation Log								
	Research develops new questions	Seeks help when needed	Helps others	On-task	Locates Resources	Solves unforeseen problems	Uses Skimming & Scanning	Uses Note Taking Strategies	Uses time provided to organize notes

Figure 13.2. Inquiry observation log.

Chapter 14

Middle School Inquiry Research Orientation

Leslie Preddy

An orientation serves to build the foundation of knowledge, which gives educators and students a point of common reference for the topic. The topic chosen for guided inquiry is found in the curriculum and standards. The classroom lessons, discussions, and lectures guide students toward inquiry research. Give students the background information necessary to successfully begin and to complete investigative activities. It is essential for students to have experienced a common foundation of topic knowledge so that they can most effectively develop thought-provoking questions that are of interest to them.

One key to building a successful foundation is for educators to agree upon a common language as they plan collaboratively. Students will easily become distracted and confused if different educators refer to the same curricular topics or instructional issues in instruction in different ways and with different key words and phrases, especially when it's a new concept. For example, what terms will you use to refer to the process of locating information in a book? What terms will you use in relation to analyzing a source for facts, opinions, bias, and understanding?

Allow students to make decisions and develop ownership. Be willing to alter the sequence and scope of activities and lessons based on the cognitive abilities of the students. Some classes may experience more success if the process is adapted to their needs by the educator facilitating class discussions and large group work instead of independent work.

Research Journal

An organizational journal is indispensable when teaching students of any age how to research. A research journal helps students develop enough structure to organize their thoughts and activities while still allowing for creativity and independent thinking. A research journal can be made out of anything: a folder, notebook, large envelope, or three-ring binder. The research journal contains the project's expressly written guidelines, expectations, activities, and deadlines. Plan together to develop a research journal that suits the educators' teaching styles and is age, grade, resource, and project appropriate.

Together, the class reviews the time line and determines the contents of the research journal before the inquiry research begins. The research journal is a tool for evaluating the process, so plan to have students turn it in for grading. It will be used to evaluate the students' organizational skills and the completion of all steps of the inquiry process, and also as a reference for educators when evaluating the process and final product.

- **Time Line:** Educators jointly develop a time line for the project. The time line clearly states for students a daily schedule of events: where they will be working, when things are due, what work to focus on, etc. Research work can be done every day, every other day, or just one day a week and includes frequent after- or before-school help sessions. When planning the time line, allow time to review the research journals and provide feedback, follow-up, and remediation as necessary. Providing time gaps may offer students the opportunity to remove themselves from the process, which is often how clarity and brainstorms occur for emergent inquirers.

- **Journal Checklist:** Students keep everything they do related to the inquiry in their research journal, which allows the educator and student to be more organized and therefore allows for more time on task. The checklist is a detailed list of what needs to be kept in the journal. It is a concrete understanding from the beginning of research of what educator expectations are: time line, classroom lecture and discussion notes, all inquiry worksheets and handouts, rubrics, completed source notes for every source used, daily reflections, primary sources, peer evaluation, storyboard, annotated bibliography, self-evaluation, and educator evaluation.

- **Rubrics:** Assessment tools in the form of rubrics are used by both the educators and the students to gauge successes and failures in the process and product. *Information Literacy Standards for Student Learning* (1998) defines rubrics as "a scaled set of criteria that clearly defines for the student and the teacher what a range of acceptable and unacceptable performance looks like." Rubrics take the guesswork out of evaluating student work and progress by describing expected behavior and action. Expectations for content and quality are established and shared with students beforehand. When reviewing the rubric, also share samples of prior students' excellent, average, and poor work. A goal for using a rubric as an assessment tool should be to give students the opportunity to clearly understand the educator's guidelines and expectations.

Inquiry lends itself admirably to assessing the research process as well as the final product and presentation. Develop the mindset that the process is important and should be evaluated. Incorporate those expectations into a rubric for evaluation purposes. The research process is more important, is more time-consuming, and should be given more weight in grading than the final product. The final product is a by-product. The actual true measure of learning should be the research process of finding, developing, analyzing, internalizing, and interpreting information in a logical and coherent fashion. It is challenging to put concrete measures, which are necessary and expected by parents, students, and fellow educators, on a process. This is why a tangible tool, like the research journal, is an invaluable measure of the process. Giving concrete significance to the process is created with a rubric or checklist that empowers and values the research process by requiring the use of a research journal and using the contents of the journal and educator observations throughout the process of on-task, age-appropriate behavior. These are standards by which to measure progress and process.

Do not share what the final product options are until the research time has almost concluded. You can give students clues to some things that they may need, like images or certain types of information, without revealing the product. In my experience, not disclosing the final product until later keeps students focused on finding the answers to their research questions instead of what they will produce. Throughout inquiry, student ownership is vital, so after students are told what the final product will be, it is possible to have each class, with the educator facilitating, develop the class's rubric for evaluating the final product.

The final product and presentation should be evaluated for accuracy, consistency, quality, analysis, supporting evidence, organization, referencing, and the ability to answer, or defend the inability to answer, the critical questions. A four-point rubric, with zero equaling no effort and four being excellent, could be used when evaluating the final product for *written*, technical and content; *oral*, technical and presentation; and *product*, artistic/aesthetics and technical content.

- **Contract:** Jointly develop a contract to share with students. The contract is a vital tool for communicating to parents the role research will be taking in their children's lives and time. The contract includes a simplified rubric with clearly stated, minimal expectations for parent and child to review together. The rubric outlines in general terms basic, satisfactory, and proficient guidelines for student work in effort, Information Inquiry, written product, oral presentation, final product, bibliography, and research journal. Knowing these expectations in advance provides another opportunity for students to take ownership of their learning. Requiring the contract be taken home, reviewed, and signed by a parent gives the guardian an advance glimpse of where his or her child's efforts will be focused.

Pre-Searching

Developed by Virginia Rankin (1999)

Students select a specific topic of inquiry following a method of pre-searching, as developed by Virginia Rankin. Pre-searching is preparing students for research with basic training and techniques, which require an instructional time commitment from educators but will improve students' success when beginning independent research and help them accept ownership of the process.

- **Brainstorming:** Brainstorming occurs after the class has been oriented to the curricular topic through instruction. It requires focusing on what is already known about the topic. As a class, direct students to think about the broad curricular topic and write down every word that comes to mind related to that topic. Some words will be very broad in scope, others will be quite specific, and a few may seem insignificant. Write down all words that students generate. Do not add or suggest any words, but instead guide as needed through a Socratic method of questioning. Next, give students a large, general encyclopedia article related to the topic and a pre-searching handout that provides practice finding citation information as well as skimming and note taking. Walk students through finding and completing bibliographic information. Follow up with a mini-lesson on how to skim a resource for information. Provide a limited amount of time for students to skim the article for more words to add to their brainstorm lists. Once the allotted time is up, come together as a class to add the new words to the list previously created.

- **Categories:** Creating categories allows students to take a large topic and look at it in smaller components. Categorizing takes the brainstormed list of words and organizes them into logical groupings. As a group, the class generates broad categories from the brainstorming list, incorporating most or all of the words . Group words by a common characteristic and give each category a name. As individuals, small groups, or a class, place the brainstormed words into the categories. Allow some words to be applicable to more than one category, and place them in the category that makes the most sense to the students.

- **Questioning:** Ownership of learning begins when students begin to develop their own researchable questions. This may be accomplished with an educator-led classroom discussion, in small groups , or by individuals. Developing a researchable question that is age-appropriate, potentially answerable with today's knowledge, and findable with the resources available is an acquired skill that requires time and patience from educators and students. A researchable question is interesting, meaningful, and challenging, and is likely to have some depth for the student. The first time in a school year that educators work with a particular group of students to develop researchable questions requires much attention and focus.

  Give students an opportunity to review the category names and contents. Students ponder which category or categories are interesting and think about what is already known about the category. Using basic question starters of who, what, when, where, why, and how, students begin to develop questions related to the two categories that are most interesting to them. The questions are ones they don't already have the answers to but would like to search for potential answers. Even though this is the developmental stage of formulating questions, students should think in terms of questions that are sufficiently appealing and will hold their interest long enough to complete the research.

If possible, educators should review the students' questions. This will allow them to gain a better understanding of a student's independent questioning level. Through this review, the educator will also develop a level of expectation for the final, strategic questions.

Figure 14.1 is a sample handout for students to complete as topic choices are narrowed, questions are developing, and advice is gathered from trusted people. The front is worked on in class. The back is worked on at home the same evening, then discussed and completed in class the following day.

Skimming and Scanning for Information

Skimming and scanning for information is a skill introduced now and reviewed and reinforced throughout the inquiry process. Skimming and scanning is important for emergent researchers. It is a strategy for more effectively using time and resources. If a researcher becomes effective at skimming and scanning, research time will be focused on learning from pertinent information instead of struggling to locate information. To teach skimming skills, develop a classroom visual with key skimming and scanning for information terms listed so that students can see, read, and listen. Allow time for a mini-lesson sharing what each applicable term is, with hands-on where or how to find it in a traditional resource. When first introducing this skill, allow each student the tactile experience of manipulating a resource while investigating each skimming and scanning term together. Allocate time in the mini-lesson for students to locate each skimming tool within the resource. Introduce skimming and scanning now, but reinforce it once the strategic questions have been developed and the investigation has begun, which is when an educator would emphasize the importance of the topic and the questions' key words with each skimming and scanning technique.

- **Contents Page:** The table of contents provides chapter numbers and the beginning page number for each chapter. A very useful contents page would also include chapter descriptions, which may help the researcher locate a specific chapter related to a question's key words.

- **Index:** An index is a list of words in alphabetical order with page numbers indicating where those topics can be located within the text. One reason key word development is so important is the use of the index. A student needs to think of the many different words for describing the same thing, looking up the same idea many different ways in the index. In order to do this effectively, an understanding of synonyms is helpful.

- **Your Topic and Question's Key Words:** Once the strategic questions have been finalized, it's important to always keep the topic and question's key words in mind. It is difficult for a student to understand that, when researching, he or she will not read everything, but instead only the sections that relate to the key words.

- **Guidewords:** Guidewords are most commonly used in a resource that is arranged in sections alphabetically. Students can quickly locate information in this type of source by following the alphabetical order of the guidewords to locate a section related to the question's key words.

- **Words in Bold or Italic:** Factual texts often has chunks of information. Students should look at the words in bold or italic that separate information and ask themselves, "Do I think this will help me with my topic, interests, or key words?" If the student cannot answer yes to any part of that question, that section should be skipped. This exercise should be repeated until the student locates a section deemed worth reading. Words in bold or italic can also be key words in the text or words that are difficult and need to be defined either in context and/or in the glossary.

NAME: _____ DATE: _____

Testing Questions for Interest & Meaning

General Topic we have been studying: _____

One category that really interests me: _____

This category interests me because _____
_____
_____

In the time allowed, list all the questions that I don't already have a possible answer to for this category:

One category that really interests me: _____

This category interests me because _____
_____
_____

In the time allowed, list all the questions that I don't all ready have a possible answer to for this category:

> **At home tonight, discuss with your family your two category choices. Listen to your family's suggestions and ideas. Think about it.**

Figure 14.1. Testing questions for interest and meaning.

Testing Questions for Interest & Meaning

| I've shown this to my family. |
| We talked about my ideas and what I am learning. |

My family thinks _____
_____
_____
_____.

In class, I learned about _____
_____
_____
_____.

I am still curious. I want to learn more about _____
_____
_____.

My friends think _____
_____
_____.

My teacher thinks _____
_____
_____.

❖   This is the very best question I can think of for now. I know it is likely to change as I read and listen more, but for now this question is my challenge. It is interesting to me and seems to be meaningful to others. I think there will be a lot more to learn in order to answer this question:

_____
_____
_____.

Figure 14.1. (*Cont.*)

- **Pictures and Their Captions:** Pictures are helpful for visualizing things that we may not be familiar with, we have not experienced ourselves, are difficult to describe with words, or help place the text into historical context. Captions often pack a wealth of information in a few words or sentences.

- **Charts and Graphs:** These are visual summaries of information and ideas. It is sometimes important to see a visual representation of key ideas and data for true understanding and meaning to take place.

- **Maps:** Maps can quickly show a variety of information, depending on their focus: political, topographical, population, historical, community, weather, etc.

- **Statistics:** Students may need to look at numbers, which often help a person understand a topic that may initially seem abstract or unconnected.

- **Summary Boxes:** Locate important facts quickly by looking for information that the eyes are drawn to because they are highlighted in a box.

- **Time Line/Chronology:** Usually found in the front or the back of the book, this is a chronological listing of events important to a specific topic, event, or person.

- **Glossary:** This is an alphabetical listing, usually toward the back of a book, of key words, words above reading level, and words not considered common knowledge for students. A glossary defines difficult or unique key words. With each word is an explanation or definition of the word and how it fits into the context of the reading.

The classroom visual in Figure 14.2 is used to let students see the words as they hear the educator's instructions and practice using skimming and scanning skills in a source. A description of each skill is given in the list above.

Skim & Scan for Information
Things to look for:

Contents page

Index

Your Topic & Question's Keywords

Guidewords

Words in Bold or Italics

Pictures & their Captions

Charts

Graphs

Maps

Statistics

Summary Boxes

Timeline/Chronology

Glossary

Figure 14.2. Skim and scan for information.

Chapter 15

Middle School Inquiry Research Exploration and Strategy

Leslie Preddy

Student inquiry in the research process begins with an orientation to research. Students learn about a theme in the curriculum and how to narrow that theme into a specific interest of inquiry for exploration. Students now move toward exploration and strategy. Research is based on an interest that has developed through curriculum and instruction. Here inquiry develops into research questions that are refined to make sure the answers to the questions are findable and that there are available resources. Remember to take into consideration the ability level of each individual as you guide the students in refining questions.

Journaling and Reflecting

Give students an occasion every day for self-analysis. Giving students this chance to personally reflect on what they are doing, what they are thinking, and what still needs to be done is an invaluable use of instructional time. Toward the end of each research session, provide ample time for detailed responses to age-appropriate and intellectually suitable questions. Allow fifteen minutes to model and go through the process of reflection together the first time or two. Once the students are completing a reflection on their own, only approximately ten minutes is needed. Ask students to respond to questions and instructions similar to the following:

- What did I do today?

- What question was I trying to answer?

- What problem, if any, did I have today?

- Explain something new I learned (for example, successfully learning a new research technique, how to use a specific resource, a new resource never used before, something I didn't know about my topic).

- New questions that I now have about my topic.

- People who helped me today and what they did to help (teacher, student, parent, sibling, library media specialist, etc.).

- How do I feel about today?

- What, specifically, do I need to do next?

Another option is to provide for students a small section for response to what resources were used and problems they had with self, others, resources, and researching to aid educators in monitoring needs. Then, leave a majority of the space for journaling a response to a text-to-self reflection question. For example, when the topic is heroes or biographies, each day one of the following questions or instructions might be selected for the reflective question:

- Pretend you are writing a note to a friend and include a paragraph about this research project. What would you say?

- Explain one or more ways the person you are researching is similar to you and one or more ways he or she is different.

- Today you were interviewed by a peer. You shared what you have learned, facts and interesting details, about your famous person. Describe how you feel about your interview. Explain what you think you did well. What did you forget to talk about and wish you had? On the back of this paper draw a picture of your person doing what you think he or she did best.

Collect the reflections every day and read through them each evening. Place at least one comment on each reflection before passing it back to the student the next school day. By not being hypercritical, allow students the comfort and personal growth experience of knowing that they may include personal feelings, even if those feelings are critical of an educator, the instruction, or the assignment. This is an opportunity for educators to quickly understand what a student's current research ability level is, as well as where weaknesses in instruction exist. Employing this step helps educators know what students need. It may show that a student is doing okay, or it may make clear that a student requires remediation of particular research techniques. It may illustrate growing frustration in a student who needs help. Other students may deserve a pat on the back for being excited about learning something new about the topic or something they learned how to do. It may highlight a student who needs some emotional encouragement and is feeling discouraged. A reflection aids an educator's understanding of the classroom research climate. It quickly establishes a need to either remediate the class with a review of a particular skill or advance to more complicated research strategies and inquiry skills.

Student Expression

An invaluable use of instructional time is allowing students to personally reflect on and self-analyze what has just been done, what needs to be done, their personal thoughts, and their feelings. Ask students to respond to writing prompts; if this is done right, you will be amazed by what an educator can learn about and from students. Include basic expectations in verbal instructions as well as on the reflection form. These might include: "Please respond to each question or statement using complete, descriptive and detailed sentences. We want to understand exactly what you're doing, why you're doing it, how you're doing it, and how you feel about it. Be honest and be sure to relate it to what you did today for your research."

Writing prompts ask the students to relate what was accomplished, what question they were trying to answer, and what needs to be done next. Responses will be as simple as reminding themselves and educators what critical question was being worked on that day, for example "what affect [his inventions] had on the colonists." Accomplishments for the day could relate to progress on research, insight about oneself, or a skill learned, like one student who stated, "I learned better skimming techniques today." Comments can be honest and lighthearted, "[I need to] keep having fun with this project!" or painful self-revelations, " . . . not talk so much." Students may use this opportunity to ask questions of educators that they are unable to ask in person: "I want to start answering my other questions, but I need to better answer this first [one] more completely. What do you think?"

Research is often a painful journey full of struggles and dead ends. Students need to acknowledge problems faced and the people who helped. They need to allow educators, through correspondence, an opportunity to help, intervene, reteach a skill, or commiserate. Sometimes there are no challenges—"Nobody helped me because it was so easy to find stuff"—but at other times there could be a source-specific problem: "The only problem I had was that one of the books was confusing," or "I had problems finding specific information because there wasn't an index in my book." The issue could be as personal as "trying to concentrate . . . ," or "I really didn't learn much because I kept reading the same thing over." Sometimes a student is able to express how he or she was able to resolve a day's challenge through finding help successfully from the peer group: "Maggie cheered me on + helped me keep going when times got rough!" or "Jeri helped me find the copywrite [sic] date." The student may recognize that an educator aided in some way: "Mrs. Moore helped me focus" or "Mrs. Preddy helped me on my strategy and finding the right book." At other times the student's response may be seen as a cry for help, a cry that would never have been expressed verbally: "I had no help from nobody" or "I feel I need to change sources since I was not finding much."

The most personal aspect is asking students to express how they feel and why. This may sound invasive, but it is often where an educator is able to recognize the danger signs of a student in trouble. These signs may not have been realized through educator observations or verbal communication and instead are written as "aargh! This is so frustrating—I can't find anything—help me!" At other times a student might express enthusiasm, which an educator would want to encourage: "This is getting really interesting!," "I feel better than yesterday," " . . . relieved that I finished one source," or "I think I worked a little better [but] I need to research more." An educator might have to burst a novice's bubble after reading, "I am so happy! I found answers to my questions," by reminding the student that he or she may be feeling a sense of accomplishment too soon and needs to continue searching for more details and answers.

Researching means continually learning. Learning how to use a specific resource. Learning how to use a new resource. Learning something not previously known about the topic. For example, relating specifically to the topic is, "I learned that some of the medicines they used were poisonous and actually killed some patients!" On a personal level a student responded with, "I learn that less conversation gets more work done." Or a student might use this as an opportunity to vent some frustrations in a safe zone, which may allow that student to get feelings out so that he or she may move forward. Reflections give the educator an opportunity to reassure the student of the true nature of the situation when he or she comments, "I feel that the teacher is very mean and doesn't like me."

It's a beautiful sight when a student has an epiphany and enthusiastically realizes that he or she has, through the process of research, touched on new questions to ask. The questions developed along the journey are often better, more challenging, more intellectually stimulating to research, and more intriguing to the student. Without journaling, a student may not recognize the benefit of these newly evolving questions. One student moved from her initial critical questions related to the fine arts in American history to this thought-provoking question: "Why was satire so big back then?" A student researching President Abraham Lincoln moved toward this question: "What did Lincoln think about slavery before his presidency, and did his opinion change during the war?" Another student, studying the music of 150 years ago, grew to realize that what the words meant to her today were different, which caused her to move toward "What did the lyrics [to the songs] mean then?" A study of slavery brought forth this emotional question: "How did slaves cope with all the beatings they received?"

Educator–Student Communication

Providing the structure and guided opportunity for students to record and communicate thoughts is invaluable. It increases the opportunity for conversations between students who need help and educators who can provide assistance. Written reflections often help students identify and organize thoughts. Written communication also helps educators manage time for constructive feedback. Daily journaling provides an atmosphere of personalized, one-on-one teaching that normally cannot be obtained in the multiple class environment of secondary education.

The Value

Journaling and reflecting builds students' self-confidence for successfully managing today's information needs. It encourages a sense of self-ownership. It provides a clear assessment tool for knowing where students are and what needs to be reinforced. Journaling and reflecting also builds a sense of ownership, which encourages students to try things never before done.

Initial indications from data collected in 2003–2004 on 140 Perry Meridian Middle School eighth-grade students are that incorporating journaling "communication" influences student commitment. Separating students into three major groupings, in which feedback from educators was limited, encouraged, or nonexistent, the following indicators were found:

- Regular opportunities for journaling provide an effective channel for students to reflect and communicate.

- Journaling provides a venue for individualized attention and an occasion to assess students' individual growth.

- Journaling leads to focus on critical problems and better management of communication between students and teachers.

Student Assessment and Grades

Reflecting and journaling is used to assess performance. As part of evaluating student effectiveness throughout the process and giving a value to the process that parents and students can understand, students complete reflections on the days specified. Each reflection is given effort points. Students receive points for each reflection that follows the instructional guidelines, uses complete and detailed sentences, answers or responds with honest relevance to that day's experiences, and uses school-appropriate language. Students develop a sense of comfort that reflections are graded only on effort. They are willing to write honestly. Figure 15.1 outlines educator guidelines for this process.

Collect student reflections immediately upon completion and read through them each evening, placing at least one comment on each student's paper before passing it back to the student the next school day. Allow students the comfort and personal growth experience of knowing that they may write any personal thoughts or feelings in the journal or reflection, even if those feelings are critical of an educator, the instruction, or the assignment. Employing this step will help educators know whether a student is doing okay, requires remedial instruction concerning particular research techniques, is growing frustrated and needs help, deserves a pat on the back for being excited about information or a skill newly learned , or needs some emotional encouragement.

Exploration

A key role in Information Inquiry is allowing each student to take a leadership role and ownership of what will be learned and researched. Students develop a personalized interest in the topic through question development. National education and state subject areas have standards written with the expectation, either clearly stated or implied, that students will develop the ability to create age-appropriate, researchable questions. This is a learned task that may be difficult to teach students whose research skills have been cultivated in a traditional environment. Traditional research, in which an assignment is handed to students with a specific topic to explore, details exactly what must be found and how findings should be reported. This scenario causes learning to occur in an artificial environment, a vacuum, that does not allow students to develop the ability to analyze, internalize, develop, and interpret information critically, efficiently, creatively, or effectively.

Exploration happens when a curricular topic is discovered as students cultivate a subject for inquiry. Fostering interest begins with learning how to develop a topic into questions. Initially this will require a lot of attention and class time devoted to the basics, but as the school year progresses, each subsequent inquiry will require less time for exploring and developing questions as students' questioning abilities advance. Work as a team to help students come to terms with a specific topic and determine what questions are of interest as well as researchable with the resources and information available.

Developing Critical Question

In the final stage of exploring, students combine and narrows down preliminary questions to those that intrigue them the most. Educators review these refined questions before the next inquiry session. Help students to understand the difference between a "thin" question, comparable to a fast food kid's meal cheeseburger, where the meat can barely be seen between the bun, and a "thick" one, a quarter-pound- of-meat-in-the-sandwich ques-

Journaling and Reflecting Dos & Don'ts

Create a secure environment. Act as a sounding board for the student who is free to voice ideas and opinions.

Do allow for ample time for students to reflect and respond.

Do allow students to be honest without recrimination or punishment.

Do respect and maintain student privacy at all times. Allow students to feel secure or they won't share.

Do place personalized comments on each student's paper. React to student's expressed needs, frustrations and joys.

Do provide immediate feedback. Return the reflection the next day at the beginning of research time.

Do make each reflection worth effort points-rewarding students for participating.

Don't be overly critical or snide in comments.

Don't allow students to "skip" the reflecting process.

Figure 15.1. Journaling and reflecting dos and dont's.

From *The Blue Book on Information Age Inquiry, Instruction and Literacy* by Daniel Callison and Leslie Preddy. Westport, CT: Libraries Unlimited. Copyright © 2006 by Daniel Callison and Leslie Preddy.

tion where the meat is just as thick as the bun. Share question stems with students to help them generate strategic questions (see Figure 15.2).

Devote an evening to reviewing all student questions. Write recommendations for changes and revisions, which will afford students nearly immediate feedback. Students use these helpful hints for success to develop a final revision of the selected, strategic questions as they move toward the strategy phase of research.

Strategy

Strategy gives students an opportunity to become more aware of the information world as they learn about a variety of resources, traditional and nontraditional, and select the most appropriate resources for answering each specific question of inquiry. To develop a strategy, students take the questions created and refined in the exploration phase, remove the least appealing questions, and refine what is left into the final, critical, strategic questions (see Figures 15.3 and 15.4). This encourages a student to engage in some personal thought and internalize research actions.

Finalizing Critical Question and Key Words

Intentionally allow students the opportunity to finalize and strategize research questions. Help students formulate key words related to each question that will be used to locate information in a resource and when skimming and scanning for information in that resource. Designing key words to questions is a skill that takes practice and training to develop. Key word development and use of key words is critical to using research time most effectively when using guidewords, an index, or a table of contents and when scanning text for topic value and meaning.

Selecting Sources

This is also an excellent opportunity to introduce or review the variety of formats of information and resources. Take the time to show students how to look at each individual question and make an educated guess as to which resource

types might be best to use initially as an answer to the question is sought. Require students to internalize decisions by explaining why they think those specific resource types might be best for answering that specific question. Keep in mind that other resources may be used, but this gives students a place to begin. (See Figure 15.5.)

Keeping Quiet: The Product

During the inquiry exploration and strategy, educators and students instinctively feel the need to discuss the outcome, or what final products will be required at the conclusion of the research. Save this discussion of what the final product will be, the expectations related to the final product, and the product rubric for when the actual research time has nearly concluded, which is when the students will actually begin working on designing and creating a product. Be prepared to respond to students who may be frustrated the first time you withhold the details of the concluding product. Holding back the details about the final product allows students to focus on attempting a thorough answer of the strategic questions to their personal satisfaction. This is important because students often try to find only what information they feel is necessary to complete the final product. This also shows that educators are serious about the value of the process rather than allowing the focus to be the product. Guide students back through the recursive process to gather specific types or forms of information needed, depending on the format of the final product chosen. They may need to find images, primary documents, audio clips, or other specifics.

Gathering information is separate from analyzing it. During exploration and strategy, reinforce with students the concept that finding the answers to the research questions should be the focus. Each student needs the opportunity to learn that research requires hard work, focus, and dedication. Allowing students to concentrate on and worry about the end product before the research has even begun is detrimental to developing information literacy and instilling a lifelong desire for and pleasure in learning for the sake of learning.

Research Question Help

- Who
- What
- When
- Where
- Why
- How

- Defend...
- Judge...
- Justify...
- In what ways...
- Imagine...
- Suppose...
- Predict...
- If..., then...
- Can I create...
- How might...
- How do...   OR   How does...   OR   How did...
- What procedures...   OR   What actions...
- What problems...
- What happens when...   OR   What happened when...
- What was the role of...in...   OR What was the role of...in...
- What is the difference between...
      OR   What was the difference between...
- What causes/caused...   OR   What caused...
- What are the results of...   OR   What were the results of...
- How did...decide to...   OR   Why did...decide to...
- What is the relationship between...and...
      OR   What was the relationship between...and...
- What are the competing sides...
      OR   What were the competing sides...
- How does...change...   OR   How did...change...
- What are some possible consequences...
- What are the effects of...   OR   What were the effects of...

References:
- Jansen, Barbara A. The Big6 Approach to Information and Technology Skills Instruction. Metropolitan School District of Perry Township Workshop. June 8, 2004.
- Rankin, Virginia. The Thoughtful Researcher: Teaching the Research Process to Middle School Students. Englewood, CO: Libraries Unlimited, 1999. Page 33.

Figure 15.2. Research question help.

NAME: _____ TOPIC: _____

STRATEGY

1.   Revise your questions based on the suggestions given to you by the teacher or media specialist.
2.   Place those improved, critical, strategic questions here.
3.   Brainstorm keywords related to your question that will help you find answers to your Inquiry questions.

A **question** I want to answer:

Keywords related to that question:

Source or sources that I think would be best for finding the answer and why I think that source would be best

---

A **question** I want to answer:

Keywords related to that question:

Source or sources that I think would be best for finding the answer and why I think that source would be best

---

A **question** I want to answer:

Keywords related to that question:

Source or sources that I think would be best for finding the answer and why I think that source would be best

---

Figure 15.3. Three-question strategy form.

TOPIC: _Underground Railroad_

Big6™
2. Information Seeking Strategies
STRATEGY

1.   Revise your questions based on the suggestions given to you by the teacher or media specialist.
2.   Place those improved, researchable questions here.
3.   Brainstorm keywords related to your question that will help you find answers to your Inquiry questions.

A **question** I want to answer:
   What was the role of the conductor and why were they disliked by the south? How did conductors free imprisoned slaves and who else helped?

Keywords related to that question:
   conductor, slaves, South, Underground Railroad, servants, African Americans, blacks, abolitionists

Source or sources that I think would be best for finding the answer (you can refer to "Information: Tools of the Trade" bookmark to help you brainstorm) and **why** I think that source would be best
   Specialized Encyclopedia because this question would be too specific to research other places.

A **question** I want to answer:
   What kind of goals had the Underground Railroad set at the beginning of their creation? How was the program started? Who were the leaders of the group and what were they like in the ways of slavery and courage? How did runaways know the route to take? Who was in charge of that?

Keywords related to that question:
   leaders, conductors, abolitionists, Underground Railroad, runaways, routes, slavery

Source or sources that I think would be best for finding the answer (you can refer to "Information: Tools of the Trade" bookmark to help you brainstorm) and **why** I think that source would be best
   Book because the question sets more on the Underground Railroad and it would be better to use a book.

A **question** I want to answer:
   As abolitionists what else was done in order to share their anti-slavery desires? What were abolitionists activities in the north, and even the south? (newspapers, speeches, etc.)

Keywords related to that question:
   Newspapers, speeches, abolitionists, anti-slavery

Source or sources that I think would be best for finding the answer (you can refer to "Information: Tools of the Trade" bookmark to help you brainstorm) and **why** I think that source would be best
   INSPIRE and specialized encyclopedias fit better with more specific information for this question.

A **question** I want to answer:
   What was the reaction of abolitionists and conductors when the Emancipation Proclamation was passed? What was the reactions of the southern slaveholders? How did each side celebrate?

Keywords related to that question:
   Emancipation Proclamation, conductors, abolitionists, Abe Lincoln

Source or sources that I think would be best for finding the answer (you can refer to "Information: Tools of the Trade" bookmark to help you brainstorm) and **why** I think that source would be best
   INSPIRE and a book would be the best because the question covers information could be found Easier In these items.

Figure 15.4. Information-seeking strategy.

From _The Blue Book on Information Age Inquiry, Instruction and Literacy_ by Daniel Callison and Leslie Preddy. Westport, CT: Libraries Unlimited. Copyright © 2006 by Daniel Callison and Leslie Preddy.

Creative Sources

Audio
CD-Rom
E-mail
Internet
Investigation
Letter
Magazine
Museum Curator or
Museum Exhibit

Newspaper
Observation
Online Database
Organizations
Person - Interview
Personal Account
Photograph/Illustration
Primary Source
Public Library
Questionnaire
Survey
Video

Books:
Biography
Non-Fiction
Specialized
Encyclopedia
Reference

Figure 15.5. Creative sources.

From *The Blue Book on Information Age Inquiry, Instruction and Literacy* by Daniel Callison and Leslie Preddy. Westport, CT: Libraries Unlimited. Copyright © 2006 by Daniel Callison and Leslie Preddy.

Chapter 16

Middle School Inquiry Research Investigation

Leslie Preddy

Investigation happens when a student is authentically in engaged using investigative research methods and attempts to find answers to inquiry's strategic questions. Think of the information inquiry task as an investigation, or systematic examination, not a traditional school research assignment. During the investigation a student should be expected to think about what is being done and learned as a variety of sources are used to try to find answers to strategy questions. Figure 16.1 shows one definition of the term "investigate."

Investigate: **To follow up step by step by patient inquiry or observation; to trace or track mentally; to search into; to inquire and examine into with care and accuracy; to find out by careful inquisition.** *Webster's Revised Unabridged Dictionary*

Figure 16.1. Definition of "investigate."

Educators and students have to look beyond the confines of a traditional research paper. Students will be expected to understand what primary sources and secondary sources are, and when it's best to use each. Students will need to receive guidance on how to interpret primary sources and how a primary source can be significant for further understanding. Train students in how to conduct an interview, survey, or questionnaire. Students should build an awareness of community resources: people, places, and things. Every research session should conclude with an opportunity for reflection.

The library media specialist and classroom teacher should observe and note students with certain abilities and have those students share their expertise with students who need help in a particular area.

Managing Resources: Effective Use of Information, Research Notes

Information inquiry means dynamically thinking about and being actively engaged in the quest for knowledge. This requires students to not only relate citation information and take notes, but also think about the usefulness of the source. As educators, we can no longer assume that students are thinking *past* gathering information; we must require them to think *beyond*. Students will use source notes to store citation information, notes, data, drawings, interpretations, analyses, hypotheses, thoughts, ideas, and concerns. The process of using a source should conclude with the student summarizing the source, what was most useful about the source, and what was most difficult about using the source. Share with students the skills necessary: reading for understanding, taking effective research notes, and evaluating whether a source is useful. These are key skills that need to be imbedded so that students can become independent learners. Allow students to reflect immediately upon the strengths and weaknesses of each source.

Figure 16.2 is a sample of a source note completed by a student working on answering one of his five strategic questions: "How did the advancements of weapons change the outcome of the war for the Union?" This source helped him partially answer two of his questions.

Based on findings and personal insights, students will meet with either the library media specialist or classroom teacher and discuss the need to adjust questions or develop new ones for further inquiry or reanalysis. As Virginia Rankin wrote in *The Thoughtful Researcher*, "Sometimes an answer itself becomes the topic for consideration."

As students use resources, build skills into the research day with mini-lessons at the beginning of the research time. For example, cover how to evaluate a source for usefulness (see Figure 16.3) and how to take notes for researching (see Figure 16.4), which may look very different compared to taking notes for other purposes.

Primary Sources

A primary source is a firsthand or direct source. Dr. Daniel Callison (2005) states that "a primary source is an 'eye-witness' to the event and one who can make intelligent inferences from what her or she observes and gains from first-hand interviews." It may be a significant or historical document without interpretation or explanation; a person to interview who was actually a participant or observer; that participant's or observer's writings or statements about the event; a person's journal, diary, letter, or memoir; an historic home, site, or artifact; or media: a film, video, audio, or photograph taken at the time or place documenting what happened. Or it may be a book, magazine, or newspaper article written and published at a particular time in history about an event occurring at that time, or correspondence or an interview with somebody who was present for the event. Primary sources can be accessed through an agency, an archive, a book,

Web/videoconferencing, e-mail, an exhibit, a government entity, an historic site, a library, a monument, a museum, an organization, a primary source Web site, a questionnaire, a report, a speech, or a survey.

When looking at a primary document, the student needs to think about the beliefs, opinions, political climate, and scientific and medical knowledge of that time and place. There are key issues to keep in mind when reviewing and evaluating a primary source (see Figure 16.5), although not every question is appropriate for every primary source.

Interview

Review interviewing etiquette and procedures before a student conducts an interview. Share interview protocol with students before the interview process begins (see Figure 16.6). Either a parent or an educator should assist a student in locating an appropriate interviewee and scheduling the interview. Approve all interviewees and interview questions before the interview takes place. The interview can be handled via Web or videoconference, letter, e-mail, fax, or telephone.

- **Whom should a student interview?** Choose somebody who is well-respected, educated, and informed about the topic. When contacting the person to see if he or she is willing to participate in an interview, identify the project, the school, and the grade level. Explain what the assignment is, why the experts input is needed, and what will be done with the information.

- **What should a student ask?** Students should ask only questions to which they have been unable to find answers. The questions should not be answerable with a simple yes or no and should never be personal or embarrassing for the interviewee. An educator should review questions for appropriateness and authenticity before the interview.

Source # 12

Source Notes
Book or Pamphlet

Author (last name, first name) __Window, Martin__

    Other Authors (in any) _____

Title of Book __The Civil War Rifleman__

City of Publication: __New York__

Publisher __Franklin Watts Limited__   Copyright Date: __1985__

Where did I find this source? IMC

If it's from the school media center, what is the call number? 973.7 Win

QUESTION: How did the advancements of weapons change the outcome of the war?
If this source is able to answer more than one question, use a separate source note for each question.

NOTES (if needed, use back of this paper):

Civil War 1st to use crude machine guns

Machine guns weren't very effective

Union Agar gun, "the coffee mill" – made from the brass funnel into which stell tubes loaded with powder, ball + percussion caps were fed

SUMMARY—in your own words (if needed, use back of this paper):
Union Agar was the best type of machine guns. Civil War was the first to use crude machine guns.

To be completed after done using source
What I found most useful about this source:
    The details of the book.

What I found difficult about using this source:
    The font was difficult to read

Figure 16.2. Sample source notes: book or pamphlet.

Is This Source Useful?

Does this resource relate to my topic and question? Does it have the information I need?

Is it important for the information to be up-to-date? If so, is the information current enough to be accurate and useful?

Can I read this information? Am I able to understand what I read?

Am I able to locate information in this source?

Is the author stating fact or opinion?

Does the author know what he/she is talking about? Has the author included a list of references?

Source:
Langhorne, Mary Jo, ed. Developing an Information Literacy Program K-12. New York: Neal-Schuman, 1998. Page 186
Rankin, Virginia. The Thoughtful Researcher: Teaching the Research Process to Middle School Students. Englewood, CO: Libraries Unlimited, 1999. Page 89

Figure 16.3. Is this source useful?

From *The Blue Book on Information Age Inquiry, Instruction and Literacy* by Daniel Callison and Leslie Preddy. Westport, CT: Libraries Unlimited. Copyright © 2006 by Daniel Callison and Leslie Preddy.

TAKING NOTES

1. Put pencil or pen down!
2. <u>Review</u> your questions & keywords.
3. <u>Find</u> a good section to read related to your questions & keywords.
4. <u>Read</u>
5. Think about what you read.
6. Now, pick up your pen or pencil & write what you think.
7. <u>Write</u> or <u>Draw</u> only important
   - Facts
   - Dates
   - Keywords
   - Your own thoughts, ideas, opinions about what you read
8. Do NOT use sentences!

> If you need to quote or copy something exactly, put it inside quotation marks. Write the page number next to it.

If all else fails:
Paraphrase
Summarize
(write the page number beside it)

Figure 16.4. Taking notes.

PRIMARY SOURCES
Evaluating

When looking at a primary document, you need to think about the beliefs, opinions, political climate, and scientific and medical status of that time and place.

Key issues to keep in mind when reviewing and evaluating a historical primary source. (Not every question is appropriate for every primary source):

1. What type/kind of primary source is it? (Photograph, Letter, Speech, etc.)

2. Who wrote, designed, built, created, or published it? What was their name(s), if you know? How were they significant?

3. Who were the key participants?

4. Who was the intended audience?

5. Who lived in, visited, read, or heard it?

6. What was its intended use? How was it used?

7. Why did they use it? What was their motive?

8. When did they use it?

9. Where was it written/designed/created?

10. What was going on locally at the time?

11. What was going on around the world at the time?

12. What impact did it have locally? What impact did it have globally?

10. How does it impact us today?

11. What are the facts about it that are important to your Inquiry Research?

Figure 16.5. Primary source evaluation.

INTERVIEW
Helpful Hints

Who do I ask?

1. Choose somebody that is informed about your topic: somebody who knows a lot about your topic.
2. Contact the person to see if they are willing to participate in an interview. You can contact him/her by phone, fax, letter, or e-mail.
   a. Identify who you are, your school, and your grade level.
   b. Explain what your assignment is, why you need their input, and what you will do with the information.
   c. Tell them how you would like to conduct the interview (in person, on the phone, through web conferencing, email, fax, etc.)
   d. If you want to videotape or audiotape the interview, ask permission in advance.
3. Agree upon a date, time, and place for the interview.

What do I ask?

1. Brainstorm questions related to your topic.
2. Which questions have you not been able to find the answer in your research?
3. Find out what resources he/she used to find information and answers.
4. Do not ask questions that can be answered with one word or a simple Yes or No.
5. Do not ask personal or embarrassing questions.
6. Ask an adult to review your questions to appropriateness and authenticity before your interview.

How do I do it?

1. Prepare your questions in advance.
2. Be on time, dress nicely, introduce yourself, and shake hands.
3. Listen carefully, don't interrupt, and take notes that include key ideas and are legible.
4. When you need to, repeat what you hear for clarification to confirm that you did understand correctly. If you need to, ask for something to be repeated.
5. Write down the words EXACTLY if you want to use it as a quote.
6. Ask for names or words you don't know to be spelled or explained.
7. Be respectful and attentive (maintain eye contact whenever possible).
8. After the interview, shake hands and thank the person for their time.

Final Thoughts

1. Review your notes from the interview and transcribe them as soon as possible.
2. Send a thank you letter detailing your appreciation and how much the interview helped you understand your topic better.

Figure 16.6. Interview helpful hints.

From *The Blue Book on Information Age Inquiry, Instruction and Literacy* by Daniel Callison and Leslie Preddy. Westport, CT: Libraries Unlimited. Copyright © 2006 by Daniel Callison and Leslie Preddy.

- **How should the interview be conducted?** All questions should be prepared in advance. The student should listen carefully to the answers given, without interrupting, and take notes that are legible and include the key ideas. Whenever necessary, the student should repeat what was said for clarification to confirm that information was not misunderstood. Students should write down the words exactly if they will be used as a quote, and should ask for names or words not known to be spelled or explained.

Immediately following the interview, the student should review all notes from the interview and transcribe them. Any interview should conclude with a thank you letter from the student detailing appreciation and explaining how much the interview helped with a better understanding of the topic.

Gathering Data with Questionnaires or Surveys

Information inquiry has close ties to scientific inquiry, including the belief that, whenever appropriate, students should gather their own data. An inquiry about the eating habits of students could include an interview with the cafeteria manager; interviews with parents of students about their dinner habits; and the development, implementation, and interpretation of data collected through a student-created survey concerning student lunch and snack content and habits. A student researching Abraham Lincoln and his administration might do "man on the street" interviews from a popular spot in town, questioning adults to gather information about what is common knowledge and what are common misconceptions. A student investigating the value of math in society might develop a survey to question adults in a variety of jobs throughout the community to evaluate what types of math are commonly used, in which jobs, and how much.

Community Resources

Educators develop and annually update a packet of resources in the community specifically created to help parents and students. The packet includes community resources, organizations, sites, museums, and Internet resources. The handout of "Resources in the Community" is an annotated list of suggested specific and general resources in the community appropriate to the topic. Include as many specifics as appropriate: address, phone, available hours, requirements and cost for admission and use, contact name, Internet address, e-mail address, etc. Before distributing the packet to parents and students, regularly update and confirm the information for each resource, as well as their willingness to work with your students. Include any necessary updates to the hours of operation, fees, and other operational details. Annotate the organization's procedures, policies, and resources available to the public that relate to the general curricular topic upon which the student's inquiries are based .

The community resource packet (see Figure 16.7) created for parents and students should be updated annually to confirm contact name, street address, phone, email, Internet address and make corrections. Update as necessary the hours of operation, fees, and other operational details. Include an annotation of related procedures, policies, and resources available to the public.

Product Options: Sharing Knowledge

Toward the conclusion of the investigation students will begin to organize their thoughts and information. As the research is drawing to a close, share with students the long-kept secret: what the final product options are for sharing and presenting the inquiry research experience and recently developed expertise.

Collaboratively, educators should guide students through the process of selecting the appropriate product to conclude the inquiry journey. Be creative about final product options to accommodate a variety of learning styles and options for student choice. Educators should want the students to share in a way that provides an opportunity for each individual student to be successful, so allow for some student choice in how to share the knowledge and research experience. Help students work out how to disseminate information (see Figure 16.8).

COMMUNITY RESOURCES: SAMPLE ENTRY
Indiana State Archives

Indiana State Archives
(near Arlington & Shadeland Ave)
6440 East 30th
Indianapolis, IN 46219
phone 591-5220
http://www.state.in.us/icpr/webfile/archives/homepage.html

Hours:
Monday-Friday 8:00-4:30

Extensive collection related to Indiana Civil War Regiments and individual soldiers. Indiana State Archives contains Civil War mustering records, including physical descriptions, when mustered in, when left, and why. It also holds regimental correspondence, clothing books, hospital records, rosters, draft enrollments, ordinance records, etc. Some of the standard reference tools they have can give you information as specific as the average height of a soldier, etc.

Sign in at the registration desk and ask for help finding the information you need. Make sure you arrive with a specific project in mind and ideas about what information you need.

Figure 16.7. Community resources sample entry.

DISSEMINATION

Topic: _____ Underground Railroad _____

1. Who is my audience? Who will I be sharing my product with?
   parent
   (teacher)
   community
   peers
   (younger students)
   older students
   other: _____

2. Thinking about my topic, the questions I had, what I've learned, and who my audience will be, what is the best way to share my knowledge? What should my product be?
   a. written

   In order to share my product in written format, I would use a display board.

   b. verbal

   Verbally, I would introduce everyone to the Underground Railroad and use a question and answer session to help them understand.

   c. visual

   As a visual aid, I could create a hide-away spot such as one at a station and use a self-created product.

3. Why do I think this will be the best way for **me** to share my expertise?
   I think these will be the best way for me to share my expertise because it would really show what I have learned. These choices could give everyone a really good picture of how the railroad worked and who worked on it. I think these would be the best choices because they could b e so detailed in many ways.

Figure 16.8. Sample dissemination form.

From *The Blue Book on Information Age Inquiry, Instruction and Literacy* by Daniel Callison and Leslie Preddy. Westport, CT: Libraries Unlimited. Copyright © 2006 by Daniel Callison and Leslie Preddy.

Storyboards and Graphic Organizers

As students select a final product format, each student will complete a storyboard for an activity, graphic, static display, or writing to help with organization. A storyboard is something that students can easily relate to when put into the perspective of how filmmakers use a storyboard to lay out the sequence of events for a film or cartoon. The storyboard provides the necessary structure a student requires when getting the research in order. A storyboard will work as a blueprint and allow a student to draft a general idea for how to present inquiry findings before actually beginning the final product. The storyboard should be completed in preparation for the peer conference, while there is still research time available. Completing and sharing the storyboard may help a student discover gaps in the information that need further investigation. Figure 16.9 is a sample activity storyboard used by sixth-grade science students to outline the events and plot for a videotaped infomercial.

Peer Conference

While thinking about themselves, students also need to think about and learn from others. They need to discover what others are learning and help fellow students through formal or informal conferencing. Students are capable of sharing what has been learned and giving advice about what needs to be done. A peer conference gives students an opportunity to verbalize their research and product in a nonthreatening setting. This process is done while there is still research time available and before the final product is created. Through sharing with a peer the strategy, source notes, and storyboard, a student synthesizes the inquiry through an informal presentation and discussion, relating what has been learned and what has been concluded throughout the investigation. Peers will interact to help the student inquirer understand what needs more clarification as well as what may be confusing to an outsider. Educators give the necessary guidance for productively and positively evaluating a peer during the conference. Students need to understand how to be respectful of a peer's feelings, ideas, and research. Teach students how to accept constructive criticism and listen to advice in a positive and accepting manner. While the peer being evaluated is summarizing

strategy, research, and storyboard, the reviewer should be thinking about the following:

1. Does your peer seem to care about and be interested in the topic? How did your peer make you feel about the topic?

2. Did your peer support the information with research? Were there supporting facts and examples?

3. What else could your peer do to help others better understand the topic? Give suggestions for improving facts and information.

4. What was organized well? What was confusing?

5. On the storyboard, what was most effective? What was least effective?

Just as a student would take notes during an interview or on a source, the student should take notes on what the peer suggests is good and bad about the research and storyboard. Upon completion of the peer conference, each student should decide what advice is worth taking: what changes the student will make and what needs further research based on the peer's advice. Figures 16.10 and 16.11 are examples of peer evaluation and peer conference forms.

Don't Lose Them!

Investigation happens when a student is most likely to become lost or lose focus. Educators should work together to reduce that risk. Incorporate before- or after-school help sessions. Conference and consult regularly with students needing guidance. Remain vigilant and facilitate impromptu help sessions and tutoring for those in need. Regularly check students' notes, research journals, and daily reflections and take action as necessary for individuals, groups, or classes who are off track.

Be observant of research challenges. Note students with inquiry questions that are difficult to answer or difficult to answer with the resources available. Information challenges should be taken into account when evaluating the final product and research process. Students who struggle to find the answers eluding them should not be penalized, but rather rewarded and encouraged for their tenacity; whether that fight concludes with answers or partial answers or no answers, it is always an experience to share.

Name: _____ Date: _____

STORYBOARD
Activity/Graphic/Visual Storyboard

When to Use: Audio, Comic Strip, Demonstration, Distance Learning, Photographs, Timeline, Tour, Video, etc.

1. Your task is to develop a storyboard to help you organize your thoughts just like you would if you were producer developing a music video, television program, or movie.
2. Lay your story out with a picture in a box of what will be happening for each major event.
3. Place a label below each picture, between 1-3 words, to represent the action that will be occurring.
4. Only use as many boxes as you need. If you need more boxes, add sheets of paper.
5. If you don't like the sequence that you've placed things, rearrange the boxes until you like the order.
6. Finally, your last event should always summarize the events in some way that brings closure for your audience.

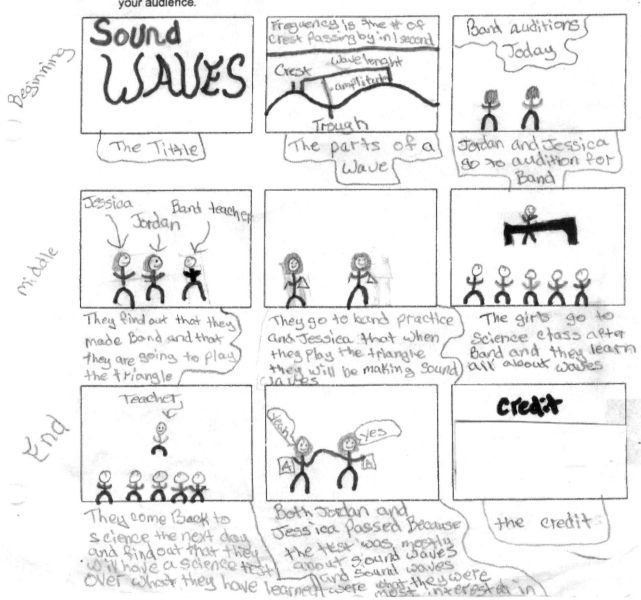

Figure 16.9. Storyboard: activity, graphic, visual.

From *The Blue Book on Information Age Inquiry, Instruction and Literacy* by Daniel Callison and Leslie Preddy. Westport, CT: Libraries Unlimited. Copyright © 2006 by Daniel Callison and Leslie Preddy.

My NAME: _____ Date: _____

Person I'm Evaluating: _____
His/Her topic: _____

Peer Evaluation Part 1

1. I will be respectful of my peer's feelings.
2. I will offer suggestions that are useful and important.
3. I will thank my peer for listening to my advice.
4. I will not work on this form until after my peer is finished presenting the topic.

Explain in one sentence what his/her topic was about:

How did he/she make me feel about the topic?

What did he/she teach me that I didn't know before?

Suggestions for improving facts and information:

Suggestions for helping the audience understand the topic and presentation better:
"I was confused when…

Most effective was:

Least effective was:

Adequate coverage of topic:	needs improvement	satisfactory	excellent
Includes supporting facts & examples:	needs improvement	satisfactory	excellent
Supported information with research:	needs improvement	satisfactory	excellent
Does he/she seem to care about topic:	needs improvement	satisfactory	excellent
Organization:	needs improvement	satisfactory	excellent
- If a thesis was required, answer the following:			
The thesis is clear:	needs improvement	satisfactory	excellent

Figure 16.10. Peer evaluation.

From *The Blue Book on Information Age Inquiry, Instruction and Literacy* by Daniel Callison and Leslie Preddy. Westport, CT: Libraries Unlimited. Copyright © 2006 by Daniel Callison and Leslie Preddy.

My NAME: _____ Date: _____

Person Helping Me: _____

Peer Conference

1. I will listen respectfully to my peer's suggestions.
2. We will meet quietly and concentrate on me.
3. I will remain positive, because my peer is trying to help me.
4. I will thank my peer for his/her help.

NOTES (what my peer said about my questions, research, and storyboard):

This is good—I did this very well: _____

_____

No matter what, I've got to fix this: _____

_____

I need to explain better or find more information on: _____

_____

I need to fix this on my storyboard before I make my final product: _____

_____

To be Completed after Meeting with Peer

CHANGES TO MY STORYBOARD I PLAN TO MAKE BASED ON MY PEER'S ADVICE:

INFORMATION I NEED TO WORK ON BASED ON MY PEER'S ADVICE:

Figure 16.11. Peer conference.

From *The Blue Book on Information Age Inquiry, Instruction and Literacy* by Daniel Callison and Leslie Preddy. Westport, CT: Libraries Unlimited. Copyright © 2006 by Daniel Callison and Leslie Preddy.

Chapter 17

Middle School Inquiry Research: Conclusion and Reflection

Leslie Preddy

Students and educators work hard throughout the inquiry process, then the time arrives to conclude the journey. Research wraps up with the logical organization of information. From that comes the development of a final product and presentation of knowledge and experiences to fellow students, parents, and possibly even community members. The conclusion of the research, product development, and presentation is followed by further reflection: reflection of peers, self-reflection, reflection of educators, and reflection on the process. Using the inquiry research process means not only doing, but always thinking, analyzing, and internalizing the who, what, when, where, why, and how in order to conclude with a sense of accomplishment.

Organization and Dissemination

For a memorable conclusion, find a way to incorporate parents and the community in the final sharing of the product and process (see Figure 17.1).

As students move toward finalizing inquiry research, they will begin to organize source notes to develop a storyboard. Organizing notes is an acquired skill that many students find difficult to master. A storyboard, a form of graphic organization, assists with organization as students design a final product layout.

No matter what the students' age, they need ongoing and repeated assistance becoming and staying organized. With a research journal in hand, which includes all source notes, a large part of the organizational aspect of this task has been accomplished. However, students must learn to prioritize and manage the material and notes collected. This is a critical step to beginning construction of the final product.

In order to develop a meaningful final product that is clearly based on the student-developed strategic questions, outline a few simple steps for students to follow:

1. Each student should choose a large space to spread out his or her work. This aids in the ability to organize and focus. The space may be a table, the floor, workspace at the public or school library, a student's bed, or the kitchen table. Whatever type and wherever the location, space that makes the student most comfortable is as important as the need for it to be free of distraction. Workspace should be large enough to be able to spread out the contents of the research journal.

2. A student's strategy clearly states the initial, critical research questions and key words. The completed strategy should be referred to in order to organize source notes, surveys, and other self-generated data into separate stacks of strategic inquiry questions. This gives students a clear indication whether each question has been answered, and answered adequately. This is also where students make decisions about whether a question that arose during research should be considered for inclusion in the final product.

PARENT and COMMUNITY INVOLVEMENT
Fun & Easy Ways to Share Your Student's Inquiry Success

1. Evening parent information meeting before major projects begin.
2. Letter home to parents before project begins. Include invitation for parents to visit school during project.
3. Thank you letter home to parents for their support after project complete.
4. Announcements in school or room newsletter before, during, and after project.
5. Back to School Night
6. Partner with other teachers to invite parents for a Family Night.
7. Display products or sample works throughout school, media center, teacher's lounge, hallways, etc.
8. Have students present at PTA meetings.
9. Host a Parent's Night.
10. Compete in Media Fair or other competition.
11. Hold a special event and invite the community and parents.
12. Students host a Distance Learning event.
13. Create and update web page showcasing student's progress, activity, and successes.

For the Best Results

Use this opportunity to share with parents the effort and time necessary to complete the process, not just the product.

Have students help parents and the community understand the work and planning involved in creating the final product by standing by the product and formally or informally discussing the energy and effort involved.

Figure 17.1. Parent and community involvement.

From *The Blue Book on Information Age Inquiry, Instruction and Literacy* by Daniel Callison and Leslie Preddy. Westport, CT: Libraries Unlimited. Copyright © 2006 by Daniel Callison and Leslie Preddy.

3. Once the source notes are organized into separate piles by strategy question, each note should be read. Direct students to read one pile at a time. The strategy question and key words should be read, then each and every source note related to that question.

4. Once all source notes for a question are read, students should place themselves in reflective mode, thinking about each note written. Give them an opportunity to digest each word, concept, thought, sketch, and fact that the they thought was important enough in the information gathering process to write it down. Students will determine that some pieces of information may or may not be important as they think of organizing the gathered data into a final product.

5. After reflecting on all the information gathered for a particular question, students will only retain for use the information that still seems important. Keeping this information answers the intended question thoroughly, thoughtfully, and with some personal insight. The question a student should be asking is whether the information that seemed important enough to write down when taking notes is still vital now that the final product is being developed. And now that the final product has been determined, is there information to align with that type of product?

6. Once the student has thoroughly weighed the information gathered, he or she should disregard any information that no longer seems useful or important. This can be done mentally, with sticky notes, or by using a pencil to gently draw a line through words or concepts on a source note.

7. Steps 3. through 6. should be repeated until all organized source note piles have been reviewed.

Students need strategies for organizing notes, as outlined in this section. Create a classroom display, using the form in Figure 17.2 or a similar one, for students to use as a visual reminder as they work.

Once the notes have been thoroughly reviewed, the final product can then be constructed based on the drafted storyboard; product rubric; information remaining in the source notes; and a student's talents, learning style, and creativity. Within the final product the student should be answering the initial strategic inquiry questions as well as any other questions they valued and researched along the way.

Expect each student to detail the research adventure. Could all questions be answered? Could they be answered to the student's and educator's satisfaction? Why or why not? As part of the reporting process, the student should be able to explain intelligently, as age-appropriate, what efforts were made, what research challenges were faced, and how the challenges were met.

Annotated Bibliography

One aspect of the concluding and reflecting phase of the inquiry process is for students to complete an annotated bibliography. A student develops a bibliography in order to appropriately give credit to information sources. The student annotates the bibliography in order to give in-depth thought to the sources' content and usefulness, and to examine personal thoughts and opinions about the sources.

Expect and plan instruction to accommodate students who are uncomfortable with constructing bibliographies. Developing an annotation may be a completely foreign experience. Devote time to introducing and reviewing how to develop a personalized and valuable annotation appropriate for each citation formulated.

Organizing Notes

1. Choose a large space to spread out your work!

2. Sort notes into piles by Inquiry Research Question.

3. Review every word and sketch you've written for a question.

4. Think about what you've written and just read.

5. Use only the information that still seems important and answers the questions you want answered.

6. Disregard, or get rid of, any information no longer seems useful, or important.

7. Repeat steps 3-6 until all question's piles have been reviewed.

Figure 17.2. Organizing notes.

Students will reflect on experiences with resources by drafting an annotated bibliography (see Figure 17.3). It is important for them to be given time to practice with format, layout, and language necessary for the successful construction of an annotated bibliography. Thoroughly explain the how-to process and circulate throughout the room during the rough drafting of the annotated bibliography to guarantee students receive the one-on-one attention necessary for success. The annotation is not intended to be complex, but instead should be thoughtful and personalized to each individual's experience with the source. Students can create an appropriate and useful annotation of a few sentences by just writing a brief paragraph that answers a few simple questions (see Figure 17.4).

Peer Evaluation

A key component to information inquiry is the opportunity to present the research quest and final product to a peer or peers, who will evaluate the final product and research openly, honestly, and critically. Ideally, peers evaluating and helping peers is a familiar activity to students, since it has been used at other stages of the inquiry research process. Dissemination of knowledge occurs with the presentation of the final product, which ideally includes an oral presentation aspect. People often learn best by teaching. Give students an opportunity to reverse teacher-student roles and become the instructor. This expands the opportunity for growth, and learning grows exponentially. A student always needs feedback from educators, but inquiry research demands a third party, a peer reviewer, to also critique the product, presentation, and process.

There are vital questions a student needs answered in order to successfully learn from the adventure, Students need to digest suggestions for ways to improve future ventures. Without this process, a means for improving future research will be lost. Students need to know not only what to improve, but also what was done well. It is important for a student to understand where his or her skills are currently. This may be different than what the student always assumed. It is also important to know where to focus improvement efforts for more successful future endeavors.

Peer evaluators should be trained and capable of responding to questions similar to the following:

- What appear to be your peer's researching strengths?

- What was done well in the presentation?

- What was done well in the final project's product?

- What did your peer seem to know best about his or her research topic?

- At the conclusion of the presentation, was the peer able to summarize the topic?

- What were your opinions of your peer's inquiry topic before the presentation?

- What were your opinions of your peer's inquiry topic after the presentation?

Self-Evaluation

Every student should complete a self-evaluation. This helps students gain a better understanding of the process and the quality of the final product. It helps students think about who they were before the inquiry, and what they have become. Self-evaluation is not a simple task. Provide students with thorough training for evaluating themselves critically, analytically, and compassionately. Students must be taught how to be detailed and use supporting evidence for the evaluation to have merit and offer the potential for self-growth. Through this training, students should be able to respond to questions similar to the following, in a thoughtful, reflective, and professional manner:

- What did I learn about my topic that I didn't know before? If I had more time, what would I still like to learn about my topic?

- What was my best and worst research question? Why do I think it was the best/worst?

- Which question helped me find really interesting information? What was it about this question that led to such interesting information? Why do I think the information was so interesting?

This sample is a direct reproduction of a student's work. It has been retyped for legibility, but all spelling, grammar, citation format, and information errors have been retained.

BIBLIOGRAPHY

General Topic we have been studying: Native Americans

Specific Topic I chose for my research: Pueblos

Citation #1

Bial, Raymond. Lifeways: The Pueblos. New York: Benchmark Books, 2000.

ANNOTATION: I got my book from looking on the cart in the IMC. This book had a lot of information on just the Pueblos. A piece of important information was that the men weaved, and the women built houses. I liked that it was all about the Pueblos. I didn't like the index.

Citation #2

Erdoes, Richard, and Martin L. Reitet. Native Americans: The Pueblos. New York: Sterling Publishing Co., 2000.

ANNOTATION: I got my book from looking on the cart in the IMC. The information in this book is only on the Pueblos. It gave a lot of information on the tools they used. The book gave lots of details. I didn't like how they talked about white men a lot.

Citation #3

Gibson, Karen. "All Roads Lead to Chaco Canyon." Cobblestone 20, September 6, 1999: 26-30.

ANNOTATION: I found this magazine by asking Mrs. Preddy in the IMC. It told me a lot about the Pueblo's pottery. A piece of important information is about what the pottery is made from. It have me lots of different information. Though the information was badly sorted.

Figure 17.3. Sample bibliography.

Writing an Annotation

What was the specific format of the source?
(encyclopedia, interview, video, etc.)

Where did I find this source?
(public library, school library media center, home, etc.)

How did I find this source?
(using the OPAC, with a teacher's help, shared by a friend, etc.)

Generally, what kind of information could be found in the source?

What information did I find in/with it that was important to me?

What did I really like about this source?

What did I find difficult about this source?

Figure 17.4. Writing an annotation.

- How did I know about what information to look for? What did I learn about how to find information that I can use again?

- What source or type of source did I find most and least useful? What was good/bad about it?

- What source or type of source did I use that I'd never used before? How did I find it? How did I learn how to use it? What was good/bad about it?

- What community resources did I use? How did it help?

- When searching for information in the future, what would I do differently, and what would I do the same?

- What part of the research journal was most useful and helped me stay on task?

- What did I do very well this time? What aspect of the instruction helped me the most?

- What could I do better next time? What would help me do a better job next time?

- Which people (students and/or adults) were most helpful? How did they help?

- What made my work better this time? When was I most creative?

- Do I like my final project? Do I like my final presentation? Why or why not? What would I do differently, and what would I do the same?

Conclude the self-evaluation segment with each student writing an essay detailing the inquiry experience. Included in the essay should be the step-by-step process of what the student did, the technical how-to of what was learned, and the personalized experiences of the student.

Students Evaluate Educators

Grant students an opportunity to honestly evaluate the inquiry research as a unit, the classroom teacher, and the library media specialist. An educator evaluation plays a pivotal role for educators and teachers. This is the opportunity for students to make judgments and give biased opinions about the topic, the inquiry process, the product, and the educators. This is a student's chance to again tell educators his or her thoughts and opinions without threat of recrimination. It is an opportunity for educators to take an honest look at the assignment and instruction through the eyes of students. It 's an opportunity to re-evaluate and reexamine instruction based on flaws and misconceptions outlined by students, based on their responses to questions such as the following:

- Should this unit be taught again? Why do you feel that way?

- What was the best thing that the classroom teacher did? What was the least helpful? @Blist = Was your teacher helpful, a little helpful, or no help?

- What was the best thing that the library media specialist did? What was the least helpful? Was your library media specialist helpful, a little helpful, or no help?

- Which research lesson was most helpful? What made it so helpful? When thinking about doing research in the future, was what you've learned and done for this research helpful, a little helpful, or no help?

- Which research lesson was least helpful? What do we need to do to make it better?

- What about the research journal was most helpful? What was least helpful? Overall, was your research journal helpful, a little helpful, or no help?

- Being honest with yourself and us, do you think there was enough time? When was there too much? When was there too little?

- What did we do well? What do we need to do better? What other suggestions and comments do you have for us?

Educators Evaluate Themselves

Just as the classroom teacher and school library media specialist require students to evaluate each other, themselves, and the unit, educators also complete a self-evaluation. This is to gain a better understanding of the process, the quality of co-instruction, and the collaborative roles. In order for the inquiry unit to have future merit, model expected behavior through an evaluation and offer further opportunity for self-, collaborative, and professional growth. Throughout the collaborative process and student inquiry, note personal opinions and observations of positive and ineffective activities and efforts. These issues can be discussed among the collaborative team throughout the process to get immediate feedback and opinions while the events are fresh in everyone's mind. Once the collaborative project has concluded, take the time to review personal notes. Privately reflect on the following questions before finally meeting with fellow collaborators to review and discuss important questions:

- Will we teach this unit again? What did I/we do very well this time? What made it work well? What do we need to do better?

- Did we allow ourselves enough unit planning and collaborative planning time?

- What did students have difficulty doing properly that I/we may need to spend more time teaching in the future?

- What aspect of instruction did I/we do successfully? Which aspect of instruction do I/we need to improve? Was the instructional time appropriate? When was there too much? When was there too little?

- What part of the research journal was most useful to me/us when helping students through the process? To students? To evaluation?

- What was my favorite experience? What was my collaborative partner's favorite experience?

- What did I learn about myself when planning collaboratively? What were my strengths and weaknesses? How will my collaborative partner's strengths make up for my weaknesses in the future? How well did I work with my collaborator?

- What did I learn about my collaborative partner? What were my partner's strengths and weaknesses? How will my strengths make up for my collaborative partner's weaknesses in the future? How well did my collaborator work with me?

- Which community resources were most helpful and accommodating?

- Which sources did I/we find most helpful when working with students? Which sources could I/we not have managed without?

- What source, or type of source, was successful that I/we had never had a student use before?

Inquiry Never Really Ends

Educator collaboration to teach information inquiry and student learning leaves all involved with a feeling of accomplishment, hard work, and overcoming worthwhile challenges. Inquiry allows for educator and student reflection and provides an opportunity to analyze what happened. This helps us make better decisions about what to do next time. Select examples of student work, both good and bad, from all phases of the inquiry process for future reference (keeping the work anonymous). Allow students to show off by placing final products and research journals on display or hosting an open house function where students can present their research process and findings to family, peers, and the community.

Using the information inquiry approach to research is a powerful, fulfilling experience for students and educators. As Julie Sumrall, freshman intensive English teacher at Jefferson High School in Lafayette, Indiana, says, "Grading the final paper was not such an overwhelming task this year because I already knew the students had been successful. I knew they had learned something. They were familiar and comfortable with the library and the inquiry process. This was what was important to me and what I had struggled with in the past. The final written paper, then, became less a measure of learning." Information inquiry lends itself admirably to assessing the research process as well as the final product and presentation. It develops skills in students that are taken to future projects and future grade levels, and continued into adulthood as lifelong learning skills. It is the process, not the final product, that is most important. As the conclusion and reflection phase of inquiry concludes, so too, does the journey, a research adventure. Jenny Moore, eighth-grade social studies teacher at Perry Meridian Middle School in Indianapolis, Indiana, sums up her thoughts on inquiry: "Teaching student[s] to find information and process it in their daily lives is one of the highest skills they can attain!"

Part II References

Brazee, Ed. (2000). Collaborating on curriculum: Why it matters, how it works. *Middle Ground* (August), 33–37.

Brooks, John I. (2001). John I. Brooks III—primary source. http://register.uncfsu.edu/f_broos/Frms/WkbkP.htm (accessed July 27, 2001).

Callison, Daniel. (1986). School library media programs & free inquiry learning. *School Library Journal* (February), 20–24.

Callison, Daniel. (2001 and 2005). Interviews. July 17 and August 22.

Carey, James O. (2001). Library skills, information skills, and information literacy: Implications for teaching and learning. *School Library Media Quarterly* (May 30).http://www.ala.org/SLMQ/skills.

Duncan, Donna, and Laura Lockhart. (2000). *I-Search, you search, we all learn to research*. New York: Neal-Schuman.

Feder-Feitel, Lisa. 2000. Rubrics are red hot!: What rubrics can do for you and your students. *Creative Classroom* (November/December), 54–56.

First steps in library research: The pre-search presented by pre-search creator Virginia Rankin. (1992). Video program. Library Instruction Round Table, American Library Association. 20 minutes.(1992).

Gordon, Carol. (1999). Students as authentic researchers: A new prescription for the high school research assignment. *School Library Media Research*, 2(May 30). http://ala.org/aasl/SLMR/vol2/authentic.html.

Holland, Holly. (2000). Reaching all learners: You've got to know them to show them. *Middle Ground* (April), 10–13.

Indiana Academic Standards. n.d. http://www.doe.state.in.us/standards/welcome2.html.

Information literacy standards for student learning. (1998). Chicago: American Library Association(1998).

Joyce, Marilyn Z., and Julie I. Tallman. (1997). *Making the writing and research connection with the I-search process*. New York: Neal-Schuman.

Kramer, Kym. (2001). Interview. January 11.

Kuhlthau. Carol C. (1993). Implementing a process approach to information literacy: A study identifying indicators of success in library media programs. *School Library Media Quarterly, 22* (1) (Fall).http://www.ala.org/aasl/SLMR/slmr_resources/select_huhlthau1.html (accessed June 6, 2001).

Langhorne, Mary Jo (Ed.). (1998). *Developing an information literacy program K–12*. New York: Neal-Schuman(1998).

Lincoln public schools guide to integrated information literacy skills. n.d. Lincoln, Nebraska: Lincoln Public Schools.

Loertscher, David V. (2000). *Taxonomies of the school library media program*. 2d ed. San Jose, CA: Hi Willow Research and Publishing.

A planning guide for Information Power: *Building partnerships for learning*. (1999). Chicago: American Association of School Librarians.

Preddy, Leslie. (2005). *Student inquiry in the research process*. August 1. http://pmms.msdpt.k12.in.us/imc/Inquiry/index.htm (accessed August 5, 2005).

Preddy, Leslie, and Jenny Moore. (2005). Key words in instruction: Student journals. *School Library Media Activities Monthly, 21* (7) (March), 32–35.

Rankin, Virginia. (1999). *The thoughtful researcher: Teaching the research process to middle school students.* Englewood, CO: Libraries Unlimited.

Stanley, Deborah B. (1999). *Practical steps to the research process for high school.* Englewood, CO: Libraries Unlimited(1999).

Stanley, Deborah B. (2000). *Practical steps to the research process for middle school.* Englewood, CO: Libraries Unlimited.

Stripling, Barbara K., and Judy M. Pitts. (1988). *Brainstorms and blueprints: Teaching library research as a thinking process.* Englewood, CO: Libraries Unlimited.

Sumrall, Julie. (2002). Interview. January 14..

Whitson, Bill. (2001). *Library research using primary sources.* Revised by M. Phillips. http://www.lib.berkeley.edu/TeachingLib/ Guides/PrimarySources.html (accessed July 27, 2001).

Wisconsin Education Media Association. (1993). With additional scenarios by Paula Montgomery. (1999). *Information literacy: A position paper on information problem solving.* American Association of School Librarians.http://www.ala.org/aasl/postitions / ps_infolit.html (accessed June 7, 2001).

Wolcott, Linda Lachance. (1994). Understanding how teachers plan: Strategies for successful instructional partnerships. *School Library Media Quarterly, 22.* (3) (Spring). http://www.ala.org/aasl/SLMR/slmr_ resources/select_wolcott.html.

Wolfe, Patricia. (2001). *Brain matters: Translating research into classroom practice.* Alexandria, VA: Association for Supervision and Curriculum Development(2001).

Wolfe, Patricia. (2003). *Brain matters: Translating research into classroom practice.* Workshop Presentation, Indianapolis, June 4–6. Sponsored by Project SEAM and M.S.D. of Perry Township.

Part III

Key Words for Instruction in Information Inquiry

The key words defined and discussed here are derived from the regular column in *School Library Media Activities Monthly* that started in 1997. Based on the articles written by Daniel Callison and edited by Paula Montgomery, the core concepts and techniques for teaching Information Inquiry are presented here. The column continues on a regular basis each month in *SLMAM*.

Readers are invited to submit ideas for key words, inquiry teaching techniques, and author guest articles to further the discussion on how instructional media specialists teach and student information scientists learn in the Information Age.

Daniel Callison
Director of School Library Media Education
Indiana University
SLIS IUPUI UL3100
755 W. Michigan Street
Indianapolis, IN 46202
callison@iupui.edu

Analysis

Daniel Callison

As defined in 1956 by a committee of college and university examiners, commonly known as Bloom's Taxonomy of Educational Objectives, "analysis" is a key category of skills at a somewhat more advanced level than the skills of comprehension and application. In "comprehension," the emphasis is on the grasp of the meaning and intent of the material. In "application," it is on remembering and bringing to bear upon given material the appropriate generalizations or principles.

Analysis emphasizes the breakdown of the material into its constituent or related parts and of the way those parts may be organized and relevant to each other. Analysis also may be directed at the techniques and devices used to convey the meaning or to establish the conclusion of a communication.

Analysis and Synthesis Contrasted

Analysis and synthesis differ in application and purpose. The information literate student uses analysis skills to critically review a document written by someone else or a task presented to the student by someone else in order to determine the merits of various elements and options.

Although there is also self-analysis, primarily we analyze documents and evidence offered by others to help satisfy our information needs. The information literate student uses synthesis to create a new or different document that includes the student's selection of key arguments, evidence, or descriptions in order to convey his or her ideas and conclusions. Although this may include, to some degree, a synthesis of ideas and evidence from others, primarily synthesis is used to convey a new and personal reflection in terms and format that best communicate to the desired audience.

Often set aside as one stage or level in models for information use processes (Eisenberg 1997, 1998), it is important to remember that analysis includes skills that permeate the entire process and are needed at a variety of levels depending on the task, ability of the learner, and the expectations of the information literacy teacher. Analysis may range from the mundane, such as determining parameters of the assignment and what can be reasonably negotiated, to the complex and difficult challenge of giving fair attention to all arguments on an issue before weighing the merits of each.

Analysis: Prelude to Evaluation

Fifty years ago, Bloom's committee concluded that analysis is best considered as an aid to fuller comprehension or as a prelude to an evaluation of material or information and is less effectively considered as an isolated technique. The committee also noted that analysis may be found in any field of study including science, social studies, philosophy, and the arts. In summary, activities that involve analysis lead to student performance of abilities to

- distinguish fact from hypothesis in a communication.

- identify conclusions and supporting statements.

- distinguish relevant from extraneous material.

- note how one idea relates to another.

- see what unstated assumptions are involved in what is said.

- distinguish dominant from subordinate ideas or themes.

Analysis involves both determining the meaning of an argument and determining the quality of the construction of the argument. Analysis skills help the mature information literate student to make wise judgments in task selection, information selection and application, and presentation of arguments to a variety of audiences. Ultimately, analysis skills are essential to determine the success or limitations of the completed communication project through self-evaluation.

Analysis involves some difficult and demanding tasks, but practice in this skill set across the curriculum and across the spectrum of the information research process should not be limited to just the gifted or advanced student groups. Practice in analysis is essential for both learners and teachers at all levels.

Becoming cognizant of when analysis should take place, is taking place, and the limits or opportunities that result from analysis is a knowledge base toward which all learners must strive, from novice to expert.

Analysis of Information Elements

A communication may be conceived as composed of a larger number of elements or several pieces of information. Some of these elements are explicitly stated or contained in the communication and can be recognized and classified easily. The communication is "taken at its face value." Conclusions may be stated along with evidence to show how one reached such conclusions.

However, there are many other elements in a communication or a document that are not so clearly labeled or identified by the author. The reader must analyze the document in terms of the following:

- **Authority.** What expertise or background does the author have to make such conclusions, or is the author simply reporting conclusions of others?

- **Source.** Are there any political, social, or economic agendas held by the institution, press, or agencies that provided the means for this communication to be distributed?

- **Context.** Relevant to what situations was this document developed? Are there issues concerning date of publication, related events, or economic or political gain for such a publication? Are conclusions of experiments reported in context of the findings of other similar experiments?

- **Method.** What methods were used by the author to gather information and were these methods reasonable for the investigation? What are the merits of various information resources such as primary sources, eye witnesses, observations, interviews, systematic experiment, and conclusions from accepted authorities?

Such questions, among others, may lead the information literate student to detect the nature and function of particular statements in a given communication or document (Grover 1993).

Statements, evidence, and conclusions must be judged on levels such as fact, value, and intent. Hidden assumptions along with unstated or misleading evidence often will lead to false conclusions. Analysis, therefore, also involves looking for what is not reported. Some examples of educational objectives that help to illustrate the skills involved in analysis of elements include the

- Ability to distinguish factual from normative statements. Is conventional wisdom, majority, or common choice at this time on this issue correct, or is such simply one snapshot of opinion?

- Ability to determine the motives for the communication. Is it to inform, to pursue, to sell, to indoctrinate?

- Ability to distinguish a conclusion from the statements that support it. Is the evidence valid and comprehensive?

Analysis of Relationships

Having identified the different elements within a communication or document, the information literate student moves on to consider the relationships among the various parts of the document. Many of these judgments deal with questions of consistency and relevance from one piece of evidence to the next and in support of a stated position, conclusion, or hypothesis. Following ar more examples of educational objectives that help to illustrate the skills involved in analysis of elements:

- Ability to recognize which facts or assumptions are essential to a main thesis of the document or central message of the communication. Are the most useful and valid pieces of evidence present to convey the desired message to the intended audience?

- Ability to distinguish relevant from irrelevant statements. Are there statements or items of evidence that detract from making a valid and well-informed conclusion?

- Ability to recognize the causal relationships and the important and unimportant details in a historical account or a current event description. Are the key points that focus the reader on the who, what, where, why, and how of an event present and constructed in an organized manner?

Analysis of Organizational Principles

While organization of evidence for arguments or events for historical description help to examine relationships among statements, organization principles also have to do with analysis of presentation mode or style for conveying the message. In order to analyze at this level, the information literate student must investigate the merits of different communication styles and patterns to consider if the arguments are best suited for the intended audience.

In doing such analysis, the information literate student will consider the merits of such communication modes for his or her own final product. Analysis involves such questions as: Has the author found the best means by which to reach the intended audience? Would such a platform be useful to me as well? Thus, documents for communication easily involve film, drama, poetry, dance, new reporting, flyers and pamphlets, advertising, and much, much more. What is the best medium to convey the message? At what level will my audience comprehend facts

and/or emotions? Do I want to get my message across to a few selected individuals who may have a higher than average awareness of the issues, or is my target audience the general masses? At this level, analysis involves practice in the

- Ability to find, in a particular work of art, the relation of materials and means of production.

- Ability to recognize form and pattern in literacy or artistic works.

- Ability to infer the author's purpose, point of view, or trains of thought and feeling as exhibited in his or her work.

- Ability to see the techniques used in persuasive materials such as advertising and propaganda.

- Ability to recognize the point of view or bias of a writer and how such bias may have influenced the means or methods used to communicate.

Task Analysis Questions

Given the parameters of the assignment, on what personal abilities can I capitalize and with what personal weaknesses will I need help to correct?

Through questioning, mapping, and brainstorming, can I determine the wide variety of elements of the overall process and the options for exploring a topic or seeking information for which I want to invest my time and energies?

In what ways will I need to expend my time personally and independently and in what ways will I need to work with others?

Information Analysis Questions

What additional background information do I need in order to identify an area for concentration and focus for my investigation and how may that focus relate to similar investigations conducted by my classmates?

What are the best sources in terms of access, authority, and age-appropriateness for me to use in addressing my information needs?

Audience Analysis Questions

What is my audience's knowledge of the subject?

What is my audience's attitude toward the subject?

What do I expect my audience to understand, consider, or accept as a result of my communication?

What seems to be the most effective and most manageable means to convey my message?

Self-Evaluation Analysis Questions

In what manner was the communication successful?

In what manner could the communication be improved?

How would the communication change for other audiences?

What new areas of inquiry are of interest to explore as a result of this communication experience?

References

Bloom, B.S. (1956). Taxonomy of Educational Objectives: The Classification of Educational Goals. McKay.

Eisenberg, M. (1997). "Task Definition: What Needs to Be Done." *Emergency Librarian* 25.

Eisenberg, M. (1998). "Use of Information: Where the Rubber Meets the Road." *Emergency Librarian* 43–44.

Grover, R. (1993, Winter). "A Proposed Model for Diagnosing Information Needs." *School Library Media Quarterly* 95–100.

Assignment

Daniel Callison

The assignment dictates the task for the student. The assignment will define parameters and identify what will be valued. Students, some more successful than others, will analyze the assignment so they can determine what should be accomplished and by when to satisfy the charge. An assignment is a very powerful item in the education puzzle. The assignment can determine the limitations or the opportunities in use of multiple resources. The lack of vision and inexperience with information resources on the teacher's part often result in an assignment tailored for quick application, quick return, quick evaluation, and little, if any, learning for the student.

Information research models that call for task analysis also should include the option to question the value of the task. If the given assignment is not much more than "drive-through research" based on straightforward ready reference efforts, the question has to be raised, "Is this a valid Information Inquiry assignment?" The teacher of information literacy, whether from the classroom or from the library media center, recognizes that assignments in the Information Age are most effective when students must make choices and justify those choices. Coming up with "something" is not a challenge in our information-rich world. Coming up with information that is relevant, precise, and authoritative can be very challenging.

The need to shift emphasis from information location to information use became very apparent during the late 1980s when new online databases and electronic reference tools were first being introduced to the schools. Callison and Daniels (1988) concluded the following after their experiences in Indiana to experiment with the first introductions of H. W. Wilson online databases with high school students in 1986:

> It may be that the value of the online search experience is not only the ground-level introduction for the high schooler with future technologies he or she will experience [in college and chosen profession], but the challenge to make information-use decisions based on facts, relevancy, currency, and authority. Such a challenge requires a great deal more be added to library instruction in the schools than "how to search online." The cost for use of online systems will need to be justified not in terms of "x" number of additional articles located, but in terms of truly challenging assignments to be placed before the student. If the objective of the term paper is to "learn how to take notes, organize notes, write a logical and readable paper, and footnote the facts," then modules that have the materials pulled and ready for student examination will meet the assignment. Such a process might be very healthy for the first experience, and common topics would allow the teacher to find a more equal base on which to evaluate the product. If the intent is to provide the student with the challenge to seek all avenues for location of information to meet a student-identified information need and to determine the quality of a document compared to other documents (to be a wise consumer of information), then the library media specialists and teachers must be prepared to expand the current typical research paper assignment at the high school level.

> Two major problems that prevent such a curricular change are: (1) too many school teachers and school library media specialists have not experienced for themselves the challenge of extensive information seeking and evaluation; and (2) uncertainty as to who is going to teach these skills and where they fit in the typical curriculum. (180–181)

David Loertscher (1996), professor of school library media at San Jose State, provides this view of the multiresource assignment:

> In the information world and the world of multimedia, we often advocate that more is better. While we have been preaching, the information pool has increased exponentially; suddenly, the Information Age has come upon many schools. Thus, a few years ago where students were able to wrest only a few tidbits of information from our collections, now they are flooded. Students accustomed to mud-puddle libraries now have Olympic size pool LMCs. Lots of young people are being thrown into the deep end of these new pools without any swimming lessons. . . . [We should] construct product assignments that require students to think rather than just cut, clip, and copy. In other words, students won't be able to find "the answer" in any source. (21)

Encyclopedic Trivia

Assignments that are encyclopedic in nature and ask the student to simply gather and report some facts will result in very limited engagement with information. Location of facts to answer given questions in reference resources around the library media center may give some practice in searching both print and electronic resources. Such trivial pursuits or treasure hunts are a stronger introduction to the information world when the students also are expected to

- discuss other ways to find the answers.

- compare resources as to which are most current, easy to use, and available at other libraries or at home.

- think about how the information found could be of real use.

- suggest what additional information is needed in order to make what was found even more useful.

- understand why different answers may be found in different sources for the same question.

Matching the assignment content to the learner's skills, needs, and interests are the complex portions of the assignment construction.

Such requires a skilled observer of the student's previous performances and regular conversations between teacher and learner.

The rest of the formula, however, is simpler. Assignments that will demand greater information-use skills and lead naturally to learning how and where to seek information should involve these characteristics:

Comparison: Information is used to compare and contrast events, items, or people. Who were the best major league pitchers of the past century? What were the three most important battles of the Civil War? What are the most critical steps in child care? What are the most important things to consider when purchasing a car? What ten photographs best illustrate the changing youth culture in America since 1950?

Process: Describe and reflect on the process you completed to gather and use the information. Information assignments should include a companion piece in which the student describes his or her choices and which were wise and which were a waste. This aspect also includes the process of seeking original information through surveys, interviews, and observations.

Justification: Support the information as the most useful evidence possible given the time and resources available. Is this justification built on selection from several information sources? Has the justification been confirmed by others who may have expertise to help you judge? Have you defined the important keys in your research question?

Solve a Problem: Based on questions designed to address information needs, the student attempts to solve a problem. Problems may include addressing information gaps for description of an event or biography; a literature review to speculate on an experiment and the documentation of the results of the experiment; and interviews and other evidence to determine perspectives and actions that might help meet the needs raised from a current social issue or conflict.

Personalize: What would you do if __? This is what the evidence from the literature and from your interview and observations leads one to conclude; however, do you agree or disagree, and to what extent do you disagree—with all or some of the conclusions? Make the situation local. Who are the best leaders in school? Why? Can you construct a method to determine an answer to this that is similar to how you and others have determined the best U. S. Presidents? Criteria might include popularity, wisdom, and/or being the right person for the situation at hand.

Thoughtful Research Projects

Barbara Stripling (1993) has supplied our profession with many valuable insights concerning how library-based assignments can be made more meaningful. Her best assignment ideas follow a progression similar to the skill development outlined by Bloom's Taxonomy for Learning (Bloom 1956). Some of these are paraphrased here:

Level 1: Recalling

- Select five accomplishments of the person you have researched and produce a "Hall of Fame" poster based on those accomplishments.

- List five dos and don'ts about a social or health issue that you have researched.

Level 2: Explaining

- Illustrate the events of your research on a map and explain the importance of each event.

- Dramatize a particularly exciting event that was part of the time period you researched. Explain why this event is the best one of those possible to dramatize. Is your choice influenced by your interests and skills, the likely audience, resources, time, and location? Is your choice of an event based on its importance to other events and therefore makes your choice the milestone or most important? How can this presentation best be accomplished? Newscast? Dramatic reading? Dance? A play? In addi-

tion to writing and staging, be ready to explain your choices.

Level 3: Analyzing

- Create a time line for the social events you have researched and correlate these to other important political, economic, and religious events.

- Rewrite a given historical event from two different points of view. After considering all sides, which do you tend to favor, and why?

- Compare your lifestyle and neighborhood to those of people living in the time period you have researched.

Level 4: Challenging

- Act as an attorney and argue to punish or acquit a given historical character for a crime or misdeed.

- Create an editorial cartoon that reflects your judgment of the key issues in a given historical event.

Level 5: Transforming

- Invite three famous scientists to dinner and predict what they are likely to discuss over the meal. Transform the conversation from the original historical context to a modern context.

Level 6: Synthesizing

- Describe either the possible evolution of or extension of an animal species and predict what effect that might have on other animals, including humans.

- Propose an ethical code for political campaigning and finance.

Pitfalls of Library Assignments

George Merrill, a high school library media specialist from Santa Rosa, California, has summarized many of the problems in assignments that are intended to engage students in the use of the library in middle and high schools. His list, adapted from Carol Kuhlthau's Guide to Teaching the Library Research Process (1985) and outlined in the Horace Newsletter (Cushman 1995), is summarized and paraphrased below.

Form over Function. The teacher overemphasizes form, especially when explaining the assignment. Discussions on length, number of sources, margins, date due, and final point value often get more time and attention than sessions to help students raise questions, consider access to resources beyond the school, or discuss research methods that may involve collection of original data.

Product over Process. Evaluation of student work is placed entirely on the final product. Little, if any, reward is based on the process or evidence that the student understood the process. Teachers fail to give value to framing a reasonable set of questions, or placing those questions within a context for the student's work and those of his or her peers. Nor is value given to selection of sources and determination from possible choices of the most useful evidence. Students often are not challenged to determine the best mode of presentation for a given audience and to consider who might read, hear, or view the product.

Information Gathering and Processing. Students often lack the skills for a full range of gathering information. Students often do not understand basic browsing skills for print and electronic collections, or potential use of indexes and abstracts. Nor do they understand the need to identify key terms and to match a controlled vocabulary that may change from one information pool to the next. Processing information from resources is also a skill that requires modeling and practice. Extracting the facts, opinions, arguments, and examples that eventually build into evidence often are not required as many library assignments can be satisfied with use of a few basic resources.

Little Interest. Students are not engaged by the subject matter of the assignment. A good research project creates a question in the student's mind that he or she wants to answer. Library media specialists and other teachers, along with the student's peers can help the student generate possible options and increase the chances that something will be of interest. Proponents of the I-Search Process would argue that student interest is the key to a successful project. Without interest and relevance, the student is simply going through the steps. With interest and relevance come challenge and self-determination.

Associated Not Integrated. The assignment is seen as something peripheral to the central concerns of the course. Ideally a research project should be integral-one of the ways students explore the essential question(s) of the course's content and objectives. Further, the assignment should require the use of multiple resources and critical choices in information selection to be integral with the library research process. Assignments should challenge the scope of information access and push the demands for more resources beyond those in the school. This, in turn, helps to drive the demand to increase school library resources and services and reduces the use of the library media center as simply a large textbook with some additional chapters. Library research projects should lead teachers and students to, what is for them, the new and unexplored, not just more of the same common ground found in most classroom texts.

Overly Emotional. A topic may be so emotional that students begin not with investigation and reflection but with simplistic conclusions that they attempt to "prove." They make no attempt to evaluate the resources found. In such cases, changing the topics may not be the problem, but giving greater emphasis to several stages in information gathering and frequent class discussions of resources and evidence can help the student to be more open to different opinions. Students should be placed in positions to voice and defend a variety of perspectives along the way. For some, this process, practiced prior to completion of the final product, will open minds to a wider spectrum of resources.

Lengthy Assignments. Students lack the skills to manage a lengthy assignment. They often procrastinate, then slap together a mush of undigested material from a few obvious sources. Library media specialists and teachers should provide graded "checkpoints" designed to bring students along in the process. Frequent practice should be relevant and rewarded. Products from these steps should be shared and displayed. Students thus will have greater opportunity to learn from each other.

Students should see "good questions;" "meaningful notes;" "clear arguments;" "examples and analogies that communicate;" and "the best Web sites, reference books, and local experts for personal interviews." Calendars should be used to plan time and to allow time for students to gain resources from beyond the school. Students need guidance, models, encouragement, and feedback at several points of intervention in order to survive and "thrive" a demanding project.

Split Roles. Without sufficient planning time, the teacher falls into the accustomed role of assigner and the library media specialist becomes the resource finder. Worse still, the assignment is made without consulting the school library media specialist at all. Sometimes, even with enough lead time, these roles don't change. The library media specialist should have a great deal to offer in the way of being an instructional specialist who recommends points of intervention, practice, and evaluation. Teachers can be powerful advocates of specific resources, and when teamed with the library media specialist to review and recommend resources together, a more meaningful research orientation will result.

Little Time for Guidance. Students receive too little time and guidance. A class is often brought to the library media center with minimal or no preparation, usually at the exploratory phase of the research process. Teachers often do not value or are not aware of the need for students to explore resources and gain a context for the possible research problems. Students should be encouraged to read background materials, both common to all and relevant to their special interests so that they build a pool of

knowledge to draw on in discussions leading to topic selection and research questions. Such exploration helps to broaden experiences and to refine notions they might raise as potential topics are considered.

Up-Front Library Media Center Orientation. Students are instructed in "using the library" before beginning the research process and seldom engaged in follow-up lessons or practice. Extended lessons prior to entering the project often do not match to the "point of need" and are better broken into several mini-lessons spread across the project. A fifteen-minute session, given every other day for library visit and research, to introduce, review, and answer problems in front of all class members is worth much more than the traditional sixty-minute heavy frontload. These brief introductions can serve to help the teaching team as well as the students to focus on teachable moments.

Final Product Not Seen by Library Media Specialist. The students' final products are often not shared beyond the classroom teacher. Some library media specialists and teachers debrief after a team lesson effort to determine different approaches for next time. These sessions should include examination of papers by the library media specialist, especially to determine what resources were used. Are there items that proved to be useful that are new to the library media specialist, and perhaps should be added to the collection? Are there items used correctly based on introduction to the resources in the school library media center? Were sources not used correctly or did the student not challenge him or herself to use a wide variety of resources?

Audience. Often there is no audience beyond the classroom teacher. Students need feedback from peers, other faculty, community representatives, and subject experts in some cases. Such may not be the case for all library-based projects, but the wider the audience possibilities, the more challenging the assignment will be for the student.

A New Prescription

Carol Gordon, head librarian of the Educational Resources Library at Boston University, has studied the attitudes and abilities of ninth and tenth grade students concerning the assignment to complete a research project. She has found that guidance focused through instructional sessions across the project, usually presented by the library media specialist, greatly helps students to become more authentic researchers as they collect data through interviews, questionnaires, and content analysis that will be displayed and analyzed as evidence. These sessions are based on the following questions, with the introduction of specific resources and search skills woven in as examples. Lessons focus on the questions, with information sources playing a secondary role.

1. What is research and how is it different from reporting?

2. What is a researchable question?

3. How do I prepare a proposal for my research?

4. How can we evaluate our own success as authentic researchers?

5. Where do I go for information?

6. How do I get data from a primary source?

7. How do I display and analyze data?

8. How do I present my paper using a style sheet?

9. How do we edit and revise our papers using the writing process?

10. How can we evaluate the success of this unit?

References

Bloom, B. S. (1956). *Taxonomy of Educational Objectives: The Classification of Educational Goals.* McKay.

Callison, D., and A. Daniels. (1988). "Introducing End-User Software for Enhancing Student Online Searching." *School Library Media Quarterly* 16 (3): 173–181

Cushman, K. (1995). "Information, Literacy, and the Essential School Library." *Horace* 12 (1): 1–8. http://www.essentialschools.org/cs/resources/view/ces_res/147 (accessed November 16, 2005).

Gordon, C. (1999). "Students as Authentic Researchers: A New Prescription for the High School Research Assignment." *School Library Media Research* 2. www.ala.org/aasl/SLMR (accessed November 16, 2005).

Kuhlthau, C. C. (1985). *Teaching the Library Research Process.* Center for Applied Research in Education.

Loertscher, D. (1996). "All That Glitters May Not Be Gold." *Emergency Librarian* 24 (2): 21–27.

Stripling, B. K. (1993). "Practicing Authentic Assessment in the School Library." In *School Library Media Annual*, edited by C. Collier Kuhlthau, vol. 11, 40–55. Libraries Unlimited.

Audience Analysis

Daniel Callison and Annette Lamb

Audience analysis involves the processes of gathering and interpreting information about the recipients of oral, written, or visual communication. Audience awareness involves the conceptions of the writer, speaker, or performer concerning the recipients of his or her communication. Regardless of whether the author is sharing an oral history, debating an issue, or writing an editorial, the writer or speaker must be aware of the needs, interests, and expectations of his or her audience.

Audience Analysis, Information Inquiry, and Curriculum Standards

The ability to analyze an audience's information needs, potential for understanding and accepting new information, and assimilating that information are skills recognized by the National Council of Teachers of English (1996) for literacy curriculum standards from elementary through secondary schools. In addition, national standards across the curriculum stress the importance of meaningful learning and connections beyond the school. For example, the National Council for the Social Studies (1994) stresses critical need for students to participate in authentic activities that call for real-life applications and audiences. The National Council of Teachers of Mathematics (2000) states that when students are challenged to communicate the results of their thinking to a real-world audience orally or in writing, they must be "clear, convincing, and precise" in their use of mathematical language.

Wisconsin University researchers (Newman, Secada, and Wehlage 1995) found that authentic achievement consists of student construction of knowledge, disciplined inquiry, and value beyond the school. They state that authentic assessment involves students in using audiences outside the school to make real-world connections. They found much higher levels of achievement on complex tasks for students in classrooms where authentic pedagogy focused on active learning, consideration of alternative perspectives, extended writing, and a real audience for student work.

Audience Analysis in Teaching and Learning

Both educators and their students address many audiences during a school day. A teacher's audience includes students, parents, community members, and colleagues. The audience of a child might include his or her teacher, parents, peers, and those outside the realm of education. Audience analysis is critical in meeting the unique needs of each of these audiences.

The closer the teacher can come to understanding the learner's abilities, experiences, and expectations, the more likely communication will be effective from the beginning of a lesson or task (Gagne and Wager 1992). Learner analysis has many parallel elements to audience analysis, and purposes may be similar. In addition, both involve motivation, persuasion, and informative communication. Teachers must be aware of the intellectual skills, subject matter knowledge, learning style, and personal characteristics of each student.

In their Instructional Design model, Dick and Carey (2000) stressed the importance of identifying characteristics of learners and the implications for each characteristic. What intellectual skills, abilities, and personality traits does each student bring to the learning environment? According to Lamb (2002), these characteristics have tremendous implications for a teacher. For example, what if there is a mixture of readers and nonreaders in a second grade classroom? How does this information impact the teacher's way of presenting learning materials?

The challenges related to Information Inquiry are twofold. The first obstacle is establishing the most effective communication channels between the teacher and each learner. The second challenge involves helping the learner understand how to identify his or her audience and select the best way to convey new knowledge to this audience. In school environments that apply authentic learning practices, the learner will face different audiences both inside and outside the school. Adjusting the message to increase the chances of communication and persuasion becomes an important skill in the information literacy curriculum.

Students develop skills in audience analysis over their academic career. Third graders may be faced with creating a picture book for their kindergarten pals, middle schoolers may develop a report for the city council on land use issues, and high school students may be writing nutritional guides for the elderly. In each case, the student author must analyze the audience carefully.

Kroll (1984) found that the letters written by nine-year-old students often lacked essential information for their readers, but they still expressed audience awareness. Strange (1986) found that young students altered their writing style for different audiences. For example, they used more slang and fewer words with their friends versus an adult audience. As students mature, they are better able to adjust their writing to meet the needs of their audience (Fontaine 1984).

Importance of Authentic Audience

From John Dewey (1916) to Howard Gardner (1991), well-known educators have emphasized the importance of authentic learning. The evidence indicates that assignments calling for more authentic intellectual work actually improve student scores on conventional tests (Newman, Bryk, and Nagaoka 2001).

Teachers who strive to instill the skills of inquiry create ways that students can write for and speak to more audiences than just the classroom teacher. The most effective teachers also share the opportunity for critical review and feedback with others so that the student can learn from a spectrum of perspectives. Learners should find the entire experience, including their final project, relevant to the real world. The most powerful aspect of authentic learning is the ability of students to transfer new knowledge and skills beyond the classroom ways to a meaningful audience (Mims 2003).

Learners in an authentic learning environment complete real-world tasks that require sustained exploration, social construction of knowledge, multiple opportunities for reflection, and real audiences. According to Brown, Collins, and Duguid (1989), these types of cognitive apprenticeships enable students "to acquire, develop, and use tools in authentic domain activities."

There are many opportunities for students to apply the results of Information Inquiry activities to real-world audiences. Government agencies, nonprofit organizations, and service groups always are interested in participating in projects. Student audiences might include developing a promotion for the local Chamber of Commerce, collecting oral histories for a local historical society, building a Web site for a local nonprofit organization, or communicating the results of a science experiment with a scholar, scientist, or government agency.

Audience Identification

Primary or Secondary

The first step in audience analysis is audience identification. Communications written in a classroom setting often have both primary and secondary audiences. For example, the primary reader of a letter to a legislator would be the public official receiving the envelope. However, teachers and peers also may read this letter as part of a classroom activity.

This dual audience can lead to confusion on the part of the learner. This is particularly difficult for students concerned about their grade. In other words, although a real-world audience may have been identified for the assignment, students also may be concerned with the reaction of their teachers, parents, or peers. These secondary audiences can be confusing particularly for novice writers. Students will need guidance in learning how to focus on their primary audience while being aware of secondary readers.

Audience Needs Assessment

Audience analysis is an important part of the communication process in any field. Not only does correct audience analysis increase the chances of being heard, but more important, increases the chances of being understood.

Needs assessment is an essential element of audience analysis. Examining what is known about the audience helps writers focus on the needs of the reader or participants. The writer or speaker must determine what the audience already knows about the topic and what they need to know. He or she also must find out about the perceptions, attitudes, values, and dispositions of the audience in order to make decisions about the best way to approach communicating information. For example, is the audience receptive or resistant, old or young, novice or expert, friendly or hostile, flexible or rigid?

Answers to the following questions can help in collecting important audience information and lead to more effective communication:

- What is the relationship of the author to the audience and how will this impact the formality of the communication or other considerations?

- What does your audience know about the topic?

- What positive or negative experiences might they have about the topic?

- What attitudes, biases, or strong feelings might your audience have toward the topic?

- What misconceptions might the audience have about your topic?

- What is the level of expertise on this topic for most of your audience members?

- What background information does your audience have about the topic?

- To what extent do you want to change the opinions held by your audience?

- To what extent do you want to inform or educate your audience?

- To what degree do you want to entertain your audience, or how will a more entertaining manner of delivery help to engage your audience and keep their interest?

- What are the expressed and perceived information needs of the audience?

- What are the important basic terms, assumptions, events, and names that your audience should know in order to gain the most meaning from your message?

- What might be confusing jargon, or overly technical terms and meaningless acronyms, that should be avoided?

- What format of communication would be most effective for this audience (i.e., report, action plan, story, persuasive essay, presentation, debate)?

- Is there a need to provide information in a visual form to help your audience understand aspects of your message that otherwise may be too complicated, too abstract, or not relevant?

- What is the most important message for this specific audience so these key ideas are emphasized in the introduction and reinforced in the conclusion?

Rather than simply a tally of the answers to these questions, an effective analyst examines the significance of this information. Hart (2001) states that writers often focus on simple, obvious issues such as gender differences. Instead, analysts must ask themselves how this information is useful in forming a communication that will be effective for this audience.

In situations that might involve debate or demand a persuasive role on the part of the speaker or writer, more advanced analysis may need to be conducted to answer these questions:

- How does the speaker or writer relate to the audience in terms of social groupings such as age, gender, religion, ethnic or cultural factors, family status, sexual orientation, educational level, and socio-economic class?

- Is your audience very small or large? What are the implications of this composition?

- Is your audience heterogeneous or homogeneous? What are the implications of this composition?

- Does your audience have a problem that you can assist in solving?

- What are the roles of your audience members (followers, leaders, decision maker s, advisors, creators)?

- How does the audience perceive your competence and confidence, character, and good will?

- What authorities or information sources will the audience most likely accept or reject?

- How does the speaker or writer relate to the audience in terms of ideology, values, beliefs, and attitudes?

- Is this a potentially friendly and accepting audience or an audience that is likely to be hostile and confrontational?

- Is your audience likely to be more receptive to analogies, testimonials, logic, minor general statistics, or complex and in-depth data?

- How does your audience feel about its past, present, and future relative to your controversial topic?

- Have members of your audience had personal experiences that may influence how they will receive your message?

- Will your audience be allowed or even encouraged to respond to your presentation?

As information about the audience is collected, generalizations begin to emerge. Some writers create an image in their mind about their "typical" audience member as they develop a communication. However, others have found it more effective to concentrate on the problem the audience is solving and the roles they play as audience members rather than the characteristics of the audience (Hart 2004).

The challenge of gathering information on audiences can be nearly as demanding as the inquiry process for gathering information on a topic. Locating and selecting information that meets a personal information need may prove to be much less demanding than gathering additional information to help one prepare to address many different situations and different audiences that may or may not be receptive to hearing or reading about the topic. Such challenges, however, are true to life and, therefore, authentic problems to address.

Obstacles to effective communication with nearly any audience have been summarized by William Pfeiffer (2002) of Southern Polytechnic State University:

- Listeners are very vulnerable to being distracted.

- Listeners can become impatient quickly.

- Listeners often lack the technical knowledge of the speaker.

- An audience will contain listeners of diverse backgrounds and different audiences will pose the challenge of different mixtures of these diverse experiences.

- Audiences will contain different levels of decision maker s and non-decision makers. Signs from members of the audience that communication is successful and the message being conveyed is welcome include:

  - Listeners become more relaxed.
  - Listeners may move closer to the presenter by leaning forward or stepping forward.
  - Listeners offer greater eye contact, and often more smiles and approving head nods.

Audience Analysis Techniques

Many of the exercises that help analyze the audience are identical to exercises that also help us think through an inquiry project. Working with a team of peers along with review and feedback from a teacher of Information Inquiry will make these exercises more useful than considerations made alone.

Brainstorming or Freewriting: In a quick outline, identify your main message. Then predict what you believe your audience is likely to know and not know. List what must be written or said to help them understand or accept your message.

Agreement Mapping: Under four headings, "Complete Agreement," "Some Agreement," "Some Disagreement," and "Complete Disagreement," list the positions that members of an audience are likely to hold on the issues you intend to present.

Devil's Advocate: Go through your script and mark terms and phrases that can be misunderstood easily or lead to argument. What are the points and counterpoints that are likely to be raised from different audiences? Put yourself in the place of your audience. What should they most likely not believe, doubt, and not accept?

Information Organization: To meet different audience needs and expertise, the presenter may want to consider a different order in which information might be presented. Should the "thesis," or main argument, be presented first or last—inductive or deductive? Consider headings, key terms, and catch phrases that will help to frame the message for the given audience. These may change with perceived differences in the ability level and background of different audiences.

Information Visualization: What portions of the speech or written document are in most need of illustration? Photographs, charts, tables, and diagrams all can add to the communication impact. For some audiences, it may work best to completely "storyboard" the message by drawing visuals on a series of pages as a set of cartoons or a picture book. From these sketches, select the few best that convey the most meaning for the intended audience.

Survey and Compare: Depending on the topic and the different audiences eventually to be addressed, it is not unrealistic to attempt to gain some demographic and opinion data from that audience before it is addressed. Gathering such information from classroom members or parent groups can be an extremely valuable learning exercise and raise the level of inquiry compared to situations in which very little is known about the audience. Pre-presentation data, gathered and analyzed several days prior to a speech, can lead to a much more constructive engagement for both the presenter and the audience.

Adjusting Style to Audience

Once the interests and needs of the audience have been examined, the writer or speaker must consider how this information impacts the design of the message and its dissemination as a plan, report, presentation, or other type of communication. How will you adjust your writing style and shape your message to meet the needs of this audience? For example, will charts be used to help the audience visualize data? Will well known research studies be cited to increase credibility? Will complex terminology be defined? Other considerations include the level of formality needed to suit the audience and message, the type of motivation needed to gain and maintain the interest of the audience, and the degree of personalization that will make the audience feel most comfortable.

Some audiences are familiar to the students, while others are not. Known audiences include self, friends, family, peers, teachers, and members of the local community. People from outside the experiences of the student may be extended or unknown audiences. Jan Youga (1998) of Gordon College, has placed adjustments for communication with different audiences on a continuum (see Figure Part3.1). Youga suggests that "as our relationship to the audience becomes more distant, we begin to change the tone of voice we use, the amount and kind of information we provide, and the mechanical features of style such as punctuation and spelling" (19).

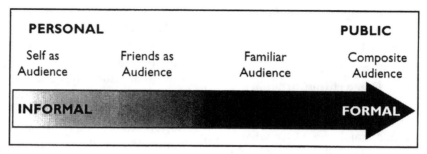

Figure Part3.1: Communication with different audiences continuum.

At each point along Youga's continuum, the speaker or writer must deal with communication and reflection in the Information Inquiry process. Although the communication may be more private and less informal at the personal or self end of the continuum, elements of persuasion, informative communication, and logic are present.

Much of what we do in order to seek and gain meaning is for ourselves and the elements of Information Inquiry apply to personal information problem solving as much as to formal information problem solving in an academic or workplace setting. Many inquirers who gain the most from their information exploration learn from personal journals they keep in order to document their investigation and questions.

Authentic Assignments and Audiences

Authentic audiences are important, but the logistics of implementing a project that uses a real-world audience can be time-consuming. When developing assignments, teachers must consider carefully the role that audience will play in the activity. In many cases, a virtual audience is an effective way to make a project more authentic. For example, the class might participate in an online forum with students from different cultures. Or, students might communicate through e-mail with a representative from a government agency such as Federal Emergency Management Agency (FEMA).

Harris (1999) states that curriculum-based telecollaboration involves students in communicating with a real audience by using written language. Projects such as Global SchoolNet (http://www.gsn.org), ePALS (http://www. epals.com/), KIDPROJ (http://www.kidlink. org/KIDPROJ), and I*EARN (http://www. iearn.org/) are a few examples.

Consider ways that technology can be used to reach outside the classroom. For example, students might write an e-mail communication rather than a "mock-letter" that might never be sent. According to Lafer (1997), e-mail communication provides students with the opportunity for authentic communication. It helps learners focus on real issues and address an audience of peers outside their local area who might have different perspectives.

For younger children, develop a guided audience analysis experience. For example, contact the recipients of the e-mail communication prior to implementing the lesson. Collect audience information that can be shared with the students to help prepare them in writing for their audience. Consider contests and competitions such as media fairs, science fairs, and writing contests. Many online projects such as ThinkQuest (http://thinkquest.org) involve sharing projects with a global audience.

Audience analysis can reduce the mystery between audience and presenter and move both to more important content exchanging levels. Addressing specific audience needs also can require the student to think more creatively in message presentation and more critically in selection of information to share. Interactions that come from audience feedback and exchanges also can lead to more originality on the part of the presenter. There are no formulas or specific steps to audience engagement, and spirited interactions can lead to truly testing the student's knowledge of and passion for what he or she has written or spoken.

References

Brown, J. S., A. Collins, and S. Duguid. (1989). "Situated Cognition and the Culture of Learning." *Educational Researcher* 18 (1): 32–42.

Dewey, J. (1916). *Democracy and Education.* Macmillan. (Available at http://www.ilt. columbia.edu/publications/dewey.html).

Dick, W., L. Carey, and J. O. Carey. (2000). *The Systematic Design of Instruction.* 5th ed. HarperCollins.

Fontaine, S. I. (1984). *Evidence of Audience Awareness in the Writing and Writing Processes of Nine- and Eighteen-Year Olds.* ERIC Clearinghouse. ED 258 183.

Gagné, R. M., and W. W. Wager. (1992). *Principles of Instructional Design.* 4th ed. Harcourt Brace Jovanovich.

Gardner, H. (1991). *The Unschooled Mind: How Children Think and How Schools Should Teach.* Basic Books.

Harris, J. (1999). "First Steps in Telecollaboration." *Learning and Leading with Technology* 27 (3): 54–57.

Hart, G. (2001). *Audience Analysis: Looking Beyond the Superficial.* STC Proceedings. (Available at http://www.stc.org/ confproceed/2001/PDFs/STC48–00006 1.PDF).

Hart, G. (2004). *Prescriptive Audience Analysis: Moving Beyond the Purely Descriptive.* TECHWR-L. (Available at http://www. raycomm.com/techwhirl/magazine/writing/ prescriptiveanalysis.html).

Kroll, B. M. (1984). "Audience Adaptation in Children's Persuasive Letters." *Written Communication* 1 (4): 407–426.

Lafer, S. (1997). "Audience, Elegance, and Learning via the Internet." *Computers in the Schools* 13 (1/2): 89–97.

Lamb, A. (2002). *Building Treehouses for Learning.* Vision to Action.

Lewis, D. (1996). *How to Get Your Message Across.* Souvenir Press.

Mims, C. (2003). "Authentic Learning: A Practical Introduction & Guide for Implementation." *Meridian: A Middle School Computer Technologies Journal* 6 (1). (Available at http://www.ncsu.edu/meridian/win2003/ authentic_learning/).

National Council for the Social Studies. (1994). *Expectations of Excellence: Curriculum standards for social studies.* NCSS. (Available at http://www.ncss.org/standards/).

National Council of Teachers of English. (1996). *Standards for the English Language Arts.* NCTE.

National Council of Teachers of Mathematics. (2000). *Principles and Standards for School Mathematics. Executive Summary.* NCTM. (Available at http://www.nctm. org/ standards/overview.htm).

Newmann, F. M., A. S. Bryk, and J. K. Nagaoka. (2001). Authentic intellectual work and standardized tests: Conflict or coexistence?" Consortium on Chicago School Research, January. (Available at http://www. consortium-chicago.org/publications/pdfs/ p0a02.pdf).

Newmann, F. M., W. G. Secada, and G. G. Wehlage. (1995). *A Guide to Authentic Instruction and Assessment: Vision, Standards and Scoring.* Wisconsin Center for Education Research.

Pfeiffer, W. S. (2002). *Pocket Guide to Public Speaking.* Prentice Hall.

Strange, R. L. (1986). "An Investigation of the Ability of Sixth Graders to Write with Sense of Audience." Ph.D. dissertation, Indiana University.

Youga, J. (1989). *The Elements of Audience Analysis.* Macmillan.

Authentic Learning and Assessment

Daniel Callison and Annette Lamb

The term authentic refers to the genuine, real, and true. Authentic learning involves exploring the world around us, asking questions, identifying information resources, discovering connections, examining multiple perspectives, discussing ideas, and making informed decisions that have a real impact. An authentic learning environment is engaging for students because the content and context of learning are accepted by the student as relevant to his or her needs and deemed by the teacher as simulating life beyond the classroom. Callison (1998) has suggested that Information Inquiry comes near authentic learning at the intersection of workplace information problems, personal information needs, and academic information problems or tasks. See Figure Part3.2.

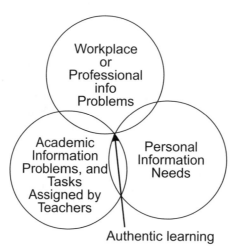

Figure Part3.2. The relationship among workplace, personal, and academic information problem sets and authentic learning.

State and national learning standards found today across disciplines often attempt to stress real world applications (Zemelman, Daniels and Hyde 2005). Students are asked to make academic connections to ordinary life experiences. Rather than surface-level, fact-based tasks, learners are asked to question, interpret, and apply information and ideas that have value in a larger social context. Many students aren't aware of how reading, writing, and mathematics are part of their daily life, and one of the challenges for educators is to help students make such real-world associations.

A specific challenge facing the library media specialist is to partner with other teachers to design learning activities and develop assessments that resemble constructive experiences beyond the school (AASL and AECT 1998). Partnering and simulating real-world situations are not easy tasks and usually fall short of any ideal implied in definitions of authentic learning. Examples and situations given here may help teams of educators to consider how to move closer to developing authentic learning environments. Moving away from heavy use of common worksheets and skill drills, multiple-choice exams, and a standard formula applied to all student research projects is an evolution toward authentic learning.

Teaching teams who engage in Information Inquiry are most likely to create authentic learning environments when they act as mentors or master-level teachers who model for their learning apprentices. They engage in inquiry with their students, not simply assign tasks. They raise questions, seek information, interpret findings and draw conclusions, and illustrate their inquiry practices as they work with students. They discuss openly for students to hear and see the inquiry process and results, and share both personal inquiry successes and failures. Cognitive apprenticeship becomes the center of the learning tasks when students grow intellectually and eventually move to a near independent learning level (Collins, Brown and Newman 1988).

Signs of Authentic Learning

Although this list probably is not exhaustive, the following are signs that teachers of Information Inquiry are reaching levels of learning that can be identified as authentic (Callison and Lamb 2004).

Learning Is Student-Centered. Probably should highlight or otherwise note these for the editor and the list. Not all of the questions for exploration are generated by the teacher, but most are raised, clarified, and become "owned" by the students working collaboratively to act more as problem-identifiers and not just problem-solvers.

Multiple Resources Accessed Beyond the School. Questions are not answered to full satisfaction of the student, library media specialist, or other teachers by information provided in the school library media center alone. While some basic background information is accessible, the library media center is a clearinghouse for contacts to more in-depth resources and expertise in the community and beyond. Electronic documents and human experts are valued, monitored

through master teacher guidance, and used extensively.

Student Acts as a Scientific Apprentice. As an "information scientist," the student is encouraged to be skeptical of the information located and seeks to corroborate facts and gain a variety of perspectives on issues and to determine credibility and authority of sources. The student learns from several systematic information exploration approaches that can be applied to meet a variety of current and future information problems. With the guidance of the master teacher, the student evaluates approaches to match to information needs and documents the results for future uses. Mapping the results of information gained from different sources becomes as important as gaining information content itself because this will help in becoming more efficient in future information seeking practices.

Student Moves toward Real Research. The opportunity for the student to gather original data through surveys, interviews, or experiments helps to enhance the project and places the student in the role of not just "library researcher," but closer to that of authentic researcher. The student moves beyond just location of documents and organized data to one who deals with analysis of findings and identification of additional information needs. The student learns how primary sources, artifacts, and observations of human behavior can all contribute to useful data. The student learns the value of documenting through a research journal their feelings and findings and to do so in a constructive manner that can be shared with others. The student learns how to analyze his or her audience in order to best communicate findings in order to inform, persuade, or engage others in their information problem-solving pursuits.

Lifelong Learning beyond the Assignment. The student finds information problems and questions to be interesting, exciting, challenging, and personally meaningful. They move toward the intersection of personal, academic, and potentially future workplace information needs. The agenda of questions continues to evolve beyond the school assignment and becomes an inquiry set that they follow outside of school as well as in future academic experiences. The agenda impacts the student's selection of reading, viewing, and discussion both for pleasure and for intellectual growth.

Process, Product, and Performance Assessment. Attempts are made by the guiding educators as well as the reflective student researcher to evaluate all aspects of inquiry. The process and product are both valued as artifacts of learning. Actions taken or performance of application of the inquiry become evidence of learning success. Has the student's thinking changed? Has the student changed the thinking of others? Has the student mastered inquiry to make a difference in some constructive manner?

Instructional Collaboration and Interchangeable Roles. Students are more likely to learn the value of inquiry and collaboration with others when they see it modeled by master teachers. Library media specialists and other teachers of inquiry demonstrate collaboration as a team to select and implement a suitable approach to information problem identification and solving. They perform as information literate educators and share with their students how they have determined quality information sources or conducted original information gathering. As a team, they freely share responsibilities for lesson planning, instructional presentation, and performance evaluation. Each member of the team is information resourceful and fluent in matching search strategies to meet information needs. Master teachers display their ideas and inquiry work along with their apprentice students. They may present findings in visuals, speeches, papers, or other media displayed for audience examination and critical discourse.

Authentic Achievement

Fred Newmann and Gary Wehlage (1993) from the University of Wisconsin-Madison stress that meaningful learning is critical to engage students and transfer learning to new situations. Their research focuses on the direct connection between authentic instruction and student achievement. In a recent study, they concluded that students in classrooms with high quality, authentic assignments scored higher on standardized achievement tests. Three criteria were used to define authentic achievement:

- Students construct meaning and produce knowledge;
- Students use disciplined inquiry to construct meaning; and
- Students aim their work toward production of discourse, products, and performances that have value or meaning beyond success in school.

Newmann and Wehlage (1993) stress two problems that often result in conventional schooling not reaching authentic levels:

- Often school work does not allow them to use their minds well.
- The work has no intrinsic meaning or value to students beyond achieving success in school.

Newmann and Whelage have identified five continuous dimensional constructs that can be used to determine the authenticity of instruction. These are

- Higher-order thinking,
- Depth of knowledge,
- Connectiveness to the world beyond the classroom,
- Substantive conversation, and
- Social support for student achievement.

There are many ways that students can demonstrate their understanding of academic content through authentic problems and projects. To demonstrate their skills in mathematics and social studies, students could develop a proposal regarding the use of a particular building or parcel of land in their city, create charts and graphs to speculate on whether racism or other factors impacted local home sales, or demonstrate the distribution of wealth and population on different continents by using ratio and proportion.

Authentic Assignments

Authentic assignments are grounded in reality and require students to create meaning from their experiences. Students are involved with communicating through e-mail, writing letters, and keeping journals. They may collect oral histories, write about current events, or conduct and report on experiments.

Molly Nicaise (1995), a faculty member in the School of Information Science and Learning Technologies at the University of Missouri, stresses that authentic learning is anchored in real-world activities. Students access the information and resources needed to address essential questions. Assessments of these activities are directly related to the task.

Authentic Context. Assignments should be rooted in a meaningful situation. Educators use simulations, scenarios, and problems to provide this context. The closer the context can be to a real-world situation, the more likely it is that students will see the connection between academic context and practical applications. Leo Vygotsky (1930) used the phrase "zone of proximal development" to describe how learners use context to understand and create knowledge. He found that cultural and historical factors impact how we learn and that learners are not always able to transfer learning to new situations.

An effective strategy is to ask students to connect local with national or international information. Students might conduct a poll in their building to collect information about whether people recycle paper, glass, or aluminum. They then could compare this to the national average. Comparisons also could be made by using local versus national population statistics or immigrant data. The same could be done by comparing the stories of local veterans with those from other countries.

Authentic Questions. Assignments begin with authentic questions generated from personally relevant concerns, issues, and topics. Questions are framed in a real context that build on personal experience and extend to the larger world.

Authentic Tasks. Learning tasks often are not explicit, requiring students to identify problems, develop strategies, make decisions, and be in charge of their own learning. Students often feel uncomfortable with these types of assignments because they require independent thinking and metacognitive skills. These types of assignments require careful guidance to help learning through the processes of problem identification.

Scaffolding is a critical element of authentic learning environments. Students must connect new information to existing knowledge and experiences. Students need guidance in making these connections in inquiry-based projects. Authentic learning activities are not easy to manage.

Elliott Soloway (Curtis et al. 2004), a professor at the University of Michigan, develops tools to provide the scaffolding needed for students to engage in authentic situations that require complicated subject matter. He stresses that teacher librarians must help learners evaluate digital content and use technology to access and use information. From handheld devices and science probes to software tools that help students with complex mathematics, he has worked with teachers to use technology to facilitate authentic learning. For example, middle school students have explored their own community environment through measuring the health of local rivers.

Tiffany Marra (2004), the Program Manager for SmartGirl.org, asks the question, "Why should students learn how to solve problems about things that will never happen, when there is so much in their lives that already involves math, reading, writing, or any other subject matter?" Each year, SmartGirl.org along with the American Library Association conducts a reading survey to identify the interests of young women as part of Teen Read Week. Marra stresses that tasks can fall on a continuum of authenticity from reading books about art and going on virtual art museum visits to actually visiting an art gallery.

Authentic tasks often involve collaboration or competition with others. Many national writing contests, local media fairs, and science fairs provide opportunities to participate in a project that is shared beyond the school. Cyberfair (http://www.globalschoolhouse.com) is a well-known Web-based authentic learning programs that focuses on youth research connecting knowledge to real-world applications in categories including local leaders, businesses, community organizations, historical landmarks, environment, music, art, and local specialties.

Authentic Activities. These activities are natural, not contrived. Rather than reading about city government in a textbook, students write questions and interview local government officials. By providing meaningful contexts for learning, authentic learning closely resembles actual situations where knowledge and skills will be used. Students read primary documents and original prose, create communications on meaningful topics for real audiences, and share work with real audiences. Students are asked to:

- Recall their prior knowledge and how it relates to a real situation;

- Articulate questions, problems, or a focus that are meaningful, relevant, and interesting; and

- Construct knowledge and discover connections in real-world contexts.

Authentic activities include working with the local chamber of commerce on promoting an annual event, natural resource, or historical building; providing nutrition and fitness information to seniors; or creating Web sites for local nonprofit agencies. Sometimes it is possible to become involved with large-scale projects such as identifying monarch butterflies, hummingbirds, or whooping cranes. In other cases, students might volunteer to participate in research being conducted by professionals at the United States Geological Survey or the National Park Service (http://www.nps.gov/ERT/). For example, a middle school class in Idaho worked on a land survey at a local cemetery and a high school class in Washington assisted in identifying wildlife habitats.

Authentic Resources

A wide variety of information resources, materials, tools, and technologies are used in authentic learning. Students increase their understanding of the world by examining primary resources, interacting with members of the community, and connecting with real-world issues. Authentic materials can be traced back to the original author or idea. Students can be involved with generating this information through e-mail interviews or original reporting of events and experiments.

The library media specialist is essential in authentic learning environments. Students are expected to go beyond teacher-directed activities and textbooks. The library media specialist can collaborate with the teacher to locate and organize authentic materials and resources from community or online experts to primary source documents or photographs. Partnerships also may be formed with the public library, community organizations, museums, natural areas, aquarium, botanical garden, zoo, or planetarium.

Rather than simply reading the work of others, learners develop meaningful questions and gather information from many sources. They often generate new data and ideas by:

• Conducting oral histories with local senior citizens,

• Developing a plan to renovate a museum exhibit,

• Comparing local and national data on air and water pollution, or

• Interviewing a NOAA oceanographer through e-mail or videoconferencing.

Technology can provide a bridge to authentic environments.

- Use webcams to videoconference with experts at remote locations.
- Go on virtual field trips to historical locations, museums, and natural places.
- Interact with experts on group discussion forums.
- Access primary sources and real-world data sources.
- Communicate with students from other cultures through e-mail.
- Watch news broadcasts from other countries over the Web.
- Use a video camera to record oral histories.

Authentic Communications and Audiences

Students need a real-world audience for their work. Authentic audiences might include the student government, local agencies, civic groups, and government offices. The oral history projects could be shared with local and national historical societies and organizations. Teachers should help students seek out stakeholders who have the authority to take action based on student recommendations. Students also should be prepared to witness the frustrations of democratic government in action (or failing to act), and be prepared to understand that not all recommendations succeed. Many voices may influence decisions in some situations while other decisions may be made unilaterally. The authentic experience, however, is one in which students are encouraged to find a voice and to participate as constructively as possible. (See Key Word: Critical Literacy.)

When examining the work of professionals across disciplines, investigators at the Consortium on Chicago School Research (Newman, Bryk, and Nagaoka 2001) found that adults rely upon complex forms of communication to conduct their work and present their results. Their tools involve verbal, symbolic, and visual communication to provide qualifications, nuances, elaborations, details, and analogies woven into extended narratives, explanations, justifications, and dialogue. When adults write letters, news articles, organizational memos, or technical reports; when they speak a foreign language; when they design a house, negotiate an agreement, or devise a budget; when they create a painting or a piece of music—they try to communicate ideas that have an impact on others. In contrast, most school assignments, such as spelling quizzes, laboratory exercises, or typical final exams, have little value beyond school, because they are designed only to document the competence of the learner.

Authentic Assessment

Assessment is a critical component of authentic learning. Students learn by applying knowledge to solve problems that mirror the challenges of tasks found beyond the classroom. Authentic assessment asks students to determine whether they've met their goal.

Authentic assessment values both the processes and products involved in learning. For example, journals, logs, and concept maps may be developed as the project progresses. Final products might include a letter to the editor, online book review, or presentation to a local nonprofit group. Students are asked to demonstrate their knowledge and skills in meaningful ways. Rather than testing isolated skills, authentic assessments effectively measure student capabilities through accurately evaluating learning by examining a student's performance in a natural situation. A variety of tools can be used in authentic assessment including checklists, portfolios, and rubrics.

Authentic assessment is used to evaluate student work as well as provide feedback for improvement. Rather than comparing students with each other, authentic assessment focuses on individual strengths and weaknesses. In other words, authentic assessment is usually criterion-referenced rather than norm-referenced. This aspect may prove to have limits however, compared to many real-world situations that are driven by human competition.

Authentic assessment is an evaluation process that involves multiple forms of performance measurement reflecting the student's learning, achievement, motivation, and attitudes on instructionally-relevant activities. Portfolio assessment is a systematic collection of student work that is analyzed to show progress over time with regard to instructional objectives. Student self-assessment offers opportunities for the student to self-regulate learning, and the responsibility of appraising his or her own progress. Integrated assessment refers to evaluation of multiple skills or assessment of language and content within the same activity. A written science report, for example, might include assessment of language skills, information selection and use skills, reasoning skills, as well as scientific content knowledge.

Other terms help to define the meaning of authentic assessment. In a broader sense, assessment is any systematic approach for collecting information on student learning and performance, usually based on different sources of evidence. Alternative assessment involves approaches for finding out what students know or can do other than or in addition to the use of multiple-choice testing. Authentic assessment, therefore, is a subset of these alternative evaluation processes, and is based on the assumption that there is a much wider spectrum of student performance that can be displayed than that limited by short-answer, standardized tests. This wider spectrum should include real-life learning situations and meaningful problems of a complex nature not solved with simple answers selected from a menu of choices.

Moving Toward Authentic Assessment

J. Michael O'Malley, Supervisor of Assessment at the Prince William County Public Schools of Virginia, and Lorraine Valdez Pierce, of the Graduate School of Education at George Mason University (1996), have listed characteristics of student performance that should be considered in authentic assessment.

- **Constructed Response:** The student constructs responses based on experiences he or she brings to the situation and new multiple resources are explored in order to create a product.

- **Higher-Order Thinking:** Responses are made to open-ended questions that require skills in analysis, synthesis, and evaluation.

- **Authenticity:** Tasks are meaningful, challenging, and engaging activities that mirror good instruction often relevant to a real-world context.

- **Integrative:** Tasks call for a combination of skills that integrate language arts with other content across the curriculum with all skills and content open to assessment.

- **Process and Product:** Procedures and strategies for deriving potential responses and exploring multiple solutions to complex problems are often assessed in addition to or in place of a final product or single-correct-response.

- **Depth in Place of Breadth:** Performance assessments build over time with varied activities to reflect growth, maturity, and depth, leading to mastery of strategies and processes for solving problems in specific areas with the assumption that these skills will transfer to solving other problems.

Types of Authentic Assessment

O'Malley and Pierce (1996) have also categorized common types of authentic assessment and the student actions that should be observed and documented. Their examples include the following:

- **Oral Interviews:** teacher asks student questions about personal background, activities, readings, and other interests.

- **Story or Text Retelling:** student retells main ideas or selected details of text experienced through listening or reading.

- **Writing Samples:** student generates narrative, expository, persuasive, or reference paper.

- **Projects/Exhibitions:** student works with other students as a team to create a project that often involves multimedia production, oral and written presentations, and a display.

- **Experiments/Demonstrations:** student documents a series of experiments, illustrates a procedure, performs the necessary steps to complete a task, and documents the results of the actions.

- **Constructed-Response Items:** student responds in writing to open-ended questions.

- **Teacher Observations:** teacher observes and documents the student's attention and interaction in class, response to instructional materials, and cooperative work with other students.

- **Portfolios:** a focused collection of student work to show progress over time.

Rubric: A Helpful, Nearly Authentic, Scoring Scale

Assessment requires teacher evaluation of student performance. To aid in making such judgments accurate and valid (teachers measure what is intended to be measured), and reliable (performances tend to be measured in the same manner from one situation to the next), a scoring scale or rubric should be established. Often the levels of evaluation in a rubric are classified as 1=basic, 2=proficient, and 3=advanced. The criteria for each performance level must be precisely defined in terms of what the student actually does to demonstrate skill or proficiency at that level.

Examples of rubric scales which reflect student progression in the use of information are as follows:

- Demonstrated indicator of student performance: integrates new information into one's own knowledge.

- Basic: puts information together without processing it.

- Proficient: integrates information from a variety of sources to create meaning that is relevant to own prior knowledge and draws conclusions.

- Advanced: integrates information to create meaning that connects with prior personal knowledge, draws conclusions, and provides details and supportive evidence.

- Demonstrated indicator of student performance: distinguishes among fact, point of view, and opinion.

- Basic: copies information as given and tends to give equal weight to fact and opinion as being evidence.

- Proficient: uses both facts and opinions, but labels them within a paraphrased use of the evidence.

- Advanced: links current, documented facts and qualified opinion to create a chain of evidence to support or reject an argument.

Role of the Instructional Library Media Specialist

Barbara Stripling (1993), past president of the American Association of School Librarians, has stated that there are several roles for the school library media specialist in the development and implementation of authentic assessment. The library media specialist is in an ideal position to help teachers shift from textbook and multiple-choice exams to alternative techniques such as projects, exhibits, and multimedia productions.

The library media specialist works with teachers in the co-role of expanding the assignment and creating a learning environment that allows authentic learning activities to become possible. Secondly, the library media specialist facilitates the activity with the teacher so that many learning environments can be made available to students including different locations for information gathering and use outside of the school beyond regular school hours.

Third, the library media specialist is versed in the authentic assessment process so that, as a professional teacher, the library media specialist provides an additional perspective to the judgment of student performance. The library media specialist provides input and evidence in the evaluation of the student's ability to process information into meaningful communication.

Making Academic Experiences More Authentic

An additional key role of the instructional library media specialist is that of curriculum consultant (AASL and AECT 1998). In this role the library media specialist, in collaboration with other teachers, examines the curriculum and the activities that compose it to expand typical academic exercises into more authentic or real-life situations. Moving from basic textbook exercises and multiple-choice exams toward more team projects is one step, but creating challenging activities which involve authentic resources should be the goal.

Authentic exercises place the student in simulations in which he or she must seek and obtain relevant information to purchase a used car; finance a college education; plan a vacation for the family; invest in the stock market; care independently for a pet; determine key resources needed to start a small business; plan a reception for visiting officials; make a proposal for new state legislation; determine which health management organization to select; and more...much more. These authentic activities require extensive use of resources that are up-to-date and often only accessible beyond the school library media center. A key message to instructional library media specialists in the implementation of authentic activities is that they must look, with their teachers, beyond locally-housed resources and into the community for access to information resources which will support real-life decision-making assignments.

Grant Wiggins (1993, 1997), well-known for his work with authentic education, places emphasis on selecting engaging problems that require students to develop effective, creative performances and products. By having a real-life context for product development, assessment has more relevance. Students are aware of the criteria used for evaluation and have opportunities for self-checking. They also have a chance to see and judge the impact of their product in the real world.

Authentic Learning and Information Inquiry

Information inquiry is at the core of authentic learning. The ultimate value of an inquiry project lies in its authenticity. Rather than exploring superficial questions and problems, students are asked to explore essential questions that require deep thinking. Students become problem-identifiers as well as problem-solvers. The skills for raising and refining meaningful questions that have depth and relevance to the real world are the skills that ultimately lead to measures of the student's ability to deal with challenging decisions.

Carol Gordon (1992), from the Educational Resources Library at Boston University, conducted an action research study with high school English teachers and the library media specialist focusing on authentic research assignments. According to Gordon, most assignments ask students to report on the findings of others and draw conclusions based on readings. She stresses the importance of placing students in an active role as researcher by conducting interviews, administering questionnaires, and journaling observations. This data then is used to construct meaning. In other words, rather than asking students to simply be reporters, Gordon suggests that students become "real researchers."

This idea has tremendous implications for teacher librarians. Rather than focusing on traditional information gathering approaches such as reading, taking notes, and summarizing, students become immersed in their research by using a variety of techniques to collect data, explore perspectives, and generate new ideas. Gordon notes that the ownership students feel for original work facilitates the construction process. Authentic inquiry may be an unreachable ideal, but the goal remains to raise the level educators should expect for student engagement and performance in meeting the information demands of their world both in and out of school.

Jinx Stapleton Watson (2003), from the University of Tennessee, has written about higher expectations relevant to student inquiry in science fair projects and summarizes how the typical library research paper fails to be authentic and often fall short of scientific method standards:

Most "research" projects assigned at the senior high school level do not provide an authentic application of scientific methods. Students who are limited to simple models that outline a linear research process will not experience the more meaningful aspects of research: personal selection of problems and research questions, application of proper methods, collection of original data, and reaching relevant conclusions. . . . [C]lean-cut exercises do not pretend to be about idea making or wondering, the essence of inquiry. Thus, teachers and school library media specialists who want students to pursue ideas that intrigue them enough to investigate must communicate different expectations from the step-by-step procedures. They must communicate that wrong turns and mistakes in thinking may offer as much information as successful efforts. They must support the approach that such inquiry might not be pursued with a single course or class schedule, but rather, across disciplines, across the day, in flexible schedules of classroom and library [access] with significant adults ready to assist at wrong turns, mistakes, and plateau periods in the investigation.

Communicating Evidence of Learning

In one of the most important recent contributions to the performance assessment literature, Violet Harada and Joan Yoshina of Hawaii, have gathered an impressive array of assessment instruments in their book Assessing Learning (2005). Samples of checklists, rubrics and portfolio structures are given, based on proven application in local classrooms and in environments where the school library media specialist has collaborated with the classroom teacher as an instructional specialist team to co-evaluate student progress.

Communication evidence of student performance provides a constructive forum to describe inquiry projects, the complexity of the processes involved and to illustrate how each student has moved forward or has yet to accomplish selected critical information skills. Harada and Yoshina broaden the audience for such communications. Conversations or reflections on student performance can take place

- between the student and teachers,

- among the instructional media specialists (classroom teacher and library media specialists),

- before the principal concerning units that are tied to state learning standards,

- before parents to discuss individual student progress, and

- before the school board to illustrate yearly progress in the standards for student learning—especially in information and media literacy skills.

What this action research team has learned is important advice for all who seek to implement authentic assessment:

The most critical uses of assessment data are to allow students an opportunity to reflect on their own progress and to provide instructors with crucial information on what students are learning and how teaching might be shaped to help students do even better. With the current emphasis on accountability, however, still another important use of assessment information has emerged: the need for synthesizing and presenting summaries of students' learning achievements to various stakeholder groups. In short, communicating evidence of what is being learned through library instruction is a valuable advocacy tool. (125)

References

American Association of School Librarians (AASL) and the Association for Educational Communications and Technology (AECT). (1998). *Information Power: Building Partnerships for Learning.* American Library Association.

Callison, D. (1998). "Authentic Assessment." *School Library Media Activities Monthly* 14 (5): 42–43+.

Callison, D., and A. Lamb. (2004). "Information Inquiry and Authentic Learning." Presented at the National Conference of the American Library Association. Orlando.

Collins, A., J. S. Brown, and S. E. Newman. (1988). "Cognitive Apprenticeship: Teaching the Craft of Reading, Writing, and Mathematics." In *Knowing, Learning and Instruction: Essays in Honor of Robert Glaser,* edited by L. B. Resnick. Lawrence Erlbaum.

Curtis, M., et al. (2004*). Palm OS Handhelds in the Elementary Classroom: Curriculum and Strategies.* ISTE.

Gordon, C. (1992). "Students as Authentic Researchers: A New Prescription for the High School Research Assignment." *School Library Media Research* 2. Available from the American Library Association Web site at http://www.ala.org/aasl/SLMR.

Harada, V. H., and J. M. Yoshina. (2005). *Assessing Learning: Librarians and Teachers as Partners.* Libraries Unlimited.

Marra, T. (2004). *Authentic Learning Environments.* Available from the University of Michigan Web site at http://wwwpersonal.umich.edu/%7Etmarra/authenticity/authen.html.

Newmann, F. M., and G. G. Wehlage. (1993). "Five Standards of Authentic Instruction." *Educational Leadership* 50 (7): 8–12.

Newmann, F. M., A. S. Bryk, and J. K. Nagaoka. (2001). *Authentic Intellectual Work and Standardized Tests: Conflict or Coexistence?* Consortium on Chicago School Research.

Nicaise, M. (1995). "Student Astronauts Blast off in the Midwest: An Example of an Authentic Learning Environment." *Space Times: Magazine of the American Astronautical Society* 34 (5): 18–20.

O'Malley, J. M., and L. Valdez Pierce. (1996). *Authentic Assessment for English Language Learning: Practical Approaches for Teachers.* Addison-Wesley Publishing.

Stripling, B. K. (1993). "Practicing Authentic Assessment in the School Library." In *School Library Media Annual,* edited by C. C. Kuhlthau, 11: 40–56. Libraries Unlimited.

Vygotsky, L. S. 1930. *Mind in Society.* Harvard University Press.

Watson, J. S. (2003). "Examining Perceptions of the Science Fair Project: Content or Process?" *School Library Media Research* 6. Available from the American Library Association Web site at http://www.ala.org/aasl/SLMR.

Wiggins, G. (1993). "Assessment: Authenticity, Context, and Validity." *Phi Delta Kappan* 75 (3): 200–214.

Wiggins, G. (1997). "Practicing What We Preach in Designing Authentic Assessments." *Educational Leadership* 54 (1): 18–25.

Zemelman, S., H. Daniels, and A. Hyde. (2005). *Best Practice: Today's Standards for Teaching and Learning in America's Schools.* 3rd edition. Heinemann.

Bias

Daniel Callison

Two challenging criteria for judging information involve bias and authority. In both cases, judgments may not be clearly possible. In both cases, there may be degrees or levels of acceptability. For students to gain experience and to demonstrate skills in making judgments, they need opportunities to consider a wide spectrum of resources under a variety of information use assignments.

Objectivity is probably never in play although often claimed. It is possible to find some level of bias in every form of communication. The bias may be clearly stated and expressed for the purpose of stating one perception or opinion in order to define a stance, make a claim, or argue for change. The bias present in some documents may be hidden and perhaps not even apparent to the author.

While eliminating bias in favor of objectivity is often stated as an information literacy goal, understanding the signs and implications of bias in conjunction with characteristics of authority may be a more reasonable expectation. The Information Age poses a complex challenge to those who teach information literacy and inquiry as they and their students face sophisticated spin on messages delivered through every media format.

Laurie Rozakis, a professor of English at Farmingdale State University and teacher of basic information research skills for many years, emphasizes that bias is not necessarily bad, as long as it is recognized as such and taken into account as the information is evaluated. The most common forms of bias, according to Rozakis (2004), are the following:

- Bogus claim. A claim can be considered false when the speaker or the writer promises more than he or she can deliver.

- Loaded term. A term is loaded when it carries more emotional impact than its context can really support.

- Misrepresentation of a fact. Such may involve wrong data, false data, and over-simplification of facts.

Research findings in every field will contain bias tied to the researcher's agenda—which questions are investigated and which are not, which populations can be investigated or not, and often in the conclusions that are selected for reporting while others are dropped. Trusted researchers will report such limitations.

To find a truly objective agenda in educational research is probably not very likely and such is a reason why one must read widely and compare findings over time and across situations. Evidence on the need for small class size, for example, may be viewed differently by different groups with different needs. School administrators may find more value in studies that indicate students meet reasonable academic standards even in classrooms with more students. Teachers and union leaders, may seek out studies that conclude more learning takes place and teacher burn-out is less likely with smaller classes. Both may be right, and both may be wrong. Bias determines the information selected and valued.

Confirmation Bias

While learning to recognize bias in resources, the information literate student must learn to recognize and manage his/her own bias behavior. Often, such behavior is not obvious to us and we all need peers and mentors who will draw attention to what can be "information blindness"—failure to keep our eyes and mind open to different data, evidence and arguments.

The Skeptic's Dictionary (Carroll 2003) defines "confirmation bias" as a type of selective thinking whereby one tends to notice and to look for what confirms one's beliefs, and to ignore, not look for, or undervalue, the relevance of what contradicts one's beliefs. The tendency to give more attention and weight to data that support our beliefs than we do to contrary data may be especially harmful when personal beliefs are not much more than a set of prejudice assumptions. Other relevant terms defined in this dictionary are

- Selective thinking—one selects evidence which is favorable or supportive of a held belief while ignoring evidence that is not favorable or supportive.

- Communal reinforcement—the process by which a claim becomes a strong belief through repeated assertion by members of a group or community.

- Ad hoc hypothesis—a notion or proposal that is created to explain away facts that seem to refute one's original theory.

- Wishful thinking—the interpretation of facts, reports, events, observations, and/or perceptions according to what one would like to be the case rather than according to the actual evidence. If such is done intentionally and without regard for the truth, it is called misinterpretation, falsification, dissembling, disingenuous, or perversion of the truth.

Other terms related to bias include

- Stereotype—an exaggerated belief, image or distorted truth about a person or a group that evolves into a generalization that allows for little or no individual differences or social variation. Stereotypes are often based on or reinforced by images in mass media, and are often established by influences from parents and peer groups.

- Hidden bias—biases thought to be absent or removed may appear in the behavior of some individuals who strive to be committed to egalitarianism and yet display hidden negative prejudices.

- Propaganda –the systematic propagation of a doctrine, ideology or idea through a planned series of communication events with the long-term goal of getting the audience to adopt a new way of thinking. Persuasion at this level is often slanted or biased in a specific direction regardless of conflicting evidence.

- Conventional wisdom—a prevailing set of beliefs about any particular subject or topic at a given point in time. The beliefs are not necessarily correct, but simply are those most widely held and seemingly respectable.

- Group-Think—the act or practice of reasoning or decision making by a group, especially when characterized by uncritical acceptance or conformity to prevailing points of view. Decision making by a group in a manner that discourages independent creativity, individual responsibility, or any suggestion of planning counter to the majority view or the commanding view held by the chair. Evidence is sought and selected to support the dominate view.

Group-think can be a phenomenon observable in the interactions among students placed in teams and charged with the task of solving an information problem. Teachers may find the following warning signs that objectivity and logic have been lost:

- Members perceive falsely that everyone agrees with the group's decision; silence is seen as consent.

- Some members withhold their dissenting views and counter-arguments, often because of peer-pressure to conform.

- The group constructs negative stereotypes of rivals outside of the group or others who might hold opinions different from the group.

- There is collective rationalization as group members discredit and explain away warnings or evidence that seems contrary to group thinking.

- Group members come to believe their decisions are morally correct and ignore ethical consequences of their decisions.

Janis and Mann (1977) have suggested, in their classic text on decision making, the following actions to avoid group-think:

- Members should be informed of the causes and consequences of group-think.

- The leader should be neutral and seek an atmosphere of open inquiry.

- The leader should give high priority to airing objections and doubts, and considering criticism.

- Unpopular alternatives should be raised with some of the stronger members playing the role of "devil's advocate."

- Outside experts, and others offering different opinions, should be included in the vital decision-making stages.

- Two or more sub-groups should deal independently with the given problem and present contracting reports for total group analysis.

- Effective leaders tend to be those who take tentative decisions to trusted colleagues who are part of the organization specifically because of their intelligence and different views.

Bias in News Media

The left-wing or right-wing bias reflected by individual newspapers or television networks is often a topic of debate, especially among those responsible for delivery of the news. Political leaders from all times and ranks have found the news media to be a challenge in conveying the message they want delivered to their followers and potential followers. Students need to know that media will hold a bias in many different ways and such may be difficult to detect. Bias may be found in the following elements of news delivery:

- **Temporal bias**—there is a bias toward the immediate, events that are new and fresh, so that attention of the audience can be maintained. Sports and athletic personalities tend to provide an ever changing set of events linked one to another, while students who score in the top-ten of their class may not be involved in activities that are as exciting or simple enough for most journalists to understand and report.

- **Bad news bias**—good news is boring, and bad news makes the world look more dangerous than it really is and politicians more crooked than they really are. Academically talented students may find themselves, if ever at all, on the inside of the newspaper while those displaying deviant behavior will make the front page.

- **Visual bias**—short time frames and limited paper space may result in only a few seconds of footage or only a single picture in the paper to cover an event. Such brief depictions can give a negative or positive slant especially for the viewer or reader who does not deal with details.

- **Narrative bias**—often news coverage forces the events into a story with a conflict and plot, completed only if there are antagonists and protagonists. In some events no real conflict exists and the "story" is that people are working toward consensus. Agreement, however, may not be exciting news.

- **Balance bias**—equal time or equal space does not mean that both sides are really equal in their arguments and evidence. Sometimes a false balance is forced on the discussion of issues with "equal time" given to minority factions that really have no relevance to the issues being debated.

Belief Perseverance

Mary Ann Fitzgerald, a professor in instructional technology at the University of Georgia, has written excellent articles on the information evaluation process and the challenge such a process brings to developing minds who may not grasp the concepts of media manipulation or deliberate lies disguised as strategic persuasion. "The difference between bias and belief is subtle," writes Fitzgerald (1999), "and writers often blur it. In the context of information evaluation, bias is the application of existing mental constructs to new information in such a way that the resulting judgment contains flawed reasoning. These reasoning flaws can be infinitesimally slight or gross. Several cognitive phenomena help to explain how these problems occur. Underlying all of them is a phenomenon called belief perseverance."

Belief perseverance is a person's refusal or inability to relinquish a belief despite new information discrediting it. Often associated to belief perseverance is confirmatory bias. Such occurs when an individual seeks information to support his or her held beliefs while ignoring information supporting opposing beliefs. Students may set out to "prove a point" by searching only for facts or "evidence" which will confirm their "hypothesis." In some cases, students will accept information or opinions as authoritative only if voiced by their candidate of choice, or favored "expert," thus often taking testimony at face value and conclusive when, in reality, such is one opinion, but not necessarily well informed.

Among many useful exercises in information evaluation promoted by Fitzgerald (1999), the following two have an excellent chance of placing students in situations where they must critically review and reflect on bias found in evidence and arguments:

- In a daily 15-minute exercise, children should find problems such as inconsistency or exaggeration in a short piece of curriculum-relevant text. These exercises should represent well-structured problems at first and progress to ill-structured problems as students become more skillful. School library media specialists can extend these classroom exercises when student perform basic research.

- Students should practice formal argumentation, which involves the evaluation of evidence. They should switch sides and argue opposite positions. Debates, mock trails, and mock or genuine editorials present excellent opportunities for this skill practice.

References

Carroll, R. T. (2003). *The Skeptic's Dictionary.* Wiley.

Fitzgerald, M. A. (1999). "Evaluating Information: An information Literacy Challenge." *School Library Media Research* 2. Available at www.ala.org/aasl/SLMR/ (accessed July 2, 2006).

Janis, I. L., and Mann, L. (1977). *Decision Making.* Free Press.

Rozakis, L. E. 2004. *The Complete Idiot's Guide to Research Methods.* Alpha Books.

Blogs and Blogging (Web Logs)

Annette Lamb and Larry Johnson

From humorous teen journals to serious scientific peer review, blogging has become a fast-growing online activity. A web-based communication tool, a blog is simply a web log. In most cases, a single author writes and posts short articles that are displayed in reverse chronological order. These blogs are generally open to the public and visitors are encouraged to comment on the author's entries (see Figure Part 3.3). However educators can easily restrict access depending on the nature of the learning activity.

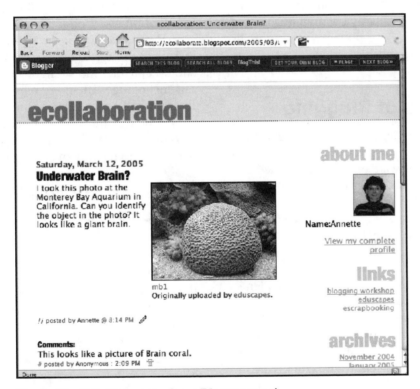

Figure Part3.3. Blog entry from Blogger.com/.

The Popularity of Blogs

According to a recent report by the Pew Internet and American Life Project (2005), over half of all American teenagers create content for the Internet including blogs. Nearly twenty percent of twelve- to seventeen-year-olds have created their own blogs and nearly forty percent regularly read blogs. Teen bloggers, particularly older girls are most likely to have experience with almost every online activity. As a result, many students are already familiar with the use of blogs.

Although often associated with news punditry and personal journaling, blogs can also provide a rich environment where students can share the process and products associated with Information Inquiry activities.

State and national learning standards stress the importance of authentic student experiences. For example, the National Council on Economics Education has identified standards regarding how economic issues affect the lives of workers, consumers, and citizens. A blog could be used to highlight members of the Chamber of Commerce and their contribution to the local economy. Students would have the opportunity to ask questions and discuss key issues with these community members.

David Warlick (2005) is an educational consultant and owner of Blogmeister, a popular blogging service for educators. He stresses that students develop better communication skills when they are authentically communicating and encourages educators to promote writing skills through student-published blogs that invite outside comments.

The Basics of Blogging

Unlike many technologies that are time-consuming to learn, blogs are easy to set up and use. No special software or skills are needed and they can be accessed anywhere, anytime from the Web. Many free or low cost online services make blogging accessible to all educators. Because blogs can be accessed from any computer with Internet, library media specialists are using them as a tool for instructional activities as well as communication with teachers, students, parents and the community.

Because blogs can contain web links, graphics, video, and audio, many educators are finding them easier to maintain than traditional Web sites for class projects. Many schools are incorporating video, audio, or podcasts (that can be downloaded to iPods and other MP3 devices) as part of blog-based electronic class or school magazines.

Blogs can be used to provide open comments and feedback to students. Because student entries are stamped with the date and time of their completion, teachers can easily monitor and trace student activities. Because all blog entries are archived, it's easy for teachers to assess student work or ask students to review and reflect on their own progress.

Multiple blogs can be created for varied purposes such as reading groups, science experiments, or school library news. A blog can be used to facilitate learning and experiences beyond the confines of the classroom such as virtual guest interviews or book discussions that extend beyond the school day.

Blogs can be used to facilitate authentic learning experiences, motivate and engage learners, and promote literacy skills across the curriculum. In addition, they encourage reading and writing for an audience, allow quick feedback from many types of readers, and encourage peer interaction and collaboration. Blogs can be used to ask meaningful questions, stimulate new questions, encourage alternative ideas, and to promote interaction and sharing of process information and products.

Before using blogs in a specific teaching or learning activity, school library media specialists should consider the strengths and limitations of this technology. Blogging requires access to the Internet and basic keyboarding skills. Students should be mindful of the larger public audience of blogs and are encouraged to write as if their parents were reading over their shoulders.

Blogs as Information Resources

With millions of blog entries available on the Web, classroom teachers and their students can easily be overwhelmed. The challenge of the library media specialist is to partner with teachers to design effective learning activities that help students locate, evaluate, synthesize, and use the information available on blogs.

Many students follow National Geographic's WildCam Africa project that includes a live video camera located at the Mashatu Game Reserve in Africa. Students can watch elephants, zebras, and other animals at a pond, then post comments and ask questions on a blog. Wildlife researchers post information and answer questions. Similarly, the FalconCam in Cleveland, Ohio is focused on the nests of peregrine falcons and students use Cecilia's Nature Blog to trace the activities of the falcons and their chicks.

Existing blogs can be used to provide information and insights related to specific subject area topics. Many government and nonprofit agencies use blogs to disseminate news about their programs. For instance, readers of the Bird Treatment and Learning Center blog are able to trace the rehabilitation of injured, sick, and orphaned wild birds.

Stephen Downes, a senior researcher with e-Learning Research Group in New Brunswick, Canada states that blogging isn't really about writing. Instead, it is about reading what is of interest to you: your culture, your community, and your ideas. Engaging with the content and with the authors of what you have read including reflecting, criticizing, questioning, and reacting.

The following categories reflect the types of bloggers and blogs students are likely to encounter.

- Diarists, storytellers, experience trackers

- Scholars, hobbyists, and enthusiasts

- Institutional outreach representatives

- Journalists and news reporters

- News pundits, advocates, and columnists

- Public figures and personalities

- Subject area and professional specialists

- Learners

Increasingly, library media specialists are using aggregators to help them organize the wealth of information generated by blogs. These aggregators let users select, categorize, and present the RSS (Rich Site Summary) feed from a blog in a blog reader rather than going to the individual blog Web sites (see Figure Part3.4). Many school library media specialists regularly follow the blogs of popular young adult authors who maintain blogs such as Laura Halse Anderson and Neil Gaiman.

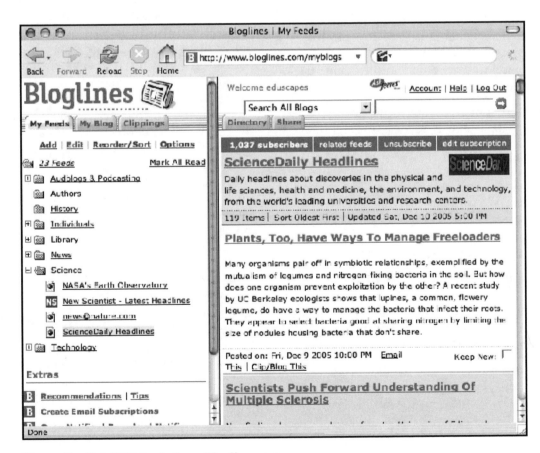

Figure Part3.4. RSS feeds from Bloglines.com.

Annette Lamb (2004) identified nine activities to promote high-level thinking using existing blogs:

- **Activate.** Motivate with blogs. Use a blog as a catalyst to generate interest in a new topic. Help students see the excitement and energy that can be found in a subject.

- **Connect.** Provide a context or establish a connection. Bring relevance to the discussion by using a "real world" situation or example found in a blog.

- **Critique.** Critically evaluate an idea or perspective by using examples to support a position. Many of these examples can be found in professional blogs.

- **Deepen.** Add depth to a learning situation by providing a detailed explanation, thoughtful observation, or new resource that provides additional information or insights. For example, use a law blog to learn more about law and ethics.

- **Expand.** Broaden thinking by providing an alternative perspective or different point of view. For example, use blogs from different countries to examine cultural differences.

- **Fresh Look.** Use blogs to provide current, immediately relevant examples. For example, get the latest science or fashion news.

- **Inform.** Provide primary sources or data that help explain an idea already presented. For example, you can track earthquakes and volcanoes. Consider a statistic or graph that illustrates a point.

- **Launch.** Look for blogs as a place for new, innovative ideas. Be the first to present a new idea rather than simply commenting on the work of others. Ask questions to keep the new idea going.

- **Synthesize.** Bring a number of ideas together. For example, consolidate these comments and draw a new conclusion.

Blogs and the School Library Media Specialist

Many teacher librarians are using blogs as a way to communicate and collaborate with their students, teachers, parents, and professional peers. They may post photographs of library activities, announce media fair opportunities, or share interesting new materials. In schools where the procedures for updating Web sites has become cumbersome, blogs are sometimes used as the virtual presence of the school library center displacing the more traditional Web site. Other school media specialists are using blogs to host online reading groups, cross-generational interactions and discussions, and to facilitate virtual expert and author visits.

Frances Jacobson Harris maintains a blog called Gargoyles Loose in the Library that provides news and views from the University Laboratory High School Library in Urbana, Illinois. She suggests that a blog can be the spot for library news, updates, and communication to the public. Harris notes that library blogs may have a single purpose such as book discussions, book clubs, library construction projects, summer reading programs, class assignments, or homework. School library blogs can also be a vehicle for active learning.

An increasing number of school library media specialists and other educators are using blogs as tools for professional communications. For example, Doug Johnson's The Blue Skunk Blog and Joyce Valenza's Neverending Search provide excellent resources and information for school library media specialists seeking ideas and professional connections.

In some cases, school library media specialists are using blogs within professional development activities. Teacher librarian Christine Maccarella created the LPS Bloggers project as part of a sustained professional development activity at Livingston Public School in New Jersey. She involved teachers with discussions such as the role of blogging in schools, young adult literature, and blog integration. Participants receive credit for completing online activities, along with implementing and evaluating their own classroom-based blog project with students.

Larry Johnson integrated blogging into a web-based course for school library media specialists. The blog, titled SLMS Bridging Theory and Practice invited experienced school library media specialists to share their expertise in areas such as grant writing, budgeting, center promotion, technology, and leadership.

Blogs in Teaching and Learning

Will Richardson, a high school supervisor of Instructional Technology and Communications in Flemington, New Jersey and author of Web Logg-ed points out that blogs are used to publish student work, collaborate with remote locations, and manage the knowledge construction activities of the learning community. Beyond traditional applications, he stresses that blogging allows a new type of writing that forces writers to read carefully and critically, demands clarity in construction, and links to sources of ideas. What he has called "connective writing" is closely aligned with the Information Inquiry activities promoted by school library media specialists.

Doug Johnson, director of media and technology for Mankato Public Schools and author of Blue Skunk Blog adds that blogging begins with reading, but may also begin with primary sources such as artifacts, surveys, experiments, interviews or personal experiences.

Rather than viewing blogging as a series of content-area writing activities, consider the specific critical and creative thinking that will occur in this learning environment. Also think about the role of students in making posting and comments. When creating learning blogs, ask yourself the following questions:

- **Purpose and learning outcomes.** What's the purpose of the blog? Why is the blog format being used?
- **Blog audience.** What is the primary and secondary audience for the blog? Are bloggers writing for themselves or a specific audience such as the teacher, other students within the class, students in other classrooms, parents or local community members, or a global audience? Is the blog intended to be use inside or outside the classroom?
- **Blog hosting.** Who will host the blog? Will that be a teacher, the school library media specialist, or will each student have his or her own personal blog? Is this blog responsibility individual, divided among small groups, or shared by the class as a whole?
- **Learning outcome.** What are the expectations and how do these reflect the learning goal? What are the specific learning outcomes? What's the objective of the lesson(s)? What standards are being addressed? When used in teaching and learning, the educational outcomes must be made clear for the students.
- **Blog content.** Will the teacher or students make the initial postings? What activities will occur within the blog? What activities will facilitate high-level thinking such as analysis, synthesis, formulating plans, or drawing conclusions? What information will be shared? Where will this information originate? Many blogs are used to share information including facts, stories, data, statistics, and links to other resources, opinions, and much more. In addition to text, the blog could contain audio, video, and visuals.
- **Process or product.** Is the blog about process, product, or both? Teachers often use blogs as a tool to document the Information Inquiry process.
- **Reflection.** Blogs can be used as a metacognitive tool to help people think about their life or learning. These reflections may be intended for themselves, their classmates, or the world.
- **Interaction.** Some blogs focus on communication between the person posting the entry and the people making comments. The responses may include additional information, expanded ideas, or critiques. Sometimes the most important aspect of the blog is questioning. With young children, the interaction is often between the child and the teacher.

- **Assessment.** How will learning be assessed? Do the learning outcomes match the assessment? Sometimes blogs are used as a tool for assessment to check student understanding. Bloggers may be asked to state facts, analyze an article, or express their understandings.

In their article titled "Scaffolding for Struggling Students: Reading and Writing with Blogs," Sara Kajder and Glen Bull (2003) describe how blogs can be used by teachers and students writers to create an engaging, rich writing space. They stress that blog characteristics particularly relevant to instruction include economy, archiving, feedback, multimedia, immediacy, and active participation. They have identified ten instructional uses of blogs in reading and writing including character journals, character roundtables, open minds, think-aloud postings, literature circle group responses, nutshelling, devil's advocate writing, exploding sentences, photoblogs, and storyblogs.

As the school library media specialist and classroom teachers collaborate on the creation of meaningful blog activities, consider some of the following assignments:

- **Analyze.** Ask students to analyze a book, article, or other posting. Then, compare their perspectives.

- **Brainstorm.** Pose problems and create a collection of ideas. Ask students to synthesize these ideas and make recommendations.

- **Chronicle.** Follow and record an event. Trace a time line; create a parallel time line.

- **Collaborate.** Work collaboratively with another class in the same school or another school.

- **Communicate.** Interact with an expert or conduct an interview.

- **Compare.** Make a comparison.

- **Critique.** Ask students to write reviews for Web sites, books, movies, games, local sights, or other topics.

- **Discuss.** Examine a problem, question, drawing, photograph, or diagram. Then,

write captions, analyze elements, speculate, or create. Some blogs focus on interaction, reaction, and discussion of a wide range of topics. While forum software is sometimes used for these, blogs can also be effective. Use the blog format for literature-rich discussions related to award nominated books, literature circles, or community book club connections.

- **Explain.** Ask students to learn and demonstrate their understanding.

- **Imagine.** Ask student to imagine a situation or scenario.

- **Inquiry.** Use the blog as a tool for questioning, exploration, and investigation. Individually or in groups, students chronicle the inquiry process and use the blog to share their experiences, reflections, and challenges. The blog is also used to interact and share ideas, provide feedback, and critique ideas.

- **Journal.** Keep a journal, log, or diary. Work individually or as a class to compose journal entries or assign groups or individual students.

- **Motivate.** Motivation is critical to learning. Sometimes a topical blog can generate passion in students who otherwise find school boring and meaningless. They may be asked to motivate others to take action.

- **Observe and log.** Observe human interactions, scientific experiments, or other activities and post a record (i.e., kindness journal, plant growth, survey results). Some blogs focus on a particular shared experience such as an annual event, field trip, or school-wide activity. The blog is used to record the experience. It might also involve connecting with students in other locations for a virtual experience.

- **Persuade.** Ask students to make a persuasive argument.

- **Predict.** Read or watch, then predict what will happen next.

- **Problem solve.** Pose a problem and discuss solutions.

- **Question.** Get students involved with asking questions.

- **React, think, act.** Connect in-class learning to blog entries. Transfer learning to new situations.

- **Read and jigsaw.** Read or use online resources and discuss (i.e., quote, Web site, poem, historical document, problem, literature circles). Then, analyze, evaluate, and create. Add a comment.

- **Remember and reflect.** Think about an activity and reflect on it.

- **Report.** Share local or global current events as a class or individually. The student or teacher posts current events articles and invites reactions, thoughts, alternative perspectives, or solutions. Use the blog format to post reports. Students can add web links to web pages, music, or videos. Some blogs also allow photographs. Categories might include key topics or it may be presented chronologically.

- **Share teacher and student work.** Any type of written work can be the focal point for a blog such as poetry, short stories, or television scripts. However, blogs can also be used to share other creative works such as artwork, musical scores, and video productions. Share materials in a digital format including documents, PDF files, photographs, charts, graphics, written work, audio, video, and presentations. Some blogs are used for maintaining a portfolio of student work.

Blogging in Information Inquiry

From journaling about the inquiry process to applying blog technology in a final product, blogging has many applications in Information Inquiry. Clarence Fisher, a middle school teacher in Canada involves his students in creating blogs. He notes that drawing information from a variety of sources, bringing it together with additional information, and thinking about the implications is not new, but placing synthesized thought online for others to access, use, and modify is new for today's students.

In her article "Blogging to Learn," Anne Bartlett-Bragg (2003), a faculty member at the University of Technology at Sydney, stresses that individual ownership of content differentiates blogging from other electronic forums like discussion boards and mailing lists. Learners control what is published and engage readers with their writing. Bartlett-Bragg has identified a five-stage process for blogging with learners:

- **Establishment.** Students recall and record learning events. Guided questions facilitate writing.

- **Introspection.** Students continue to record events, but also reflect and evaluate these experiences.

- **Reflective monologues.** Students take more responsibility for topics, develop questioning techniques, and write for themselves rather than the teacher.

- **Reflective dialogue.** Students consider their style of expression, intended audience, and publication of their thoughts. They move away from surface level reporting to personal knowledge publishing.

- **Knowledge artifact.** Students move to reflecting on the knowledge learned and providing guidance to readers who may use the information to enhance their own learning.

Blogging activities can be integrated throughout the inquiry process. Blogs can be used in both individual and collaborative inquiry environments. One of the advantages of blogs is the ability to extend postings through the use of comments. In an inquiry activity, these comments may come from the individual conducting the investigation, the supervising teacher, peers, or outside participants such as students in other schools, local volunteers, or members of the virtual community (see Figure Part3.5).

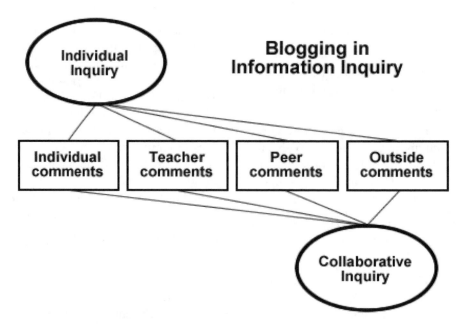

Figure Part3.5. Blogging in Information Inquiry. Annette Lamb and Larry Johnson. Copyright 2006.

Ask students to track their inquiry experience by using blog entries to record their activities, thoughts, and reflections as they move through each aspect of the inquiry process. Students may reflect on their activities identifying a topic, solving a problem, answering questions, or conducting research. They may even go back and comment on their own postings as they reflect on their progress.

To extend this metacognitive activity, the teacher librarian may comment on student progress and provide helpful feedback and suggestions. Students often wait to the last moment to do a project. A blog can keep students on-track and allows the teacher to provide guidance and encouragement throughout the Information Inquiry process.

In addition, classmates may become involved in peer sharing, support, encouragement, mentoring, or cognitive apprenticeships. In other words, if a peer finds that a classmate is having difficulty focusing on a topic, he or she may add a comment that suggests a direction or source to consider.

Consider ways to move these virtual activities beyond the walls of the school. For example, local senior citizens may be asked to provide their insights into inquiry projects through posting comments in a student blog. Members of scientific community may be willing to share their

professional insights related to an environment investigation.

Beyond individual inquiry activities with outside contributions, use blogging as a tool for collaborative inquiry experiences. A blog may serve as the gathering place for Information Inquiry. In other words, students may brainstorm questions, categorize their ideas, and come to consensus on a project direction. Later in the project, this online community may share and evaluate resources, identify varied perspectives, and synthesize their findings. While initial postings may be used to structure activities, students may also use the blog as a free flowing environment for sharing and discovery.

Danny Callison, professor in the School of Information and Library Science at Indiana University at Indianapolis states that inquiry can be viewed as controlled, guided, modeling, or free. These levels are useful in planning blog-based activities. For example, in a controlled inquiry environment, the teacher librarian may create the initial blog postings and ask students to respond by telling stories, evaluating, sources, or comparing approaches. In the free inquiry environment, students create their own blog postings and control the level of outside interaction their wish.

Callison states that meaningful information application comes from analysis of information need, analysis of information gained, and synthesis of information to address the need in the most efficient and effective manner possible. The interactive components of Information Inquiry are questioning and exploring, assimilation and inference, and reflection.

Figure Part3.6 visualizes how a student conducting an individual Information Inquiry might go through this recursive process making initial blog postings and subsequent comments on his or her own work as the inquiry progresses. In the illustration, numbers are used to indicate the order in which the entries were made. The student began with a posting brainstorming questions. Then, an experience related to information exploration was recorded as a posting. Next, the learner returned to the first posting and added a comment sharing a thought. The student eventually made seven postings and ten related comments.

Inquiry, Connectiveness, and Synergy

George Siemens, an instructor at Red River College in Manitoba, Canada has developed a learning theory focusing on the idea of connectivism stressing that learning is a process of connecting ideas and concepts. Siemens has observed that learning is no longer simply an internal, individualistic activity. He points out that the additional value of blogs comes from the ability for learners to teach and learn from each other.

Konrad Glogowski, an elementary language arts teacher in Canada states that learners need more than blogging tools and time to write. In addition, students must become members of an online learning community and view writing and reading as cognitive tools for learning. Being plugged into a social network allows a simple student posting to have added meaning when it gets interpreted, re-interpreted, commented on and discussed by other members of the group. Students soon begin to see patterns and connections. The blog becomes a catalyst for inquiry.

References

Bartlett-Bragg, A. (2003). "Blogging to Learn." *The Knowledge Tree* 4 (December). Available at http://www.flexiblelearning.net.au/knowledgetree/edition04/pdf/Blogging_to_Learn.pdf.

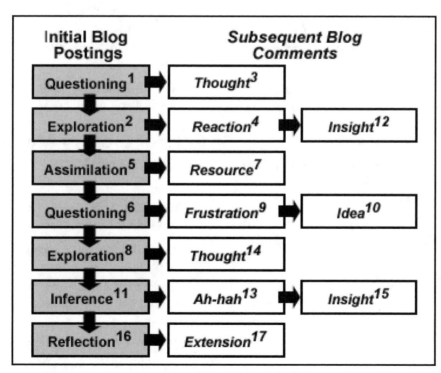

Figure Part3.6. Visualizing the Information Inquiry process. Annette Lamb and Larry Johnson. Copyright 2006.

Callison, D. (1999) "Inquiry." *School Library Media Activities Monthly* 15 (6): 38–42.

Downes, S. (2004). "Educational Blogging." *EDUCAUSE Review* 39 (5): 12–26. Available at http://www.educause.ed_Hlt532800574uBM_4_/apps/er/erm04/erm0450.asp.

Embrey, T. R. (2002). "You Blog, We Blog: A Guide to How Teacher-Librarians Can Use Weblogs to Build Communication and Research Skills." *Teacher Librarian* 30 (2). Available at http://www.teacherlibrarian.com/tlmag/v_30/v_30_2_feature.html.

Harris, F. J. (2005). *What's a Blog Doing in My Library?* Available at http://www.uni.uiuc.edu/library/blogging/.

Harris, F. J. (2005). *I Found It on the Internet: Coming of Age Online.* ALA Editions.

Hastings, P. B. (2003). *Blogging Across the Curriculum.* Available at http://mywebspace.quinnipiac.edu/PHastings/bac.html.

Kajder, S. and G. Bull. (2003). "Scaffolding for Struggling Students: Reading and Writing with Blogs." *Learning & Leading with Technology* 31 (2): 32–35.

Lamb, A. (2004). "Blogs and Blogging." *Escrapbooking.* Available at http://escrapbooking.com/blogging.

Pew Internet and American Life Project. (2005).*Teen Content Creators and Consumers.* Available at http://www.pewinternet.org/PPF/r/166/report_display.asp.

Richardson, W. (2006). *Blogs, Wikis, Podcasts and Other Powerful Web Tools for Classrooms.* Corwin Press.

Warlick, D. (2005). *Classroom Blogging: A Teacher's Guide to the Blogosphere.* LuLu.

Educator Blogs

2 Cents Worth by David Warlick http://davidwarlick.com/2cents/

http://classblogmeister.com/

Blog of Proximal Development by Konrad Glogowski http://www.teachandlearn.ca/blog

Connectivism Blog by George Siemens http://www.connectivism.ca/blog

Educational Bloggers Network http://www.ebn.weblogger.com/

Blue Skunk Blog by Doug Johnson http://doug-johnson.squarespace.com/

Connectivism Blog by George Siemens http://www.connectivism.ca/blog

Kathy Schrock's Kaffeekatsch http://kathyschrock.blogspot.com/

Librarian in the Middle http://www.beiffert.net/wordpress/

LPS Bloggers by Christine Maccarella http://classblogmeister.com/blog.php?blogger_id=5336&new_display_count=1000

Marc Prensky's Weblog http://www.marcprensky.com/blog/

Neverending Search by Joyce Valenza http://joycevalenza.edublogs.org/

One Trick Pony by Bernie Dodge http://webquest.org/bdodge/

Remote Access by Clarence Fisher http://remoteaccess.typepad.com/

SLMS Bridging Theory and Practice by Larry Johnson http://slmsbridge.blogspot.com/

Web Logg-ed by Will Richardson http://www.weblogg-ed.com/

School Library Media Center Blogs

Armstrong Library at Neil Armstrong Elementary School by Mr. Fritz http://armstrong-library.blogspot.com/

Book Break from Berkley High School Library Media Center by MS Spear http://www.bookbreak.blogspot.com/

Gargoyles Loose in the Library by Frances Jacobson Harris http://www.uni.uiuc.edu/library/blog/

Grandview Library Blog by Sarah Chauncey http://www.grandviewlibrary.org/

Mabry Middle School—Media Center Blog by Mrs. Hendrix http://mabryonline.org/blogs/media/

The Reading Room from Northfield Mount Hermon School http://nmhlibrary.typepad.com/

Other Blogs to Explore

Laura Halse Anderson http://www.livejournal.com/users/halseanderson/

Bird Treatment and Learning Center http://birdtlc.blogspot.com/

Cecilia's Nature Blog http://falconcam.apk.net/blog/

Neil Gaiman http://www.neilgaiman.com/journal/journal.asp

WildCam Africa http://www9.nationalgeographic.com/ngm/wildcamafrica/

Cognitive Apprenticeship

Carol L. Tilley

Apprenticeship is a traditional mode of teaching and learning in which the skills and knowledge of a trade such as tailoring or healing are passed from master to apprentice. In an apprenticeship, the apprentice spends time observing the master in action and practicing increasingly complex components of the skill being observed. The master guides the apprentice throughout the learning process, offering hints, suggestions, and critiques, until the apprentice demonstrates competency and is ready to go out on his own.

In the past two decades, educational theorists and researchers have proposed and tested a similar method of apprenticing the mind: cognitive apprenticeship. Like traditional apprenticeship, cognitive apprenticeship works by providing students with the opportunity to observe experts and practice skills while receiving expert guidance. Unlike traditional apprenticeship, however, cognitive apprenticeship is focused largely on teaching and learning tacit skills and knowledge.

Information literacy and its components such as information problem solving and reading are examples of complex sets of skills and knowledge that are amenable to teaching and learning through cognitive apprenticeship. In each instances, the knowledge (e.g. the difference between fact and opinion), strategies (e.g. when to use a magazine index instead of the OPAC), and processes (e.g. how to draw inferences) required to be competent and literate are implicit, hidden in the minds of the teacher and student. The cognitive apprenticeship approach provides a model for making this knowledge visible and, as a result, making teaching and learning more successful.

Cognitive Apprenticeship

Collins, Brown, and Newman (1989) proposed one of the best-known frameworks for cognitive apprenticeship. In their model, instruction is all about making the invisible—that is, knowledge and strategies—visible, so that novice learners develop expertise whether it's in reading, writing, scientific inquiry, or information problem solving. Teaching and learning occurs through interactions similar in form to traditional apprenticeship with teachers modeling, coaching, scaffolding, and fading knowledge and strategies in a specific sequence for students. As much as possible, instruction using this model depends on creating real-world contexts and tasks that emphasize social interaction. In traditional apprenticeships, novices would not be expected to learn how to build a house by completing a worksheet; in cognitive apprenticeships, students do not learn to solve information problems by participating in a library scavenger hunt.

Modeling is the process of demonstrating behavior in order to provide a model for imitation and learning. In cognitive apprenticeship, modeling is thinking made visible. By having teachers (N.B. media specialists are considered to be teachers throughout this article) demonstrate a task, students develop a rich, conceptual model of the task to be performed. This model allows students to see what expert performance looks like and it provides a guide for feedback. Modeling is more than making available a finished product such as a sample composition or multimedia presentation; modeling requires that teachers allow students to witness the mental wrangling that goes into creating an end product. It means teachers and library media specialists as information media specialists complete inquiry processes and products too.

As an example of modeling in action, consider how a teacher might model expository reading skills. While much of young people's expository reading is limited to textbooks, they read a wide variety of expository texts such as Web sites, magazines, nonfiction trade books, and even exams; each of these texts makes use of different conventions (see Burke 2001 for examples). As teachers, we must remember that reading—for us, an expert process—is for students, even in high school, still a developing skill set. One way to help students become more savvy, strategic readers is through modeling our own expert reading processes across a variety of texts.

In *Strategies That Work: Teaching Comprehension to Enhance Understanding,* Harvey and Goudvis (2000) suggest that helping young people become more strategic readers is best accomplished by focusing on a single skill at a time. So, through several instructional periods, a teacher might take a variety of expository texts such as magazine articles, pages from a book chapter, or encyclopedia articles, and read these aloud to students. As he reads the texts aloud, the teacher might focus on the questions that the texts raise. For instance, one question this paragraph might raise for you is "How will I find the time to do this?" The goal is to make these questions explicit for your students, so that they see that expert readers interact with texts. Similarly, in other modeling sessions, a teacher might focus on making inferences.

Coaching is the process of guiding behavior through incremental skills practice in the form of scaffolding as well as through giving feedback. Scaffolding involves breaking a skill into its components and then supporting students—just as scaffolding supports construction workers—as they practice the components. As students become more competent, scaffolding decreases, and students are empowered to do more on their own. Coaching requires knowing what support is necessary for each student and when each student's needs change, so that coaching, like scaffolding, lessens (this is 'fading'). Coaching also compels teachers to assist students in understanding how their performance differs from the expert model and to provide strategies or guidance so that the students' performance becomes more expert.

Reciprocal teaching (e.g., Palinscar and Brown 1986) is one example of how coaching can be to used to develop expository reading skills. Reciprocal teaching is a dialogic form of teaching, often initiated by a teacher with a group of students, but with practice, it can be shifted to student-only groups or pairs. Initially, the teacher models the strategies of predicting, questioning, summarizing, and clarifying—all skills used by expert readers—as she reads a text. Through the prompting (scaffolding) of a discussion leader or even cards, students learn to initiate these strategies as they read texts in order to improve their understanding. As students gain practice and begin to internalize these behaviors, the prompts are removed.

Cognitive apprenticeship also encourages students to improve their metacognition, the act of thinking about thinking. By providing students with opportunities to articulate, reflect, and explore what they are learning they gain better control over the knowledge, strategies, and processes that comprise expert practice. As a result, they may be better able to monitor their own progress and performance. Dialogue between teacher and student is one way to promote metacognition, but cooperative and competitive student group learning activities are equally useful.

One of the key ideas underlying cognitive apprenticeship is the notion that learning occurs primarily through social interaction. The work of Vygotsky (1978) and others suggests that knowledge, strategies, and processes are 'learned' only after students have opportunities to try them out, talk about them. Just as young children mimic language long before they understand what the words and patterns mean, students of all ages try out ideas and actions before true understanding occurs. Dialogue between teacher and student as well as interactions between and among students provide a means of testing out ideas and actions.

A second key idea underlying cognitive apprenticeship is the importance of placing learning in an authentic context with authentic activities. Lave and Wenger (1991), among others, refer to this as situated learning and it allows students to become acculturated to real-life expertise. Although schooling invariably has artificial elements, the more authentic the task, the audience, the tools, and the practice are, the better. If expert practice does not include worksheets and tests of recall or recognition, then ideally activities for students should not include them either.

Information Literacy and Cognitive Apprenticeship

Studies of students' information seeking and use suggest that students could benefit greatly from a cognitive apprenticeship approach to teaching and learning information problem solving and information literacy. For example, McGregor found that students focus on the final product of information seeking, often to the exclusion of the process that goes into creating it. A possible reason for this is that students lack an explicit model for the knowledge, strategies, and processes that information seeking and use requires: the product is something tangible on which to focus. Research by Pitts (1995) upholds this supposition. The students in her study not only lacked models to guide their information seeking and use, but when they asked their teachers for guidance, the help they received never extended beyond directional assistance in using the media center.

When students lack expert models, they flounder in their attempts at information seeking and use. The result is often that they produce (and often are rewarded for) products that are little more than the result of cut-and-paste strategies. In these instances, the inquiry or research assignment becomes an activity where incidental items such as bibliographic form, preliminary outline, and internal citation receive higher value than the ability to demonstrate expertise in information seeking and use. Ultimately, it is the apprenticeship of form instead of function.

Several authors have suggested implicitly and explicitly the utility of a cognitive apprenticeship approach to teaching information problem solving and encouraging information literacy. Kuhlthau (2003) writes about the importance of teachers mentoring students information seeking through mediation and guidance in a way that meets the needs of individual students; this tactic is similar to coaching in cognitive apprenticeship. Sheingold (1987) also suggests that features of cognitive apprenticeship such as modeling and scaffolding are valuable techniques to develop inquiry skills. Callison (1994) suggests that features of cognitive apprenticeship provide a useful structure for developing any program of instruction that works to improve students' thinking and critical information use skills, while Mancall, Aaron, and Walker (1986) similarly emphasize the role of metacognition.

Practicing Cognitive Apprenticeship

McGregor (1993) suggests that teachers and media specialists have the enrichment and extension of students' thinking skills as a central goal of their jobs. While teachers typically encourage students to think about information as argument, media specialists emphasize thinking about information as artifact. Cognitive apprenticeship calls for a more fluid definition of labor between teachers and media specialists with regard to teaching thinking. A full-scale cognitive apprenticeship approach to teaching information literacy—together with information literacy and content-area or expository reading—takes time and support to develop. Most teachers, though, can begin to implement some aspects of apprenticeship with minimal effort combined with basic cooperation and collaboration.

Some ideas to begin implementing an apprenticeship approach in the media center include the following:

- Strive toward authentic tasks and contexts. Knowledge, strategies, and processes need to be taught as they pertain to specific tasks in progress, not as isolated entities. Worksheets, games, and tests seldom fit the definition of "authentic" and therefore are of questionable benefit.

- Practice modeling your own thinking (metacognition) about information literacy, as well as information problem solving and reading, in both group and individual teaching opportunities. If trying this in front of an audience initially makes you nervous, practice alone: pose an information problem and start talking aloud as you work to solve it. Becoming fluent and comfortable with verbalizing one's mental processes takes time and repetition. You will likely learn something about your own thinking and problem solving that surprises you.

- Divide big tasks into authentic and manageable components for students. Two important considerations here: first, not everyone goes about solving information problems in the same way, so be open to alternatives; second, not everyone works on the same time-table, so be flexible in providing students with support and guidance.

- Provide students with tools and strategies for developing their own metacognitive skills. For example, webbing (or similar graphic organizers) may be useful for helping students refine information needs, planning a course of action, or visualizing the relationships among pieces of information. Double-entry note taking in which students elaborate or reflect directly on the notes they take may help them evaluate and integrate information. Also, teaching students how to summarize or paraphrase may encourage them to go beyond directly copying information as well as serve to improve their comprehension.

- Allow time for students to learn from each other. Recognizing the social nature of learning does not automatically require the development of group projects. Instead, give students opportunities to talk to each other about their projects, both to share and to evaluate other's work. Peer conferencing may help students evaluate information, determine a course of action, or even identify information needs.

References

Burke, J. (2001). *Illuminating Texts: How to Teach Students to Read the World.* Heinemann.

Callison, D. (1994). "Expanding the Evaluation Role in the Critical-Thinking Curriculum." In *Assessment and the School Library Media Center,* edited by C. C. Kuhlthau. Libraries Unlimited.

Collins, A., J. S. Brown, and S. E. Newman. (1989). "Cognitive Apprenticeship: Teaching the Crafts of Reading, Writing, and Mathematics." In *Knowing, Learning, and Instruction: Essays in the Honor of Robert Glaser,* edited by L. Resnick. Erlbaum.

Daniels, H., and S. Zemelman. (2004). *Subjects Matter: Every Teacher's Guide to Content Area Reading.* Heinemann.

Harvey, S., and A. Goudvis. (2000). *Strategies That Work: Teaching Comprehension to Enhance Understanding.* Stenhouse.

Kuhlthau, C. C. (2003). *Seeking Meaning: A Process Approach to Library and Information Science Service.* 2d ed. Libraries Unlimited.

Lave, J., and E. Wenger. (1991). *Situated Learning: Legitimate Peripheral Participate.* Cambridge University Press.

Mancall, J. C., S. L. Aaron, and S. A. Walker. (1986). "Educating Students to Think: The Role of the School Library Media Program." *School Library Media Quarterly* 15: 18–27.

McGregor, J. (1993). "Cognitive Process and the Use of Information: A Qualitative Study of Higher-Order Thinking Skills Used in the Research Process by Students in a Gifted Program." *School Library Media Annual* 11: 124–133.

Palincsar, A. S., and A. L. Brown. (1986). "Interaction Teaching to Promote Independent Learning From Text." *Reading Teacher* 39: 771–777.

Pitts, J. (1995). "The 1993–1994 AASL/ Highsmith Research Award Study: Mental Models of Information." *School Library Media Annual* 13: 187–200.

Sheingold, K. (1987). "Keeping Children's Knowledge Alive Through Inquiry." *School Library Media Quarterly* 15: 80–85.

Tilley, C. L., and D. Callison. (1998). "The Cognitive Apprenticeship Model and Adolescent Information Use." In *Instructional Interventions For Information Use: Proceedings of Treasure Mountain VI,* edited by J. H. ___, M. D. Callison, and R. V. Small. Hi Willow Research and Publishing.

Vygotsky, L. (1978). *Mind in Society: The Development of Higher Psychological Processes.* Harvard University Press.

Collaboration

Daniel Callison

Collaboration is one of the most frequently used words in the 1998 revision of the national guidelines for school library media programs, *Information Power: Building Partnerships for Learning* (AASL 1998). The term appears over sixty times-three dozen times alone in Chapter 4 "Learning and Teaching." Therefore, collaboration must be an important instructional term.

Collaboration is defined very briefly, however, as "working with others." While a three-word definition serves as a beginning, there must be more to the meaning of collaboration. The authors of Information Power do provide several word associations to extend the context for instructional actions: collaborative inquiry, collaborative planning, and collaborative teaching.

While examples and guiding principles are clearly given in the 1998 national guidelines, collaboration will be given a wider context here in order to extend its meaning and applications. Collaboration should involve a broad range of partnerships, from various planning levels and across the many groups who comprise the learning community (Callison 1995). At its entry or beginning levels, collaboration may represent at least a willingness to converse and discuss possibilities. At its highest and most effective levels, collaboration should involve interactive trust and support (Cook and Friend 1999). Collaboration at the interactive levels means that while members of instructional teams may have some specific unique tasks, they serve equally in many areas of teaching and evaluation, and share in leadership roles with their common focus always being on improving the learning environment (Callison 1987; Harvey 2002).

At the highest levels of collaboration, there are few distinctive differences between the school library media specialist and the classroom teacher. Both possess and practice curriculum development-information literacy integrated across the curriculum-and both possess extensive knowledge of information and literature resources. Collaboration does not take place because one educator needs the other's expertise as much as the collaboration is built on shared goals and knowledge that are enriched by a partnership for instruction. There will be different levels of expertise in some subject content areas depending on the participants, but in terms of instructional strategies and implementation of information literacy, all collaborative educators carry a similar focus and skill base to the tasks of teaching students to be effective users of information.

Collaboration can be related to various roles of the instructional library media specialist. Cooperation with the local public library (Callison 1997), for example, may involve routine borrowing and returning of materials and the courtesy to inform public library staff of upcoming student projects that will demand use of local materials beyond those of the school library media center. Collaboration levels, however, imply joint long-range collection development between school and public librarians and coordination of efforts to be certain that the institutions reduce duplication of resource titles whenever possible and together provide local students a wider array of materials. Levels of planning and extent of interactivity best define collaboration in the instructional arena as well as in cooperation for provision of joint library services within the same community.

Meeting in the Middle

In 1996, Barbara Herrin, then AASL Director of Professional Development, brought teams of teachers, administrators, and library media specialists together to develop teaching plans based on collaborative efforts. The gathering in the nation's center, Kansas City, was sponsored by the U. S. Department of Education and titled "Meeting in the Middle." Geographically and pedagogically, educators found consensus and enthusiasm through collaboration. The lesson planning at Kansas City was based on the premise that collaboration is essential for successful integration of information skills instruction into curriculum subject areas. But collaboration is often used to mean cooperation or coordinating, and there's a big difference among the three terms. Reporting on lessons learned from the project, Robert Grover of Emporia State University edited an AASL brochure summary with the following definitions issued in 1996:

> Cooperation is informal, with no commonly defined goals or planning effort: information is shared as needed. A library media specialist and teacher in a cooperative relationship work loosely together. Each works independently, but they come together briefly for mutual benefit.

> [Coordination] suggests a more formal working relationship and the understanding of missions. Some planning is required and more communication channels are established. In a library media program, the teacher and the library media specialist make arrangements to plan and teach a lesson or unit, and a closer relationship is [therefore] required. Collaboration is a much more prolonged and interdependent [interactive] effort. Collaboration [results from the following shifts in actions on the part of all involved]:

> • Moving from competing to building consensus.

> • Moving from working alone to including others from different fields and backgrounds.

> • Moving from thinking mostly about activities and programs to thinking about larger results and strategies.

> • Moving from focusing on short-term accomplishments to requiring long-term results.

> In summary, collaboration is a working relationship over a relatively long period of time. Collaboration requires shared goals, derived during the partnership. Roles are carefully defined, and more comprehensive planning is required (Grover 1999).

Communication is conducted at many levels to ensure success. Leadership, resources, risk, control, and results are shared. As a result of collaboration, there is substantial benefit because more is envisioned and likely accomplished jointly than can be done individually.

Gail Bush (2003), from Dominican University and creator of the collaborative school buddy system, emphasizes how important it is for school library media specialists to be knowledgeable in many areas in order to have credibility in collaboration. These are the essential basics:

- Have a mission, know it and be ready to fit it into conversations.

- Know Information Power (AASL 1998) and other relevant national guidelines.

- Understand and practice information literacy.

- Be familiar with local school improvement plans.

- Acquaint yourself with your school's accrediting agency.

- Critically examine your school's and your district's curriculum structure.

- Read, study and experiment with instructional materials.

- Support and conduct action research to test instructional methods locally.

- Network with other educators, online and at conferences.

- Accept opportunities to educate other educators through professional development participation.

Cognitive Styles Influence Collaboration

Several years prior to the "Meeting in the Middle" conference, Paula Montgomery (1991) presented her dissertation findings to the AASL Research Forum. Her work established the thesis that differences in cognitive styles of library media specialists are related to perceived levels of cooperation (between teachers and library media specialists) when planning and teaching library media skills.

Montgomery's study was based on, among other factors, a working definition of the difference between cognitive styles of field-independent and field-dependent individuals. Field-independent individuals perceive objects as separate from the field, abstract figures from a field, impose personal structures on the environment, state self-defined goals, work alone, choose to deal with abstract subject matter, are socially detached and rely on their own values, and are self-reinforcing.

In contrast, field-dependent people tend to rely on the field for clues about an object, prefer a structure provided by the environment, experience the environment more globally, are interested in people, use externally defined goals, receive reinforcement from others, focus on socially-oriented subject matter, and prefer to work with others. Montgomery's data showed that library media specialists who perceived their roles based on field-dependent characteristics were more social in their cooperative actions and tended to engage more frequently in collaborative efforts with classroom teachers. Such social interaction may tend to take place more frequently by those who are field-dependent regardless of commonly raised limitations of time, resources, and classroom teacher resistance to team efforts.

Montgomery relates her findings to a comprehensive research literature that tends to support the notion that socially interactive people-those who are willing and enjoy sharing ideas and responsibilities including the leadership role when necessary-are likely to be more successful in collaborative efforts. Certainly subject content expertise for the school library media specialist should include a wide knowledge of resources and literature, an understanding of curriculum development, and use and application of technologies for instruction and information access. However, moving school library media professionals into a more interactive mode is dependent on development and practice of effective social skills.

Beyond "love of books," those entering the profession should possess the ability to diagnose information and instructional needs and comprehend the value of helping people. For some, such skills are natural, but the opportunity to practice and enhance such skills should be given a more formal place in pre-service education and professional development (Callison 1995).

According to Jean Donham (2004), professor and library director at Cornell College, clear communication skills enhance collaborative teaching. She has outlined the following strategies that will help the constructive flow for collaborative planning:

- **Pose questions using nonthreatening language.** To protect the no-risk atmosphere, phrasing questions so that they do not put others on the defensive is important. No one wants to speak in a group where ideas are at-risk of being criticized or attacked; yet, open discussion demands that disagreement be voiced.

- **Ensure that all team members are heard.** Some people tend to be cautious about speaking up even in small groups. Someone must take responsibility for seeing that all voices are heard.

- **Clarify terms.** Careful communication is important for team work, so think about assumptions and see that they are explicit.

- **Keep the discussion focused.**

- **Engage in active listening.** Paraphrase what others say, ask probing questions, jot down important points, withhold advice until all information is shared, and listen to advice in full before reacting. (102)

Schedules and Collaboration

Julie I. Tallman and Jean Donham reported in 1994 that in elementary school settings, a flexible schedule allowed for a substantial amount of additional time to be devoted to team planning and such resulted in over twice the number of collaborative teaching efforts between classroom teachers and school library media specialists. They found that library media specialists managing flexible schedules were able to devote substantially more time to the collaborative planning process than those on fixed schedules. That extensive increase in time spent allowed the library media specialist to contribute considerably more to the planning process, and provide access to more resources.

In situations where there was a combination of flexible time management available to the library media specialist and team planning was frequent, the number of collaborative units was five times that of situations in which the library media specialist had to meet a fixed schedule of meeting classes without any level of cooperation with classroom teachers.

Strategies for Successful Collaboration

Linda Lachance Wolcott (1994), from the Department of Instructional Systems Technology at Utah State University, has outlined several useful strategies leading to a greater chance that instructional partnerships will be successful. Conversations at many different levels and many different opportunities, some when least expected, can lead to constructive plans (Bush 2002).

- Together, reflect on teaching and learning. Let the commonalities of experience and mutual concerns serve as the basis for an ongoing dialogue. Occasions for such conversations can be formal or informal. The key is to establish such engagement as high priority.

- Approach the planning process from the teachers' perspective. Planning, as prescribed by numerous instructional design models, is not the same as the manner in which most teachers plan. While design models may be prescriptive and will likely provide some framework for some discussions, they are not representative of how many classroom teachers approach planning. Written lesson plans will help

to clarify communication and planning based on prescribed instructional stages may help to monitor progress, but be flexible and ready to engage in planning on a recursive basis. Engage successful teachers at their point of reference and elaborate from there.

- Accommodate various types and styles of planning. Planning is often a solitary activity for teachers and many may not welcome or be familiar with partnership approaches. Identify both comprehensive and incremental planners among the faculty and approach them accordingly.

- Provide the leadership. Library media specialists need to be active in raising expectations about their involvement in the development of curriculum and instruction. Don't wait to be asked. Assume partnership and look for opportunities to plan with teachers. Openly model the process whenever possible.

Diagnosis for Collaboration

Phil Turner (1996), dean of library and information science at North Texas University, has been a long-time leader in systematic development of instructional planning. His research and models have served as a key basis for methods to help teachers teach. Turner has proposed communication techniques that help teachers of information literacy (classroom teachers and instructional library media specialists) identify areas for close collaboration efforts. Turner recognizes that some team efforts may be met at lower levels of cooperation. Initial levels may include exchanging lesson plan ideas or collecting possible instructional materials for examination by teachers. Such cooperative efforts may or may not lead to more extensive collaboration.

Information to diagnose instructional needs can be gathered through brief written surveys (managed easily today with e-mail), interviews (with student assistants possibly helping to make contact with all teachers), or brainstorm sessions as a portion of regular teacher meetings. Results given in Turner's experience include the following areas in need of in-depth collaboration:

- In-service training in use of the newest multimedia;
- Workshops on the latest instructional techniques, especially model teaching and critical thinking; and
- Workshops on motivational strategies.

New Models for Collaboration

In a recent exhaustive and insightful review of collaboration, Patricia Montiel-Overall (2005), assistant professor at the University of Arizona, offers this conclusion on the potential for higher levels of instruction and curricular partnerships:

> Collaboration has the potential for creating a renewal in education by combining strengths of two or more individuals in productive relationships that can positively influence student learning. Moving toward powerful collaborative relationships involving greater intensity and commitment, as reflected in Models C and D (below), may propel improvements in education because of powerful symbiotic relationships between school library media specialists and teachers, one that arguable creates far more interest in teaching and learning than current practices. Collaborators may feel a particular sense of accountability to their working partner, which affects the quality of instruction created for students. Perhaps the power of collaboration lies in students' greater understanding of material from being exposed to diverse opinions and distinct teaching and communication styles. Students may develop a sense of importance in the collaborative effort when they witness deep commitment to innovative instruction from those responsible for their education.

See Figure 7.6, the integrated instruction model (page 122) and Figure 7.7, the integrated curriculum model (page 122).

References

American Association of School Librarians and Association for Educational Communications and Technology. (1998). *Information Power: Building Partnerships for Learning*. American Library Association.

Bush, G. (2002). "Something to Talk About: Six Collaborative Conversations." *Knowledge Quest* 31 (2): 34–37.

Bush, G. (2003). "Do Your Collaboration Homework." *Teacher-Librarian* 31 (1): 15–18.

Callison, D. (1987). "Evaluator and Educator: The School Library Media Specialist." *Tech Trends* 32 (5): 24–29.

Callison, D. (1995). "Restructuring Pre-Service Education." In *School Library Media Annual (1995),* edited by B. J. Morris, 100–112. Libraries Unlimited.

Callison, D. (1997). Expanding Collaboration for Literacy Promotion in Public and School Libraries. *Journal of Youth Services in Libraries* vol. 11, 37–48.

Cook, L., and M. Penovich Friend. (1999) *Interactions: Collaboration Skills for School Professionals*. Addison-Wesley.

Donham, J. (2004). *Enhancing Teaching and Learning*. Neal-Schuman.

Grover, R., ed. (1996). *Collaboration: Lessons Learned Series*. American Association of School Librarians.

Grover, R. (1999). "Planning and Assessing Learning Across the Curriculum." *Knowledge Quest* 28 (1): 10–16.

Harvey, C. (2002). "It Takes Two: Collaboration, Media, and You!" *School Library Media Activities Monthly* 18 (7): 27.

Montgomery, P. (1991). "Cognitive Style and the Level of Cooperation between the Library Media Specialist and Classroom Teacher." *School Library Media Quarterly* 19 (3): 185–191.

Montiel-Overall, P. (2005). Toward a Theory of Collaboration for Teachers and Librarians. *School Library Media Research* 8. Available at www.ala.org/aasl/SLMR (accessed November 16, 2005).

Tallman, J. I., and J. Donham van Deusen. (1994). "Collaborative Unit Planning-Schedule, Time, and Participants: Part Three." *School Library Media Quarterly* 23 (1): 33–37.

Turner, P. M. (1996). "What Help Do Teachers Want, and What Will They Do to Get It?" *School Library Media Quarterly* 24 (4): 208–212.

Wolcott, L. L. (1994). "Understanding How Teachers Plan: Strategies for Successful Instructional Partnerships." *School Library Media Quarterly* 22 (3): 161–165.

Concept Mapping

Daniel Callison

Concept mapping is a heuristic device that has proven to be useful in helping learners to visualize the relationships or connections between and among ideas. Of equal usefulness, mapping of term relationships helps to demonstrate to the teacher what the learner is constructing or assimilating. Thus, while mapping is a method to organize the pieces taken from a new piece of information (article, chapter, lecture, etc.), it presents a visual for the learner and teacher to further discuss the merits of what the learner believes to be the new knowledge gained.

Joseph D. Novak (1998), a science educator and professor at Cornell University, is credited with developing the technique of concept mapping. A teacher who practiced constructivist theory and related much of his own work to the assimilation theories of David Ausubel (1968), Novak stressed the importance of determining what the learner already knows as a strong factor leading to providing meaningful learning tasks. Novak and Ausubel believe that meaningful learning involves the assimilation of new concepts and propositions into existing cognitive structures. In order for learning to take place the material to be learned must be conceptually clear with examples understood by the learner, the learner must possess relevant prior knowledge, and the learner must be serious and motivated to make the choice to learn in a meaningful way. Concept mapping provides a tangible representation to guide, document and evaluate this process.

Computerized Revision of Concept Maps and Relationships

Computer software has enhanced the ability of students and teachers to construct various levels of concept maps. Inspiration Software, Inc., for example, has developed several programs that allow even elementary school students to web terms in a manner that illustrates initial ideas for inquiry (Inspiration Software 2005). Building on their early webs, students can expand their web each time new contributions are made by classmates or new information found in the library, the Internet, or through interviews. Whether for novice information explorers, graduate school scientists, or team planners for corporations, "it is important to recognize that concept a concept map is never finished." According to Novak (2005), "After a preliminary map is constructed, it is always necessary to revise the map. Good maps usually undergo three to many revisions. This is one reason why computer software is helpful."

Advanced (in advance of lesson or project, not necessarily of high complexity) organizers, help to visualize a connection of ideas offered during brainstorming. This visual map may be constructed by the individual as he or she considers all possible associated terms, events, people, or questions related to a central theme. Such becomes a visual web and can represent shared ideas when produced by a small group or the entire class.

Purists who apply Novak's techniques are quick to note that concept mapping differs from just general webbing of ideas in that there is a purposeful attempt in concept mapping to arrange concepts in a hierarchy and to show relationships among various sets of concepts. Concepts are often connected with labeled arrows, in a downward-branching hierarchical structure. The relationship between concepts is articulated in linking phrases such as "gives rise to," "results in," or "contributes to." Concept maps constructed by students in Novak's science classes often included references to relevant diagrams, spreadsheets, reports and other concept maps making the product highly complex and yet providing a visual framework allowing many students to gain insight on problems they could not previously manage (Novak and Musonda 1991). (See Figure Part3.7.)

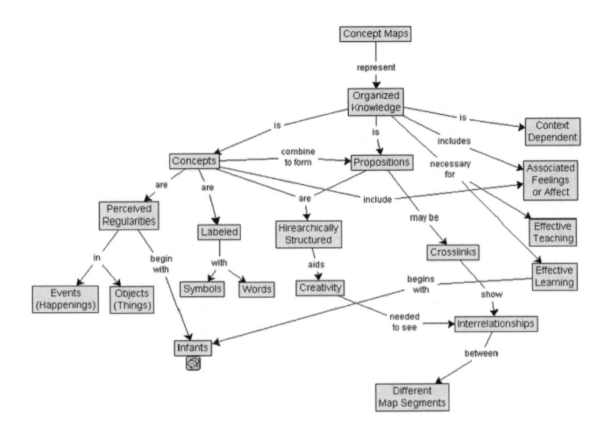

Figure Part3.7. Elements of a typical concept map.

Concept Maps and Notes

Concept mapping has been used to describe a variety of visual modeling activities that range from note taking and summarizing, to collaborative modeling for shared understanding among teams, to advanced organizers used to represent a string of tasks that much be completed and understood before new objectives or goals are introduced to the learning situation.

Concept mapping serves the purpose of helping the learner clarify what he or she has just read or heard. Concept mapping involves a short-hand or visual sketching of key terms around a central idea or concept. The learner visually maps what he or she believes best represents the message from the new information and may place such within a visual context of what he or she already knew about the concept. The concept map thus will focus on those points and relationships that are most important and can most likely be retained for a longer duration than other items.

Because the process involves choices and a focus, along with some organization of terms, the learner becomes engaged with the content derived from the reading or lecture. Through the process, the learner gains some ownership. As a result, the student creates visual notes that are more meaningful than attempts to compose lengthy notes. Focus, selection, relationships, and visual representation strengthen the image for the new mental model (Novak and Gowin 1984; Kinchin 2001).

How to Begin a Map

Select a term that represents the main idea of a reading, book, or lecture. Often this comes from the title. On a clean sheet of paper, preferably without lines, write the term in the center. Quickly, without pausing, write terms and phrases that come from the new information and are associated with the central concept. Do so without analyzing, judging, or editing.

Concept mapping, at this point, may seem very much like brainstorming. Both mapping and brainstorming may be used to encourage the generation of new material, different interpretations, and viewpoints. Mapping, however, relies less on intentionally random input.

Brainstorming attempts to encourage highly divergent lateral thinking. Mapping, by the structure that will be imposed, provides opportunity for convergent thinking, i.e., fitting ideas together.

After the sheet is filled or there are no more terms that come to mind to write on the sheet, examine the content and begin to link or organize the terms. Group similar terms together through similar colors or connecting with lines or arrows. Those items that seem to be very clearly associated may be rewritten as lists and others may look more like a series of branches that grow from the central concept. Advantages of this mapping process include:

- Helps to define the central idea and give it perspective.

- Helps visualize relationships and subsets.

- Key or essential concepts emerge and become trigger words or phrases that are remembered, and later will serve to help the learner recall the minor or detailed points that emerge from these major ones.

- Gaps will become apparent, which will lead to new questions that will guide what to read next or lead to new questions.

Map Applications to Information Inquiry

The concept mapping process can be applied to document or information summaries by creating various visual representations of ideas. The act of creating visualization of document can both help the creator retain more information from the document and synthesize messages that have a higher chance of being communicated (Hyerle 1996). Some advocate the use of this method as a more focused, yet free-thinking, way to take notes during a lecture. Others find the process more powerful when used to summarize the lecture content over several class sessions in a way to find areas of emphasis and association.

Some writing instructors encourage concept mapping as a way to generate an essay layout or plan. Following background reading and discussion of possible essay themes, students may find they move much faster into the construction of the essay if they spread the pieces out through terms and phrases on one sheet. Allowing the ideas to get out and on paper will open the opportunity to grouping and clustering as a foundation to the working outline for the essay.

Carol Gordon (2000, 2002), Associate Professor and Librarian at Boston University, has documented how a small group of high school students that were engaged in concept mapping of terms related to their term paper topic were more likely to focus on their project in an efficient manner than those students who did not construct such maps. The most dramatic differences seem to show during electronic searching for information, as those who had practiced concept mapping

- spent less time searching;

- searched for fewer and shorter sessions;

- preferred subject heading to key word searching; and

- performed a larger percentage of depth searches rather than breadth or exploratory searches.

Mind Mapping Strengthens Note Taking

Mind mapping is a process developed by Tony Buzan (1990). As president of the Brain Foundation, Buzan has authored books and produced tapes on his method for corporate training. Much of his research has concerned how students take notes in lectures. Buzan has concluded there are four major disadvantages of standard notes.

- They obscure the key words. Important ideas are conveyed by key words. In standard notes, these key words often appear on different pages, obscured by the mass of less important words. These factors prevent the brain from making appropriate associations between the key concepts.

- They make it difficult to remember. Monotonous (usually single color) notes are visually boring. As such, they will be forgotten. Standard notes often take the form of endless similar- looking lists.

- They waste time. Standard note-taking systems waste time at all stages:

  - by encouraging unnecessary noting,
  - by requiring the reading of unnecessary notes,
  - by requiring the re-reading of unnecessary notes, and
  - by requiring the searching for key words.

- They fail to stimulate the brain creatively. By its very nature, the linear presentation of standard notes prevents the brain from making associations, thus counteracting creativity and memory. In addition, especially when faced with list-style notes, the brain constantly has the sense that it has "come to the end" or "finished."

This false sense of completion, according to Buzan, acts almost like a mental narcotic, slowing and stifling our thought process. Buzan proposes "radiant thinking" or a more organic process for note taking. The emphasis is on letting the key elements grow and connect and to be highlighted in some manner either through color, size, position, or relation to other items. Unlike the structured organizers with boxes and circles positioned for students to fill in for purposes of comparing terms or listing terms without discriminating as to which are more valuable than others, Buzan calls for conscious effort to give visual weight to that which is most important. This is necessary in order to pull to the forefront that which must be remembered and assimilated. Some of Buzan's guiding principles for mind mapping are:

- Use emphasis—highlight or bold the most important.

- Use one central image.

- Use several colors per central image.

- Use dimension in images.

- Use variations of size of printing and line.

- Make associations with arrows and other connectors.

- Print all words.

- Print key words on lines.

- Make central or more important lines thicker and organic.

- Develop a personal style with signals you immediately understand for skimming at quick revisits-the more personal, the better the information retention.

See Figures Part3.8 and Part3.9.

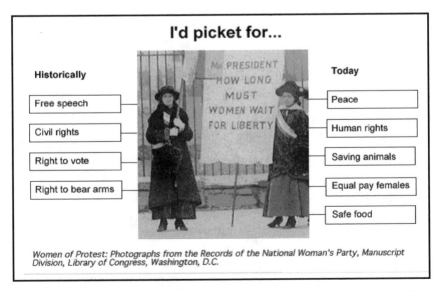

Figure Part3.8. Concept Map turned into a Graphic Organizer and illustrated with a photo from the public domain.

Gas vs Hydrogen Fuel Cells

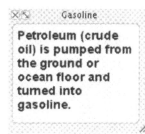

Gasoline

Petroleum (crude oil) is pumped from the ground or ocean floor and turned into gasoline.

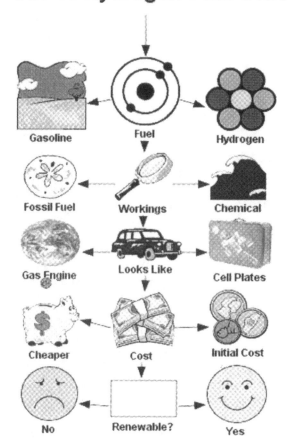

Hydrogen

Although abundant in nature, hydrogen is expensive to produce, store, and transport.

Gasoline — Fuel — Hydrogen

Fossil Fuel — Workings — Chemical

Gas Engine — Looks Like — Cell Plates

Cheaper — Cost — Initial Cost

No — Renewable? — Yes

Figure Part3.9. A visual concept map using generic clip art.

References

Ausubel, D. P. (1968). *Educational Psychology: A Cognitive View.* Holt, Rinehart and Winston.

Buzan, T. (1990). *The Mind Map Book.* Plume. (Mind Map is a registered trademark of the Buzan Organization.

Gordon, C. A. (2000). "The Effects of Concept Mapping on the Searching Behavior of Tenth Grade Students." *School Library Media Research* 3. Available at www.ala.org/aasl/SLMR (accessed November 14, 2005).

Gordon, C. A. (2002). "Methods for Measuring the Influence of Concept Mapping on Student Information Literacy." *School Library Media Research* 5. Available at www.ala.org/aasl/SLMR (accessed November 14, 2005).

Hyerle, D. (1996). *Visual Tools for Constructing Knowledge.* Association for Supervision and Curriculum Development.

Inspiration Software, Inc. (2005). http://www.inspiration.com/ (accessed November 14, 2005).

Kinchin, I. M. (2001). "If Concept Mapping Is So Helpful to Learning Biology, Why Aren't We All Doing It?" *International Journal of Science Education* 23 (12): 1257–1269.

Marzano, R. J., D. J. Pickering, and J. E. Pollock. (2001). *Classroom Instruction That Works: Research-Based Strategies for Increasing Student Achievement.* Association for Supervision and Curriculum Development.

Novak, J. D. (1998). *Learning, Creating, and Using Knowledge: Concept Maps as Facilitative Tools in Schools and Corporations.* Lawrence Erlbaum Associates.

Novak, J. D. (2005). "The Theory Underlying Concept Maps and How to Construct Them." In *Concept Map Software: A Knowledge Construction Toolkit.* Available at http://cmap.coginst.uwf.edu/info/ (accessed November 14, 2005).

Novak, J. D., and D. B. Gowin. (1984). *Learning How to Learn.* Cambridge University Press.

Novak, J. D., and D. Musonda. (1991). "A Twelve-Year Longitudinal Study of Science Concept Learning." *American Educational Research Journal* 28 (1): 117–153.

Web Sites That Illustrate Concept Maps

The Graphic Organizer: Concept Maps. http://www.graphic.org/concept.html (accessed November 14, 2005).

Kinds of Concept Maps. http://classes.aces.uiuc.edu/ACES100/Mind/c-m2.html (accessed November 14, 2005).

Constructivism

Daniel Callison

Constructivism is a theory about the nature of reality and how people understand the world around them. Constructivists argue that humans make or construct their own knowledge based on their experiences. Ideas are not held to be absolutely true or false. Instead, ideas explain and predict in ways that are better or worse than other ideas. Therefore, some ideas are more viable than others. Solutions to problems will depend on the situation and the factors involved. The extent to which the learner moves forward in considering ideas and the potential for solutions to problems depends on what experiences the learner brings to the situation. The potential for learning is relative to the factors involved in the given learning environment and those experiences and expectations brought to the situation by both the learner and the teacher.

Constructivist teaching is one form of "discovery learning," a term generally applied to any learning environment in which the student is actively involved in problem solving. The dominant learning theory for the past century has been behaviorism, or the learner as a passive reactor to the teacher. Learning, especially simple skills, can be effectively and efficiently managed through control of stimulus and response. The learner is more or less helpless and whatever he or she learns and does is a function of his or her environment.

Behaviorist theory fails to explain more complex learning behaviors and does not provide a meaningful framework for how learners can and should be engaged in development of higher order thinking skills. Constructivism seems to offer a theory to move in the direction of learning processes that center on such skills as analysis, synthesis, and evaluation. Although defined in several different ways, according to Tom Duffy and Don Cunningham (1996) of Indiana University, the definition of constructivism usually includes:

- learning is an active process of constructing rather than acquiring knowledge; and

- instruction is a process of supporting that construction rather than simply communicating knowledge.

John Zahorik (1995), professor of curriculum at the University of Wisconsin, writes "Knowledge is constructed by humans. Knowledge is not a set of facts, concepts, or laws waiting to be discovered. It is not something that exists independent of a knower. Humans create or construct knowledge as they attempt to bring meaning to their experience. Everything we know, we have made" (2).

Constructivist Assumptions about Learning

David Jonassen, a leader in instructional design from Pennsylvania State University, has offered several assumptions about learning that are made by those who accept constructivist theory (Jonassen, Peck, and Wilson 1999). The process of making meaning, as theorist Jerome Bruner (1990) has called it, assumes that we learn from experiencing phenomena (objects, activities, events, interactions, conversations, processes); interpreting those experiences based on what we already know; reasoning about them; and reflecting on the experiences and the reasoning in order to assimilate those experiences as new knowledge.

1. Constructivists believe that knowledge is constructed, not transmitted. Knowledge construction, according to those who support this theory, is a natural process. Whenever humans encounter something they do not know but need to understand, their natural inclination is to attempt to reconcile it with what they already know in order to determine what it means. Constructivists believe that knowledge-the richness and fullness of knowing- cannot be simply transmitted by the teacher to the student. Portions of lower levels of knowledge can be transmitted so that the student becomes aware or comprehends meaning as conveyed by the perspective given from the teacher.

   Transmission of knowledge is never pure. The teacher's personal context is always different from that of the student. Because of those differences, the fullness of what the teacher knows cannot be transmitted completely to the student. The greater the understanding between teacher and learner of their experiences and abilities, the higher the potential for more meaning that can be communicated. The initiative to learn more about what the student brings to the learning situation is clearly the responsibility of the teacher. In the constructivist approach, creating situations so that the teacher can gain more understanding of the learner is essential. Although there are some common behaviors among most students, the teacher resists application of general assumptions to the student group and finds ways to explore for individuality. Construction of knowledge, therefore, will differ with each learner, and will certainly differ for that of the teacher.

2. Knowledge construction results from activity, so knowledge is embedded in activity. Facts about a state capital will have more meaning when the student has been guided to apply his or her personal knowledge to that gained from a well-planned and implemented field trip to the capital. Construction of meaning, however, will vary from student to student and from student to teacher as each has a different experience level on which to build or construct knowledge.

3. Knowledge is anchored in and indexed by the context in which the learning activity occurs. Knowledge construction consists of not only the ideas, but also the context in which the ideas or content is experienced. Rules and formulas are more likely to make sense when applied to concrete problems or real situations with which the learner identifies.

4. Meaning is in the mind of the knower. Knowledge is not an external item or object to be gained, but an internal process that evolves based on the interactions with the outside world and the interactions within the mind.

5. Therefore, there are multiple perspectives on the world. Jonassen and other constructivists conclude, since no two people can possibly have the same set of experiences and perceptions of those experiences, each of us constructs our own knowledge, which in turn affects the perceptions of the experiences that we have and those we share.

6. Meaning making is prompted by a problem, question, confusion, disagreement, or dissonance (a need or desire to know) and so involves personal ownership of that problem. The degree to which the learner constructs meaning based on higher-level skills depends on the challenge and extent of authentic problem solving in which the learner is engaged for his or her ability level. Problem solving at its lowest level may simply be an exercise and the learner is guided through the process. Practice or drill situations may be useful, but do not take the student into higher-order learn-

ing. A good teacher should be able to model problem-solving methods, and such examples are essential to help the student create a vision for his or her own approach. At higher levels of problem solving, emphasis is on student application of the skills to address a problem-to "enter the game and play," rather than simply to practice the shots.

Common sense suggests that all experience levels, including basic skills practice, are needed. But the constructivist would argue that too much of what we call teaching today never goes beyond that basic level, and we must move into more authentic situations without fear for student or teacher as both are able to learn new problem-solving techniques.

7. Knowledge building requires articulation, expression, or representation of what is learned (meaning that is constructed). In order to evaluate or reflect on learning, it must have some tangible form. The learner demonstrates or shows what he has learned through speaking, writing, or doing some observable act. Those who support management of learning through objectives would argue that learning is not present until there is an observable, measurable change in the direction defined by the teacher.

More important to the constructivist, however, is the notion that processes of learning, as well as the products of learning, should be gathered in concrete form for the learner to analyze. Reflection by the student on what he or she has learned is more powerful than the reflections of the teacher. More powerful, in that self-reflection can result in internal as well as external change in terms of attitude and motivation. Ability often is limited by the lack of motivation.

Self-reflection is also a key element for sustained or transfer knowledge. It can serve to help the student retain a greater portion of the new knowledge and also may serve to help the student approach new problems on his or her own without teacher guidance.

8. Meaning also may be shared with others, so meaning making also can result from conversation. Learning is formed when the individual is placed in the position to communicate to others. Learning is reformed by the feedback from or conversations with others.

9. Meaning making and thinking are distributed throughout our tools, culture, and community. Meaning, as it develops over time and experiences, influences what groups with which we communicate, what discourse in which we engage, what tools for communication we use, and in what culture and community we decide to mix. In most cases, this is a process of finding a position that is comfortable and low in conflict. In other cases, the learner finds that in order to continue to learn, he must challenge himself and place himself in contexts that are alien.

10. Not all meaning is created equally. Although a common constructive approach to engage the learner is through brainstorming exercises in order to help identify what the learner brings to the situation, not all learning is equal. Even though brainstorming often includes no value judgments in order to encourage all to share in the process, ultimately learners will progress at different paces from different places and reach different levels. Evaluation, therefore, must include measurement of these differences for each individual. Learning becomes not just reaching a goal or an objective set for all, but also the degree and level of individual growth and development.

The Constructivist Teacher

The Association for Supervision and Curriculum Development (ASCD) has endorsed the following actions that define the constructivist teacher (Brooks 1999):

1. Constructivist teachers encourage and accept student autonomy and initiative. The student is encouraged to be a "problem finder" as well as to be a "problem solver." Looking beyond the given task, to find questions of personal interest that are challenging and relevant to the subject content, is a student behavior valued by the constructivist teacher. Robert Marzano states for ASCD, "Robbing students of the opportunity to discern for themselves importance from trivia can evoke the conditions of a well-managed classroom at the expense of a transformation-seeking classroom" (1992, 10).

2. Constructivist teachers use raw data and primary sources, along with manipulative, interactive, and physical materials. Collaboration between the classroom teacher and the resourceful instructional library media specialist is very important in this area. Use of multiple resources, access to primary and local documents, and activities that require the student to gather information through survey, observation, or tests take learning to authentic levels.

3. When framing tasks, constructivist teachers use cognitive terminology such as "classify," "analyze," "predict," and "create." Marzano writes for ASCD, "The teacher who asks students to select a story's main idea from a list of four possibilities on a multiple choice test is presenting to the students a very different task than the teacher who asks students to analyze the relationships among three of the story's characters or predict how the story might have proceeded had certain events in the story not occurred" (1992, 21). School library media specialists who promote a heavy dose of computerized reading tests, accelerated or not, should ask if such exercises are really of merit (Everhart 2005). Do we allow such routine, computerized book reviews to take the place of more valuable, but more time-consuming, book discussion groups and reading circles?

4. Constructivist teachers allow student responses to drive lessons, shift instructional strategies, and alter content. This does not mean that students and their opinions alone determine course content. It means that their questions, and what they do and do not bring to a learning situation, influence the content. Effective teachers use this analysis of their students to identify quickly "a series of teaching moments" and move to address them so that student interest can be captured. Successful interactions on these moments can result in further motivation of students and deeper content understanding based on a common teacher-student learning experience. The teachable moment does not take place when just "the student is ready to listen," but occurs when teacher and student are both ready to listen.

5. Constructivist teachers inquire about students' understandings of concepts before sharing their own understandings of those concepts. Too many inquiry opportunities are cut short by teachers who deliver what students tend to accept as the dominate perspective or accepted conclusion. The opportunity to freely explore then becomes a challenge to authority and difficult to initiate by most students. An open opportunity to question and consider alternatives should come very early in the lesson. Frequently teachers do have the "correct answer" and often neither teacher nor student want to "waste time." The constructivist teacher looks for opportunities to open inquiry from the beginning, and recognizes that not all engagements are meant for full inquiry. In some cases, delivery of basic facts or background become necessary in order to establish the groundwork for more meaningful inquiry to follow.

6. Constructivist teachers encourage students to engage in dialogue with the teacher and with one another. Learning involves not only reading and doing, but talking about what is read, heard, and performed, or is in the process of being performed. Talking provides a shared communication so the teacher may respond, and peers also may provide suggestions. Most of all, the student "hears" himself/herself and often learns by thinking through what needs to be said as well

as thinking about the responses received. Conversations initiate nearly all demonstrations of learning performance. These conversations must take place in an active manner in all learning environments, including libraries once thought to be quiet reading coves only.

7. Constructivist teachers encourage student inquiry by asking thoughtful, open-ended questions and encouraging students to ask questions of each other. As models for inquiry learning, teachers must be ready and willing to accept questions from students that lead to open discussion and often no quick solution, if there is a solution at all. Instructional specialists who also manage information centers need to model reference services that are beyond "ready reference" and help students move beyond just the facts found in almanacs, encyclopedias, and handbooks.

   Practice exercises that place students in the position of seeking answers through the use of library media center materials should be developed by students asking each other questions rather than a school library media specialists who alone always formulates a "trivia treasure hunt." Turn a set of encyclopedias over to a group of fifth graders and instead of dictating questions, ask them to raise all the questions they can come up with that can be answered in the set. Ask that they also list as many questions as they can that probably can't be answered, and why. After one hour of such activity, the instructional library media specialist will have a full agenda to discuss with students concerning what they should and should not expect from the encyclopedia and where to go for leads to other information resources.

8. Constructivist teachers seek elaboration of students' initial responses. Initial responses should be verbalized and shared. They serve as the foundation from which we can raise additional questions. Elaboration means reading more, listening more, exploring multiple resources, and building on and revising the original response. Learning is a constant process of elaboration. Typical library-based research projects are more effective when the student can demonstrate growth from the initial idea to more complex findings that are shared with the class.

9. Constructivist teachers engage students in experiences that might engender contradictions to their initial hypotheses and then encourage discussion. The student is challenged to defend or reject his or her personally-held assumption or belief. This is an important process as the student searches and examines information for facts or evidence to accept or reject. Too often, the student determines relevance or authority based on content that agrees with his or her original assumptions. Acceptance of opinions or statements that come from individuals the student accepts as an authority on all matters, regardless of expertise, is a sign of novice information selection. A constant pattern of accepting or rejecting evidence based on assumed authority without question usually will lead to false conclusions. Such action certainly will not broaden the student's perspective on the issues.

10. Constructivist teachers allow wait time after posing questions. Allow students to think about the posed situation. In some cases, teachers have given a great deal of thought to asking the question and have probably asked the questions dozens of times before. Suddenly students are supposed to be ready with a response within a few seconds. Complex questions may need some small group discussion time so that students may talk among themselves and test out possibilities before presenting responses before the entire class.

11. Constructivist teachers provide time for students to construct relationships and create metaphors. Metaphor and analogies allow for creative expressions and lead to new visions on an event or problem. Marzano writes, "Metaphors help people to understand complex issues in a holistic way and to tinker mentally with the parts of the whole to determine whether the metaphor works." Formulation of potential cause-and-effect and other patterns or relationships require several attempts. Any of these require time for the student to write or state possibilities and to place them side by side for comparison and analysis.

12. Constructivist teachers nurture students' natural curiosity through frequent use of a learning cycle model. The first step is discovery through the interaction with purposefully selected materials in order to raise questions and hypotheses. In the second step, the teacher facilitates concept introduction aimed to focus the students' questions and to give meaning to new terms or vocabulary needed for the lesson. The third step is concept application, a series of attempts to apply solutions to the problem or test the hypothesis. From this third step, new questions arise and the cycle begins again.

Student discovery at its first level may be guided by the teacher so that basic concepts often are gained from what the teacher already holds and understands. Higher-level discovery is not uncovering what the teacher "has hidden" or knows and hopes the student will find out for himself. Ultimately, discovery at its highest levels will involve new learning for both the student and the teacher as collaborative learners.

References

Brooks, J. Grennon. (1999). *In Search of Understanding: The Case for Constructivist Classrooms.* Association for Supervision and Curriculum Development.

Bruner, J. (1990). *Acts of Meaning.* Harvard University Press.

Duffy, T. M., and D. J. Cunningham. (1996). "Constructivism: Implications for the Design and Delivery of Instruction." In *Handbook of Research for Educational Communications and Technology,* edited by D. H. Jonassen, 170–198. Simon & Schuster, Macmillan Library Reference.

Everhart, Nancy. (2005). "A Crosscultural Inquiry into the Levels of Implementation of Accelerated Reader and Its Effect on Motivation and Extent of Reading." *School Library Media Research* 8. Available at www.ala.org/aasl/SLMR (accessed November 14, 2005).

Jonassen, D. H., K. L. Peck, and B. G. Wilson. (1999). *Learning with Technology: A Constructivist Perspective.* Merrill.

Marzano, R. J. (1992). *A Different Kind of Classroom: Teaching with Dimensions of Learning.* Association for Supervision and Curriculum Development.

Zahorik, J. A. (1995). *Constructivist Teaching.* Phi Delta Kappa Educational Foundation.

Content Literacy

Daniel Callison

Anthony Manzo and Ula Manzo (1997) introduce their ideas for interactive teaching strategies and content area literacy with the assumption that acquisition of large amounts of information is less important than the acquisition of effective strategies for accessing and evaluating information. The movement to place learners in educational environments that challenge students to analyze, reflect, communicate, create, and critically review has parallel strands in reading education and information literacy education.

Content literacy seems to imply integration of strategies and experiences in at least two ways. First, effective strategies for reading, writing, speaking, listening, and thinking are more likely to develop more naturally and easily when tasks are integrated than when isolated. Second, meaning is enriched across subjects and experiences when content literacy embraces discourse and text from several distinct disciplines. Ultimately, the student who is content literate has a heightened awareness and use of the organization and structure of distinct texts in diverse fields of study and knows how to read in strategic ways to obtain important knowledge from them. The strategic reader knows, for example, the value of doing an initial preview of a research article in order to become familiar with the focus, scope, general findings, length, and level of complexity of the materials before doing a more thorough analytical reading of the text.

A less informed and strategic reader, on the contrary, is apt to approach diverse texts in a generic fashion, covering the assigned pages once, with limited comprehension and recall, perhaps highlighting but failing to consolidate the information in some form of manageable and meaningful study notes. This underprepared reader is also likely to cling to a single inefficient and ineffective method of chapter previewing or reviewing, regardless of the actual assignment demands or subject area. Furthermore, students who lack content literacy skills frequently exhibit passive and dependent learner behavior, avoid assigned readings, and rely upon peer tutors or class lectures to access needed information from texts. Students who lack content literacy skills or who are in educational environments that fail to provide such opportunities across the curriculum may gain general reading proficiency but will not function well on tasks required of the independent information-literate learner.

Manzo and Manzo (1997) contend that the basic approach to content literacy is based on interactive methods for teaching reading-thinking concurrently with subject area knowledge and application. Regular use of such methods from grade to grade and across subject areas supports student development of independent reading-learning strategies and empowers even relatively poor readers to read and learn from materials that they otherwise would find difficult.

Content Literacy Expertise

Reading comprehension is enhanced greatly, according to those who support content literacy, when students strive to obtain the expert level strategies. These techniques also serve the student striving for more meaningful levels of information literacy. Expertise is refined by analyzing purpose, questioning content and experiences brought to the text or new information, and reflecting on what is found in order to assimilate new information for new understanding. This is illustrated by Manzo and Manzo (1997) in three phases and one of the thinking strategy sets practiced by proficient readers:

- Before reading, expert readers activate schema and set a purpose for reading. This involves:

  – looking for organizing concepts

  – recalling related information, experiences, attitudes, and feelings

  – deciding how easy or difficult the reading selection is likely to be

  – setting a purpose for reading

  – trying to develop a personal interest

- During silent reading, readers continuously monitor comprehension and use fix-up strategies as needed. Doing this involves:

  – translating ideas into own words, and ideas to personal experience

  – trying to identify main ideas, and stop and question when this is unclear

  – noting important details

  – rereading whenever necessary for clarification

  – consolidating ideas into meaningful groups

  – noticing unfamiliar vocabulary

  – forming mental pictures

  – evaluating the author's purpose, motive, or authority when appropriate

  – inventing study strategies as needed

  – managing time to sustain concentration

- Following reading, expert readers check basic comprehension, build schema, and decide on relevant applications of the new information. Elements of this process include:

  – checking basic comprehension by reciting or recall, "What did I learn?"

  – organizing information into chunks of manageable size, "How can I remember it?"

  – deciding what is important, "How much should I understand of this?"

  – evaluating new information in terms of previous knowledge and experience, "Does this make sense?"

  – developing study strategies according to class demands or personal purposes, "What should I do to remember this?"

  – reviewing material periodically, "How much do I remember now?"

Thematic Approach to Content Literacy

Marian Tonjes, Ray Wolpow, and Miles Zintz (1998) have promoted integrated content literacy for years. Their approach to reading and use of new information for making meaning, reflecting, and remembering is based on this philosophy:

- Strive for integrating knowledge—blurring borders between subjects, rising above our individual content area ruts, and bringing a fresh perspective to learning.

- Reading, thinking, writing, and studying are not separate subjects or entities but flow across the entire curriculum.

- Support cooperative teaching and learning and allow for freedom of choice when feasible.

- Everyone has the potential for creativity, but for many it has been downplayed in early years. To flourish it must be encouraged and practiced often.

- Create a nonthreatening, stimulating classroom environment in which students feel free to risk, experiment, and make mistakes without ridicule.

- Believe in the innate dignity and worth of every student, no matter what the student's background, culture, or ability.

- The process, or keys to opening avenues of learning, is as important or even more so than the product or knowledge gained. When we feel comfortable with how and when to perform the process, we will be more apt to continue learning on our own, and then the knowledge gained will be more personally meaningful.

- Teach through modeling and guided practice of what you preach and use exemplars when possible. To best teach information literacy, practice and converse about information literate habits of your own.

- Because we organize, store, and retrieve information by categorizing data into patterns, we should make it a common practice to construct a cognitive map of our learning.

- Teaching is not just telling, nor is it an easy task if performed properly. Teaching takes continuous effort, study, and willingness to try the unknown-a combination of curiosity and a caring heart.

Thematic approaches to reading and information research projects may create the most options leading to integration of content literacy across the curriculum. Montgomery (1992) has reminded library media specialists and other teachers that they must be sensitive to the students and what they may bring to the thematic literature approach. The approach assumes that the student can easily comprehend general information when reading; most prevalent is the ability to generalize. The student must be adept at and probably enjoy examining bits of information, rearranging those information bits, and drawing general conclusions about the information. The student's experience base or prior knowledge is extremely important, according to Montgomery, and the student must be able to advance in practice of skills to summarize and analyze both the concrete examples and the more abstract ideas provided in a variety of texts.

Advantages of the thematic approach to techniques and strategies in practice of content literacy include the opportunity to introduce different literary forms that are centered on the same idea so that students can compare and contrast the presentation of the same theme. Montgomery also suggests that thematic approaches naturally promote instruction across curriculum areas. Thinking, speaking, listening, reading, and writing may be incorporated into a meaningful context. Such may increase the chance that the content of the work becomes key to the motivation for reading and students increasingly may feel, as the varied projects are initiated and they return to the original text, more emotion and per-

sonal involvement. Options across the curriculum in the thematic approach create opportunities for self-identification.

A Content Literacy Cross-Curriculum Sample

Content literacy exercises may involve reading and selection of relevant information from different disciplines. Meaning may be found through narrative, graphs, tables, charts, or illustrations depending on the subject content and the manner in which data, opinion, or emotions are best displayed for that subject. Information may be displayed differently by literature genre as well and students extract meaning from poetry, diaries, and dramatic scripts, along with novels and short stories. A basic approach to constructing a content literacy experience may be similar to the following content literature web or outline proposed by Tonjes, Wolpow, and Zintz (1998):

Central piece of literature and (theme): Island of the Blue Dolphins (Survival)

Related student activities to engage content literacy might include:

- Literature-Compare and contrast to Swiss Family Robinson.

- Geography-Describe a good choice for the location of this island.

- Music-Compose or select music that would serve to set the theme or mood for different chapters.

- Health-What would be the most healthy diet possible on the island?

- Science-Chart and classify the wildlife likely on the island.

- Social Studies-Who are the Aleuts and what are their customs?

- Mathematics-What are the dimensions for a typical shelter, and what would be a sketch for a basic plan?

- History-Explore the history of how wild dogs eventually became pets.

References

Manzo, A. V., and U. C. Manzo. (1997). *Content Area Literacy: Interactive Teaching for Active Learning.* Merrill.

Montgomery, P. K. (1992). *Approaches to Literature through Theme.* Oryx.

Stephens, E. C., and J. E. Brown. (2000). *A Handbook of Content Literacy Strategies: 75 Practical Reading and Writing Ideas.* Christopher-Gordon Publishers.

Tonjes, M. J., R. Wolpow, and M. V. Zintz. (1998). *Integrated Content Literacy.* McGraw-Hill.

Cooperative Learning

Daniel Callison

Cooperative learning refers to instructional situations in which students work together in small groups and receive rewards or recognition based on their group's performance. This has been the standard definition since the 1980s, with recent linkage of associated terms. Over the past decade, these concepts have been related in theory and practice to cooperative learning: activity units, group dynamics, interpersonal relationship, peer teaching, social integration, and teamwork.

Many educators who believe that they are using cooperative learning are, in fact, missing its essence. There is a critical difference between simply putting students in groups to learn and structuring cooperation among students. Cooperation is also more than a student being physically near other students, discussing material with other students, helping other students, or sharing materials among students, although each of these aspects is important in cooperative learning. No single method for structuring the learning environment should be awarded the prize as the most effective in all situations; however, there is much to be said for the positive aspects of cooperative learning applied to library and information literacy activities.

Cooperative learning receives more discussion and consideration than actual application in classroom settings. Effective teachers of library and information skills, however, will be quick to note that there is a growing awareness of the merits of cooperative learning in situations where students are to deal with multiple resources, address a variety of issues and perspectives, and present information using a variety of formats. Put simply, assignments that require multiple resources tend to result in richer processes and products from groups of individuals who share a variety of skills than from most students who face such assignments on an individual basis. Beyond the academic activity, students are placed in situations in which they must participate in effective interpersonal communication in order to be successful. The process, the product, and social skills all benefit from cooperative interactions.

Beyond Bloom

Bloom's Taxonomy of Instructional Objectives has been the predominant influence on identification of cognitive, affective, and motor skills for the past half Century. The cognitive domain is the root for the skill stages often listed for current information problem-solving activities. Knowledge, comprehension, application, analysis, synthesis, and evaluation have provided the standard pattern since the mid-1950s for a wide array of instructional objectives across all areas of the curriculum. A fourth skills set, extending from overlaps within the cognitive and affective domains, is gaining attention (Heinich, Molenda, & Russell 1993). The emerging interpersonal domain is foundational to the student skills that can be observed and measured in cooperative learning.

Interpersonal skills can be classified in six categories:

1. Seeking/giving information. Asking for/offering facts, opinions, or clarification from/to another individual or individuals.

2. Proposing. Putting forward a new concept, suggestion, or course of action; providing evidence of support.

3. Building and supporting. Extending, developing, enhancing another person, his or her proposal, or concepts.

4. Including. Involving another group member in a conversation, discussion, or action.

5. Disagreeing. Providing a conscious, direct declaration of difference of opinion, or criticism of another person's concepts; providing counter evidence.

6. Summarizing. Restating in a concise and clear form the important items from the content of previous discussions or considerations.

Circles of Learning

David Johnson and Roger Johnson (1998), brothers, co-researchers and the most prolific writers on cooperative learning have identified five essential components that must be in place for "circles of learning" to be successful (Johnson, Johnson, and Holubec 1994). These are not easy components for the teacher to implement, and even if we assume that humans are naturally social creatures, the components are not easy for students to practice. These components must be modeled, structured, and rewarded by teachers and by peers. As with other instructional approaches, cooperative learning groups may be challenged by parents who want to be certain that their child receives justified credit for excellent academic performance without being "brought down" by student group members who do not excel. These critical components are:

1. Positive interdependence. Group members must perceive that they are linked with each other so that one cannot succeed unless everyone succeeds. Students must realize that each other's achievement results from sharing resources, assisting each other's efforts, providing mutual support, and celebrating their joint success.

2. Promotive interaction. Time and reward must be provided for students to communicate. Activities should be based on orally explaining to other students how to solve problems, discussing what information has been gathered or concepts learned, sharing gained personal knowledge with classmates, and expressing how new knowledge connects with past assumptions.

3. Individual accountability. Evaluation can be facilitated by the teacher and/or group peers, with the goal being to provide some level of individual accountability for each group member. Evaluations are shared, adjustments are made so that an individual is not allowed to "hitchhike" on the work of others.

4. Interpersonal and small-group skills. Cooperative learning provides an environment in which social skills can be demonstrated, observed, and corrected. Strategies for teaching constructive social skills must be employed along with those for teaching the academic task. Leadership, trust-building, and conflict management are taught just as purposefully and precisely as academic skills.

5. Group processing. Group members discuss how well they are achieving their goals and determine what actions are helpful to improve future cooperative efforts.

Meaningful-Use Tasks

One of the major decisions in planning for the meaningful use of knowledge (beyond memorization and reciting of facts) is whether students will work in cooperative groups. The meaningful-use tasks (decision making, investigation, experimental inquiry, problem solving, and invention) are probably completed more efficiently by a cooperative group than by an individual. Meaningful-use tasks require gathering a lot of information, and a cooperative group can naturally gather more information than an individual can. A long project can easily exhaust the energy and resources of one person, whereas the energy and resources of a properly trained and supported cooperative group can "go the distance."

When meaningful-use tasks are performed in cooperative groups, two special aspects evolve: group reward and task specialization. Group rewards based on every group member's performance increase instructional effectiveness because such rewards are likely to motivate students to do whatever is necessary to make it possible for the group to succeed. No individual can succeed unless the group succeeds. Task specialization inherently enhances the quality of the meaningful-use tasks because it maximizes the knowledge, ability, resources, and energy available for each component of the task. Where one student might not have the knowledge necessary to complete a component of an experimental inquiry task, another would. Where one student might not have the ability to set up an experiment, or conduct a complex electronic search for information, others in the group may be able to initiate such tasks and are likely to be key instructors, teaching peers in their group.

Applications to Library Information Projects

Several strategies used by language arts teachers have direct application to increasing cooperative activities that are based on school library media center projects. The strategies outlined here are intended to help one consider greater cooperative learning during the process of library information research. Frequently, there is cooperative effort in such activities as producing a video news program, constructing a hypercard database, giving oral reports on world religions, and so forth. Students are placed in groups, territories and responsibilities are sorted out, and eventually, in most cases, a role is identified for each student to play. Listed below are suggestions of cooperative activities that are matched to the interpersonal skill domain. Activities have been suggested that lead to observable behavior, and therefore such student actions could be included in performance criteria to be graded by teachers of information literacy (Hilke 1990; Golub 1994).

1. Seeking/giving information. While it may be more and more common for students to be encouraged to help each other seek information, openly giving information within a structured manner that can be rewarded is not so common. In fact, conventional wisdom suggests that exercises in library information skills should lead to developing students who can search well on an independent basis and to become self-sufficient.

   Modern technologies applied to cooperative efforts, however, allow for students to gather evidence, classify it, reference it, and submit it to a database established for the student's group or for the entire class. Thus, "electronic note cards" are shared with everyone in the group, and gaps showing information needs are easier for the group to detect and discuss. At the very least, even without the advantages of computerized storage, members of a group should be given time and direction to describe their success and failures in information searching so that other group members can provide suggestions as well as be sensitive to such information needs for others while they browse for their own sources. Such discussions can be initiated if the group has a deadline for each member for presenting to the rest of the group all of the note cards compiled to date and describing the story or argument their evidence justifies to date.

2. Proposing. One of the most difficult tasks for students in the information search and use process is to define focus and to eventually state the hypothesis, purpose, or main message of the product. Oral sessions in which group members are expected to verbalize to other members the state of their focus and related issues that may shift that focus should be placed in the list of regular tasks, perhaps as frequently as a twenty-minute focusing session for each four-member group every third day. One specialized task may be for one member of the group to compile and map a record of these sessions so that the group can visualize progress as well as problems.

3. Building and supporting. A student who offers his or her talent to assist others has a high-level interpersonal skill. Although students live and learn in an interactive social environment, they may not know all of the skills held by members. Each member who is strongest in grammar, spelling, argument construction, evidence linkage, editing, illustrating, or conceptualizing story lines has a talent that should be applied for the purpose of teaching other members and raising the overall ability level of group. Evidence of shared expertise may be gathered in student journals if students are encouraged to document occasions in which they felt they received special assistance from another group member.

4. Including. Seeking out hidden talents or making progress in respecting talents of an individual who is not normally accepted into group situations should be encouraged and rewarded. This skill may be the most difficult to activate, even painful for some to demonstrate, and yet may be the most intrinsically rewarding. Again, through compiling a journal in order to reflect on the investigative experience, students may be encouraged to write about situations in which their talents were valued by others who had not known of or noticed these skills before. Journals might also include entries in which the student describes observing talents of another student. It may be necessary for the teacher to interview younger student groups in order to obtain an impression of the practice of this skill.

5. Disagreeing. It is unlikely that there will be any difficulty in members of the group to disagree on something, but such conflict can be counterproductive. Disagreeing in constructive, measured ways can be managed. Learning how to make a motion, submit discussion, and vote is a common method to settle group disagreements.

Learning that there are degrees of disagreement also helps, in that many arguments become cooler once parties understand that there are also areas of agreement. While applying library information activities, learning how to identify constructively group opinions on the issues related to the academic content at hand will be necessary as well. The attention of the group should be directed toward identification of the major content issues related to their topic and demonstration of how to categorize those issues with supporting and counter evidence. Practice sessions in which they make such cases within their group obviously help to polish what the group will present to the class or some other audience.

6. Summarizing. Can each member of the group state what they learned from others during the process of constructing the project? While each member would also be expected to state or write what they knew or assumed prior to the project compared to their knowledge at the close of the project, they should also be expected to identify and summarize any changes in the impressions they hold about members of their group. In addition, academic measurement can be taken in this skill area as well. Based on the cognitive skills of analysis and synthesis, can the student extract from a group's discussion for the day the key issues, related evidence, and what needs to be done over the short term to fill information gaps? An end-of-the-week summary check, written in 100 words or less, will provide teachers a snapshot of this skill and may help teachers of library information skills identify groups that need special attention during the week ahead. Group cooperative projects can be enhanced if students are placed in specific roles to match either their skill strengths or placed in roles for which they need to practice

specific interpersonal skills in order to improve their cooperative behaviors and improve their communication. In an authoring cycle mode, for example, students can role play the tasks of managing editor, copy editor, illustrator or layout designer, reviewer, or publisher. These roles easily transfer to webmastering. In production of video programs, roles include story board consultant, script writer, producer, director, and even promoter of the final student product.

Regardless of the cooperative processes and final product, a major concept to govern such projects is that school library media centers are not only places for information, but one of several places for constructive conversations. Moving the student within an isolated and narrow environment in which he or she concentrates on only his or her content and talent alone limits the possibilities of the student gaining a wider and richer perspective of the issues, arguments, and alternatives for communication. Interpersonal skills, practiced through cooperative learning, can greatly deepen the meaning of information literacy and inquiry.

References

Golub, J. N. (1994). *Activities for an Interactive Classroom*. National Council of Teachers of English.

Heinich, R., M. Molenda, and J. D. Russell. (1993). *Instructional Media and the New Technologies of Instruction*. Macmillan.

Hilke, E. Veronica. (1990). *Cooperative Learning*. Phi Delta Kappa.

Johnson, D. W., and R. T. Johnson. (1998). *Learning Together and Alone: Cooperative, Competitive, and Individualistic Learning*. Allyn & Bacon.

Johnson, D. W., R. T. Johnson, and E. Johnson Holubec. (1994). *The New Circles of Learning: Cooperation in the Classroom and School*. Association for Supervision and Curriculum.

Creative Thinking

Daniel Callison

Thinking creatively is the cognitive process we use to develop ideas that are unique, useful, and worthy of further elaboration (Chaffee 1997). When a question is posed to a critical thinker, analysis of the question, definition of terms in the question, and degree or boundaries for acceptable answers may be included in their response. When a question is posed to a creative thinker, multiple options for other ways to ask the question are likely to be raised along with placing the question in various situations or contexts to see if these variations might lead to new insights before any attempt to answer the question directly is made.

The Artist in Each of Us

People often confuse being creative with only being artistic-skilled at art, music, poetry, creative writing, drama, or dance. Although artistic people are certainly creative, there are many ways to be creative that are not artistic. John Chaffee, director of the Center for Critical Thinking and Language Learning at the City University of New York, suggests that we each consider all of the activities we enjoy: cooking, creating a wardrobe, raising children, playing sports, or cutting or braiding hair. Whenever you are investing your own personal ideas or putting on your own personal stamp, you are being creative.

Howard Gardner (1993, 1995, 1997), in his examination of selected prominent creative minds, concludes that creators differ from one another not only in terms of the dominant intelligence but also in terms of breadth and combination of intelligences. Sigmund Freud and T. S. Eliot had strong scholastic abilities, reflecting linguistic and logical aspects of intelligence, and they presumably could have made contributions in many academic areas. Pablo Picasso, on the other hand, was weak in the scholastic area, while exhibiting quite strongly targeted strengths in spatial, bodily, and personal intelligence spheres. Igor Stravinsky and Mahatma Gandhi were indifferent students, but one senses that their lackluster performances arose more out of lack of interest in school than out of any fundamental intellectual flaw. Stravinsky, while weak in scholastic aspects had strengths in musical aspects. Gandhi, while weak in artistic aspects, was creative through personal and linguistic intelligences. Martha Graham had broad intellectual strengths-weak in logical-mathematical aspects, she was never fully engaged in the creative process until she encountered the world of dance.

Chaffee (1997) concludes that thinking critically enables humans to identify and accept a given problem. When humans generate alternatives for solving a problem, they are using creative thinking abilities. When they evaluate the various alternatives and select one or more to pursue, humans are thinking critically. Developing ideas for implementing solutions and alternative approaches, if necessary, involves thinking creatively. Constructing a practical plan of action and evaluating the results depends on critical thinking.

Teaching for Thinking

Good creative and critical thinking take place in a context of questioning and open inquiry that requires a certain spirit of thought manifested in certain attitudes and dispositions like being open-minded and considering points of view other than one's own. Creating a classroom or establishing the school library media center as an information laboratory, rather than teaching for specific skills, is the most difficult aspect of teaching to generate thinking. Development of such learning environments requires continual experimentation and self-monitoring.

Robert J. Swartz (1987) of the Critical and Creative Program at the University of Massachusetts summarizes a brief taxonomy for creative thinking skills:

- Fluency of thought: generating ideas in a multitude of different categories.

- Originality of thought: coming up with new ideas.

- Elaboration of thought: generating as many details as possible.

These skills are typically viewed as nonjudgmental and therefore different from critical thinking skills, which are based on evaluative judgments and choices. These creative attributes or dispositions are basic to inventiveness. Thomas Edison explored thousands of alternatives for filament fiber before creating a workable light bulb. Hundreds of lab technicians and a competitive marketplace have served to refine Edison's invention to increase its durability and to adjust its composition to meet specific needs.

There is a danger, Swartz warns, in separating critical thinking from creative thinking, separating each into sets of skills, and then structuring lessons that involve students in using these skills piecemeal. In developing good thinking skills, students also must develop a sense of when and where they can be used most appropriately and effectively. Creative alternatives and critical selections work best in tandem.

Common Techniques to Spark Creativity

It seems that as school children grow older, there is greater need for encouraging creative thinking. It may seem that the typical school experience actually stops natural curiosity and creativity. It may be that creative thinking is more difficulty to manage and to evaluate than the demonstration of critical thinking. But in order for either to exist, students must be encouraged to challenge conventional wisdom and standard academic knowledge. Techniques which help to

"grant a license to question authority" include the following:

- **Fractionation.** An established pattern is usually taken for granted. To create new patterns, it is necessary to separate the whole into the smallest parts possible and then reconnect the pieces in a different manner. Consider breaking apart a model of a school and creating a structure for future facilities with more ties to the community and technology; evolution of future automobiles; the common structure of a reference book in print moving to electronic format; or rewriting the United States' Constitution for 2010.

- **Reversal.** In the reversal method, one takes things as they are and then turns them around, inside out, upside down, back to front. Then one sees what happens. How does this painting sound? How does this song look?

- **Suspended judgment.** The need to be right all the time is the biggest barrier there is to new ideas. To explore new ideas, one needs to delay judgment, avoid making summary evaluation of an idea, and consider even an obviously wrong idea to see why it is wrong. This technique is necessary in brainstorming.

- **Analogy:** This often involves translating a problem into an analogy and then relating similarities back to renewed consideration of the original problem. Consider folk tales and legends as models for new stories created by students. Ask learners to compose a scenario that describes an event for a future school, or describe how one might approach homework differently if a proposed technology plan is funded. Analogies allow the creative thinker to illustrate, elaborate, and eventually sooth or excite an audience.

Activities to Create the Mind's Museum

The critical thinker moves through a museum to consider factual information presented. How relevant? How authoritative? The critical thinker will tend to review and evaluate the evidence displayed. The creative thinker will see what is not displayed and raise questions that lead to new exhibit ideas. John B. Bunch (2005), associate professor at the Curry School of Education at Virginia University, has collected several sets of questions related to creative and critical thinking activities that can serve to prime students for constructive field trips to museums:

- **Compare and Contrast.** The ability to see similarities and differences between two or more concepts. How is this artifact like a puzzle? How is this painting like a party, a song, or a mathematical formula? In what ways are the visuals produced by Mathew Brady and Frederic Remington similar and different? And how might each, if alive today, illustrate future space exploration?

- **Analysis.** The ability to take apart and understand the interrelationships and structure of the whole. Name one thing that you could delete from this painting that would not alter the artist's intent. What does this object tell us about the artist's attitude toward war?

- **Elaboration.** The ability to expand and embellish ideas with intensive detail. Select two or more musical pieces to accompany this object. Pretend you are a character in this painting and tell us as much as you can about your life. Describe the events of the day leading up to and following Mr. Brady taking this picture of President Lincoln and General Grant. Describe any technical problems Mr. Brady might have had in taking these photographs.

- **Fluency.** The ability to produce a quantity of possibilities, ideas, consequences, or products. Describe all of the feelings you derive from this object. What other formats for expression are necessary in order to represent those feelings? If you were to paint two panels that would be placed on either side of this portrait of General Washington, what would you illustrate and why?

- **Originality.** The ability to produce unusual, unique, or highly personal responses, ideas, or solutions. If this object could fly, where would it go? If the paintings in this gallery were viewed as a storyboard, what would be the content of a play or movie that might result? How would your interaction with the objects of this museum change if they were electronically displayed through multimedia and accessed as a "virtual museum" collection?

- **Evaluation.** The ability to draw conclusions by interpreting data and appraising alternatives. If you could select one object to take home with you for display in your house for a year, which would it be and why? Would your parents select the same object or something different? Why? If you could rearrange the manner in which objects are displayed here and add new displays, what changes would you make? Which items should be on permanent display, always available for people to view each day?

- **Flexibility.** The ability to view something in many different ways with a variety of ideas or products. If this scene was painted to depict different lighting because of time of day or weather conditions, what would differ from the original? This exhibit on the use of the first atomic bomb seems to express one viewpoint, but what other ideas, events, or opinions should be represented? This painting depicts Westward expansion for American in the 1880s. What else does it depict?

Synectics: Where Critical and Creative Mix

"Synectics" is derived from the Greek word synecticos, meaning "understanding together that which is apparently different." Synectics is a process that uses group creative processes to create new insights-a creative group energized without restrictions and results in synergy (Gordon 1961). The synectics process was first widely employed about forty years ago by groups of individuals responsible for developing new products. Think tanks thrive in this process as members often play out "what if" scenarios.

From synectics have come several techniques useful for the stimulation of creative thinking. Mary Alice Gunter, Thomas H. Estes, and Jan Schwab (1995) describe these techniques in their text *Instruction: A Models Approach*. The assumption is made that the human mind is not able to understand something new unless the new concept is associated with something that is already familiar to the learner. In synectics, "metaphor" is broadly defined to include all figures of speech such as simile, personification, and oxymoron. These join together different and apparently irrelevant elements through the use of analogy. Three forms are stressed in the synectic model:

- **Direct Analogy:** a direct comparison between two objects, ideas, or concepts. How is a classroom like an anthill? How is math like a crowded bus? Within such questions is an implied metaphor or an analogy by metaphor. Students, with guided practice and comparison of ideas, are usually able to eventually give elaborate responses beyond the obvious.

- **Personal Analogy:** an invitation to students to become part of the problem to be solved. How would you feel if you were a tree attacked by acid rain? The goal here is empathy.

- **Symbolic Analogy:** a compressed conflict involving descriptions that appear to be contradictory. When is silence deafening? How can love nurture and smother? When is duty both ennobling and unkind?

Detached observation and analysis are essential to solving problems, but the ability to use empathy, imagination, and feelings are equally essential, perhaps most important in presenting a proposed solution to others and gaining acceptance. The flashes of insight and creativity that come from nonrational thinking create unique and extraordinary images and solutions. The critical thinker will center on quantitative measures for precise comparisons. The creative thinker will concentrate on elaborations through qualitative measures based on case studies in order to find the contrasting perspectives. One offers concise arguments while the other offers elaborations and detail.

Creating Meaning Through Story and Reflection

Creative thinking also provides the narrative, the description, or the story necessary to express meaning for the emotions that compose our lives. Howard Gardner's 1995 study of eleven world leaders suggests that what they had in common was the fact that they arrived at a story that worked for them and, ultimately, for others as well. They told stories-in so many words-about themselves and their groups, about where they were coming from and where they were headed, about what was to be feared, struggled against, and dreamed about. They created meaning.

Gardner's 1993 study of leading creative minds tells us that individuals can differ enormously in terms of energy. What struck Gardner about his subjects was that they were each productive every day. Eliot may not have written poetry each day, but he wrote hundreds of reviews, edited major publications, and issued books on a wide range of subjects. Gandhi's literary output fills ninety volumes. Einstein worked on questions of physics until the last years of his life. Picasso may have made a thousand paintings over a five-year period, but in his own mind one or two of them were far more important than the others. Freud may have written a dozen papers a year, though he could be repetitive in these essays, and he stressed his own need to search actively for new ideas. Each found meaning through revision and elaboration-reflection based on various perspectives imagined at different stages in their personal intellectual growth and development.

Questions for Creative Inquiry

Robert Harris (2002) has raised dozens of situations that require creative thinking in order to address the problems he poses. Often team work is necessary to consider possible options and solutions. One answer is never enough. Questions similar to those that follow can raise

Key Words for Instruction in Information Inquiry

challenging inquiry projects for students and require a great deal of investigation and information, perhaps more so than the typical academic questions normally used for the student term paper.

- Invent a new game for the Olympics.
- Create a new snack food that is really nutritional.
- How can the time on school buses be used by kids more constructively?
- How can we reduce health care expenses and still provide good services?
- What if gasoline cost $25 a gallon?
- What if a citizen could serve only one term in one office during a lifetime?
- What if everybody looked almost exactly alike?
- What if each home could have their television on for only one hour each day?

Questions and problems that challenge the creative mind often rest with making tasks or services safer, more simple, easier, more accessible, more flexible, more elegant, less expensive, more efficient, more powerful, longer lasting, more understandable and/or more widely accepted. The critical mind will ask why? The creative mind will ask why not?

References

Bunch, J. B. (2005). *Going to a Museum? A Teacher's Guide.* Available at http://curry.edschool.virginia.edu/go/museums/Teacher_Guide/Mail/home.html (accessed September 19, 2005).

Chaffee, J. (1997). *Thinking Critically.* 5th ed. Houghton Mifflin.

Gardner, H. (1993). *Creating Minds: An Anatomy of Creativity Seen through the Lives of Freud, Einstein, Picasso, Stravinsky, Eliot, Graham, and Gandhi.* Basic Books.

Gardner, H. (1995). *Leading Minds: An Anatomy of Leadership.* Basic Books.

Gardner, H. (1997). *Extraordinary Minds: Portraits of Exceptional Individuals and an Examination of Our Extraordinariness.* Basic Books.

Gartenhaus, A. R. (1997). *Minds in Motion: Using Museums to Expand Creative Thinking.* Caddo Gap.

Gordon, W. J. (1961). *Synectics: The Development of Creative Capacity.* Harper & Row.

Gunter, M. A., T. H. Estes, and J. Schwab. (1995). *Instruction: A Models Approach.* Allyn and Bacon.

Harris, R. A. (2002). *Creative Problem Solving.* Pyrczak Publishing.

Swartz, R. J. (1987). "Teaching for Thinking: A Developmental Model for the Infusion of Thinking Skills into Mainstream Instruction." In *Teaching Thinking Skills*, edited by J. Boykoff Baron and R.J. Sternberg, 106–126. W. H. Freeman.

Critical Literacy

Daniel Callison

Rule number one: Don't believe everything you read.

Rule number two: Don't read only what you already believe.

Most progressive educators believe if either rule is not followed, learning will not occur.

Rule number three: Through critical selection of what you read, hear and observe, apply actions to change your self and/or society's status quo in order to move closer to the common good.

Most teachers of critical literacy and inquiry believe if rule number three is not followed, meaningful learning of any real value has not occurred.

Learning That Empowers

Advocates of critical literacy emphasize the empowering role that literacy can and should play in reshaping the environment in which one lives and works. Through mastering the skills of critical literacy, students apply the inquiry process and knowledge gained as a means for political or social action. By gathering appropriate information, organizing, and defining specific objectives, literacy serves as a method to change the status quo. More than an academic exercise, critical literacy is not complete unless change is proposed, contested, debated and ultimately determined by the power of evidence and argument.

Information resource professionals, such as school media specialists, must understand the goals of critical literacy and judicial inquiry if they are to collaborate effectively with teachers who want to promote critical thinking. In elementary school settings this means access to books that raise and provide examples for discussions on social issues. In secondary schools, it means access to factual documentation that will help students contend with local social issues. Information literacy is not complete unless students understand how to identify issues, gain a context for the arguments surrounding an issue, and move through information as intelligent selectors of evidence in order to dialogue, debate and propose change.

More than seeking meaning through the selection and use of information, critical literacy is the process for seeking self. The student who has reached mature levels in critical literacy will challenge, de-construct, and re-construct information in terms of arguments to justify social and political reform. Through this process, the student defines himself or herself. In authentic application, critical literacy is the strongest form of due process and judicial review in a democratic society.

Patrick Shannon (1990), Professor of Education at Pennsylvania State University relates critical literacy to the public education setting. He writes in response to Kathleen Jongsma (1991), column editor, in *The Reading Teacher*:

> Critical literacy education pushes the definition of literacy beyond the traditional decoding or encoding of words in order to reproduce the meaning of text and society until it becomes a means for understanding one's own history and culture and their connections for fostering an activism toward equal participation for all [in] the decisions that effect and control our lives. This type of education has a distinguished history in America. When led by teachers who demonstrate the power of critical literacy, students of all ages have learned to read and write both the word and the world as perceived through multiple-symbol systems.

For example, intermediate grade children in Chicago at the turn of the [last] century were able to read why technological change in industry always causes new social problems. In McDonald County around 1920, children were able to read about typhoid problems of local farmers and to write a plan for a community health cooperative. During the 1920s and the 1930s, at the Work Peoples College in Duluth, Minnesota, workers were reading about the advantages of organized labor and writing a union of the Farmer and Labor Parties. Throughout the southeastern United States in the late 1950s and early 1960s, disenfranchised blacks were learning to read the Constitution in Citizenship Schools and were writing an end to apartheid in America.

Critical literacy has a rich history in development of education settings. From John Dewey to Lev Vygotsky to Paulo Freire, progressive education has been based on providing students not merely with functional skills, but with the conceptual tools necessary to critique and engage society along with its inequalities and injustices. Horace Mann, known as the Father of the Common School and free public education, challenged his students to, "Be ashamed to die until you have won some victory for humanity." (518)

Critical Literacy in K–6 Classrooms

Powerful case studies about elementary classrooms where teachers integrate inquiry methods to increase student conversations based on their own questions derived from critical literacy are illustrated in *Learning Together Through Inquiry* (Short et al. 1996). These cases, however, also document elementary school library collections that contain many out-of-date resources, fail to provide depth to support student inquiry, and do not describe a collaborative role for professional school media specialists as co-teachers of the inquiry process. While students eventually are successful through classroom collections and community resources, true teachable moments for critical discussion of social issues and supporting materials are lost without the support of the school librarian.

A more recent series on critical literacy in elementary classrooms has been published by the International Reading Association (Vasquez 2003; Hefferman 2004). While the school librarian is still not shown as a collaborating professional, this series highlights several useful trade books that trigger critical inquiry and set the stage for student questions concerning local and historical social issues. Successful methods to help students journal, discuss, and seek community resources to address these questions are clearly outlined. The collection of fiction, nonfiction and biographical resources should be extensive in both the classroom and the school library, with duplicate copies of key books that will stimulate social issue conversations. Examples include the following:

> Bartoletti, S. (1999). *Kids on Strike!* Houghton Mifflin.
>
> Cronin, D. (2000). *Click, Clack, Moo: Cows That Type.* Simon & Schuster.
>
> Fradin, D., and J. Fradin. (2001). *Ida B. Wells: Mother of the Civil Rights Movement.* Clarion Books.
>
> Loribiecki, M. (1996). *Just One Flick of a Finger.* Dial.
>
> Ringgold, F. (1999). *If a Bus Could Talk: The Story of Rosa Parks.* Simon & Schuster.

Regular communication between classroom teachers and the school media specialist, perhaps also involving the local public librarians from youth services, could generate an extensive list of quality resources to give a rich foundation for elementary level critical inquiry (Bush 2003; Bush 2006b). Such titles provide the basis for regular book and curriculum discussions among these professionals. Teachers and librarians practicing critical literacy themselves can generate lesson activities tailored to meet local issues and historical events that will open greater perspectives than those often summarized and limited in scope as outlined in standard textbooks (Bush 2002).

In collaboration with the National Council of Teachers of English, the International Reading Association has compiles several examples of lesson plans through their online

ReadWriteThink series and *Focus on Critical Literacy* (accessed May 22, 2006). These lessons, if supported with a rich information base of books, reference materials, links to quality online documents, and contacts with local experts for interviews and provide for engaging social action experiences. These lessons include:

Critical Literary: Point of View

Magazine Redux: An Exercise in Critical Literacy

Critical Media Literacy: TV Programs

Critical Media Literacy: Commercial Advertising

Identifying and Understanding the Fallacies Used in Advertising

Persuasive Essay: Environmental Issues

Analyzing the Purpose and Meaning of Political Cartoons

Supporting Critical Conversations in Elementary Classrooms

As students work with critical literacy, they learn the power of literacy. This is a very insightful lesson beyond the mechanics of literacy. They learn how to be literate, what it means to be literate, what one can do with literacy to define and shape impressions of others, and how the literate control the content of text and recorded history across society (Dozier, Johnston, and Rogers 2006). Jerome Harste (1999), retired professor at Indiana University and past president of the National Council of Teachers of English, has been a longtime advocate of starting and sustaining critical inquiry conversations across elementary classrooms stimulated by key books for children. Harste chaired a group of educators who selected dozens of titles for K–6 classrooms that can spark conversations for critical discussions on contemporary issues. To be selected by the panel, a book had to meet at least one of the following criteria:

- It doesn't make difference [among people] invisible, but rather explores what differences make a difference.

- It enriches our understanding of history and life by giving voice to those who traditionally have been silenced or marginalized—those we call "the indignant ones."

- It shows how people can begin to take action on important social issues.

- It explores dominant systems of meaning that operate in our society to position people and groups of people.

- It helps us question why certain groups are positioned as "others." (Harste 1999, 507)

Some notable titles from this review committee are listed below to illustrate the range of titles available in the 1990s, and many more have been published over the past decade. Teachers and school library media specialists will want to consider age appropriateness when presenting some of these titles to readers, but each will spark questions for conversations and inquiry on social action.

Breckler, Rosemary. (1996). *Sweet Dried Apples: A Vietnamese Wartime Childhood.* Houghton Mifflin.

Dash, Joan (1996). *We Shall Not Be Moved: The Women's Factory Strike of 1909.* Scholastic.

Forrester, Sandra. (1997). *My Home Is Over Jordan.* Lodestar.

Hesse, Karen. (1998). *Just Juice.* Scholastic.

Jimenez, Francisco. (1998). *The Circuit: Stories from the Life of a Migrant Child.*

Kaplan, William. (1998). *One More Border.* Groundwood.

Lorbiecki, Marybeth. (1996). *Just One Flick of a Finger.* Dial.

Lorbiecki, Marybeth. (1998). *Sister Anne's Hands.* Dial.

Martinez, Victor. (1996). *Parrot in the Oven: Mi Vida.* Harper Collins.

McGuffee, Michael. (1996). *The Day the Earth Was Silent.* Inquiring Voices.

Mochizuki, Ken. (1997). *Passage to Freedom: The Sugihara Story.* Lee & Low.

Rapp, Adam. (1997). *The Buffalo Tree.* Front Street.

Springer, Jane. (1997). *Listen to Us: The World's Working Children.* Groundwood.

Wyeth, Sharon Dennis. (1998). *Something Beautiful.* Bantam Doubleday Dell.

In summarizing recent research projects on critical literacy at the IUPUI School of Education, Professor Christine Leland (Leland, Ociepka, and Stoughton 2004, 1) stated:

Critical literacy practices encourage people to use language to question the everyday world, interrogate the relationship between language and power, analyze popular culture and media, understand how power relationships are socially constructed, and consider actions that can be taken to promote social justice. The goal of a critical literacy curriculum is to help children learn to analyze spoken, written, and visual texts to uncover bias and identify whose interests are served as well as whose are being marginalized. These practices are substantially different from what are commonly referred to as critical thinking approaches. While critical thinking approaches have focused more on logic and comprehension, critical literacies have focused on identifying social practices that keep dominant ways of understanding the world in place Critical literacies are rooted in principles of democracy and justice, of questioning and analysis, of resistance and action – all uncommon in traditional pedagogies that define a teacher as transmitter of knowledge. Even though democratic principles are highly touted in textbooks and political rhetoric more general, they are not often taken up in classroom routines or enacted in daily school life.

Maureen McLaughlin, a professor of reading at East Stroudsburg University, and Glenn DeVoogd, an associate professor of literacy at California State University (2004), contend that use of critical literacy is at its best when students challenge and are critical of text, explore different identities of characters, and struggle to see beyond the bias in the text and in themselves. They believe that critical literacy in K–8 classrooms is needed for students and teachers to

- establish equal status in the reader-author relationship;

- understand the motivation the author had for writing the text (the function) and how the author uses the text to make us understand in a particular way (the form);

- understand that the author's perspective is not the only perspective;

- and become active users of the information in texts to develop independent perspectives, as opposed to passive reproducers of the ideas in text. (2004, 7)

McLaughlin and DeVoogd believe readers need to understand that they have the power to envision alternative ways of viewing the author's topic, and they exert that power when they read from a critical stance. Ultimately, critical literacy focuses on sociopolitical issues. Informed readers, both students and teachers, may eventually take action to promote social justice and act to change an inappropriate, unequal power relationship between people. Actions, if organized and implemented at all, are usually managed to impact the local community. Information Inquiry is, in such cases, a method to raise and define issues and to gather specific evidence locally to justify a plan for action and change. McLaughlin and DeVoogd recommend many book titles to start discussions concerning disruption of the commonplace and routine, offer insights into identities, and provide multiple viewpoints. Among their recommendations are the following:

Adler, D. A. (2003). *Mama Played Baseball.* Gulliver Books.

Avi. (2002). *Crispin: The Cross of Lead.* Hyperion.

Choi, Y. (2001). *The Name Jar.* Knopf.

Fama, E. (2002). *Overboard.* Cricket Books.

Hidier, T. (2002). *Born Confused.* Scholastic.

Hoyt-Goldsmith, D. (2001). *Celebrating Ramadan.* Holiday House.

Jones, C. (2002). *Every Girl Tells a Story.* Simon & Schuster.

Lasky, K. (2002). *A Time for Courage.* Scholastic.

Montes, M. (2003). *A Crazy Mixed-Up Spanglish Day*. Scholastic.

Park, L. S. (2002). *When My Name Was Keoko*. Clarion Books.

Turner, A. (2003). *Love They Neighbor*. Scholastic.

Whelan, G. (2000). *Homeless Bird*. HaperCollins.

Wittlinger, E. (2002). *Gracie's Girl*. Alladin.

Wood, R. W. (2003). *Goodbye Vietnam*. Omonomany.

Dialogue, Discussion, and Debate for Secondary School Students

As with other literacy applications, critical literacy can be found in poems, essays, dramatic narratives, documentaries, and even autobiographical or biographical texts. Such often rely on emotion as well as reason and may be tied to historical contexts that reflect some social or political injustice. The most common form of critical literacy, however, rests in informal and formal formats for discussion and debate. Formulations of proposals for change, based on evidence and argument, require the student who practices critical literacy to gain expertise in selection of evidence to support a targeted cause. Critical literacy asks the student to consider the politics of the authors or evidence read and to decide on which side of the debate the student is as he or she communicates or presents responses.

Critical debate asks students to make the strongest possible case for a position that is diametrically opposed to their own. It's the kind of exercise, according to Stephen Brookfield and Stephen Preskill (1999), that may help them strengthen their own argument by anticipating the claims of opponents, or it may cause them to look at the issue in a new light and bring about a shift in their point of view. Here's how critical debate works:

1. Find a contentious issue on which opinion is divided among participants. Frame the issue as a debate motion.

2. Propose the motion to participants. Ask people to volunteer by a show of hands to work on a team that is preparing arguments to support a motion or one that is preparing arguments to oppose it.

3. Announce that everyone will be assigned to the team opposite the one for which they volunteered.

4. Conduct the debate. Each team chooses one person to present the arguments. After initial presentations, the teams reconvene to draft rebuttal arguments. A different person presents these.

5. Debrief the debate. Discuss with participants their experience of this exercise. Focus on how it felt to argue against positions to which you were committed. What new ways of thinking about the issue were opened? Did participants come to new understandings? Did they change their positions on this issue at all?

6. Ask participants to write a follow-up reflection paper on the debate. Students should address the following questions:

   – What assumptions about the issue were clarified or confirmed for you by the debate?

   – Which of these assumptions surprised you during the debate?

   – Were you made aware of assumptions that you didn't know you held?

   – How could you check the validity of these assumptions?

   – What sources of evidence would you consult?

   – In what ways, if any, were your existing assumptions challenged or changed by the debate?

Formal Debate

Formal debate follows three styles:

- **Lincoln-Douglas Debate.** This style is modeled after the famous debates between Abraham Lincoln and Stephen Douglas. This type of debate is also known as "values" debate. Debaters focus on competing values inherent in the proposition and are expected to argue on the basis of the underlying principles of their side of the resolution or motion. For example, an affirmative argues that "Government ought to provide for the needs of the poor," and would make a broad philosophical case for this government obligation. The affirmative would not have to prove the effectiveness of any particular government program. In general, Lincoln-Douglas Debate centers on the ideas, values, and spirit governing the political, economic, social, moral, and aesthetic positions held.

- **Parliamentary Debate.** This style is modeled on the British House of Parliament. One team represents the Government and the other the Loyal Opposition. A Speaker of the House officiates and judges. A specific resolution is offered with a definition of terms. Usually two debaters represent each opposing side and debate may center on specific practical approaches to solve a problem or change the status quo. Audience members are free to interject opinions, insights, questions, or even provide a good heckle.

- **Policy Debate.** The focus is on a specific plan to meet a resolution (Hensley and Carlin 2001). Such may be statements as "Government should provide public works jobs for the unemployed" or "Government should ban all tobacco advertising." Each term of the resolution must be defined, a series of needs to justify change must be introduced and defended, and a plan to resolve the issues must be detailed. While the affirmative must provide evidence for such change, the negative side will seek to show that there is no real need for change and that the affirmative team's plan may actually cause more problems than it solves. Specific time limitations are placed on each speaker. Often time is set aside for face-to-face cross examination. Usually a single judge determines the winner with feedback provided on value of the arguments presented and the merits of the evidence offered.

In policy debates, arguments are usually based on specific data that can support a claim. The affirmative team, in favor of the resolution for change, will try to present evidence (facts, observations, or opinions from experts) that allow them to make a claim for a new approach rather than the status quo. Based on a series of claims, the affirmative will tie these to a warrant for revision of the current way things are being done and present a plan for addressing the problems raised.

The Negative side will show evidence that the claims or not valid or exaggerated. They will also attempt to show that not only is change not necessary, but to adopt the affirmative plan can cause more problems and perhaps also be more expensive, inconvenient or even more dangerous than the current practice.

Debaters mature in their abilities to apply argument to social action and find that the true information search is not so much for a gathering of impressions and descriptions, but for hard evidence that supports or rejects specific arguments and plans. Further, they learn the use and meaning of the following terms:

Ad hominem: attacking your opponent personally rather than his/her argument; fallacious argumentation.

Argument: a conclusion supported by proof that may consist of analysis, reasoning, and evidence.

Assertion: an unsupported statement or claim.

Burden of Proof: the obligation to prove the need for change and establish a prima facie case.

Causal Link: analysis that is based on cause and effect; the affirmative must identify and remove the causes of the supposed problem without creating a new set of significant problems.

Counter Plan: accepting there is a need for change, the affirmative's plan may be rejected in favor of a different approach to solve the problem which may not be as costly or disruptive to the status quo.

Operational Definition: beyond what is offered in the dictionary or expert opinion, but defining terms as they specifically relate to how things operate or will be managed in a proposed plan for change.

Prima facie Case: a case that would convince the average reasonable and prudent person that a proposal for change is warranted.

Refutation and Rebuttal: counterargument to a proposal, opinion, evidence, or need for change based on reasoning and a line of argument with its own set of evidence to justify its merits.

Jurisprudential Inquiry

Bruce Joyce and Marsha Weil (2000) outline jurisprudential inquiry as a key instructional method for learning to think about social policy. Participants should be versed in three competency areas:

1. Familiarity with the values of the American creed. Understanding of principles embedded in the Constitution and the Declaration of Independence. These principles form the values framework or basis for judging public issues and making legal decisions.

2. Skills for clarifying and resolving issues. This will involve coming to terms with value differences, clarification of facts, and definition of key terms of any proposal or resolution.

3. Knowledge of contemporary political and public issues. Although a broad understanding of the history, nature, and scope of contemporary issues is important, in the jurisprudential inquiry model, students explore issues

in terms of a specific legal case rather than in terms of a general study of values.

Introduction of this critical education method often rests with the use of Socratic dialogue. In the Socratic style, the teacher asks the students to take a position on an issue or to make a value judgment, and then he or she challenges the assumptions underlying the stand by exposing its implications. For example, according to Joyce and Weil, if a student argues for freedom in some situation, the teacher will test whether the argument is meant to apply to all situations.

The function of the teacher is to probe the students' positions by questioning the relevance, consistency, specificity, and clarity of the students' ideas until they become clearer. Practice in this method should help both teacher and student to become skillful in the following:

- pose worthwhile questions;

- evaluate the adequacy of an argument;

- recognize facts, inferences, and opinions and use each appropriately;

- deal with quandaries and ill-formed problems that have no pat or unique solutions;

- give and receive criticism constructively;

- agree or disagree in degrees (based on common definition of terms, students may find they do not totally disagree but will find portions of issues on which there is common ground);

- extend a line of thought beyond the range of first impressions; and

- articulate a complex position without adding to its complexity, but begin to understand a wider range of opinions.

Constructive Dialogue and Socratic Circles

Matt Copeland (2005) teaches English in Topeka, Kansas. His strategies for fostering critical learning through open questioning and dialogue in secondary level classrooms guides students to find common ground as well as to challenge conventional wisdom. Copeland broadens the debate over social issues to include the more constructive aspects of open dialogue. He draws on the comparison between dialogue and debate as established in a law curriculum guide from Saskatchewan Learning (Accessed 2006). Selected comparisons include the following:

- Dialogue is collaborative. Two or more sides work together toward common understanding. Debate is oppositional. Two sides oppose each other and attempt to prove each other wrong.

- In dialogue, finding common ground is the goal. In debate, winning is the goal.

- In dialogue, one listens to the other side(s) in order to understand, find meaning, and find agreement. In debate, one listens to the other side in order to find flaws and to counter its arguments.

- Dialogue enlarges and possibly changes a participant's point of view. Debate affirms a person's own point of view.

- Dialogue complicates positions and issues. Debate simplifies positions and issues.

- In dialogue, it is acceptable to change one's position. In debate, it is a sign of weakness and defeat to change one's position.

- Dialogue creates an open-minded attitude, an openness to change. Debate creates a close-minded attitude, a determination to be right.

- Dialogue assumes that many people have pieces of the answer, and that together they can put them into a workable answer. Debate assumes there is a right answer and that someone has it.

Social Action and Information Literacy Standards

In one of the most important essays published in *School Library Media Quarterly,* Karen Sheingold (1987) detailed how even a small group of students in a large city can have an impact on the regulations that might improve their local environment based on their inquiry and presentation skills.

The American Association of School Librarians (AASL) produced a series of video programs through Great Plains National Broadcasting in 1997 with several examples of students taking the initiative to change opinions and regulations in their community that resulted in better parks, safer bike paths or other improvements that city council members were willing to consider.

Gail Bush (2006a), associate professor at Dominican University, has recently proposed a tenth learning standard be added to the AASL (1998) list of nine for information literacy. This standard would place students in situations where they seek information that has real world use, especially in application to meeting social and political issues locally, or assisting in civic service to improve local living conditions (Kay 2003).

Social action learning is often a direct result of an increase in both student and teacher abilities to exercise critical literacy (Lewis, Espeland, and Pernu 1998). The school media center can serve as a clearinghouse for such projects with information on social organizations and contacts nationally as well as locally. Student projects that demonstrate application of information to make a difference in their own school or community can be tangible artifacts that show how debate, planning and application of critical knowledge are authentic learning experiences (Shor and Pari 1999).

References

American Association of School Librarians and the Association. (1998). *Information Literacy Standards for Student Learning.* American Library Association.

Brookfield, S. D., and S. Preskill. (1999). *Discussion as a Way of Teaching.* Jossey-Bass.

Bush, G. (2002). "Something to Talk About: Six Collaborative Conversations." *Knowledge Quest* 31 (2): 34–37.

Bush, G. (2003). "Walking the Collaborative Talk: Creating Inquiry Groups." *Knowledge Quest* 32 (1): 52.

Bush, G. (2006a). "Social Action Learning." *School Library Media Activities Monthly.* 22 (7): 38–41.

Bush, G. (2006b). "Walking the Road between Libraries: Best Practices in School and Public Library Cooperative Activities." *School Library Media Activities Monthly* 22 (6): 25–28.

Copeland, M. (2005). *Socratic Circles.* Stenhouse Publishers.

Dozier, C., P. Johnston, and R. Rogers. (2006). *Critical Literacy Critical Teaching.* Teachers College Press.

Focus on Critical Literacy. International Reading Association. Available at http://www.ira.org/resources/issues/focus_critical.html (accessed May 22, 2006).

Harste, J. (1999). "Supporting Critical Conversations in the Classroom." In *Adventuring with Books,* 12th ed., edited by K. M. Pierce, 506–554. National Council of Teachers of English.

Hefferman, L. (2004). *Critical Literacy and Writer's Workshop.* International Reading Association.

Hensley, D., and D. Carlin. (2001). *Mastering Competitive Debate.* Clark Publishing.

Jongsma, K. Stumpf. (1991). "Questions and Answers: Critical Literacy." *The Reading Teacher* 44 (7): 518–519.

Joyce, B., and M. Weil. (2000). *Models of Teaching.* 6th ed. Allyn and Bacon.

Kay, C. B. (2003). *The Complete Guide to Service Learning.* Free Spirit Publishing.

Know It All: Saying It Another Way. (1997). Video program number 5. 20 minutes. Great Plains National Broadcasting in collaboration with the American Association of School Librarians.

Langford, L. (2001). "Critical Literacy: A Building Block Towards the Information Literate School Community." *Teacher Librarian* 28 (5): 18–21.

Leland, C., A. Ociepka, and E. Stoughton. (2004). *Using Critical Literacy to Support ALL Children.* Report for the IUPUI School of Education. Available at http://education.iupui.edu/CUME/docs/Anne%20ciepka-monograph.pdf (accessed July 3, 2006).

Lewis, B. A., P. Espeland, and C. Pernu. (1998). *The Kid's Guide to Social Action: How to Solve the Social Problems You Choose—and Turn Creative Thinking into Positive Action.* Free Spirit Publishing.

McLaughlin, M., and G. L. DeVoogd. (2004). *Critical Literacy: Enhancing Students' Comprehension of Text.* Scholastic.

Saskatchewan Learning. *Dialogue vs. Debate Chart.* Available at http://www.sasked.gov.sk.ca/docs/social/law30/unit02/02_05_sh.html (accessed May 21, 2006).

Shannon, P. (1990). *The Struggle to Continue: Progressive Reading Instruction in the United States.* Heinemann.

Sheingold, K. (1987). "Keeping Children's Knowledge Alive Through Inquiry." *School Library Media Quarterly* 15 (2): 80–85.

Shor, I., and C. Pari, eds. (1999). *Critical Literacy in Action.* Heinemann.

Short, K. G., et al. (1996). *Learning Together Through Inquiry: From Columbus to Integrated Curriculum.* Stenhouse Publishers.

Vasquez, V. (2003). *Getting Beyond "I Like the Book": Creating Space for Critical Literacy in K-6 Classrooms.* International Reading Association.

Critical Thinking

Daniel Callison

John Chaffee (1997), director of the Center for Critical Thinking and Language Learning at the City University of New York, offers two useful and contrasting definitions of critical thinking:

- Thinking critically is the cognitive process we use to carefully examine our thinking (and the thinking of others) in order to clarify and improve our understanding.

- Thinking creatively is the cognitive process we use to develop ideas that are unique, useful, and worthy of further elaboration.

Related term descriptors from the Educational Resource Information Clearinghouse (ERIC) serve to provide additional notions for contrasting critical and creative thinking.

Both critical and creative thinking are subsets of cognitive processes.

- Critical thinking is associated with the more narrow terms convergent thinking and evaluative thinking, while creative thinking is associated with the more narrow terms divergent thinking and productive thinking. Critical thinkers seek the best or most reasonable solution from available options to solving a problem. Creative thinkers raise alternatives that lead to new or unique solutions.

- Critical thinking is related to citizenship education, consciousness raising, controversial issues, decision making, heuristics, inferences, problem solving, and logic. Creative thinking is related to concept formation, discovery processes, heuristics, imagination, improvisation, intuition, inventions, problem solving, and visualization. Thus, there are areas of overlap as well as contrast.

Chaffee concludes that thinking critically enables humans to identify and accept the problem. When humans generate alternatives for solving the problem, they are using creative thinking abilities.

When they evaluate the various alternatives and select one or more to pursue, humans are thinking critically. Developing ideas for implementing solutions and alternative approaches, if necessary, involves thinking creatively. Constructing a practical plan of action and evaluating the results depends on thinking critically (Browne and Keeley 1990; Elder and Paul 2002).

Goals in the Critical Thinking Curriculum

Robert H. Ennis (1987), whose work for the University of Illinois Critical Thinking Project during the 1980s provided much of the initial critical skill identification, argued that critical thinking is influenced by five key ideas: practical, reflective, reasonable, belief, and action. These ideas combine, according to Ennis, for the working definition: critical thinking is reasonable reflective thinking that is focused on deciding what to believe or do. Influenced by Bloom's taxonomy of educational objectives, Ennis outlined the basic student dispositions and abilities that must be evident in the critical thinking curriculum. He did not equate such student actions with higher order thinking skills, but was satisfied to state that these skills represent the more cognitive material to be acquired in school than banks of memorized and soon-to-be-forgotten facts.

Following are selected items from the Ennis curriculum, many relevant to information literacy skills:

- Seek a clear statement of the thesis or question.

- Try to be well informed.

- Use and mention credible sources.

- Take into account the total situation.

- Look for alternatives and seriously consider other points of view.

- Withhold judgment when the evidence and reasons are insufficient.

- Take a position and change a position when the evidence and reasons are sufficient to do so.

- Seek as much precision as the subject permits.

- Deal in an orderly manner with the parts of a complex whole.

- Be sensitive to the feelings, level of knowledge, and degree of sophistication of others.

Student Abilities

- Focus on a question: formulate a question and criteria for judging possible answers.

- Analyze arguments: identify arguments, stated and unstated reasons, and handle irrelevance.

- Ask and answer questions for clarification and/or to challenge: Why? What is your main point? Please give me a specific example. What difference would that make? What are the facts? Would you say more about that?

- Judge the credibility of a source including expertise, lack of conflict of interest, agreement among sources, and reputation.

- Judge observation reports or witnesses, testing with corroboration.

- Make correct application of either deductive or inductive logic.

- Infer conclusions and hypotheses.

- Determine an action to address the problem.

- Interact with others through presentation of a position, oral or written.

A Newer List of Critical Thinking Skills

In 1995, the National Center for Education Statistics (NCES) published a study in which the perceptions of selected undergraduate instructors and managers that hire college graduates at entry level professional positions were compared. Critical thinking skills for online education were added in 2002 (U.S. Department of Education NCES 95-001). The following is a list of student abilities highly rated by those from either academic or employer ranks and provides more precision of student actions than the Ennis guide from the previous decade. More refined description of critical thinking skills can lead to more precise measurement of student performance. While this list describes critical thinking abilities of college graduates, lower level scope and sequence skills can be extracted and reworded for K–12 levels. Academic faculty, business managers, and policy makers agreed it is extremely important that the college student be able to demonstrate adequate performance of each of the following critical thinking skills.

Student Disposition

- Be curious and inquire about how and why things work.

- Persevere and persist at a complex task willingly.

- Be flexible and creative in seeking solutions.

- Be inclined to arrive at a reasonable decision in situations where there is more than one plausible solution.

- Exhibit honesty in facing up to prejudices, biases, or tendency to consider a problem solely from one's personal viewpoint.

- Find ways to collaborate with others to reach consensus on a problem or issue.

Interpretation Skills

- Formulate categories, distinctions, or frameworks to organize information in order to aid comprehension.

- Translate information from one medium to another to aid comprehension without altering the intended meaning.

- Make comparisons: note similarities and differences between or among informational items.

- Classify and group data, findings, and opinions on the basis of attributes of a given criterion.

- Detect the use of leading questions that are biased towards eliciting a preferred response.

- Recognize the use of misleading language, such as language that exaggerates or downplays the importance of an issue or neutralizes a controversial topic.

- Detect instances where irrelevant topics or considerations are brought into an argument that divert attention from the original issue.

- Recognize the use of slanted definitions or comparisons that express a bias for or against a position.

- Recognize confusing, vague, or ambiguous language that requires clarification to increase comprehension.

- Ask relevant and penetrating questions to clarify facts, concepts, and relationships.

- Identify and seek additional resources, such as resources in print, that can help clarify communication.

- Develop analogies and other forms of comparisons to clarify meaning.

- Provide an example that helps explain something or removes a troublesome ambiguity.

Analysis Skills

- Identify the ideas presented and assess the interests, attitudes, or views contained in those ideas.

- Identify the background information provided to explain reasons that support a conclusion.

- Identify the unstated assumptions of an argument.

Evaluation Skills

- Assess the importance of an argument and determine if it merits attention.

- Evaluate the credibility, accuracy, and reliability of sources of information.

- Determine if an argument rests on false, biased, or doubtful assumptions.

- Assess statistical information used as evidence to support an argument.

Inference Skills

- Determine what is the most significant aspect of a problem or issue that needs to be addressed, prior to collecting evidence.

- Formulate a plan for locating information to aid in determining if a given opinion is more or less reasonable than a competing opinion.

- Combine disparate pieces of information whose connection is not obvious, but when combined offers insight into a problem or issue.

- Judge what background information would be useful to have when attempting to develop a persuasive argument in support of one's opinion.

- Determine if one has sufficient evidence to form a conclusion.

- Seek the opinion of others in identifying and considering alternatives.

- Seek evidence to confirm or disconfirm alternatives.

- Assess the risks and benefits of each alternative in deciding between them.

- After evaluating the alternatives generated, develop, when appropriate, a new alternative that combines the best qualities and avoids the disadvantages of previous alternatives.

- Use multiple strategies in solving problems including means-ends analysis, working backward, analogies, brain storming, and trial and error.

- Seek various independent sources of evidence, rather than a single source of evidence to provide support for a conclusion.

- Note uniformities or regularities in a given set of facts, and construct a generalization that would apply to these and similar instances.

- Employ graphs, diagrams, hierarchical trees, matrices, and models as solution aids.

Presenting Arguments Skills

- Present supporting reasons and evidence for conclusion(s) that address the concerns of the audience.

- Negotiate fairly and persuasively.

- Present an argument succinctly so as to convey the critical point of an issue.

- Cite relevant evidence and experiences to support a position.

- Formulate accurately and consider alternative positions and opposing points of view, noting and evaluating evidence and key assumptions on both sides. A skill rated as important by most evaluators, but for which there was considerable disagreement as to the degree of importance (faculty ranked it higher than employers) is:

- Illustrate control concepts with significant examples and show how these concepts and examples apply in real situations.

Reflection Skills

- Apply the skills of self-analysis and evaluation to arguments and confirm and/or correct reasoning and conclusions.

- Make revisions in arguments and findings when self-examination reveals inadequacies.

Application across the Curriculum

Critical thinking skills are best employed in learning situations if

- they are modeled by teachers, especially teachers of information literacy;

- they are not taught as a separate or special set of skills, but taught as normal expectations integrated in many areas of the curriculum;

- they are practiced and refined based on shared reflections among learners and teachers;

- they are linked to real life situations as well as the demands of academic exercises.

While each of the critical thinking skills given above may seem impossible for the average student and far beyond the usual performance of most students in the K–12 setting, these statements should serve as descriptions of behaviors for which all learners and teachers strive. Application of these statements can result in evaluation stages or rubric measures of student performance. Consideration for these levels and discussion between learner and teacher about the meaning of such performance can set the stage for increasing the proportion of college students and other secondary school graduates who are knowledgeable in the practice of critical thinking.

Mel Levine (2002), founder of the All Kinds of Minds Institute, has outlined his steps for parents to engage their children in critical thinking and problem solving (p. 204–205). His philosophy is based on the assumption that children at all levels can engage in these steps with some guidance.

Step 1—Enumerating the Facts. Report the facts as known, objectively.

Step 2—Uncovering the Author's or Creator's Point of View. Help the child determine the point of view, intention, or motive behind the information.

Step 3—Establishing What the Child Thinks. What are the child's feelings and thoughts and how do they relate to the facts? What are the options to explore?

Step 4—Searching for Errors and Exaggerations. Evaluate, with the child, to find false claims and misleading information.

Step 5—Getting Outside Help. Search for and explore lots of related outside resources. Get guidance from the local public or school librarian and explore information resources.

Step 6—Weighing the Evidence. Pull together what you have found and consider the additional facts and opinions as objectively as possible.

Step 7—Communicating. Once an evaluation of the evidence is concluded, the child should be guided in framing and stating a conclusion.

The child will learn from communicating what new information they have learned and identifying new questions or areas they have discovered which will need more information to address. These critical thinking steps are common to most models for information literacy and inquiry.

ICT Literacy

In 2005, the Educational Testing Service (ETS) launched its version of assessment of critical thinking skills for Information and Communication Technology (ICT) Literacy. Developed and field tested through a consortium of universities, this assessment aims to measure student critical thinking competencies in use of computerize information and evaluation of data found in electronic documents. The objective is to measure both cognitive and technical skills necessary for successful academic performance in the Information Age.

More than a multiple-choice test, the ETS ICT assessment presents what it describes as real-time, scenario-based tasks. These tasks center around seven key critical thinking skills identified by those who have consulted with the testing service:

- **Define.** Appropriately represent an information need—a research topic, asking questions, completing a concept map.

- **Access.** Collect and retrieve information in digital environments—search databases, browse linked Web sites, access information through online help systems, download multimedia such a video-based programs.

- **Manage.** Apply an existing organizational or classification scheme for digital information—sort e-mails into appropriate and useful folders, prioritize information in tables, document information relationships using an organizational chart.

- **Integrate.** Interpret and represent digital information—synthesize information, compare and contrast information.

- **Evaluate.** Determine the degree to which digital information meets a need—selecting best databases, determine sufficient level of meeting information need, ranking quality of Web pages, determine relevance of digital information accessed.

- **Create.** Generate information by adapting, applying, designing or inventing information in ICT environments—create a graph that displays information to support a point of view, select specific text or graphics that support a point of view.

- **Communicate.** Communicate information properly in its context and gear electronic information for a particular audience—recasting an e-mail, adapting presentation slides, prepare a text message for a cell phone.

While the successful implementation of the ETS ICT Literacy Assessment is yet to be seen, this effort is a clear example of taking steps to apply critical thinking to the management of data and written communication now over-flowing and seldom reviewed in the electronic Information Age.

High school teachers may be in need of such assessment as implied from a study funded by the 2003 Highsmith Research Award (Williams, Grimble, and Irwin 2004). Senior high school teachers tended to consider information from subscription electronic databases to be more reliable and better focused than the information students generally retrieved from the Internet. However, quality information that required more time to assess and verify was viewed as too time-consuming an effort for students to undertake.

Further, most teachers reported they were aware of the specialized databases, but did not know how to use them. Therefore, research assignments usually were not marked down for citations linked to questionable information from the Internet. Teachers promoted the use of the Internet because it was faster, easier to use, and led to a greater scope of information immediately than did the commercial databases. Quality of information took a backseat to speed in completion of the research assignment. Findings from the research have resulted in new objectives for information orientation sessions, including more in-service training for teachers.

References

Browne, M. N., and S. M. Keeley. (1990). *Asking the Right Questions: A Guide to Critical Thinking*. 3d ed. Prentice Hall.

Callison, D. (1994). "Expanding the Evaluation Role in the Critical-Thinking Curriculum." In *Assessment and the School Library Media Center*, edited by C. C. Kuhlthau, 43–57. Libraries Unlimited.

Chaffee, J. (1997). *Thinking Critically*. 5th ed. Boston: Houghton Mifflin.

Educational Testing Service (ETS). (2005). ICT Literacy Assessment. Accessed November 17, (2005). www.ets.org/ictliteracy.

Elder, L., and R. Paul. (2002). "Critical Thinking: Distinguishing Between Inferences and Assumptions." *Journal of Developmental Education* 25 (3): 34–36.

Ennis, R. H. (1987). "A Taxonomy of Critical Thinking Dispositions and Abilities." In *Teaching Thinking Skills*, edited by J. B. Baron and R.J. Sternberg, 9–29. W. H. Freeman.

Levine, M. (2002). *A Mind at a Time*. Simon & Schuster.

National Center for Education Statistics (NCES). (1995). *National Assessment of College Student Learning: Identifying College Graduates' Essential Skills in Writing, Speech and Listening, and Critical Thinking*. U. S. Government Printing Office and Superintendent of Documents.

U.S. Department of Education NCES 95–001. (2002). "Teaching Critical Thinking Online." *Journal of Instructional Psychology* 29 (2): 53–77.

Williams, T. D., B. J. Grimble, M. Irwin. (2005). "Teachers' Link to Electronic Resources in the Library Media Center: A Local Study of Awareness, Knowledge and Influence." *School Library Media Research* 7. Available at www.ala.org/aasl/SLMR (accessed November 17, 2005).

Evidence

Daniel Callison

Evidence—What Is it?

While it is too high an expectation for elementary and secondary school students to be legal or medical judges of evidence, they are never too young to be legal and authority-minded. At the very least, they should be encouraged to question the validity of information they retrieve and presented to them by others. Does this mean "questioning authority"? It means respecting authority that is trustworthy and relevant, and often that can not be assumed. As the student matures in Information Inquiry, proof of an argument or a claim should become a natural reaction to any opinion, observation or data, regardless of the original source. The student as information scientist will "test" information by seeking verification, second opinions and validation of content by checking credentials, publishers and impressions from his peers (fellow students) and mentors (instructional media specialists).

Amy Bruckman (2005), assistant professor in the College of Computing at Georgia Tech, offers this view on why it is important for students to learn to deal with evidence at an early age and continue through college:

> . . . one college student e-mailed me to say he was worried; most of the sources he was finding on his topic seemed "old" to him. Would it be OK, he asked, assuming at least some of his sources were from this year? Talking with him further, I determined that for him old meant "three or four years old." I tried to explain that "recent" and "relevant" are not synonyms, and that I could think of things more than 100 years old that would be important to his topic. With the barrage of the latest information available online, it's not surprising that students begin to equate newness with value and credibility.
>
> This is not meant to disparage today's students. Quite the opposite. Writing college research papers 20 years ago, I had a limited source of material—the contents of my university's library—to choose from. Library materials are vetted by trained professionals. However, just because it's in print, and a librarian bought it, doesn't mean it's true, of course. But on the whole, the quality of the materials available in a library is pretty good.
>
> Contrast this situation with the amount of information available to today's paper-writing student. The quantity has increased exponentially, and the range of subject and quality of the information as increased in both directions. . . . How are students to make sense of this complexity if we don't teach them to evaluate and use what they read online?
>
> Peer review and the social construction of knowledge are key concepts students need to understand. However, there are other approaches to the nature of truth, and it's important for all students to understand competing theories.
>
> If students are to make sense of the information that increasingly surrounds them, their teachers and their parents need to start this kind of practical, epistemological education earlier, before they arrive in my class a college seniors. (35–37)

The Time Line Structure of Emerging Scientific Information

Until this past decade, the common evolution of an idea or testable thesis to debate, review and assimilation into the discipline on a wide scale was commonly seven to ten years. And that is a generalization up for clarification as many ideas in science never make it to the stage of being widely accepted as some level of fact and depending on the questions being addressed may take generations before emerging in standard science textbooks.

The Information Age has changed that to a large degree as ideas and papers without peer review can appear in online conversations or self-produced Web sites. While this has probably given speed to the creation and testing processes and links to a wider knowledge base to reduce duplication of experiments, it has also opened a wider problem—self-publication sometimes masked as legitimate research. Knowledge in testing for authoritative electronic discussion areas has become an essential skill for today's scientist in all research disciplines (Henninger 2005). This is illustrated in the time line represented in Table Part3.1. Adapted from Reed (1991), Table Part3.1 illustrates how much slower, but perhaps more reviewed and tested information was at point A before the Internet than today at point B with the Internet. Others might argue that information today is open to more critical review, faster, and to a wider audience than in pre-Internet days.

This is not to say all information in electronic discussion form is wrong or misleading, nor to say that all information that has gone through a ten year review period is valid. The changes of the reviewed information to add meaning to evolving thought and to have been more widely accepted by experts is greater under the progression to the public at point A. Others might argue, however, that we live in an electronic age that will allow new discoveries to change our notions quickly through immediate mass discussion and distribution. The information literate student is one who realizes that these patterns for emerging evidence, especially in the scientific communities, continue to evolve with the expanding capabilities of telecommunications. Learning who are the experts in a field may no longer depend on longevity and tenure as much as checking qualifications of those who add frequently and convincingly to electronic discussions concerning emerging notions and ideas. Expertise can rise and fall rapidly in the Information Age. While modern electronic communications allow for self-publication, it also demands that the researcher be ready to make his or her case and defend it with the rest of the world watching.

Table Part3.1. Structure of Emerging Scientific Information Pre- and Post-Internet Introduction

Time	Content	Publication Level	Internet
0	Idea		Posted, Blogged
1–2 Years	Research		Draft Findings

B. General public access can begin here in the Information Age with the Internet and with little review or refereeing of content—but openly debated and documents can be quickly challenged for all to consider.

Time	Content	Publication Level	Internet
2–3 Years	Invisible College		Discussions
2–4 Years	Conference	Refereed Proceedings	Article Drafts
3–5 Years	Journal Articles	Primary Literature Review	Online Articles
		Original Literature	
4–6 Years	Indexed, Reviewed		
5–7 Years	Monographs	Secondary Literature	
6–10 Years	Textbooks	Tertiary Literature	

A. General public access has been here pre-Internet, after extensive review and referring.

Filtering Techniques

High school and college students can be introduced to the use of several filtering techniques that help them increase the chances of identifying relevant data and valid information in the Information Age. According to Leslie Stebbins (2005) at Brandeis University Libraries, the following techniques can greatly increase the student's ability to identify quality resources:

- Use a specialized article database that covers scholarly journal articles and screens out popular magazine articles or any unpublished writings that have not been edited or fact-checked.

- Use bibliographies listed at the back of scholarly books, journal articles, or subject encyclopedias. The authors of these sources have provided authoritative screening for you by selecting key articles. A great deal of scholarly research is conducted by tracing the bibliographies of other researchers.

- Ask for recommendations from professors or other experts. Their years of knowledge and extensive reading provide a valuable human filter that can point to key resources.

- Use the Web of Science, a database that traces which journal articles are heavily cited by other researchers. Google Scholar, a new free service developed by Google, and Scopus are developing similar products, but currently they are significantly small than Web of Science.

- Use the "invisible college," a loosely defined network of scholars all working on similar research. The Internet has made this "invisible college" of scholars more accessible to student researchers by opening up listservs, e-mail, blogs, and conference proceedings to anyone who is interested. Through interactions with [selected portions of] this network, important articles can be found. (56)

Variances in Evidence

The medical world, over the past decade, has established standards for research clearly showing that not all evidence is created equal and certainly not accepted on an equal basis in application (Dorsch 2004). Depending on the type of question and the specific medical field, evidence may not be accepted as legitimate unless it is derived from studies that are based on a double-blind, randomized controlled trail, or cohort case studies over a substantial amount of time to see variations in results based on interventions combined under different situations and multiple combinations of treatment. Health information clericals as well as medical school students seem to make selections of journal articles that are more clearly evidence-based after they understand the importance of such criteria and learn how to search electronic databases using filtering techniques to locate studies that meet high standards (Schilling et. al. 2006).

Different treatment profiles can result in more effective treatment if researchers extend studies over time and various populations. Student inquirers will not have the time, resources or expertise to master such levels of research. But they should understand that such issues in research exist and that gleaning information from secondary and third level sources in Information Inquiry will involve gaining an understanding of how clinical research is reported in the popular media of news magazines and trade journals.

Popular media surrounds us daily with survey results and rankings. The information literate student will seek an understanding of how the data for such reports was gathered. It is common knowledge from the 2000 and 2004 Presidential elections that even the most sophisticated survey processes can be wrong. In these two very close elections, exit interviews ill-timed and poorly worded brought about misleading conclusions.

In more general terms, surveys conducted by television stations concerning some local or national issue are often faulty, especially if they request listeners to respond to the survey before the end of the broadcast. Questions are often stated in a leading manner, with definition of terms. Questions are offered to those watching the program and perhaps already biased in the direction of the political standing of the local broadcasters. Often responses are limited to only a few extremes without any allowance for justification of a response based on exceptions to the given situation. And the characteristics of those who respond, other than they are willing to respond within a very short period of time, are seldom known. In short, such surveys are misleading and to further add to their wasted efforts, the television broadcasters will often announce the results as being "unscientific," but report their anyway findings with some expectation that something in all of the effort is valid because it is on television (Hernon and Schwartz 2002).

Surveys, even when conducted well, are usually a measure of opinion on a very specific topic at a very specific time. Data gathered across different populations and over time can be of some value, but evidence from surveys is descriptive at best, and seldom useful as evidence to justify action other than the likely reaction from various audiences. As student inquirers practice survey techniques and present their findings, they will need to learn how to also describe the situation in which their data was gathered and the limits of the data as reasonable evidence.

Legal evidence will also mean different things to different people in different situations. Seldom is documentation of an argument, especially when dealing with a controversial issue or competing set of issues, conclusive. Bias, perspective, experience, self-interests will tend to shade the acceptance and assimilation of information as reasonable evidence. Thus, when the much respected *Black's Law Dictionary* defines "evidence to support findings" as "substantial evidence or such relevant evidence as a reasonable mind might accept as adequate to support a conclusion . . . ," the question remains, "who determines what is reasonable?" In our modern legal system, either a judge or panel of judges so determine based on their legal expertise, or a jury of peers interprets such based on their understanding of the facts and situation and their level of identification with the peer on trail.

Each time we encounter new information, do we take it through a trail by judge and jury? Each time we learn of a new perspective or opinion, do we wait until a scientific survey is conducted to accept or reject it? Each time a health or medical issue is before us, do we commission a series of controlled studies to determine our final choices?

While Information Inquiry can involve basic research methods to gather original data, the essential skills involve techniques to help the information consumer select the best information

to address the given task they possibly can under the given situation and limitations. Such increases the chances that better information will lead to better choices. Over time and with practice, the mature information and media literate student will reach higher levels of correct, or at least near correct, decision making and sense-making. Even when one has applied to be best of his or her ability the selection of what seems to be the best information possible at that time, mistakes will still occur. Good information can be poorly interpreted and poorly applied. Good information today may not be good information in the future. Decisions may rest not so much on "the fact" but on the logic that comes with experience and wisdom from learning from decision-making situations.

Sources of evidence and their level of acceptance or rejection by different audiences is also an experience base accumulated over time by the information literate student. Scholarly journals may have more authority than trade journals or popular magazines. Trade journals, however, may be a valuable source for finding expert summary of research finding applied to practical and more understandable situations.

Kinds of Evidence

It is not useful to list every possible type of evidence here, but several common types of evidence will help to illustrate that evidence is seldom clear and conclusive, especially one fact, one observation, or one scientific study in and of itself. Those who say they have found the absolute truth, have probably not read, listened, and conversed widely on the issue. An adage, that might be worth testing for validity itself, is the more you read, the more you know, but the more you know the more you become aware of many uncertainties. It is the wise person who often begins his or her reply to a complex question or a controversial issue with "it depends."

Testing the relevance and validity of information includes making judgments while identifying content for notes. Julie Coiro (2005), a member of the New Literacies Research Team at the University of Connecticut, suggests the following format for selective "cut and paste" of notes by high school and college students working from electronic documents:

My research questions:

Paste selected text or image with URL:

The most salient points of the text are:

The information connects to other information located in the following ways:

This information changes my thinking in the following ways:

My original synthesis, which considers significant points from my sources, is:

My supporting statements, informed by at least two of my summaries and at least two of my connection statements are:

A Closer Look to Challenge Evidence

A sample of different types of evidence defined in *Black's Law Dictionary* include:

* Evidence—Testimony, writings, material objects, or other things presented to the senses that are offered to prove the existence or nonexistence of a fact.

* Expert evidence—Testimony given in relation to some scientific, technical, or professional matter by persons qualified to speak authoritatively by reason of spe-

cial training, skill, or familiarity with the subject.

* Tangible evidence—Physical evidence; evidence that can be seen or touched such as documents or weapons.

* Testimonial evidence—Communicative evidence from a witness or expert.

* Demonstrative evidence—Tangible objects that help to illustrate or explain oral evidence.

Other terms associated to evidence defined by Black include "beyond reasonable doubt," "extraneous evidence," "partial evidence," "hearsay," "weight of evidence," "presumption," and "prima facie evidence." These terms raise questions about the value of various levels of evidence. For the novice, judgments on evidence extracted from print and electronic media can be challenging. Nearly all statements may seem to be acceptable unless the student begins to challenge what he reads and hears with questions such as those given in Table Part3.2. Practice in application of the "Capital Cs to Challenge Evidence" can start in elementary school and build across the student's academic career. These are basic challenges any wise information consumer should make as a responsible citizen in a free society.

Table Part3.2. The Capital Cs to Challenge Evidence

Common	Is this information Common knowledge and not in need of verification?
Conventional Wisdom	Is this information a Commonly held assumption or belief, but in need of verification as majority opinion is not necessarily Correct? Conventional wisdom will Change over time and across events and is very much influenced by political Correctness.
Corroboration	Does this new evidence Corroborate previous information from another source and help to Confirm the notion held by the inquirer? As a second or third source, does it add strength to an argument by validating the earlier opinions or evidence gathered?
Circumstantial	Although not direct and tangible proof, does this evidence provide Convincing observations or facts that one can reasonably infer in support of a Conclusion? Is this substantial evidence drawn from logical reasoning?

Cherry Picked

Has the evidence presented in this resource been selected to argue only one side of the issue? While some of the facts and opinions may be relevant, is it clear the author has selected only the evidence that agrees with his side of the argument? Are you giving Care to the selection of your own evidence so that you do not become closed minded to other options and weigh the evidence from several perspectives. Cherry picking is often a technique to gather evidence that an underling believes his or her boss wants to hear or to support a decision already made, no matter how poorly Conceived.

Comforts

Does this evidence give Comfort to the inquirer because it supports the Current held notion? Should the inquirer beware of accepting evidence simply because it seems to agree with what the inquirer believes, wants to believe or wants to be true?

Chains or Connects

Is the evidence a useful part of the Chain of evidence linking facts and observations Collectively to make an argument in support of a Claim or notion? Does it Clarify and add value to the meaning of the other evidence? Are there a reasonable number of good sources Cited in the document to at least believe the author has reviewed many documents relevant to the issues and has Connected them to make his or her Case?

Counters, Convincing, and Changes

Does this new evidence Counter previous information found from an earlier source or opinion held by the inquirer? Is it more Current or more Convincing? Will this piece of evidence Convince naysayers that are unlikely to be swayed by the other evidence found so far? Is this evidence so strong and so conclusive, that it is likely to support a particularly difficult to accept point of view? Is this new information so impressive that it Changes the notions held by the inquirer in some manner? It may stand alone an independent, but very Convincing piece of evidence.

Credible

Based on the credentials given of the source and author of the evidence, the methods used to establish the evidence and, if necessary, the respect held for the information source and author by the inquirer's mentors, is it reasonable to accept the evidence as Credible? In the case of opinions, credibility may rest with the position of the person expressing the opinion. Remember that politicians and editorial writers are not necessarily experts on the many subjects for which they offer their opinion. These Comments may represent the viewpoint of a certain group or position, but options can be expressed widely in our society without providing evidence, and sometimes, without being logical.

Critical or Counts Highly

In comparison to other information gathered, does this information Count for more in that it is a Core or Critical piece to Construct and justify a Conclusion? Does this new evidence provide a Critical piece of information that makes the argument or discussion of the topic more or less Convincing? Is this evidence the "missing link" to show a Clear path for documenting an argument or describing an event in great detail?

Creative

Can the information be transformed into an entirely new or innovative way of thinking about the topic or support or rejection of an argument? Does the evidence Cause a paradigm shift on the part of the student, does it cause the student to look at the topic very differently? Could Conventional wisdom be Challenged by synthesizing information in a new way or viewing from a perspective that is new to the inquirer and his or her audience?

Controversial

Is this information or evidence that is at a level the student inquirer is not prepared to handle? Does the evidence offend to the degree that for this inquirer and his or her audience the language, specific example and/or illustration takes away from the focus of the issues to be addressed in the paper or presentation? Controversial evidence may also mean information that is highly questioned as legitimate by a few or nearly all parties involved in discussion of the issue. Is this evidence so questionable that it will Cast doubt on the other evidence you have gathered to make your Case? Depending on the audience and the issue some evidence is best left behind, or Cast aside.

Copy, but give Credit

Is this evidence so important in the manner it is presented and stated in the original source that is should be Copied or quoted word-for-word, as originally stated or illustrated, or in its original table or chart of data? Credit should be given to any authoritative evidence, but always to information that is presented specifically from the original source and selected because authority of that source is meaningful.

Classic

Is this evidence standard for the field of study? Is it documented or linked to the major authoritative names and assumptions in the field? Has this evidence become the foundation for the Content written on this subject in tertiary resources that are the encyclopedias, handbooks and textbooks of the field?

Convey and Communicates

Does this new piece of evidence help to Communicate ideas in a way not possible with evidence gathered so far? Does it illustrate or translate issues in some manner that the target audience is more likely to understand? Is the new evidence in some format that might serve to help Convey the massage to various audiences—visual, motion, sound, animation, graphic, table, chart, motion? Does new media lead to a new message?

Council and Confidence

Does this evidence provide support for an emotional point of view? Does this evidence help to create sympathy or empathy for the argument? Does it help the inquirer to understand emotional reactions that may overshadow reasonable evidence? Does it give the inquirer Confidence that they are on the right track, making a meaningful case, telling an important story, and making information Choices that will be useful to solve the Information Inquiry task, need or problem? The inquirer will gain Confidence in his or her Capability to succeed.

Table Part3.2. (*Cont.*)

| Continues | Does this information give evidence that Creates excitement and helps to motivate the inquirer to Continue the search for more evidence to help focus a Conclusion. Does it help to elaborate or Complete the description of a phenomena? |

The Argument Curriculum

Deanna Kuhn (2005), professor of psychology and education at the Teachers College of Columbia University, has recently summarized her critical observations of student practice in public schools to justify the need for typical student research reports to move to a higher level of engagement with inference, evidence, and justification of argument. According to Kuhn, most of what is expected of students simply does not meet the test of reasonable argument, critical application of evidence, and drawing meaningful conclusions. Student presentations are usually limited to uninformed opinion, organization, and neatness of presentation, and seldom address issues that make much difference in learning or life. Kuhn argues eloquently that inquiry and argument based on the best information as the most relevant evidence possible are the elements for education for life. Her summary of the activities associated with cognitive goals constitutes her proposal for the "argument curriculum." Her outline, given below, deserves serious consideration by all teachers of information literacy and inquiry, K–college:

Generating Reasons—Reasons underlie opinions; different reasons may underlie the same opinion.

Elaborating Reasons—Good reasons support opinions.

Supporting Reasons with Evidence—Evidence can strengthen reasons.

Evaluating Reasons—Some reasons are better than others.

Developing Reasons into an Argument—Reasons connect to one another and are building blocks of argument.

Examining and Evaluating Opposing Side's Reasons—Opponents have reasons too.

Generating Counterarguments to Others' Reasons—Opposing reasons can be countered. We can fight this.

Generating Rebuttals to Others' Counterarguments—Counters to reasons can be rebutted. We have a comeback.

Contemplating Mixed Evidence—Evidence can be used to support different claims.

Conducting and Evaluating Two-sided Arguments—Some arguments are stronger than others. (2005, 153–154)

References

Black, H. C., ed. (1990). *Black's Law Dictionary*. 6th ed. West Publishing.

Bruckman, A. S. (2005). "Viewpoint: Student Research and the Internet." *Communications of the ACM* 48 (12): 35–37.

Coiro, J. (2005). "Making Sense of Online Text." *Educational Leadership* 63 (2): 30–35.

Dorsch, J. (2004). *Evidence Based Medicine: Is All Evidence Created Equal?* University of Illinois at Chicago. Available at http://www.uic.edu/depts/lib/lhsp/resources/levels.shtml (accessed January 23, 2006).

Foster, L. F. (2006). *Student Guide to Research in the Digital Age: How to Locate and Evaluate Information Sources*. Libraries Unlimited.

Henninger, M. (2005). *The Hidden Web: Finding Quality Information on the Net*. University of South Wales Press.

Hernon, P., and C. Schwartz. (2002). "The Word Research: Having to Live with a Misunderstanding." *Library and Information Science Research* 24: 207–208.

Kuhn, D. (2005). *Education for Thinking.* Harvard University Press.

Reed, C. (1991). "Teaching the Structure of Scientific Information." In *Judging the Validity of Information Sources: Teaching Critical Analysis in Bibliographic Instruction,* edited by L. Shirato, 89–95. Pierian Press.

Schilling, K., et al. (2006). "An Interactive Web-Based Curriculum on Evidence-Based Medicine: Design and Effectiveness." *Family Medicine* 38 (2): 126–132.

Stebbins, L. F. (2005*). Student Guide to Research in the Digital Age.* Libraries Unlimited/Greenwood Press.

Facilitator

Daniel Callison

The term facilitator is generally not recognized as a standard instructional term, but it is often related to such actions as intervention, planning, guidance, and mediation. The term has gained popularity over the past decade with increased agreement that teachers should act more as facilitators of learning and less as the sole fountain of knowledge.

Just as facilitation of managerial responsibilities requires actions at the stages of planning, implementation, and evaluation, specific actions are also necessary at the same three stages of facilitation of instruction. Knowledge in how to collaborate in planning, intervene and mediate during instructional implementation, and constructively give feedback for purposes of evaluation are essential skills for today's facilitator of information literacy and inquiry (Callison 1995).

Intermediary Process

Kathy Brock (1994) has suggested a model to depict the actions of the teacher-librarian involved in the information search and use (ISU) process. In her model, facilitating occurs through six phases of the student's information search and use experience:

- **Defining the Problem:** the library media specialist helps students select topics, suggests sources for topic overview, and consults as students develop authentic topics and research questions.

- **Developing Information-Seeking Strategies:** the library media specialist suggests specific resources and explains strategies that lead to a variety of information formats.

- **Locating Information:** the library media specialist helps students become independent in locating resources and may provide guidance and personal contact in helping students obtain resources beyond the library media center.

- **Gathering and Assessing Information:** the library media specialist helps students make decisions in evaluating, assimilating, selecting, and rejecting information and become independent in making and recording such decisions.

- **Synthesizing Information:** the library media specialist helps students become independent in organizing information selected for presentation.

- **Evaluating and Refining Results:** the library media specialist provides constructive feedback concerning the product or presentation and gives suggestions for revision.

Prompting for Elaboration

Much of the current research related to reading-to-write/writing-to-read implies the importance of the role of the teacher as facilitator for extending the student's consideration of a topic or argument through prompts. This technique places the facilitator in the position of asking the student to consider options. The teacher of information literacy can adopt such prompting as well.

Normally the library media specialist raises options by asking if the student has considered other resources. Beyond resources, however, are prompts that the library media specialist should employ to facilitate with other teachers a greater student consideration of the content to be synthesized and eventually incorporated into the student's paper or presentation.

Michael Zellermayer (1991) has outlined two categories for prompting. The first is prompting for increased quantity of facts, opinions, and ideas. The second is prompting for quality or better consideration of the evidence or opinions located in order to establish linkages among evidence and to derive conclusions.

- Quantity

  - Facts: Could you add more details?

  - Thoughts: Do you have further thoughts on this issue?

- Quality

  - Evidence: What evidence do you have? From whom, where, how recent?

  - Personal View: What is your opinion?

  - Deduction: What are your conclusions?

  - Hypothesis: What would happen if . . . ?

  - Explanation for Clarity: What exactly do you mean when you say . . . ?

  - Relation: Why is this important or more important than other facts, evidence, or issues? Why is this point relevant and how does it relate to others?

  - Cohesion: How does this relate and enhance what you said before?

  - Judgmental: Why is this interesting to you? Why would this be interesting to your audience?

  - Creative: Tell me a story or analogy based on this information.

  - Audience Analysis: How would you revise this information to make it more meaningful for your intended audience?

When the library media specialist moves from the limited role of facilitating resource options and access and into the cooperative facilitation role with other teachers of prompting selection and use of evidence, the librarian becomes a true teacher of inquiry—an instructional media specialist. Raising meaningful questions, using inclusive strategies to hear from all involved, and encouraging thoughtful reflection in the inquiry process and in the evaluation of inquiry products are all roles for meaningful discussion lead by the instructional media specialist (Rankin 2006).

Conversations in the Constructivist Role

Kuhlthau (1997) tells us that library media specialists and other teachers play a central role in facilitating learning in the constructivist approach. Based on her research, it is clear that while transmission of information may rely on textbooks and packaged materials (including multiple resources through libraries and the Internet), guiding the learning process through construction calls for expertise that only skillful sensitive professionals can provide.

Skilled facilitators know not only how to intervene in order to prompt and guide, but know when to do so. Kuhlthau refers us to the Russian psychologist, Vygotsky, and his concept of the zone of proximal development. The zone of intervention, and the best time for facilitating learning, is when the learner can use guidance and assistance in what he or she cannot do alone. She tells us that help within this zone moves the student along in the information search process. Intervention on both sides of the zone is inefficient and unnecessary, and attempts to facilitate become meaningless or overwhelming. Timely intervention within this zone is efficient and enabling. How does the facilitator determine the best time to intervene?

Kuhlthau's list of coaching strategies help the skilled facilitator place the student in situations where the student voices, writes, or performs in some manner in order to give the facilitator clues leading to identification of student needs in the information search and use processes.

- **Collaborating:** students move from isolated information searching and use to sharing the effort with other students, and in the mix of seeking and selecting information together, voice to the group and the teachers their successes and frustrations; often students become facilitators themselves as they teach each other.

- **Continuing:** voicing when there is or is not enough information; to move out of the exploration stage of the information search and into an area of focus with assurance that there is enough information to continue the process.

- **Conversing:** describing the information search and use experiences with everyone who will listen and provide feedback; other teachers and sometimes even parents can facilitate, but usually the mere act of verbalizing the needs and progress along with the intended direction of the project helps the student focus.

- **Charting:** providing a visual representation of the search process to date and organizing the evidence located helps to convey what has and has not been accomplished; diagrams, categorizing note cards, outlining, or sequencing the task in some visual manner helps the facilitator identify both gaps and areas that seem near completion.

- **Composing:** journals and logs help the student record actions and thoughts about those actions; pre-writes or pre-speaks may help the student formulate pieces which eventually are linked for the product and they also provide tangible items to which the facilitator can provide feedback.

References

Brock, K. T. (1994) "Developing Information Literacy through the Information Intermediary Process." *Emergency Librarian* 22 (1): 16–20.

Callison, D. (1995). "Expanding the Evaluation Role in the Critical Thinking Curriculum." In *Information for a New Age: Redefining the Librarian,* 153–170. Libraries Unlimited.

Kuhlthau, C. C. (1997). "Learning in Digital Libraries: An Information Search Process Approach." *Library Trends* 45 (4): 708–724.

Rankin, V. (2006). "Talk About It! Using Discussion to Extend and Enhance Student Research." *Teacher-Librarian* 33 (3): 8–12.

Zellermayer, M. (1991). "The Development of Elaborative Skills: Teaching Basic Writing Students to Make the Commitment to Audience and Topic." *Linguistics and Education* 3 (4): 359–383.

Gender

Carol L. Tilley and Daniel Callison

Girls Rule, Boys Drool

Perhaps you've seen the t-shirts emblazoned with this motto above or maybe the ones that proclaim "Boys Are Stupid—Throw Rocks at Them." While the slogans have generated some controversy—enough to encourage some retailers to pull products that bear them for fear of generating anti-male bias—recent reports in both the popular and academic press bear witness to adult concerns that these slogans may not be far off the mark.

Take, for example, a widely publicized report from the National Center for Education Statistics (NCES 2004). Among other things this report shows the gap between girls and boys when it comes to plans to attend a four-year college (girls, 62%; boys, 51%) and that girls are more likely than boys to see school learning as something important to adult life (girls, 43%; boys, 37%). Likewise, consider the article in Business Week (Conlin 2003) that carries the subtitle: "From kindergarten to grad school, boys are becoming the second sex."

The images of girls as educational stars and boys as underachievers are not limited to the United States. The introduction to the British book (Rowan et al. 2002), *Boys, Literacies, and Schooling*, begins: "Educating boys is currently seen—both globally and locally—to be in crisis." Another British publication, the journal *Literacy Today*, recently published a report of a study on gender stereotypes and achievement (Myhill and Jones 2004). This provocative report suggests that the emphasis on underachieving boys masks problems that girls face in school:

> By contrast, the high-achieving girls were seen as typical girls, while underachieving girls appeared to be almost invisible, with no typical description attributed to them. The children revealed in interview that, regardless of their own gender, they thought that girls were cleverer than boys and more likely to succeed. (21)

So, what's the real story with girls? Do girls really rule?

Girls and Early Literacy

Early (or emergent) literacy, simply defined, is the notion that literacy is a developmental process, beginning at birth, and that children benefit from meaningful verbal and print interactions with adults. In essence, young people are not magically turned into readers when they start school at age six; instead, readers are created—a page, a story, a conversation at a time—from birth.

The NCES (2004) report mentioned above includes three measures of early literacy—being read aloud to, being told stories, and being taken to a library. Although the percentage differences are small, girls come out ahead in each indicator. Take a look at the figures below for children ages three to five.

	Read to three or more times in past week	Told a story at least once in past week	Visited a library in the past month
Girls	86.1	84.7	37.1
Boys	82.1	82.4	35.2

Young girls tend to have greater exposure to new words, story structure, and print conventions—all components of early literacy—through these activities. While the relationship between a four-year old hearing a story and later success in reading may seem difficult to imagine, studies consistently show that early literacy activities matter.

The *PIRLS 2001 International Report: IEA's Study of Reading Literacy Achievement in Primary Schools* (Mullis et al. 2003) demonstrates that in each of the 35 countries (including the United States) which reported data, a positive correlation exists between early literacy activities and reading achievement levels at fourth grade. Children who have parents who read to them, who have access to extensive collections of children's books at home, who have parents who model reading, and who engage in activities like playing with alphabet toys and singing songs tend to be better readers as they progress through school. Because girls are more likely to experience these activities, girls are likely to be better readers. In fact, in all 35 countries in the PIRLS study, girls outperformed boys in reading.

All girls are not created equal, though, when it comes to early literacy. The NCES (2004) data indicates that girls—and boys—who come from white, not black or Hispanic families, are more likely to have parents and caregivers who engage them in early literacy activities. Were the data reported in terms of socioeconomic levels as well, girls—and boys—from higher socioeconomic groups would likely show higher early literacy engagement as well. Ethnicity and income matter.

Girls and School Achievement

As the NCES (Freeman 2004) report notes, girls outpace boys when it comes to standardized tests of reading. For the past decade, girls have, without fail, scored higher than boys at reading at fourth, eighth, and twelfth grades—the three points measured by the National Association of Educational Progress (NAEP). The most recent scores shown below, are consistent with those from previous years.

	Fourth Grade (2003)	Eighth Grade (2003)	Twelfth Grade (2002)
Girls	222	269	295
Boys	215	258	279

While there are clearly gender differences in the scores at each grade level, what is less clear is what these differences actually mean. Given that the NAEP scores reading achievement on a 500 point scale, what exactly does a difference in 7, 11, or 16 points signify?

The NAEP examines reading achievement in particular ways. It examines both reading contexts—reading for literary experience, for information, to perform a task—and reading aspects—forming understanding, developing interpretation, making reader/text connections, and examining content and structure. While the NAEP does not provide any breakdown for scores by context or aspect, the assessment guide indicates that at the eighth grade level based on the average scores reported above, girls are more likely than boys to be able to "recognize appropriate description of character," "identify purpose of stylistic device," "use context to identify meaning of vocabulary," and "identify causal relation between historical events."

Beyond these differences, it is important to note at least two things. First, the average scores shown above for girls and boys at each grade level place are at the "Basic" level in terms of reading achievement according to the scoring guides; so, the average young person, regardless of gender, is not able to perform at the "Proficient" level that would indicate mastery of basic skills and competence. Second, as with early literacy, the biggest gaps in reading achievement are not between girls and boys, but among racial and ethnic groups (e.g., the average reading score of white eighth graders is 272; for black eighth graders, 244; for Hispanic eighth graders, 245) and among socioeconomic levels (e.g., the average reading score of fourth graders who are not eligible for free/reduced-price lunch is 229; for those who are eligible, 201).

Girls and Recreational Reading

In recent years, books such as *Reading Don't Fix No Chevy's: Literacy in the Lives of Young Men* (Smith and Wilhelm 2002) and campaigns such as Jon Scieczka's *Guys Read* have popularized the notion of the boy who doesn't like to or will not read. There are no similar titles or efforts to encourage girls to read. After all, girls like to read for fun, right?

Generally speaking, girls do have a more positive attitude than boys do when it comes to recreational reading. A 1995 study (McKenna, Kear, and Ellsworth) published in *Reading Research Quarterly* that examined national attitudes towards reading did find that throughout elementary school, girls indicate more positive feelings for reading than do boys. Although the warm-fuzzy feeling that girls demonstrate for recreational reading declines at each grade level, the falloff is not as sharp as it is for boys. This fits the general trend that researchers like Guthrie and Wigfield (2000) note for a decline in reading motivation as young people approach puberty.

A 1999 study by the Kaiser Family Foundation (Roberts et al 1999) titled *Kids & Media @ The New Millennium* examines how young people between the ages of 2 and 18 interact with electronic, video, audio, and print media for recreational purposes. For young people between the ages of 8 and 18—when independent reading is most likely possible—on average, girls do use print media (i.e. books, magazines, and newspapers) for more minutes during the day than boys (48 minutes versus 41 minutes).

As with other research on young people and reading, gender is not the only factor that determines attitude and ability. The Kaiser Family Foundation study data indicates differences in the use of print media related to age (e.g., 8–13 year olds spend an average of 50 minutes daily; 14–18 year olds, 37 minutes), race/ethnicity (e.g., white and black children average 45 minutes daily; Hispanic children, 37 minutes), parents' educational attainment (e.g., children of parents with high school educations average 38 minutes daily; with college education, 50 minutes), and income (e.g., children from low-income areas average 41 minutes daily; from higher-income areas, 47 min-

utes). So, again, ethnicity and socioeconomic levels are important.

Now What?

Girls do have some advantages over boys when it comes to reading. On average, girls have more exposure to early literacy activities, they achieve higher scores on standardized tests, they express a more positive attitude towards reading, and they spend more time interacting with printed materials. It is important to remember, though, that young people—regardless of age or gender—are individuals. Certainly there are still high achieving boys and low achieving girls. More important, though, these gender-based differences turn out to be minor in comparison to differences found by ethnicity or income.

As instructional media specialists (teachers from all levels and subjects and library media specialists), we need to do what we can to motivate all readers—girls and boys. We must first start with ourselves, modeling for young people what it means to be readers. We must work in our schools, getting coaches, teachers, administrators, and support staff to read more and to read in view of our students. We must work in our libraries and classrooms, making sure we have materials available that engage our young people—nonfiction, magazines, comic books, fantasies and other "genre" books, series books—not just the books we think they need. We must work with our students, helping them to see that reading is a viable and enjoyable way to spend time, not just a way to earn points for prizes.

Yes, budgets are tight. Yes, schedules are tight. But, when we do these things, we will be able to spend less time talking about whether girls read better than boys and more time talking about books and ideas with young people—all young people.

Gender Differences and Information Inquiry

A few studies have attempted to identify differences between girls and boys on a range of information access and use skills. Recent national reports (Callison 2004) indicate the gap is gone when it comes to ability and willingness to use computers to access information and to display or report through use of multimedia. Other studies (Agosto 2001; Akin 1998; Brown 2001) over the past decade, but limited to local situations without true national implications, imply that:

- girls identify and deal with personal information overload sooner than boys;

- girls tend to manage information overload by limiting their search by format (not giving time to magazines and newspapers, for example), while boys seem to not demonstrate any consistent strategy to manage overload;

- in general, when boys are behind girls in development of basic language skills, they also have problems in conducting successful online searches (poorer spelling and more limited vocabulary);

- when involved in use of computer-based instruction, girls tend to prefer collaboration, while boys seem to prefer competition;

- when faced with solving online information search problems, girls tend to be open to options, while boys favor finding a single path.

- girls tend to score higher on tests of ability to locate information in traditional reference books.

A summary published by the Association for Supervision and Curriculum Development (Gurian and Stevens 2004) on recent research involving gender learning behavior comparisons, greatly influenced by differences identified in brain development observations based on new brain imaging technologies, indicate that:

- girls tend to multitask better than boys, with fewer attention span problems.

- girls have, in general, stronger neural connectors in their temporal lobes than boys and this leads to better listening skills, and better detail in writing assignments.

- the male brain is better suited for symbols, abstractions, diagrams, pictures, and objects moving through space than for the monotony of words.

- boys tend to need more physical space than girls to deal with multiple resources.

While some gender differences have been detected little has been tested to determine best practice to meet these differences when students are involved in student research and inquiry projects. Should practice follow suit in what Scieszka (2005) suggests in order to engage males more in reading?

- Guys should be able to choose what they read. Should there be more choice in research topics and a wider array of inquiry methods promoted?

- Guys should be able to pick from and have valued all different kinds of reading formats. Should a larger number of information sources be introduced to students in order to engage a higher portion of student researchers? Should there be options to only gaining information from text? Should there be more opportunity to gain information from interviews, field trips, experiments, and tangible application of information to address local issues?

- Guys should find out what other guys read. Is there need for male students to see more men utilize methods for searching, extracting, applying and presenting information? Perhaps modeling of effective information selection and use is needed for all students, regardless of gender, to see teachers who understand the applications of information literacy in order to be a wise information consumer.

National standards for school library media centers have always described the school library as a location where spaces, resources, and guidance can be found at varied levels to meet all learner needs. The flexibility that so many call for in library access scheduling often over-rides the flexibility originally envisioned for school libraries as an environment that can address a wide spectrum of learning needs.

Teachers of information literacy and inquiry must be fluent in addressing these differences, but guarded about applying solutions simply based on what seem to be gender differences alone.

Key Words for Instruction in Information Inquiry

Gender research should not narrow our target for learning support, but open our minds as educators to the wide variety of learning barriers we all face—cognitive, physical, social and emotional.

References

Agosto, D. E. (2001). "Propelling Young Women into the Cyber Age: Gender Considerations in the Evaluation of Web-based Information." *School Library Media Research* 4. Available at www.ala.org/aasl/SLMR (accessed June 1, 2005).

Akin, L. (1998). "Information Overload in Children: A Survey of Texas Elementary School Students." *School Library Media Quarterly Online* 1. Available at www.ala.org/aasl/SLMR (accessed June 1, 2005).

Brown, G. (2001). "Locating Categories and Sources of Information: How Skilled Are New Zealand Children?" *School Library Media Research* 4. Available at www.ala.org/aasl/SLMR (accessed June 1, 2005).

Callison, D. (2004). "Digital Divide." *School Library Media Activities Monthly* 20 (6): 37–40, 51.

Conlin, M. (2003). "The New Gender Gap." *Business Week* (May): 74–81.

Freeman, C. E. (2004). *Trends in Educational Equity of Girls & Women: 2004* (NCES 2005–016). U.S. Department of Education, National Center for Education Statistics. U.S. Government Printing Office.

Gurian, M., and K. Stevens. (2004). "With Boys and Girls in Mind. *Educational Leadership* (November): 21–26.

Guthrie, J. T., and A. Wigfield. (2000). "Engagement and Motivation in Reading." In *Handbook of Reading Research*. 3d ed. Longman.

McKenna, M. C., D. J. Kear, and R. A. Ellsworth. (1995). "Children's Attitudes Toward Reading: A National Survey." *Reading Research Quarterly*, 934–956.

Mullis, I. V. S., et al. (2003). *PIRLS 2001 International Report: IEA's Study of Reading Literacy Achievement in Primary Schools.* Boston College,

Myhill, D., and S. Jones. (2004). "Noisy Boys, and Invisible Girls?" *Literacy Today,* 21–22.

National Center for Education Statistics (NCES). (2004). *Reading: The Nation's Report Card.* Available at http://nces.ed.gov/nationsreportcard/reading/results2003/ (accessed February 24, 2005).

Roberts, D. F., et al. 1999). *Kids & Media @ the New Millennium: A Kaiser Family Foundation Report.* Available at http://www.kff.org/entmedia/1535–index.cfm (accessed February 24, 2005)

Rowan, L., et al. (2002). *Boys, Literacies, and Schooling: The Dangerous Territories of Gender-Based Literacy Reform.* Open University Press.

Scieczka, Jon. (2005). *Guys Read.* Available at http://www.guysread.com (accessed February 24, 2005).

Smith, M. W., and J. D. Wilhelm. (2002). *"Reading Don't Fix No Chevy's": Literacy in the Lives of Young Men.* Heinemann.

For Further Reading

Abilock, D. (1997). "Sex in the Library: How Gender Differences Should Affect Practices and Programs." *Emergency Librarian* (May/June): 17–18.

Brozo, W. G. (2002). *To Be a Boy, to Be a Reader.* International Reading Association.

Gurian, M. (2002). *Boys and Girls Learn Differently: A Guide for Teachers and Parents.* Jossey-Bass.

Knowles, E., and M. Smith. (2005). *Boys and Literacy: Practical Strategies for Librarians, Teachers, and Parents.* Libraries Unlimited.

Schwartz, Wendy. (2002). *Helping Underachieving Boys Read Well and Often.* ERIC Clearinghouse on Urban Education. ED467687. Available at http://www.vtaide.com/png/ERIC/Boys-Read.htm (accessed March 21, 2005).

Sullivan, M. (2003). *Connecting Boys with Books.* American Library Association.

Thomas, N. P. (2004). *Information Literacy and Information Skills Instruction.* Libraries Unlimited.

Tovani, C. (2000). *I Read It, But I Don't Get It.* Stenhouse Publishers.

Idea Strategies

Daniel Callison

Strategies for ideas and composition help the maturing, information-literate student deal with the complexities of the communication process. Idea generation involves not only "what do I want to learn and what do I infer from this new information," but also "what do I want to convey to others and how?"

Interwoven from idea to communication are the complexities of information evaluation. Each element of the process is fundamental to the assimilation of new knowledge, both for the learner who gathers and conveys and for the audience which receives. Tasks in the process are not always sequential steps, and they often do not flow easily from one to the other, especially for the novice. Often simple strategies are necessary to solve problems that block progress. These strategies often ask the student to step back and rethink, take a different perspective, relate to previous experiences and thoughts on a concrete basis, or listen to feedback from others. Testing portions of the message along the way will help to clarify how to best deliver the final communication.

This is why conversations with others about ideas and information needs are so important during the inquiry process. In building the message to be communicated, purpose will determine the strategies. Purpose, or goal of the communication, is influenced by learner abilities, previous knowledge of the learner, quality of information available, and the level of learner comprehension. Strategies for communication are influenced by the purpose of the message, the means of communication, and the perceived level of audience reception. The learner will assimilate knowledge for him or herself, but find that such may need to be revised or modified in some manner in order to move a message through different communication channels and to offer it to different audiences. Writing, speaking, use of media, and other formats may alter the message. It is possible during such adjustments to enhance the message for clarity in order to successfully persuade, or to cloud the message resulting in miscommunication.

The format also may influence the continued assimilation of the communicator's knowledge as he or she faces revision tasks to fit the medium. Audience analysis is a learned craft leading to comprehending as best as possible what the audience will understand, accept, or reject-can result in change of both the message and clarity of the communicator's assimilation as well. (See Key Word "Audience Analysis") The goal of employing strategies for idea and composition is to offer a menu of strategies to adjust communication in different ways to meet different needs.

Idea strategies, therefore, imply methods that help the learner to both comprehend and communicate. Ideas help us to move forward, to explore, and to frame questions that are meaningful to us and hopefully to others. Composition strategies can be applied to not only writing for communication, but to a wide array of formats (oral, audio, visual, multimedia), genres, and modes that serve as channels in delivery of the intended message.

Thought Starters

Many college and university writing labs provide guides to strategies that help the novice jump-start the communication process. One of the best is the Owl Online Writing Lab through Purdue University. Among their more useful guides is a list of thought starters based on asking the right questions. These are adapted from Jacqueline Berke, Professor of English Emerita and Director of the Drew University Program from 1965 to (1985) (Berke and Woodland 1996):

Definition—What does X mean?

Description—What are the different features of X?

Simple Analysis—What are the component parts of X?

Process Analysis—How is X made or done?

Directional Analysis—How should X be made or done?

Functional Analysis—What is the essential function of X?

Causal Analysis—What are the causes of X, or what are the consequences of X?

Classification—What are the types of X?

Comparison—How is X like or unlike Y, or what is the present status of X compared to previous status?

Interpretation—What is the significance of X?

Reporting—What are the facts (who, what, when, where, and how) about X?

Narration—How did X happen?

Characterization/Profile—What kind of person is X?

Reflection—What is my personal response to X?

Reminiscence—What is my memory of X?

Evaluation—What is the value of X?

Summary—What are the essential major points or features of X?

Persuasion—What case can be made for or against X?

In each case, as the writer matures in information literacy, "why" should be linked to the initial questions. Why is this important? Why did this happen? Why are these causes and consequences relevant to us today? The goal of inquiry is to address or to infer why X seems true, valid, conclusive, or predictable for similar situations. The "what" and "how" questions provide the foundation to assimilate knowledge and to move toward the more demanding questions.

Information Evaluation Phases

The work of Mary Ann Fitzgerald (1999), associate professor at the University of Georgia, has resulted in some important guidelines and strategies for effective evaluation of information. Fitzgerald reminds us that information is a complex and challenging task. Although it can be assumed that children are more likely to take information at "face value" than most adults, the skills necessary to select information that is authoritative, understandable, and relevant for a given situation requires practice, guidance, and feedback, at any age. Such skill practice should begin in early grade levels and continue through the student's academic career, including graduate school if applicable.

Fitzgerald (2000) identifies three phases of information use and strategies for evaluation (selecting or discarding) information at each phase. Some of her original titles and terms have been paraphrased below:

Phase 1: Search and Initial Contact. The student makes selections based on abstracts or key words that indicate likely relevance. The item (article, chapter, book, Web site, etc.) is noted, retrieved, and copied for further examination and later study. Common evaluation strategies are relevance of key words, author, and title; length of item (too short may be too general, too long may be too specific and overly detailed); and context meets need (opinion, fact, narrative, investigative study).

Phase 2: First Complete Reading. Complete reading may not be reached until the student has skimmed subheadings, and closely examined the lead paragraphs and concluding paragraphs as well as any illustrations, tables, or graphs. The more mature reader also may look for author qualifications and examine the references cited, if any. If the item meets basic tests for quality (clear, focused, interesting, relevant, perhaps contains new information not seen before), it is likely to be selected for specific highlighting of information and taking of notes. Assimilation of the information, or acceptance by the reader, may depend greatly on his or her maturity level in being open to considering both supportive as well as nonsupportive content.

Kuhlthau (1993) identified the "uncertainty principle" and the idea that the reader may have problems with information that is unfamiliar to him or her is important to remember at this stage. Information that seems to match the knowledge (opinion, bias, basic assumptions) of the reader may be accepted more readily than information that is not familiar. Problems in assimilation may be tied to new terms unknown to the reader as well as opinions or arguments that are not acceptable. The more mature information literate and critical thinker will pause at this point to give as much consideration as possible to new information and may seek additional advice in order to make certain judgments for moving into phase three.

Phase 3: Reconsidering Information. The item has reached the level of thorough examination. Re-reading leads to comparison of information to previous information as well as personal entry level knowledge on the topic. More critical questions are raised to make a final acceptance of the content. Is this evidence trustworthy? Fitzgerald (2000) offers several strategies to help students make judgments concerning information.

Although exceptions to these strategies could be noted easily, in general they will help the student make wise decisions. Note that one factor for downgrading or upgrading usually does not lead to a conclusion to reject or accept the information. A combination of factors often will be needed and some negative factors actually may cancel out other positive factors. The combination of factors that lead to a final selection or rejection of the information may differ from one communication situation to another. Audience, learner bias, resource availability, and time limitations all come into play as well. Some of the decision factors Fitzgerald (2000, 21) has observed in use among secondary and college students are that they:

Downgrade information which:

- is blatantly persuasive,
- contains personal attacks,
- contains sarcasm,
- includes vocabulary that does not suit context,
- seems without purpose,
- is not clear,
- is not organized,
- is not current for the issue,
- is essentially an advertisement,
- has errors in grammar or spelling, and/or
- contains inappropriate repetition.

Upgrade information which:

- is organized into tables or clear graphics,
- has clear purpose and audience,
- is supported by other authoritative sources,
- provides fair consideration of other opinions,
- states conclusions based on logic and fact,
- is from an author who admits and explains personal bias,
- is relevant and current to issues, and/or
- suggests new perspective or new evidence worth considering.

Strategies in Writing Management

Although many students depend on the last-minute adrenalin rush to complete a composition, those who tend to succeed best are usually those who manage the process over time. Everyone who composes a video script, play, editorial, research paper, or nearly any other kind of communication will find the pressure of the deadline will influence their concentration. Those who have practiced the following strategies, however, will find they have a much richer base to work from when crunch time comes.

Break up writing sessions into small periods. Write portions of the project when an idea is fresh or just budding, even if it may not make it to the final piece. Such parts may be used for either the beginning, middle, or end. Successful writers strive to get things down on paper or into electronic files and worry about fitting the chunk into the whole later. Short writing periods also lead to identification of and time for retrieving additional information.

Many of the gaps that otherwise would appear at the deadline will become apparent sooner and can be filled. Writing and reading information feed each other and small steps allow this interaction to take place:

Analyze your audience. Communication will not be complete unless you have a good idea of who will receive your message. Understanding the expectations, biases, and generally held notions of the person or group who will view, hear, or read what is presented is at least half of the communication process. It can greatly influence the other half—seeking, selecting, and composing information.

Define your purpose. Such may evolve, but stating a goal or working thesis from the beginning helps to organize both the information search as well as the writing. As new information is explored, the working thesis likely will change as the final thesis may not become apparent until most of the information from reading, observation, and interviews have been concluded and analyzed.

Outline and organize. Work with guiding questions and subheadings from the beginning.

Make these the topics for note cards or for electronic files. As ideas and information are gathered, sort them into these areas and consider new questions and subheadings. The brainstorming exercises that may have helped to identify the branches of an initial topic continue through to the end, but in a more focused manner.

Let it sit for a while. Spend this time on some other tasks that help you relax. Exercise, such as walking, bike riding, or taking a drive, will help to rearrange things in the writer's mind. Letting the draft distill for a couple of days will allow sleep to work its magic as well. New ideas will generate from rest. New ideas also may come from further exploratory reading or discussion of your ideas with peers and mentors. While additional reading and conversations help, an extended stagnant consumption of television programming is more likely to hinder. Short selected viewing, however, can serve as a reward to completion of segments.

Seek a routine. Some writers seek a specific location and setting. Most agree that discipline includes placing yourself in front of the word processor at a regular time each day, and writing something (one thought, one line, one paragraph, or one page) relevant to your topic, whether it is eventually used or not.

Read it out loud. Read it to trusted friends and peers. Free write whenever possible to get something on paper. Seeing some pieces will help generate relationships and ideas that will grow into a full composition. Draw it, if you don't feel at the time you can write it.

Seek help from a qualified editor. Depending on your level of writing, the person who serves as editor will change. The point is that another set of eyes, especially to look for understanding and meaning based on organization of ideas, always will be beneficial. If for no other reason, successful writers find they verbalize thoughts differently in response to questions of the editor. Copy editing is a different process and comes at the final stages of the communication. Concentrate on logic, organization, and clarity of ideas first. Standards of grammar and style come later.

Conference Strategies for Draft and Revision

Intervention strategies are very important as a means for the mentor or peers to help move the writer along when stalled or off track. Good composition teachers seek such interventions and even create conference times to converse with the student about problems. Similar interventions are important for assisting the novice information searcher, user, and presenter.

Randy Bomer (1995) has refined these strategies as a middle school and high school teacher. Now codirector of the Teachers Writing Project at Columbia University, Bomer has learned from his students some smart ways to confront composition snags during draft and revision:

Problem: Student has written a beginning and can only imagine the piece going this one way.

Strategy: Write three very different possible beginnings for this same piece.

Problem: Student has written in an order that no longer makes sense to him or her.

Strategy: Outline what has been written and rearrange the chunks.

Problem: Student is having trouble deciding how much background to explain.

Strategy: List what the student assumes the reader knows and what the reader needs to learn.

Problem: Student can't decide what should come next.

Strategy: Outline four possible options.

Problem: Student's character is really just a name on the page, and the reader hasn't gotten a chance to know the character.

Strategy: Make at least three pages of notes about each character as a person.

Problem: There is no way the reader can imagine the place the student is writing about.

Strategy: Draw the place in detail from different angles, or describe it for two pages.

Problem: The story seems sappy because it only has one simple feeling to it.

Strategy: Write the incident from several different points of view.

Problem: The student hates what he or she has written-the whole thing. It's not saying what he or she means.

Strategy: Write a page of the piece in two other possible genres.

Problem: It's hard to make decisions about what is important because the student is just stringing together entries.

Strategy: Write, "what I want the reader to believe about my topic" at the top of a page and write a half page in response to that.

Problem: What the student is trying to say seems too simple or too obvious.

Strategy: Interview someone who feels differently about the topic. Write down what is said and list new questions.

Problem: The student has blurted out everything he or she has to say in the first two paragraphs and has nothing left to say.

Strategy: Divide a page into three sections, corresponding to sections of the piece, and jot notes about what information to release to the reader and what will remain a mystery for now.

Problem: The student is explaining too much and is having a hard time helping the reader to "see" what he or she is writing.

Strategy: Write a section of the piece as if someone were going to make a movie of it, including directions to designers and dialogue for actors.

Problem: The student feels like he or she doesn't have anything else to say.

Strategy: Read and respond to literature about the topic.

Problem: The student believes his or her writing feels flat and boring, and can't think of how to make it better.

Strategy: Read, copy out good bits, and make notes about the craft of pieces of literature he or she admires that is written in the same genre.

Problem: The whole experience is not working; it's hard and boring, and the student hates it and has no energy to write.

Strategy: Write about a time when he or she has written successfully (compared to now), especially if it was a similar kind of piece, and think on paper about what worked before.

Beef Up the Middle

Stephanie Harvey and Anne Goudvis (2000) have devised strategies that work to help students extract ideas from text. These ideas, often posted on sticky notes placed directly on the text read, provide the content for detail, extending and connecting thoughts with other texts, or, in short, getting some meat on the bones of the skeleton outline. Although Harvey and Goudvis have refined their exercises for upper elementary students reading nonfiction, these strategies can help the reader make connections and create meaning at any age.

Text-to-Self Connections: Identify information where you connect your life to the text. Think about your past experiences and prior knowledge. Further state words or draw images that represent this connection.

Text-to-Text Connections: Identify information in this text that connects to previous texts (book, movie, article, script, song, or any information that has been formerly composed). Extend this connection in your own words or visuals.

Text-to-World Connections: Using the same techniques as given above, how does the text you have encountered connect to events, people, or issues you know?

Further connections with text become elaborations when the reader can begin to display ideas as a composer in response to challenges such as the following:

- Write as many new questions as possible that come to mind, organize them, and predict possible solutions or answers.

- Draw your ideas so that you can visualize something that enhances and extends your understanding of the text.

- Synthesize the most important ideas gained from the text and list them in phrases.

- Midway through the text (article, story, play, book), predict the possible conclusions.

- Infer what the information so far might lead to as a solution or a more difficult problem.

The Intro and the End

How to start and how to conclude seem to remain the two most difficult portions of the composition. Some find that writing a conclusion as one of the first chunks and an introduction as one of the last portions seems to work. Others find assurance in starting in the middle and working in both directions, toward the beginning as well as the end. Still others find comfort in the organization of following the sequence of beginning, middle and end, especially in these days of word processing and the ability to revise and extend easily. Laurence Behrens of the University of California and Leonard J. Rosen of Harvard University (1997) promote these proven strategies:

For Introductions:

- **Quotation:** Use the words of the hero, a victim, the wise person with insight beyond that of the story, or other quotation that can "set the stage."

- **Analogy:** Similar to quotation use. Suggest something similar to the larger idea of the event to be detailed, but when used as an introduction, an analogy can provide something with which the audience may identify easier.

- **Historical review:** What are the situations and events that have led to this story?

- **Review of a controversy:** What are the issues and people who represent the arguments?

- **From the general to the specific:** What is the greater moral dilemma before specific examples are detailed?

- **From specific to general:** What specific event illustrates the greater issues to be discussed?

- **Question:** The key questions that motivated this investigation are stated early and may serve as an outline for the rest of the composition.

– **Statement of thesis:** What is the key question tested or to be addressed and what assumptions are made?

For Conclusions:

– **Statement of the subject's significance:** Conclude with a clear answer to the "so what?" question. Show that this story or study has meaning for others and future situations.

– **Call for further research:** No investigation is completely conclusive, and pure scientific method begs for replication and further examination beyond any given study. A general statement that more work should be done is not enough. A list of what should be explored is necessary.

– **Solution or recommendation:** Based on the information and evidence gathered, or based on the experiment conducted, it is logical to conclude the answers or directions for action.

– **Anecdote:** Is there a brief story, joke, or ironic situation that can either leave the audience with some common insight or raise new questions beyond what has been written or presented?

– **Quotation:** Just as an insightful statement may entice the reader at the introduction, so may quotations give a more universal ending. Quotations may be remembered when the rest of the essay may not, and often a few memorable lines help to climax emotions.

– **Questions:** What questions remain? What new questions come from this study or story and are suggested for future compositions, investigations, or dramatic presentation?

– **Speculation:** Although not a firm conclusion, why do mysteries remain and what seems likely because of this study?

What future themes are likely to be explored by the writer or the audience because of what has been communicated with this piece?

References

Behrens, L., and L. J. Rosen. (1997). *Writing and Reading across the Curriculum.* 6th ed. Longman.

Berke, J., and R. Woodland. (1996). *Twenty Questions for the Writer: A Rhetoric with Readings.* 6th ed. Harcourt Brace.

Bomer, R. (1995). *Time for Meaning: Crafting Literate Lives in Middle and High School.* Heinemann.

Fitzgerald, M.A. (1999). "Evaluating Information: An Information Literacy Challenge." *School Library Media Research* 2. Available at www.ala.org/aasl/SLMR (accessed August 21, 2005).

Fitzgerald, M.A. (2000). "Critical Thinking 101: The Basics of Evaluating Information." *Knowledge Quest* 29 (2): 13–24.

Harvey, S., and A. Goudvis. (2000). *Strategies That Work.* Stenhouse.

Kuhlthau, C. C. (1993). "Principle of Uncertainty for Information Seeking." *Journal of Documentation* 49: 339–355.

Owl Online Writing Lab. Purdue University. Available at http://owl.english.purdue.edu (accessed August 26, 2005).

For Further Reading

Forney, M. (1996). *Dynamite Writing Ideas: Empowering Students to Become Authors.* Maupin House Publishing.

Parker, S. M., M. C. Quigley, and J. B. Reilly. (1999). *Improving Student Reading Comprehension through the Use of Literacy Circles.* Heinemann.

Rankin, V. (2000). *The Thoughtful Researcher: Teaching the Research Process to Middle School Students.* Libraries Unlimited.

Rose, M., and M. Kiniry. (1997). *Critical Strategies for Academic Thinking and Writing.* Bedford/St. Martin's.

Stephens, E. C., and J. E. Brown. (2004). *A Handbook of Content Literacy Strategies: 125 Practical Reading and Writing Ideas.* Christopher-Gordon Publishers.

Topping, D. H., and R. A. McManus. (2002). *Real Reading, Real Writing: Content-Area Strategies.* Heinemann.

Informal Learning

Daniel Callison

Chautauqua

The Chautauqua Institute, founded in 1874 as an experiment in out-of-school, vacation learning, does not show as a term in current standard indexes and dictionaries related to instruction and education. And yet, this term, so neat to say, and this concept, so inspiring for lifelong learning, should be a part of our modern information literacy vocabulary. An environment in which people of all ages are free to present talents, knowledge, and ideas to audience members who are free to engage in discussions with a given presenter or move on at their own will and pace is clearly a companion concept to the library as a learning laboratory.

It is not simply an ideal, impossible to reach. The free-learning mode of Chautauqua is the heart blood necessary for meaningful learning in informal learning environments such as museums, zoos, and libraries. Chautauqua took a traveling form in the late 1900s and through the 1920s until the Depression stopped most such events in mid-America. I remember stories from my mother about experiences she enjoyed at Island Park in a small southern Kansas town. She and her sisters roamed the park to enjoy music, plays, debates, and even major political figures of the day, including William Jennings Bryan of Nebraska, three-time nominee for President of the United States.

What was learned in this environment? There was not a set of state standards, nor performance instruments based on a rubric of acceptable behavior. There was not the expectation that at the end of the week, one would apply new skills and demonstrate some level of mastery that resulted in a greater degree of literacy than before. There was, however, learning because learning was enjoyable, both something to be valued intrinsically and to be shared with friends and family.

What are the tangible characteristics of Chautauqua? It includes the oldest continuous book club in America, the Chautauqua Literary and Scientific Circle with nearly a half-million members. It is the Chautauqua Platform, founded in 1880, and continues to be the forum for open discussion on international issues, literature, and science. And Chautauqua includes the arts with expression through dance, symphony, and theater.

Imagine, and the image is very vivid to me, school library media programs in cooperation with public libraries, historical societies, museums, zoos, and other public learning institutions providing celebration of inquiry and learning! A special spring or summer event, perhaps, that for a week or at least a weekend provides the opportunity for young and old to make speeches, demonstrate special talents, debate local and national issues, and exchange ideas and questions. And imagine the opportunity to guide these learners to additional resources to read, view, and think more. Some of our best school library media programs are active participants in career fairs and science fairs. Why not Chautauqua?

What follows is a traditional review of some nontraditional key terms in instruction. This is a structured look at the more unstructured modes for learning. Please do not, however, forget the potential and promise of Chautauqua.

Informal Learning

"Informal learning" is the British term for a wide spectrum of continuing education options beyond the structured classroom. Educators from the United Kingdom (McGiveney 1999; Dale and Bell 1999) have defined informal learning to include the following:

- Learning that takes place outside a dedicated learning environment and which arises from the activities and interests of individuals and groups, but which may not be recognized as learning.

- Non-course-based learning activities (which might include discussion, talks or presentations, information, advice, and guidance) provided or facilitated in response to expressed interests and needs by people from a range of sectors and organizations.

- Planned and structured learning, such as short courses organized in response to identified interests and needs, but delivered in flexible and informal ways and in informal community settings.

- Learning that takes place in the work context, relates to an individual's performance of his or her job and employability, and is not formally organized into a program or curriculum by the employer.

Professional development is, therefore, a part of the informal learning spectrum, but most of the discussions on the lifelong value of informal learning are centered on events, which are unorganized, unsystematic, and even unintentional at times. Some believe that informal learning accounts for the bulk of any person's total lifetime learning. Informal learning involves the lifelong process by which every individual acquires and accumulates knowledge, skills, attitudes, and insights from daily experiences and exposure to the environment—at home, at work, and at play.

This broader perspective of education outside of the classroom, sets the stage for a more recent focus on a powerful component of informal learning, choice. The opportunity to select for oneself the learning agenda, learning mode, and learning application is an extremely powerful motivator. The ability to make such choices and to apply the results to solving personal information needs and interests is a sign of a mature, information-literate, lifelong learner. Free-inquiry and free-choice can be viewed as subsets of the Informal to Formal Learning Spectrum identified by John Ellis in 1990 (see Figure Part3.10).

Inquiry often is introduced within the curriculum as a set of recurring steps leading from questions and back to more questions. Students are engaged in practice of several techniques to raise questions and to gather information or data and to make sense from it all. Teachers of Information Inquiry know these techniques as wondering, question asking, key term webbing, concept mapping, observation, note taking, interviewing, data analysis, and so forth.

Several formal curricular approaches to inquiry have attempted to establish strategies that help the student apply inquiry to real world or

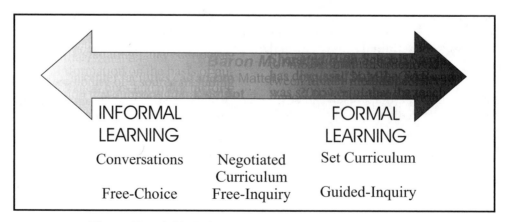

Figure Part3.10. Informal to formal learning spectrum.

more student-relevant issues. Such strategies are often contrived and are heavily literature-based. They do, however, serve to give a foundation for practice in social research and inquiry, and can serve to instill the skills needed for the mature information-literate student to eventually engage in free-inquiry. Richard Beach of the University of Minnesota and Jamie Myers (2001) of Pennsylvania State University have identified six inquiry strategies for engaging students in what they call inquiry-based English instruction within a practice-oriented curriculum:

- Immersing. Entering into the activities of a social world, experiencing the social world as a participant, or observing a social world.

- Identifying. Defining concerns, issues, and dilemmas that arise in a social world or from conflict across multiple social worlds.

- Contextualizing. Explaining how the activities, symbols, and texts used in one or more social worlds produce the components of a social world—identities, roles, relationships, expectations, norms, beliefs, and values.

- Representing. Using symbolic tools to create a text that represents a lived social world or responds to a represented social world.

- Critiquing. Analyzing how a representation of a social world privileges particular values and beliefs; analyzing how particular literacy practices within a social world promote certain meanings while marginalizing other possibilities.

- Transforming. Revising one's meaning for the components of a social world; changing one's actions and words within a social world to construct more desirable identities, relationships, and values (17–18).

Free-Choice Learning

Those who follow the principles of student-centered education and the Montessori tradition have long provided for educational situations in which the student moves at his or her own individual pace. Opportunities for hands-on application for learning are abundant and the teacher facilitates learning by providing a learning context that will challenge the student. Creative learning and critical thinking are reinforced when the student demonstrates such. Free-choice is encouraged so that the student grows in the understanding of his or her own abilities and limitations. This is free-choice education within a curriculum and structure, although much more flexible than found in the traditional school. New thinking on free-choice learning rests outside the school and on what is learned outside the curriculum.

According to the Institute for Learning Innovation (2006), free-choice learning is the type of learning guided by a person's needs and interests—learning that people engage in throughout their lives to find out more about what is useful, compelling, or just plain interesting to them. Much of the modern world has moved from the industrial society to the information society and the shift has made learning across the lifespan more important and possible. Both leisure time and optional learning modes have increased. Adults and children are spending more and more of their time learning, but not just in classrooms or on the job—through free-choice learning at home, after work, and on weekends. Free-choice learning is an essential component of lifelong learning. Surfing the Internet, participating in a book discussion group, watching a documentary, selecting books at the library, and visiting the museum are all free-choice learning actions.

The term "free-choice learning" is, therefore, used to refer to the type of learning that occurs when learners have control over what, when, why, and how they learn. Typically, free-choice learning refers to the type of learning regularly facilitated by museums, science centers, zoos, and aquariums; a wide range of community-based organizations including libraries, youth groups, environmental and health-related organizations, and faith-based groups; as well as print and electronic media.

Freedom to select from any area of the entire collection, fiction or nonfiction, and to read at leisure has been documented by Krashen (1993) to be extremely beneficial for advancing reading achievement across all ability levels.

Different levels of choice also can appear in the multitude of library-based exercises and projects students experience. Christine Somers (2001), a library media specialist at Indian Creek Middle School in Trafalgar, Indiana, and co-teacher in a graduate level course at Indiana University in Information Inquiry for school teachers, summarized the options for choice as follows:

- **General Topic.** Students are introduced to a general topic, such as the Civil War, and may find a specific person, event, or other more focused subtopic of their choice.

- **Related Concepts.** Students are exposed to a concept such as biomes and are allowed to select from one of seven biomes to explore in more detail.

- **Demonstrate Proficiency.** The teacher may identify several options for project exploration and presentation, each fairly equal in time and effort, and the student may select the mode they prefer.

- **Free Will.** The student has near total control over topic selection and methods to explore and present results. Seldom, if ever, open to middle grade students, but a likely avenue in more progressive and alternative high school environments.

- **Consensus.** Students working as a group on an inquiry assignment may have the option to come to agreement or justify their own choices as a group. Collaboration often is determined through democratic or majority vote processes.

- **Illustrations.** Students often will have a great deal of choice in how to illustrate, present, or package a report.

- **Grade Options.** Some teachers favor defining the requirements for different final grade levels and contract with students on their choice for time and effort invested in return for potential level of evaluation.

The Contextual Model for Learning

Over the past decade, John Falk and Lynn Dierking (2000, 2002), associated with the University of Maryland's College of Education and founders of the Institute for Learning Innovation, have conceptualized free-choice learning in a contextual model. Learning begins with the individual and is reformulated by the physical and sociocultural contexts that interact on the personal context.

Much of their work has centered on how young and adult museum visitors learn by choice. Falk and Dierking's Contextual Model for Learning has implications for all learners in many other environments beyond the classroom. Although "library" seldom appears in their recent books, they acknowledge the freedom of choice posed by thousands of books and other information items open for the patron to explore and to learn by free-choice.

The components and implications of the Falk/Dierking Contextual Model for Learning include the following:

Personal Context

- Most human learning is self-motivated, emotionally satisfying, and very personally rewarding. Humans are highly motivated to learn when they are in supporting environments; when they are engaged in meaningful activities; when they are freed from anxiety, fear, and other negative mental states; when they face choices and control over their learning; and when the challenges of the task meet their skills.

- Learning, particularly intrinsically motivated learning, is a rich, emotion-laden experience, encompassing much, if not most, of what we consider to be fundamentally human. At its most basic level, learning is about affirming self.

Sociocultural Context

- All communication media (television, film, magazines, books, museum exhibitions, the Internet, etc.) represent a socially mediated form of culturally specific conversations between the producers of that medium and the user or receiver.

- Knowledge, rather than being the same for all individuals, is shared within often delimited communities of learners.

In other words, there exist myriad communities of learners, defined by the boundaries of shared knowledge and experience.

- Universally, people mentally organize information effectively if it is recounted to them in a story or narrative form.

The Physical Context

- Learning appears to be not just "enveloped" within a physical context but rather "situated" within the physical context.
- For humans, the search for meaning, to make sense of the environment, to find pattern and make order out of chaos, to make sense of experience are innate processes.
- Humans automatically form long-term, emotion-laden memories of events and places without deliberately attempting to memorize them.

Falk and Dierking summarize findings on several research studies, which are based on observations of zoo and museum visitors. Most of the studies concern the free-choice, actions, and learning of young visitors, but free-choice is a powerful motivation for learning and exploring for all age groups and several studies reinforce the need for all learners to have some control over their agenda for visits to such free-exploration centers. Many of these findings can be associated with free inquiry learning through the school library media and information literacy program:

- Learning from interaction with or observation of others also seems to involve longer examination of exhibits, more questions asked of guides or docents, and a greater opportunity for adults to interact with children to exchange observations, and this includes teacher with students as well as parents and their children.
- Pre-field trip orientations seem to influence the amount of learning that results from a visit to the zoo, museum, or historical site, but of most promise for retaining of learning and discovery was the opportunity for students to have input in the orientation agenda. The child-centered orientation set the children's minds at ease so that they could concentrate on the experience of the visit. Orientations tended to settle concerns about food, restrooms, returning home, and how to associate with friends. A notion that can be drawn from such a finding is that library and information skill orientations that concentrate more on an overall model for the inquiry or research project and less on specific rules and tools are likely to have the same result of easing anxiety if the model presented demonstrates that the task at hand will be manageable and in many respects enjoyable.

- Visitors to museums do not come as blank slates. They come with a wealth of previously acquired knowledge, interests, skills, beliefs, attitudes, and experiences, all of which combine to affect not only what and how they interact with educational experiences but also what meaning, if any, they make of such experiences. This finding has powerful implications for the free-inquiry environment in exploration of resources in the school library media center.

- Parents can be effective facilitators of their children's learning when exhibitions are designed with collaborative learning in mind and when adults feel comfortable with the content and experiences provided in museums. How much time and effort goes into informing parents about information search models, access to resources beyond the encyclopedia, and the rubrics for research performance placed before their children?

- Parents are far more willing to take advantage of in-house library materials, family activity kits, and other opportunities . . . if they know that these materials are available and understand their role in providing assistance to their children. Parental guidance can lead to a deeper and more meaningful level of learning.

References

Beach, R., and J. Myers. (2001). *Inquiry-Based English Instruction: Engaging Students in Life and Literature.* Teachers College Press.

Cecil, N. L. (1995). *The Art of Inquiry: Questioning Strategies for K-6 Classrooms.* Peguis. Chautauqua Institute. Available at http://www.ciweb.org (accessed February 26, 2003).

Dale, M., and J. Bell. (1999). *Informal Learning in the Workplace.* Department for Education and Employment (London).

Ellis, J. (1990). *Informal Education.* Open University Press.

Falk, J. H., and L. D. Dierking. (2000). *Learning from Museums: Visitor Experiences and the Making of Meaning.* AltaMira Press.

Falk, J. H., and L. D. Dierking. (2002). *Lessons Without Limit: How Free-Choice Learning Is Transforming Education.* AltaMira Press.

Institute for Learning Innovation. (2006). *What Is Free-Choice Learning?* Available at http://www.ilinet.org/freechoicelearning.html (accessed July 2, 2006).

Krashen, S. (1993). *The Power of Reading.* Libraries Unlimited.

McGiveney, V. (1999). *Informal Learning in the Community.* NIACE.

Somers, C. (2001). "Class Presentation on Choice in Assignments, L551 Information Inquiry for School Teachers." School of Library and Information Science, Indiana University.

Information Search Strategies

Daniel Callison

Strategy is a term often linked with information searching as well as instructional methods. Associated with either search or instruction, "strategy" infers a plan of action, or a systematic way to accomplish a goal and to meet a need. Instructional strategies are overall plans for implementing instructional goals, methods, or techniques. Reading strategies, for example, are methods that can be used or taught to facilitate reading proficiency. Therefore, strategy is also something that can transfer from teacher to learner so that the strategy becomes a skill or process the learner will employ on his or her own as the teacher fades from the situation.

Search strategies are not new to the teaching tasks faced by instructional media specialists and other teachers of information literacy as they attempt to orient the user to the information environment and to establish a framework the student may apply generally to their information search problems. "Search strategy" often is defined as a comprehensive plan for finding information and includes defining the information need, determining the form in which it is needed, if it exists, where it is located, how it is organized, and how to retrieve it. Such a definition has both positive and problematic aspects. It is positive in that it moves search strategy beyond the traditional linear decision-making process that has been used to introduce most students to the library. It is problematic in that the definition assumes a great deal of entry level knowledge on the user's part, and the process still concentrates on location of the source rather than on location of specific information (Hirsh 1997).

In the context of student learning through information literacy, there is a need to give more attention than has been provided previously to the strategies for understanding information and how to use what is extracted in a meaningful and constructive way. This is not to say that search strategies that lead to more efficient ways to locate sources and introduce key resources should not be taught also. It is to state that the information search process does not stop there and the responsibilities of those who teach information literacy are just beginning when the student obtains and is encouraged to question the nature, validity, usefulness, or relevance of the information located.

Purpose Determines Strategy

The intended goal or purpose of the instruction will determine the strategy most suited to accomplish that goal. This can be illustrated by the evolution of library instruction over the past thirty years (Thomas 1999; Kuhlthau 1987, 2003).

Orientation to Sources and Services. The traditional search strategy concentrates on information tools and services offered within the given library. The student is introduced to a linear progression of information sources and services, not so much to tailor these to meet the students' needs, but to acquaint the students with nearly all the library has to offer. Too often the emphasis is to make the patron fit the collection. Student assignments are often contrived in order to "teach the use of the library" rather than to "teach how to meet information needs." The search strategy is generic and fits the way the institution is organized, and often is not flexible to deal with true inquiry projects.

Thus, the student works from indexes, to reference materials, to general book and periodical collections, to nonprint and electronic sources, to special collections such as local history or government documents. The purpose is to show what is owned, where it is housed, and what must be done to get to the information. The strategy may acquaint the student with the library, but does little to meet his or her specific information needs. Thus, there is frequent use of the reminder, "Ask a librarian."

Awareness of Key Literature. The purpose is to introduce the literature that best supports a given theme or discipline. In school library media center situations, this might involve the best resources for consumer information and students will be introduced to key magazines, annual reports, useful Web sites, and perhaps how to contact the Better Business Bureau. In the K–12 setting, this approach is often used in those resource-based experiences in which a specific pool of gathered resources allow the student to explore topics related to a theme.

The purpose is to read extensively beyond the limits of textbook summaries or classroom discussions. In the academic setting, this strategy is based on a conceptual framework, commonly called a pathfinder. Detailed in theory and practice by Mary Reichel and Mary Ann Ramey (1987), undergraduate and graduate students are introduced to the publication sequences, subject structures, and key reference and index resources as a conceptual framework for information in a field or discipline. The Ohio State University Library Gateway displays examples of such pathfinders (http://www.lib.ohiostate.edu/gateway/subjects.html).

The goal of the framework or pathfinder strategy is for the student to learn key classification numbers, key controlled vocabulary terms, key specific reference materials, core periodicals and textbooks, and the standard or most cited books and people in the discipline at hand. Thus, from knowledge of this central literature, on anthropology for example, the student becomes acquainted with the accepted ideas, trends, and history of a field. This strategy provides the foundation for future exploration, but does not place the student in situations in which he or she must deal with new or unique information problems. Both the source and pathfinder strategies do not typically deal with evaluation of sources or the analysis of information need and do little to teach problem-solving skills.

Critical Thinking and Problem Solving. The strategy best used to meet the information needs at this stage is the process approach. The student, usually selecting from a theme or set of given issues, must determine a topic or problem to explore, determine appropriate resources, extract information, synthesize findings, and present a solution. The process approach is most effective if the student is given time and guidance to read widely about the given theme in order to move beyond the core resources and central issues. While this strategy moves the student through stages of thought and reflection, it is recursive in that movement back to indexes and reference resources will cycle through again and again as the student struggles to find focus.

Inquiry. At this level, the student is challenged with the task to set his or her own research agenda as much as possible. Near mastery of the preceding strategies must be reached as the student faces greater responsibility in formulation of his or her own personal investigation questions. Inquiry is driven by strategies that encourage framing, sharing, and testing ideas. Thus, there is a great deal of reading, discussion, and visualization of thoughts and options. Further, inquiry is driven by evidence. Depending on the nature of the inquiry, evidence can be facts, elaborations, different perspectives, and/or original data. The foundation for evidential considerations comes from a review of associated literature. Here the student traces citations, both from indexes and from bibliographies of valued initial readings, and critically examines information that has been written by others considering similar issues and problems. Here the student concentrates on what has been examined and reported before he or she moves into investigations, creative writing, or illustrations that are in some manner unique to the student.

In the previous information search process situations, problems and tasks often come predefined. At the inquiry level, the student's major task is to identify the problem and associated questions. Strategies must allow for exploration of all possible avenues for ideas and evidence, and these may be outside of standard indexes and literature guides. The goal is for the student to comprehend the value of potential evidence or other pieces of information and determine quality based on relevance and authority specific to the message to be communicated or the argument to be supported.

Search Tactics

Marcia J. Bates (1979), from the University of Washington, defines a "search tactic" as a move to further refine a search. Combinations of these tactics become an important set of techniques that often come to play within the overall search strategy. Bates (1989) defined her list of search tactics in 1979 to assist the professional online searcher and secondarily in teaching fledgling searchers how to increase their search sophistication. Although the orientation of her techniques was toward the professional, search technologies have evolved and are somewhat more manageable for the lay person. Nancy Thomas (1999), associate professor at Emporia State University, has taken many of the tactics listed by Bates and refined them as strategies that help student searchers rethink their searches.

Intervention and guidance from the teacher of information literacy is usually necessary in order to illustrate these search options. As an apprentice learner, the student must gain an understanding of not only how to employ the tactics, but when and why to apply them.

Bibble—to look for a bibliography already prepared; to see if the search work one plans has already been done in a usable form by someone else; to examine the bibliography of a valued source and select key reference leads.

Record—keep track of trails one has followed and of desirable trails not followed up on or not completed. This can be part of a journal in which the student documents success and frustrations in various search situations. Most modern databases build a search record for the novice to examine and gain understanding of alternatives.

Brainstorming—getting ideas and considering alternative ideas to enrich understanding by talking through the possibilities with others prior and during the search; read widely during the topic formulation stage so terms and ideas flow easily.

Consulting—testing ideas with others, usually mentors or experts who have useful insights to offer, to obtain valuable information and feedback on initial search terms.

Rescuing—being persistent and thorough in order to prevent premature conclusions or bias that may eliminate useful evidence that does not seem to fit preconceived notions.

Wandering—browsing in a variety of resources to stir the imagination and ignite thinking; look for synonyms and antonyms.

Breaching—considering a different subject area or domain, database, or discipline when a given search strategy is exhausted; gaining insight from a different area of discourse.

Reframing—reexamining the question to get rid of distortions or erroneous assumptions.

Jolting—changing the point of view by looking at the question as it has been addressed by different age groups, different cultures, different presentation or communication formats, or different disciplines.

Focusing—narrowing the search or the concept, or looking at only one part of it to give depth and greater meaning.

Dilating—expanding the search to widen the focus or to include larger issues and provide a more meaningful context for the central question.

Neighboring—cluster terms to be located within the text; consider associated terms that help to broaden the context or narrow the focus.

Reflection—stopping at several points in order to determine what else might come to mind; using revision stages to determine if all aspects have been covered.

Parallel—to make the search formulation broad or broader by including synonyms or otherwise conceptually parallel terms.

Contrary—to search for a term logically opposite from that describing the desired information.

Tracing—using the subject tracings that tag relevant citation hits during searching in order to find additional information classified by the database under such terms or subjects; examine information already found in the search in order to find additional terms that can be used to further the search.

Linkage—from the best sources located and read, identify what may be especially valuable such as reoccurring citations to authors (Callison and Daniels, 1988), articles, books, or Internet documents. New sources are found through linkage to the referenced documents and tracing of names in indexes or on the Internet.

Comprehension to Enhance Understanding

Reading for meaning is key to advancing in the information literacy processes (Axelrod and Cooper 1999). Useful strategies for reading text critically include first making a photocopy of the pages that seem to contain the most relevant information. Once the pages are copied or printed from the Internet, a highlight pen and a dark lead pencil are used to

- Highlight or underline key words or sentences.

- Be selective and highlight no more than 20% of the information on the pages; 10 percent if possible.

- Bracket important passages and write notes near the passages that paraphrase and/or link to items from other sources that have been photocopied or printed.

- Connect related ideas with lines, a number code, or key term code.

- Circle words to be defined further.

- Outline the main ideas in the margin.

- Write brief comments and questions in the margin.

- From these pages, construct note cards or place information pieces in a database for future sorting, linkage, and summary.

- Always note the correct citation for the records.

One of the most useful publications that contains comprehension strategies based on use of nonfiction literature for children and young adults is *Strategies That Work* by Stephanie Harvey and Anne Goudvis (2000). The authors define "strategic reading" as thinking about reading in ways that enhance learning and understanding. Strategies that help the student focus on important ideas, drawing inferences, and asking questions can improve the student's overall comprehension of text. It is not enough, however, for the student to simply understand a given strategy. Harvey and Goudvis remind us that students also must understand when and how to use such strategies.

Levels of Comprehension

David Perkins (1992), author of *Smart Schools,* suggests that learners can be categorized by the following four levels in reading ability. These levels may also apply to information seekers and users:

- **Tacit Learner:** The student lacks awareness of how to think about what he or she is reading. No association is made between the information being read and information need or associated information need possibilities.

- **Aware Learner:** The student realizes that meaning has broken down and confusion has set in, but does not have a sufficient set of strategies to remedy the problem. New information is different from or in conflict with that which was expected and the learner may not know how to deal with the content other than to ignore it.

- **Strategic Learner:** The student understands and applies basic strategies to think about and comprehend what is read. He or she applies systematic methods to assimilate new information and track information gaps, and thus is more likely to identify new information needs and how to address them.

- **Reflective Learner:** A reader who is strategic about his or her thinking and is able to apply strategies flexibly depending on goals and purpose for reading. Search and information analysis strategies are transferred easily by the learner to meet new information needs and different information formats so the learner also may be strategic in listening, viewing, speaking, and writing.

Strategies Used by Proficient Readers

Seven strategies that Harvey and Goudvis (2000) find key for practice and will result in students becoming more proficient readers:

- Making connections between prior knowledge and the text—Readers naturally bring their prior knowledge and experience to reading, but they comprehend better when they think about the connections they make among the text, their lives, and the larger world.

- Asking questions—Asking questions will keep readers engaged, especially if they discover some answers and raise more questions in a continuous learning cycle. When readers ask questions, they clarify understanding and forge ahead to make meaning.

- Visualizing—Active readers create images in their minds based on the words they read in the text. Enhancement of these visions can come from sharing with peers and parents.

- Drawing inferences—Inferring is at the intersection of taking what is known, garnering clues from the text, and thinking ahead to make a judgment, discern a theme, or speculate about what is to come. Inference must occur in order for the teacher to conclude that the student has "used the information."

- Determining important ideas—Thoughtful readers grasp essential ideas and important information when reading. Readers must differentiate between less important ideas and key ideas that are central to the meaning of the text. Such discrimination will help the learner move through large amounts of information by skimming for that which is most relevant.

- Synthesizing information—Synthesizing involves combining new information with existing knowledge to form an original idea or interpretation. Reviewing, sorting, and sifting important information can lead to new insights that change the way readers think.

- Repairing understanding—If confusion disrupts meaning, readers need to stop and clarify their understanding. Often guidance and support from the teacher are necessary, but students' independent abilities to reflect and clarify come with practice.

Harvey and Goudvis (2000) insist that the reading strategies they find worthwhile are most likely to influence learner behavior if these strategies are modeled and clearly practiced by the classroom teacher. Teachers of information literacy also should be model learners and illustrate, vocalize, and share with students how they use strategies to think through information searching, selection, analysis, and application. The information literate teacher is also a strategic, reflective learner.

References

Axelrod, R. B., and C. R. Cooper. (1999). *Reading Critically, Writing Well.* Bedford/St. Martin's.

Bates, M. J. (1979). "Information Search Tactics." *Journal of the American Society for Information Science* 30 (4): 205–214.

Bates, M. J. (1989). "The Design of Browsing and Berrypicking Techniques for the Online Search Interface." *Online Review* 13 (5): 407–425.

Callison, D., and A. Daniels. (1988, Spring). "Introducing End-User Software for Enhancing Student Online Searching." *School Library Media Quarterly* 16 (3): 173–181.

Harvey, S., and A. Goudvis. (2000). *Strategies That Work: Teaching Comprehension to Enhance Understanding.* Stenhouse.

Hirsh, S. G. (1997, Spring). "How Do Children Find Information on Different Types of Tasks?" Library Trends 45 (4): 725–746.

Kuhlthau, C. C. (1987, Fall). "An Emerging Theory of Library Instruction." *School Library Media Quarterly* 16 (1): 23–28.

Kuhlthau, C. C. (2003). *Seeking Meaning: A Process Approach to Library and Information Services.* 2d ed. Libraries Unlimited.

Ohio State University Library Gateway to Information Subject Guides. http://www.lib.ohio-state.edu/gateway/subjects.html (accessed August 10, 2005).

Perkins, D. (1992). *Smart Schools: Better Thinking and Learning for Every Child.* Free Press.

Reichel, M., and M. A. Ramey. (1987). *Conceptual Frameworks for Bibliographic Instruction.* Libraries Unlimited.

Thomas, N. P. (1999). *Information Literacy and Information Skills Instruction.* Libraries Unlimited.

For Further Reading

Ercegovac, Z. (2001). *Information Literacy: Search Strategies, Tools, and Resources for High School Students.* Linworth Publishing.

Harvey, S. (1998). *Nonfiction Matters.* Stenhouse.

Tovani, C., and E. O. Keene. (2000). *I Read It, But I Don't Get It: Comprehension Strategies for Adolescent Readers.* Stenhouse.

Interview

Daniel Callison

The interview can be a valuable tool used in the inquiry process to gain primary information that will help to clarify and add meaning. The information literate student who has gained a mature sense for seeking evidence will use the personal interview in order to

- Verify evidence from written sources. It is not uncommon to find, as one discusses issues based on what is written in popular magazines and newspapers, that some facts may depend on specific situations or no longer be true and relevant at all. An interview with a person of expertise related to the issue can add weight to the evidence or explain how new knowledge counters what is "conventional wisdom."

- Add color and story. Personal interviews can often lead to testimonials, descriptions of life experiences, and even embellishments of extreme opinion. Interviews can give context to the information that the student takes to the interview. The interviewee may give detail to events so that the student begins to understand various situations over time or in different cultures.

- Extend a line of inquiry. Interviews can make the topic more local and personal and, while doing so, lead to new questions for further exploration.

Techniques for successful interviews must be practiced and refined just as with other skills involved in information searching and application. Knowing when to seek an interview, with whom, what questions to pose and how, and how to listen for the most relevant information are elements that are not easy to master. The mature information literate student will seek out interviews often and even return to the same source to get further explanation and elaboration, just as he or she might return to re-reading basic reference materials on a topic. Teachers of information literacy skills will find that interventions for modeling such skills will be important, and should realize that the school library media program has as much an obligation to provide an environment that encourages use of human resources as it does provision of print and electronic materials.

Encouraging the use of interviews means thinking of such events as being as much a part of the center's collection as books, magazines, and the Internet. Teachers of information literacy may maintain a file or database of good resource people in the community who are willing to be interviewed and who are authoritative, but also able to communicate with students. Such a list may correspond to the typical controversial issues many students research concerning drug abuse, peer pressures, capital punishment, or the environment. Interviewing can take the shape of individual face-to-face questioning or e-mail and written correspondence.

Afraid to Make the Most of Interviewing

Ken Metzler (1989), a journalism teacher, has written extensively about student fears of interviewing and such anxiety is at the core of what Metzler calls "unseen problems":

- An aversion to asking questions for fear of being shown up as ignorant. Metzler notes that a natural, childlike curiosity unfortunately seems to go out of style as people reach a certain age-the teens, perhaps. He reminds us of a Chinese proverb, "He who asks is a fool for five minutes; he who does not is a fool forever."

- Failure to define clearly and state the purpose of the interview, or general lack of preparation. Ability to define purpose is not likely to come early in the student's inquiry process, but later as they begin to gain focus. There should be a need for the interview, and if one cannot be stated, then using the expert's time for specific answers should wait until unique questions can be identified.

- A lack of enthusiasm and natural curiosity about people and the world at large. Lack of interest on the part of the interviewer lessens the likelihood of an enthusiastic responder and increases the likelihood that answers will be short and without the rich details that can make an interview a key source of information.

- Failure to listen. Elements of a professional listener include getting ready to listen, giving attention and eye contact, avoiding prejudgment of people, listening for major points and supporting evidence, and evaluating what is said and not said or only half-articulated. Interviewers who are more secure in their craft will offer encouragement and direction and show that they are listening through interview etiquette, which may even include dressing in proper attire to demonstrate that the interviewer is serious about the situation.

- Failure to probe, vagueness, and convoluted or over-defined questions.

Opening questions should set the interviewee at ease and allow them to demonstrate what they know or believe. Follow-up questions help the interviewee to further define and give specific examples or illustrate their thoughts in some manner. The mature interviewer knows that this is not the time to demonstrate all of his or her knowledge about a subject through expansive questions, but to demonstrate enough knowledge to be credible and yet curious for more information.

Interviews for Inquiry

Interviewing is a skill that can be introduced very early in the student's academic experience. Some would agree that most two-year-olds are natural interviewers and that their first experience in school, unfortunately, is to learn not to ask too many questions. Paula Rogovin (1998), an elementary school teacher at the Manhattan New School, believes in and practices inquiry through interviews as the foundation for her curriculum. Based on her experiences growing up in a family life rich with conversations around the dinner table, field trips to museums and art galleys, and open debate concerning the progressive issues of the day, Rogovin has drawn from those experiences to create a classroom full of questions.

Working with students from five to seven years of age, Rogovin has constructed a learning environment around children who interview their parents and other relatives, local neighborhood workers and personalities, and even a celebrity from time to time. But the emphasis is on learning from people with whom we live and see. Learning about different cultures and careers is driven by interviewing, listening, reflecting, and asking again and again. Insightful information, as well as moments to learn correct spelling and grammar, are facilitated through her guidance of thirty young inquiring minds. Interviews may involve several guests each week along with field trips.

Interviews usually take place first thing in the morning, when students are fresh and alert. Writing accompanies the interviewing as students use personal journals to write what they have heard and what they think about what they have heard. Pages of notes eventually evolve into class-produced books that are accumulated for reading and story time during other parts of the day. Parents, grandparents, and others who have had their thirty minutes in the interviewee's seat often autograph the book compiled and illustrated by the children.

Rogovin has perfected several strategies for successful interviewing over years of experimentation and hundreds of contacts in her community:

- Acknowledge prior knowledge. Just as students bring knowledge to any other situation, so they have prior knowledge they bring to an interview situation. By creating a context for the interview prior to the person being present, students can share such knowledge and thus can help to form and practice question building. Prior knowledge may come from knowing the person to be interviewed, having read or heard stories relevant to the occupation of the interviewee, or remembering similar information from previous interviewing experiences.

- Help guests feel at ease. For some adults, the thought of being interviewed by children is scary. Rogovin leads her class in a friendly and polite "good morning" and emphasizes that sometimes the most significant issues of the interview come from informal discussions to help the guest relax. While being prepared is essential, being flexible and alert to comments that may have special interest to the children is important for successful facilitating of the interview.

- Focus the interview in questions about facts and feelings. What kind of work do you do? How did you learn to do that job? How did you feel when the customer was rude to you?

- Model the questions and the sequence. While children will have many questions, the interview bears more fruit if children see from the teacher that questions should be open-ended at first and then move to the specifics as the discussion progresses. Often questions are rehearsed or practiced and students may role play prior to and even during an interview.

- The teacher serves as an interpreter and one who helps to link information to help the students find meaning.

Constantly alert for the "teachable moment," Rogovin will capitalize on new words, emotions, and surprise comments in order to explain the spelling of a new term, location of a different country, or ask students to think or write about how they might feel in a similar situation just described by the interviewee. Interviews also open the opportunity to make connections with literature and music as a rich collection of cultural heritage is available in this metropolitan neighborhood.

Rogovin does not elude to a school librarian or media specialist. Hopefully there are many helpers who supply additional learning resources and collaborate on ideas. Her classroom is filled with books, records, maps, and illustrations. Resource "cubbies" house books, illustrations, toys, and artifacts gathered by the children. These resource shelves are labeled by the children in terms that they use to describe the careers or other topics being explored. These collections of items serve on a continuing basis for linking interviews together, both in reference to previous interviews and in preparation for the next. Interviewing becomes not only a method to extract information, but an experience for children to explore the world.

Oral History Interviews

One of the best uses of good interviewing techniques is to capture the stories and dialects of relatives, friends and other community citizens who have experiences they are willing to share on tape, audio or video. (See Key Word: Oral Histories.) Some suggestions that will lead to successful oral history interviews follow:

- Inform the interviewee in advance and in clear terms of the purpose and subject of the interview.

- Gain permission from the interviewee that they are willing to have their stories and observations made a part of the oral record you are gathering. The interviewee should have the right to decline responding to any questions.

- Learn efficient operation of equipment, effective placement of microphones, and be ready for technical problems with extra batteries, lights and even a back up recorder.

- Use a quality recording medium—tape or digital disc.

- Do a brief pre-interview over the phone so that you can determine if the interviewee has stories of value and so the interviewee has a better idea of the sort of questions that will be asked.

- Be on time and be courteous.

- Record the name, date and location of the interview without fanfare prior to beginning the interview.

- Keep the interview to 30 minutes and allow time for both the interviewee and interviewer to rest and think before proceeding to additional follow-up questions.

- Try not to record near air conditioners and heating vents that cause background noise. Try to record inside in a setting that is comfortable for the interviewee.

- Try to have interviewee personal photographs and other memorabilia available for the interviewee to respond to as such will "jog" the memory. Do background research concerning the general areas about which you have questions so you may ask intelligently for details on childhood chores, schooling, occupations, world and local events, and other areas that are typical for comparison among those interviewed.

- Remember that a good interview is more a monologue than a dialogue. Make questions short and direct and let the interviewee tell their story. Practice interviewing techniques with more experienced interviewers in several sessions prior to taking the time of those you plan to interview and not being prepared.

- Learn to edit oral history interviews so that important comments pertaining to similar events from several interviewees can be compiled. Maintain, however, the complete original interview in its full unedited form for those who may want to have access to such a full record.

- Be certain that the interviewee's name, age and address are correctly written on the tape or disc.

- Send a thank you message to each person interviewed.

- Instructional media specialists, other teachers and students should work together to establish an event at which the best segments of oral interviews can be presented to others and be enhanced with visuals that illustrate the content of the interviews.

References

Metzler, K. (1989). *Creative Interviewing: The Writer's Guide to Gathering Information and Asking Questions*. 2d ed. Prentice Hall.

Rogovin, P. (1998). *Classroom Interviews: A World of Learning*. Heinemann. With companion 50-minute video on VHS from Heinemann Videos.

Lesson Plan

Daniel Callison

A "lesson plan" may be either an informal or formal set of actions taken by a teacher or a group of teachers to determine what their students are to learn, how the teaching activity will be implemented, and how the acquisition of new skills or knowledge may be demonstrated and evaluated. This process is illustrated in several basic questions paraphrased from the lesson plan outline provided through AskERIC. Each teacher should ask and answer the following:

What do my students bring to the learning situation?

Where are my students going?

How are they going to get there?

How will I know when they have arrived?

How will I assess and document degrees of achievement?

Collaborative lesson planning among the instructional media specialist and other teachers can involve more complex questions in order to move through a systematic method for shared teaching roles. As with most processes, the lesson plan will reach higher levels of effectiveness when communication channels are open for interactive input among the educators. Although often illustrated in a linear fashion, the spark to initiate the plan or to elaborate on new potential areas for the plan may come at any juncture of the elements that are discussed here.

The Instructional Consultant Role

Patricia Pickard's (1993) study of the instructional consultant role for school library media specialists in DeKalb County, Georgia, provides insight on the classic issues faced over the past four decades concerning the potential for leadership from library media specialists in lesson planning and curriculum development. Her survey is based on an extensive literature review to establish these key points:

Actions for the library media specialist to play a key role in curriculum development include the following:

- Be aware of the total instructional program in the school.

- Visit and participate in classes as much as possible.

- Know current trends in successful teaching methods.

- Become involved in curriculum planning, not just responding to the established curriculum.

- Conduct in-service for teachers. Teach teachers whenever possible.

- Establish, read, and promote a current collection of professional materials, including texts and quality Web sites.

- Join and participate as a member of instructional teams. Create the instructional plan and act as leader when beneficial to the project.

Depending on the situation, the library media specialist may take active or proactive steps to engage in the lesson planning and curriculum development processes. At the highest levels, inter- active steps are taken so that the library media specialist acts as co-educator, listens to and evaluates ideas and input from other teachers, and provides his or her own insights. Such input moves beyond "knowing resources" to knowledge of teaching and evaluation methods. Callison wrote in 1987:

> The [instructional] media specialist acts, not only as a leader, but also begins to examine the educational system in terms of evaluating its successes and failures. The [instructional] media specialist becomes an important force for curriculum development. This impact involves not only integrating information skills into all areas of the curriculum, but working to revise lessons and activities to the degree that such lessons require the use of [resource-based education] through the media center and guided by the [instructional] media specialist (24)

Nearly two decades after Craver's (1986) extensive review of the library media specialist's instructional role, the primary challenge remains: to narrow the gap between theory and practice and between internal and external perceptions and expectations (Callison 2002). In the early 1990s, Pickard (1993) found, as continues to be true across the nation, a small portion (10 percent) of the practicing library media specialists perceived their instructional role to be important. When accepted at all, it was in a supporting role and seldom in a leadership position. Tasks that involved the library media specialist in evaluation of student performance were viewed as too time-consuming and reserved for the teacher, even though such responsibilities move the library media specialist into a stronger co-educator role. Such engagement with student performance also provides essential feedback concerning the effectiveness of bibliographic instruction and the degree to which students may effectively select and use information. Without such evaluation, the library media specialist continues on a blind track in faltering attempts to teach information literacy.

How Teachers "Plan"

Linda Lachance Wolcott (1994), from the Instructional Technology Department of Utah State University, has made the case that a greater understanding on the part of library media specialists as to how teachers plan or don't plan will strengthen instructional partnerships. Certification programs in many states are moving beyond basic teacher certification for library media specialist to require successful classroom teaching experience as well. Evidence of successful teaching practice is now seen in many position announcements for new media specialists. Knowledge of technology and resources as they can be applied to instruction, along with management of information access and control, have become more common job descriptors than ten years ago.

Wolcott noted that when planning does take place between library media specialist and classroom teacher, it is seldom formal. Often spur-of-the-moment plans take place because of lack of time, lack of awareness for the need of collaborative participation, or because the "library lesson" may be seen as peripheral to the major learning task. Certainly, some library media specialists are in familiar territory with teachers who have worked with them before and there are tasks that are quick and routine to plug in. Formal planning, however, can increase interaction and effectiveness in the long run (Turner 1991, 1993). Formal planning is more likely to lead to integration of information literacy skills for units that support inquiry learning.

Wolcott describes two types of planning. "Incremental planning" is characterized by a short problem-solving stage, brief unit planning, and reliance on trying activities in the classroom. "Comprehensive planning" gives more attention to the unit as a whole and attempts to specify plans thoroughly prior to teaching. Her review of the research on teacher planning practices indicates that:

- Planning is a mental activity. Very little of what teachers plan is committed to paper. Teachers form a "mental image" of the lesson and activities often based on routines or sets of procedures. Objectives often are conveyed verbally, if at all. This practice increases the chance of the students misunderstanding the intent of a lesson especially when written statements are not available, explained, or practiced.

- Planning in practice is nonlinear. Ideas or lessons may originate from several of the stages often described in a more formal model. Textbook outlines, schedules, and personal interests may influence the origin of the lesson more than any reflective thoughts on evaluation or analysis of student learning needs.

- Planning is influenced by published curriculum. Although teachers may not tend to write their own plans, those which have been written for them through state, district, or textbook guides often are employed. Tailoring curriculum to meet local needs and custom design of lessons based on predetermined entry level skills for the specific students at hand usually is not attempted. To engage teachers in the planning process, Wolcott identifies several strategies. These are based on the assumption that the library media specialist will be in tune with the normal planning habits of the teachers and thus engagements may be more likely after the teacher is into a unit, rather than pre-planning a unit far in advance. Wolcott's suggestions are paraphrased and elaborated on here:

- School library media specialists should seek occasions to talk with teachers about what they are teaching and enjoy teaching. Informal moments may arise concerning specific resources the teacher is seeking for today's or this week's lesson. A quick follow-up with the teacher may open possible collaborative teaching when the lesson is presented again.

- School library media specialists should involve teachers in weeding of resources as well as selection and purchase of resources. Often through the weeding process, teachers can see gaps in the resource collection and conversations can begin as to how these might be filled, along with resource-based units in the future.

- School library media specialists should think of planning as a series of increasingly broader-reaching centric circles radiating out from a central focus. From the instructional task at hand, what stages might evolve, over time, that will move the activity into a more resource based experience? Build from where the teacher is and together modify as the teacher learns of more resource options and the library media specialist learns of the specific instructional objectives intended.

- School library media specialists should accommodate various types and styles of planning. Often planning and teaching is a solitary activity. Teachers need to be offered teaming approaches that will prove to be not only more successful for the students, but also save time and concentrate on objectives the teacher finds meaningful. While the library media specialist will introduce additional information literacy skills to a lesson, these should be seen as integrated with the other skills and not simply add-ons. Some teachers just may not be open to teaming and success may be limited to showing the teacher information skills they can incorporate on their own. On other occasions, success may be finding a teacher who becomes a team player for the first time.

- School library media specialists should provide leadership. Often scheduling, resource management, and consolidation of ideas and objectives must be completed by one team member who has a vision of where the lesson can go in the future as a unit to involve different areas of the curriculum and several teachers. Instructional media specialists are at their best when they take this leadership role.

Models for Formal Planning

While it is reasonable to become acquainted with common teacher planning practices, analysis of local teacher planning behaviors and needs is critical. Just because most teachers push aside planning methods as cumbersome jargon, the conclusion should not be that haphazard lessons are successful ones. The instructional media specialist also will want to become well-versed in the elements of more formal planning. These elements, while not always used in a linear or sequential manner, still provide the context for the questions, ideas, and conversations (informal or formal) to engage teachers in the possibilities. More important, these models serve as a map to make more meaningful lesson planning a reality.

If we stay in a world of fragmented solitary planning, with no communication of objectives, or verbal communication only, and curriculum guided by forces outside of the creativity of our best local teachers, we remain in a very narrow, textbook-dominated educational environment. We waste the reason why we exist, regardless of how much principals, teachers, and other library media specialists may not realize the potential of our instructional role. Much depends on attitude as well as expertise. Without the desire to make a difference in the educational structure, time for planning and meaningful conversations don't stand a chance.

Multidisciplinary Planning: Elements of the Instructional Resource Plan (IRP)

Movement from a basic lesson to a series of activities coordinated with several teachers takes instruction into a full unit of study. Talents of the teachers involved must be organized and managed, just as resources are, by the instructional media specialist. There is a fundamental difference between the reactive levels of the library media specialist and the interactive levels of the instructional media specialist. Management of ideas, talents, expertise, methods, analysis of needs, and evaluation are as important, if not more important, than management of access to resources.

The fourteen elements listed and discussed here are based on my twenty-five years of teaching the development of Instructional Resource Plans (IRP) at Indiana University and other schools, as well as seven years of experience as a high school instructional media specialist. Nearly all of these elements I have learned from others, practicing library media specialists and other teachers. Not all of the elements must be in place for a unit to be successful, nor would the

planning process always follow the order in which the elements are listed.

Each element can tie to many others. The spark for a more formal unit plan can come within any element as noted several times in the following detailed description.

- **IRP Objectives.** Objectives, clearly stated in observable terms to direct student performance and evaluation, are essential. These may be drawn from proven local classroom objectives, district or state guides, or national standards. Information Power provides not only nine standards for student performance in information literacy, but also specific objectives or indicators along with statements that illustrate levels of proficiency and relevance to different areas of the curriculum. Are there entry-level skills that need to be mastered prior to introducing these objectives? Are these objectives reflected in lessons, activities, and other elements of the plan that follow? New standards can and should spark new ideas for lessons and units as well as bring together previous successful lessons that stood alone, but gain strength as skills can be connected through a full unit.

  – Learning objectives should be tied to information literacy learning indicators whenever possible (AASL 1998).

  – Learning objective should be tied to knowledge content standards found in the teacher's state guide. Several national Web sites will like the teacher to these standards:

  Mid-continent Research for Education and Learning http://www.mcrel.org/standards-benchmarks/

  Developing Education Standards http:// edstandards.org/Standards.html

  StateStandards.com http://www.statestandards.com/

- **IRP Context.** Think about and discuss the context for the unit. What interests and excites the students, you, and other teachers? Do you know critical characteristics about the students to be involved?

Are they more or less creative than previous groups? Do some important skills seem in need of reinforcement? Are there teachers who have interests and expertise along with a willingness to experiment with a teaming unit? Have they demonstrated in the past the willingness to commit to a project and share ideas? For the first attempts at such units, a small team of two to four will be plenty. Do not force all areas of the curriculum to be represented in the unit or project. Select those that seem most likely to cooperate, and plan to add more teachers as the unit matures through several intervals of implementation. Extensive units that place the instructional media specialist in a lead role are likely not to number more than three or four for a given semester even in the hands of the most skilled and efficient specialist. First timers may want to begin with one such unit for the first year or two.

- **IRP Time Frame.** Schedule the important events that come to mind for brainstorming, resource considerations, lesson planning, implementation, and evaluation. Through e-mail communication or on a calendar posted in the teachers' lounge for all to see, block and reserve times. Common lunch periods and evenings will come into play. Some school corporations pay for additional summer days for in-depth planning.

- **IRP Lessons and Roles.** Usually a full unit of study will involve several lessons and activities. Determine which teacher takes the lead for each lesson and what joint roles, if any, other team members will play. In some cases, this will mean individual teachers will facilitate different groups of students on either different skills to meet different ability levels or to provide for small group interaction. In other cases, one teacher may take the lead for full- or large-group presentations. In such cases, other teachers may have time to work on other elements of the unit. In all cases, the instructional media specialist and other teachers may find that teaching in tandem is beneficial. This does not

mean one teaches while the other sits. It means both or several have presentation roles in the lesson and all engage the learners. In hands-on skills practice, for example, one teacher may present the steps and methods to the entire group while other teachers serve as "rovers" to work with individual students and their specific problems. Sample lessons should be sketched out with individual objectives and necessary resources noted. Different orders of the deliveries of these lessons may depend on scaffolding of objectives and skills. Although never exact, some attention should be given to how practice of some skills is necessary and must be mastered before moving on to higher or more complex skills.

- **IRP Questions.** As a teaching team, brainstorm the questions you would expect the average student to be able to answer following their participation in the unit. Do these questions represent all of the key content? If the list becomes very long, determine the five or ten most critical questions. These should tie back to the objectives and standards. In some cases, these questions may create new objectives, lessons, and activities. The brainstorming involved in generating these questions may serve as a model for one of the early exercises in any unit with students, to engage them in the generation of questions they want to explore over the coming unit. Who, What, and How questions are often the first to be raised. Remember, for strong inquiry units, there should be lots of Why questions.

- **IRP Resources.** This element includes the traditional role the library media specialist has played in the tie with instruction. What resources are available to support the unit? What access is possible to additional materials through other schools, the public library, or other libraries in the area? Are there good Internet resources suitable for the age group involved? Are there new materials on the market that should be considered, or previewed, and ordered? The less traditional use of resources, but more important in the plan development, involves idea generation. What have you read or seen that gives you good ideas for this unit? Read widely, explore and be open to ideas from all media. Reading a good book or magazine article or ideas from viewing that PBS special last week often spark further unit planning. In some cases, that special resource is the seed of the idea for beginning the planning for the possible unit, so stage one might be right here. In other cases, immersion in unit planning triggers a more sensitive awareness of potential resources. This may happen even without a great deal of systematic searching as newspaper articles, television news, or discussions with friends will suddenly include notice of items that would have been ignored before.

- **IRP Search.** A more systematic search for additional resources may be necessary. Time invested under the management of the instructional media specialist may include examination of both resource guides used to locate library media materials as well as journals and guides used by classroom teachers for resources. These are not the same, and both should be explored as there is often little duplication and both will contain potentially useful materials. Examination or preview of additional resources available at other schools and libraries should be a task for a team member or two.

- **IRP Packaging.** Gathering the resources and materials for the unit can involve most of the team members, although, again this is a traditional role often played by the library media specialist. It should not be the only role, nor should it be one isolated for the library media specialist alone. Arrangements to alert the local public library of the up-coming unit can be a responsibility of a classroom teacher on the team. The local children's or youth public librarian may be willing to serve as a community member on the team and provide readers with advisory and reference services specifically in support of

the unit. For some units, special resource corners in the library media center that highlight the unit serve to not only provide a central place to gather the resources in a convenient location, but bring attention to the unit and publicize such multidisciplinary collaboration. Packaging also may involve composing a webography along with the usual bibliography so that primary sites can be located quickly and provide a jump start for students. Some instructional media specialists construct a WebQuest, an online package of resources to support many elements of the plan as well as instructional activity links. Human resources who are willing to be interviewed by students or come as guest speakers may be included in this packaging. At the end of the unit, a compilation of quality resources should be available in a local resource kit, ready for use the next time the unit is implemented, and available for loan to other schools. The objective is to manage information resources for efficient access and to help learners move quickly beyond the location stage and into the information use stages.

- **IRP Common Piece of Literature.** Many resource-based lessons, and eventually units, spring from a strong and emotional piece of young adult literature. This can serve as a common base for all involved in the unit, teachers and students. From this piece can come strands for a broader theme and ties to other relevant literature pieces to promote. Centered on this piece can be teacher and student read-alouds in class, and often serves as the basis for dramatic outlets to student products in stories, essays, plays, and multimedia. Students who have not had the desire to read before often are engaged when this one title drives an exciting unit. Although not always the case, and not required for a resource-based unit to be successful, a good young adult novel can stimulate a great many themes for learning. A classroom set or a copy for all students involved often is provided if the budget will allow. Clusters of children's books, a major motion picture, or even a classic nonfiction book are all candidates for a common base of information from which grows the purpose for the unit. If the materials are of quality and engage learners in thoughtful questions, the tie to many of the standards is natural. While the usual approach is to identify the learning objectives first, some young adult titles are so powerful that they deserve not only promotion for reading for pleasure but have a place in driving the curriculum as well.

- **IRP Community.** Community involvement is high on the list of most school districts, but such ties should be considered not just because of the insistence of the administration. Community experts can provide valuable information on some topics as guest speakers or by responding to student questions over e-mail. Parents may help with field trips and some may play the role of tutor. Depending on the theme of the unit, local businesses and organizations may have resources to contribute. Recruiting such community support should be based on a clear vision as to how it will enhance students' learning.

- **IRP Evaluation.**

  - At least two types of evaluation should be considered, with the first being the task of evaluating student performance. Specific criteria should come from the standards and objectives. A checklist or a rubric of criteria with levels of performance may be useful. Clear understanding on the part of the teaching team and the students as to what will be evaluated and by whom is important to convey. Student performance in such a unit should be reported within the context of how students are graded for the given school. Often multidisciplinary units allow for evaluation of multiple skills. Some students who struggle with initial phases of the unit will shine at the performance and presentation stages. A composite of the evaluations based on different skills from different evaluators should generate a comprehensive judgment of the learner's accomplishments.

  - The second type, evaluation of the unit and its lessons and activities, is essential. Depending on the length of the unit, there may need to be a mid-point, formal evaluation by the team. Adjustments are thus made for the next implementation with emphasis on identification of new resources that will support the unit in the future. Should roles be combined, eliminated, or expanded in some manner? Are there new areas for future student evaluation, and who will develop the evaluation method and take the lead?

- **IRP Budget.** While it may seem very much out of place in lesson planning, there can be expenses that stand in the way of moving an otherwise strong resource-based unit into action-expenses for materials, duplication, field trips, guest speakers, and classroom sets of common literature pieces. While the library media center budget and departmental budgets may cover some of these expenses, a well-organized unit plan will attract dollars from the principal's budget, and from the local parent/teacher associations as well. The elements addressed in this Instructional Resource Plan are the common elements normally required to detail in a formal grant application. Practice in development of the IRP can lead directly to seeking additional funds through school district and state agencies.

- **IRP Celebration.** A resource-based unit that involves several teachers and dozens of students in a special theme deserves celebration. Often a special evening or open house in the library media center will provide the opportunity for students to display what they have accomplished. Other classes in school may visit during the day and parents and friends in the evening. Often students remain with their displays to explain and talk about what they learned, similar to the science fair format.

- **IRP Modeling Inquiry.** These multidisciplinary units provide the opportunity for the instructional media specialist and other teachers to model how they learn. Create segments in which teachers raise questions they want to explore. They should ask and talk through information problems and how they plan to find solutions as clear examples for the students. They should explore and participate in the projects as much as the students and share their successes and frustrations. Instructional media specialists and other teachers become co-investigators in inquiry projects. They explore and reflect as well as facilitate and evaluate.

The Dream Weavers Model

The Dream Weavers are composed of a group of eleven teachers in the Pike Township School Corporation of Indianapolis. Led by a cadre of specialists in library/media, art, music, and enrichment, these educators base their planning at the Fishback Creek Public Academy on the ICAN learning philosophy ,learning through multiple skills. ICAN is a state experimental program that provides a computerized interdisciplinary curriculum to developmental benchmarks and allows the compilation and analysis of individual student records. As a part of the mission of this academy, all learners are involved in meaningful activities that address their strengths and provide opportunities for growth.

The Dream Weavers Model has been illustrated (see Figure Part 3.11) and outlined by Kym Kramer, library media specialist, and Nicole Rose, art teacher.

- **Align and Combine.** Begin with classroom curriculum. Brainstorm and align additional areas. Approximately eight to twelve weeks prior to the next grading period, the Dream Weaver Team meets to share what they have planned in their classroom. A list is made of key lessons and activities. The specialist cadre members chime in and list from their areas ideas for providing common learning threads based on media, literature, stories, art, and music projects.

- **Design and Define.** Core planners design the project, weaving the curriculum together. Define each area's responsibilities.

- **Time line.** Create calendars and a linear flow chart. Show responsibilities. List benchmarks and critical due dates of the project. These are provided for all to see so that, at any point, team members can easily see what is going on in any room. Due dates make team weavers accountable to others.

- **Refine.** Meet with the team, review calendars, and make final changes just a few weeks prior to implementation.

- **Assign Baselines.** Discuss what will be graded. Decide who will be responsible for grading specific skills. Set due dates.

- **Implement the Divine! Just Do It!** But communicate frequently to be sure things are on track! The specialists weave their activities among the classes to support, enhance, and extend the classroom activities.

- **Shine! Celebrate!** After weeks of work, give children and teachers the chance to shine and enjoy the products of their learning efforts.

- **Assess for Next Time.** Debrief as a team on how program goals were met or not. Did the weaving activities strengthen classroom activities and support learning objectives?

- **No Confines!** Continue to weave. Projects are never ending-poetry, bookmaking, insect kits, play and story creation, multimedia, and storytelling festivals with the kids as stars!

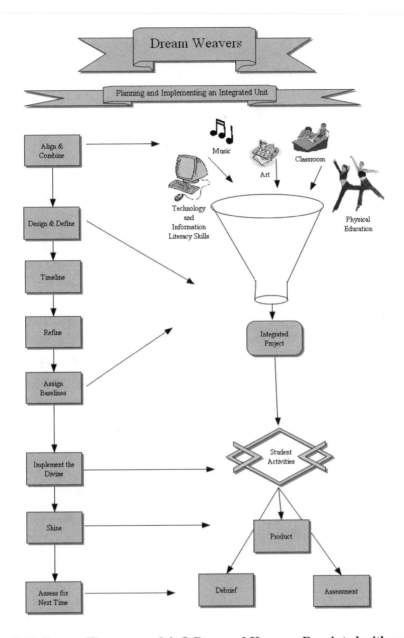

Figure Part3.11. Dream Weavers model. © Rose and Kramer. Reprinted with permission.

Key Instructional Strategies During the Lesson

The Association for Supervision and Curriculum Development provides many current guides to help implement instruction. One of their most popular is the 2001 *Classroom Instruction That Works* (Marzano, Pickering, and Pollock). To improve instructional effectiveness and to help make nearly any lesson plan a success, keep in mind these recommendations for instructional strategies during delivery of the unit:

- Guide students in identifying and articulating what they already know about the topics.

- Provide students with ways of thinking about the topic in advance.

- Ask students to compare the [their] new knowledge with what was known prior to the lesson.

- Have student keep notes on the knowledge addressed in the unit.

- Help students represent [and share] knowledge in nonlinguistic ways.

- Ask students to work individually, but also at times in cooperative groups—[depending on the activity and the need for interaction].

References

American Association of School Librarians and the Association for Educational Communications Technology (AASL & AECT). (1998). *Information power: Building Partnerships for Learning.*. American Library Association.

AskERIC Education Information. "Lesson plan." http://ericir.syr.edu/Virtual/Lessons/Guide.shtml (accessed November 15, 2004).

Callison, D. (1987). "Evaluator and Educator: The School Media Specialist." *Tech Trends* 32 (5): 24–29.

Callison, D. (2002). "The Twentieth Century school Library Media Research Record." In *The Encyclopedia of Library and Information Science,* edited by Allen Kent, 70: 339—368. Marcel Dekker.

Craver, K. W. (1986). "The Changing Role of the High School Library Media Specialist: 1950–(1984)." *School Library Media Quarterly* 14 (4): 183–191.

Marzano, R. J., D. J. Pickering, and J. E. Pollock. (2001). *Classroom Instruction That Works: Research-Based Strategies for Increasing Student Achievement.* Association for Supervision and Curriculum Development.

Pickard, P. W. (1993). "Current Research: The Instructional Consultant Role of the School Library Media Specialist." *School Library Media Quarterly* 21 (2). Also available in *School Library Media Research* at http://www.ala.org/aasl/SLMR/slmr_resources/select_pickard.html (accessed November 10, 2004).

Turner, P. M. (1991). "Information Skills and Instructional Consulting: A Synergy." *School Library Media Quarterly* 20 (1): 13–18.

Turner, P. M. (1993). *Helping Teachers Teach.* 2d ed. Libraries Unlimited.

Wolcott, L. Lachance. (1994). "Understanding How Teachers Plan: Strategies for Successful Instructional Partnerships." *School Library Media Quarterly* 22 (3). Also available in *School Library Media Research* at http://www.ala.org/aasl/SLMR/slmr_resources/select_wolcott.html (accessed November 10, 2004).

Literacy

Daniel Callison

Modern applied research and educational theory have combined to broaden the meaning of literacy as we should view it today. A true understanding of literacy is certainly more than basic reading and writing. The dynamics of literacy across learning environments also is much more than what has been sparked by the technologies of the Information Age. Literacy has several rather traditional aspects that are now emerging in new ways as we gain a greater understanding of interactive learning.

Shirley Brice Heath (1996), professor of Anthropology, English, and Education at Stanford, voiced several aspects of the new literacy during a recent interview at Indiana University. Heath places her definition in the more powerful learning contexts outside of the school room. Literacy is knowing how to get information that is needed in order to get around within your environment and to get things done. Literacy is knowing how to select, reject, or revise information from a variety of access points for use in a host of different communication channels. Literacy is a dynamic skill requiring fluency in a variety of decoding situations.

"Information fluency" would counter the common core of national cultural literacy described in 1987 by E. D. Hirsch Jr. In addition to an understanding of a common series of names, events, facts, values, and ideas, information fluency involves the ability to move from one community of literacy to another. The maturing, information-fluent student sees value in the differences and relationships from the literacy of one environment to another. That student applies the process skills to become productive and communicative across a variety of audiences. This does not necessarily mean the student is "multilingual" but that the information-fluent student is "multiliterate" and understands the information search, analysis, and synthesis necessary within and across a variety of settings.

Heath (1991) says that today's youth would scoff at limited definitions of literacy based only on a common set of reading and writing mechanical skills. Literacy is both fluid across disciplines and ever-changing with the growth and maturation of the learner. Therefore, what is a strong measure of "being literate" will change and evolve with the learning content, physical and mental growth of the learner, and the variety of audiences and contexts with which the learner must deal, especially in the workforce or "real world." Schools continue to do students the disservice of limiting the scope of literacy skills and regimenting learning experiences to the point that such environments are not authentic, but isolated from critical thinking that really matters for survival and success.

Beyond the ability to read the modern codes and icons of the electronic age, students may begin to reach new levels of literacy when literature is presented in a more challenging and dynamic manner. According to Heath, literature response and text interactions should mean that literature never says the same thing twice. The growing and changing literate student moves from the common meaning given in text to adding his or her own personal meaning. Each time one returns to text, even the same text, one has changed and holds new experiences ready to trigger new meaning. The mark of a quality or classic literary writer is that he or she has layered within the text the figures of speech and nuances necessary for the reader to discover new thoughts with each revisit. Critical thinking in this context involves not only problem solving but the insight to find richer linkages to historical and contemporary issues through literature.

Quality text is not stagnant, but turns on the reader, and actually interacts with the maturation of the learner. Heath concludes that literacy is not acquired in a vacuum. Nor does it spring fully formed from our minds, like Athena from the head of Zeus. It is an evolutionary process changing from generation to generation and from life to life.

Emergent Literacy

Stuart McNaughton (1995), professor of Education at University of Auckland, has written of the socialization model of emergent literacy and argues that child development should be seen as occurring through complex and dynamic exchanges between its parts. The parts are, on the one hand, children and their actions to make sense out of their world (their constructions); and, on the other hand, the social and cultural process in everyday activities, such as what guidance is given, and how that guidance is given. All factors are dependent on each other as well as a part of each other, hence the term "co-construction."

According to McNaughton, one of the central functions of the family is to socialize children into the ways of thinking and acting that are appropriate for the community of which the family is a member. His model involves ambient, joint, and personal activities to engage the child in the expertise and relationships of literacy. Jean M. Casey (1997) has summarized these elements in more tangible terms as the basic ingredients for early literacy:

- a positive attitude toward writing and reading what they have written,

- listening to adults reading to them, and

- being surrounded by interesting books.

The Multitude of Literacies

The new *Literacy Dictionary* (Harris and Hodges 1995) defines "literacy" as the minimal ability to read and write in a designated language, as well as a mindset or way of thinking about the use of reading and writing in everyday life. It differs from simple reading and writing in its assumption of an understanding of the appropriate use of these abilities within a print-based society. Literacy, therefore, requires active, autonomous engagement with print and stresses the role of the individual in generating, as well as receiving and assigning, independent interpretations to messages.

In current usage, the term implies an interaction between social demands and individual competence. Thus, the levels of literacy required for social functioning can and have varied across cultures and across time within the same culture. Today literacy is understood as a continuum, anchored at the bottom by illiteracy. Of equal importance to illiteracy, however, is aliteracy—the unwillingness to use literacy even though the capability is present.

Representative Types of Literacy

Adult literacy: A level of literacy that enables a person in or about to enter the workforce to function effectively both as an individual and as a member of society.

Autonomous literacy: Independent literacy; the individual's ability to make independent judgments of meanings in text.

Community literacy: Reading, other than that done in school, associated with participation in neighborhood activities, local government, church, and social organizations.

Computer literacy: Possession of the skills and knowledge necessary for operating a computer. Generally thought of as familiarity with the personal computer and the ability to create and manipulate documents and data via word processing, spreadsheets, databases, and other software. Understanding of the importance and implementation of electronic technologies to communication and learning.

Craft literacy: Knowledge of the skills, tools, and procedures for meeting the standards of a given craft.

Critical literacy: The use of language in all of its forms, as in thinking, solving problems, and communicating solutions; the ability to participate in challenging and changing power structures.

Family literacy: Literacy efforts or activities that involve more than one generation; activities may range from study skills to reading aloud to foster appreciation for literature.

Functional literacy: A level of reading and writing sufficient for everyday life but not for completely autonomous activity.

Information literacy: The ability to identify an information need or question; the ability to find, evaluate, and use information effectively in personal and professional situations; the ability to locate, analyze, evaluate, synthesize, and selectively use information from different sources regardless of format and to effectively communicate or present results to relevant audiences.

Intergenerational literacy: The efforts of second- and third-generation adults in a family, usually an extended family, to help themselves or others in the family learn to read and write.

Media literacy: The ability of a citizen to access, analyze, and produce information for specific outcomes. Those who advocate media literacy recognize the influence that television, motion pictures, recorded music, and other mass media have on people daily. The media literacy movement also recognizes the fact that educators have traditionally spent a preponderance of time teaching reading, and little time focusing on decoding media. Education aims to increase students' understanding and enjoyment of how media work, how they (media) produce meaning, how they are organized, and how they construct their own reality.

Network literacy: Awareness of the range and uses of global, networked information resources and services; understanding by which networked information is generated and managed; ability to retrieve specific information from a data network by using a range of information mining or discovery tools.

Quantitative literacy: Fluency in reading and writing computational data; numeracy.

Real-world literacy: The literacy and numeracy skills needed to survive in the nonacademic world.

Survival literacy: Minimal reading, writing, and often numeracy skills needed to get by in everyday life in the target or local community language.

Technology literacy: A complex, integrated process that involves people, procedures, ideas, devices, and organization for analyzing problems and devising, implementing, evaluating, and managing solutions to those problems, involved in all aspects of learning.

Television literacy: Competence in using television to enhance daily life and to acquire social power; competence in interpreting the successive patterns, or mosaics, of television stimuli that are characterized by low visual orientation and high involvement with maximal interplay of all the senses; teleliteracy.

Vernacular literacy: The ability to read, write, and sometimes speak the common language of a speech community; popular literacy.

Visual literacy: The ability to understand and use images, including the ability to think, learn, and express oneself in terms of images; the ability to interpret and communicate with respect to visual symbols in nonprint media, as visual literacy in viewing television, art, and nature.

Workplace literacy: Literacy that focuses attention on individuals in relation to the societal and economic concerns of a nation; on a more local application, knowledge and command of the communication tasks to be successful on the job.

References

Casey, J. M. (1997). *Early Literacy: The Empowerment of Technology.* Libraries Unlimited.

Harris, T. L., and R. E. Hodges, eds. (1995). *The Literacy Dictionary.* International Reading Association.

Heath, S. Brice. (1991). *Children of Promise: Literate Activity in Linguistically and Culturally Diverse Classrooms* NEA Professional Library.

Heath, S. Brice. (1996). *Ways with Words: Language, Life, and Work in Communities and Classrooms*. Cambridge University Press.

Hirsch, E. D. (1987). *Cultural Literacy: What Every American Needs to Know*. Houghton Mifflin.

McNaughton, S. (1995). *Patterns of Emergent Literacy: Processes of Development and Transition*. Oxford University Press.

For Further Reading

Spitzer, K. L., M. B. Eisenberg, and C. A. Lowe. (2004). *Information Literacy: Essential Skills for the Information Age*. Libraries Unlimited.

Tyner, K. (1998). *Literacy in a Digital World: Teaching and Learning in the Age of Information*. Lawrence Erlbaum Associates.

Wolf, A. Shelby, and S. Brice Heath. (1992). *The Braid of Literature: Children's Worlds of Reading*. Harvard University Press.

Literature Circles

Maureen Sanders-Brunner

The literature circle is one form of emergent literacy instruction that encourages students to become information literate, independent learners, and socially responsible citizens. Emergent literacy is centered on the concept that the ability to read, analyze, and understand literature always is evolving as one continues to explore and experience literature throughout one's lifetime. Literature circles also are referred to as reading circles, literature discussion groups, and even book clubs. Edna Brabham, Assistant Professor, and Susan Villaume, Associate Professor, Department of Curriculum and Teaching, Auburn University, refer to literature circles as the "grand conversation" (2000). This term, coined by Mary Ann Eeds in 1989, describes a specific and thoughtful discussion of literature as opposed to the more one-dimensional question-and-answer sessions often practiced in the classroom for the purpose of assessing reading comprehension (Eeds and Wells 1989). Literature circles combine the idea of the grand conversation with individual responsibility, small-group participation, and theme-related activities.

Regardless of the term used to define literature circles, the basic concept behind this form of literacy instruction is the ability of a learner to choose and read a piece of literature and then within the structure of a small group cooperatively discuss the literature in critical, thoughtful, and personal ways. The literature used is often a novel, but it can take any form. Picture books, trade books, poetry, newspaper or magazine articles, and professional literature all can be read and discussed in critical and creative ways within a literature circle. Often, each member of the group has a specific role to play, excerpt to read, or related presentation to create.

Writing activities such as reflective journals and vocabulary exercises also play an important part in the process. Depending on the needs of the group, the library media specialist and classroom teacher may assume a limited role, such as facilitator or active listener, or a more authoritative role, such as participant or mediator.

Multiple books and articles have been written on the procedural aspect of literature circles. Several "Literature Circle Guides" for popular juvenile and young adult novels also are available for teachers, some on the Internet free of charge. The methods of implementation are as varied as the possible selection of topics and literature. Of course, the "how-to" of literature circles is important and provides educators a practical frame of reference; however, Brabham and Villaume (2000) caution against the quest for a prescriptive model. The implementation of literature circles should be student centered and reflect the curricular and personal needs of the learner at a specific time. As the needs change and the participants become increasingly self-sufficient, some methods may become obsolete and hinder growth if not revised or abandoned.

Alignment with Standards

As teachers of information literacy, we should be concerned first with why literature circles are important and how they encourage the effective use of ideas and information. By nature, literature circles provide a diverse and valued learning environment. In literature circles, students become information literate by reading authentic literature, thinking about the messages and intent of the author, listening to peers discuss their own interpretations, cooperatively participating in discussions with others, and reflectively drawing their own personal and relevant connections. Often literature circles are a catalyst for questions and further inquiry on a specific theme or genre of literature. The practice of effective literature circles can be the instrument for ensuring that information literacy standards, as set forth in *Information Power: Building Partnerships for Learning* (AASL and AECT 1998), are achieved at the highest level of proficiency. Depending on the application of the literature circle, each Information Literacy, Independent Learning, and Social Responsibility standard is potentially addressed in varying degrees and at different times within the framework of the curriculum.

Information Literacy Standards

Information literacy standards require that students access information effectively and efficiently, evaluate information critically and competently, and use information accurately and creatively. Literature circles provide a rich and relevant process to achieve these abilities. Brabham and Villaume (2000) discuss how students involved in literature circles can have continuous opportunities to make predictions, construct visual images, create connections, make decisions about the relevance of information, solve word and text problems, and creatively construct meaning. Allowing students to practice and become increasingly skilled in reading, reflecting, discussing, and internalizing meaning, teachers ensure that students will take ownership of their learning and understanding of the literature. Many times, literature circles include the opportunity for students to present the information and ideas generated within the discussion group. When students are empowered to choose the format of the presentation, they are held accountable for their learning while encouraged to use information creatively.

Independent Learning Standards

According to *Information Power,* students who are independent learners pursue information related to personal interests, appreciate literature and other creative expressions of information, and strive for excellence in information seeking and knowledge generation. Lit-erature circles can promote independent learning standards when students are allowed the freedom to choose information that they find interesting or relevant. Whether students make decisions about the theme or subject they will study, or which title they will read, the power to choose motivates students to continue to be vested personally in future information seeking. According to Joseph Sanacore (1999), assistant professor at Long Island University, students experience growth and confidence as readers when they are given the ability to self-select their reading material, or at least the themes that are most interesting. Bonnie Burns (1998), Reading Specialist and Elementary Principal, River Forest Illinois Public School, references Linda Gambrell (1996), Associate Dean, College of Education, University of Maryland, that research has consistently shown that the reading material students find most interesting are those they self-select.

Social Responsibility Standards

Social responsibility is achieved when students contribute positively to the learning community and society, recognize the importance of information in a democratic society, practice ethical behavior, and participate effectively in groups to pursue and generate information. Burns (1998) states that the study of literature in the small group environment moves students from individually creating meaning to socially negotiating that meaning with others. The ability to work with others and collaboratively generate information is inherent to the process of the literature circles.

In literature circles, students often are grouped according to their interest or literature choice rather than their reading level or ability. Kathryn Mitchell Pierce (1998), a teacher at Glenridge Elementary in Clayton, Missouri, finds that this type of group mix makes learning more equitable. The personal and close setting of a literature circle provides a safe opportunity for more participation by each group member, whereas a discussion in a larger class setting might be dominated by a select group of students. Children have an opportunity to learn about their own unique strengths and recognize the strengths of others. When groups have a mix of cultures, gender, abilities, and socio-economic backgrounds, literature circles become the training ground for responsibly contributing to a culturally diverse and global community.

Conversations about what students deem relevant within the literature can open up dialogue with other peers about their culture thereby drawing a personal connection between reading and real life. Sandy Kaser, teacher, Robins Elementary in Tucson, Arizona, and Kathy G. Short, associate professor at the University of Arizona, find that when students are given the opportunity to relate to literature by collaboratively reflecting on their own experiences and through dialogue with fellow students about their thoughts, literature has a greater and more permanent impact on their lives (1998).

Literature circles provide an educationally relevant and authentic form of reading and literacy instruction that is long lasting and meaningful by allowing students of all ages and abilities control over literature choice, time for discussion, accountability for what they learn, and a personal connection to the world in which they live and work.

Opportunities for Collaboration

At the heart of *Information Power* is the directive for library media specialists to implement and support literacy initiatives through collaboration and instruction. According to Kathy Latrobe, professor, University of Oklahoma, and Anne Masters, director of Media Services and Instructional Technology, Norman (Oklahoma) Public Schools, the library media program should ensure the

- Continuous development and maintenance of a collection of both professional and student level material that supports instructional excellence;

- Design and implementation of instructional activities that reflect current research and practice;

- Evaluation, acquisition, provision, and promotion of information resources to meet the learning needs of all learners;

- Effective and enthusiastic use of books, videos, films, and other multimedia;

- Encouragement of reading for enjoyment and information;

- Analysis of individual learning needs;

- Activities that address the diverse needs of the learning community; and

- Demonstration of the attitudes and skills of an independent lifelong learner. (Latrobe and Masters 1999)

The implementation and success of literature circles can be improved greatly by the involvement of the school library media specialist. Alongside traditional library support such as collection development, selection training, professional development, and technology instruction, library media specialists can incorporate their expertise in facilitating, budget and funding issues, and collaborative planning and instruction to provide a well-rounded literacy curriculum that includes the implementation of literature circles.

Literature circles allow for virtually unlimited opportunities for collaboration between library media specialists and classroom teachers. Depending on the willingness of the classroom teacher, collaboration can happen on the most basic level, such as providing materials, to the most advanced level of collaborative curriculum planning and instruction. For example, even though literature circles are viewed primarily as a holistic form of instruction, research demonstrates the ability to mix literature circles with more text-based, basal type instruction. According to Pierce (1998), new teachers as well as established teachers may be somewhat nervous about accountability factors when implementing literature circles and find it better for their classrooms to ease into discussion groups during free reading periods while allowing language arts time to continue to be devoted to basal activities. These teachers also may be cautious of or resist the idea of collaborative teaching.

Kathryn Au (1997), professor, College of Education, University of Hawaii, states that implementing literature circles will be most effective when there is a full implementation; however, small steps should be made toward the total emersion of this type of instruction when a different method has been the norm. In this case, the library media specialist could work cooperatively with the classroom teacher to help build text sets for the classroom library or by providing professional literature on the implementation and benefits of literature circles.

The implementation of literature circles is most effective when modeled by the teacher or library media specialist. When offering students a variety of literature choices, the library media specialist can collaborate with classroom teachers by giving booktalks on the different choices offered to the students. During the booktalk session, the library media specialist and classroom teacher together can model effective reading techniques and acceptable group discussion. When this is done prior to initiating student-driven activities, students are given the framework for expected behavior and can practice in a safe environment before they take control. Also, when library media specialists regularly read aloud in the classroom or media center, students are exposed to a variety of literature selections and may begin to form genre and subject matter preferences.

The library media specialist also can provide instruction on how to make independent and informed decisions on how to choose quality literature that fits the specific needs, interests, and reading levels of the students. To ensure a good fit between reader and literature, Sanacore (1999) suggests that the teacher or library media specialist show children selection skills through "think aloud" instruction. Walking students through a literature selection demonstrates how to determine if the topic is interesting or if the material is too difficult and also empowers students to become better consumers of information and to avoid pitfalls that may lead to reading aversion.

The use of media center facilities can add an aspect of collaboration that supports literacy circles. By collaboratively planning, library media specialists and teachers could encourage students to go beyond the classroom exercises and begin an inquiry project based on questions that were uncovered during group discussions. In this case, the library media specialist can assist the classroom teachers through content specific bibliographic instruction.

Literature circles, like most forms of reading instruction, are most effective when children are allowed quiet time to read in school. In this case, the library media center also can be a refuge for silent reading time when needed. The students, teachers, and library media specialist all can take advantage of the comfortable atmosphere of the media center to delve into their reading materials and afterwards discuss what they read with the class or write their experiences in a journal.

Teachers as Readers

One of the most powerful ways a library media specialist can support and encourage literature circles within the school is to implement and facilitate a "Teachers as Readers" (TARs) group within their school. The mission of the library media program includes the goal of ensuring that staff as well as students are effective users of information and ideas. By taking a leadership role in professional level literature circles, library media specialists help teachers become better readers and encourage them to teach their students the same skills more effectively.

As the organizer of a TARs group, the library media specialist might lead the group in discussion, instruct teachers on how to select the literature for the reading circle, help find funding for materials, incorporate the idea into a "students as readers" group, promote the program annually, share their group experiences with students during library time, and show teachers how to share their experiences with their students.

Within the TARs group, classroom teachers, administrators, and other staff members voluntarily get together to read and discuss books for personal and classroom activities. Maribeth Carmichael (2001), library media specialist, Sherando High School, Stephens City, Virginia, has discussed how the TARs group in her school was so powerful that the teachers began to argue about which books they would include in classroom units. During the reading of one selection, the principal was so influenced by a book about the handicapped (Ron Jones, *The Acorn People*, Abingdon, 1978) that he bought a copy for each student in the entire ninth grade to read during English class.

During TARs groups, the library media specialist can encourage teachers to share their experiences and insights about literature with their students. Au (1997) states that when teachers share their own literacy experiences with students, they reveal themselves in a more personal light which can have a profound impact on their students. By discovering their own concepts of literacy, teachers establish a starting point for successful student-directed literature circles and writing workshops. Likewise, by actively reading and discussing their own literature experiences on a regular basis, educators are in a better position to recommend and discuss different titles with students. A TARs group gives teachers the forum that leads to sharing with their students regularly and also the environment to forge new partnerships and relationships between school educators of different grade levels and subject matter expertise. Au finds that by networking with other educators who hold similar teaching beliefs, a teacher can be more effective and confident in his or her instruction of literacy.

Collaborative Grant Writing and Funding

Library media specialists can ensure the successful implementation of literature circle instruction by securing funding for the purchase of multiple copies of literature that will be used in the literature circles and TARs groups. After finding grants and mini-grants that are available, the library media specialist can assemble the needed information and help each teacher individually or as a group apply for and secure funding.

Support for literature circles also can come from outside organizations such as local universities, other schools, or the public library. Sometimes institutions that fund activities and materials with grants will give more funds to organizations that team up and submit joint applications. School and public libraries also might be able to pool resources to offer students and instructors a more complete collection without the additional costs. Pierce (1998) suggests that library media specialists build relationships with consultants and educators from universities. These consultants can lead discussions on the implementation and ongoing assessment of literature circles during professional development sessions. By supporting teachers with relevant research from a nonevaluating third party, teachers are free to discuss their concerns, successes, and failures, as well as get educated and informed feedback.

Literature circles are shown to be a very effective method of teaching information literacy in a way that encourages students and teachers to become lifelong learners and readers. Literature circles encourage the development of skills in reading, listening, thinking, and reflecting while fostering high self-esteem and acceptance of others.

While literature circles can be incorporated easily and slowly into any curriculum, regardless of teaching beliefs and practices, there is much planning and consideration that must go into the full and successful implementation. By actively participating in collaborative planning and instruction, and providing expertise in collection development, budgeting, and professional development issues, the library media specialist can ensure that students and classroom teachers have access to the best possible literature and information literacy instruction through the effective use of literature circles.

References

American Association of School Librarians and Association for Educational Communications and Technology. (1998). *Information Power*. American Library Association.

Au, Kathryn. (1997). "Literacy for All Students: Ten Steps Toward Making a Difference." *The Reading Teacher* 51: 186–194.

Brabham, Edna G., and Susan Kidd Villaume. (2000). "Continuing Conversations about Literature Circles." *Reading Teacher* 54 (3): 278–280.

Burns, Bonnie. (1998)." Changing the Classroom Climate with Literature Circles." *Journal of Adolescent and Adult Literacy* 42 (2): 124–129.

Cambourne, Brian. (1995)."Toward and Educationally Relevant Theory of Literacy Learning: Twenty Years of Inquiry." *The Reading Teacher* 49: 182–190.

Carmichael, Maribeth. (2001)."Creating a Teachers as readers Group in Your School." *Teacher Librarian* 28 (5): 22–24.

Eeds, Mary Ann, and D. Wells. (1989)."Grand Conversations: An Exploration of Meaning and Construction in Literature Study Groups." *Research in Teaching of English* 23.

Gambrell, Linda. (1996). "Creating Classroom Cultures that Foster Reading Motivation." *The Reading Teacher* 50: 14–25.

Kaser, Sandy, and Kathy Short. (1998). "Exploring Culture Through Children's Connections." *Language Arts* 75: 185–192.

Latrobe, Kathy, and Anne Masters. (1999). "Assessing the Library Media Program and Its Partnerships: The Implementation of Information Power." *Teacher Librarian* 27 (2): 8–13.

Leu, Donald J., and Charles K. Kinzer. (1999). "Literature Discussion Groups or Book Clubs." In *Effective Literacy Instruction*, 4th ed. Prentice-Hall.

Pierce, Kathryn Mitchell. (1998). "Initiation Literature Discussion Groups: Teaching Like Learning." In *Talking About Books,* edited by Kathy Short and Kathryn Mitchell Pierce. Heinemann.

Sanacore, Joseph. (1999). "Encouraging Children to Make Their Own Choices about Their Literacy Learning." *Intervention in School & Clinic* 35 (1): 35–39.

Short, Kathy, Gloria Kaufman, Sandy Kaser, Leslie H Kahn, and Kathleen Marie Crawford. (1999). "Teacher Watching: Examining Teacher Talk in Literature Circles." *Language Arts* 76: 377–385.

Recommended Readings and Resources for Implementing Literature Circles

Brown, Mary Daniels. (2001). "Literature Circles Build Excitement for Books!" *Education World.* Available at http://www.education-world.com/a_curr/curr259.shtml (accessed July 2, 2006).

Daniels, Harvey. (2002). *Literature Circles: Voice and Choice in the Student-Centered Classroom.* 2d ed. Stenhouse.

Day, Jeni Pollack, ed. (2002). *Moving Forward with Literature Circles: How to Plan, Manage, and Evaluate Literature Circles That Deepen Understanding and Foster a Love of Reading.* Scholastic Professional Books.

Hill, Bonnie Campbell, Nancy J. Johnson, and Katherine L Schlick Noe, eds. (1995). Literature Circles and Response. Norwood, MA: Christopher-Gordon.

Hill, Bonnie Campbell, Katherine L. Schlick Noe, and Nancy J. Johnson, eds. (2001). *Literature Circle Resource Guide.* Christopher-Gordon.

LiteratureCircles.com. http://www.literaturecircles .com

Literature Circle Resource Center. http://facstaff.seattleu.edu/kschlnoe/LitCircles/index.html

Noe, Kathryn L Schlick, and Nancy J. Johnson. (1999). *Getting Started with Literature Circles.* Christopher-Gordon.

Roser, Nancy L., and Miriam G. Martinez, eds. (1995). *Book Talk and Beyond: Children and Teachers Respond to Literature.* International Reading Association.

Samway, Katharin Davis, and Gail Whang. (1996). *Literature Study Circles in a Multicultural Classroom.* Stenhouse.

Mental Models

Daniel Callison

The term "mental models" must rest in jargon vocabulary at the current time because the term is not recognized in the vocabularies of educational indexes and databases. Acceptable related terms are "mental representation" and "cognitive mapping." The most common related term is "schemata" which concerns mental images and concepts that provide a cognitive framework by which the individual perceives, understands, and responds to stimuli. There is a growing interest in the process, intuitive and guided, that learners employ to construct meaning. "Mental modeling" has been the term of choice in recent discussions concerning student abilities to visualize or comprehend the demands of the information research process.

Evolution of Perspectives on Learning

Over the past fifty years, there has been a clear evolution in the perspectives held by most leading educators concerning "how we learn." This evolution is simplified in the outline below.

Behaviorist Perspective

In the mid-1950s there was a shift from research on communication stimulus to learner response to stimuli. Behaviorists, such as B. F. Skinner, were interested in voluntary behavior rather than in reflexive behavior. Behavior could be modified, based on reinforcement theory, through reinforcing [learning] and leading the learner through a series of specific instructional steps.

Behaviorists refuse to speculate on what goes on internally when learning takes place. They rely solely on observable behaviors. As a result, they are more comfortable explaining relatively simple learning tasks. Information processing is too complex to be limited to this single perspective.

Cognitivist Perspective

Cognitivists make their contributions to learning theory and instructional design by creating models of how information is received, processed, and manipulated by learners. Cognitivists create a mental model of short-term and long-term memory. New information is stored in short-term memory where it is considered, rehearsed, and examined relevant to held knowledge until it is ready to be stored in long-term memory, in relation to previous knowledge. If the information is not rehearsed it is not likely to be retained. Learners then combine the information and skills in long-term memory to develop cognitive strategies for dealing with complex tasks.

Jean Piaget identifies three concepts for such mental development:

- Schemata: mental structures by which learners organize their perceived environment.

- Assimilation: process by which the learner integrates new information and experiences with existing schemata.

- Accommodation: the process of modifying or creating new schemata.

Experienced learners have a broader network of schemata, refined over time as the learner progresses through natural maturation.

Constructivist Perspective

This current movement extends beyond the usual stages of ability, to advocating the engaging of students (regardless of age) in meaningful experiences that will accelerate and enhance the construction of schemata. The shift is from passive transfer of information to active problem solving. Constructivists emphasize that learners create their own interpretations of the world of information. The constructivist will argue that the student situates the learning experience within his or her own experience and that the goal of instruction is not to teach information, but to create situations so that students can interpret information for their own understanding. Learning is a search for meaning.

The constructivist believes that learning occurs most effectively when the student is engaged in authentic tasks that relate to meaningful contexts. The ultimate measure of learning is based therefore on the ability of the student to use knowledge to facilitate thinking in real life. The ultimate role of the teacher is to facilitate situations in which the student finds relevance and constructs meaning through observation, interviewing, debate, conversations, evidence selection, and other skills that are practiced in an authentic context.

Applications to Interactive Technology

Early use of the term "mental models," over fifty years ago, was often connected to the thesis that advocated that humans construct internal models of the environment around them, and from these models humans reason and predict outcome of events. Just as an engineer may build a scale model of a building so as to see the effects of applying various stresses prior to building the real thing, humans build models that enable us to make predictions about an external event before carrying out an action. Mental models are considered essentially as internal constructions of some aspect of the external world that can be manipulated, enabling predictions and inferences to be made. Various applications of mental modeling have evolved and today the term is used in reference to applied problems of human-computer interaction (HCI)

and human-machine systems (HMS), and a variety of planning sequences for development of interactive information systems (IIS).

Defined within the interactive software development world, a mental model is a conceptual cognitive structure within a specific domain that a student develops and uses to explain and confront novel situations and problems. Different forms of mental models have been derived from the three levels of knowledge used to represent domain specific skills required for success in use of computer programs. These three discrete knowledge levels are

- **Declarative:** information is described as factual information;

- **Procedural:** information is the compilation of declarative knowledge into functional units; and

- **Conditional:** knowledge is described as the understanding of when and where to employ procedures.

The knowledge levels have been applied to use of a CD-ROM encyclopedia, and mental models describing development of knowledge levels have been formulated by Ron Oliver.

The three mental model descriptions corresponding to the discrete knowledge levels follow:

- **Management.** This mental model describes the user's understanding of the control and guidance of a program. It influences the decisions and choices made by the user in interacting with the software to display specific information. It represents the user's construction of the protocols and procedures of the CD-ROM encyclopedia interface.

- **Navigation.** The navigation mental model describes users' constructions and schemata of moving within the information base between discrete elements and nodes. This mental model differs from management in that it pertains to users' understanding and concepts of information access, rather than simple interactions with the interface.

- **Organization.** This mental model describes users' understanding of the manner is which the information is organized within the CD-ROM encyclopedia. This mental model is dependent on users' information skills and mental constructions of the information base. It differs from navigation in that it is less specific to an individual CD-ROM, and represents broad and transferable skills and knowledge. Mental modeling is useful in attempting to address the most common problems in design and development of interactive information systems:

- **Disorientation:** difficulty knowing where one is in the product.

- **Navigation:** difficulty moving from one point to another.

- **Cognitive Overload:** exposure to information that vastly exceeds that required to answer a given question.

Student Information Decision Making

The concepts related to mental models have been used to attempt to address the question: When students are seeking and using information, why do they make the decisions they make? Limited research is attempted to determine answers to these related questions:

- What prior learning do students have (established mental models) that influences the decisions they make while seeking and using information?

- How is that prior learning the same as or different from what students need to address their information task?

- If differences exist between what students need to know and what they do know, how do they cope?

One proposed notion in response to these questions is that a student will bring several mental models to a problem or project and will rely on those models he or she has developed and practiced in the past to apply to the new situation. In terms of meeting information problems, the student has two options. First, the student may hold a previous mental model based on facts, concepts, and opinions about the subject-matter content that may be closely related to the new problem. (What do I know about other historical events that will help me address the questions I need to answer about a new historical event?) A second model involves information access skills. (How have I accessed information on previous topics which I can now apply to finding necessary information on this new topic?)

In one study, conducted by Judy Pitts (1995) at Florida State University, concerning senior high school science students assigned the task of producing video programs on a variety of subjects, the researcher concluded that incomplete subject-matter mental models led to incomplete identification of information need. The analysis of the students' information- seeking activities showed that most were driven by very general information needs.

When asked what kind of information they were seeking, students frequently responded by restating their topic or with a shrug and phrases such as "I don't know," "Anything we can put on the video," and "Whatever." Pitts went on to speculate that it is probably true that most people who begin a new research project are at first novices in the subject matter involved. If those people have expert information-seeking-and-use understandings, however, they know how to use the information skills to strengthen the subject understandings. They might, for example, know how to find general, overview information as a first step and thus obtain the expertise necessary to identify clearly the information needs. This idea can be expressed in the following equation: novice subject understandings + expert information skills = students who may use information skills to find information necessary to strengthen subject understandings.

In the opposite case (people with expert subject understandings but novice information skills), students know enough about their topics to articulate their information needs clearly to an information professional. This situation can be represented by another equation: expert subject understandings + novice information skills = students who may articulate information needs clearly to those who can help them.

But, concludes Pitts, if both subject understandings and information skills are weak (as was the case with most students in her study), students have little chance of being able to progress on either (mental model) strand. One strand cannot support the other. A third equation represents this dilemma: novice subject understandings + novice information skills = students who are not likely to make progress on either strand.

A second study, conducted by Joy H. McGregor (1994), concluded that most students do not make intuitive shifts from one mental model to another, or stated in another way, students do not instinctively operate in a metacognitive manner. McGregor made the following recommendations for practice:

- A metacognitive environment in which thinking strategies are discussed, modeled, monitored, and evaluated in a supportive atmosphere could help students as they learn to think about using information more effectively.

- In order to monitor thinking processes, it is necessary for students to have a vocabulary they can use to talk about such processes.

- The process of doing a library research paper provides many opportunities for practice in analyzing, synthesizing, and evaluating information and practice in mental model construction and mental model transfer.

References

McGregor, J. H. (1994). "Cognitive Processes and the Use of Information." In *School Library Media Annual 1994*, edited by C. Collier Kuhlthau, M. Elspeth Goodin, and M. J. McNally, 124–133. Libraries Unlimited.

Pitts, J. (edited by J. H. McGregor and B .K. Stripling). (1995). "Mental Models of Information." In *School Library Media Annual 1995*, edited by B. J. Morris, J. L. McQuiston, and C. L. Saretsky, 187–200. Libraries Unlimited.

For Further Reading

Fasick, A. M. (1992, February). "What Research Tells Us about Children's Use of Information Media." *Canadian Library Journal,* 51–54.

Jin, H., and T. Reeves. (1992). "Mental Models: A Research Focus for Interactive Learning Systems." *Journal of Education Training Research and Development* 40 (3): 39–53.

Jonassen, D. H., and P. Henning. (1999). "Mental Models: Knowledge in the Head and Knowledge in the World." *Educational Technology* 39 (3): 37–42.

Rogers, Y., A. Rutherford, and P. A. Bibby. (1992). *Models in the Mind*. Academic Press.

Metacognition

Daniel Callison

Metacognition is a term that gained acceptance in educational research and instructional design circles in the 1980s. In a narrow sense, the term refers to meditation or reflection on what one thinks. In a broader sense, metacognition involves all of the cognitive processes and places emphasis on the process of learning more than the products the student generates to display what he or she has learned. Metacognition is thinking about thinking; knowing what we know and what we don't know.

Understanding metacognition is essential for those teachers who want to facilitate effectively the creation of learning environments in which the student learns how to learn and extends much of that learning activity primarily through the student's abilities to instruct himself. This term is key to lifelong learning.

Strategies

Several studies have suggested that increases in learning have resulted from direct practice of metacognitive strategies. Elaine Blakey and Sheila Spence (1990) have outlined several strategies for developing metacognitive behavior, in a publication for the U.S. Office of Educational Research and Improvement:

- **Baseline Knowledge.** At the beginning of a research activity, students need to make conscious decisions about their knowledge. It is useful to write or voice "what you know" and "what you want to learn."

- **Talking about Thinking.** Students need a thinking vocabulary. During planning and problem-solving situations, teachers should model and talk through the process so students can follow demonstrated thinking procedures. Teachers can facilitate student thinking by labeling thinking processes and telling students when they are effectively employing them.

- **Paired Problem Solving.** Peers, parents, and others can help to extend the process by listening as the student talks through the problem and potential options for solutions.

Students can take turns establishing and refining questions and gaining focus by eliminating information that is not relevant.

- **Keeping a Thinking Journal.** This is now widely accepted in situations where the student is expected to monitor his or her thoughts over a lengthy time span based on what the student reads, hears, and writes in a formal manner. The journal provides a concrete record of student reflection for all to review at various steps in the thinking experience.

- **Planning and Self-Regulation.** Assuming that such responsibilities are modeled correctly by the teacher, the students should be expected to assume increasing responsibility for regulating their learning. Students can be taught to make plans for learning activities that include estimating time requirements, organizing materials, and scheduling procedures necessary to complete an activity.

- **Debriefing the Thinking Process.** A three-step method is useful. First, the teacher guides students to review the activity, gathering impressions on thinking and feelings. Then, the group classifies related ideas, identifying the thinking strategies used and the strengths and weaknesses of each as related to the recent information research (or other learning) activity. Finally, students and the teacher evaluate their success, discard inappropriate strategies, and discuss application of the best strategies for future applications.

- **Self-Evaluation.** Guided self-evaluation can be introduced through individual conferences and checklists that focus on the thinking processes. As students begin to recognize that some learning activities in different disciplines are similar, they will begin to transfer self-guided learning strategies.

Educating Students to Think

In 1985, a select group of educators was called together by the National Commission on Libraries and Information Science. A concept paper evolved from those discussions and the ideas expressed by the authors (Mancall, Aaron, and Walker 1986) are foundational to the models which have evolved over the past decade concerning the instruction of information literacy skills across our nation.

"Educating Students to Think" is an essay every teacher of school library media should read and reflect on frequently. Citing several learning and information theorists, the authors of this concept essay describe concerns related to the novice-expert dimension. Elizabeth Robinson is quoted, "Novices at any task not only lack the skills needed to perform it efficiently, but are also deficient in self-conscious participation and intelligent self-regulation of their actions" (19).

If instruction based on metacognition theory is to be effective, two conditions must be met. First, the student must be developmentally ready to learn the skill. Second, the student must realize that use of the skill will be effective in solving a personal cognitive problem. The teacher of literacy information is a critical player in facilitating the "learning to think" environment. Unless that teacher is able and willing to model, council, and evaluate the student's information selection and use process, moving the student from the child novice levels to higher order thinking skills will falter. .

Implications for Information Skills

Linda H. Bertland (1986) conducted an extensive review of research in cognitive psychology. Her report was key to the essay mentioned above. Bertland's insightful conclusions help us understand some of the implications for the timing and structure related to teaching information skills:

- Research in comprehension indicates that greater attention needs to be paid to the level at which children are processing information. Shallow processing of information will probably lead to rote copying from sources without any perceived need to evaluate and relate the material into a meaningful whole.

- More attention must be paid to the way children perceive the task parameters of reading and viewing. Children in early grades do not seem to be aware of the various goals of reading, nor of strategies appropriate to the realization of those goals.

- Children who perceive little need to invest mental effort in television viewing may be learning less from instructional audiovisual material than would be anticipated, regarding it more as a source of amusement rather than instruction.

- Metacognitive strategies that apply to information skills instruction include the need to teach students question analysis, practice careful definition of the topic, manage the consideration of time and task parameters, and gain practice and feedback leading to the most effective strategies for use of resources in order to gain meaningful evidence.

References

Bertland, L. H. (1986). "An Overview of Research in Metacognition: Implications for Information Skills Instruction." *School Library Media Quarterly* 15 (2): 96–99.

Blakey, E., and S. Spence. (1990). *Developing Metacognition*. Office of Educational Research and Improvement.

Mancall, J. C., S. L. Aaron, and S. A. Walker. (1986). "Educating Students to Think: The Role of the School Library Media Program." *School Library Media Quarterly* 15 (1): 18–27.

Motivation

Daniel Callison

Students are learning all the time. It is not possible to stop them from learning. An important task for the teacher of information literacy is not so much to teach students how to learn, but to motivate them to learn at times that may not seem immediately rewarding to the student. Motivation helps to increase the chances that students will learn what is needed even when they may initially classify the activity as being overly demanding or of no interest. Motivation approaches are varied and in many ways common sense, but often left out or given little attention as teachers concentrate on academic goals to meet cognitive performances. Attitudinal performances toward the learning situation are just as important to consider.

The Motivation to Learn

Alfie Kohn (1993) outlines these "facts" pertaining to motivation of students to learn in his book *Punished by Rewards*:

Fact 1: Young children don't need to be rewarded to learn. The children who arrive at school every weekday morning represent a range of interests and abilities and circumstances. Some come from homes where intellectual curiosity is encouraged, some from places where it is a challenge just to survive. But the fact that children are not equally receptive to what the teacher is doing at any given moment should not distract us from recognizing that the desire to learn itself is natural.(144)

Fact 2: At any age, rewards are less effective than intrinsic motivation for promoting effective learning. The point here is quite simple: just as adults who love their work will invariably do a better job than those goaded with artificial incentives, so children are more likely to be optimal learners if they are interested in what they are learning. (144)

Fact 3: Rewards for learning undermine intrinsic motivation. It would be bad enough if high grades, stickers, and other Skinnerian inducements just weren't very good at helping children learn. The tragedy is that they also vitiate the sort of motivation that does help. (148)

Reading Rewards

Stephen Krashen (2005), reviewer of hundreds of studies on reading programs, is avid in his conclusion, "AR [Accelerated Reading] consists of four components, which include providing interesting books, time to read (one hour a day), quizzes on the content of the books (with an emphasis on the facts), and rewards for points earned on the quizzes. There is strong evidence that the first two components are effective: children who have access to interesting reading material and time and place to read will read more and make more progress in literacy development. There is no direct evidence that tests the efficacy of the third and fourth components" (48).

Characteristics of Motivation

Wilbert McKeachie (1978), former president of the American Association for Higher Education and Director of the Center for Research on Learning at the University of Michigan, has classified his observations on motivation in the following categories:

- **Curiosity.** People are naturally curious. They seek new experiences; they enjoy learning new things. Although derived at different levels and various formats, humans find satisfaction in solving puzzles, perfecting skills, and developing competence. Asking students questions, rather than presenting statements of fact, not only improves learning, but increases interest in learning more about the topic in discussion.

- **Competence.** In addition to natural curiosity, another intrinsic motive for learning is competence or self-efficacy. Students will receive pleasure from doing things well and knowing they have done things well. Teachers may need to link success with the perception that the success was due to the student's own ability and effort. For students who lack a sense of efficacy, teachers must not only provide situations where success occurs, but to prove that they have themselves mastered the task without special help.

- **Affiliation.** Most students want to be accepted and liked. Approval from the teacher may be an important reward, but may also lead to being ostracized as the "over achiever." In addition, motivation may be complicated by conflicting needs for independence and dependence. While students are likely to resent the teacher who directs their activities too closely, they are also likely to be anxious when given independence. McKeachie suggests that the solution is to find ways to simultaneously satisfy both needs.

- **Grades.** In most educational environments, this is the most tangible and, for many, the most important motivation. Grades represent an expert's appraisal of performance and such are recorded for others to see and consider for future advancement or rejection. Because grades are important to them, most students will learn whatever is necessary to get the grades they desire. If instructors base grades on memorization of details, students will memorize the facts or even the text as given. If the student believes grades are based upon the ability to integrate and apply principles, he or she will attempt to do this. Too often, however, tasks related to the selection and use of information are not demanding enough and adequate grades can be achieved with location of a minimum number of required resources without reward for making wise choices and discarding poor information. In such cases, the grade is unwisely based on quantity and not quality. Getting the citation format correct is not motivating. Expressing why a source is "the best that can be located" can be motivating.

- **Achievement.** Some research suggests that students with high achievement motivation are more likely to remain highly motivated in highly competitive environments where their chances of success are about fifty-fifty. Some tests have shown that in such environments the students not only excelled, but reported greater interest in school work. The conflict remains today on the advantages and disadvantages for individual students or the common good as decisions are made concerning tracking or inclusion. The latter approach may present more motivational challenges.

- **Modeling.** Perhaps the key source of stimulation for motivation, or the major controlling agent for motivation factors, is the teacher. McKeachie stresses the obvious, but as teachers of information literacy, we should never forget that our own enthusiasm and values have much to do with our students' interest in the subject matter. Nonverbal as well as verbal methods are used to communicate such attitudes. Smiles and vocal intensity may be as important as the words we choose.

Legendary Teachers

Playing strongly on techniques used by successful coaches, David Scheidecker and William Freeman (1999), both successful public school teachers, have recently summarized how "legendary teachers" bring out the best in their students. Their approaches to motivating high student achievement include:

- **Convey Enjoyment.** Even on the worst days, motivational teachers convey to their students that they enjoy being with the students and having them in class.

- **Take the "We" Approach.** The teacher does not separate him or herself from the student when failure occurs, but finds a way to partner with the student to determine what went wrong and to help guide the student to improve for better results.

- **Build Safety Nets.** It seems more and more students face conflicts and failures within their home environments.

Students who are willing to take the risk to achieve at school should find safety in celebration of victories. Scheidecker and Freeman also recommend such systemic safety nets as ungraded pretests for practice prior to exams, mandatory make-up exams for below average performance, and additional review sessions for those testing below average. Motivation grows from legendary teachers who are available when needed and provide the time and guidance for students to correct mistakes.

Motivation in the Multigenre Research Paper

Margaret Moulton (1999), a high school teacher, reports that she has found the multigenre research paper to lead to greater interest by her seniors in the process to gather and present information. Defining her approach closely in terms of the I-Search model, Moulton's students were encouraged to select a topic of their choice and also to select multiple ways to present their findings.

Seniors presented a portfolio of artifacts that represented different aspects of their information research. Encouraging alternative presentation modes, usually formats other than paper (such as video), is not new to teachers of information literacy. However these seniors were expected to express themselves in multiple genres to match varied emotions and communication levels. Thus, a portfolio might include original sheet music, a eulogy, a wedding invitation, a list of trivia facts and quotations, journal entries, a student-designed poster (wanted poster, playbill, concert, movie, etc.), or student-created newspaper tabloid front page. A variety of artifacts are selected and created that best reflect the theme or character chosen and may range from a few to more than a dozen. Students were motivated through choice and variety.

One of Moulton's students reported, "Throughout doing all these multigenres I realized that I learned more than doing a regular research paper. I really got to know the person I had to write about and at some point the person I had to be. I enjoyed this assignment. The only thing that I did not like was all the typing because I wrote more than a regular research paper and because of that my wrists hurt. Besides that, this was the best and most educational report I have ever had to do. To think about it, it is kinda sad to know a senior did a great report only once."

Reading Motivation

Education literature is filled with useful methods designed to motivate students to read. An Indiana collaborative team (Closter and Thomas 1998) representing the classroom, the school library media center, and the local public library has elaborated on the "original recipe" to motivate reading in the middle schools. Programming is designed around a theme and includes the following:

- **A Design Team.** School teachers, school library media specialists, and public librarians plan, read, discuss, and support each other.

- **Quality Book Selection.** Multiple copies of well-written books with genuine dialogue and strong characters, with heavy investment in paperbacks.

- **Funding.** Encourage community groups to donate to the cause so that there is a local investment in the activity.

- **Food.** Tie the eats to the theme and the content of the key books selected for the theme. This age group, grades six to ten, will come into the activity if they have a role in food selection too.

- **Publicity.** Enthusiasm is contagious! Excited students can create more excitement if they are engaged in the promotional activities.

- **Connections.** Attempt to make thematic connections with the local environment including historical sites, community organizations, and colorful personalities.

- **Mood.** Re-create a mood that is built on the key elements of the novels selected to support the theme.

- **Facilitators.** Kids are more motivated to read and communicate if facilitators are good listeners rather than constantly offering a critique of what the kids have to offer.

Motivation and Information Skills Instruction

Ruth V. Small (2004), professor at Syracuse University, initiated a series of studies to explore motivational strategies used by school library media specialists during information skills instruction. She has based her work on the ARCS Model of Motivational Design. Motivation is enhanced when the learner values the task and believes that he/she can be successful in completing the task. These strategy components are necessary:

- Attention

  - Perceptual Arousal—provide novelty, surprise, incongruity or uncertainty.

  - Inquiry Arousal—stimulate curiosity by posing questions or problems.

  - Variability—incorporate a range of methods and media to meet different styles and needs of the learners.

- Relevance

  - Goal Orientation—present the objectives and useful purpose of the instruction and specific methods for successful achievement.

  - Motive Matching—match objectives to student needs.

  - Familiarity—present content in ways that are understandable and that are related to the learner's experience and values.

- Confidence

  - Learning Requirements—inform student about learning and performance requirements and assessment criteria.

  - Success Opportunities—provide challenging and meaningful opportunities for can be completed for success.

  - Personal Responsibility—link learning success to students' personal effort and ability.

- Satisfaction

  - Intrinsic Reinforcement—encourage and support intrinsic enjoyment of the learning experience.

  - Extrinsic Rewards—provide positive reinforcement and motivational feedback.

  - Equity—maintain consistent standards and consequences for success; be fair.

Promoting the Potential for Learning Satisfaction

Small (1999) has found that school library media specialists tend to use attention motivational strategies more than three times as often as relevance, confidence, and satisfaction strategies combined. At least among the actions of the elementary and middle school library media specialists that Small documented, most of the attention strategies could be classified as inquiry arousal or questioning and problem-posing strategies to spark curiosity. Small also reported that her test group used significantly more rewards than punishments.

Small has teamed with Marilyn Arnone (2000) to apply motivational theory to "turning kids on to research." Their approach is based on confidence builders as strategies to provide extra incentives for students as they find their best medium for investigation and presentation through posters, music, storytelling and other options. Traditional library orientations also become more exciting with the use of mystery questions and competition.

References

Closter, K., K. L. Sipes, and V. Thomas. (1998). *Fiction, Food, and Fun: The Original Recipe for the Read 'n' Feed Program*. Libraries Unlimited.

Kohn, A. (1993). *Punished by Rewards: The Trouble with Gold Stars, Incentive Lans, A's, Praise, and Other Bribes*. Houghton Mifflin.

Krashen, S. (2005). "Accelerated Reader: Evidence Still Lacking." *Knowledge Quest*, 48–49.

McKeachie, W. J. (1978). *Teaching Tips: A Guidebook for the Beginning College Teacher*. D. C. Heath.

Moulton, M. R. (1999). "The Multigenre Paper: Increasing Interest, Motivation, and Functionality in Research." *Journal of Adolescent & Adult Literacy* 42 (7): 528–539.

Scheidecker, D., and W. Freeman. (1999). *Bringing Out the Best in Students: How Legendary Teachers Motivate Kids*. Corwin Press and Sage Publications.

Small, R. V. (1998). "Designing Motivation into Library and Information Skills Instruction." *School Library Media Quarterly Online*. Available at http://www.ala.org/aasl/SLMQ/small.html (accessed April 13, 2003).

Small, R. V. (1999). "An Exploration of Motivational Strategies Used by Library Media Specialists During Library and Information Skills Instruction." *School Library Media Research*. Available at http://www.ala.org/aasl/SLMR/motive.html (accessed April 9, 2003).

Small, R. V. (2004). *Designing Digital Literacy Programs with Impact: Information, Motivation, Purpose, Audience, Content, and Techniques*. Neal-Schuman.

Small, R. V., and M. P. Arnone. (2000). *Turning kids on to Research: The Power of Motivation*. Libraries Unlimited.

Nonfiction

Daniel Callison

Have you seen a presentation by Beverly Kobrin (1988) when she shows you the multitude of possibilities for engaging kids with nonfiction? It is an eye-opener! We boys especially listen to her. She defines nonfiction to include newspapers, magazines, cookbooks, small appliance manuals, phone books, and much more. The most important message from Kobrin is that nonfiction can be just as engaging and emotional as fiction. Yes, even books with world records, baseball's best and all those things that are hard to "believe it or not." Kobrin (1995) also promotes nonfiction as the source for answering kids' questions and raising many more. Nonfiction is at the core of inquiry.

Nonfiction plays a dominant role in the wide range of signs and signals that kids must handle in order to make meaning of their world (Baxter and Kochel 1999; Cianciolo 2000). A child's decoding starts from the very beginning of his or her life. Parents, Kobrin insists, should be the first and foremost guides for their children as both parent and child discover that practical nonfiction can be both fascinating and enlightening.

Nonfiction, representation in text, sound, and/or visuals of real events is a key stimulant for early development of writing skills. Nonfiction captures aspects of the world with which students may gain understanding of authentic happenings that pertain to their lives. Tony Stead (2002), a facilitator for the Balanced Early Literacy Project of the Boston Public Schools, has documented how children in early elementary grades learn how to write nonfiction when they

- See a purpose for writing and have an audience in mind. Children need to be given authentic purposes for writing nonfiction and be aware of why authors write different types of nonfiction.

- See many models of different types of nonfiction writing for a variety of purposes. Teachers need to provide children with an abundance of nonfiction texts as part of both shared reading and read-alouds as well as books in the classroom [and school] library for children's independent reading.

- See demonstrations of how to write different text types for different purposes. Teachers need to provide demonstrations on author's craft, research skills, and language mechanics to make explicit what writers do when they are working with specific genres [journalists, historians, engineers, travel guides, government agents, and scientists]. These demonstrations need to be in individual, small-group, and whole-class settings according to identified needs.

- Are given time and opportunity to engage in working with nonfiction texts. Schedules need to allow adequate time for children to engage in the process of writing nonfiction pieces. These engagements should not be one-day wonders but rather comprehensive units of study that will help children learn from ongoing engagements.

- Are allowed to take on responsibility for their learning. Children need to be part of the decision-making process when selecting the content of what they wish to write about independently.

- Are given opportunities to learn from each other. The classroom [and library] should be structured to allow frequent opportunities for children to discuss and share their writing pieces with each other. (15)

Nonfiction writing ideas are enhanced by information drawn from nonfiction visuals such timelines, posters, photographs, charts, tables, and graphs. Students should be engaged in extracting information from such materials and placed in learning situations where they present their own nonfiction facts in such visual formats.

Betty Carter, at Texas Woman's University, tells us that high interest in nonfiction crosses ability levels and grows and expands as the child moves into adolescence and young adulthood. Teenage boys read more nonfiction than teenage girls. Much of the nonfiction read by young adults is read for pleasure, diversion, and entertainment (Carter and Abrahamson 1990).

Carter believes that knowing books translates into reading books. There's a strong tendency for librarians and teachers to equate reading books with reading fiction. Textbooks on young adult literature heavily favor fiction, the content of young adult literature courses typically stresses fiction, lists of teen favored books contain fiction, and awards traditionally go to fictional works. Many teachers and librarians are drawn to their particular profession because they themselves enjoy fiction. Yet, the undisputed fact remains that young adults read nonfiction (Colman 1999). And since teachers and librarians accept the charge to help young adults grow into mature readers, they must read widely in all areas of literature-in the multiple genres of fiction as well as poetry, drama, information books, and biography.

Many school library media center collections reflect the strong selection of quality fiction and the lack of useful nonfiction. Surveys in twelve key states in the mid-1990s by the American Library Association (Lynch, Kramer, and Weeks 1994) showed both elementary and secondary collections to be adequate to excellent in fiction, but poor and out-of-date in nonfiction areas such as mathematics, multicultural education, science, technology, geography, fine arts, and careers.

New Collections and Radical Change

The computer technologies that now bring reams of nonfiction information to students through the Internet also have led to a revolution in the design and printing of thousands of new nonfiction titles for children and young adults over the past two decades. This explosion of quality nonfiction, often graphically illustrated, creates new opportunities for school library book collections to be revitalized. If funded and managed properly, the adventure to weed out the old and to select the new leads to exciting collaborative planning in thematic lessons and information literacy education.

Dianne McAffee Hopkins (1999), from the University of Wisconsin, found this to be true through the recent evaluation of the national Library Power project. She reported that in situations where collections were updated based on collection mapping that targeted selected areas of the curriculum:

- New collection development practices led to improved collections and expanded use of collections in instruction.

- Changes in collection development practices were well regarded by librarians, teachers, and principals.

- Strong connections were established between library collections and instruction.

- Up-to-date collections selected by both teachers and librarians represented the basis for most collaborations between librarians and teachers. The wide availability of appropriate resources was clearly the first basis for collaborative efforts.

Eliza Dresang (1999), professor at Florida State University, has recently illustrated how nonfiction books for young adults are undergoing radical change. Hypertext and digital design are enhancing nonfiction in ways that make engagement with text more exciting than ever. Students may rewrite text or story to suit different audiences, move text and compare facts, or skim and highlight with electronic key term searching. These changes in literature for children and young adults will open new discourse levels on social and political issues as access to data will be more extensive and placed within richer contexts that include interviews and motion illustrations. Formats will become more interactive as well as

- nonsequential in organization and format; and

- interlaced with multiple layers of meaning.

Research on Reading Related to Nonfiction

The research on reading education and skill development (Hansen and Graves 1991) has provided several new insights that also pertain to how a student makes meaning from information. The teacher of information literacy processes should give attention to the following findings from studies completed over the last twenty years (Sweet 1995).

- Children who engage in daily discussions about what they read are more likely to become critical readers and learners (Cazden 1988).

Students' discussions in classrooms are important to their learning. Research shows that students' verbal exchanges about content improve learning and increase their level of thinking. The social nature of learning implies that, because each context is different, participants must always evaluate what to say, when and how, consider options, and make choices. Learning rests in taking these actions.

Discussion concerning information needs, quality and relevance of information located, and optional leads to more information are activities that teachers of information literacy skills can lead, model, and support to increase critical thinking at any grade level. Given the importance of discussion for effective learning, effective teaching involves providing students with ample opportunities to engage in daily discussions with one another. Small-group and peer-to-peer interactions are valuable in promoting academic and social learning. Some researchers have concluded that children who rely on each other for help learn more than children who work alone.

- Expert readers have strategies that they use to construct meaning before, during, and after reading.

As students become proficient readers, they develop a set of plans or strategies for solving problems they encounter in their reading experiences. These strategies include (Cazden 1988; Saul 1994; Saul and Dieckman 2005):

- **Inference:** The process of reaching conclusions based on information within the text and the cornerstone of constructing meaning. Inference includes making predictions by using prior knowledge combined with information available from text.

- **Identifying important information:** The process of finding critical facts and details in narrative (story) or expository (informational, nonfiction) text. The tasks may differ from narrative (plot, character, theme) to expository (background facts, arguments, warrants a thesis or prediction, evidence, and conclusions), but both will include identification of key text items. The student will mature in his or her information fluency through both seeking more demanding reading experiences and an increased sophistication in accessing information.

- **Monitoring:** A metacognitive or self-awareness process that expert constructors of meaning use to help themselves overcome problems as they read. For example, when good readers have difficulty understanding a paragraph, they become aware of the problem and stop immediately to fix it by employing a technique such as rereading, and in some cases, rereading prior paragraphs for context, not just the problematic paragraph.

- **Summarizing:** Process that involves pulling together important information gathered from a long passage of text.

- **Question generating:** Involves readers asking themselves questions they want answered from reading that require them to integrate information while they read.

- Children's reading and writing abilities develop together (Langer 1986).

Both reading and writing are constructive processes. Current research also suggests that a similar, if not the same, level of intellectual activity underlies both reading and writing: interactions between the reader/writer and text lead to new knowledge and interpretations of text. Just as thoughtful readers read for a specific purpose by activating prior knowledge about the topic at hand, writers activate prior knowledge that relates to the topic and has a purpose for writing-to impart meaning to a reader.

While reading, readers reread and modify meaning accordingly. While writing, writers think about the topic and the more they think, the better developed their writing becomes. They also think about what they've written, reread it, and make revisions to improve it. This process of reading and writing not only unfold in similar ways, they tend to be used together. It remains to be shown if those who manage access to more information and learn how to identify pertinent information efficiently may accelerate the reading and writing processes more than those who rely on a few common knowledge information resources (i.e., those who never move past basic encyclopedia sets and popular news magazines). Effective management of multiple sources of information depends on growth and maturation beyond basic reading and writing skills.

- Children increase their ability to use language by becoming involved with language that is somewhat more mature than what they currently use.

Canadian educators Terry Johnson and Daphne Louis (1987) contend that children need to be introduced to literacy through somewhat simplified language, but they believe the unconscious simplification used in creating stories and poems the young mind can appreciate to be infinitely preferable to the conscious mechanical simplification that comes from word counts and sound/symbol regularities. Where the Wild Things Are will serve children better than demanding that they "see Dan run" or that they get their mouths around "ack," "ile," "ump," or "og." Engaging in story opens more meaning than simply engaging in sound.

The introduction to information resources is also, at times, too remedial. Treasure hunts may provide practice in searching, but are more effective if used as tools to open discussions about what the found information means:

Are there other ways to find the same information?

How might you use this information to solve a problem?

Are there similar sources of information available at other libraries or likely to be found at home?

Students at any age should be challenged to apply information, not just hunt for unrelated facts. Students at any age should be encouraged to talk aloud about their perception of the potential usefulness of several information resources. Voicing meaning from text provides the practice and opens the opportunity for feedback. As the student gains confidence, he or she will move to more challenging resources. Discourse about information findings leads to meaningful conversations concerning information seeking and information application.

- The most valuable form of reading assessment reflects our current understanding about the reading process and stimulates authentic reading tasks (Stiggins and Conklin 1992).

Until very recently, reading assessment focused on measuring students' performance on a hierarchy of isolated skills that, when put together, were thought to compose "reading." Now it is known that the whole act of reading is greater than the sum of its parts (i.e., isolated skills). Moreover, these parts are interrelated within a literacy context and do not always develop in a hierarchical way.

The same should be extracted for the information search and use processes. Growth in the students' abilities to access and process multiple nonfiction texts and to derive meaning through the process is recursive, interactive, or a dynamic evolution, not just a step-by-step skill sequence. Information as evidence may change in meaning and value depending on its context with other data, additional primary and secondary sources explored, considering how to present to different audiences, and frequent conversations with others (peers, parents, library media specialist, and other teachers) to verify it. Reflection at any point in the information search and library research process may send the student back to rethink previous experiences before moving forward.

Teaching Students to Read Nonfiction

Virginia Rankin's collection of practiced and refined strategies for teaching the research process in middle schools, *The Thoughtful Researcher* (1999), is a must-read and reread for anyone who strives to implement an effective information literacy instructional program. Many of her activities can be used by classroom teachers. Rankin recommends that most of her lessons will have even more impact in raising student interest, and perhaps student performance, when the library media specialist presents them in conjunction with an actual research project. The following portion of questions from her handouts illustrate key questions that students must address as they gain practice and grow in becoming mature users of nonfiction text information. (Questions in brackets have been added to Rankin's list.)

Judging Suitability of the Information Resource

Is there confusing vocabulary? If only a word or so, work on finding an understandable definition. [Several difficult words? Source seems new and interesting but difficult to read? Seek guidance from peer, parent, teacher, or librarian before you give up on the source.] If many difficult words, move on to another source. Does it contain references to persons, places, or things with which I'm familiar? Skim it for a quick overview to seek new information which may relate to your current knowledge. Does it assume I already know too many things? Skim to look for new information or it may be an item which will have more meaning later after you have read other resources.

Understanding and Comprehending Information

Is a concept confusing? Try to tell it in your own words to someone or see if you can write a summary without a great deal of rereading the text. Can I sum up the main point? Look at the introduction, conclusion, topic sentences, and section headings.

Evaluating and Extracting Information

Do I know what I want from this source? Does this relate to my research questions? Make value judgments-this is an important piece of information to record; this is not. Make comparisons with what you read to what you already know. Does this expand my idea? Does this make a complete new point I have not yet considered? Does this disagree with something I thought I knew or with a previous source?

Following Up or Linking to Other Information

Has the author mentioned other authorities on my topic? Should I try to find material by them? Is there a bibliography that might give me ideas for further reading? Which seem interesting, most relevant, most likely to be accessible? After completing some reading on this topic, I seem to be more sensitive to it and note items on television, in the newspaper, and even in conversations with peers and parents; which of these information leads should I follow up and how? Are there some new questions I have as a result of this reading? Do I seek answers? [Do I shift my research questions to these new ones? How do I move in the research process from this point? Does it move me forward to restart the information search process for this new portion of my study?].

Cris Tovani (2005, 2004), an English teacher from Colorado, summarizes these points that help her senior high school students read nonfiction with purpose (brackets include additional notes from the author of this chapter):

- Study the front and back covers and table of contents of the book and skim through the pages. Jot down four [or more] questions you have about the topic.

- Decide which parts of the book you will read [you don't have to read the entire book; the index may guide you to key pages]. As you read, jot on sticky notes [that can be placed on the text] information you learn that helps you address your questions. [You should try to have at least two notes for each question.]

Key Words for Instruction in Information Inquiry

- Write down what you have learned about this topic [try to paraphrase in your own words if possible]. Include any new questions and any new connections you've made about the subject.

Similar reading for purpose strategies that secondary school level students can master include (Coutant and Perchemlides 2005), on a printout or copied pages from original texts:

- **Coding**—note confusing, surprising, important items with highlighted question marks, exclamation points, and asterisks or stars.

- **Highlight repeated words**—key words, important names, titles of events all help to summarize and serve as terms to trace in indexes, databases and other reference materials.

- **Summarizing**—in a few words, show how this portion of the text relates to your thesis statement. Paraphrasing should a third of the total words, preferably much less, than the original text (Everhart 1994).

- **Interpreting**—organize pertinent facts; relate them to key questions; prioritize as to most effective, most current, or most relevant; identify what the facts in this source have failed to answer.

Strategies That Don't Engage Readers— Especially Adolescents

Gay Ivey from James Madison University and Douglas Fisher from San Diego State University have compiled a list of key strategies that tend to have little effect on teens to read more. These educators believe that strategies alone are not enough to engage students to read, but good practices include self-efficacy, interest, and strategic knowledge for meaning and purpose relevant to the reader (2005). Their list of ineffective strategies, with descriptions that correct such poor approaches, includes the following:

- Don't let students read. Principals who have helped to establish, support and participate in all school Sustained Silent Reading over time have seen student reading comprehension scores rise compared to neighboring schools that do not

engage in such activities on a consistent basis. A full discussion on the merits of access to a large and high quality collection of reading materials is provided by Stephen Krashen of the University of Southern California (2004). Support by all educators at all levels to provide a rich reading environment that includes free and convenient access to books, magazines, newspapers and quality online resources will result in better student academic achievement and greater appreciation for reading. Such access does not mean that all students become high achievers, advanced placement candidates or national merit finalists. It does mean that students at all levels from a variety of social and economic backgrounds will be given a reasonable chance to explore and learn both independently and socially if engaged in culture for reading (Dreher 2003).

- Make students read what they don't know about and don't care about. Self-selected and self-directed reading, supported by instructional media specialists who provide plenty of reader's advisory, will result in a wider spectrum of reading. Often, once the student's initial interests are satisfied, the knowledge base gained is a platform to accept and explore materials recommended or even required. When teachers understand student interests, they are more likely to make connections with advocating quality literature choices. Discussion and interaction create teachable moments for readers' advisory (Burgin 2004).

- Make students read difficult books. Engaging students at their ability level with appropriate materials will build a foundation to move into more difficult texts that may come from a wide selection of titles offered through the school library media center. Students reading choices may move up in difficulty as instructional media specialists and other teachers read aloud, especially with those who display reading skills below their age level.

- Interrogate students about what they read. Questions raised to interpret text should come from students as well as teachers and should relate to contexts and knowledge the students bring to the text. Cross-examination on plot and character development can take the richness out of exploring text from the variety of perspectives students have to offer. Instructional media specialists may want to create and engage in book discussion groups with fellow teachers in order to experience interactive discussions outside of the classroom. Such conversations, rather than drilling for facts, can help to establish a aptitude for interactive discussions.

- Buy a computer program and let it do all the work. Too many school library and classroom book collections are being developed based on the strict recommendations of reading lists that come from commercial computerized programs that promise a quick quiz and prizes for students (Cordova and Lepper 1996). Skills lab settings that do not include the option for open class reading discussions, cut short the opportunity for students to gain an appreciation and growing understanding for text. Meaningful intervention and feedback remain the primary realm for the teacher and student peers. Instructional media specialists greatly enhance reading motivation by providing additional and new reading materials (books, magazines, quality Web sites) that reward student inquiry rather than reinforce simple multiple-choice quizzing (Everhart 2005).

References

Baxter, K. A., and M. A. Kochel. (1999). *Gotcha! Nonfiction Booktalks to Get Kids Excited About Reading.* Libraries Unlimited.

Burgin, R., ed. (2004). *Nonfiction Readers' Advisory.* Libraries Unlimited.

Carter, B., and R. F. Abrahamson. (1990). *Nonfiction for Young Adults from Delight to Wisdom.* Oryx Press.

Cazden, C. (1988). *Classroom Discourse: The Language of Teaching and Learning.* Heinemann.

Cianciolo, P. J. (2000). *Informational Picture Books for Children.* ALA.

Colman, P. (1999). "Nonfiction Is Literature, Too." *The New Advocate* 12 (3): 215–223.

Cordova, D. I., and Lepper, M. R. (1996). "Intrinsic Motivation and the Process of Learning." *Journal of Educational Psychology* 88 (4): 715–730.

Coutant, C., and N. Perchemlides. (2005). "Strategies for Teen Readers." *Educational Leadership* 63 (7): 42–47.

Dreher, M. (2003). "Motivating Struggling Readers by Tapping the Potential of Information Books." *Reading and Writing Quarterly* 19: 25–38.

Dresang, E. T. (1999) *Radical Change: Books for Youth in a Digital Age.* H. W. Wilson.

Everhart, N. (1994). *How to Write a Term Paper.* Franklin Watts.

Everhart, N. (2005). "A Crosscultural Inquiry into the Levels of Implementation of Accelerated Reader and Its Effect on Motivation and Extent of Reading." *School Library Media Research* 8. Available at www.ala.org/aasl/SLMR/ (accessed February 8, 2006).

Fisher, D. (2004). "Setting the Opportunity to Read Standard: Resuscitating the SSR Program in an Urban High School." *Journal of Adolescent and Adult Literacy* 48 (10): 138–150.

Ivey, G., and D. Fisher. (2005). "Learning from What Doesn't Work." *Educational Leadership* 63 (2): 8–15.

Hansen, J., and D. H. Graves. (1991). "The Language Arts Interact." In *Handbook of Research in English Language Arts,* edited by J. Flood, J. M. Jensen, D. Lapp, and J. Squire. Macmillan.

Hopkins, D. M. (1999). "The School Library Collection: An Essential Building Block to Teaching and Learning." *School Libraries Worldwide* 5 (2): 1–15.

Johnson, T., and D. Louis. (1987). *Literacy Through Literature*. Metuchen.

Kobrin, B. (1988). *Eye-openers: How to Choose and Use Children's Books about Real People, Places, and Things*. Penguin.

Kobrin, B. (1995). *Eye-openers II: Children's Books to Answer Children's Questions About the World Around Them*. Scholastic.

Krashen, S. D. (2004). *The Power of Reading: Insights from the Research*. Libraries Unlimited.

Langer, J. A. (1986) "Reading, Writing, and Understanding: An Analysis of the Construction of Meaning." *Written Communication* 3 (2): 219–267.

Lynch, M. J., P. Kramer, and A. Weeks. (1994) *Public School Library Media Centers in 12 States: Report of the NCLIS/ALA Survey*. U. S. Commission on Libraries and Information Science.

Methe, S. A. (2003). "Evaluating Teacher Modeling as a Strategy to Increase Student Reading Behavior." *School Psychology Review* 32 (4): 617–622.

Pappas, M. L., and A. E. Tepe. (2002). *Pathways to Knowledge and Inquiry Learning*. Libraries Unlimited.

Rankin, V. (1999). *The Thoughtful Researcher*. Libraries Unlimited.

Saul, E. W. (1994). *Nonfiction for the Classroom*. Teachers College Press.

Saul, E. W., and D. Dieckman. (2005). "Theory and Research: Practice of Choosing and Using Information Trade Books." *Reading Research Quarterly* 40 (4): 502–513.

Stead, T. (2002). *Is That a Fact? Teaching Nonfiction Writing K-3*. Stenhouse Publishers.

Stiggins, R. J., and N. F. Conklin. (1992). *In Teacher's Hands: Investigating the Practices of Classroom Assessment*. State University of New York Press.

Sweet, Anne P. (1995). "State of the Art: Transforming Ideas for Teaching and Learning to Read." *Indiana Media Journal* 17 (4): 128–142.

Tovani, C. (2004). *Do I Really Have to Teach Reading?* Stenhouse Publishers.

Tovani, C. (2005). "The Power of Purposeful Reading." *Educational Leadership* 63 (2): 48–52.

Additional Recommended Resource

Loertscher, L. D., and D. V. Loertscher. (2005). *My Reading and Writing Log*. LMC Source.

Oral History

Daniel Callison

An Information Inquiry project that often employs aspects of both information and media literacy, along with critical and creative thinking, and can engage learners from many community groups in an oral history. Student teams, trained in correct interview methods and strategic methods for recording interviews, can experience excitement from documenting original local history. Intergenerational communication opportunities become reality. Young inquiring minds gain the chance to learn from information artifacts and to generate a variety of memorabilia displays.

Sometime a daunting task, oral history projects can be bogged down in too much emphasis on written transcription. While a written record should be a portion of the project, video and audio technologies now managed my even elementary school students, can provide a rewarding and challenging learning experience. Such projects also lend themselves to multiple disciplines as language arts and history merge to reinforce their complementary skills sets.

Formally defined by the Institute for Oral History (2003) at Baylor University, the term oral history refers to 1) a qualitative research process based on personal interviewing, suited to understanding meanings, interpretations, relationships, and subjective experience; and 2) a product—an audio- or videotape recording—that is an original historical document, a new primary source for further research.

Think Local and Practice

Students even at the lower elementary school level can practice raising questions and participating in interviews of classroom guests (Callison 1999). Best practice tends to suggest that such guests should be from the students' neighborhood and have experiences that will be of interest to the students. Forming questions so that the students share in "tell me more" is the process for nurturing inquiry.

Young, curious minds have a natural drive to gather information from other humans. Managing this process so that questions are asked with a specific purpose and responses are recorded to be analyzed for information can also involve peer interviews. The purpose of practice sessions can include questions which ask a student to describe a special event, tell what was special or a surprise to them, and to describe how the event compared to other similar happenings they have observed. Tell me about your birthday party? What was the biggest surprise? How was your party different from your sister's?

Oral histories are usually based on recollection of events in a person's life and how those events might be linked to major events of the greater society (Terkel 1970). Personal experiences during a war or conflict are often involved. Labor workers who recollect a strike or other dispute generate both elaborations on such events as well as personal opinions. Comparing life then to today is also a common questioning track.

Practice in asking questions, answering questions, operating equipment and taking notes, all done locally and under instructional media specialist supervision, can pay off when students move to the field application of these skills. Teachers helping the total class identify common themes from class interview sessions can set the stage for analysis of later collected oral histories. Are there descriptions that we can classify as common to the given kind of event? Are there special or unique stories that give us a wider spectrum or greater insight as to the total experiences we can relate to an event?

Depending on the age group involved, common practice questions can include world events and recollections of where you were, what you were doing, and what you though about the event in relation to your life.

Questions Drive the Inquiry

Students should consider the difference between open and closed questions:

Open: How did your family usually spend Christmas?

Closed: Did your family go to church on Christmas Eve?

Open: Why did your family come to the United States?

Closed: Was your family persecuted in your native country?

Open: Describe your feelings about leaving Vietnam.

Closed: Were you sad to leave all of your friends behind?

Open questions: often begin with what, why, how.

Closed questions: have only yes or now answers.

Students should know the difference between primary and secondary questions. Primary questions introduce topics or new areas within a topic. Secondary questions are attempts to get more information. They are also "follow-ups" to primary questions or to closed questions.

Examples of primary questions:

- Tell me about a typical day you spent at school?

- Tell me about the worst day you had at school?

- Tell me an example of a family joke or special story.

- What kind of jobs did you do to help earn money for you family?

Examples of secondary questions:

- Go on.

- And then?

- Tell me more about . . . .

- What happened next?

- How did you feel about that?

- What did you do after that?

The Greater Class Project

In 1972, Eliot Wigginton wrote in the introduction to his classic collection of student-gathered oral histories from Georgia:

Daily our grandfathers are moving out of our lives taking with them, irreparably, the kind of information contained in this book (Foxfire). And it isn't just happening in Appalachia. The big problem, of course, is that since these grandparents were primarily an oral civilization, information being passed through generations by word of mouth and demonstration, little of it is written down. When they're gone, the magnificent hunting tales, the ghost stories that kept a thousand children sleepless, the intricate tricks of self-sufficiency acquired through years of trial and error, the eloquent and haunting stories of suffering and sharing and building and healing and planting and harvesting—all go with them, and what a loss. If this information is to be saved at all, for whatever reason, it must be saved now; and the logical researchers are the grandchildren.

Most classroom projects will not result in saving a generation of stories nor publication of a dozen best sellers. But classroom oral history projects can place students in teams where they must plan and cooperate in order to deal with the complexities of documenting their local community and presenting the results to others. It should also be remembered that although we often think of the older generation as being the subject for oral histories, generations at all stages have memories and stories to share.

Thad Sitton (1983) has listed many options for classroom projects. These ideas were identified over three decades ago and based on the use of audio cassette recorders. Consider his ideas in light of current technologies that have become manageable and affordable for even the youngest public school student to use. Compact video cameras and computerized editing have opened new possibilities for these tried and true class projects:

- **Living History—Classroom Interviews of Community Informants.** Students locate community people with unique life experiences, special skills, and other valuable firsthand knowledge about the community past. The living history project is an exploration of local history through direct, face-to-face interaction with the persons who lived it. Students might recruit these resource persons from among their own relatives and acquaintances.

- **An Oral History of the Home Neighborhood.** This could be a study of a complete neighborhood or of some segment of one, such as a block or a street. The object is to find out how the neighborhood has developed and changed across time, as perceived by long-term residents.

- **A Memory Book.** Students brainstorm the questions to include in a memory book with which to interview one or both of their grandparents. The idea is to come up with a series of good questions common for all students to write down their grandparent's answers.

- **Researching the Origins of Local Place Names.** Using a topographic map of the home county as a basic reference, students use the oral history to discover the origins of local place names and learn the history of their area. These names would be those of the community, roads, city streets, streams, hills, and other natural and artificial features.

- **An Oral History of the School.** Based on review of old school newspapers, questions can be generated to ask former students, teachers, principals, secretaries and custodians. Students will have special interest in championship athletic events, faculty and student dress, student pastimes and social events.

- **Oral Histories of Local Buildings.** Photographs located in books on the local city history may show blocks and buildings as they were over 100 years ago. Students can gather photographs of the same locations today and interview past owners and occupants.

Oral Interview Steps

The Utah Statehood Centennial Commission (KBYU 2000) and the Institute for Oral History (2003) at Baylor University, along with others (Sommer and Quinlan 2002), have provided clear guidelines concerning the interview process:

Preparing for the interview. The interviewing team should demonstrate that they have an adequate knowledge background that will lead to intelligent questions. Although the interviewee will give responses that will lead to new questions and give new information and insights, they should not be interviewed in a void. Student interviewers should know the context for terms, events, people linked to the social and historical environments being explored. Background knowledge will result in a much richer interaction with the interviewee. Inquiry functions from the beginning to the end of the project with questions driving each stage.

Arranging the interview. Contact the potential interviewee both in writing and over the phone. Make it clear why his or she is of value and interest to those gathering the oral histories. Establish a rapport that is open and caring. Describe the purpose of the oral history project and give specific examples of typical questions that will be asked. Elderly subjects tend to prefer to be interviewed in the morning when they are fresh for a new day of conversation.

Setting up at the location. Select a location that is convenient for the interviewee. Often this will be at their home or apartment. Be very respectful of their property, pets and time. Take some time, 15 minutes or so, to get acquainted and to ease into the recorded interview. Select a quiet spot and seat them in a chair they find comfortable. Use an external microphone or clip-on microphone and encourage all individuals involved in the recording to speak up. Try to record away from clocks, telephones (turn off cell phones), air conditioner vents and other items which may cause background noise problems.

Equipment. Be familiar with all features and controls on audio and video recording equipment. Test all equipment before leaving to conduct the interview and test all equipment again after setting up on location. Try to use natural light as much as possible without the use of harsh additional lights for video recording. Be sure to bring back up batteries for all equipment. Planning on a thirty minute interview? Bring along at least ninety minutes worth of blank tape. Work as an interviewing team. One member may operate equipment, two others pose the questions, and another listens with interest and reassures the interviewee that they are providing interesting and useful information.

The interview process. The principal interviewer should state on tape the location, date, name of the interviewee and interviewer(s), and name of the project. An oral history interview is not a general dialogue. The purpose of the interview is to listen to what the interviewee has to say and to stimulate the narrative with understanding comments and intelligent questions. Ask open-ended questions first, waiting to see where they lead. The interviewer should tailor their reactions and follow-up questions to the responses of the interviewee. Ask the interviewee for details and examples for elaboration. Let the train of memory run its course before shifting to new topics.

The interview rapport. One member of the interview team may want to take notes, while others who are asking questions maintain eye-contact and interest. An oral history is not the time for the interviewer to voice his own opinion or to share his own stories. Participate in the interview with nods of encouragement, smiles, short phrases of understanding. Do not feel compelled to interrupt silences. Give the interviewee time to answer each question fully. If they feel they want to move on and return to the topic again later, let them. Be aware of the interviewee's race and economic background and of their culture.

Information artifacts and stimulation. The use of items from the time period being explored will help to generate stories and for the interviewee to elaborate with details. Family scrapbooks and photo albums will help. Toys, trading cards, old newspapers, furniture, appliances, clothing representing the styles of the day all help to stimulate memories and lead to more questions. Gathering examples of these social artifacts so that copies or photos can be made will help to enhance displays that help to illustrate the oral history project. In some cases, students may construct memory boxes that contain visual representation of artifacts and these are clearly labeled or numbered so that as the oral history is hear by others they can recognize the items being described on tape. Of course, with the use of video tape, these artifacts can be edited into the visual program.

Time and exit. Ninety minutes is likely to be the absolute maximum time to be spent on any one interview regardless of the age group, location, subject and experience level of those involved. If more time is needed, give it at least a full days rest if possible and record again the next morning. Memories refresh themselves with sleep. A general release form should be signed by the interviewee granting permission for use of the interview for historical and educational purposes. In some cases, the interviewee may need to be contacted again in order to verify or clarify statements given in the recording. A thank you should be expressed as the interviewers exit and should be sent in writing to the interviewee within one week following the interview. If there is a formal record or presentation that results, the interviewee should be invited to see such.

Evaluating the Oral History Interview

Over thirty years ago, Sitton (1983) offered the following criteria for evaluating an oral history interview. His questions remain valid today.

Is the topic of the interview identified?

Does the tape include name of interviewer, interviewee, date and location of the interview?

Does the interview start with the interviewee providing a brief biographical sketch?

Does the interviewer

- ask clear, singular questions?
- avoid asking leading questions?
- seem willing to ask for elaboration?
- ask questions that elicit extended answers?
- avoid making biased comments?
- have a good knowledge of the subject?
- allow the interviewee time to think and respond?
- avoid interrupting the interviewee?
- seem willing to use some well-timed flattery?
- start and stop the tape unnecessarily?

Is the interview environment free of anticipated distractions?

Is the tape free of audible difficulties?

Editing for Presentation

Oral history purists correctly argue that the entire oral record should be maintained both in recorded form and transcribed into a written manuscript. For projects produced by school children and young adults, editing may be not only a necessary process in order to keep the final presentations concise and interesting, but selection of the key portions of interviews linked together to support various topics and opinions can prove to be an important practice of media literacy skills.

Final presentation "products" can come from a set of oral histories and can be in the form of video programming or a series of digital projected visuals with a recorded narrative. Depending on the age and ability levels of the student producing the presentation, a ten minute to thirty minute final product is usually sufficient. This shorter format forces editing choices so that the message stays on track and the audience will remain interested. Visuals should change at least every 15 seconds.

Other presentation modes can include original plays based on the "characters" interviewed. A special program guide to the can include some examples of brief stories and quotations from those interviewed. School newspapers and Web sites are good places to publish in-house selected portions of oral histories. Some projects may reach the stage of detail and verification that they are acceptable records for local historical societies. Some public libraries are also establishing oral history collections if the content is relevant to the county or region and its local history. National efforts have been made to interview veterans of World War II as a portion of that generation is dieing away each day, and should be an indicator that other, younger, generations should be recorded now with fresh perspectives on the 1960s and 1970s.

The end result can be an evening of memories and stories on events pertaining to community happenings twenty to fifty years earlier. These events are "brought back to life" through oral recording, photographs, maps, and various other artifacts. Students may select the best three or four projects for final presentation and also be available to answer questions as to how this human record was gathered, analyzed and selected for sharing with the community. Wonderful school open house events can center on posters, dress, events and memories of previous decades.

References

Callison, D. (1999). "Interview." *School Library Media Activities Monthly* 15 (7): 40–41.

Institute for Oral History. Baylor University. (2003). http://www3.baylor.edu/Oral_History/Workshop.htm (accessed September 30, 2003).

KBYU. (2000). *Capturing the Past: How to Prepare and Conduct an Oral History Interview.* Brigham Young University, the Utah Statehood Centennial Commission and Wisteria Pictures. Distributed by Direct Cinema Limited, Santa Monica, CA. 31-minute videotape.

Sitton, T. (1983). *Oral History: A Guide for Teachers.* University of Texas Press.

Sommer, B. W., and M. K. Quinlan. (2002). *The Oral History Manual.* AltaMira Press.

Terkel, S. (1970). *Hard Times: An Oral History of the Great Depression.* Pantheon.

Wigginton, Eliot, ed. (1972). *The Foxfire Book.* Doubleday. Subsequent volumes of the same title.

Young, K. S., and B. A. Bernum. (2001). *Teaching Interview Skills without Full-Fledged Interviewing: An Alternative Exercise.* Annual meeting of the National Communication Association, Atlanta. ED 469 774.

Additional Relevant Web Sites

American Folklife Center: Folklife and Fieldwork. http://www.loc.gov/fieldwork/howto.html (accessed September 30, 2003).

Countdown to Millennium: An Oral History Collection Project. Ohio University. http://www.tcomschool.ohiou.edu/cdtm/index.htm (accessed September 30, 2003).

Using Oral History: Lesson Overview. The Library of Congress Learning Page. http://memory.loc.gov/ammem/ndlpedu/lessons/oralhist/ohhome.html (accessed September 30, 2003).

What Did You Do in the War Grandma? South Kingstown High School. http://www.stg.brown.edu/projects/WWII_Women/tocCS.html (accessed September 30, 2003).

Organizers

Daniel Callison

"Organizers" are tools or techniques that provide identification and classification along with possible relationships or connections among ideas, concepts, and issues. Organizers are useful to the learner when given in advance of instruction and often serve as clues to ideas that the instructor plans to introduce. Such organizers seem to have a positive influence on the learner's ability to focus on new information and may increase the portion that is eventually assimilated as new knowledge for the student (Johnson 1989; Clarke 1991; Fisher 2001).

Organizers also may help to illustrate potential student research topics that derive from brainstorming a given theme. When student ideas are connected through some graphic means, the organization of these often random thoughts may show how eventual student projects will relate and support each other. Such visual mapping of concepts and questions also can illustrate the need for students to be more open and cooperative in the research process as they discover facts and resources that overlap with the information needs of others in the class.

In addition to serving as primers, objectives, outlines, and mental maps, organizers also may prove useful to enhance summaries and conclusions. Here, ranking and rating may enter the process more strongly than in the planning stages as the learner displays new knowledge in the form of conclusions and findings. The learner may have gained enough entry-level expertise not only to organize information, but also to make decisions as to which findings are more important or more relevant than others. Organizing such thoughts in order of importance is one sign that the maturing information literate student is becoming a critical thinker.

Advance Organizers

David Ausubel's (1967) research and ideas concerning organizers given in advance of lessons have become fundamental aspects for modern discussions of learning theory. He defined "teaching" as the deliberate guidance of learning processes for the purpose of enhancing learning outcomes. An advance organizer is a statement given before instruction of new material that relates it to existing knowledge. To enhance the instructor's guidance toward meaningful information, Ausubel offered the following proposal as to the power of an effective advance organizer:

> If an [advance] organizer can first delineate clearly, precisely, and explicitly, the principal similarities and differences between the ideas in a new learning passage on the one hand, and existing related concepts in [the student's] cognitive structure on the other, it seems reasonable to postulate that the more detailed ideas and information in the learning task would be grasped with fewer ambiguities, fewer competing meanings, and fewer misconceptions suggested by the learner's prior knowledge of the related concepts; and that as these clearer, less confused new meanings interact with analogous established meanings during the retention interval, they would be more likely to retain their identity. (2)

Bruce Joyce and Marsha Weil (1980), co-authors of the classic educational text *Models of Teaching,* provide one of the more clear descriptions of Ausubel's work and application of his ideas to instructional practice. Joyce and Weil compare and contrast a wide variety of approaches to instruction.

The strongest advance organizers are those that provide a conceptual framework through which students, with some variety in backgrounds and experiences, each may connect and construct an intellectual scaffold. Through the use of specific models, examples, and analogies, the teacher helps students identify elements of a new concept in concrete ways. The organizer is broad, however, and conceptual in nature so that it provides a large umbrella under which many more specific items can be identified, discussed, and related. The organizer must be new to the audience if learning is to take place. The advance organizer sets a stage for a new experience-one that can be linked to experiences brought to the situation by the students. The effective teacher, in Ausubel's view, directs such linkage. A growing body of modern constructivist theory would suggest, however, that such linkage becomes stronger and more likely to be retained when the students are emerged in a social environment among themselves and the resources in order to build additional linkages for themselves.

The Implications of Ausubel's Theory

Joyce and Weil (1980) have summarized implications to educational structures that are derived from Ausubel's insights.

Curriculum:

- Progressive differentiation. The most general ideas of the discipline are presented first, followed by a gradual increase in detail and specificity.

- Integrative reconciliation. New ideas should be consciously related to previously learned content.

Teaching:

- Expository organizer. Provides a general model for introduction of new facts or ideas, but broad enough to move the learner up a notch or so on the complexities of the material to be learned. Ausubel recommended this type of organizer for completely unfamiliar learning material in which it is necessary to furnish an expository organizer consisting of more inclusive or superordinate ideas that could subsume or provide anchorage for the new material.

- Comparative organizer. Provides a more specific model closer to that which is already familiar and very similar to concepts just mastered. Ausubel recommended this approach for introduction of relatively familiar learning material, organized along parallel lines to that already held by the learner, but designed to increase discriminability between new and existing ideas, to refine differences with precision and detail.

See Figure Part.3.12 for common graphic organizers.

Webbing: Organizing Information to Visualize Ideas and Relationships

Organizing techniques have always been effective for teachers who want to bring meaning out of information overflow and sort out misinformation and irrelevant information. Kay Vandergrift (1994), professor of library and information science at Rutger's, gives attention to a specific technique, "webbing," in her guide to the teaching role of the school library media specialist. A web may be a visual representation of different subsets of names, events, concepts, or questions related to a more general topic or theme. A web may serve as a visual representation of characters, events, conflicts, and new vocabulary with a novel serving as the center for the web and one result being identification of additional similar books to spark young reader interest. The web may have been constructed by professional educators as a guide to illustrate the wide choice of topics possible for a given theme. For student research topics, exploration of basic classification systems such as Dewey Decimal and Library of Congress can provide, to some degree, the "lay of the land" for organized information. Textbook outlines, tables of contents, and glossaries sometimes provide the same initial, but expertly formal, approach.

The more effective approach, supported by Vandergrift, is to use webbing as an engaging technique to bring students into the creation of the research agenda. Students brainstorm expres-

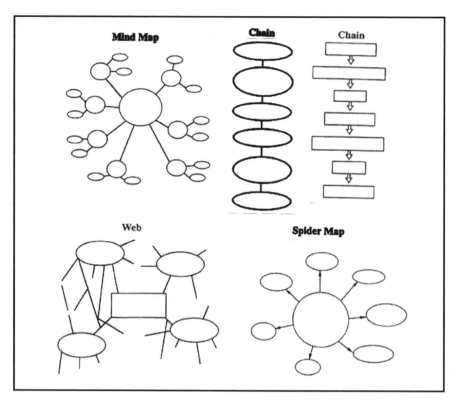

Figure Part3.12. Common graphic organizers.

sions of experiences, events, and questions, and place these ideas on a large board or overhead. No initial judgment is made as to value or relevance, although as items are clustered and related, students begin to see that some subtopics offer more potential depth than others. Some see webbing as a free-flowing outline that allows ideas to be expressed and captured without the constraints of an ordered progression. Webbing seems to work best with groups of students as they are encouraged to express ideas for themselves and for peers to learn of the variety of possibilities for their classmates. Formal outlining, however, will eventually have its place in the research process, especially in the presentation stage that requires judgment and order.

Vandergrift (1994) reminds us that large-group semantic webbing is a triggering device that will need to be followed by continued background reading and likely a series of webs created by the individual student before he or she gains focus for the project. "They reconsider what they already know, identify what they want to find out, and formulate spe-

cific research questions or hypotheses. Even if a teacher has assigned the broad topic, this activity can help students see possibilities within that topic, encourage their personal ownership and involvement with the assigned task and, most importantly, get them excited both about what they already know and what is yet to be known." (p. 15)

Graphic Organizers

The KWL Table, created by Donna Ogle (1986) and illustrated by James Bellanca (1990, 1992) in his collection of graphic organizers for cooperative thinking, has become a common tool for students to individually map their research agenda. By using this simple three-column structure, the students list what they Know, Want to learn, and have Learned. The visual organizer again helps students see relationships, but also helps learners see personal progress and initiates self-evaluation. (See Figure Part3.13.)

Key Words for Instruction in Information Inquiry

K	W	L
Smallpox: - is contagious - can be fatal - is serious - infects people People get vaccinated so they don't get it People with smallpox get covered with bumps	Where did smallpox originate? What makes it so bad? How is it spread and treated? When was a vaccine created? Is there more than one form of smallpox? Do people still get smallpox?	Smallpox has been around for 1000s of years. It's particularly harmful to virgin populations. There is no treatment; only vaccine for prevention. It is spread from direct contact with infected person. One in three inflected will die. The last case was in 1949, but people fear its use in bioterrorism.

Figure Part3.13. Sample KWL Organizer with sample comments on the topic smallpox.

Leticia Ekhaml (1998), professor of research at State University of West Georgia, has described how graphic organizers have recently evolved from traditional charts and tables to specific designs associated with different tasks in problem solving and critical thinking. Some of the benefits of such organizers listed by Ekhaml include

- seeing connections, patterns, and relationships
- facilitate recalling or retelling of literature
- ranking ideas
- listing causes and effects
- improving comprehension skills and strategies

Ekhaml (1998), based on Bellanca's cooperative think tank ideas, illustrates four basic patterns for graphic organizers: sequential, conceptual, hierarchical, and cyclical. Although each of these organizers is likely to be more formal than the less structured brainstorming, such as webbing, each represents an effective visualization of showing steps, decision points, relationships, and rankings. Creating visuals that personalize such organizers may well be a new trend in summaries and visual presentations we will expect from students as they demonstrate their information literacy skills. Visual organizers can convey the core of the essential or critical message that student researchers are expected to discover.

References

Ausubel, D. P. (1967). *Learning Theory and Classroom Practice*. Bulletin No. 1. The Ontario Institute for Studies in Education.

Bellanca, J. (1990). *The Cooperative Think Tank: Graphic Organizers to Teach Thinking in the Cooperative Classroom*. Skylight Publishing.

Bellanca, J. (1992). *The Cooperative Think Tank II: Graphic Organizers to Teach Thinking in the Cooperative Classroom*. Skylight Publishing.

Clarke, J. H. (1991). "Using Visual Organizers to Focus on Thinking." *Journal of Reading* 34 (7): 526–534.

Ekhaml, L. (1998). "Graphic Organizers: Outlets for Your Thoughts." *School Library Media Activities Monthly* 14 (5): 29–33.

Fisher, A. L. (2001). "Implementing Graphic Organizer Notebooks: The Art and Science of Teaching Content." *Reading Teacher* 55 (2): 116–120.

Johnson, L. Lee. (1989). "Learning Across the Curriculum with Creative Graphing." *Journal of Reading* 32 (6): 509–519.

Joyce, B., and M. Weil. (1980). *Models of Teaching.* Prentice-Hall.

Ogle, D. (1986). "K-W-L: A Teaching Model That Develops Active Reading of Expository Text." *The Reading Teacher* 36 (6): 564–570.

Vandergrift, K. E. (1994). *Power Teaching: A Primary Role for the School Library Media Specialist.* American Library Association.

Web Sites for Graphic Organizers

Freeology—Free Graphic Organizers. http://www.freeology.com/graphicorgs/ (accessed August 29, 2005).

Houghton Mifflin English—Graphic Organizers. http://www.eduplace.com/kids/hme/k_5/graphorg/ (accessed August 29, 2005).

The Graphic Organizer. www.graphic.org (accessed August 29, 2005).

Inspiration Software, Inc. http://www.inspiration.com/home.cfm (accessed August 29, 2005).

Kathy Schrock's Guide for Educators—Graphic Organizers. http://school.discovery.com/schrockguide/assess. html#go (accessed August 15, 2004).

Region 15 Graphic Organizers. (English and Spanish Versions) http://www.region15.org/curriculum/graphicorg.html (accessed August 29, 2005).

Web English Teacher—Graphic Organizers. http://www.webenglishteacher.com/graphic.html (accessed August 29, 2005).

Write Design Online—Graphic Organizers. http://www.writedesignonline.com/organizers/ (accessed August 17, (2005).

Parent

Daniel Callison

"Parents: The Anti-Drug" is a public service campaign developed on the premise that parents are the most influential adults in a child's life, at any age. Action is the operative term in these announcements. The parent is not influential in a quiet, reserved role nor as one who moves aside for others to deal with education of the child. The parent takes action to meet the problem.

In support of literacy and Information Inquiry, is there a role for the parent? Assuming that the parent has an understanding of his or her child's abilities and that the parent has a basic understanding of the emerging challenges of the Information Age, are there actions the parent can take to be a constructive contributor to the student's growth in selection and use of information?

Stepping aside while the child faces information selection may not be on the same critical level as failing to be involved in drug education. Yet, there are valid reasons for parents to practice information literacy and model such skills for their child. How might professional educators provide the opportunity for parents to gain a greater understanding of the information needs their child will face? How might the parent serve to mentor many of the information search and use processes? Are there reasonable support techniques the parent can employ that fall someplace between driving Susie to the public library and the temptation to write the final paper for Johnny?

"Parent" often will be used in the singular here, but not at the exclusion of the "parenting team" or the potential for strengths that might come from collaborative father and mother roles. At least one adult who is committed to that child's well-being and delivers by being available in nearly all situations is, perhaps, the most powerful single factor for increasing the chances that a child will feel safe, will strive to achieve, and will contribute to society. Many studies over the past fifty years have tied the strength of the parent or guardian relationship to the potential for social acceptance and academic success for the child (Mallen 1995; Morrow 1995; Fredericks 1997; Catsambis 1998; Epstein 2002).

The roles of two parents or two guardians may increase the chances or diversify the opportunities for the child to be successful. Collaboration can be powerful in any team-teaching situation, formal or informal. However, the discussion here on "parent" as a key instructional word assumes that at least one parent can make a tremendous difference. The techniques and strategies mentioned can help lead to effective actions on the part of at least one parent or guardian. The educational impact of the parent also assumes that the parent can and will give the time and attention to a child on an individualized basis. Demands from work, social life, and even other children can, obviously, influence the quality of the parent/child relationship.

What Works: Curriculum of the Home

The United States Department of Education released a summary of "what works" in successful teaching and learning situations in (*What Works* 1986). While the list of research findings remains valid for K–12 education environments today across many disciplines, the document led off with specific findings that relate to parents as teachers. "Parents are their children's first and most influential teachers. What parents do to help their children learn is more important to academic success than how well-off the family is" (7). The following comments were made by the Education Secretary to clarify this research finding:

Parents can do many things at home to help their children succeed in school. Unfortunately, recent evidence indicates that many parents are doing much less than they might. For example, American mothers on average spend less than half an hour a day talking, explaining, or reading with their children. Fathers spend less than 15 minutes.

Parents can create a "curriculum of the home" that teaches their children what matters. They do this through their daily conversations, household routines, attention to school matters, and affectionate concern for their children's progress.

Conversation is important. Children learn to read, reason, and understand things better whey their parents:

- read, talk, and listen to them,

- tell them stories, play games, share hobbies, and

- discuss news, TV programs, and special events.

- In order to enrich the "curriculum of the home," some parents:

- provide books, supplies, and a special place for studying,

- observe routine meals, bedtime, and homework, and

- monitor the amount of time spent watching TV and doing after-school jobs.

- Parents stay aware of their children's lives at school whey they:

- discuss school events,

- help children meet deadlines, and

- talk with their children about school problems and successes.

Research on both gifted and disadvantaged children shows that home efforts can greatly improve student achievement. For example, when parents of disadvantaged children take the steps listed above, their children can do as well at school as the children of more affluent families.

What was defined in this message from the U. S. Department of Education was the "wealth factor" that dominates nearly all of the attempts to find items and actions that correlate to improving student achievement. The wealth of the family setting, with at least one parent who engages the child for the motivation to learn, is not based on high financial income, but on elements of security. There is stability for the child and the wealth is found in a steady, reasonable income that allows the family to plan on a future that is predictable and likely to improve for all members. Children do not have to be concerned with problems associated with nutrition, clothing, safety, comfort, warmth and caring. These needs are met and children can concentrate on, and greatly enjoy, the learning processes.

Factors in Parent Partnerships

Lesley Farmer (2001), school library media certification supervisor at California State University Long Beach, writes, "Parents usually want the best for their children, but they may not get involved in education. Several factors affect the likelihood of establishing a partnership and maintaining it. The more quickly library media teachers recognize the following issues and address them, the better will be the results" (89). Farmer identifies the following specific concerns:

- **Low expectations.** Some parents will need positive models from other parents and samples of quality student work in order to better understand their own role and their child's potential to meet basic academic performance.

- **Personal issues.** Some parents may fear the unknown and may believe they have little to contribute to the school or to their child's education. In some situations, a volunteer training program, sponsored districtwide, can help. On the other hand, some parents may believe they are overqualified to participate in school projects. Again, a coordinated volunteer program can help these parents gain a more realistic idea of in-school and at-home roles they can play.

- **Family issues.** Children in secondary schools may not want to have others see their parent involved in school activities or for others to know that the parent provides additional assistance at home. Getting parents involved "behind the scenes" is more challenging but possible when planned and coordinated.

- **Logistics.** Even with the best intentions, some parents may be limited in their involvement because of work schedules, lack of transportation, lack of home technology, and/or language barriers. Each of these, however, may open special challenges for library media specialists and other teachers to coordinate efforts and address local problems.

What the Parent Can Do That the School Can't

In the "best case" situations, the parent knows and understands to a large extent the child's experiences, potential, and limitations. A parent who wants to build on this knowledge and understanding will seek opportunities to share with, as well as listen and learn from, their child's teachers and counselors. The parent has many opportunities to influence the child's development, often more extensive than what is offered in school. The parent can (*Building Successful Partnerships* 2004)

- provide a consistently safe and nurturing environment, tailored to the child's reasonable wants and most important needs;

- create, associate, and therefore capitalize on hundreds of "teachable moments" because of frequent, close, and individual association with the child in many different situations;

- listen, encourage, and give guided practice and critical review, acting as both an appreciative audience and an inspiring coach;

- create a learning environment with books, computer access, and office supplies specifically identified for the child and allow for both formal (desk) and informal (couch) study areas;

- schedule a regular daily time for conversations and reading, regardless of there being a specific academic assignment or task, in order to make learning routine;

- visit many formal and informal learning environments, especially music festivals, museums, public libraries, and community events, and make the child a sharing companion in the experience;

- learn through social, active, informal events, such as recreation and camping, as well as visits with neighbors and other members of the family;

- model and articulate specific political, social, and religious values held by the parent and, perhaps, the wider family base;

- reward positive child behavior through affection;

- seek out local content experts when needed for elaboration on some topics as well as critical feedback on the child's academic work when appropriate; and

- display the child's accomplishments within the home in a prominent location and over an extended time.

Helping with Study Skills

John Hoover (1989, 1993), director of Research and Evaluation at the University of Colorado, has written extensively about methods parents can adopt to help their child become more successful in school. A few of his helpful homework techniques, selected from dozens, are given here and updated to reflect access to electronic resources.

Time Management

- Develop semester and monthly schedules, showing deadlines and personal goals.

- Develop and enforce a time schedule for after-school events that includes time for family, recreational activities, and homework, and which manages access to television based on selection of mutually agreeable programs.

- Eventually, the child should set his or her own schedules, justify his or her plan, and place it into a computer-monitored calendar.

Reference Materials

- Build access to ready reference resources through a personal collection, the public and school libraries, and marking favorites over the Internet.

- Parent and child should review how reference materials can be used and how information is accessed and might be of value both to stimulate ideas and to complete academic assignments.

- Critique notes taken and applied for completion of reports, papers, or exams.

- Review feedback on graded assignments, especially written and oral reports, to ensure inclusion of better information, better organization, and other corrections for future work.

- Discuss the value and meaning of different resources and the information drawn from those sources, including print, electronic, and human expertise.

- Encourage the child to use basic reference sources to solve problems such as maps for travel, schedules for transportation, and price guides for purchase of clothes, communication equipment, or other items relevant to the age group.

Oral Reports

- Demonstrate, guide practice, and listen to different ways for the child to deliver and enhance oral presentations.

- Help the child elaborate on a topic of interest while discussing events and happenings at mealtime. Exchange stories and give personal meaning to events. The parent should listen at least as much as he or she talks.

- Give time over several days to rehearse portions of a presentation so that it can be revised and polished rather than a last-minute, overwhelming event the night before it is due to be presented in school.

Note Taking/Outlining

- Review with the child notes they have taken. Ask the child to verbalize orally the events of the class to help clarify the notes for an exam or major assignment.

- Help the child develop a format that works for him or her personally to take meaningful notes efficiently.

- Have the child apply outlining to plan events out of school such as a party, shopping, repair of a bike, searching for information on the Internet, or predicting what is hoped to be seen in a movie.

Visual Material

- Discuss graphs, charts, and photographs shown in catalogs, the newspaper, and on television. What is the intended message and is it effectively conveyed?

- Encourage use of a digital camera, computer graphics, and free drawing to help express a story or to document an event such as a vacation, summer camp, or a visit to see grandparents.

Library Usage

- In addition to learning how to access and borrow resources, encourage and support building a personal library at home.

- Compare and contrast different libraries as well as libraries to the Internet and discuss differences, options, and limitations of each.

- Encourage the child to seek out and to read widely on a topic of personal interest. Maintain this special interest over time with the opportunity to visit places and events relevant to the topic. Purchase books and magazines for the child on the topic of interest as rewards for constructive learning behavior or to celebrate a birthday.

Using the Library—Explore and Question Together

Approaching the library can be as foreboding for the parent as it often is for the child. Most public and school librarians work very hard to make the library an inviting place and strive to provide personal assistance. The least productive scenario for effective student learning and least likely to create the opportunity for the parent and child to learn together is for the parent to ask all of the questions concerning the information need, resource access, and library use. Two stronger scenarios for productive learning experiences follow:

- The child is encouraged by both the librarian and the parent to raise his or her own questions, although the parent should listen and converse to help clarify access procedures when absolutely necessary.

- The parent does some background exploration and reading on his or her own prior to a visit to the library with the child so that they gain enough understanding of the environment to provide useful guidance and still have a good sense of when to return to the librarian for professional assistance. Those parents who have some successful library use experiences may find that they are helpful in assisting their child in the use of online indexes. Some parents also may be helpful with skimming information sources and helping the child select from many resources beyond the standard encyclopedia. Access to specialized materials, perhaps rare or historic in nature, may need the parent to provide adult permission to access and to help the child interpret.

Inquiry and other project assignments that involve use of multiple resources in order to gain information beyond the textbook can present several occasions for parent and child interactions (Eisenberg and Berkowitz 1996). Assuming that the parent has access to the given inquiry assignment and has an understanding of the teacher's expectations, limitations, and deadlines, conversations between parent and child can involve:

- **Question Generation.** Exchange ideas on questions that might be of interest to explore on several potential topics the child has raised. The parent can give value to the child's questions by commenting on how intriguing the topic seems to be and raising other questions that might be added to the information exploration that will follow.

- **Explore and Read.** Both parent and child can read widely about a given topic in order to build a background knowledge based on terms, names, and events. This establishes a common information pool from which to raise additional questions and to begin to clarify the inquiry project's potential.

- **Surfing the Internet.** Both parent and child, often searching together, will want to turn to the Internet as one of the important resources to explore background on nearly any topic. Surfing together can help parent and child build a joint vocabulary that serves to refine the topic and to give both focus to the project, and will help them gain some idea of the limitations of the resources located through the Internet.

- **Planning.** If this is a major inquiry project that will involve many resources, interviews, data-gathering, and more, the parent can help the child work out a calendar and set deadlines for different stages of the project. Such a schedule may have been given by the teacher and the child should be encouraged to share such with the parent. Communication concerning such deadlines can help to avoid last-minute panic, but also can clue some parents in as to when they may want to ask about progress on the project and be available to assist on difficult phases.

- **Revisit Sources.** As the child moves through the project and gains focus, relevant resources should be visited again for detail and clarification. Parents should continue to have students raise new questions and to reflect with their child on concerns they may have on gaining the best information possible to answer those questions.

- **Arrange for Special Resource Access.** The parent may be especially helpful as an adult who may assist the child in contacting local experts on a given subject or gaining access to special or academic collections that would only be loaned to an adult.

- **Revisit the Librarian.** Often the best questions and more precise needs can be expressed by the child after he or she has progressed through the basic information search, background reading, and initial question raising. Moving into these latter exploration stages, the child will be ready to ask very specific questions and express specific information needs.

- **Read and Listen to Drafts.** The parent is probably most valuable as a patient and objective audience. Both are extremely difficult tasks for the parent, but both are essential. The parent listens to drafts of paragraphs read aloud or to segments of oral presentations so that constructive feedback can be given along with encouragement. The child gains important practice, discipline, and self-confidence.

- **Continue the Interest.** In very fortunate situations, the parent and child may find through inquiry a topic of mutual interest and they can continue to read, talk, and travel together to explore places and events pertaining to the topic in the future, long after the school assignment has been completed.

A Nurturing Environment for Reading

The Northwest Regional Education Lab (Davis and Lewis 1997) has published an extensive guide for parents. Techniques are outlined that help to promote and refresh reading as the child grows from preschool to middle school. "Children learn to read best when they have books and other reading materials at home and plenty of chances to read. This means not only having lots of books around—from libraries, bookstores, and book clubs, as gifts, and as treats—but many chances to read and talk about what they are reading" (3). Selected examples are given here to illustrate the strong role the parent can play to model the value of reading for pleasure and meeting information needs.

Things Parents Can Do with Infants and Toddlers:

- Read books over and over again. Make sure that the child-care providers read and talk to your child.

- Talk about the pictures and ask questions.

- Make talking to your infant or toddler part of everyday life.

- Link reading to real life and tangible examples the child will see, touch, smell, hear, and understand.

Pre-K through First Grade:

- Read daily to your child—even if all you have is ten minutes.

- Reread stories and as your child gets to know the story pause and let the child finish the sentence.

- Have plenty of markers, crayons, pens, paper, and other materials on hand and encourage kids to make books, write, and draw.

- Ask your child to tell you a story about what he or she has drawn. Write the child's words on paper and read it back.

Second and Third Grade:

- Follow and encourage your child's interests and find reading materials relevant to those interests.

- Have your child help you with recipes from cookbooks or mixes. Ask him or her to read ingredients, measure, mix, and clean up.

- Help your child become a more fluent reader by having him or her read to younger brothers and sisters.

- Get blank books or help make one so your child can write his or her own words and symbols or paste in cut-outs to compile a book.

- Limit television to shows that you and your child select together and try to hold viewing to under a dozen hours per week.

- Play games that involve reading.

- Have the child help you compile a grocery shopping list and read it off at the store as he or she helps you collect items.

Fourth and Fifth Grade:

- Keep reading aloud to your child even if they can read alone.

- Link movies and television shows to books, but continue to limit television watching to under fourteen hours per week. Many of those hours should include watching programs with the child and discussing what is shown.

- Encourage children to read more by letting them stay up fifteen to thirty minutes later if they are reading.

- Give a magazine subscription as a gift that will keep giving all year.

- Ask the child to read schedules for television, transportation, or local events in the newspaper.

Sixth through Eighth Grade:

- Look closely at how you and your child spend time and consider ways to read at the same time both separately and together.

- Be sure the child observes you reading for pleasure and for information and talk with the child about what you are reading. Read aloud small excerpts.

- Give gifts that encourage reading and writing such as a reading lamp, stationary, and books to build their own home library collection. While the child will value a personal collection in his or her room, he or she also will value some of the books being placed on a family bookshelf along with titles read by the parent.

- Encourage the child to read aloud to others at all ages, including grandparents, in order to experience reading as a form of entertainment, learning, and socializing.

Media Literacy—Watching Television Together

According to studies summarized for the United States Office of Educational Research and Improvement (OERI), children typically learn far less from television than they do from a comparable amount of time spent reading. In addition, what children tend to learn from television without selective guidance and discussion tends to not be beneficial.

Television viewing is nearly always an "out of school" experience. Although impossible to monitor always, the most likely teacher at the point of need for discussion of televised events is the child's parent.

Television programs often present a very selective view of life, with glamorous, witty, and powerful characters. This often stands in contrast to the real people with which children come into contact. In 1994 Sweet and Singh summarized twenty years of research for OERI:

> About eighty percent of all [television] programs contain some violence with an overall average of slightly more than five violent acts per hours (this has very likely increased over the past ten years with the addition of cable and satellite options). Settings and time patterns are often contrived and condensed into a brief time slot. Problems are often resolved quickly and violently, and the violent or other antisocial behavior often goes unpunished and without comment.
>
> . . . Research shows that parents can protect their children from potentially harmful influences and can even use television for learning when there are age-appropriate developmental activities. Parents can teach children critical viewing skills. For example, children can be taught to recognize stereotypes, distinguish fictional from factual portrayal, and identify scenes portraying behavior and values that conflict with their own and their family's values, and think about and describe alternative, nonviolent means of resolving problems. (3)

The reporting of news on television, radio, or the local newspaper can provide an opportunity for meaningful discussions between the parent and child, especially when there has been a major event that likely has received attention at school. Some discussion might involve considering why a certain story is on the front page or leads off the news broadcast, while others get less attention in later pages or at the end of the broadcast. What visuals are used to enhance the story in print and on television? What sounds or interviews are selected on radio news reports and what might one speculate as to why these items were edited into the report?

Other issues to raise for discussion (always depending on the child's readiness and the age appropriateness of the event and news forum) are the following:

- Compare and contrast different types of news, features, sports, and editorials.

- Identify facts and opinions and the reason for both.

- Discuss time and space limitations for presenting news.

- Discuss different formats for presenting news—headlines, commentary, debate, and historical analysis, and the options to locate these different formats.

- Does there seem to be a strong political bias on the part of some news broadcasts, broadcasters, stations, or newspapers?

- How would you summarize the important points of an extensive news story?

- How would you find more details behind a brief story or series of headlines?

- How would you locate additional opinions and facts on a story that contains issues on which people clearly disagree?

- Parents may find important moments when their own feelings, values, and beliefs should be shared with the child, especially if the child asks.

Library Media Specialists and Parents Teaching Technology

Eileen Faucette (2000), coordinator and founder of PTA Live Online, promotes the posi-tive cooperation between teachers and parents in the application of today's computerized technologies to improve communication between the school and the home. She stresses the need for joint parent and teacher understanding because of these issues:

- Families have concerns because they have heard lots of distressing things about technology, but parents tend to be more accepting the more they learn about technology and the options to manage it.

- Family members of the student may have technology experience and contacts that can be useful for the educational program if schools can tap into such expertise.

- Teachers should showcase what students are accomplishing in school with computer technology and encourage parents to discuss how they might extend such learning and computer applications at home.

Faucette concludes that "library media specialists are uniquely placed to support and encourage [parent] involvement, especially technology efforts. [T]he library can be the parent involvement hub" (61).

Workshops, evening seminars, and even outreach programming in cooperation with the public library can lead to many opportunities to teach the parent how to use technology to support the child's academic needs. As a library media specialist, consider the following titles for a parent workshop and what you would provide for leading a evening of interactive instruction:

- Effective Ways Parents Can Communicate Electronically with Teachers: Assignments, academic achievement, classroom behavior.

- Booktalks for Parents: What your child likes to read and good titles to help you become an even better parent (supported with a special collection ready for loan to parents from either the school or public library).

- How to Search the Internet and to Select the Most Relevant Resources: Judgments on meaningful content and age appropriateness.

- Electronic Resources Available at School and at the Public Library: How to access and how to get help from the local librarian.

- Homework Assistance: Evenings at the school and public libraries with teachers and librarians available.

References

Building Successful Partnerships: National PTA Involvement Initiative. Available at http://www.pta.org/programs/bsp/ (accessed June 14, 2004).

Catsambis, S. (1998). *Expanding the Knowledge of Parental Involvement in Secondary Education.* Center for Research on the Education of Students Placed at Risk. ED 426 174.

Davis, D., and J. P. Lewis. (1997*). Tips for Parents about Reading: Information and Ideas for Helping Children Through Eighth Grade Succeed with Reading.* Northwest Regional Educational Lab. ED 412 525. Fulltext online.

Eisenberg, M. B., and R. E. Berkowitz. (1996). *Helping with Homework: A Parent's Guide to Information Problem-Solving.* ERIC Clearinghouse on Information and Technology.

Epstein, A. S. (2002). *Helping Your Preschool Child Become a Reader: Ideas for Parents.* High Scope Educational Research Foundation.

Farmer, L. (2001). *Teaming with Opportunity: Media Programs, Community Constituencies, and Technology.* Libraries Unlimited.

Faucette, E. (2000). "Are You Missing the Most Important Ingredient? A Recipe for Increasing Student Achievement." *Multimedia Schools* 7(6) (November-December): 56–61.

Fredericks, A. D. (1997). *The Librarian's Complete Guide to Involving Parents Through Children's Literature.* Libraries Unlimited.

Hoover, J. J. (1989). *Helping Children Develop Study Skills.* Hamilton.

Hoover, J. J. (1993). "Helping Parents Develop a Home-Based Study Skills Program." *Intervention in School and Clinic* 28 (4) (March): 238–245.

Mallen, T. (1995). *Taking Charge of Your Child's Education: Nine Steps to Becoming a Learning Ally.* Acumen Press.

Morrow, L. M., ed. (1995). *Family Literacy: Connections in Schools and Communities.* International Reading Association.

Sweet, D., and R. Singh. (1994). *TV Viewing and Parental Guidance.* Office of Educational Research and Improvement (OERI). ED 374 922.

What Works: Research About Teaching and Learning. (1986). United States Department of Education.

Additional Recommended Resource

Champlain, C., D. V. Loertscher, and N. A. S. Miller. (2005). *Raise a Reader at Any Age: A Librarians' Toolkit for Working with Parents.* LMC Source.

Plagiarism

Daniel Callison

I want to give Doug Johnson credit. Even though at many times during my thirty years as an educator I am certain I have stated and written phrases and concepts that match Mr. Johnson's (2003, 2004) recommendations concerning the prevention and management of plagiarism. Probably I've made similar statements even before Mr. Johnson became a media specialist. It seems our approaches are very similar: Encourage what can be done rather than concentrate on what should not be done. Student research should be presented as an opportunity to explore and share, not just learning how to follow another set of rules. Engage students in projects that reward original thought and discourage the need to copy or cheat.

Now, I know I have "paraphrased" Mr. Johnson and have interpreted what I understand from his comments and writings on plagiarism, but he will still receive "credit" even if his presentations and articles come along several decades after my own similar ideas. Why? He deserves credit because he has published such ideas in much respected and widely read sources, including his own books. He has achieved a respected status as a director of library media and as a national speaker. He has synthesized some ideas and concepts that remain insightful, even though we both probably wish they were common knowledge and hope they become common practice.

In addition to the standard citation, I give him credit within the text of my writing (or speech, or video, or Web site). Thus, I practice the opportunity to share with others my findings, my resources, my links to what I have read and I think others should read. Within my text I give you some measure of the value of the experts, opinions and evidence I have worked hard to locate and organize. I give credit to those with which I share ideas, have gleaned ideas, and combined ideas for new insights of my own.

I give credit both within my text and my references to help the reader identify my own knowledge trail so that they may learn more beyond what I write. By identifying experts, I give the reader the key link to other resources of value that I may not even know about or that have not been written yet. As examples—I would cite Carol Simpson, associate professor at North Texas University and Kenny Crews, law professor at Indiana University—Indianapolis in nearly any paper or presentation on copyright issues because their names trace to an established literature and can be counted on to lead the reader to future discussions. I would take the time to find relevant evidence from them to deliver through me to my audience, but deliver such with much more in mind that a simple quotation. Links to experts help us keep on learning beyond the issues at hand.

Documentation of work, regardless of format, not only verifies that much has been examined, analyzed and synthesized, but experts described and sources cited express a judgment on those sources. The writer or speaker passes along to the audience their evaluation of the sources of evidence and expertise. Sources of evidence can be more than just cited, they can be given value by the author stating relevance of the evidence and authority of the expert.

The information literate student knows that giving credit in not only the right thing to do, but such strengthens his/her own communication. It serves to validate arguments and ideas. Plagiarism hides this and keeps the communication product from becoming three-dimensional: what I bring to the question, what I assimilate from other sources, what I now know and raise as new questions. So who helped me get there? Give them credit.

When and How to Cite

Robert Harris (2002) has taught students how to cite materials in their compositions at the college level for the past thirty years. In addition to avoiding plagiarism and evidence that the student has been exploring resources widely, he adds these two reasons to cite sources:

- Such leaves a literature trail for others to read beyond the essay; citations are a help and guide to the reader.

- Citations show respect for those who have proceeded you with providing the knowledge base for your essay.

Harris also identifies what content should receive specific quotation (47):

- Expert declaration—an expert whose authority requires his/her exact words.

- Direct support—provides crisp response to a sense of immediacy and the exact quotation reinforces the key point.

- Effective language—elegant, clear, direct, and can't be stated better.

- Historical flavor—or regional or cultural flavor; the statement reflects the times or the culture.

- Specific example—as a brief personal anecdote the entire quotation tells a special story.

- Controversial statement—makes an outrageous claim or shocking opinion.

- Material for analysis—analyzes or criticizes and exact words are needed so the issue or resolution is clear to defend or attach.

Harris also recommends that quotations carry a sense of qualification of the author within the text. Thus, more authority, context or relevance can be added by noting the person cited with some organizational affiliation, job description, or accomplishment.

Peer Pressure, Procrastination, Publish or Perish Often Equals Plagiarism

Plagiarism in the higher education circles has been wide spread even before the temptations of electronic "cut and paste" (Hansen 2003). Macabe (1996) relates much of the plagiarism in by college students to peer pressure and procrastination. Surveys of college faculty indicate that nearly one third of college professors admit they have plagiarized at some time in their scholarly career; another third indicate they have likely plagiarized but are not certain (Genereux 1995). Note that these pieces of information are cited, but the experts in each case are not of high relevance to my audience. They receive due credit, but not additional value by my description of their authoritative standing within my text.

Recent charges of plagiarism against two prominent historians, Doris Kearns Goodwin and Stephen Ambrose are common knowledge in the popular reading circles. Their relatively minor transgressions are of much less importance than the extensive contributions that both have made, through primary interview and tremendous first-hand research, to the record of American presidential history. My opinion here carries no reference as it is similar to most others, and can be easily traced in the popular news. However, if I were presenting the detailed arguments to debate the issues pertaining to the Goodwin and Ambrose cases, I would cite resources extensively. I note them here to illustrate that even the best historians are at times not always our very best role models, but such should not destroy the value of their contributions to our knowledge base.

This is not to say that plagiarism is not a serious ethical offense. "Plagiarius" is Latin for kidnapper. Not a minor crime. One who copies or even closely imitates another composer, artist, writer or speaker without permission steals from the originator, assuming the true original author can be identified for certain. Paraphrasing does not make an idea one that can be claimed by a new owner. Intellectual property in our society can be held by the creator for many years and for a profit.

Of course, the computerized cut and paste information world we live in today has increased the ease to lift chunks of information from others and call them our own. The same computerized world, however, provides us with ease to identify authoritative documentation and to include such in our communications ranging from the most basic of school reports to the most complex scholarly works.

Applying Principles of "Giving Credit"

Doug Johnson, director of Media and Technology for the Mankato Public Schools and international speaker on a wide spectrum of school media management issues, proposed the following in Phi Delta Kappan (2004):

> Much effort is expended in education trying to "catch" plagiarism in student work. Teachers and library media specialists are using various web services and techniques using search engines to determine if or how much of student writing is lifted from online sources. Such tools are necessary and can be effective.
>
> But our time as educators is better spent creating assignments, especially those that involve research, that minimize the likelihood of plagiarism in the first place. Rather than making assignments that can be easily plagiarized and then contriving methods for detecting or reducing copying, whey not do a little work upfront to design projects that require original, thoughtful research? (549)

Johnson has quoted Carol Tilley, then a school media specialist in Danville, Indiana, that a good approach to discouraging electronic plagiarism is to "Change the nature of the research assignment to utilize a higher level of thinking skills" (Johnson 1996). Johnson has built on Tilley's summary with examples that "Lower [the] Probability of Plagiarism" or LLP projects. A selected listing of some of his ideas (Johnson 2003, 76–80) is paraphrased below, and related to inquiry-based approaches described in previous key instructional word columns (Callison, 2000; Callison and Lamb 2004a; Callison and Lamb 2004b):

- Projects are based on student-raised questions associated with real-world questions concerning local issues. If students are engaged in the process with guidance, such can result from topics that have relevance, meaning and purpose.

- Evidence will need to include interviews, personal observations, experiments or other primary source data. Answers can not be found based on simple reference source searching—such is not research. Strategies for location are searching. Data analysis, synthesis, application of evidence to form conclusions is the elements of research.

- Students are expected to use narrative style writing for at least a portion of the project, including a description of how they formulated their questions, gathered information and determined the value of the information. The I-Search process originated by Macrorie (1988) and refined by Joyce and Tallman (1997) proves useful here.

- Students have authentic assessment outlets that include a variety of methods to present their report, including multimedia. They have a variety of audiences to which they can present their report beyond the teacher alone and must adjust for different ages and abilities in their audiences. They document how they reflect and revise to meet different audience needs.

- Students gather evidence and opinions from which they can rank people, events and opinions as they relate to themselves personally. What are the ten inventions that most influence your life and why? Who are the ten people that have influenced how you live and why? The ten events in history that have most effected how you live today are and why? Or nearly any assignment where the student must make judgments, evaluations, make choices and give justification.

Teaching More Than Location and Citation

Joy McGregor, then assistant professor at Texas Woman's University, and Denise Streitenberger, then a doctoral student at TWU, observed high school juniors and found that they reduced their amount of copying when taught how to paraphrase and correctly cite resources, but not by a great deal (1998). In a few cases, they suspected that students who "copied" and provided a more clear and organized paper than students who had messy, yet original papers were graded higher. They concluded that teacher interventions regarding the format and rules of correct citations seemed to limit the amount of blatant copying, but did not help students learn from the sources or construct their own understanding of their research topics.

Their recommendations include more time should be invested by the teacher collaborating with the media specialist to work with students to understand the research process and to explore topics in more depth. Unfortunately, the most common instructional role of school librarians remains "how to look up information and how to cite it."

Instructional media specialists who approach projects based on inquiry principles know that their role with the teacher is to help stimulate lots of student-generated questions, to encourage students to read and explore background resources widely, and to demonstrate how such exploration leads to meaningful research project ideas from which students can make a choice. Proper citation style is taught at the point of need, when evidence is being gathered and documented.

In order to reduce the amount of cheating, teachers at the Lake Placid Central School of New York have adopted these ideas as part of their instruction with the school media specialists. Specifically, with permission, they use the "Insider's Guide to Cheating" developed by the Battle Creek, Michigan schools. Sara Kelly Johns, director of school library media at Lake Placid Central, presented (at ALA in 2005) a summary of the guidelines and guidance she and other teachers give to students:

- The best way to avoid cheating and plagiarism is to find ways to personalize your assignments. React in your writing about how your topic might personally affect you, your family, your school, or your community. An original conclusion supported by facts from other works that are properly cited is never cheating. Write in your own voice [style], not just in your own words.

- Organize your work so that you don't run into a last minute time crunch that keeps you from studying, writing, creating, revising, reflecting and making your work your own.

- Keep good records as you do research of where you found your supporting ideas.

It's easier than doing research twice—once for finding the information and again for doing the bibliography.

- Always include a bibliography, list of resources, or acknowledgements whenever you use the work or ideas of others. If you can't provide a citation, don't use the source. If giving a presentation, credit your source verbally.

- Understand that using the work of others IS permissible and usually necessary to create a well-supported set of arguments, conclusions or specific answers to questions. Giving credit to the source of this work will help to avoid plagiarism.

- Make a large percentage of your work original as possible. Use direct quotes or paraphrasing only when what you find is written in such a way that it clarifies or makes the idea expressed more understood.

Shared Credit in the Media

Kym Kramer, library media specialist at Fishback Academy in Indianapolis, has engaged her elementary students over the years in lots of multimedia productions. At her annual celebration of the student products, she explains to an audience of parents all of the work that goes into planning and producing each individual student video. Above all, she and her students make sure parents and others know who was involved in each production and the resources that were used for scripts—especially student documentaries of local events and institutions.

Credit is given to the source of information, both within the narration of the student video and in print as credits role at the end. Students who carried out technical duties are also credited. Kym's students learn at an elementary school level the value and courtesy of giving credit to others who influence the product in any manner.

One of Kym's graduate interns, Michelle Ward (2005), recently assisted a group of students write a script to help them identify those who should receive notice in a "video bibliography." This was the script for two students who had completed a team effort to report on the zoo:

My name is _____ and my name is _____.

We have been studying _____.

We got our live footage from the Indianapolis Zoo.

We got our information from _____.

We got our still shots from _____.

We got additional information from Indyzoo.com, SIRS Discover, and

EBSCO Animal Encyclopedia.

[and some suggested additions to Michell's script]

Zoo keepers interviewed were _____.

Video Director _____.

Script by _____.

Final Editing by _____ and _____.

As these elementary school students mature and experience additional projects for science fairs, debates, formal speeches, even plans to solve local community problems, they can build from their early experience to give credit where credit is due both within the text of the presentation and at the end—"for the record." If you don't believe there is lots of credit to go around, take the time to stay and view the credits as they role after any recent major motion picture. Probably going that far is too far, but encouraging students to practice the courtesy of acknowledging the work of others can certainly extend to all student products, not just the senior term paper.

References

Callison, D. (2000). "Assignment." *School Library Media Activities Monthly* 17 (1): 39–43.

Callison, D., and A. Lamb. (2004a). "Audience Analysis." *School Library Media Activities Monthly* 21 (1): 34–39.

Callison D., and A. Lamb. (2004b). "Authentic Learning." *School Library Media Activities Monthly* 21 (4): 34–39.

Cheating: An Insider's guide to Cheating at Lakeview High School. (2002). Battle Creek, Michigan Schools. Available at www.infotoday.com/MMSchools/jan02/Cheating.pdf (accessed August 18, 2005).

Genereux, R. L. (1995). "Circumstances Surrounding Cheating." *Research in Higher Education* 36: 687–704.

Hansen, B. (2003). "Combating Plagiarism: Is the Internet Causing More Students to Copy?" *CQ Researcher* 13(32): 773–795.

Harris, R. A. (2002). *Using Sources Effectively: Strengthening Your Writing and Avoiding Plagiarism.* Pyrczak Publishing.

Johns, S. K. (2005). "Information Ethics for the Net Generation." Presented at the American Library Association National Conference, Chicago.

Johnson, D. (1996, January). *Head for the Edge—Past Columns from* Technology Connection, The Book Report, *and* Library Talk *Magazines.* Citing Carol Tilley from an LM-Net posting in 1995). Available at http://www.dougjohnson.com/dougwrit/cut.html (accessed August 16, 2005).

Johnson, D. (2003). *Learning Right from Wrong in the Digital Age.* Linworth Publishing.

Johnson, D. (2004). "Plagiarism-proofing Assignments." *Phi Delta Kappan* 85 (7): 549–552.

Joyce, M. Z., and J. I. Tallman. (1997). *Making the Writing and Research Connection with the I-Search Process.* Neal-Schuman.

Macabe, D. (1996). "The Relationship Between Student Cheating and Fraternity Membership." *NASPA Journal* 33: 280–291.

Macrorie, K. (1988). *The I-Search Paper.* Heinemann.

McGregor, J. H., and D. C. Streitenberger. (1998). "Do Scribes Learn? Copying and Information Use." *School Library Media Research* 1. Available at www.ala.org/aasl/SLMR (accessed August 16, 2005).

Ward, M. (2005). "Journal of Internship with Kym Kramer for Certification as a School Library Media Specialist." Indiana University School of Library and Information Science at Indianapolis.

Web Sites

(each accessed August 15, 2005)

Following are three useful Web sites to help you determine when and how to cite sources, avoid plagiarism, and present authoritative information as credible evidence:

Indiana University Writing Tutorial Services. http://www.indiana.edu/~wts/pamphlets.shtml

Purdue University Online Writing Lab. http://owl.english.purdue.edu/handouts/research/r_plagiar.html

NoodleTools. http://www.noodletools.com/

Portfolio

Daniel Callison

A portfolio is a purposeful collection of a student's work that exhibits the student's personal and academic efforts, progress, and achievements. The purpose of the portfolio determines the content. Digital portfolios have the potential to meet several goals (Niguidula 2005). They may showcase the student's best products and should show also the processes the student mastered to come to the final product. They can justify the achievements to meet requirements for graduation. Portfolios showing a visual display of progress over the years, in elementary or secondary school, can be a powerful communication devise among teachers, parents and the student. In some cases, the portfolio can become the tool by which the student self-analyzes his academic standing and future potential. Often the portfolio will include

- evidence of the student's participation in selecting content to meet a specific purpose,

- the criteria for selection of artifacts,

- the criteria for judging merit, and

- evidence of student self-reflection.

The intent is to provide a more complete and richer display of a student's abilities to deal with complex problems. The portfolio is one answer to those who feel that the traditional evaluation of student performance, limited to letter grades or points for academic work and behavior, is too narrow to depict other possible student talents. New developments in the application of portfolios include emphasis on self-reflection, portfolios for professional educators and teachers in training, and management of artifacts through multimedia means. Perhaps, some educators believe, portfolio evaluation can make formative and summative evaluation closer to authentic evaluation. They see portfolios as an opportunity to view multiple dimensions in student performance, richer than the measures on standardized exams. Others believe the portfolio process to be cumbersome and complex and not as precise as the standardized exam process.

Constructive Conversations

While grades seem cold and conclusive, portfolio collections often can open constructive conversations among teacher, parent, and student about the processes that have brought the student to the conclusion of the most recent product and raise plans for future possibilities. Portfolios can, if gathered and maintained in a systematic manner, provide a record that

- has been compiled with the participation of the student through self-reflection and selection of the pieces to represent his or her record;

- is tangible and can be compared to others in the class and to previous work by the student to clearly show areas of progress or need for attention;

- leads to a progressively more complex and demanding set of academic requirements, tailored to the student's individual talents and needs. (Clemmons 1993; Chatel 2001)

Portfolios can, if not valued as a valid means for evaluation and if not regularly groomed and up-dated, become space-consuming clutter, vulnerable to those who are quick to criticize educational fads.

The means for evaluation and the potential content for the student portfolio have been given reasonable attention over the past decade (Chang 2001). Implementation of portfolio assessment is still at the experimental stage, but some schools are making progress. Composition and science seem to be the frontline curricular areas to adopt this approach. Progressions in student grammar, spelling, sentence structure, and communication of meaning are clearly composition elements that can be demonstrated and compared from one year to the next. Defining terms, practice in basic experiments, documenting observations in narrative and numeric methods, and drawing conclusions or making predictions offer scope and sequence that can be reflected in science portfolios.

The portfolio approach opens evaluation to richer descriptive records (Valencia and Paris 1991; Rousculp and Maring 1992; Callison 1993). Reading performance, for example, becomes more than a number of titles read or reading ability at, below, or above a specific grade level. Reading teachers and library media specialists can comment on the student's ability to make reading selections and the student's growth in discussion about the content of what has been read. The portfolio record may even document the student's reflections on what he or she has selected and favored over the years and can define a goal for reading more in terms of questions to be explored and personal interests rather than just mastering basic phonetic skills. Such reflection can truly set the stage for life-long learning. The same may be true for portfolios in information literacy. Will they be used to document basic steps or to illustrate critical thoughts?

The Portfolio and Information Literacy

What is the potential for use of portfolios to document the information literacy performance of students? Should this be a record compiled by classroom teachers, by library media specialists, or both? Can such records be realistically gathered and maintained in a timely, efficient, and understandable manner? These are demanding and largely unexplored questions for the school library media field. Library media specialists who have established information skills instruction integrated at the point of need with specific assignments, collaboratively planned and implemented with the classroom teacher, are clearly on the cutting edge for instruction today. They may feel that there is no need to expand this instructional role into the evaluation of student performance through portfolio records. Some schools have adopted a scope and sequence curriculum that includes identification of specific information skills; however most have not coordinated such efforts so that information literacy is a performance to be evaluated in a variety of curricular settings across the student's academic career.

Without such a curricular framework it is difficult to illustrate the degree of proficiency of a student's information selection and use skills. To add an evaluation process that requires documentation of student work; conversations with student, teachers, and parents; and writing a constructive judgment may be asking too much of the library media specialist.

And yet, we must speculate on the possibilities if the teaching role is to be implemented fully. Conducting evaluation completes the teaching cycle. Evaluation can take many forms, including the assessment of student information needs through reference interviews, determining reading options through reader's advisory, and feedback to classroom teachers for purposes of revising collaborative lessons. Evaluation of student performance, however, is the key to becoming a full player in the information literacy educational process (Callison 1987).

Such evaluation can tell us much about what students really select as valid information, when and how they make those judgments, and what library media specialists and other teachers should do to encourage or correct various information use or misuse behaviors. It seems that the most reasonable approach for introducing the potential for portfolio assessment in the information literacy curriculum is to further expand the basic principles that provide the foundation for the collaborative instructional activities. Information literacy becomes a component of the assessment criteria for the portfolio, and this component can appear in a record related to any area of the curriculum. The criteria, however, remain the same across the curriculum. These criteria can be introduced to teachers with the hope that they will adopt them as part of the established evaluation process, or these evaluation criteria can become an extension of the collaborative teaching role now seen as key to ensuring that students are effective users of information.

The Colorado Model

Work in development of information literacy rubrics in Colorado has led to identification of some of the evaluation criteria measures that should be applied in portfolio assessment for information skills.

A rubric is a descriptive measurement, given on a progressive scale. Often the rubric defines in a set of related statements what the learner should know and be able to demonstrate for self-evaluation or evaluation by others.

The progressive scale usually ranges from basic skills to advanced skills relative to the age group being measured. Target indicators are used to show the skills to be considered. Measures range from entry-level actions such as "in the process of making progress toward this skill" to "showing signs of being proficient in this area" to "demonstrating advanced, creative, exceptional performance compared to peer group."

The Colorado Information Literacy Rubric (Colorado Department of Education and Colorado Media Association 1996) provides one of the first systematic frameworks for documenting the ability of every student in how he or she

- constructs meaning from information;

- creates a quality product;

- learns independently;

- participates as a group member;

- uses information and information technologies responsibly and ethically.

As with any pioneering document, there is still room for refinement and greater specificity,

but the Colorado instrument goes a long way in introducing some skill development strands which can be converted to evaluation criteria applicable to student portfolios of information use, composition, and critical thinking. One rubric strand is illustrated below.

Target Indicator: The student acquires information. Progressive, observable actions for the student to reflect on and for others to consider in evaluation of performance:

a. **In Progress:** "Someone helps me extract details from information."

b. **Essential:** "I can extract details and concepts from one type of information resource."

c. **Proficient:** "I extract details and concepts from different types of resources."

d. **Advanced:** "I extract details and concepts from all types of resources."

Taking this one example from the Colorado plan, in isolation, does not illustrate the full range of information literacy skills contained in their proposed rubric framework. However, this one sequence, as others from the rubric, can give rise to ideas concerning evidence necessary for the components in a portfolio that would represent information literacy. Examples from the student's work would be sought to indicate that the student:

a. Follows specific steps concerning what to read and what information to look for to answer a given question. Guidance may be given by the library media specialist, classroom teacher, parent, or other student. A worksheet with pre-stated questions and specific examples for guidance may be evidence of the practice of this first-level skill.

b. Knows the difference between fact and concept. Along with this, the student can demonstrate how to extract facts and concepts from an information source which is commonly accepted as a resource for the student's ability level: an almanac table and summary, an encyclopedia article, a magazine article. Exercises in practice of fact and concept identification from an information source may serve as evidence of this ability.

c. Examines several resources for identification of related information, similar or conflicting, from several sources and links these pieces together to construct aspects of an argument, to expand perspective by listing several related issues, or to describe in detail an event or phenomenon.

This is a jump to sophisticated skills. Demonstration of the ability to move through a variety of information sources for such purposes may be difficult to document. One option is a collection of note cards that contains both direct quotations and paraphrasing of information extracted by the student. In addition, the student needs to show evidence from a variety of sources and to document which sources were most useful and why. Therefore, notes should include room for the student to document judgments concerning the adequacy of the source and information extracted.

d. Can determine which resources are most likely to provide the information necessary to confirm, contradict, and therefore expand a line of argument; provide association and clustering of issues; or enrich a description of an event. Evidence at this point is more than simply showing that the student can extract information from a personal interview, a self-conducted survey, a televised debate of experts, a primary source, or any other type of resource we might identify. Extracting information from any one resource is basic and doesn't change the skill level, even through the student may now be able to demonstrate how to extract information from an almanac, a journal, and a personal interview. Evidence that the student has used three different sources is simply one skill times three-a repetition of level one-unless newly introduced sources require a different set of skills for extracting information. Assignments in which the student has been required to use three sources, whether necessary or not for the completion of the report, do no more to document advanced skills than do basic worksheets for practice use of one source. Knowing why other sources are necessary and best in predicting where, when, and how to approach those sources for gathering the potential evidence to meet a specific information need are the advanced skills to be documented in a portfolio based on information literacy.

While these may be reflected in a student's product, such as a report based on use of multiple resources, these advanced skills are best documented by a reflection paper or a critical discussion by the student in which he or she explains why certain resources were selected and what limitations as well as merits each resource provided in helping the student accomplish his or her desired communication goal.

The Colorado Information Literacy Rubric does not get into the details for specific student products for portfolios, nor does it expand on each indicator suggested above. It is, however, an invaluable collection of potential evaluation categories from which can be extracted checklists, questions, and evaluation criteria for student portfolio review. Moving from this given rubric to information literacy portfolio evaluation criteria will result in additional consideration as to what critical skills are worth the time and effort to document.

Guided by Indicators and Standards

Getting started in the complexities of information literacy portfolio construction and review may require some consideration of a rubric that illustrates the roles and actions of those involved. Division of time and effort among other tasks is certainly a key factor that will delay full implementation of portfolio review for information literacy skills; however, the potential is enormous if the review process is established in relation with successful portfolio programs for student composition, reading, and critical analysis skills across the curriculum.

Target Indicator: The School Library Media Specialist as Evaluator of Student Information Literacy Performance

In Progress: The teacher of school library media collaborates with the classroom teachers to integrate information literacy with various assignments requiring the use of multiple resources. Specific student performance skills for information use have been identified and organized in a scope and sequence across the academic program for typical, special need, and gifted students K–12.

Essential: The school library media specialist and the classroom teacher collaborate to present, facilitate, and coach students as they develop skills in the selection, analysis, synthesis, and application of information to solve problems. Both the school library media specialist and other teachers feel comfortable in conversing with students about their information needs, interpretation of information content, and alternatives for further information.

Exercises in information use are evaluated by both teachers from the library media center and from the classroom. Student information literacy performance has an influence on the overall evaluation of the student.

Proficient: Evaluation of the student's product includes evaluation of the information selection and use process. Criteria for this evaluation have been established and provided to the student prior to the beginning of the process, and the application of the criteria has been modeled by the school library media specialist and the other teachers. Application of the criteria for evaluation includes student self-evaluation as well as feedback from the library media specialist and other teachers.

Advanced: Examples of communication products, including those electronically recorded with narrative and visuals, are gathered to reflect the progression in information literacy by the student. A record of the evaluation of student performance by the library media specialist, other teachers, student peers, and the student are contained in checklists and descriptive notes. The student's progress is mapped against the scope and sequence measures for the school's information literacy curriculum.

Joie Taylor (2006), a school media specialist from Nebraska, has summarized typical artifacts for a portfolio representing the student's research process skills:

- Brainstorming concerning the task or critical question.
- What resources were considered and the thought process to determine which would be used.
- A time line showing progress on the work.
- A learning log of successes and difficulties
- Actual notes that were taken.
- Feedback along the way from the library media specialist.
- Drafts of the final project.
- The finished project or CD-ROM or videotape of actual project.
- Student reflection on the overall project.

Information Skills Tied to Portfolios from Subject Disciplines

Barbara Benson, Susan Barnett, and Susan P. Barnett (1999), high school teachers who have promoted "student-led conferencing" as a powerful technique to showcase student portfolios have compiled questions from various academic disciplines for students to address.

Electronic Portfolios

Portfolios are being used more and more to support college graduates in job interviews or to summarize a student's high school academic career through a personal presentation or exit interview prior to graduation. The use of multimedia technologies has advanced to the level that most students can gather and maintain a collection of artifacts electronically. In addition, most adults (teachers, administrators and parents) have the equipment to access such documents. The multimedia evolution will move through floppy and zip disks, CDs and eventually rest on the Internet.

Web-based storage and access to student portfolios are already expanding from K–12 settings to colleges and graduate schools. Samples can be found at Tammy Worcester's Soderstrom Elementary School in Kansas http://www.essdack.org/port/ and The Teaching Learning Center at Indianapolis http://www.iport.iupui.edu/teach/teach_studenteport.htm.

Preservice teachers are housing online portfolios at the Center for Technology and Teacher Education at the University of Virginia. Carol Brown and Robin Boltz (2002) of East Carolina University have shown how gathering electronic artifacts aligned with program objectives and national standards can be effective portfolio evaluation tools for library professionals, both as library managers and library science educators.

Marilyn S. Heath (2004), formerly of East Tennessee State University, has identified four types of professional portfolios that lend themselves to electronic compilation:

- **Resume**—documents previous work experiences, skills, and recommendations with links to visuals and Web sites.

- **Showcase**—a selected set of the very best work and may show process as well as products through the use of slide shows and motion clips.

- **Evaluation**—organized to match to a set of standards or criteria for a profession.

- **Professional Development**—centers on examples of continued professional growth with artifacts that reflect a wide variety of new skills both in content of disciplines taught and the technology skills associated with effective instruction.

Helen Barrett (2000) of the School of Education at the University of Alaska is the most of-

ten cited expert for the emerging discussion on professional electronic portfolios. Portfolio construction may gain effectiveness if the compiler follows a theme or metaphor such as a mirror, a map, a story, a journey, a laboratory, a kaleidoscope of accomplishments. Barrett stresses two major assumptions:

1) a portfolio is not a haphazard collection of artifacts (such as a scrapbook), but rather a reflective tool which demonstrates growth over time; and

2) as education moves to a more standards- based performance assessment, new tools are needed to organize and easily access meaningful evidence of successful teaching. (1)

Barrett concludes that electronic portfolio development draws on two bodies of literature:

1) multimedia development—decide, design, develop, evaluate; and

2) portfolio development—collection, selection, reflection, projection.

Portfolio experiences for students and teachers become most effective when they have not only documented accomplishments, but can help focus on a future course of achievement based on improved communication and information management skills.

References

Barrett, H. (2000). *Electronic Teaching Portfolios: Multimedia Skills + Portfolio Development = Powerful Professional Development.* Association for the Advancement of Computing in Education. Available at http://electronicportfolios.org/portfolios/site2000.html (accessed August 9, 2005).

Benson, B. P., S. Barnett, and S. P. Barnett. (1998). *Student-Led Conferencing Using Showcase Portfolios.* SAGE Publications.

Brown, C. A., and R. Boltz. (2002). "Planning Portfolios: Authentic Assessment for Library Professionals." *School Library Media Research* 5. Available at www.ala.org/aasl/SLMR (accessed August 2, 2005).

Callison, D. (1987). "Evaluator and Educator: The School Library Media Specialist." *Tech Trends* 32: 24–29.

Callison, D. (1993). "The Potential for Portfolio Assessment." In *School Library Media Annual 1993*, Vol. 11, edited by Carol C. Kuhlthau, 30–39. Libraries Unlimited.

Chang, C. (2001). "Construction and Evaluation of a Web-Based Learning Portfolio System: An Electronic Assessment Tool." *Innovations in Education and Teaching International* 38 (2): 144–155.

Chatel, R. G. (2001). *Portfolio Development: Some Considerations.* ED 459 437.

Clemmons, J. (1993). *Portfolios in the Classroom: A Teacher's Sourcebook.* Scholastic Professional Books.

Colorado Department of Education and Colorado Educational Media Association. (1996). "Rubrics for the Assessment of Information Literacy." *Indiana Media Journal* 18: 50–61.

Heath, M. S. (2004). *Electronic Portfolios: A Guide to Professional Development and Assessment.* Linworth Books.

Niguidula, D. (2005). "Documenting Learning with Digital Portfolios." *Educational Leadership* 63 (3): 44–47.

Rousculp, E. E., and G. H. Maring. (1992). "Portfolios for a Community of Learners." *Journal of Reading* 35: 378–385.

Taylor, J. (2006). *Information Literacy and the School Library Media Center.* Libraries Unlimited.

Valencia, S. W., and S. G. Paris. (1991). "Portfolio Assessment for Young Readers." *Reading Teacher* 44: 680–682.

Electronic Portfolio Web Sites

Center for Technology and Teacher Education at the University of Virginia. http://curry.edschool.virginia.edu/class/edlf/589–07/sample.html (accessed August 25, 2005).

Electronic Portfolios for Elementary Students and Teachers, presented by Tammy Worcester at Soderstrom Elementary. http://www.essdack.org/port/ (accessed August 25, 2005).

Ideas Consulting. www.richerpicture.com and www.efoliominnesota.com (accessed February 6, 2006).

Indiana University Purdue University Portfolio Development at the Teaching and Learning Center. http://www.iport.iupui.edu/teach/teach_studenteport.htm (accessed August 25, 2005).

Mt. Edgecumbe High School Student Portfolios. http://www.mehs.educ.state.ak.us/portfolios/body.html (accessed August 1, 2005).

This Week's Tips from Teaching Today: *Creating Professional Portfolios.* http://www.glencoe.com/sec/teachingtoday/weeklytips.phtml/21 (accessed August 29, 2005).

Primary Sources

Daniel Callison and Maureen Sanders-Brunner

Primary sources are original objects or records that have survived the past. Some times referred to as "raw history," they represent a direct personal experience of a specific time in the past. Primary sources are artifacts such as official documents (birth certificates, marriage licenses, and property contracts), journals (diaries and letters), clothing, toys, tools, visuals (sketches, paintings, and photographs), and more.

Thousands of documents too valuable for the general public to handle are being placed on Web sites for electronic access, many containing public domain resources now offered free to researchers and educators. The Library of Congress Web site is perhaps the most exciting example (www.loc.gov). And new tools help novice researchers deal with barriers such as illegible handwriting of ancestors (Allen and Dutt-Doner 2006). For example, the Memorial Hall Museum Online offers a Magic Lens that superimposes a typed manuscript over a primary source written in elaborate script.

Primary sources are nonfiction, first-person items, whereas secondary sources, such as biographies and trade books, are created as a result of documenting or interpreting events at some time after the actual event. Third-level, or tertiary sources, such as encyclopedias and textbooks, are a compilation and interpretation from a broad spectrum of selected documents that have gained conventional acceptability and usually set the norm for the content taught in public education (Holt 1995; Kammen 1995).

Why Use Primary Sources?

History can be reconstructed through critical analysis of primary sources (Coatney and Smalley 2005). In the hands of an expert historian, primary sources may give evidence that uncovers clues to what "really happened" in the past. When applied to our common American heritage through local history and the wider spectrum of the everyday lives, a new breadth and richness emerges beyond the official records left by government bureaucrats that often give us a one-sided view of history through military and legislative actions. For students in elementary and secondary school settings, primary sources serve to give context and more personal meaning to historical events (Levstik and Barton 2001). Family artifacts can give an emotional connection between present and past. Great-great-grandparents can be placed within historical events (Carey and Greenburg 1983).

Within the inquiry-based learning environment, primary sources lead to interesting questions and reflections often more exciting than the cold facts and figures recited in the typical textbook (Coatney and Smalley 2006). People telling family stories or giving an eyewitness account also can be considered primary sources as long as such oral history is a testimony to events experienced personally. Reflections on the greater meaning of historical events, however, serve as "an informed opinion" and slip into the secondary resource category to be accepted in the context of other, often more authoritative, records (Potter 2002; Seidman 2002).

It is important to use critical evaluation of primary sources, especially autobiographies and oral histories. Oral histories can be seductive and persuasive because it may be easy to accept what seems to be an "eyewitness" account. But such primary records can carry strong biases, misinterpretations and misunderstandings of happenings even though experienced first hand. As students grow in their skills for applying inquiry methods to information literacy, they will understand these criteria that should be considered in order to determine validity of the descriptions and stories found in recorded interviews (Stebbins 2006):

- Understand the social and cultural biases of the time period of the interview.

- Determine the mission of the oral history interviewer—are questions leading or open and unbiased?

- Check oral history accounts against other documented accounts if necessary—although much of oral history value can be first person accounts of how an event effected the subject emotionally.

Authoritativeness often is defined in historical narratives not so much by "firsthand account" as by the ability, experience, and knowledge to provide a meaningful interpretation. Yes, it is possible for some historians to provide greater meaning and insight to the Normandy invasion than General Eisenhower could himself.

To fully understand why educators should use primary sources in the classroom, we should examine why we teach history and what the most important aspects of history are for students to comprehend. After all, primary source lessons can be very messy, and the resources are difficult to access and use without a firm, unbiased conviction for their curricular importance. First and foremost, studying history tells the story of who we are, how we came to live in our communities, and what knowledge and experiences are important to pass along to future generations.

Rewriting History for Kids Based on Primary Sources

Understanding how history is written helps students appreciate their own personal and family history and how it relates to larger, current global events. Young people may develop empathy for the struggles and triumphs of those from diverse cultures and make better decisions for their own lives based on greater understanding of past events. Through a personal understanding of history, not just the facts and figures, but the stories, events, and motives of individuals, helps young people become informed and active citizens in a global community.

An emerging trend in nonfiction for children and young adults are books that frankly report, based on primary documents, how presidents and other "heroes" really behaved. Not intended to shock or destroy our heritage, these "New Age" books show young readers that there are several perspectives on the importance of a given historical event and that they can gain pride in a wider spectrum of leaders. Rather than believing in the myths that have been constructed of a few so-called heroes, respect for the sacrifices made by "common" men and women of all ages and economic levels can be gained.

Jim Murphy, author of the Newbery Honor book *The Great Fire,* continues his skillful use of primary sources in his newest and highly honored book for young people, *An American Plague: The True and Terrifying Story of the Yellow Fever Epidemic of 1793.* Murphy (2003) interlaces stories of true human sacrifice based on diaries and other documents that tell of those who remained in Philadelphia to care for the dying and clean the diseased city while others, many major names in American history, left town and offered little assistance.

Original records also are used by Murphy to document final chapters to illustrate, without holding back in any manner for young minds to comprehend, how disastrous plagues can happen again today and in the future. Moving history closer to reality and away from myth will stimulate discussions that require practice in logic and reasoning. Such sets the stage for students to practice critical literacy. Debates over the merits or characteristics of "revisionist historians" may come down to understanding that all historians, except for whoever the first one might have been, are revisionists. Adding perspectives and new insights is the basic role of the historian.

Suzanne Jurmain's *The Forbidden Schoolhouse* (2005) is an excellent example of using primary sources to establish the role of a true, enlightened educator in American History that is so often dominated in textbooks by politicians and military leaders. Her story of Prudence Crandall, who accepted Black American girls into her school at the risk of her life and complete ostracism in a Northern society that believed itself to be anti-slavery, but was clearly bigoted, is wonderful example of stories students can aspire to write. Although not likely to be as detailed and as finely documented as Jurmain's first professional work, just examination of her layout and organization of information is worth study by young social science inquirers.

Critical Thinking Through History and Information Literacy

Many public school educators often miss the larger meaning of the importance of history and fail to engage students in the pursuit of asking and answering their own questions about the past. Some students dread history class, starting at a very young age. Most lessons, although carefully planned, can be boring and meaningless. Human history is largely a mystery that must be uncovered, realized, and then fully explored before an educated guess can be offered and discussed with others. When history is taught as a hard science, as a series of absolute facts without room for debate, there is no need for students to invest themselves in critical learning. Educators already have made consideration and interpretations for students, and meaningful practice in information literacy skills is lost.

Most states include the use of primary sources in their academic standards for K–12 social studies curriculum. Primary sources build analytical skills because they necessitate the need for the interpretation and juxtaposition of often conflicting information. Students must organize new information chronologically, place artifacts within a context of a time other than their own, and develop their own questions and make predictions as to what new information from primary items might bring when compared to conventional historical records (Craver 1999).

Teaching with Primary Sources

Susan Veccia (2004), former manager of educational outreach services at the Library of Congress (LC), has written an impressive guide for busy library media specialists and other teachers to manage the complex task of teaching with primary sources. *Uncovering Our History,* published recently by the American Library Association, provides a realistic path to nearly eight million primary resources now accessible online for public use for everyone from professional historians to the elementary school student's first introduction to the Mayflower. Because of this expansive access not possible before the Internet, new opportunities now exist for incorporating primary sources into all grade levels.

Veccia gives many examples from the Learning Pages of the LC American Memory Web site and integrates these across curricular areas. Clued into the power of collaborative teaching, she identifies the following characteristics of the library media specialist as an instructional partner:

- **Proactive School Leader.** Initiate a building level history study group that will work together to compile leads to primary sources, local and national, that are related to specific areas of the curriculum. Provide in-service sessions on the potential uses of the American Memory Project.

- **Cheerleader for Primary Sources.** Participate in regional and state workshops and associations that promote primary resources. Promote primary sources through displays of artifacts from the local school district's history and photographs of the community and residents from previous generations. Add examples of questions that may help students consider why their local history is relevant to their lives.

- **Teacher of Students and Online Coach.** Explore the potential primary resources sites and search along with students as they attempt to work with online primary resources.

- **Arbitrator of Difficult Materials.** Primary resource documents reflect the social setting of their time. Language used reflects the social values of the period and may be offensive in today's world.

- **Program Administrator and Instructional Partner.** Experiment with activities that have potential for enriching social studies curriculum such as oral histories, photograph and artifact analysis, creating a museum, field trips to historical sites, and re-enactments of local historical events.

Levels of Story and the Interpretation of Primary Sources

The potential use of primary sources is mentioned within the standards of the social studies curriculum in each state. Specific activities vary, but in each case the intent is to "bring history to life" and make it relevant to the student at his or her learning stage. At all levels, students can become engaged in gathering local and personal artifacts in order to create a "museum" of historical personalities, events, and issues. Library media centers are perfect places to house such displays over several weeks.

- **Elementary.** The student should be able to identify common historical artifacts. Such artifacts may be presented along with telling a family story—"how my grandfather farmed" or "how my grandmother made bread." Favorite toys such as dolls and action figures of today have relevant similar or companion artifacts found in all previous generations.

- **Middle School.** Students can begin to see personal relationships between artifacts representing their current lives and the lives of their ancestors. These common historical artifacts can lead to creating stories of the past that mirror the present. Consider music, cars, hairstyles, ball caps, jeans, class rings, and letters from war times or other situations when family members were far from home because of major events. Local natural disasters such as floods, tornadoes, and illnesses also may trigger stories that tie the generations together.

- **High School.** The student begins to understand that artifacts help to tell us something about how ancestors made a living and socialized. Some students at this level will begin to document stories that generalize about why ancestors came to their local community and what individuals were needed in order for the community to be established. In some cases, a photograph from the past will help to create a story that ties the past with the present. A series of photographs, showing evolution of the community from past and present, can illustrate final Web sites, displays, or dramatic presentations developed by students.

- **Advanced Placement.** Students at this level can hypothesize from artifacts some aspects of how social, economic, and political structures impacted everyday life. Stories about health care, social activism, political movements, trade unions and working conditions, and educational opportunities and limitations are a few of the possibilities. These students may find interactions with local historians from colleges and historical societies to be enriching.

When Does the Past Become History?

Ruth Sandwell (2003) of the University of Toronto believes that as much as primary sources are needed to help students in secondary schools understand history, the process for evidence-based critical inquiry is stymied by the reluctance of students to open their minds to the elements that make the past into history. Students believe history, including examination of primary sources, is directed at finding what truly happened. Such is not possible, argues Sandwell. History is an open dialogue about, or critical engagement with, evidence from the past. History is not a set of absolute facts and conclusions, but rather a set of reasonable interpretations of available evidence. Of major importance among the pieces of evidence are primary sources. Sandwell has these insightful observations about how history is created. In order for the past to become history:

- There has to have been a record (document, artifact, memory) created.

- The record has to be preserved over time.

- The record has to be found by someone, and considered significant—worthy of analysis, interpretation, and fitting into the historical puzzle.

- What has been documented has to be interpreted.

- It has to be incorporated into a meaningful historical narrative.

Happenings from the past still can become lost without gaining a place in history if these five stages are not concluded with the narrative (written and read, spoken and heard) being shared among present and future generations. Thus, an additional stage should state that a portion of the past becomes history if it is engaged with open discussion and debate in order to share perspectives and enrich meaning of multiple personal experiences.

Sandwell also notes that each of these stages involves bias. All decisions for selection and interpretation of information include some degree of bias. Individuals had to make a decision at each stage to discard or record, preserve, and interpret the happening and the extent to which such would be recorded while other aspects of the past events are left out. At each decision point, truth becomes less and less possible to regain, assuming it ever was possible from the beginning. No commentary at any stage can possibly portray exactly what happened because no one could possibly see or understand everything for any one event or set of events, no matter how many primary sources might be available.

"After students have been introduced to the idea that historical truth is not absolute, but instead is constructed by historians," writes Sandwell (2003, 169), "they usually feel uneasy. If there is no absolute truth, if we can never know what 'really happened,' they ask, is not any interpretation as good as any other? Is not everything just someone's opinion, then, or just an interpretation? Why should we believe them?" While students are overly concerned with "is it true," most historians, most of the time, according to Sandwell, are involved in asking of primary historical evidence, "What does it mean?"

To gain insight on meaning, students must think as historians concerning the circumstances of a primary source or document's production. To gain historical context, perspective, and some glimmer of meaning, they must place primary sources within their time period and ask just what was going on when that particular source, document, or artifact was being created. Critical thinking and information literacy are essential teaching techniques that help move students to these higher levels of understanding, interpretation, and evaluation of primary resources.

References

Allen, S. M., and K. M. Dutt-Doner. (2006). "Using Digitized Documents in the Classroom." *Educational Leadership* 63 (4): 66–70.

Carey, H. H., and J. E. Greenberg. (1983). *How to Use Primary Sources.* Franklin Watts.

Coatney, S., and R. Smalley. (2005). "Inquiry and Living History, Part I." *School Library Media Activities Monthly* 22 (4): 24–27.

Coatney, S., and R. Smalley. (2006). "Inquiry and Living History, Part II." *School Library Media Activities Monthly* 22 (5): 28–31.

Craver, K. W. (1999). *Using Internet Primary Sources to Teach Critical Thinking Skills in History.* Greenwood Press.

Holt, T. (1995). Thinking historically: Narrative, imagination, and understanding. College Entrance Examination Board.

Jurmain, S. (2005). *The Forbidden Schoolhouse.* Houghton Mifflin.

Kammen, C. (1995). *On Doing Local History.* Rowman & Littlefield.

Levstik, L. S., and K. C. Barton. (2001). *Doing History: Investigating with Children in Elementary and Middle Schools.* Erlbaum.

Murphy, J. (2003). *An American Plague: The True and Terrifying Story of the Yellow Fever Epidemic of 1793.* Clarion Books.

Potter, L. A. (2002). "Teaching with Documents." *Social Education* 66 (7) (November/December): 390–399.

Sandwell, R. (2003). "Reading Beyond Bias: Using Historical Documents in the Secondary Classroom." *McGill Journal of Education* 38 (1): 168–186.

Seidman, R. F. (2002). "Making Historical Connections: A Historian Shows How Documents Can Be Used to Teach Critical Inquiry." *School Library Journal* 48 (7): 36–37.

Stebbins, L. F. (2006). *Student Guide to Research in the Digital Age: How to Locate and Evaluate Information Sources.* Libraries Unlimited.

Veccia, S. H. (2004). *Uncovering our History: Teaching with Primary Sources.* American Library Association.

Internet Web Sites for Primary Resources and Lesson Plans

(each accessed November 20, 2005)

Many sites based on recommendations from Joanne Troutner, director of technology and media, Tippecanoe Public Schools of Indiana and frequent contributor to selection of Internet resources in *Teacher-Librarian.*

AEA 262 Curriculum Integration Links. Primary Source Materials. http://www. aea267.k12.ia.us/curriculum/ primarysources.html

American Historical Association. *Teaching Methods.* http://www.theaha.org/teaching

Berkeley Digital Library SunSITE Digital Collection. http://sunsite.berkeley.edu/ Collections/

Digital Historical Inquiry Project. http:// dhip.org/pihn.shtml

Documenting the American South. http://docsouth.unc.edu/EDSITEment.

The Best of the Humanities of the Web. http://edsitement.neh.gov/

Eye Witness to History. http://www. eyewitnesstohistory. com/

George Rarey's World War II Air Force Cartoon Journals. http://www.rareybird. com/

Historical Newspapers. http://historynews. chadwyck.com/

History Channel. *Classroom Lesson Plans.* http://www.historychannel.com/classroom/ classroom.html

History Channel. *Speech Archives.* http:// www.historychannel.com/speeches/archive1. html

John W. Hartman Center for Sales, Advertising, and Marketing History, Duke University. Ad*Access. http://scriptorium.lib. duke.edu/adaccess/

Letters from an Iowa Soldier in the Civil War. http://www.civilwarletters.com/home.html

Library of Congress. *The Learning Pages.* http://memory.loc.gov/learn/index.html

Making of America. http://www.hti.umich. edu/m/moagrp/index.html

National Archives. Digital Classroom. http://www.archives.gov/digital_classroom/ index.html.

National Archives and Records Administration. *Education Program.* http://www. OurDocuments.gov

National Museum of American History. *You Be the Historian.* http://www. americanhistory.si.edu/hohr/springer/index. htm

New York Public Library Digital Library. http://digital.nypl.org/

Persistent Issues in History Workshop. http://crlt.indiana.edu/research/pih.html

PBS Online. *American Experience: War Letters.* http://www.pbs.org/wgbh/amex/ warletters/index.html

Repositories of Primary Sources. http://www. uidaho.edu/special-collections/Other. Repositories.html

Smithsonian Education. *Lesson Plans and Artifact Analysis.* http://www. smithsonianeducation.org

Spy Letters of the American Revolution. From the Collections of the Clements Library, Ann Arbor, Michigan. http://www. si.umich.edu/spies/

Teaching Politics. *Images of American Political History.* http://teachpol.tcnj.edu/ amer_pol_hist/index.htmWorld War II Resources. http://www.ibiblio.org/pha/

Teaching Politics. *Techniques and Technologies.* http://teachpol.tcnj.edu/

Professional Assessment

Daniel Callison

Too often school library media specialists shy away from program assessments and fail to seek out the opportunity to participate in the review of their school or district for accreditation purposes. On a smaller scale, but just as critical, is the school library media specialist's reluctance to be judged professionally as his or her fellow teachers are assessed—on classroom management and effective instructional delivery.

The claim is often stated that the school library media specialist has many other roles and duties than those of the classroom teacher. And yet, what role could be more important to demonstrate than the professional instructional role? Those who seek status as a teacher of Information Inquiry will seek out assessment of their instructional role and welcome the opportunity to be judged as a leader in curriculum development.

Exemplary Teaching and Learning

Goals

The American Association of School Librarians promotes "Teaching and Learning" as the first cluster of target indicators for school library media program assessment. At the exemplary level, these indicators represent very high expectations. Documentation to show that the library media specialist, in collaboration with other teachers, has developed a program at this level will be challenging to establish. The following statements paraphrased from the AASL Planning Guide for Information Power (Adcock 1999) can serve as a foundation for a progressive teaching philosophy and should be regarded as long-range goals:

- Because the library media program is a catalyst for intellectual inquiry, students learn to incorporate information literacy skills into their work and they become proactive users of information.

- The library media specialist coordinates the development of an information literacy program that is coordinated with the school's broader instructional program.

- Teachers at different grade levels and in most subject areas collaborate in the planning and implementation of this integrated and information-rich learning environment.

- Student evaluation strategies employed by the school library media specialist and collaborating teachers often involve reflection and authentic assessment.

- The library media specialist is an active participant in providing a schoolwide culture and greater community learning environment that encourages viewing, reading, writing, speaking, and listening for the intrinsic rewards of learning, enrichment, and personal pleasure.

- The library media specialist collaborates with other teachers to offer programs and activities that enable and encourage students to employ their abilities to solve information problems and to present their solutions in order to help others.

- The library media specialist applies effective teaching strategies to meet the needs of student groups or individual learners.

- The library media specialist takes an influential role in the assessment of student application of information literacy skills and helps to establish audiences in which students may demonstrate such skills in school and in the greater community.

National Board Standards

Criteria for school library media specialist certification through the National Board for Professional Teaching Standards were approved in (*NBPTS Library Media Standards* 2001). Since then, hundreds of experienced library media specialists have documented their value and impact on their local learning environment with evidence presented on videotape and documents in portfolios. The NBPTS criteria are high and also may seem a little abstract to many library media specialists. Concrete examples are given after each abstract criterion here to help envision how such high goals might be addressed on a regular basis.

These national standards can be applied to annual performance review to demonstrate the broader influence the library media specialist can have on the local community of learners. NBPTS expects the accomplished library media specialist to

- Have knowledge of learning styles and of human growth and development: Examples of identifying a variety of instructional materials to match different learning needs; development of literature sets to meet age appropriate needs.

- Know the principles of teaching and learning that contribute to an active learning environment. Application of such knowledge has increased the frequency and depth of collaborative planning with other teachers.

- Know the principles of library and information studies needed to create effective, integrated library media programs: Re-evaluation of the collection in cooperation with other teachers who have expressed curricular needs and an understanding of the students' right to read have resulted in higher book circulation, meaningful book discussions, and more demanding assignments.

- Integrate information literacy through collaboration, planning, implementation, and assessment of learning: New units of study have been introduced that call for team-teaching and student assessment of information and inquiry skills, including the library media specialist as an evaluator of student selection and use of information.

- Provide equitable access to and effective use of technologies and innovations: Training of students in the use and care of digital cameras has led to loan of these items to students who need to document field trips and local interviews.

- Plan, develop, implement, manage, and evaluate library media programs to ensure that students and staff use ideas and information effectively: A long-range plan that includes steady growth in the number of teachers who learn and practice information literacy is in place.

- Engage in reflective practice to increase their effectiveness: The library media specialist devotes more time to debriefing with other teachers on how collaborative information literacy lessons can be better presented and evaluated than in the past.

- Model a strong commitment to lifelong learning and to their profession: The library media specialist has completed advanced training in WebQuest authoring and will instruct other teachers in such skills in a series of workshops.

- Uphold professional ethics and promote equity and diversity: The library media specialist negotiated agreements allowing greater flexibility for in-class use of selected instructional video programs and a license for access to a greater number of online databases.

- Advocate for the library media program, involving the greater community: The library media specialist has served on the local public library board of directors and has served as a homework helper during two evenings a week.

School Library Impact Studies

Since 2000, more than a dozen state studies have been conducted in order to measure some degree of impact that school library media programs have on student achievement. Many of the findings relate the amount of holdings to higher student achievement. Other aspects of these studies, however, show a slightly moderate relationship between the instructional performance of the library media specialist and higher student achievement. Prior to such studies, Marilyn Miller and Marilyn Shontz (1998) identified the characteristics of "high performance" library media specialists in programs where technology was clearly advancing. High performance was shown in terms of

- Communicating clear long-range planning on a regular basis with the principal;

- Offering curriculum-integrated information skills instruction;

- Conducting workshops for teachers;

- Collaborating with curriculum committees;

- Coordinating in-school production of media, including television production;

- Devoting ten percent or more time each day to co-planning and co-instruction; and

- Supporting access to information in a variety of formats including electronic and beyond the school.

Indicators of Quality

The National Study of School Evaluation (Fitzpatrick 1998) has established its own list of indicators of quality library media specialist performance as a professional educator. Along with indicators similar to those mentioned above, NSSE's professional assessment instruments suggest instructional effectiveness is most strongly indicated by

- Fostering authentic assessment of student learning;

- Constructing collections cooperatively with teachers in support of learning standards;

- Fostering individual and collaborative inquiry; and

- Engaging students in reading, viewing, and listening for understanding and pleasure.

Agents of Learning

A recent profile of the successful school library media specialist has been outlined by Ross Todd and Carol Kuhlthau based on recent interviews of elementary school students in Ohio who testify to the help provided by their library media specialist. Ironically, *School Library Journal* (Whelan 2004) tends to give credit to the library media center as the place or program rather than to the person or professional who Todd and Kuhlthau characterize as an essential agent of instruction:

- **Resource Agent:** Provides up-to-date and diverse materials and guides students to make meaningful and relevant resource choices.

- **Literacy Development Agent:** Engages students in an active and meaningful search process, enabling them to explore, formulate, and focus their searches.

- **Knowledge Construction Agent:** Develops lessons that support information literacy scaffolds that lead to construction of new knowledge and understanding.

- **Academic Achievement Agent:** Helps the student achieve better grades, especially on project assignments.

- **Independent Reading and Personal Development Agent:** Fosters independent reading and is an advocate for meeting personal reading needs and interests.

- **Technological Literacy Agent:** Provides up-to-date software and assists in effective use of computer-assisted instruction.

- **Rescue Agent:** Helps students and teachers solve last-minute information crises.

- **Individualized Learning Agent:** Learns individual characteristics of learners and provides information advice to meet special needs at critical times on a personal basis.

Principal or Peer Assessment

Evaluation of teacher performance has been the principal's domain for as long as public schools have been in place. The complexities of the role of the high performing library media specialist, especially one who has moved to the levels of instructional media specialist, are so demanding and intricate that more observation and evaluation are necessary than just that of the principal. Collaborative instructional efforts among professionals open the opportunity for peer review and evaluation. Library media specialists who wish to document their instructional performance and effectiveness may want to gather a portfolio of examples that include aspects of the following observations from their fellow teachers. Collaborative teaching also can include collaborative professional assessment.

Organization:

- The library media specialist is well-prepared for class.
- Objectives are clearly stated and relevant to learning standards.
- Relationships to class content and information literary are evident.
- Class time is used effectively.
- Learning activities are well-organized and lead to meaningful discussions.
- Students are encouraged and motivated to remain focused on intended objectives.

Strategies:

- Choice of teaching technique is appropriate for the learning goals.
- The library media specialist shows good questioning skills and models inquiry.
- The library media specialist raises stimulating and challenging questions.
- The library media specialist encourages and rewards constructive questions from students.
- The library media specialist mediates discussion well.
- Class schedule proceeds at an appropriate pace.

- The library media specialist uses multimedia effectively.
- Visuals and handouts are legible, pertinent, and understandable.
- The library media specialist provides clear directions for group work and other forms of active learning.
- The library media specialist helps students learn from each other.
- The library media specialist effectively holds class attention.

Field settings and practice work:

- Procedures and techniques (for information searching) are clearly explained and demonstrated.
- The library media specialist is thoroughly familiar with most likely results of different information search techniques.
- The library media specialist provides individual attention when necessary.
- Search exercises clearly develop important skills for future application.
- The library media specialist assists in interpretation of search findings.

Content knowledge:

- The library media specialist is knowledgeable about the subject matter (information access and information evaluation).
- The library media specialist is confident in explaining the subject matter or search process.
- The library media specialist uses vocabulary and examples to meet appropriate age level.
- The library media specialist uses a variety of illustrations or analogies to explain content, needs, and information problem situations.
- The library media specialist is open to considering new ideas and different approaches when relevant.
- The library media specialist is sensitive to the need to be as inclusive as possible in terms of age, ethnic group, and gender representation.

Key Words for Instruction in Information Inquiry

Presentation skills:

- The library media specialist is an effective speaker.
- The library media specialist employs an appropriate rate of speech that is clear and not boring.
- The library media specialist uses class space well.
- The library media specialist attempts to make the content interesting as well as relevant.
- The library media specialist relates subject content to practical situations and likely student needs.
- The library media specialist uses proper grammar.

Rapport with students:

- The library media specialist welcomes student participation.
- The library media specialist models good listening habits.
- The library media specialist motivates students.
- The library media specialist responds well to student differences and potential conflicts.
- The library media specialist demonstrates a sense of humor.
- The library media specialist demonstrates effective classroom management techniques, including acceptable discipline when necessary.
- The library media specialist demonstrates flexibility in responding to student concerns or interests.
- The library media specialist welcomes multiple perspectives.
- The library media specialist anticipates likely student problems in dealing with new content.
- The library media specialist is able to help a diverse spectrum of students including those with a disability.
- The library media specialist accepts constructive criticism.

- The library media specialist does not display or express sexist or racist attitudes.

Value of Student and Teacher Impressions

The use of impressions gathered in surveys and interviews of students and teachers was employed by Ross Todd and Carol Kuhlthau in the examination of school library media services in thirty-nine high performing schools in Ohio (2003). Before engaging in similar evaluation processes, a review of the limitations of such research and evaluation methods as described by Melissa Gross (2006) is a wise investment of for planning how to gather the opinions of students and colleagues. Gross warns:

> In qualitative research, it is always important to ask what the impact of the researcher is on the context being studied. Inserting a new presence into any context changes the interpersonal dynamics and can affect the way people behave, what they say, and how they feel. When researchers are working with children, they must consider how their presence is perceived and to what extent they are able to develop a good working relationship with children participating in the study. The danger is that unless children feel comfortable, understand the purpose of the research, and are voluntary participants, the validity of the data may be in question. There is also the danger to validity in that children are often eager to do and say what they think is expected. (14–15).

The Ohio study gathered responses from more than 13,000 students and nearly 900 teachers. The survey and interviews covered seventy-five questions, to which students could respond through an electronic database. The information garnered, along with the additional teacher stories of collaboration with and assistance from school librarians, helped to establish an exciting model of the modern effective school media program as a service-oriented center that can transform learning in very positive ways. Strategically, the researchers wanted to glean the best examples and best impressions from exemplary schools to illustrate a best-practice learning environment. Combined with their years of experience and knowledge concerning constructivist learning approaches, Todd and Kuhlthau were successful. The options for student response and the method for reporting the survey data from students, do, however, raise some issues:

- Response options for students were limited to positive ranges.

- Any positive response was tabulated to mean the student believed the school library helped them learn better, no matter how much or how little.

- Student responses were not analyzed by grade level to the degree that one might be able to see differences in the expectations of younger students compared to more demanding and critical older student groups.

- The survey and interviews indicated some areas of need, such as greater readers' advisory and more open hours for access before and after school.

Unfortunately, trade magazine publications (Whelan 2004, Kenney 2006) tended to hype the student responses to the extent that journalists implied that nearly all students, regardless of their age and true quality of the library program, believe the school library helps them learn better. The refereed research reports were more guarded and reasonable (Todd 2005; Todd et al. 2005). The point, however, is that if data from children are to be gathered for evaluation purposes, they should be gathered systematically, reported fairly, and examined to use them to the extent they can be of value, to examine shortcomings as well as success. A misinterpreted 99 percent approval rate does little to help the local school media specialist to determine what areas are in need of more attention, and embellished ratings, in the end, do little to impress local administrators, especially if not well founded.

The most important aspect of the Ohio study is what Ross and Kuhlthau introduce as questions to measure the degree of information use assistance and guidance. This is a substantial move added to the basic common question, "Did the librarian help you find materials?" Among the new measures tested in Ohio are: "The school library has helped me know when I find good information" and "The school library helped me find different opinions about my topics." These are examples of measures that assess the degree to which the school librarian is adding value to the information evaluation process. These questions address teaching, not just the service of locating materials. For these questions, as with many others posed to students from the thirty-nine exemplary Ohio schools, it was clear that a majority of the students believed that yes, the school librarian was very helpful in considering the value of the information located.

For application of this approach locally, the school library media specialist will want to select a few key questions to measure, probably not more than a dozen. Student impressions should be gathered prior to the semester and measured again after a semester of inquiry units in which reasonable information guidance is provided. Teachers should be involved in the process so that as instruction in the processes for search, use, and evaluation of information take place, they reinforce what is being taught and the value of such skills. Measures may be much lower than those reported in the Ohio Study at first, but the successful teaching team will find that as they work with students to help them ascertain the value of various information and evidence, the percentage of students who agree they are getting quality guidance for inquiry and for learning will go up. An increase in teaching effectiveness is the evidence that will be a basis for positive reports to the administration and to parents.

References

Adcock, D. C., ed. (1999). *A Planning Guide for Information Power with School Library Media Program Assessment Rubric for the 21st Century*. American Association of School Librarians.

Fitzpatrick, K. A. (1998). *Program Evaluation: Library Media Services*. National Study of School Evaluation.

Gross, M. (2006). *Studying Children's Questions*. Scarecrow Press.

Kenney, B. (2006). "Ross to the Rescue." *School Library Journal* 52 (4): 44–47.

Miller, M. L., and M. L. Shontz. (1998). "More Services, More Staff, More Money: A Portrait of a High-Service Library Media Center." *School Library Journal* (May): 28–33.

NBPTS Library Media Standards. (2001). National Board for Professional Teaching Standards. Available at http://www.nbpts.org (accessed June 1, 2002).

Todd, R. J., and C. C. Kuhlthau. (2003). *Student Learning Through Ohio School Libraries: A Summary of the Ohio Research Study.* Ohio Educational Library Media Association. Available at http://www.oelma.org/studentlearning.htm (accessed July 5, 2006).

Todd, R. J. (2005). "Listen to the Voices: Ohio Students Tell Their Stories of School Libraries." *Knowledge Quest* 33 (4): 8–13.

Todd, R. J., et al. (2005). "Student Learning Through Ohio School Libraries, Part 1: How Effective School Libraries Help Students." *School Libraries Worldwide* 11 (1): 63–88.

Whelan, D. L. (2004). "13,000 Kids Can't Be Wrong: A New Ohio Study Shows How School Libraries Help Students Learn." *School Library Journal* (February): 46–50.

Additional Sources on Professional and Program Assessment

Dresang, E. T., M. Gross, and L. E. Holt. (2006). *Dynamic Youth Services through Outcome-Based Planning and Evaluation.* American Library Association.

Everhart, N. (1998). *Evaluating the School Library Media Center.* Libraries Unlimited.

Kryder-Reid, Elizabeth, et al. (2006). *Shaping Outcomes: An Online Course on Outcome Based Planning and Evaluation.* The School of Liberal Arts Museum Studies at IUPUI and the Indiana University School of Library and Information Services, Washington, DC. Available at http://www.sahpingoutcomes.org/ (accessed July 6, 2006).

National Center for Restructuring Education, Schools and Teaching. http://www.tc.edu/centers/ncrest/ (accessed August 13. 2006).

Todd, R. J. (2003). "School Libraries Evidence: Seize the Day, Begin the Future." *Library Media Connection* 22 (1): 12–18.

Project-Based and Social Action Learning

Daniel Callison

The project approach to learning is a method of teaching in which an in-depth study of a particular topic is conducted by a child or a group of children (Helm and Katz 2001). Of course, projects provide adults the opportunity to learn and to work together also. But the review of theory and practice here will be based on methods that move the child to the center of the project as it emerges and as decisions need to be made.

Gifted teachers who can manage this level of instruction engage the students at as many decision-making junctures as possible because learning from choice is as important as learning from subject content. Project-based learning has the potential to increase a student's feeling of responsibility for, and control over, his or her own learning.

According to the Advanced Learning Technologies in Education Consortia Web site at the University of Kansas, allowing students to choose personal approaches to problems simulates real-world tasks in which multiple views and methods compete in the search for a solution. ALTEC provides a useful instrument from which students can consult with teachers in constructing their own evaluation checklist. The checklist can be converted to a rubric format to match a progression of performance expectations.

Several Offer Definitions

Helm and Katz (2001) have defined the degree of child initiation and decision making in different approaches to teaching:

Single Concept: Teacher instructs, determines content; limited to single skill.

Integrated Concepts: Teacher instructs, determines content, integrates skills and content.

Units: Teacher instructs, determines content; unified exploration of several content areas on a narrow topic.

Thematic Teaching: Teacher instructs, determines content; or child-initiated with learning experiences are integrated over a broad topic.

Teacher-Directed Inquiry: Thematic approach with teacher directing and planning in-depth research and exploration by children.

Projects: In-depth investigation; may be child- or teacher-initiated; research focused on finding answers to student questions; direction of inquiry follows children's interests. (2)

Additional characteristics of project-based learning are that

- The amount of time or length of the learning experience will be determined by the project progression, student interest, resource and community support and may last over several weeks, even months.

- Activities focus on investigation, finding answers to questions, using resources, especially human experts to demonstrate skills and be interviewed.

- Teachers and school media specialists (teaming as instructional media specialists) support by facilitating and debriefing students after field trips, interviews and other times for all to freely read and consider information from a variety of resources.

- Resources are brought to the project by students, parents, and other community members, not just teachers and school library media specialists.

- Teachers and school library media specialists (teaming as instructional media specialists) observe children's investigations, and use student interest and questions to determine the next steps of the project, often based on discussion with students to help in the planning.

- Concept maps or webs are written at various steps in the project to illustrate how the progression in the project changes what the children know, learn and still have left to explore.

- Artifacts and other objects (model cars, pretend space ships, tools, fossils, or other items relevant to the investigation) are collected or created by the students to represent the project and what has been learned, and are displayed for all children to view and handle.

- The burden to demonstrate learning will often rest on the student in final presentation or demonstration of the success or failure in implementing the project.

- Celebrations should involve students in a showcase of projects open to parents and other community members to visit and praise.

At highest learning levels in secondary schools, project-based learning should be based on challenging questions or problems, that involve students in design, problem solving, decision making, or investigative activities that give students the opportunity to work relatively autonomously over extended periods of time and culminate in realistic products or presentations (Jones, Rasmussen, and Moffitt 1997).

In 1999, the Autodesk Foundation added these criteria to define meaningful projects:

- are central, not peripheral to the curriculum.

- are focused on questions that drive student to encounter and struggle with the central concepts and principle of a discipline.

- involve students in a constructive investigation.

- are student-centered.

- are realistic, not "school-like."

The Family 4-H Approach

A true American educational innovation, the 4-H youth development program originated over 100 years ago to address the vital need to improve life in rural areas. Based in many ways on a hands-on apprenticeship approach traditional to training in basic farm operation, the 4-H has expanded its project oriented approaches to include today opportunities for young people to explore mass communications and media literacy, consumer information, and management of multimedia technologies. The Iowa State University 4-H Extension Web site illustrates the wide variety of projects and steps for planning successful implementation.

Head, heart, hands, and health continue to be a valid combination for project-based learning. The 4-H approach that combines the community, extension office and family support structures offers a positive model for public school educators who want to apply a greater student selection for learning from constructive activities that contribute to personal growth.

The Ohio State 4-H Extension office illustrates a model to support project learning. In the center, the project helper's role includes responsibilities for focus, support, feedback and debriefing—very similar to the teacher or school media specialist as facilitator for information projects. The young 4-H member's role includes (4-H Project Learning 2005):

- **Experience:** become familiar with the content

- **Reflect:** explore deeper meaning of the content

- **Generalize:** connect what is learned from other examples

- **Apply:** apply content to real world situations

Problems with Project-Based Learning

As expected, the complexities involved in implementing project-based learning in public school learning environments can result in many frustrations. The process can be time-consuming, difficult to clearly show student learned measured against standards, and can prove to be expensive in provision of reasonable resources support. While such independent learning projects certainly are a part of the student learning standards promoted by the American Association for School Librarians (AASL and AECT 1998), they may be prime territory only for instructional media specialists who are exceptionally flexible and innovative. Project-based learning, when successful, can provide a wonderful showcase for administrators to take pride in, but it takes administrators who have patience and an open pocketbook to get such projects to the celebration stage.

Limited research on project-based learning, most of it concentrated on math and science students in the middle grades, indicate that most students will demonstrate proficient skills in generating plans and carrying out procedures. However, most students had difficulty in

- generating meaningful scientific questions,

- managing complex processes,

- managing time,

- transforming data,

- developing a logical argument to support claims.

Students pursued questions without examining their merits, and pursued questions based on personal preferences rather than questions warranted by the scientific content of the project. Students also had difficulty understanding the concept of controlled experiments, and created inadequate research designs and poor data collection plans, and often failed to carry out their plans systematically. When presenting results, students tended to present data and state conclusions without describing the link between the two, or drew conclusions based on incomplete data (Krajcik et al. 1998).

Such are not surprising findings as most students will need a great deal of guidance and modeling for scientific projects, especially for their first experience. The findings tend to underscore the need for collaborative efforts between science teachers and library media specialists who together facilitate as instructional media specialists and provide frequent interventions to advise, model and provide comparison to previous successful student projects. Resource assistance may also be needed, but guidance in critical review of data and evidence is most important.

Project-based instruction was also found to be taxing for teachers (Marx et al. 1997). Teachers, especially in elementary school settings, reported lack of time, difficulties in classroom management, poor access to necessary technology, and inability to provide meaningful assessment. Most reported difficulties associated with striking a balance between the need to maintain order in the classroom and the need to allow students to work on their own.

Some Positive Observations from Research

With all of the factors in place that work against project-based learning, a few studies have concluded the efforts can be worthwhile. When students are involved over an extended period of time (several semesters) in a variety of project-based experiences a few studies have indicated greater development of the ability to raise complex and insightful questions, higher gains in math word problem performance, more positive attitudes toward mathematics, and stronger performance on math portions of standard exams than compared to students who were not involved in projects (Boaler 1998).

Other studies have reported that low ability students gain the most in critical thinking skill performance based on challenges presented in project-based activities (Horan, Lavaroni, and Beldon 1996).

Steps to Successful Projects

Researchers for the Buck Institute for Education (Mergendoller and Thomas 2002) have identified several practices that should increase the chances for successful project-based application. A few of these are paraphrased below:

- Schedule projects and end-of-term assignments at different times.

- Give lots of advance discussion and planning to projects.

- Give students a rubric that communicates their responsibilities.

- Reach an agreement with students on grading criteria before the project begins.

- Require frequent checkpoints and smaller products that build to the larger one to facilitate a sense of mission.

- Involve students in project design, goals and evaluation.

- Use examples of previous successful projects to illustrate and define high quality work.

- Combine standards with scaffolding to help students reach milestones and to take more responsibility gradually upon successful completion of initial steps.

- Group projects should include members representing a variety of skills relevant to the project and allow for novice students to learn from experienced students.

- Use scaffolding (Callison 2001) to acquaint learners with different levels of

inquiry (Callison 1999), and build experiences from controlled, to guided, to modeled to free discovery.

- Establish frequent but short conferences with the entire group to discuss progress.

- Use planning sheets, group folders, and other concrete devices to record evidence of progress and notes on next steps.

- Make group progress a public matter for all members of the class.

- Teachers should facilitate group discussions on the consequences of different various options and choices as the project progresses.

- Communicate progress on the process as well as final product to parents and administrators.

- Find effective ways to involve parents as resource participants and even as content experts.

- Experts and other resources have the most impact when introduced at the "point of need."

- Involve information content expertise at "point of need" when it is applicable to the student needing to determine information choices.

- Have student master complex technologies before including such in projects.

- Use a variety of assessment methods, all clearly understood by teacher and student.

- Give both individual and group grades, with emphasis on how the individual contributes to the success of the group.

- Reflection is an important part of the assessment process for the student and for the teacher; both should write and speak about what they learn from the process.

Social Action Projects

An approach that can lead to authentic learning experiences is to engage students in projects that will address critical issues locally. Often these issues have a national appeal as well and local efforts can be tied to national organizations, but for students to have an authentic learning experience in which they see results or experience frustrations directly from their efforts, local projects preferred.

Gail Bush (1997), director of school library media education at Dominican University, has advocated social action learning at several stages of public education. She has made a strong argument that information management skills related to social actions projects are so important they should be among those promoted as standards for student learning of information literacy (Abilock 2006, Bush 2006). "Standard 10: The student who contributes to the learning community and to society is information literate and seeks opportunities to use knowledge to create a more socially just and humane world" (Bush 2005).

Social action projects are featured in the video Know It All series (1997) produced by the Great Plains Network in support of *Information Power*. Karen Sheingold (1987) provided eloquent examples of student social action to meet local water pollution problems in her speeches and articles promoting inquiry methods in public education.

In social action learning projects, students identify a real cause and must develop information presentation strategies that are target and convincing in order to address the problems they confront. Therefore, delivery of a poster for teacher evaluation is minor compared to presenting a series of posters, speeches and displays to the city council that something must be done to address some specific environmental, recreational, or social problems selected as a "cause" by the student inquirers. Selection and presentation of valid arguments is "on the line" in such presentations to local authorities being asked to change the statue quo.

Issues in social action can range from voter registration, tolerance in gender, age and ethic differences, to recycling, and animal welfare. Some guides (Lewis 1998) provide tips on writing resolutions for change, methods for mediation of issues, lobbying and mailing campaigns, and even organized protest marching. The line between social action projects and civil disobedience can become blurred if the issues are emotional and high profile. Instructional media specialists, however, should be aware of the potential for some social action projects to represent meaningful application of information literacy and inquiry skills.

Useful organization contacts that can provide materials and structure in print, multimedia or over the Internet for social action projects include:

- Boys & Girls Clubs of America www.bgca.org

- 4-H Youth Development www.4-h.org

- National Youth Development Information Center www.nydic.org

- Volunteers of America, Inc. www.voa.org

- American Society for the Prevention of Cruelty to Animals www.aspca.org

- Humane Society of the United States www.hsus.org

- EcoNet www.igc.org/igc/en

- Environmental Defense Fund www.edf.org

- Defenders of Wildlife www.defenders.org/index.html

- Sierra Club www.sierraclub.org

- National Audubon Society www.audubon.org

- Facing History and Ourselves www.facinghistory.org/

- Gay, Lesbian and Straight Education Network www.glsen.org/

- Youth Activism Project www.youthactivism.com/

- Rethinking Schools www.rethinkingschools.org/

- Institute for Global Communications www.igc.org

- The American Promise www.pbs.org/ap

- Center for Civic Education www.civiced.org

- Global Kids, Inc. www.globalkids.org

- Human Rights Watch www.hrw.org

- CARE www.care.org

- Amnesty International www.amnesty.org

- Webactive www.webactive.com

- Kids Voting USA www.kidsvotingusa.org

- Youth as Resources www.yar.org

- National Network for Youth www.nn4youth.org

- Habitat for Humanity International www.habitat.org

- Teaching Tolerance www.tolerance.org/teach/

References

Abilock, D. (2006). "Justice, Equality, and Social Responsibility: Envisioning Standard 10." *Knowledge Quest* 34 (5): 9–16.

American Association for School Librarians and the Association for Educational Communications Technology (AASL and AECT). (1998). *Information Power: Building Partnerships for Learning.* American Library Association.

Advanced Learning Technologies in Education Consortia. *Project-Based Checklists.* (2005). The University of Kansas. Available at http://altec.org/index.php (accessed September 14, 2005).

Autodesk Foundation. (1999). *Kids Who Know and Do:* 7th National Conference on Project-Based Learning.

Boaler, J. (1998). "Open and Closed Mathematics: Student Experiences and Understandings." *Journal for Research in Mathematics Education* 29: 41–62.

Bush, G. (1997). "Let It Begin with Me: Advocating for Youth Activism." *Voice of Youth Advocates (VOYA)* 20 (4): 229–231.

Bush, G. (2005). "A Discussion for the Standard Bearers." Presented at the National Conference of the American Library Association, Chicago.

Bush, G. (2006). "Envisioning Information Literacy Standard 10." *Knowledge Quest* 34 (5): 19–21.

Callison, D. (1999). "Inquiry." *School Library Media Activities Monthly* 15 (6): 38–42.

Callison, D. (2001). "Scaffolding." *School Library Media Activities Monthly* 17 (6): 37–39.

Extension to Youth & 4–H. Iowa State University. (2005). http://www.extension.iastate.edu/4H/homepage.htlm (accessed September 10, 2005).

4–H Project Learning. (2005). The Ohio State University Extension. Available at www.ohio4h.org/product/publications.html (accessed September 10, 2005).

Helm, J. H., and L. Katz. (2001). *Young Investigators: The Project Approach in the Early Years.* Teachers College Press.

Horan, C., C. Lavaroni, and P. Beldon. (1996). *Observation of the Tinker Tech Program: Students for Critical Thinking and Social Participation Behaviors.* Buck Institute for Education.

Jones, B. F., C. M. Rasmussen, and M. C. Moffitt. (1997). *Real-life Problem Solving.* American Psychological Association.

Know It All: Information Literacy Series: K–8. (1997). Great Plains Network. Thirteen video programs.

Krajcik, J. S., et al. (1998). "Inquiry in Project-Based Science Classrooms: Initial Attempts by Middle School Students." *The Journal of the Learning Sciences* 7: 313–350.

Lewis, B. A. (1998). *The Kid's Guide to Social Action.* Free Spirit Publishing.

Marx, R. W., et al. (1997). "Enacting Project-Based Science: Challenges for Practice and Policy." *Elementary School Journal* 94 (5): 341–358.

Mergendoller, J. R., and J. W. Thomas. (2002). *Managing Project Based Learning: Principles from the Field.* Buck Institute for Education. Available at www.bie.org (accessed September 15, 2005).

Sheingold, K. (1987). "Keeping Children's Knowledge Alive Through Inquiry." *School Library Media Quarterly* 15 (2): 80–85.

Questioning

Daniel Callison

Probably the most frequently-stated reason for using a library, besides finding a good book, is to "find an answer." I accept both of those, but I want you to give some additional thought to "the library media center is the best place for students to raise questions." Questioning is the first element of Information Inquiry. Questioning seeds all other processes. Without questions, the inquiry cycle stops and learning regresses into read and recite without testing for relevance and meaning.

The ability to question is the ability to see beyond the facts and opinions placed before you. The ability to see that most answers are only partial solutions and there are many more questions to explore, is a sign of a lifelong learner—whether aged two or ninety-two.

Conversations with parents at home, in the evening around dinner, may include such statements as "I got an A on my history paper" or "I answered 90 of 100 math questions correctly today." Good bragging rights, no doubt. But the conversation could also be sparked by Johnny telling his parents what he has read about ancient Egypt and all the questions he now has about mummies. Why did they preserve bodies so well? Who got selected and why? What modern preservation methods do we use today that are the same as 3,000 years ago?

Not good dinner conversation, you say? Anything with questions, leading to more reading, or more net-surfing, or for Mom and Dad to join in the exploration is the best chatter of all. While interesting questions can lead to interesting discussions, mastering the formulation of questions in a manner that leads to organizing how information is to be searched, retrieved, and sorted is the primary step leading to critical thinking. Questions, voiced or written, can reveal thoughts and help organize thinking.

The Art of Questioning

Dennis Palmer Wolf (1987) offered insights on how teachers influence inquiry through their questioning behavior. His comments were delivered to the College Board in Santa Cruse California and drawn from developmental theorist Erik Erikson (1975, 2):

The very way in which teachers ask questions can determine, rather than build, a shared spirit of investigation. First, teachers tend to monopolize the right to question—rarely do more than procedural questions come from students. Second, the question-driven exchanges that occur in classrooms almost uniformly take place between teachers and students. Moreover, classroom questioning can be exclusive. It can easily become the private preserve of the few—the bright, the male, the English-speaking.

Wolf paraphrases a common Chinese proverb: Ask a man a question and he may inquire for a moment or perhaps a day; teach a man to question (encourage him, guide him, reward him, allow him ownership of more questions, give him the intellectual freedom to continue questioning) and he will practice inquiry for life. Questioning through inquiry becomes the very foundation of "lifelong learning."

Types of Questions

Questions can be limited to recall of factual responses. Questions may also involve processes (critical thinking):

- How are these alike or different?
- Which is best and why?
- Which path do we take? Why?
- What are the advantages and disadvantages?

Questions may stimulate imagination (creative thinking):

- What if you could change things?
- What will things be like in the future?
- What is your plan for action?

The Foundation for Critical Thinking (2005) describes various questions in the following manner:

- **Questions of Relevance**—discriminate what does and what does not bear on an original question.
- **Questions of Accuracy**—force evaluation and testing for truth and correctness.
- **Questions of Precision**—lead to details, the specifics.
- **Questions of Consistency**—examine for contradictions.
- **Questions of Logic**—consider the synthesis of the whole and ask if conclusions make sense.
- **Questions of Interpretation**—examine the organization and meaning derived from information.
- **Questions of Assumption**—make us examine from several different perspectives what we are taking for granted.
- **Questions of Implication**—test possible interpretations and challenge where evidence and arguments may be taking the investigation, and may raise the value of the impact of our work. Are these questions worthwhile? Or, do these answers cause more harm than good?

- **Questions of Point of View**—force consideration of other relevant perceptions, opinions and evidence.
- **Questions of Depth**—take the investigation under the surface level evidence and deal with hidden complexities.
- **Questions of Purpose**—define the task and keep the investigation on target.
- **Questions of Information**—force examination of the sources of information and the quality of the information selected or rejected.

When to Question and When Not to Question—That Is the Question

When students learn and practice effective questions, most of the following actions take place: They have the opportunity to hear for themselves what they want to know; to express to other students what they think is important to know; and to see how their questions are similar to the concerns of many others and yet discover those questions they have that might be different or even insightful:

- Questions voiced by students help them identify issues, frame parameters for argument, and determine points that must be explored further for more convincing evidence.
- Student ownership of the questioning process leads to students becoming content experts if they continue to question, probe, and explore. An expert discovers the questions that are "central to the issue;" questions that are of more interest currently; questions that have "haunted humankind for ages."
- Renovated and revised questions, documented in journals, voiced on a regular basis, will give the library media specialist one important indication of the student's progress through the information selection, analysis, and synthesis processes.

Look for evidence that the questions evolve in detail and complexity, but questions should not end there. Detail and complexity show that new information is driving the thoughts. Simplicity and clarity show that these questions have been reconsidered in order to construct a focus for all further investigation.

Look for new questions that have come from reading, viewing, Internet surfing, and discussion—questions that were not possible for the students to consider before such activities.

Are there new questions now being asked by the student that show that new information is needed, that the student has consumed the materials immediately available, and that new questions can only be addressed with access to resources and people beyond the school library media center?

The school library media program moves into higher levels of service when such questions become the driving force for further student inquiry:

- Questioning and talking reduce the prewriting tension related to not knowing what to write about. Brainstorming ideas, constructing topic webs or concept maps, or just basic outlining of the topics related to a given theme can help the student get a better grasp on what may eventually be the focus of his or her work. Library media specialists and other teachers should encourage students to state questions related to each new topic as it is placed before the class for consideration.

- Questioning should be recursive and reflective because new questions will arise and old questions will become revised as the student explores additional information. For quick factual reference questions, one information source might be acceptable, but for nearly all questions of value, many sources should be explored. The result will be a cycle of new questions, discarding of old no longer interesting questions, and claim to new exciting questions. As this process generates new lines of inquiry, students will need to learn how to cluster questions, link them to other questions, and identify those that are most relevant to their interests or as-

signment, those with highest potential to be addressed, and those that will likely remain a mystery.

Instructional media specialists, as teachers of information processing, should practice the following actions related to questioning (Brown and Keeley 1990; Christenbury and Kelley 1993):

- **Model questioning.** As reference materials are introduced, the library media specialist should state questions that might be addressed by these tools, and state questions that will not be. This gives you a chance to link to other reference tools and show a pattern of question raising and possible question answering.

- **Engage students in sharing questions and resources.** Ask students to describe sources (reference materials, magazine articles, a Web site) in terms of what questions might be answered from the source. This is an important way to help the student practice synthesizing what the document has to offer in his or her own words and to determine why the document is or is not useful.

- **Look for a variety of questions that demonstrate various levels of thinking.** Do not, however, expect questions to build in a progressively more complex and precise manner. Even though we might look for such examples to determine maturity in the questioning process, questions (just as thinking) usually scatter and jump about without immediate linkage to other questions. Thus, students need to keep track of questioning thoughts. The teacher is an important coach to help them cluster, organize, map, and associate these questions in order to move along on finding meaning.

- **Information comes from text.** Meaning comes from questions organized within a context. Who, what, where, when, why, and how give a start toward construction of this context.

- **Reward questioning.** Tell students when you hear a good question and why the question is good. Use questions to stimulate conversations by asking the students questions for which you know they can deliver the answer and then lead them into new questions, many for which the students and library media specialist may not know complete responses.

- **Display questioning.** Often bulletin boards display a "general idea" but do not really raise new questions. A rewarding and interactive method to display questioning is to allow students to post their questions on bulletin boards (traditional or electronic) and expect peers and teachers to respond.

  Often library media specialists will give guided practice in reference skills by posting a weekly list of questions that can be answered with facts located in the general reference collection by students. Allow such given questions to be extended by students and let the challenge begin.

- **Organize by questions.** Signs over various book shelves often give the classification number and the general topic. Could questions be added to these signs? Government: How are laws written? Sociology: What is special about how other people live? Biology: What animals live in the Wetlands? Such question-displays help elementary school students understand the meaning of the more general categories. They may be encouraged to compose such questions for display over the course of the school year.

Promote Reading with Questions

Bibliographies and pathfinders can often be organized under question-headings. What general books will give me an overview of this topic? What materials in addition to the book collection will help me? What local people in the community are willing to tell me more about this topic?

- **Promote reading with questions.** Many good booktalks end with questions that invite the audience to read the book being promoted. Questions can be used to head a book list or a poster that lists several books that help answer questions such as "What will be the best job for me when I am twenty-five? or "How can I start my own business?"

- **The most effective use of questions to promote reading,** however, is again related to student-generated questioning. Students at all levels (and teachers, too, but that really leads to another instructional term to define at a later date) should read on a regular basis, sustained through time and reading collections provided by the school. But even with a library of 20,000 titles before many students, the haunting question comes, "So, what shall I read?" Book lists and recommendations from fellow students help. A major item that will jump-start reading is a list of questions I want to find answers to (not an answer, but answers). From five to ten stated questions will come a plan for reading and viewing for the semester. Materials should vary in format, and much nonfiction will begin to show in the form of magazines and newspapers. The reading record (once "a list of books I have read this year") is compiled to show the materials used to answer the first set of questions and material that spun new questions. In closing, there are two actions that library media specialists and teachers should not take in the questioning process:

- **Do not ask all the questions.** The more student-centered, student-generated the questions and information discussions, the more powerful the learning process.

- **Do not expect immediate answers** nor immediate questions every time. Wait time is probably the most abused segment of the academic day. It is difficult to wait thirty seconds before a response comes from the class. It is very frustrating to wait several days before students, often struggling with information on a given subject for the first time, begin to identify questions of merit. Getting focus takes time, and often after several failed attempts.

While many of our best questions, from students and teachers, come in almost a natural way, the rest of our best come from reading, writing, listening, debating, and interacting with each other and information texts. (Rubin and Dodd 1987)

To Wonder, To Learn

Jamie McKenzie (2005), former school administrator and current international lecturer on educational technology innovations and other actions to improve student learning, draws his reader's attention to the questioning by comparing it to yeast. Questioning is to thinking as yeast is to bread making. Unleavened bread is flat, hard and unyielding. Unleavened thinking is uninspired. Questioning is what converts the stuff of thinking into something of value, acting as leaven to transform matter into meaning.

McKenzie often models the questioning process in order to allow the student's path for exploring information to become more challenging. Questions that will make the typical biographical assignment more personal and will lead to more insights about both the personality and the student writer push the extreme:

- In what ways was this person's life remarkable, despicable, admirable?

- What are several important lessons you or any other young person might learn from the way this person lived?

- An older person or mentor is often very important in shaping the lives of other people by providing guidance and encouragement. Two what extent was this true of the personality you are exploring?

- Did this person make any major mistakes or bad decisions? If so, what were they and how would you have chosen and acted differently?

McKenzie has also rounded up one of the most diverse collections of different kinds of questions. A sample from his examples, some modified for sake of space, helps us see how much McKenzie's questioning process can enrich any standard school curriculum:

Clarification questions—How did they gather their data? Was it a reliable and valid process?

Sorting and Sifting Questions—Which parts of the information gathered through the survey are worth keeping?

Elaborating questions—How could I take this farther? What is the logical next step?

Planning questions—What have other groups before us done to address these issues?

Strategic questions—How can I best approach this next step? What resources do I have at hand and what others do I need to acquire?

Unanswerable questions—How can I maintain my ideal when there is so much wrong with the world and some many greedy, evil people? What is the perfect solution that will bring world peace?

Irreverent questions—What can we do to changes things? What social action can we take? Can we really trust the government?

Divergent questions—Beyond the information gathered so far, what else do we need in order to make our argument convincing?

McKenzie encourages educators to move from trivial questions, to essential questions to engage students in learning that can be more authentic and meaningful. Traits of an essential question include that it

- probes a matter of considerable importance (relative to the learner's ability, environment and needs);

- moves the learner beyond mere understanding and toward action to solve a problem;

- cannot be addressed with a simply yes or no;

- endures and shifts or even turns and leads to larger questions as the inquiry progresses;

- is very likely one that can not be answered completely; and

- creates frustration and mystery, but maintains the interest of the inquirer.

Testing Your Research Questions

The Canadian instructional team of Koechlin and Zwann (2001) have developed a rubric to test the value of typical research questions raised by students:

- Focus—Does your question help to focus your research? At the highest level, focus will target a defined investigation and serves to examine all relevant perspectives.

- Interest—Are you excited about your question? Interest can inspire further investigation, more questions, and keep the student on task in difficult and confusing events in the inquiry process.

- Knowledge—Will your question help you learn? This can be a strong motivator as well as meeting academic standards.

- Processing—Will your question help you understand your topic better? At the highest level the question should be challenging and require analysis and synthesis actions to apply the information gained.

Questioning as Scientist and Information Scientist

Students who are guided by the scientific method will be problem-identifiers as well as problem-solvers (Harada 2003). The student scientist and the student information scientist will both apply the systematic steps of the scientific method to their project. The student scientist will test his research question or hypothesis, and ask questions such as the following:

1. What are the key research questions?

2. What is the best method to test my hypothesis?

3. What are the conclusions that I can infer?

4. What audience needs do I address with my conclusions?

The student information scientist will experiment with information to see if it is convincing, entertaining, and/or understandable for the intended audience. The student information scientist will need space to draft, edit, rehearse and receive criticism on information selected.

The student information scientist will test the information and address questions such as the following:

1. Is this project meaningful and does it meet a need or interest? Have I identified an important question or information need that merits my time and the time of others for me to explore possible answers?

2. Are there likely to be useful sources that can be accessed and understood by me?

3. Have I read widely and in the most relevant literature to inform myself for this project? Has this experience generated additional relevant questions, names, events and other terms that will help in my information search?

4. Have I found the most credible and authoritative information possible? If necessary, is this the most recent information available?

5. Is my use of information to support my ideas the most convincing, understandable and meaningful I can possibly make it for the audience I am to address or for my own personal satisfaction?

6. What information search paths and sources were most useful and perhaps likely for me to use again in similar information need situations?

7. What information (book, Web site, magazine, person) was so important that it inspired me or convinced me I was learning and gaining excitement about what I would be able to report to others?

8. What information have I found in this process that I enjoyed enough to return to for reading pleasure in the future?

9. What information sources did I discover that were least useful and not authoritative enough for me to return to in the future for any reason?

10. In what effective manner might I present or display the message I want to convey from my inquiry experience?

Brainstorm Questions

Students often need help and validation in development of questions. Exploring possible questions related to several typical student research topics can help students understand that it is possible to "test" questions with these criteria in mind:

- high interest to themselves and their peers—is this something I really want to spend time with and is relevant to what others are exploring as well?

- potential for resource support—are resources available within the time and location allotted for the project? Will others help me acquire special resources if necessary?

- age and ability level—does this topic and related questions meet my own level of understanding. Does it challenge me to move to the next level of exploration so that I will really learn not only new facts but also new investigative techniques as well?

Further, students may work in groups as well as with the guidance of the instructional media specialist and other teachers to raise issues to explore from the following question stems:

- Which one (or more)? Questions that force an informed choice. Which is the best or most recommended cure? What event influenced the final outcome the most? What five inventions during the past 100 years have changed the most how you live today?

- Who? Questions often ask who were most or least in given situations. Who was the President that promoted civil rights the most effectively? (Hint: It was probably not Mr. Lincoln.) What three people in American History have most influenced the sort of job you may hold at your age today?

- How? Questions are raised to address action. How might we address the problem of wasting water in our community? What are the best specific steps and how should we take them?

- What if? Questions that pose a possible different path and raise different consequences. What if the authors of the United States Constitution had decided to abolish slavery?

- When? What are the milestone events leading to a cure for polio? Which were by accident and which were according to scientific methods? When was the Civil War actually started? Was it by started because of policy or because of armed conflict; when did one lead to the other?

- Should? Questions that often pose moral debate. Should we allow humans to be cloned? When should we go to war and when should we not?

- Why? Perhaps the first and last stem for all inquiry questions, and often the most difficult to answer. Why, however, often leads to questions of real value.

References

Brown, M. N., and S. M. Keeley (1990). *Asking the Right Questions: A Guide to Critical Thinking.* Prentice Hall.

Christenbury, L., and P. P. Kelley. (1993). *Questioning: A Path to Critical Thinking.* National Council of Teachers of English.

Foundation for Critical Thinking. (2005). *The Role of Questions—the Critical Thinking Community.* www.criticalthinking.org (accessed August 15, 2005).

Harada, V. (2003). "Empowered Learning." In *Curriculum Connections through the Library,* edited by B. Stripling and S. Hughes-Hassell, 41–64. Libraries Unlimited.

Koechlin, C., and S. Zwann. (2001). *Info Tasks for Successful Learning.* Pembrook.

McKenzie, J. (2005). *Learning to Question, to Wonder, to Learn.* FNO Press.

Rubin, D. L., and W. M. Dodd. (1987). *Talking into Writing.* National Council of Teachers of English.

Wolf, D. P. (1987). "The Art of Questioning." *Academic Connections* (Winter): 1–7.

For Further Reading and Viewing

Barell, J. (2003). *Developing More Curious Minds.* Association for Curriculum Supervision and Development.

Dontonio, M., and P. C. Beisenherz. (2000). *Learning to Question, Questioning to Learn.* Allyn & Bacon.

Erikson, E. (1975). "Gatekeeping and the Melting Pot." *Harvard Educational Review* 45 (1): 40–77.

Freedman, R. L. H. (1993). *Open-ended Questioning.* Addison Wesley.

How to Improve Your Questioning Techniques. (1998). Association for Supervision and Curriculum Development. Video. 15 minutes.

Reflection

Daniel Callison

Reflection is key to both the student process for learning effective use of information and for the teacher who wants to evaluate his or her own techniques for instruction in information literacy. To be reflective is to consider options and to make judgments intended to improve future performance.

For the emerging information literate student, this may involve selective use of evidence, knowledgeable use of authority, experimentation with the plausibility of an argument, and self-evaluation of final selection of information for presentation. For the teacher, reflection involves the approaches that model and guide students in the information literacy process.

At the highest levels of reflection, the mature information literate student will demonstrate these actions:

- The student draws extensively on evidence from multiple resources (human, print, nonprint) to support conclusions and the conclusions clearly show a coherent use of the evidence.

- The student has significant recognition of authority and has shown some attempt to investigate and document the authority's credibility or point of view.

- The student recognizes all sides of an issue, is able to weigh the pros and cons of all sides, and recognizes the strengths and limitations of each position in taking a stand.

In addition to these skills, the mature information literate student will demonstrate fluency in application of different information seeking strategies to meet different needs. At these high levels, the student has considered the strategies modeled by teachers of information literacy as well as behavior of his or her successful peers. Through reflection, the student has applied critical review of his or her own previous performance and matures in the ability to move from one information seeking strategy to another based on experience.

Reflection has a powerful impact on student learning when implemented as part of the process of dealing with inquiry to address ill-structured problems, i.e., those situations in which there is no clear right or wrong set of answers or conclusions. Reflection may involve critical analysis beyond any formula provided by a learning guide or evaluation rubric. In time, the mature information literate student will reflect on each piece of information gathered, the manner in which information is linked as evidence, and the strength of conclusions derived from the evidence. Intelligent decision making can be taught, but wisdom can not.

The Elementary Levels for Student Reflection

Linda Hoyt (1999), an elementary school teacher and curriculum specialist, has provided a recent guide to strategies for improving reading comprehension through reflection and application of skills for elementary students to revisit, reflect, and retell. Her list of questions for students to ask each other about books are also questions that elementary level students should ask as they engage with new information and attempt to assimilate that information with previous knowledge and experiences:

- What did you notice?

- What did you like?

- What is your opinion?

- What did you wonder?

- What does this mean?

- What did you learn?

- How did it make you feel?

- What parts of the story seemed especially important to you?

- As you read, were there any places where you thought of yourself, people you know, or experiences you have had?

- What did you read that gives you new ideas?

- What do you know now that you did not know before?

Hoyt's (1999) strategies to engage young learners in conversations about books and to manage personal and social exploration of meaning have applications for placing elementary students on tasks to become selective and critical of information from nonfiction materials as well. Students must select the key or most important elements which summarize the message of a story. "Two-Word Strategy," for example, asks each student to select and justify just two words that reflect their understanding, feeling, or related experience to a thought-provoking selection from a story, newspaper article, or passage from a resource book. As students share their selections, Hoyt notes that a rich tapestry of various understandings, visions, and feelings emerge.

Other strategies place young readers in the position to rank characters and events from a story or news happening. They demonstrate the ability to concentrate on the most important issues. Such skills eventually lead to the ability to center on the key arguments so that limited time and resources can be directed to address these while minor characters, events, or meaningless evidence can be discarded.

Her use of "book commercials," similar to "booktalking," places the student on the task of gleaning for the most interesting or intriguing elements in order to provide excitement as they sell the story through a variety of formats, similar to advertising in mass media.

Retelling expository text is a practiced skill that will build to more mature critical analysis of documents at higher grade levels. For the elementary school student, Hoyt poses these questions for student reflection on information documents such as magazine articles, encyclopedia articles, or newspaper features:

- What is the topic?

- What are the most important ideas to remember?

- What did you learn that you did not already know?

- What is the setting for this information?

- What did you notice about visuals such as graphs, charts, and pictures?

- Can you summarize or retell what you learned?

- What do you think was the author's purpose for writing this article?

Hoyt's (1999) recommended techniques also place younger learners in situations to practice paraphrasing or claiming the key message in their own words after they have identified important information clusters:

READ only as much as your hand can cover.

COVER the words with your hand.

REMEMBER what you have just read. (It is okay to take another look.)

RETELL what you just read inside your head or to a partner.

Reflection on Processes for Older Learners

Carol Collier Kuhlthau's (1994) steps to the library research process culminate in application of self-evaluation techniques designed to cause the high school student to reflect on the research experience. Two important areas for reflection are "use of time" and "use of sources."

The mature student researcher learns to pace him(her)self and through the use of a time line or diary can visualize actions that took more time than necessary and the need to allow for more time in critical areas. These critical areas may include time to compare and contract evidence in a variety of ways before launching into the writing or preparing to present tasks. More time may be necessary to acquire materials from distance loan or to establish a useful interview with an expert in the community.

Knowledge of their own limitations in management of time and correcting for such helps the maturing information literature student to both conserve and concentrate time and energies in order to arrive efficiently at the focus of their research. Testing and confirming focus is crucial to the eventual development of presentation of meaningful findings.

Kuhlthau's (1994) recommended techniques are as follows:

- **Time Line.** Plotting the stages initiated and completed during library research and recalling when focus seemed to emerge.

- **Flowchart.** Decision boxes show the linkages and recursiveness through the process and may highlight "ah-ha" experiences when key ideas and key resources emerged.

- **Conferences.** Debriefing sessions involving the student or small groups of students along with the library media specialist and other teachers can lead to recall of key decision and inspiration points. These conversations can help identify important times for interventions by the library media specialist and other teachers in future research assignments.

- **Writing a Summary Statement.** A clear abstract of the process and product can help the student convey to him(her)self and others the focus or meaning of the research experience. In this technique, as in the others, students should be expected to be critical as they select and summarize their best ideas and resources.

Reflection in the I-Search Process

Marilyn Joyce and Julie Tallman (1997) have placed reflection at several strategic points within the I-Search process. Their approach is to create intervention experiences along the research path so that teachers and students are constantly raising questions about decisions and actions so that research topics become manageable as well as personal.

Students are expected to journal and or vocally state their reflections on such questions as

- What are some of the research projects you have completed prior to this?

- From these previous experiences, what does "research" mean to you?

- Describe one of your research successes. Why was the experience positive?

- Describe one of your research failures or frustrations. Why was the experience negative?

Small group and individual conferences are held to help generate, expand, and clarify research question formation. Students generate potential areas to explore based on interest and resource availability and pre-notetaking reflection can serve to gain an initial focus so that eventual information selection and gathering becomes more targeted and meaningful.

Joyce and Tallman recommend that students address the following kinds of questions as they reflect on pre-notetaking and background reading:

- Describe how the pre-note taking sheet helped you find both a focus for your topic and research questions to investigate.

- Summarize what happened during your conference. What problems or obstacles did you identify during your conference? What strategies will you use to overcome them?

In true application of the I-Search process, the student may demonstrate emerging information literacy skills by composing a report or paper on the research process itself. This may serve as a companion piece to the final research product and becomes a document that should be read and evaluated by both the library media specialist and collaborating teacher. Sample questions given below could be used in peer or teacher evaluation of the student product as well as self-assessment by the student as they report on their experiences.

Presearch

- Has the student chosen a personally meaningful topic?
- Did the student create original and demanding research questions that move the need for evidence beyond simply fact gathering and into evaluation of evidence in terms of relevance, authority, and display of various perspectives?
- Did the student show organizational strengths through an ability to prioritize potential topics, clarify search questions with key terms for more precision, make quality resource choices, and consider alternative solutions to problems through extensive background reading?

Search

- Did the student examine a sufficient variety of relevant sources including interviews and use of electronic documents?
- Did the student show the ability to apply relevant evidence and to discard irrelevant sources or misleading evidence?

Presentation

- Is the presentation organized and based on the key issues relevant to the audience addressed?
- Is the presentation based on relevant information and the use of multiple resources and multiple perspectives where necessary?
- Can the student articulate a likely personal information search and selection strategy to be used in similar future assignments?

The Reflective Teacher

Virginia Rankin (1999), a school media specialist who has demonstrated how to help students reflect on their projects through both presearch and post evaluation processes, defines her own reflective manner in the following terms:

- **Hopefulness**—a positive state of mind helps one take on nearly any inquiry, you know you can be successful;

- **Persistence**—success is exhilarating and worth the struggle;

- **Inquisitiveness**—determining the right question can be as rewarding as finding the right answer:

- **Flexibility**—look at the problem in many ways and be open to many possible solutions;

- **Risk Taking**—do not be afraid to seek answers that may be difficult or impossible, the process often uncovers new areas of inquiry that will be even more rewarding.

Stevens and Levi (2005) in their guide that is an introduction to developing rubrics in secondary schools and colleges list these important and practical questions a teacher should consider as they build a lesson and determine how student performance will be judged:

- Why did I create this assignment?

- Have I given this assignment or similar assignment before?

- How does this assignment related to the rest of what I am teaching?

- What skills will students need to have or develop to successfully complete this assignment?

- What exactly is the task assigned?

- What evidence can students provide in this assignment that would show they have accomplished what I hope they would accomplish?

- What are my highest expectations for student performance on this assignment overall?

Kathleen Blake Yancey (1998) of the University of North Carolina at Charlotte states:

If we want students to be reflective, we [teachers] will have to invite them to be so, [and] may need to reflect with them. Reflection, like language itself, is social as well as individual. Through reflection, we tell our stories of learning; in the writing classroom, our stories of writing and of having written and of [what we] will write tomorrow. . . . I suppose I think this reflection is so important because without it, we live the stories others have scripted for us, in a most unreflective, unhealthy way. And I think the stories we make-whether inside the classroom or out, whether externalized or not, construct us, one by one by one. Cumulatively. So I think it's important to tell lots of stories where we get to construct many selves. (11)

Yancey's statement is important in at least two ways. First, reflection on writing and research processes helps the student to construct a personal identity derived from the choices made, questions fashioned, presentations scripted, and assimilations to previous personal experiences. Student reflection on these actions is essential to the growth and maturation of the information literature student.

Second, the teacher of information literacy and inquiry needs to participate in reflection as well, not only as a coach or model of the reflection process, but to be one who reflects on teaching style, purpose, and actions. "Reflective teaching" has become a generic term referring to a range of efforts intended to prepare teachers to be more thoughtful.

Some advocates hope to engage teachers in becoming more thoughtful about the educational/cultural context, with the assumption that teachers are or should be agents of social change. Others wish to focus teachers' thoughts on the art of teaching, in the hope that through inspection, introspection, and analysis, teaching can be enhanced. The reflective teacher monitors, invites peers to monitor with him or her, and may even journal thoughts in response to questions such as:

• How do I interact with students?

• How do I respond when they ask questions?

• What kind of classroom atmosphere do I create?

• What kinds of questions do I ask?

• Is my classroom spontaneous or is it predictable?

• Are my students involved?

• Why didn't a lesson go over well?

• Why did a lesson work?

More precise areas for reflection have been identified by the National Council of Teachers of Mathematics (1989), but these apply across the curriculum including those who teach library research processes and information literacy:

Nature of Task

– Is the task a problem or an exercise for my students?

– Is it possible to make the problem realistic and grounded in real-world experiences?

– Is it possible to represent and respond to the problem concretely, pictorially, and abstractly on several levels of learning and intelligence?

Teacher's Communication

– Am I determining what the students "know" or bring to a situation?

– What kinds of questions do I ask?

– Genuine questions for which I do not know the answers?

– Testing questions to find out what my students know or have learned?

– Focusing questions that encourage students to think about some idea, to explain, to justify, to hypothesize or predict?

– Am I using wait time before and after I receive responses to questions?

– Am I exploring alternative strategies posed by different students?

– Am I using various forms of communication—reading, writing, listening, speaking?

– Am I modeling creative and critical thinking?

Students' Communication

- What kind of questions are my students asking?
- Are my students talking to each other constructively-disagreeing, challenging, debating?
- Are my students willing to take risks?
- Are my students listening to each other?
- Are my students taking time to think about problems fully?
- Are my students able to explain their ideas clearly and precisely?
- Are my students able to reflect on the experience and identify that which was hard or easy for them, what worked and what didn't, and what they liked and disliked?

Tools That Enhance Discourse

- Am I making use of the technology available?
- Are meaningful and representational models for process and product available for my students?
- Do I encourage and reward by using various tools to communicate ideas?

References

Hoyt, L. (1999). *Revisit, Reflect, Retell: Strategies for Improving Reading Comprehension*. Heinemann.

Joyce, M. Z., and J. I. Tallman. (1997). *Making the Writing and Research Connection with the I-Search Process*. Neal-Schuman.

Kuhlthau, C. C. (1994). *Teaching the Library Research Process*. 2nd ed. Scarecrow Press.

National Council of Teachers of Mathematics. (1989). *Curriculum and Evaluation Standards for School Mathematics*. NCTM.

Rankin, V. (1999). *The Thoughtful Researcher*. Libraries Unlimited.

Stevens, D. D., and A. Levi. (2005). *Introduction to Rubrics: An Assessment Tool to Save Grading Time, Convey Effective Feedback, and Promote Student Learning*. Stylus.

Yancey, K. B. (1998). *Reflection in the Writing Classroom*. Utah State University Press.

Rubrics

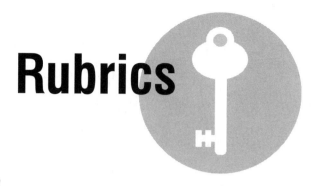

Daniel Callison

The rubric strategy is one of several assessment methods recommended in the student performance assessment section of *Information Power: Building Partnerships for Learning*. A "rubric" is a set of scaled criteria, usually ranging from performance that is considered unacceptable to minimal through progressive stages which eventually defines that which is observable superior performance. Language is used, in terms that both the student and teacher understand, so that precise actions are defined for what the student must do to demonstrate a skill or proficiency at a certain level.

Dannelle Stevens and Antonia Levi (2005), both from Portland State University, define the basic reason for rubrics as a scoring tool that lays out the specific expectations for an assignment. Rubrics, according to this team of undergraduate educators, divide an assignment into its component parts and provide a detailed description of what constitutes acceptable or unacceptable levels of performance for each of those parts.

Grant Wiggins (1998), director of programs for the Center on Learning, Assessment, and School Structure, proposes that rubrics should answer the following questions:

- By what criteria should performance be judged?

- Where should we look and what should we look for to judge performance success?

- What does the range in the quality of performance look like?

- How do we validly, reliably, and fairly determine what score should be given and what that score means (so that a score means the same from one similar task performed by a similar group to another but evaluated by different instructors, or the same instructor, over time)?

- How should the different levels of quality be described and distinguished from one another?

Some rubric models allow for points at each level so the point totals can be translated into standard grades, if necessary. Some rubric models show a relationship between the percentage or degree of proficiency and the action demonstrated. In these cases, lower performance may be at the 50 percent level implying that the student has demonstrated only half of the skills in the given area evaluated, or that the student is below the norm in this area. The percentage gradually increases until, at the highest level, the student has demonstrated 95–100 percent proficiency.

Such numeric guides, however, should not take away from the purpose and value of rubrics: to write in clear statements those performances that are not acceptable and those that are acceptable as measured against the expected standard performance for the task and age group. A rubric provides phrases to translate for the student, teacher, and parent explaining why the student has failed, needs more practice, has performed in a satisfactory range, or has excelled.

Classification of Performance

Rubrics may provide classification of performances in several ways. Usually the rubric is constructed on a grid with the evaluation skill levels or target indicators listed down the left-hand side and the levels of performance classified across the top of the grid. The skill levels may range from "basic knowledge," followed by "analysis skills," and then "synthesis skills." Or, the skills may simply be clustered in such categories as "written," "oral," and "social." Some evaluators cluster the skills by Gardner's multiple intelligence categories which include linguistic, logical, spatial, musical, kinesthetic, intrapersonal, and interpersonal.

Some rubric designers cluster skills by those which reflect critical thinking and those which match more to creative thinking. Thus the student may be evaluated on his or her skills in selecting the best information to prove a point in a logical manner and be evaluated again on the ability to create a plan that will address the given problem. Still other rubric designs allow for skills that are essential or required and allow space for elective skills. This is similar to judgments made in some Olympic competitions in which the performance is compared very closely to others in the required or compulsory elements, but there is room for judgment of individual initiative as well in the "free style" section.

The rubric also will display the progression or range of quality of performance (Donham 2005) in terms of "novice" to "apprentice" to "expert." Other terms used to classify the progression are "beginning," "developing," "accomplished," and "exemplary." Usually no fewer than three levels are given and often room is provided for notes from the teacher and student that describe actions to be taken to improve future performance.

In cases where students are truly involved in self-evaluation, space is provided on the grid in both the list of skills and columns for levels of criteria so students may add their own expectations beyond those listed as common for the entire class. Rubrics can be constructed for any area of the curriculum, across all grade levels and entry ability levels. Thus, a given rubric should be labeled as an evaluation instrument for a specific set of learners and for a specific lesson or task. It also is useful to provide a list of entry level skills, those the student should have mastered prior to this lesson.

Also useful, and likely to be similar to the proficient level for the instructional performance indicators, will be exit objectives, the minimum basic skills the student will demonstrate during and as a result of the given lesson.

Other Evaluation Methods

The rubric method is most useful when applied to a lesson that will require multiple skills to be demonstrated over time and during which the student will be evaluated on both process and product. Checklist methods help to keep the student on track and to make certain all tasks are completed, but little evaluation really takes place.

Conference and journal methods allow for more extensive intervention and teacher direction, and as outlets for self-reflection. Rubrics, therefore, take objectives for student performance and provide an evaluation grid or map so the learner knows what is expected and what will be valued.

The rubrics for a given lesson should be provided as an opening organizer for the lesson, a midpoint check or evaluation so adjustments in performance are possible, and serve as a menu, guide, or agenda for the final evaluation or exit conference concerning student performance among several groups that may include student, library media specialist, other teachers, and parents.

Advantages and Frustrations

Rubrics allow for evaluation of academic and social skills. As Jean Donham (2005) at Cornell University suggests, one rubric set can be applied to one task and result in an examination of a portion of a performance set, or rubrics compiled over time and across several lessons will lead to a more complex or holistic view of the student's progression in skill mastery.

For rubrics to work effectively, especially applied to student self-assessment, there are, according to Donham (2005, 265), three critical attributes:

1. Explicit criteria. The criteria provide enough description that students know what successful performance looks like.

2. Structured feedback. The criteria are ordered to show students how close to excellence they are at the time of evaluation. Feedback is not hit-or-miss-all students get feedback.

3. Front-end information. The criteria for success are provided as the student begins the work, not at the end.

The advantages of rubrics in assessment are that

- Assessment is more likely to be reasonably objective and consistent from lesson to lesson and from student to student, especially useful in team teaching situations that involve collaboration among the library media specialist and other teachers.

- Teachers focus on the essential criteria and performances.

- Students have a more clear visual of their progress and what is necessary to achieve a higher rating than is reflected in simple letter grades.

- Feedback is easy to convey and can provide a benchmark from one lesson to the next. Communication with parents is often more constructive.

- If applied correctly, rubrics come close to assuring that inadequate, satisfactory, and excellent mean the same thing on the same skill set from one group of students to a similar group regardless of who makes the evaluation.

Frustrations of rubrics include the following:

- Construction of good rubric statements takes time and practice. There is still a great deal of room for experimentation.

- Although the rubric instrument as an assessment innovation has been given a great deal of attention, letter grades remain the standard. Even the best rubric matrix eventually melts back to A, B, C, D, or F, unless the school district is committed to archiving portfolios.

- Although consistency can be provided within a lesson, the more teachers, grade levels, and subjects involved, the wider the range and definitions of acceptable performance criteria, and evaluation suddenly becomes very complex and confusing.

- When rubrics do define a standard performance, such is often resisted and viewed as taking true evaluation out of the hands of the individual teacher.

- Poorly constructed rubrics give emphasis to quantity rather than quality; the student does something more times rather than doing something better.

Process and Product

The Minnesota Department of Children, Families, and Learning (2005) has developed a set of evaluation rubric guides for application across the curriculum and at all grade levels. Sample exercises are provided on their Web site along with possible evaluation criteria. Two key elements are present in many of these state recommended examples:

- Both teacher and student identify where they believe the learner stands on a given performance level.

- Elements of the process are listed for evaluation as well as elements of the final product or final performance.

Thus the student makes judgments along with the teachers of information literacy and inquiry on such process stages as the following:

- Research questions are relevant to the topic and are adequate to lead to sufficient and appropriate kinds of data.

- The investigation plan allows for adequate and feasible collection of data.

- Data chart/matrix/note cards include bibliographic information.

- The interview questions are designed to get the needed information, clearly relate to research questions, and lead to responses that are complete and detailed. The interviewer is adequately prepared to ask additional questions for clarification.

Midpoint evaluations, or multiple checkpoints, in the progress of the student toward completion of a complex research project can be guided by the process portion of the evaluation rubric. Often teachers of information literacy and inquiry can guide a student who is off track back to a focus and direction if inadequate preparation is discovered during these debriefings.

Types of Rubrics

Despite the variety of rubric formations that have been described here, Germaine Taggert (1998) of Fort Hays State University has categorized rubrics as three types:

Holistic. Holistic rubrics are criterion-referenced, which show what a student knows, understands, or can do in relation to specific performance objectives of the instructional program. How does one perform overall?

Analytic. Criterion-referenced analytic rubrics assess summative or formative performance along several different important dimensions. How does one perform on several individual tasks?

Primary trait. These define the essential traits that must be observed for successful performance. How does one perform on the specific essential elements for success in this lesson or activity?

Although the current literature generally agrees that the rubric approach is clearly criterion-referenced and must be tied to a standard for acceptable performance, room also should be given for objective evaluation of personal growth. Within the series of evaluation conversations, students and teachers need to consider progress that is evident and reward such progress in order to motivate more constructive action. Some students will not achieve at the adequate or excellent level on most criteria, but rubrics that allow for a wide enough range to show some progress will serve to encourage a wider spectrum of students. Movement for some from "inadequate" to the basic "in need of improvement" or "emerging" levels will prove helpful in some performance phases.

Any evaluation rubric should allow space for additional comments that will address individual traits and special characteristics of the learner so that such information is not lost in rigid standards. These additional principles should be kept in mind:

- Rubrics are texts that are visible signs of agreed-upon values. They cannot contain all the nuances of the evaluation community's values, but they do contain the central expressions of those values:

- Rubrics need to grow out of and be accompanied by discussion. A core set of rubrics should be available to the learner from the beginning, but options for additional criteria should be present as the activity unfolds.

- Rubrics provide a map and guide for student assessment. More importantly, a record of the discussion concerning student performance should be included in the student portfolio to show areas of progress over time.

Rubrics for Information Literacy

Several creative groups, under the guidance of the Colorado Department of Education in 1996, provided some excellent examples of rubrics in information literacy. Two are illustrated here:

---

1. Target Indicator: Student is a self-directed learner.

In progress: I have trouble choosing my own resources and I like someone to tell me the answer.

Essential: I might know what I want, but need to ask for help in solving information problems.

Proficient: I choose my own resources and like being independent in my information searches.

Advanced: I like to choose my own information resources. I am comfortable in situations where there are multiple answers as well as those with no answers.

---

2. Target Indicator: Student as a group contributor.

In progress: I need support to work in a group. I have trouble taking responsibility to help the group.

Essential: I usually participate with the group. I offer opinions and ideas, but cannot always defend them. I rely on others to make group decisions.

Proficient: I participate effectively as a group member. I help the group process, and evaluate and use information with the group.

Advanced: I am comfortable leading, facilitating, negotiating, or participating in a group. I work with others to create a product that fairly represents consensus of the group.

A Rubric for Rubrics

Given the trends in current development of the rubric strategy for evaluation of student performance, one can consider this rubric to help test the degree to which new instructional rubrics have been constructed for effective use:

Target Indicator: Write a meaningful rubric statement set.

In progress: Statements are not clearly tied to a standard for student performance and fail to provide a reasonable range to reflect progress in student performance.

Essential: Statements are tied to a common standard, but define student progress only in terms of increased quantity and not in terms of quality.

Proficient: Statements are clearly relevant to several accepted standards for student performance and are illustrated in terms of progressive criteria for increased quality of student performance.

Advanced: Statements illustrate a broad range of tasks to demonstrate student performance measured against acceptable standards in terms of appropriate quantity and/or quality, and allow for the learner to explore additional criteria for evaluation if both student and teacher see merit in such options.

A Framework for Rubrics

Stevens and Levi (2005) have established an excellent guide to introduce secondary school teachers and college instructors to the rubric construction process. Their ideas are based on proven application in their curriculum development courses at Portland State University. Their framework, however, is generic and standard to rubric design over the past decade found in many elementary and secondary schools. They identify four basic parts to rubric construction:

- Task definition or statement of the assignment in measurable objective terminology.

- An evaluation scale of the levels of possible achievement, usually in terms of points or grades.

- The dimensions of the assignment, a specific listing of the skills or knowledge to be demonstrated by the student in completion of the assignment.

- Level of performance and what constitutes each level, usually shown in a progression from unacceptable to exemplary.

A typical framework for a rubric is shown in Table Part3.3. Each the scale level for each dimension may also have a subscale to help further define where the student's performance level is even within a given scale. Evaluators may want to circle or highlight specific phrases that best express the performance of the specific student from the general statements provided. For those students who are required to perform the task again in order to improve their grade or pass the minimum expectations, new highlights in a new color can indicate progress. For complex projects that may take students several weeks to complete, multiple rubric instruments may need to be developed.

Table Part3.3. Simplified Typical Rubric Format

The Task or Assignment: The student shall complete an inquiry into the job opportunities for teens in our local community and present findings as to training and educational requirements necessary to meet such opportunities successfully. Findings shall be presented to members of the student's class in both a written and oral report.

	(Scale) Lacking 0—1—2—3—4—5	(Scale) Proficient 6—7—8—9—10	(Scale) Exemplary 11—12—13—14—15
(Dimension) Ability to define the task.	a. Has not raised meaningful questions. b. Has not defined jobs and opportunities. c. Has not identified training or educational options.	a. Has written and tested useful questions to gain necessary information. b. Has validated likely local job opportunities. c. Has validated limitations and opportunities for local training and education.	a. Has extended questions into a useful outline to organize information gathering. b. Has contacted several local employers and agencies who can enhance information on local jobs. c. Has contacted valuable human resources on local training and education programs.
(Dimension) Ability to present findings.	a. Does not display adequate skills for use of presentation formats. b. Has not organized findings in a meaningful way. c. Is uncertain of the message to be presented.	a. Has mastered at least one presentation method to present findings from options that include poster, brochure, computerized slides, Web site, or video. b. Findings are organized for understanding by most of the student's peers. c. Has identified specific elements of the message to be conveyed.	a. Has mastered a variety of presentation methods involving various media in order to present findings most effectively. b. Has analyzed the interests and needs of his audience in order to deliver the most meaningful conclusions and to answer likely questions from the audience. c. Has an identifiable theme and over-all principles to convey that will help the audience understand and remember findings.
(Dimension) Others can be added as teachers and students see the need.			

Comments: (Regardless of how complete a rubric instrument may be, there should always be room for specific and unique comments.)

References

Colorado Department of Education. (1996). "Rubrics for the Assessment of Information Literacy." *Indiana Media Journal* 18 (4): 50–71.

Donham, Jean. (2005). *Enhancing Teaching and Learning: A Leadership Guide for School Library Media Specialists.* Neal-Schuman.

Minnesota Department of Children, Families and Learning. n.d. Minnesota Electronic Curriculum Repository. http://mecr.state. mn.us/home (accessed July 12, 2005).

Stevens, D. D., and A. J. Levi. (2005). *Introduction to Rubrics: An Assessment Tool to Save Grading Time, Convey Effective Feedback, and Promote Student Learning.* Stylus.

Taggart, Germaine, ed. (1998). *Rubrics: A Handbook for Construction and Use.* Technomic.

Wiggins, Grant. (1998). *Educative Assessment: Designing Assessments to Inform and Improve Student Performance.* Jossey-Bass Publications.

Additional Web Sites

Chicago Public Schools. *Instructional Intranet: The Rubric Bank.* http://intranet. cps.k12.il.us/Assessments/Ideas_and_Rubrics/ Rubric_Bank/rubric_bank.html (accessed February 25, 2006).

Rona's Teacher Tools—Rubrics. www. rubrics4teachers.com (accessed June 15, 2001).

University of Northern Iowa Professional Development. www.uni.edu/profdev/rubrics. html (accessed July 15, 2005).

Region 20 Education Center. www.esc20. net/etprojects/rubrics/Default.htm (accessed June 15, 2001).

Project Based Learning—Checklists. www. 4teachers.org/projectbased/checklists.html (accessed June 15, 2001).

Schrock, Kathy. *Assessment Rubrics.* http://school.discovery.com/schrockguide/ assess.html (accessed July 15, 2005).

Scaffolding

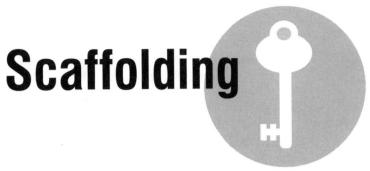

Daniel Callison

Scaffolding is a term that has gained popular use as a metaphor for support, reinforcement, learning sequence, and similar phrases which infer that learning is constructed. Similar to a building under construction, student learning is constructed based on a sequence of skills with meaningful activities that are presented by a teacher to help the student climb to the desired educational goal or behavior.

Scaffolding is most commonly associated with Jerome Bruner and his colleagues in the 1970s and 1980s as they attempted to describe the role of the tutoring process in problem solving. Used most often in the preschool and elementary school setting, scaffolding is a useful concept for describing nearly any situation in which a novice and an expert are engaged in the learning process. Scaffolding is a temporary device in construction or building repair and eventually removed when the desired work is accomplished. So too in learning construction the expert fades from the situation as the novice masters the necessary skills and takes on a new set of mental models or mastered skills.

Laura E. Berk, Distinguished Professor at Illinois State University, and Adam Winsler, assistant professor at Alabama University, have provided an excellent guide (1995) to understanding scaffolding as a changing quality of support over a teaching session, in which a more skilled teaching partner adjusts the assistance he or she provides to fit the child's current level of performance. More support is offered when a task is new; less is provided as the child's competence increases, fostering the child's autonomy and independent mastery.

The Scaffolding Analogy

A more detailed discussion and diagram of scaffolding moves the metaphor into an analogy as additional similarities between construction of learning and construction of buildings become apparent. (See Figure Part3.14.)

The purpose of the scaffolding is to help the learner or builder reach higher tasks than can be performed at just the base level. The base level is extremely important, however, as a firm, secure, foundation is desirable for both learner and builder. The base may be composed of several associated skills to give it a broad foundation upon which to build higher skills sets. Strength is derived from linking these foundational or entry level skills together and through practice.

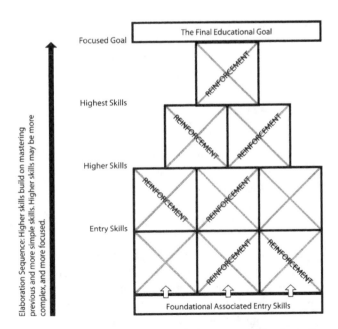

Figure Part3.14. Skills and reinforcement illustrated as scaffolding to achieve the final educational goal.

Success is reinforced by the teacher and by the learner's growing awareness and/or understanding when the task has been achieved. Reinforcements tie the task together and often help to link to other tasks.

Scaffolding can be deconstructed as well as constructed. In some cases, this would imply changing unacceptable behavior or modifying out-dated information, changing the mental model through assimilation of new knowledge leading to a different understanding.

Scaffolding also can be thought of as deconstructed when similar parts are moved, or transferred, to new learning situations. Hopefully the maturing learner, begins to recognize how portions of the previous scaffold apply to a new learning task and may move forward with self-construction of much of the scaffold without the assistance of the expert. Practice in and observation of likely transfer of learning is an important part of movement toward what many describe as "lifelong learning skills." Setting up scaffolding in either learning or building construction is hard work, often messy and repetitious. The final result just as often can be frustrating as rewarding, and both can be exhausting.

As the scaffolding is built higher, the skill set may become both more complex and more refined or precise. A focus often will take place so the learner can meet the final educational goal. The focus may change from one situation to another and, therefore, the scaffolding structure or design may change to meet those different needs.

Elaboration Theory

Professor Charles Reigeluth of Indiana University is a leader among many instructional designers who believe elaborations of content in courses of study are based on concepts, principles, and procedures (1983). The sequencing of lessons is best designed when based on the simple and then move toward the more complex.

The first lesson, the epitome, is followed by successive layers of complexity and associated lessons that provide illustration and practice. Within the lesson design, easiest or most familiar organizing concepts are presented first. Summaries are important as a means to provide content review. Summaries may serve to reinforce demonstrated performance as the teacher explains what has been achieved by the student. The student may signal his or her readiness to move on to the next level by the ability to summarize or synthesize for him or herself. Increased learner control of the learning situation is desirable. More confident learners are more likely to move to the highest levels.

A sequence of skills, or elaboration sequence, as noted in Figure Part3.11, is based on moving to higher and more complex skills only after mastering of the basic or simpler ones. The difficult role for the teacher is to find the balance between moving the learner through this sequence too slowly and creating boredom, or moving too quickly and creating anxiety.

Effective use of scaffolding is more than just breaking down a task into substeps offered by the adult or expert to the novice. Such a limited approach reduces the novice or child to a passive recipient of the adult's didactic efforts. Scaffolding should involve a series of social communication efforts, likely to become more complex and detailed just as the elaboration of the skill set content grows. Elaboration may, therefore, be best described as interaction as both parties involved need to communicate for purposes of testing out examples, analogies, predictions, and possible solutions depending on the task at hand.

Reaching the desired levels of performance, however, will bring on a dramatic reduction in such communication as the novice-become-expert may begin to dominate the conversations. Such is a strong cue to the teacher to fade from the learned lesson.

Other Elements of Scaffolding

Berk and Winsler (1995) identify several additional elements that should be present in an effective scaffolding process:

Joint problem solving. Scaffolding will have more chance of being on a firm foundation if the learner is engaged in a culturally relevant problem that has meaning to him or her.

Intersubjectivity. This is when two people begin a task with a different understanding and arrive at a shared understanding. The final goal must be clear for both novice and expert. Different methods and different perspectives can be adjusted as the two learn to communicate, but the goal or final learning objective should be common to both.

Warmth and responsiveness. Engagement of the novice will be more likely when the expert displays attitudes that are pleasant, warm, and responsive to the learner.

Promoting self-regulation. Encourage the learner to take the role more and more to regulate the information intake. This will provide indications that the learner is growing in his or her understanding of how he or she learns and matures in the knowledge of his or her limits. While the expert continues to find ways to challenge, the healthiest approach includes an increased role on the part of the learner to recognize his or her own abilities.

Keeping the Learner in the ZPD

Although it is unlikely Lev Vygotsky ever used the scaffolding metaphor or the analogies that could be derived from the building or construction tasks, scaffolding is often associated with his notion of the Zone of Proximal Development (ZPD). Vygotsky (Leong and Bodrova 1996) viewed education as leading development-placing learning within the zone just beyond the learner's proven skills so that the challenge to grow and move forward was always present until the learner had reached full mastery of the skill.

As shown in Figure Part3.15, the novice moves, ideally, with the help of the expert, closer and closer to the final performance goal over a sequence of practice sessions, with each employing strategies to move the learner higher. In a social learning environment, through collaboration and interaction with teachers, parents, and other children, the child actively constructs new cognitive abilities.

According to Berk and Winsler (1995), Vygotsky originally introduced the ZPD in the context of arguing against standard intelligence and achievement testing procedures and against the view of development and education that emerges from the use of such tests. He regarded the traditional tests of intellectual functioning of his time as extremely limited because they only assessed static or fossilized abilities, leaving out the dynamic and every-changing quality of human cognition. Vygotsky suggested that what we should be measuring is not what children can do by themselves or already know, but rather what they can do with the help of another person and have the potential to learn.

Therefore, he defined the ZPD as the distance between the actual developmental level as determined by independent problem solving and the level of potential development as determined through problem solving under adult guidance or in collaboration with more capable peers. Moving the learner into the ZPD and supporting the learner to move beyond it is an essential part of scaffolding.

Inner Speech and External Speech

Vygotsky also saw a developmental relationship between thought and language (Leong and Bodrova 1996). His observations of preschool children convinced Vygotsky that children use private speech to bring new concepts into their minds; they move their mouths to do so. Inner speech, sentences spoken silently, help the child formulate the thought as his own. Eventually the child will use external speech to test his

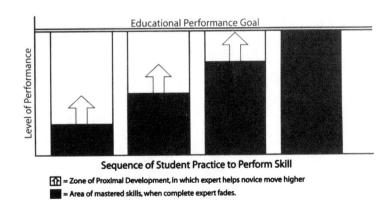

Figure Part3.15. Sequence of student practice to perform skill illustrating progressive closure of ZPD.

or her thought. Inner speech is often both more concise and more complex than external speech. The mind knows cues, images, and relationships that may be difficult or impossible to be expressed to others. With time, the child, or novice, finds ways to elaborate on communications so that thoughts become more expressive and relevant to a growing spectrum of social events.

This process follows the scaffolding pattern just as many other skill sets. In the information search and information use processes, the novice may need to be encouraged to externalize his or her thoughts. Composing visual search strategies with different key terms helps the school library media specialist and other teachers mediate the need to expand, refine, or combine in some other fashion the terms that may lead to the most useful information. Students need to read materials, internalize the major points, and verbalize them before moving on to an external paraphrasing or linkage of the new information to other information gathered.

References

Berk, L. E., and A. Winsler. (1995). *Scaffolding Children's Learning: Vygotsky and Early Childhood Education.* National Association for the Education of Young Children.

Leong, D. J., and E. Bodrova. (1996). *Tools of the Mind: The Vygotskian Approach to Early Childhood Education.* Merrill Prentice Hall.

Reigeluth, C. M. (1983). *Instructional Design Theories and Models: An Overview of Their Current Status.* Erlbaum.

For Further Reading

Holliday, W. G. (2001). "Scaffolding in Science." *Science Scope* 25 (1): 68, 70–71.

Larkin, M. J. (2001). "Providing Support for Student Independence Through Scaffolded Instruction." *Teaching Exceptional Children* 34 (1): 30–34.

Wray, D. (2001). *Developing Factual Writing: An Approach Through Scaffolding.* ED 454 534.

Silent Sustained Reading

Ann Marie Moser

Pappas and Tepe (2002) are correct that wide engagement with literature in many formats and genre can be a powerful foundation for inquiry learning if such is enhanced through open discussion, a culture for consistent reading habits, and modeled by mentors (Methe 2003) such as older students, teachers and the school media specialist as instructional media specialist. The more we read, the more we know, the more we question and explore, and the greater the options for inquiry projects, directed and free.

A method that has been applied across all grade levels over the past fifty years (and very likely was common in one room school houses even earlier) is Silent Sustained Reading (SSR). In some urban school settings, SSR is an initiative being resurrected by students, but success requires commitment of time and resources from the entire school community (Fisher 2004). Anne Marie Moser (2006), as a graduate student in youth services at Indiana University—Indianapolis, has summarized the merits of this method in the following essay.

Sustained Silent Reading: What Could It Look Like in Your School?

(Reprinted with permission from "Sustained Silent Reading: What Culd It Look Like in Your School? Indiana Libraries 25 (1) (2006): 33–35, the Indiana Library Federation)

"Reading is a skill for life, and if students do not learn to enjoy reading, they are cheated of a vital part of their education." Steve Gardiner (2005, p. 69)

Enjoy reading? Unless we are living within a bubble of enthusiastic student readers, the answer to this question may be a resounding "no." Children who love to read seem to enjoy it almost inherently, while most other students tend to become distant when asked to read, whether it is for class or for pleasure. How can we, then, as school librarians engage our students and partner with teachers to help students enjoy reading?

Basic Principles of Sustained Silent Reading

Sustained silent reading (SSR) is one way that has been tried and tested in schools across the United States as a way to encourage reading. Proposed over 30 years ago by Lymon C. Hunt, Jr. (Trelease, 2001, p. 109), SSR in its purest form has eight main factors or components:

1) Access—materials in a variety of formats are provided for students

2) Appeal—reading materials are of interest to the students

3) Environment—comfortable, quiet setting is provided for reading

4) Encouragement—teachers model the reading behavior, recommend appropriate materials, and explain the benefits of reading

5) Staff Training—learning the philosophy of SSR and creating practical guidelines for individual classrooms

6) Non-Accountability—SSR should be non-threatening, and a time for pleasure reading, not earning credit or a grade

7) Follow-up Activities—activities that carry over students' excitement about reading onto other subjects

8) Distributed Time to Read—SSR time should be offered on a regular basis (even for small blocks of time), rather than large blocks of time every so often. (Adapted from Pilgreen, 2003, p. 43)

Although this model may seem daunting, it comes down to offering interesting and level appropriate reading materials, modeling reading behaviors by reading while the students read, and helping teachers interact with their students through conversation or extension exercises. As Gardiner (2005) states, "We don't need to spend a lot of money or design complicated programs to help students learn to enjoy reading; we just need to give them time to learn that reading can be enjoyable" (p. 67). Too often it seems that reading in the classroom is a means only to an end: a student reads to gain information on a certain topic. The joy of the process of getting that information, essentially reading, is overlooked in the hurry to complete assignments and "check things off a list."

Criticism and Praise for SSR

Despite recent criticism, SSR has proven to be an effective tool in today's classrooms. One of the most recent attacks against SSR was the 2001 National Reading Panel (NRP) report that states that research:

> " . . . has not yet confirmed whether independent silent reading with minimal guidance or feedback improves reading achievement and fluency . . . the research suggests that there are more beneficial ways to spend reading instructional time than to have students read independently in the classroom without instruction." (p. 3–1)

However, critics of this report, including panel members themselves, immediately spoke out against the methods used to make such statements and have since written several articles debunking the argument of a lack of research supporting SSR. Stephen Krashen (2005) has defended SSR most vocally, stating that the NRP simply missed substantial evidence of the successfulness and utility of SSR. In his own research, Krashen determined that 93 percent of the SSR students did as well as or even better than students having no SSR time (Trelease, 2001, p. 110). Jim Trelease (2001), author and well-known literacy advocate, asserts that SSR is a way that educators can expose children to the written word in context: "Until students spend more time meeting words in context (reading), there can be no improvement in comprehension or reading speed" (p. 111). When children spend more time reading material of their choice, their learning experience becomes more enjoyable.

Alternative Forms of SSR

There are other variations on SSR that have proved to be effective. Jodi Crum Marshall instituted a program in her school called Supporting Student Literacy which incorporated sustained silent reading, sustained silent writing, and reading aloud together in order to instill the qualities of literacy in students. She has found that these three elements working in tandem help students truly connect with what they are reading, and in turn, engage with the text and with each other during the class periods. Marshall (2002) asserts that reading aloud especially helps create incentive for reading: "Hearing short stories, poems, newspaper and magazine articles and excerpts from books provides the spark struggling readers need to explore reading on their own" (p. xvi). In her opinion, allowing children the time to read, in isolation of other activities, will not work with every student so it is important to use more structured literacy program to provide tools for those reading experiences (Marshall, 2002).

In 2005 Leslie Preddy collaborated to pilot a program of SSR that included students writing a response to their reading based on a prompt provided by the teacher. Teacher intervention strategies included reading aloud to students, holding personal conversations with students about their reading, incorporating factual text into the weekly routine, writing a personal response in student's journals, and maintaining a teacher's log and observation checklist. Through the incorporation of these intervention strategies, there was greater growth than the previous average increase in students' reading comprehension scores from Spring to Fall for the first year of the program compared to several previous years. (Preddy, 2005).

What Does This Research Mean for Your School and Library?

Matching Readers with Books

School librarians can play a major part in the SSR program at their schools. One of the main components, and perhaps one of the most difficult to fulfill, is the need for teachers (and librarians) to recommend and provide appealing and level-appropriate reading materials for their students. This cannot happen effectively if the professionals do not know what their students enjoy. Many students, not being avid readers themselves, do not know where to begin when given the choice to choose a book. As librarians, we can help our students and our fellow teachers decide what book is "just right." In her article "Perfect Match," Rebecca Clements (2002) discusses her experiences as a teacher trying to link her students with that "perfect" book. Some of the methods she incorporates in her classroom are reading surveys and class discussions on what students liked and disliked in books. Initiating a conversation with students about their interests, what they like to do at home, watch on TV, or read about, is often the first step in deciding what type of book they would like to read. School librarians can offer this vital service to students by building conversations around books and topics in which the students are interested.

Being a role model

School librarians have the unique opportunity to promote reading in their schools simply by doing what many of us love the most, by reading. Students who see and hear about the adults in their lives reading are more likely to perceive the importance of the activity. In line with the role modeling theory of Albert Bandura, Yoon (2002) states that "a given behavior modeled by parents, teachers, peers, or celebrities may facilitate their learning of it. For this lens, showing a reading behavior to them may be one of the most important sources of developing their attitude toward reading" (p. 188).

Conclusion

In conclusion, to get a resounding "yes" from students who are asked if they enjoy reading, try the following concepts of SSR:

- Modeling—students see you read, they hear you talk about reading (personal interest material—not necessary what you are SUPPOSED to read)

- Encouraging and initiating conversation—encourage students to talk about what they read, about what they like or dislike about particular books, and share with them what you enjoy reading

- Providing stability in the schedule—a stable schedule encourages students to anticipate reading time

- Experimenting with the types of books and materials that are offered—you might find a winner in an unlikely source such as a magazine, comic book, newspaper, or graphic novel

Knowing your students. Yes, research is good and will tell you what other people have tried and succeeded with, but each classroom is distinctive and you have the opportunity to provide unique teaching strategies. Adapt the suggested programs with what you believe will work for your school and/or classroom and, most especially, for individual students.

References

Clements, R. (2002). "Perfect Match." *PEN* 134, 2–7.

Gardiner, S. (2005). "A Skill for Life." *Educational Leadership* 63 (2), 67–70.

Krashen, S. (2005). "Is In-school Free Reading Good for Children? Why the National Reading Panel Report Is (Still) Wrong." *Phi Delta Kappan*, 444–447.

Marshall, J. C. (2002). *Are They Really Reading? Expanding SSR in the Middle Grades.* Portland: Stenhouse Publishers.

Pilgreen, J. (2003). "Questions Teachers Are Asking about Sustained Silent Reading." *California Reader* 37 (1), 42–53.

Preddy, L. B. (2006). "Sustained Silent Reading with Intervention Project." *NetWords* (Winter), 6–7.

Trelease, J. (2001). *The Read-aloud Handbook.* 5th ed. New York: Penguin.

Yoon, J. (2002). "Three Decades of Sustained Silent Reading: A Meta-analytic Review of the Effects of SSR on Attitudes Toward Reading." *Reading Improvement* 186–195.

Additional Readings on the Topic

Gardiner, S. (2005). *Building Student Literacy Through Sustained Silent Reading.* Alexandria, VA: Association for Supervision & Curriculum Development.

Krashen, S. D. (2004). *The Power of Reading.* 2d ed. Westport, CT: Libraries Unlimited.

Trelease, J. (2001). *The Read-aloud Handbook.* 5th ed. New York: Penguin.

Story

Daniel Callison

For over one hundred years, many librarians and classroom teachers have found the art of storytelling to be a useful technique to promote reading. Stories stimulate the imagination. A good storyteller who engages the audience to envision a different time and place also will increase the desire to read more about similar characters and events. Story is a powerful method, and often more powerful than the medium (voice, actions, illustrations) used. When relevant to the needs of a receptive audience, story can promote, persuade, instruct, soothe, and excite (Simmons 2002). Story can, with the right mix of interaction, enchant.

From the very beginning of human communication, story has provided a way to document human history, events, and behavior through the oral tradition of family or tribal storytelling. Recent studies on cultures that depend on oral family history suggest that males establish story based on memories of personal mischief and challenge, while females tend to center story on family conflict, change, and personal crisis (McCormick and Lipka 1998).

Folktales help us seek within a richer context an understanding of the culture of others and give depth to our own personal culture. Some have found folktale storytelling can be used, in school and group settings by teachers, mental health workers, and other group leaders, as a means of increasing self-awareness and building self-esteem. Promoting enjoyment of stories can include audience acceptance of messages for positive social growth (Wolfe 1995).

On another level, story can be one of the most persuasive tools for leadership (Denning 2005). Of the many political skills held by Abraham Lincoln, his ability to express a vision for what should be and to convey that to his audience through story is often listed as his most enduring characteristic. This ability to communicate and lead through story did not seem to be diminished by a rather high and often unpleasant voice. Lincoln, and hundreds of other leaders, found that strength lies in the content, sincerity, and vision of the message, although such can be enhanced with voice control and other techniques that often appeal to the listener.

Story is necessary when reality for an audience does not exist or is not enough.

Telling Tales

Connie Rochman (2001), a professional storyteller for the past three decades and advocate for librarians to engage children and young adults in story through the oral telling tradition, has offered these tips for those who wish to prepare an effective story:

- Choose stories you sincerely love and have a strong desire to share.

- Allow time to learn a story.

- Visualize the setting and the audience.

- Divide the story logically into parts.

- Master the style of the story.

- Tell the story to yourself several times.

- Timing is crucial to a well-told tale. Include pauses for suspense and dramatic intensity. Change the pace of your voice as the action dictates.

- Find someone to listen to your story and give you feedback.

- The goal is to connect to the imagination of another.

- Find an audience and tell, and retell, the story again and again.

Do Listeners Learn?

The degree to which story helps to instruct has a mixed record in the research. The National Council of Teachers of English (n.d.) suggests that story should be an important part of the curriculum and teachers' instructional tools. Listeners encounter both familiar and new language patterns through story, according to the NCTE position statement. Students learn new words or new contexts for already familiar words. Perhaps even more powerful, learners who regularly "tell" stories become aware of how an audience affects a telling, and they carry that awareness into their writing.

Some researchers (Bygrave 1994; Smith 1998) suggest that the concept of story schema offers a framework for the mental organization of a story. Children use this framework, or story structure, to aid in listening comprehension and recall. Retelling a story is a constructive process and requires the use of a story structure as a method for the organization of a story from beginning to end. Story schema expands with age and experience with story, thus storytelling and storylistening from early preschool age through young adulthood seem to help expand memory and mental organization skills to accept more and more complex visions.

Direct impact on reading, comprehension, and composition skills through the use of story seems to be more positive in the lower grades on those students who are below-average readers. Average to above-average readers tend to be successful regardless of the introduction of story to their learning environment, although they often enjoy the entertaining aspects of storytelling.

Enchanting the Listener's Imagination

Brian Sturm (1999), associate professor in children's literature at the University of North Carolina at Chapel Hill, has studied the storylistening trance as it pertains to professional storytellers and members of their adult audience. Many of the actions that seem to trigger enchantment for the adult listener are likely to be similar for listeners at younger ages as well. He illustrates the elements that lead to the entrancing experience with a model composed of three concentric circles representing the baseline state of consciousness, the transitional period, and the discrete altered state of consciousness (see Figure Part3.16).

The d-ASC (see Figure Part3.16), or storylistening trance, is placed within the baseline state of consciousness. The spokes of the wheel are portals from the baseline to the altered state of consciousness. Sturm proposes that one element of storytelling has remained nearly unconsidered over recent years while storytelling has flourished. This element is perhaps the most profound part of the communication process-the change in the listener's experience of reality. Through enchantment, the normal, waking state of consciousness changes as the story takes on a new dimension. Listeners seem to experience the story with remarkable immediacy, engaging in the story's plot and with the story's characters, and they may enter an altered state of consciousness- a "storylistening trance." The trance has the following characteristics:

- Realism—the sense that the story environment or characters are real or alive.

- Lack of Awareness—of surroundings or other mental processes.

- Engaged Receptive Channels:

  - visual (both physical watching and mental visualization;

  - auditory (both physical hearing and mental "chatter;"

  - kinesthetic; and

  - emotional.

- Control—of the experience by the listener, or someone or something else.

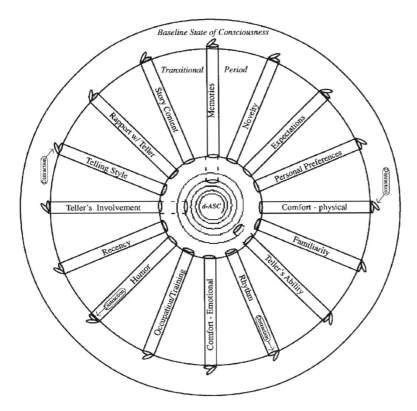

Figure Part3.16. The story wheel. Copyright 1999 Brian Sturm. Reprinted with permission.

- "Placeness"—the sense that the listener goes somewhere or into another space.

- Time Distortion—the sense that subjective time moves at a different speed than objective, clock time.

The actions that influence the storylistening trance reflect a list of techniques that are often practiced and perfected by those who seek to use storytelling as a powerful method to convey vision and meaning. Sturm identified these elements based on observations and interviews with adult storylisteners at professional storytelling events. He found the listener to be more likely to move toward entrancement if some of the following were present in the telling/listening interaction:

- Storytelling Style
- Activation of the Listener's Memories
- Sense of Comfort and Safety
- Story Content
- Storyteller's Ability

- Storyteller's Involvement
- Expectations (of enjoying the experience)
- Personal Preferences (matching style between teller and listener)
- (relevance to) Training or Social Roles (of the listener)
- Rapport with the Storyteller
- Novelty and Familiarity (of the story)
- Rhythm
- Humor
- Recency

Do Tellers Teach and Learn?

Use of story seems to be a common teaching technique among those who are successful in engaging their students in more than factual information. (Clark 2000) They are able to create a mood with verbal illustrations that can transport the student to the intended event. The art, practice, and perfection of storytelling for the classroom may be more of a learning experience for the teller than for the listener. Gathering the information needed for the story and developing the context for the story adjacent to the curriculum are powerful learning experiences for the presenter. (Green 1996)

Storytelling for teachers has been shown to be an important and valuable skill in several studies testing different communication methods. Undergraduate teacher preparation curricula, however, seldom provides room for adoption of this method. Storytelling has often been identified as a key leadership skill for Chief Executive Officers, including school principals and superintendents. One recent study (Kempton 1997), for example, demonstrated the importance of using storytelling skills to construct and share information in interdistrict magnet schools. Storytelling involved the ability to detail specific events and needs and to illustrate these with stories about relevant individuals involved. Storytelling encouraged constituent participation in the magnet school. Carefully selected words resulted in stories that allowed the leader to market the school and to increase participation of important stakeholders.

Storytelling, thus, is an important option in the menu of methods for student presentation of information for inquiry projects, as well as an entertaining way to pass along culture and heritage.

Digital Storytelling

In the third edition of a guide to multimedia projects for teachers and students, Ivers and Barron (2006) define digital storytelling as video products in which student act out a self-composed story, or interpret a story from literature experienced in a language arts class. Normally such projects include tasks that meet learning standards in speaking, reading, writing and theatrical interpretation of literature. Social studies students might also tell a nonfiction story as a documentary on an historical event by re-enacting such events as Lee's surrender to Grant, invention of the light bulb, or the events surrounding the 9/11 tragedy. Science students might "tell the story" of the life cycle of a butterfly, stages of a basic experiment or explain a

winning science fair project. More than just a journalistic report, these nonfiction stories should include analysis and interpretation of such events.

Through creating electronic personal narratives, students become active creators, rather than passive consumers of multimedia, and they develop the power of their own voices. Such is the philosophy of Jason Ohler (2005), professor of distance learning at the University of Alaska. He recommends that students and teachers use more than "story-boards" to plan their multimedia stories. Story maps allow young story creators to identify the true call to adventure, illustrate how characters meet and solve problems, and bring the story to a meaningful closure. Ohler concludes:

> Creating digital stories is a perfect opportunity to engage students in media literacy, in learning about how the media influence our perceptions of the world. Stories are enjoyable because we give ourselves over to them; this is also what makes them dangerous. By their very nature, stories require us to suspend our disbelief and be swept away by their narrative. Yet students need critical media skills in a world overwhelmed by story-based media, much of which views their age group in terms of commercial market share. We want students not only to learn with media, but also to learn and think critically about media. We want students to understand that the difference between a successful digital story and an effective advertisement is largely one of purpose. (47)

Bernajean Porter's (2004) self-published guide to telling digital stories brings the personal approach back into the process with modern multimedia techniques added to highlight and focus on emotion. Porter's elements for a good digital story are valid for any media format the storyteller might use:

- **Living inside your story.** The perspective of each story is told as a personal experience with the content using your own voice to narrate the tale.

- **Unfolding lessons learned.** Each story can express a personal meaning or insight about how a particular event or situation touched your own life.

- **Developing creative tension.** A good story creates intrigue or tension around a situation that is posed at the beginning of the story and resolved at the end, sometimes with an unexpected twist.

- **Economizing the story told.** A good story has a destination—a point to make—and seeks the shortest path to its destination.

- **Showing not telling.** Good stories use vivid details to reveal feelings and information rather than just saying something was tall, happy, scary, or difficult to do.

- **Developing craftsmanship.** A good story incorporates technology in artful ways, demonstrating exemplary craftsmanship in communicating with images, sound, voice, color, white space, animations, design, transitions, and special effects.

References

Bygrave, P. L. (1994). "Development of Listening Skills in Students in Special Education Settings." *International Journal of Disability, Development, and Education* 41 (1): 51–60.

Clark, R. W. (2000). "Teachers as Storytellers." Dissertation, Saint Louis University.

Denning, S. (2005). *The Leader's Guide to Storytelling: Mastering the Art and Discipline of Business Narrative.* Jossey-Bass.

Greene, E. (1996). *Storytelling: Art and Technique.* Bowker.

Ivers, K. S., and A. E. Barron. (2006). *Multimedia Projects in Education.* 3d ed. Libraries Unlimited.

Kempton, L. J. (1997). "Leaders as Storytellers: An Investigation of Leadership Practices Used in Implementing an Elementary Interdistrict Magnet School for Integration." Dissertation, University of Hartford.

MacDonald, M. R. (1993). *The Storyteller's Start-up Book.* August House.

McCormick, K., and C. Lipka. (1998). *Reading Our Histories, Understanding Our Cultures: A Sequenced Approach to Thinking, Reading, and Writing.* Allyn & Bacon.

National Council of Teachers of English. (n.d.). *Position Statement from the Committee on Storytelling.* Available at www.ncte.org/positions/story.html (accessed August 28, 2005).

Ohler, J. (2005). "The World of Digital Storytelling." *Educational Leadership* 63 (4): 44–47.

Porter, B. (2004). *DigiTales: The Art of Telling Digital Stories.* Bernajean Porter.

Rochman, C. (2001, August). "Tell Me a Story." *School Library Journal,* 47 (8): 46–49.

Simmons, A. (2002) *The Story Factor: Inspiration, Influence, and Persuasion Through the Art of Storytelling.* Perseus Books.

Smith, P. L. (1998). "A Qualitative Investigation into the Educational Benefits of Storytelling: Teaching Through Storytelling." Dissertation, Washington State University.

Sturm, B. W. (1999). "The Enchanted Imagination: Storytelling's Power to Entrance Listeners." *School Library Media Research* 2. Available at http://www.ala.org/aasl/SLMR/vol2/imagination.html (accessed August 25, 2005).

Wolfe, P. (1995). "Traditional Folktales: Exploring Wants and Needs." *School Library Media Activities Monthly* 9 (9): 29–30.

For Further Reading

Hughes, C. (1998). *Museum Theatre: Communicating with Visitors Through Drama.* Heinemann.

Mooney, W., and D. Holt. (1996). *The Storyteller's Guide: Storytellers Share Advice for the Classroom, Boardroom, Showroom, Podium, Pulpit and Central Stage.* August House.

National Storytelling Network. http://www.story.org (accessed August 25, 2005).

Rodari, G., J. Zipes, and H.R. Kohl. (2000). *The Grammar of Fantasy: An Introduction to the Art of Invention Stories.* Teachers and Writers.

Student Journals

Daniel Callison

Student journals have taken many formats and have increased in their use over the past decade at all education levels from grade school to college. These journals may be called day logs, diaries, and even think-books. Although still usually documented with pencil and paper and in loose-sheet formats so that portions can be shared with peers and teachers without sharing the entire journal, more and more use of personal laptops allows for students to process their thoughts.

Assumptions about Language and Learning

"Some teachers encourage students to write about whatever they want, while other teachers carefully specify topics. In most cases, students are encouraged to express honestly their personal opinions, take some risks with their thoughts, and write in their own natural voices" (Fulwiler 1987, 5).

These general characteristics of student journals were summarized by Toby Fulwiler, director of the writing program at the University of Vermont and Chair of the National Council of Teachers of English Commission on Composition in the 1980s. His group constructed guidelines for assigning journals based on the following assumptions about language and learning:

- When people articulate connections between new information and what they already know, they learn and understand the new information better.

- When people think and figure things out, they do so in symbol systems commonly called languages, most often verbal, but also mathematical, musical, and visual.

- When people learn things, they use all of the language modes to do so—reading, writing, speaking, and listening. Each mode helps people learn in a unique way.

- When people write about new information and ideas—in addition to reading, talking, and listening—they learn and understand them better.

Journals Begin in Elementary Grades

Jana Stanton, an instructor from George Mason University, conducted research on the use of dialogue journals in counseling and family communication with the Fairfax County Schools. She has applied her findings to methods that best introduce and manage journals with elementary school students.

To introduce the idea of journaling:

- Discuss the natural need to communicate and understand each other in the classroom; use the analogy of phone conversations in which each person gets a turn. Do not talk about dialogue as a way to "improve your writing."

- Discuss the importance of privacy: each dialogue journal belongs to two writers, to be shared only with consent.

- Brainstorm possible topics and functions for writing the first day or two. Topics that might help to facilitate this practice are evaluating a story, describing playground activities, expressing opinions on an event, requesting help, complaining, or expressing feelings.

- Stress that entries can vary in length.

- Students should write each day.

- Don't worry about the content of the first entries—what matters is getting students into the routine of writing and expecting response from the teacher.

To manage journals in an elementary classroom:

- You can start gradually, with a few students who seem ready or with one group at a time, to gain experience in responding to children's entries before doing it with the whole class.

- Provide a journal for each student, preferably one with a cover that can be individually decorated.

- Set aside a brief time in the morning for students to read your responses and write back. Often this is done in a period before the class formally begins. At first you also may need to set aside a five- to ten-minute period later in the day for a new entry. Later, older students can use independent work time to write entries.

- Create a special place where students can leave their journals for you when they are finished for the day.

- Use positive reinforcement strategies to encourage regular entries. Teachers should express interest in what students are writing. Do make clear that this kind of daily communication is expected, even though the writing is not graded.

Student Journals in Science and Language Arts

Pat D'Arcy (1987), an advisor for writing projects in the United Kingdom, has summarized the purpose for journals in science classrooms based on collected observations of her co-teachers:

- Journal s enable students to collect ideas and information together before they embark on a continuous piece of writing.

- Writing in journals can help students to "rediscover" the information that they have already absorbed.

- Journal s can help students to come up with their own questions about what they still need to learn.

- Journal ing allows students to express their feelings about the work they have been doing with honesty to the teacher.

- Journal s make two kinds of internal conversation possible: a conversation that the writer carries on with him/herself; and a conversation that the writer can have with the teacher without the rest of the class hearing.

- The journal can provide the student and the teacher with a personal map of the progress the student is making.

- Journal ing does not demand a special writing style. The student is free to think on paper as the words come. For this reason, journals often carry a strong sense of the writer's voice (and often will allow for a larger number of students involved to express themselves eventually over time).

Les Parsons (1990), author of the classic handbook on response journals and a leader in implementation of whole language programs, has summarized what a student journal is and is not. A student journal has these characteristics:

- A convenient, familiar, and flexible method for students to explore and reflect on their personal responses to such experiences as independent reading, viewing a film or television program, listening to a read-aloud, and/or a small-group discussion.

- A sourcebook of ideas, thoughts, opinions, and first drafts that can be mined for later use in other contexts for writing.

- A place to record observations and questions prior to a reading conference and comments and suggestions derived from the conference.

- A simple tracking device for students to record what and how much they've read, and, after a small-group discussion, individual perspectives on what was discussed or their roles in the discussion dynamics of the group.

- A reference file to help both student and teacher monitor individual development and progress for both formative and summative evaluation purposes.

- Another way for individual students to dialogue in written form with their teachers and peers.

According to Parsons, a response journal is not

- A personal diary containing lists of favorite rock songs, breakfast menus, and "what I did last night";

- A book in which students write responses that are never read, never discussed, and never evaluated;

- A compendium of reactions to silent reading that has little connection with the rest of the language arts program; or

- Another add-on to an already burgeoning curriculum!

Journals and the Information Search Process

Journals have been identified as a method to help students record and reflect on their information search process in several of the models used to teach information literacy and inquiry. Carol Kuhlthau (2002) provided sample guide sheets for this process in her classic guide to the student library research process. An important key to student management of the Information Search Process, as defined by Kuhlthau, is the opportunity for the student to deal with the anxieties of approaching a large multiple-task writing project. Journals can help convey and address that anxiety through both self-reflection and communication with the library media specialist and the classroom teacher.

Marilyn Joyce and Julie Tallman (1997)described in detail how important the journaling in "learning logs" is to the I-Search Process, especially in consideration of the relevance of new information obtained and how it might or might not address the student's needs. Students were given time to reflect on information they gathered from initial reading, viewing, and listening so that a focus could be determined for their personal research projects.

References

D'Arcy, Pat. (1987). "Writing to Learn." In *The Journal Book,* edited by Toby Fulwiler, 41–46. Heinemann.

Fulwiler, Toby, ed. (1987). *The Journal Book.* Heinemann.

Joyce, Marilyn Z., and Julie I. Tallman. (1997). *Making the Writing and Research Connection with the I-Search Process.* Neal-Schuman.

Kuhlthau, Carol Collier. (2002). *Teaching the Library Research Process.* Scarecrow Press.

Parsons, Les. (1990). *Response Journals.* Pembroke/Heinemann.

Staton, Jana. (1987). "The Power of Responding to Dialogue Journals." In *The Journal Book,* edited by Toby Fulwiler, 47–63. Heinemann.

Student-Talk

Daniel Callison

Mary Frances Zilonis, as director of Library Media Services in Cambridge, Massachusetts, tells viewers in the *Kaleidoscope* (1993) video produced for the American Association of School Librarians that library media specialists and other teachers should give more attention to "student-talk." The implication is that too often student needs and interests are prejudged without a deeper understanding of individual differences. In addition, more student-talk implies a greater responsibility and opportunity placed before the student to take a teaching role themselves-to demonstrate, present, and voice their knowledge. The result should be less dictating of knowledge from the teacher's voice alone, and more teacher facilitation for student self-learning.

While more attention to student-talk does not mean that children create a student-centered curriculum in which they become dictators of the objectives and evaluation, it does imply that teachers listen more to what students have to say about their experiences, interests, and ambitions. Student-talk can lead to important shifts in how children and adolescents can be engaged in learning. It can also lead to dramatic changes in how library media centers provide access to information and to space for student work. Collection development becomes more student-need directed. (Hughes-Hassell and Mancall 2005) More work areas for active voices are created in library media centers and classrooms when student-talk is increased.

Social Curriculum

"Student-talk" can be defined as a "social curriculum" in which the student is placed in a variety of problem-solving situations and must express himself or herself in order to gain needed information and to share information. In the social curriculum, students are evaluated on their interactive and interpersonal performances. Their abilities to communicate, negotiate, speculate, and debate verbally and constructively are seen as primary skills.

In the social curriculum, student-talk is at least as valuable as adult-talk. Adults tend to use talk to think aloud, to tentatively explore the beginnings of an idea, to hitchhike on what others have said, to clarify and modify the personal knowledge base, to affirm thoughts to others, and to acknowledge and enable speakers to continue groping for meaning. However, as David Booth and Carol Thornley-Hill (1991) suggest in *Classroom Talk,* children traditionally have been rewarded for using talk in a much more structured, formal way and often only in a question-and-answer pattern where hesitation and change are not rewarded. To observe children engaged in activities that require conversation is to understand the nature of learning. Interactive, voiced problem solving can lead to enhancements for thought and language development and stimulate both intellectual and emotional growth.

Frequent Talking

Students need frequent opportunities to talk. (Yes, you read that sentence correctly.)

Establishing situations so that the talk can be constructive and on target takes a great deal of creativity and patience. The nature and size of groups in the classroom, according to Curt Dudley-Marling of the University of Wisconsin and Dennis Searle of the University of London (1991), can significantly affect students' use of language. The larger the group, the fewer the opportunities that individual students will have to use language. They conclude that whole-class discussions will never be a good way to encourage language use for many students, even though learning to talk in large groups is one of the skills students need to acquire in school. Large-group discussions tend to be dominated by more capable or outgoing students.

One of the best ways to encourage students to engage in discussions is to bring them together in small groups. Students who lack confidence in their verbal abilities may be shy about speaking in front of more fluent classmates. Teachers can provide opportunities for students to use language for different purposes by creating situations that encourage all kinds of talk. Dudley-Marling and Searle remind us that how teachers ask questions is an important factor in how students respond. Open-ended, probing questions, for example, invite students to speculate, imagine, and analyze. In contrast, narrow questions with predictable answers only encourage students to use language to demonstrate factual knowledge without the challenges of elaboration and exploration.

Varied Experiences Increase Vocabularies

Students come to school with a wide range of experiences and backgrounds. In part, these experiences will account for differences in vocabularies for both abilities of expression and reception. Children whose families travel a lot learn words associated with travel ("exit," "motel," "billboard") . Children who enjoy baking with their parents learn words such as "rise," "yeast," and "mix" through direct practice and application. Assume that parents engage their children in conversations during such experiences as the children grow older and the vocabularies should become more precise and more complex.

In general, the more varied people's experiences, the richer and more varied their vocabularies. Some experiences, of course, may not match the normal expectations of teachers. Students' vocabularies, like their experiences, aren't necessarily impoverished, only different. But these differences can interfere with their ability to get along in school.

Talking as You Read

The opportunity to read widely, to read for pleasure, and to share with others what you have read is one of the most powerful techniques to build vocabulary. It may be the best way to enrich experiences so that meaningful discussions can take place through more student- talk. Children have a natural sense of wonder about things and teachers can learn a great deal about how children make sense of their world through careful observation and lots of listening. Construction of meaning can take place through the interactions among a small group of students. This happens when talk is a natural part of their reading and not just the calling-out of words from the printed page.

Children are naturally interested in books. Given time, opportunity, free access to a variety of books, and the security of "discussion buddies," attitudes toward learning improve, depth of discourse gets richer, and those once shy begin to come forward with stories that have expression and meaning.

Storytelling

Most teachers, especially primary teachers, are interested in getting students to construct a good narrative-to relate stories or events in their lives-in a clear and orderly manner. For students to learn how to exploit the narrative function of language, at least two things have to happen. They have to be exposed to regular demonstrations of how narrative works. They need models from older students, parents, teachers, and others who can "tell a good story." And, they have to have frequent opportunities to try out the narrative function themselves.

Practice should range from brief and concise descriptions (learning to convey a message in precise terms) to practice in giving detail and colorful elaboration (expression of clarity, wit, opposition, linkage of ideas, and drawing conclusions). (See also Key Word: Story.)

Information Talking

The list of potential oral verbal skills is as extensive, and perhaps more so, as those that can be listed for written communication. Opportunities to practice oral communication skills can be expanded through gathering and considering information. School library media center nonfiction collections and access to World Wide Web sites can certainly enhance many of the following situations:

- **Experience Talk:** using background experiences, knowledge, and previous information to add to discussions or to assist in problem solving

- **Working Talk:** giving suggestions, manipulating materials, sharing ideas

- **Get Things Done Talk:** an organizer, who knows there is a solution or solutions, acts as a motivator for the others in the group

- **Asking Questions Talk:** asking questions in order to clarify the problem or to gain more precise information

- **Exploratory Talk:** describing the materials, time, or other variables involved in the problem-solving situation

- **Thoughtful Talk:** attempting to work things through, and provides initial efforts to solve the problem

- **Social Talk:** may be counterproductive, but may also provide the means to relax, reflect, release tension with humor, and attack the problem in a new way

- **Frustration Talk:** can be abrupt short phrases, voiced louder than normal, and may signal the need for intervention from someone outside the group, or anyone who can mediate talk

- **Troubleshooting Talk:** informed speculation that leads to solving some problem or aspect of the problem

- **Dominating Talk:** will continue in any environment until there is full group access to information and passive members gain confidence through opportunities to express themselves

Student-Talk and Collection Development

Mancall (1994) has proven to be one of the leading voices in principles of collection development for school library media centers. The relationship between "greater analysis of the user" and "listening more closely to student-talk" is very strong. Mancall recommends that school library media specialists observe more, listen more, and interact more in order to refocus the management of information access and align it more closely with user needs. To refocus, the developer of the library media center collection must

- place the users at the center of all considerations;

- define the user's perspective on the problem;

- isolate learner tasks to be accomplished;

- know the learning preferences that may control what access and resources you suggest;

- identify the content that must be accessed and the characteristics of the knowledge required; and

- expand possibilities for retrieval beyond the local collection, especially to meet varied and unique learner needs.

To realign from ownership to access, the collection developer must

- become an active partner in the teaching/learning process and part of planning teams for curriculum and resource sharing;

- think subject and learner access parameters (abilities, entry skills, time limits for access and use);

- renegotiate budget lines to relate to the redefined process (change from resource format lines to lines that reflect curricular and information need areas); and

- monitor usage trends so that informed adjustments can be made in collection operation and justification can be based on demonstrated need.

Where to Student-Talk

The locations for practicing constructive student-talk include the library media center as well as the classroom, field trips, and the home. Areas for small group active discussion and verbal communication practice have long been included in library media center facilities. Such "conference rooms" have allowed groups to be isolated and away from disturbing the main area of the library media center reserved for reading and searching for materials.

If student-talk is to be given the opportunity it needs in order to become constructive, observed, and mediated when necessary by library media specialists and other teachers, it may be that the small areas reserved for "conferencing" should be those reserved for "reading and independent study." The wider spaces of the library media center (from the reference areas, to media production spaces, to computer labs, to open areas providing large tables for groups to cluster) should be open for extensive student-talk. An open invitation to students to take a lead in their learning agenda through oral expression makes the school library media center a natural part of a student-centered curriculum.

References

Booth, D., and C. Thornley-Hall. (1991). *Classroom Talk*. Portsmouth, NH: Heinemann.

Dudley-Marling, C., and D. Searle. (1991). *When Students Have Time to Talk: Creating Contexts for Learning Language*. Heinemann.

Hughes-Hassell, S., and J. C. Mancall. (2005). *Collection Management for Youth: Responding to the Needs of Learners*. American Library Association.

Kaleidoscope: New Visions for School Library Media Programs. (1993). American Association of School Librarians and Follett Software Co. Video program. 29 min.

Mancall, J.C. (1994). "Refocusing the Collection Development Process: Collecting, Cooperating, Consulting." *Taproot* (Spring): 8–13.

For Further Reading and Viewing

Roth, K .J. (1986). *Curriculum Materials, Teacher Talk, and Student Learning*. Institute for Research on Teaching.

Rubin, D., and W. M. Dodd. (1987). *Talking into Writing*. National Council of Teachers of English and ERIC.

Rudder, M. E. (1999). "Eliciting Student-Talk." *Forum* 37 (2). Available at http://exchangesstate.gov/vols/vol37/no2/p.24.htm (accessed July 2, 2006).

Synthesis

Daniel Callison

Synthesis is the fusion of separate elements or substances to form a coherent whole. In research, synthesis is the combination of thesis and antithesis in the dialectical process, producing a new and higher form of being. A synthetic product is usually produced from extracting natural elements to create a new compound that is stronger and directed to solve a more specific problem than the original elements allowed one to address. Analysis must take place prior to and in conjunction with synthesis as the synthesized product is the result of analysis.

As defined in 1956 by a committee of college and university examiners, commonly known as "Bloom's Taxonomy of Educational Objectives," synthesis is a process of combining elements or parts in such a way as to constitute a pattern or structure not clearly there or seen before. This is the category in the cognitive domain that most clearly provides for creative behavior on the part of the learner. However, it should be emphasized that this is not completely free creative expression since generally the student is expected to work within the limits set by particular problems, materials, or some theoretical and methodological framework.

Bloom's committee also determined that comprehension, application, and analysis, in some ways, are each similar to synthesis in that these skills also involve the putting together of the elements and the construction of meaning. But the lower order skills tend to be less complete and final than the higher demands of performance in the synthesis domain.

In synthesis, on the other hand, the student must draw upon elements from many sources and put them together into a structure or pattern not clearly there before, either new to the student or on an original research level new to the human knowledge base. The student's efforts, according to Bloom's committee, should yield a product—something that can be observed through one or more of the senses and which is clearly more than the materials with which the student began to work. It is to be expected that a problem which is classified as a task primarily involving synthesis also will require all of the previous categories to some extent. Thus, synthesis is the stage for the product that represents, often, the culmination of knowledge, comprehension, application, and analysis.

Synthesis is not just the act of summarizing, paraphrasing or abstracting information from a document as several models for information search and basic student research imply. Synthesis should also include extracting inferences that link selected findings together in a logical and meaningful pattern.

Kinds of Synthesis

Unique Communication. A synthesis of facts, opinions, perceptions, emotions, and/or other elements identified through analysis of information artifacts and experiences. The intent of the author is to synthesize a message in order to inform, describe, persuade, impress, or entertain. Such products may include dramatic readings, poetry, posters, critical essays, news articles, musical compositions, and many other tangible items that reflect a selection of information to communicate a message within parameters that the intended audience can access and understand.

Plan of Operation. Although not complete until the intended outcome is accomplished, a proposed set of operations represent a category of synthesis which illustrates skills to combine ideas, resource availability, and techniques or methods that will likely lead to accomplishing the final product. Such operative plan products include scripts for video productions or live stage presentations, lesson plans, specifications for a new house, HTML script or other programming plan tested and modified to meet audience need, an outline for a report or essay, a long-range plan or policy development, a diagram for a football play, and many other items that provide tangible representation of a plan for action.

Abstract Relations. Following analysis of issues and consideration for what problem is to be solved, question answered, or working hypothesis tested, synthesis provides clear definition of what is deduced to be primary and concluded. Synthesis takes place at all stages. The student is to synthesize the key questions that need to be answered, meaning that questions are to be written in a manner that will allow for operational means to find complete or partial answers. A working hypothesis is a synthesis of the predicted result of the investigation. A final hypothesis and conclusion is a synthesis of key, relevant findings and the original contribution to the knowledge base.

There are levels of performance for each of these kinds of synthesis depending on student ability and expectations of student performance within the context of the learning environment. For example, elementary students (Breivik and Senn 1998) may synthesize a comparison and contrast of facts found from a variety of sources on the lifestyle and behavior of bears. Such data can be illustrated in tables, charts, posters, multimedia programs, and even student-written plays.

Many secondary students will have the ability to synthesize issues and information into more sophisticated products, and some will grasp the skills necessary to synthesize plans for operation. Fewer will really understand and apply fully the synthesis of abstract relations; however, activities and practice with demanding synthesis exercises and questions may help to increase the portion of students who grasp the higher levels of synthesis. Such learner growth is certainly a goal of those who believe in the value of modern information literacy.

At any level, synthesis can be conducted over a range of challenges, from a quick micro-level to

a very large scale and complex creation task (Chaffee 1997). James Potter (2001) illustrates this range to his students at the University of California at Santa Barbara by describing the micro-level as when a television program breaks for a commercial, and we sometimes reassemble the characters and elements in the plot line to imagine what is coming next or to imagine ourselves in the teleplay. This type of synthesis can take only a few seconds and be more emotionally guided, according to Potter, than intellectually complete.

On a larger scale, Potter continues, we may one day be inspired to write an episode of our favorite show. In order to do this we need a deep knowledge about all the elements in the previous episodes. We need to know all the quirks about each character and have an intimate sense of what each would do or say in any situation. Then, in writing our script, we would need to evaluate the appropriateness of dialogue, plotting points, character interactions, and more. The final product depends on our complete command of all these elements assembled in a new creative manner.

Synthesizing Information Pieces

It is important to remember that actions, such as paraphrasing or rearranging blocks of information from other sources, do not represent the more demanding levels of analysis or synthesis. Expressing data or refining terms into phrases that are more understandable for the student or his/her intended audience is more a reflection of demonstrating comprehension than analysis or synthesis. Writing assignments that call for manipulation of chunks of information extracted from various sources are not demanding enough to provide true synthesis experiences. Such recall, rearranging, rewriting, or scribing exercises, without student reflection on what are the key questions and important conclusions emerging and perhaps now understood by the student and how the student came to that understanding, should not be offered as a synthesis product in the information research process.

Brenda Spatt (2002) has described a detailed method to confront multiple sources of information and to truly synthesize the content efficiently and effectively. Her steps are more demanding than the simple jigsaw methods which too often stop with the student shuffling information chunks into some order without extracting and comparing the key information. Spatt illustrates that analysis and synthesis are overlapping stages of a single, larger process. She suggests these steps to draw synthesis from analysis:

- **Chart Common Ideas.** Extract specific facts or various opinions from the multiple sources analyzed. For some issues this may involve a dozen or more sources and "authorities." Group or cluster similar facts or opinions. The process of synthesis, according to Spatt, starts as soon as the list is started, and the task is to look for new patterns that may lead to new discussions in the essay or report.

- **Distinguishing Between Reasons.** It may take several readings and some assistance before the student begins to see where some opinions may overlap and where others are actually two distinctly different ones. Charting should be a continuous process as new information is engaged and assimilated, and charting should be a product for intervention and review by the guiding teacher of information literacy skills.

- **Sequence of Topics.** After facts or opinions have been worked into reasonable clusters, they may eventually become key topics or subtopics relevant to the overall working thesis of the project. Further analysis and evaluation will lead to decisions for selecting the most relevant, most illustrative, or most entertaining clusters for presentation. Thus, refining stages in synthesis methods leads to identification of that which is key or essential and that which can be let go. Ordering those which remain into a logical sequence is often the concluding task.

Summary Practice Leading to Synthesis

There are several activities that can be used with groups or during individual interventions with students to help them practice skills that will lead to effective synthesis of information. These exercises tend to emphasize choice of key terms, central concepts, or essential information that will best illustrate or convey a message in a concise manner. We see attempts at and often practice ourselves some form of synthesis every day. Assuming we have analyzed the parameters involved and screened the information necessary, how do we deliver the most effective message in the most efficient manner?

Examples of activities that center on summary and evaluation skills (Stripling 1993), and can lead to discussions about synthesis follow:

- **Headlines and Media.** Given the local newspaper, read and analyze the stories, summarize as key terms, and synthesize new headlines. In what manner is CNN Headline News a summary and the PBS Lehrer Report an analysis of the news? Are there news programs, or portions within the programs, that provide a synthesis? Does Jim Lehrer attempt to synthesize in some manner before the program ends?

- **Annotation.** In your own words, give a brief description of a source and identify the reasons why it is relevant to the topic or working thesis of your paper. In what manner does the source relate to others in providing new information, confirming previous information, or countering previous information? In what manner did the source answer your previous questions and in what manner did this key source raise new questions?

- **Key Sources.** As a part of reflecting on the quality of your term paper, identify the key sources you used and justify why these sources could be defended as such. Through this evaluation exercise, summarize the reasons why you would probably not be able to conclude the assignment without the use of these few most important sources. Synthesize the key issues and conclusions supported by these key sources.

- **Evidence.** Read each statement several times and look at the evidence in several sequences. Label evidence (cards or electronic files) with terms or phrases that are meaningful to you and relevant to the issues of the project. Again, this paraphrasing and jigsaw approach will be effective if the final step is taken, and that is to write in your own words a description of the events, issues, arguments, or insights represented by the cluster of evidence. Strongest and most information-rich clusters are likely candidates for the synthesis as the final product.

The Questions of Analysis and Synthesis

Questions involving analysis are intended to separate an entire process, event, or situation into its component parts and to help seek an understanding of the relationship of these parts to the whole. Analysis, a critical skill gaining more and more importance as students have wider access to electronic resources that have not been edited or validated, centers on questions of argument logic, evidence quality and unbiased selection of evidence to support arguments. Questions of synthesis have as their goal a combining of ideas to create a new whole. The synthesis may be seen in the creation of a prediction, a proposed solution, or a design for action. Synthesis involves such questions as

- Based on opinions voiced by members of the group, what should be the steps to be taken next?

- Based on the analysis of your observations, what do you predict will happen next?

- Given the basic background necessary and an understanding of the relationship among the characters, how would you rewrite this act?

Key information literacy skills (Breivik and Senn 1998) that are synthesis-based include the following:

- Construct and organize key questions in operational terms so that they support the central question or working hypothesis, and reconstruct the questions and hypothesis as warranted.

- Create a plan for information searching based on analysis of needs and parameters such as resources available and time allotted.

- After analysis of various methods, select and plan the best method to gather information from primary resources.

- Taking into account an analysis of the audience and other elements of the final presentation, plan the manner for most effectively and efficiently conveying the intended message.

References

Bloom, B. S., ed. (1956). *Taxonomy of Educational Objectives: The Classification of Educational Goals.* David McKay Co.

Breivik, P. S., and J. A. Senn. (1998). *Information Literacy: Educating Children for the 21st Century.* National Education Association.

Chaffee, J. (1997). *Thinking Critically.* 5th ed. Houghton Mifflin.

Potter, W. J. (2001). *Media Literacy.* 2d ed. Sage Publications.

Spatt, B. (2002). *Writing from Sources.* 5th ed. St. Martin's Press.

Stripling, B. K. (1993). Practicing Authentic Assessment in the School Library. In *School Library Media Annual 1993,* edited by C. C. Kuhlthau, 40–55. Libraries Unlimited.

Taking Notes

Daniel Callison

Different Notes for Different Research Stages

One of the many important observations Carol Kuhlthau (1994) has contributed to the study of the student research process is that more successful student inquirers (and adult researchers) take notes differently for at least two different stages, exploration and collecting information. (See Table Part3.4 and Figure Part3.17.) According to Kuhlthau, "The exploratory library search should be separated from the collection search when teaching students to do library research. Skilled library researchers go to the library to read about a topic and reflect over a period of time. After some ideas have formed, they return to the library to gather information specifically related to their developing ideas and how they will present the topic" (1994, 61).

Table Part3.4. Note Format Changes Across Information Seeking and Use Stages

Stage:	Brainstorm	Explore Sources	Focus Ideas	Present Information
Note Format:	Web	Notebook/Journal	Index Cards	Database/References
Need:	All Ideas Related	Test Ideas and Explore Options	Elaborate or Detail Ideas for Final Message & Manipulative Format	Illustrate/Give Credit Authoritative Support

Subject _____ Date _____

Main Idea Inferences New Questions	Details

Summary: brief abstract of meaning to you and your judgment on quality of the information. Do you need to find additional supporting evidence or clarification?

The 3 R's of the Cornell System: Record meaningful facts and ideas; Reduce to main ideas and summarize; Recite later the most important terms, concepts, ideas, conclusions.
This system is similar to a Box Score for any athletic event. Some students will quickly understand this analogy as sports pages and television sports reports are filled with one box or one screen on which you will find the most important players, plays, scoring events, and team totals.

Figure Part3.17. The Cornell note format.

If two different note-taking strategies are beneficial, it is best to introduce these at separate times, each at point of need. Journals or note-books are best for the exploration stage. Here students may keep notes on many areas such as

- General topics; is there an information pool related to these topics locally or can materials beyond local access be obtained within the time period for the project?

- New topics that become apparent and of interest but had not come to mind before—is there something more focused, of more interest to me and to others who may hear or read my report?

- Additional research questions and how they may cluster to form a pool of questions that link together—the inquiry process involves a continuous process of rethinking and rewording questions to make them more meaningful and more operational; i.e. possible to manage and address.

- Important names which keep re-appearing either associated with the topics or as a frequent author of related information— names, events and other nouns become the basic search terms in later more in-depth exploration.

- Linkages to other potential resources based on sources sited in materials read and viewed at the exploration stage; mature inquirers will see authors and perhaps book titles referenced several times and seek out such sources through extensive library searching or interlibrary loan because these items may prove to be core or central items upon which general knowledge about the considered topics has been constructed.

Thus, the journal may be divided in to several sections in which notes are written to keep track of ideas and construct possible foci that might emerge from exploration. It should be emphasized that the true inquirer will, of course, explore far beyond the library for ideas and information. Discussions with teachers, friends, and family are important at this stage. Initial conversations with possible "experts" in the field might take place for some topics. The chance to verbalize ideas or to complete short free-writing exercises can also help the student to have content upon which to write about and to reflect on in the journal.

Notes at this stage may appear very messy and unorganized. In some cases, the student will return to these exploration notes and use a color marker to circle or highlight items, cross out others and link ideas, names, and resources together. The journal should be a reflection of the thought processes with space toward the back for the student to analyze what has been found and to synthesize a plan to move toward a workable focus.

Highlight + Write + Recite + Cite = Focus

Actions taken to "make notes" may differ in the styles that work best for individuals. Computer printers and copy machines are often very useful in gathering pages from Internet and print reference tools that can later be highlighted with color pens. While teaching hand written note taking strategies for students to use in journals and on note cards may be less expensive and may be more ecologically-minded, such may not always save money, time or trees. Printing selected pages, including the page providing the necessary information for later reference citation and bibliography, can prove to provide a workable pool of preliminary information chunks in a shorter amount of time.

On these printed pages the inquirer may circle and highlight selected pieces of information, write over text or in columns with bold key terms near the statements or ideas, and sort and re-sort the pages to help form a preliminary vision for the direction one wants to take toward topic focus. These marked pages, sorted and resorted, can serve as the basis for exercises in "testing" ideas. After work with several dozen sources (fewer for younger age groups) the inquirer may want to "quick-write" a paragraph or two in which is summarized what has been discovered so far. In other cases, it can be useful for the inquirer to try to verbalize in two to three minutes of reciting to a friend what has been drawn from these sources so far and point to several highlighted items to show support (Rankin 1999).

These printed pages can later be some of the items from which more formal note cards or information databases are created, but they can serve as very useful rough construction tools as the search for a focus takes place. The likelihood of notes being paraphrased or "in the student's own words" is greater if they practice written and oral summaries. Direct quotes, however, should not be "outlawed" as long as credit is given. There are times when a concept or a perspective is best worded by the original author and should be kept as given.

Different Notes for Different Topics and Formats

Live and Media

As Marjorie Pappas and Ann Tepe (2002) tell us, "Students engaged in inquiry-based learning often discover that they need to gather information from authentic sources. These sources include people who are experts in the chosen subject area, community information providers such as [directors and curators from] land labs or a museum, . . . so [students] should develop strategies to enable them to gather information from people" (14).

Although the processes described here pertain more to students in secondary schools and college situations, elementary school students can be introduced to the basics of note taking. Modifications for young learners might include asking that they state, in writing or orally, the one idea they learned from a field trip, an in-class guest speaker, an encyclopedia article, or a short film. These pieces combined on a chart or web to show contributions as a class will quickly illustrate the variety of messages and will also show repetition of the major messages retained by many students. Elementary school students can engage in combining information to strengthen ideas and order ideas to show a flow for main to minor. By the fourth grade and up, students are probably ready to take on some form of gathering individual notes from different sources. (Stanley 2000a, 2000b)

Early efforts in taking notes from text, lectures, or interviews may involve some form of

double-entry as recommended by Marilyn Joyce and Julie Tallman (1997, 50–51) so that the student gains practice in recording both content and personal response. Sometimes referred to at a "T-Format" (See Figure Part3.18), the student will place the topic or question at the top of the page or card and have two divisions under, one for summary of content and the other for personal response. This simple response format has implications for journal notes, exploration notes, and final note cards.

The Question or Topic	
Content Summary (What it says)	Personal Response (What it means to me.) Tie to previous content. Why enlightening to me? Why it is so important? A new question generated.

Figure Part3.18. T-Form notes.

Taking notes from a lecture, presentation, televised news event, interview or other source for which it may be difficult to have the content repeated places the note taker in the position of getting content down as quickly and as efficiently as possible. To scribe every word and every detail is not possible physically nor desirable intellectually. Of course, recorded presentations allow for rewinding and repeating of the information. Taking notes from media or live presentation modes requires concentration and a system of short-hand. Gleaning the notes later to analyze and synthesize aids in learning while simply re-copying the notes is usually a waste of valuable study time. Analysis and synthesis will help to highlight the notes that may eventually be associated with the topic for the term paper or inquiry project in the class. In some cases, notes from one course or presentation may serve to provide information for an inquiry project in another class or a project for a later semester.

Recommendations for note taking in these media or live situations include the following:

- Date your note-taking session and give full name of the person lecturing, being interviewed, or media source; note the actual production title and date of the media item if pre-recorded.

- Take notes on one side of paper in a spiral notebook so that the notes do not "bleed" through and so the notes remain together for future reference.

- Divide the page into two parts, usually with a line drawn down one third of the way in on the left side. Following the classic Cornell format (see Figure Part3.17), the smaller left side is used later to synthesize main ideas, while the wider left side is used to gather details during the event. Often one page following the session is used to free-write a summary of the session, usually no more than 100 words per 30 minutes of the presentation; an abstract of the major message.

- As notes are taken, leave space between details, usually one inch for every two inches of notes taken. This allows for clearer notes and for returning to interject new information presented later but associated with ideas presented earlier. If the presentation is interactive (allowing for questions), this allows for noting areas with a question mark as well as fitting in responses to the later questions if given the opportunity.

- Be an effective listener. Concentrate on the message and listen for key words and main points. Try to be selective in the information you take the time to write down. Such may come with practice and with experience as to what information tends to be useful later. Information that is written on the blackboard, on digital slide presentation, on the television screen should be summarized in notes in a selective manner. Such presentations are often an outline of phrases or key words and the note taker must be even more selective and record only the most important items, often less than a third of what is shown on a given screen.

- Write in a shorted form that you understand. Use abbreviations, numbers, and symbols as long as they are common for your own understanding.

- Look for important clues that may indicate valuable information such as definition of terms previously not familiar to you; introductions that indicate the "most important reasons for," or "the most influential person was," or "the major cause of this change was."

- Note terms and definitions given and check definitions later of unfamiliar terms, as well as names, events, dates, steps, or directions.

- Ask for clarification of ambiguous statements and answers to questions you have noted if possible.

- Within 30 minutes following the interview, lecture, presentation, or television (media) broadcast complete the left hand column with a summary of main ideas written phrases, key terms, or a semantic map or web.

- Within the same day as hearing the information presented, write a summary or abstract in space provided either at the bottom of the page or at the end of the notes.

If this information is gathered from an interview with an expert relevant to your topic of inquiry, obtain how you may contact the person later through a phone call or electronic mail in order to clarify or elaborate on additional information if necessary.

Sources and Transfer from Notebook

Index note cards, at least three inches by five inches, are the standard and recommended pieces for gathering information that is relevant to a focus, thesis, and related sub-topics. Laptop computers now allow us to gather such information on individual frames and sorted by files as we work with resources in the library, at home or "in the field." The general guidelines given below for note cards probably still hold true with emphasis on "one central idea to one note card." The task is to make information decisions and to force those decisions into manageable pieces of relevant information.

The principles for selection of information and transfer to notes generally apply the growing use of capturing text from electronic documents and transfer to an electronic file. Those who use such methods, through word processing or written note cards, should keep in mind:

a. Be very selective of information for capture and transfer and the ease of "cut and past" can lead to compiling a large amount of material that makes final selection of relevant information difficult.

b. Be certain to capture and transfer the URL and other location information as well as the date the information was located as electronic documents may be removed from or moved around in the Internet.

c. Attempt to also capture and transfer information from the document that shows how authoritative, bias, and/or current the information is. Authoritativeness can be confirmed by the status of the author or agency of the Web site and that such is clearly stated on the site, references and links from the site to other authoritative sites, as well as links from authoritative sites back to the site noted. Apply "Find: URL" searches to check if authoritative Web sites are linked to the one you are considering. The degree of bias may be determined, to some extent, based on the purpose and reputation of the author or association responsible for posting the site or document. The actual date of the information should be clearly stated, but may be more likely to be stated at the end of the Web site or following the title and author's name at the beginning of the document. Credentials of listed authorities may be cross searched on the Web, or your library's print or online reference collection may lead you to confirmation of the credentials for an author or other individuals mentioned in the document. Instructional media specialists can be effective models of how to select authoritative Web sites by talking through out loud with students the clues from URLs, links, interactive features, dates of revision, the site map and results of any internal search options (Coiro 2005).

d. Creating specific subtopic files from further organization of downloaded information is a good practice for those who want to begin to find information patterns and linkages among pieces of information found from various documents. Paraphrase as much as possible and reduce text to key terms and ideas. If several notes provide the basic same facts, select the most current and eliminate the others. Print-outs of many information chunks spread out across the living room floor and resorted to show, links, associations and other relevant connections, will help the inquirer see important patterns and consider new ways of approaching an old thesis or creating a new one.

e. If possible, print out documents or make copies so that specific marks can be made on the copy to highlight and connect facts, opinions, names and events. Highlight important paragraphs of discussion, data in charts and even information from photos or illustrations. When narrowing the final selection of information, paraphrase to note cards or word processed notes and files. At the least, paraphrasing should reduce the number of words to be transferred to notes to one third of the original and even more if possible.

f. Gain an understanding of copyright guidelines, as extensive use of some documents will not be allowed, even for educational exercise purposes. Photographs, charts and tables may be available to download, but their content will also have some copyright restrictions. It is best to summarize data from a selected chart or table to so specifically the relevant statistics needed and to give full credit to the publication containing the original data or the agency responsible for gathering the data.

g. Whenever possible, information and ideas should be paraphrased for final notes as this will reduce the chances of plagiarism. There are, however, often quotations or opinions what should remain exactly as stated because of the importance of the specific message and the status of the person who has made the statements. Notes should clearly show when such an exact, word-for-word quotation has been selected so that full credit to the author of the paragraphs, tables, or figures is clearly given in the final paper or presentation.

h. Clearly note full bibliographic information, including the date Web sites are accessed, and keep a running bibliography of sources along with noting citations on the note cards or word processed note pages.

As with electronic documents, this is a transfer process from information found in print resources including books, magazines, as well as transcribed from the notes gathered through interviews, lectures and media described above. The transfer should involve not only the mechanical means to move notes into a format that allows one to manipulate the information (resorting cards, move or matching data on electronic files) but to make some additional critical decisions as to the information which is worth retaining. This selection process should include "ranking" information pieces to retain and review those most relevant and to discard or place in a secondary file those items which have merit, but are not critical to writing or producing the final product.

Standard Library and Term Paper Guides Provide Good Fundamentals

Dozens of handbooks and library research guides illustrate how an index card can hold the essential information such as sub-topic, citation abbreviation with page number, and key words and phrases. New publications written by Deborah Stanley (2000a, 2000b) provide useful guides and Virginia Rankin (1999) also has published step-by-step procedures for students to extract information and compile notes.

An excellent guide to the basics of information searching for term papers common in elementary and secondary schools is *How to Write a Term Paper* by Nancy Everhart (1994). Some of her many "super strategies" are selectively paraphrased below:

- See if there is access to previous term papers so you will have an idea of what one looks like. Find those judged to be excellent and make a list of what seems to have made them good. Keep the list handy when working on your own project. Remember, this is for the purpose of gaining insight on projects that were judged to be excellent before you, not to copy information or to "steal" ideas or even entire papers.

- Whenever possible, make that case that you will do your best work when you have selected a topic that is of interest to you and others as well as meeting the parameters of the assignment. Select a topic you want to spend some time with, because a good inquiry project will be challenging and result in the best experience if you explore the topic widely as well as focus on a final thesis.

- Keep a list of key terms, names and events and expand the list as new sources are explored. Some library tools such as Sears List of Headings and Library of Congress Subject Headings will help you identify important related terms and the manner in which the terms may be used in standard databases. Use these terms to check indexes in possible relevant books, because important insights can be found in a page or two on people or events not listed in larger databases.

- Generally speaking, books and other print resources that have extensive (two or more per page) references are more authoritative sources.

- Certain authors, publishers and organizations are considered experts (or at least are associated with the issues of your topic) in specific fields. See if they show across several resources.

- It is usually better to interpret graphs or charts in your own words, rather than just put them in your paper. Illustrations will often help clarify ideas, but relate factual information in your text to the illustrations.

Information extracted for note cards should pertain to one idea, concept, fact, or argument (see Figure Part3.19). Information should be summarized or paraphrased to fit on one side of the card if at all possible along with the space to label or code the card in the upper corners. The code of key words in the corners usually includes sub-topics that allow for clustering the notes later and eventually noting some order of the information for a logical flow of the story, description, or evidence for an argument on issues. A separate set of index cards or database is maintained with complete bibliographic information of the sources consulted and becomes the basis for eventual citations and reference lists. Usually the author's last name and date of the source is used as part of the code on the note cards.

As the inquirer matures in examination of sources and evidence, he or she will want to be certain they note the original source of the data, opinion expressed, or conclusion. Reference sources are usually third level, tertiary compilations derived from secondary works and ultimately trace back to primary work. Almanacs, encyclopedias, news magazines and the common newspaper are each often sited as the "source" when in reality some primary agency noted by the chart, table, or within the article is responsible for the original gathering of the data. A true date of the information may be several years prior to the publication date of the reference book. Younger students may not be able to engage this concept, but maturing inquirers should eventually learn to site the original source and true dates on data and other information gathered.

Number of Source or Author's Last Name & Date	(+ or other symbol indicating extremely high information value)	Key Word for Subtopic or Question

The Most Important Facts

Summary of information written in terms and phrases meaningful to the inquirer.

Usually such information is paraphrased and written in a shorthand.

Use direct quotation when it is the best means to communicate the opinion, thought or conclusion and note specific location of the quotation, who made the statement and their qualifications. Place the direct quotation within quotation marks on the card and within the final product and note any special qualification of the author of the quotation so that such may be used within the text of the report or presentation, "Chair of the committee . . . , Lead scientist on the expedition . . . , First astronaut on the moon . . . , Award-winning teacher . . . , Nobel Prize Winner . . . , Inventor of . . . , Author of many books on the subject . . . .

In some cases, the primary source of the information needs to be noted especially for information gained from common reference sources; i.e. is the source the 2002 World Almanac or is the source the U.S. Department of Transportation, 1999?; or information from a research review and it is not the reviewer who should be cited for a conclusion or recommendation, but the author of the original research report—check the references.

Figure Part3.19 Note card content.

Forming Focus with Final Transfer Notes

"Forming," writes Kuhlthau (1994), "is the creative activity of thinking of a focus for research based on what students already know about a topic and what they want to learn about a topic. It requires attention, interest, and concentration" (85). "As a focus is formed, the purpose of the library research turns from exploring to collecting, and the materials used go from general to specific, and the information sought changes from relevant to pertinent" (86). As the student, or any inquirer, gathers specific information, the note-taking task becomes focused to locate such pieces as

- data from text, charts, tables which are relevant to the situation and may help prove a point; sometimes data from several charts will be summarized into one note

- data which are relevant to the situation and may help disprove or counter a point, proposal or plan

- key facts, especially not commonly known

- key names associated with issues, events, happenings and their role

- key terms and definitions, especially if not know prior to this research effort

- opinions and observations of experts; any of these first three can be the basis for information becoming evidence

- events or happenings which illustrate, give context, provide an example case relevant to the topic

- a chain of sources which give support to the need to show similar evidence from more than one or two sources; pieces which substantiate previous information

- an item which fills in a gap and may be unique data or a different observation then found anyplace else

- information which is either more current than previous information, or provides historical context for chronological comparison of information

- above all, the information item is relevant, authoritative, and understandable and will help clarify issues, events and happenings that must be described in final report or presentation

Discussion about information changes at this stage as well. In exploration, the inquirer will converse about the potential of a topic or argument. The intent may be to determine audience interest, help determine one's own interest, and to gain a sense for how well one can identify and express the ideas, events and concepts related to a potential topic. Conversations at the data gathering stage may be more to one's self to paraphrase information and to see if it can be expressed in meaningful terms to fit or assimilate to one's needs. In some cases, new data and new

opinions may actually change the thinking of the inquirer, and often for the open-minded researcher, change the message originally intended for the final product.

Practice in paraphrasing does not make the idea the property of the researcher. Credit still belongs to the original source. Paraphrasing can, however, make the new information manageable, understandable, and workable as relevant supporting information for a line of reason or story. Reflection on collected information is a test for the inquirer to think through the value of the information and to make decisions on assimilating or discarding.

Among other recommendations, Rankin (1999, 106) lists these strategies for middle grade inquiring students to take into consideration as they select information to extract from text and transfer to note cards:

- Preview for indicators of key information in subtitles, topic sentences, table of contents, pictures [and picture captions], and charts.

- Select relevant information through skimming and scanning for items clearly relevant to your topic and subtopics

- Read [in more detail] information that is relevant

- Evaluate the reading in terms of how it may address your [inquiry] questions, relate to main ideas, or provide supporting details

- Write to summarize with lists, phrases, key words, main idea on one card

- Review the note cards to see if they lead to new questions, raise the need for more information, begin to lead to something new and exciting you have not considered about your topic before.

Thus the student inquirer through selecting, summarizing, sorting, and sifting uses the note-taking process to organize the essential pieces which will eventually lead to his or her written report, digital slide presentation, poster session, storyboard, or what ever is the final format for conveying the findings. Some students find it to be useful to write transition cards that can be used to link together evidence card clusters. This can serve as a concrete map from one item to the next and helps in the flow that will follow in word processing the final report or script (Kramer and Largent 2005).

How many notes can transfer from one source onto index cards? The range probably depends on the topic, the source and the sophistication of the student inquirer. In early practice exercises, there may be some set guidelines to help the student select the three to five most relevant items of information for a given source. But one would hope, over time and maturation of the student as being more and more information literate and information fluent, that such teacher and library media specialist imposed limitations would give way to the student making such decisions. Just as no true inquiry project should be restricted by "three sources, each from a different format" so too must the decision-making process for information extraction and transfer be left to the experienced student inquirer rather than be a dictated task from the teacher.

References

Coiro, J. (2005). "Making Sense of Online Text." *Educational Leadership* 63 (2): 30-35.

Everhart, N. (1994). *How to Write a Term Paper.* Franklin Watts.

Joyce, M. Z., and J. I. Tallman. (1997). *Making the Writing and Research Connection with the I-Search Process.* Neal-Schumann.

Kramer, K., and C. Largent. (2005). "Sift and Sort: The Answers Are in the Questions." *School Library Media Activities Monthly* 21 (8): 33–37.

Kuhlthau, C. C. (1994). *Teaching the Library Research Process.* Scarecrow Press.

Pappas, M. L., and A. E. Tepe. (2002). *Pathways to Knowledge and Inquiry Learning.* Libraries Unlimited.

Rankin, V. (1999). *The Thoughtful Researcher.* Libraries Unlimited.

Stanley, D. B. (2000a). *Practical Steps to the Research Process for High School.* Libraries Unlimited.

Stanley, D. B. (2000b). *Practical Steps to the Research Process for Middle School.* Libraries Unlimited.

Technology

Daniel Callison

Heinich, Molenda, Russell, and Smaldino (1996) define "technology" in their standard instructional media text as

1. A process of devising reliable and repeatable solutions to tasks.

2. The hardware and software (i.e., the products) that result from the application of technological processes.

3. A mix of process and product, used in instances where the context refers to the combination of technological processes and resultant products or where the process is inseparable from the product. (416)

Healy (1998) defines and editorializes a little in her best seller, *Failure to Connect: Technology and Power:*

Throughout history, new technologies have altered the existing social order, economy, and power structure. "Technology" is any tool or medium that helps people accomplish tasks or produce products more efficiently, and computers are only the latest in a long line of innovations-going back to axes and fire-that have changed the way humans interact with the world and with each other. Computers, like all technologies that introduce new information or alter the format of information, are changing the balance of power in schools. Increasingly, the "techies" rather than the educators, hold the power to make educational decisions. (30–31)

The Association for Educational Communications and Technology released a set of definitions for basic terms in that field in 1977. According to the AECT Task Force on Definition and Terminology:

Instructional Technology is a complex, integrated process involving people, procedures, ideas, devices, and organization, for analyzing problems, and devising, implementing, evaluating, and managing solutions to those problems, in situations in which learning is purposive and controlled. [Design of instruction may involve components such as] messages, people, materials, devices, techniques, and settings. Purposive learning is learning in which someone else has determined that learning is to occur within the learner. Further, the purpose of such learning can, and must be, specified in advance [objectives that can be observed and measured]. Controlled learning is learning in which the contingencies of the learner's behavior are determined and managed by someone else [much in step with the principles outlined by B. F. Skinner (1968) for the technologies of teaching]. (76–77)

Inquiry and Technology

A quarter of a century later, little has changed in defining the purpose of technology in instruction. A great deal, however, has been added to our considerations as to how and by whom technology will be applied to learning. Inquiry includes the guided and purposive learning techniques when some aspects require a training or exercise mode. To hold at that level, though, destroys the potential for the learner to experience self-motivation, self-direction, and to mature as one who can manage the technologies of learning for him or herself.

Therefore, as a tool, technologies can help make some aspects of inquiry more manageable or efficient. Information access can be faster. Information records can be stored easier and sorted or accessed in more combinations. Information communication can be packaged in presentation modes that are designed by the student. While the teacher may master some aspects of instructional design through the latest evolution in hypermedia, the more powerful strategy is the technology in the hands of the learner.

Inquiry can be made more efficient through the application of one of the many models for the information search process or for information problem solving. It is likely, however, to be more effective when there is time given to information exploration, sharing of ideas, and demonstration of how new information has been assimilated. While technologies are tools that lead to more efficiency, as teachers of Information Inquiry we also should consider how technology might make learning more effective. Pleasure, motivation, and self-reflection are powerful aspects of a more welcoming learning environment. Perhaps modern technology hardware and software also should be developed to help enhance these behaviors in a positive way.

Curriculum and Technology

A key question is: Where does inquiry enter into the design of learning environments compared to instructional technology? It enters at the foundation. Some would say "inquiry is the curriculum."

Robert Heinich, professor of Instructional Systems Technology at Indiana University, shifted the educational technology field in 1970 when he moved instructional technology into a planning phase for curriculum development. Thus, instructional media specialists were moved, in his model, to the role of curriculum design rather than reactors to curriculum and simple audiovisual classroom support. In many cases, there was no professional in place in the

traditional audiovideo approach. Use of technology in the 1960s, as too often today, was used as an add-on or afterthought. Audiovisual often meant an item that would pass the time faster or relieve the teacher of some talking time.

Programmed instruction in the 1970s was designed to make teaching more efficient, rather than to make learning more effective. The more important agenda was that of the teacher or trainer. Learner needs and entry abilities often were measured only for the purpose of helping the instructional designer. Little consideration was given to the opportunity for the learner to understand his or her own entry abilities and potential.

Heinich moved technology, and it continues to apply today in a world of computers, as tools to help plan and deliver curriculum. The principles of inquiry that place the student at the center of the purpose of curriculum will set the foundation for experiences that are more authentic and meaningful to student needs. This teaching philosophy builds from what the learner brings to the situation, and then applies information-seeking and use models that seem to best fit the situation. (See Figure Part3.20.)

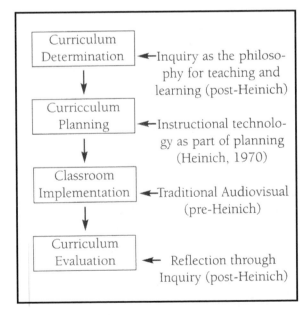

Figure Part3.20. Modification and updating of the entry of instructional technology into the instructional process model by Heinich.

Reflection, the component of inquiry that examines the merits of the process and products of instruction, is important to add in the string of events illustrated in Figure Part3.17. Continuously, technology should be evaluated and modified to serve the curricular and instructional needs of teachers and students. Technology is a tool set that can be reconfigured. The purpose is not just efficiency, but to restructure interactive instructional delivery systems so that the accepted principles of learning can be achieved effectively.

Debbie Abilock (2001), curriculum coordinator and director of Technology and Library at the Nueva School in Hillsborough, California, models this approach in one of several essays gathered by Lebaron and Collier. She "puts technology in its place" as a tool to alter curriculum based on sound learning principles that do not change. Abilock coordinates the application of modern information technologies for her school so her students have efficient access to a wide selection of information in electronic, multimedia, and print formats. The information selection tasks remain the same, however, regardless of the technologies employed.

Abilock (2001) writes, "The science program at Nueva is hands-on, minds-on, feet-in-the mud, which means that it consists of experiments, simulations, and activities from which students construct an understanding of science concepts. In problem-based learning, students are confronted with ill-structured problems that mirror an authentic situation. It is important for them to recognize that just as in real-world problems, there are not simple right and wrong answers. The challenge for students is to understand complex issues, develop an informed and defensible position, locate data supporting [or rejecting] their point of view, recognize information that is relevant, and evaluate the authority of sources" (6).

The Right Questions and Criteria

Healy (1998) has generated a list of questions that administrators and teachers should answer prior to investing in the next generation of computers:

- How can computer technology help achieve our educational goals? Are these goals compatible with the interests, abilities, and needs of today's students?

- How and why will this experience [based on the technology to be acquired] improve the quality of learning sufficiently to justify the cost and the time involved?

- What will it have to replace (family activities, silent reading, social playtime, art, music, gym, recess, foreign language) and is the trade-off acceptable?

- Who makes software decisions and on what criteria?

- Are we willing to loosen traditional top-down structures of education and produce students who will think and question?

- What content can be taught, and how do we measure the outcomes? Are computers the best, not just the trendiest, way to do this particular job? (67)

Healy (1998) also understands the power of a technological innovation and provides this criteria for methods that will increase the motivation to learn. In the best practices, this motivation is enhanced, allowing the student to explore computers as well as learning specific applications:

- Let the child be an active agent rather than just a button-pusher. Offering the child reasonable choices within limits builds internal controls.

- Avoid programs that give "rewards" for completing tasks, particularly easy ones. Emphasize that pleasure should be found in using one's mind to solve problems and feeling good about success.

- Corrective feedback develops thinking skills and confidence by helping a student understand a mistake and how to correct it.

- Cultivate the notion that learning is inherently interesting, rather than something so boring that one must be externally rewarded to do it.

- Well-designed hypermedia programs can enhance motivation, especially for youngsters with more visual and kinesthetic learning styles.

- Check whether the program requires only convergent answers or whether it allows the child to do some original thinking. Is it possible to come up with a solution that even the programmer didn't anticipate?

- The depersonalized computer may help uncertain students to take more risks in the service of learning because there is no one there to make fun or criticize.

- Insist that the child take reasonable responsibility. Don't let him or her believe that the computer does the work or blame it for making the mistakes. (188–189)

Technology Foundation Standards and Computer Skills

The most recent standards for student performance from the International Society for Technology in Education (2000) reflect a multidisciplinary approach. Before computer skills are identified, a clear vision for establishing new learning environments is illustrated. ISTE advocates technology connections to the curriculum based on a learning environment that prepares students to

- communicate by using a variety of media and formats.

- access and exchange information in a variety of ways.

- compile, organize, analyze, and synthesize information.

- draw conclusions and make generalizations based on information gathered.

- know content and be able to locate additional information as needed.

- become self-directed learners.

- collaborate and cooperate in team efforts.

- interact with others in ethical and appropriate ways. (5)

Doug Johnson, district media supervisor for the Mankato, Minnesota Schools, and Mike Eisenberg, professor at the Information School of the University of Washington (1999), have listed computer skills that they feel reflect each stage of the Eisenberg and Berkewitz (1990) information problem-solving approach. They identify the following skills for Synthesis. (Students must organize and communicate the results of the information problem- solving effort.)

Students will be able to

- Classify and group information by using a word processor, database, or spreadsheet.

- Use word processing and desktop publishing software to create printed documents.

- Create and use computer-generated graphics and art in different print and electronic presentations.

- Generate charts, tables, and graphs by using electronic spreadsheets and other graphing programs.

- Use presentation software to create electronic slide shows.

- Create hypermedia and multimedia productions with digital video and audio.

- Create World Wide Web pages and sites by using hypertext markup language (HTML).

- Use e-mail, ftp, and other telecommunications capabilities to share [information and ideas].

- Properly cite and credit electronic sources.

Impact of New Technologies on School Library Media Centers

Nearly every current school library media specialist can give examples of how information access has become frequent "uploading or downloading." Electronic searching and fulltext access are now common not just in the library media center, but in classrooms and homes. More and more teachers and students are not only users of electronic products, but are the creators of many instructional presentations.

Many of the following features suggested by Callison in 1993 are becoming common today:

- electronic continuous access to information, 24/7;

- computers on teachers' desks with software to support grading, student records, professional development programs, and access to the Internet and other electronic databases and libraries worldwide;

- provision for cable and satellite reception in every classroom, with distance education coordinated through the library media center;

- homework hotlines, collaborative writing labs, and immediate contact among school library media centers and local public and academic libraries;

- technologies that have been modified to meet the needs of students with physical and learning disabilities; and

- technologies that extend staff development conferencing throughout the year, including summers.

Instructional Technology Software

Callison and Haycock (1988) field-tested early microcomputer software designed for instructional purposes in the 1980s. They found students tended to prefer programs that were simulations with challenging tasks to solve in order to "take a journey" or solve a problem with different possible resolutions. Teachers tended to favor computer software that supported already established curriculum and learning objectives. They tended to look for and approve computer software that reinforced what they were already teaching, and it has not been until the past decade that more and more teachers have been adapting some of the advantages that new technology software has to offer to modify their lessons. Interactivity and student ability options have gained wider acceptance over the two decades since the first computer-assisted instruction packages were introduced.

In the late 1990s, Haughland and Wright (1997) provided the foundation for the following guidelines for selection of instructional software for children:

- Is the child in control, an "actor not a reactor"?

- Does the child set the pace of the activity?

- Are instructions clear?

- Does it teach powerful ideas, not just trivia?

- Can the child operate it independently?

- Does it feature discovery learning, not skill drilling?

- Does it capitalize on the child's intrinsic motivation rather than using external rewards?

- Is the process more important than the product?

- Does it reflect the child's experience in the real world?

- Are technical features well-designed responds quickly, saves child's work, and has uncluttered graphics?

- Does it display gender role equity?

Future Trends in Technology

Ann Barron of the University of South Florida and Gary Orwig (1997, 2002) of the University of Central Florida have provided an excellent guide to the technology terms and formats of emerging media. (Barron et al. 2006) Subtitled "a beginners guide," their publication gives excellent outlines for such technologies as CD-ROM, interactive video, digital audio, digital images and video, hypermedia, local area networks, telecommunications, teleconferencing for distance education, and assistive technologies for those with special needs (on-screen keyboards, screen enlargement, Braille displays, speech synthesis, text-to-speech conversion).

Through the many editions of the Heinich, Molenda, Russell, and Smaldino (2004) (Smaldino et al. 2005) text *Instructional Media and Technologies for Learning*, the authors have attempted to predict future trends in media and technology. These three seem to be most clear:

- **Merging of media**—away from the 1950s media as separate entities, sometimes combined as multimedia, to the seamless combinations made possible by digitization of print, images, and sound.
- **Convergence of telecommunications technologies**—high-speed networks for telephone and broadcasting.
- **Convergence and disappearance of the computer as we know it today.**

Theodore Frick's essay for the Phi Delta Kappa Education Foundation in 1991 gave a vision for future technological systems that will restructure educational settings and result in more community-based learning. Rather than tied to the classroom, students will gain from more direct interaction with cultural, governmental, business, and industrial institutions with technology providing more direct contact with people, events, services, and mentoring. Technology provides two key functions; it

- extends the communication and interaction options; and
- makes simulations more realistic and demanding, leading to meaningful learning experiences.

Thus Frick argues that technology will play a large role in restructuring education so that it gains meaning through an environment that consists of the surrounding community and its culture.

One of the most exciting recent discussions concerning future technologies has been written by George Gilder (2000), Senior Fellow at the Discovery Institute. He contends that the computer age is over and a new age of telecommunications, "telecosm," is emerging. Infinite bandwidth will revolutionize our communication and education world again. Delivery of audio and video data will be "instant." Control over what the user wants, when, how often, and at what ability level will be realized as never before. Telecosm entails the domains of technology unleashed by the discovery of the electro-magnetic spectrum and the photon, with fiber optics, cellular telephony, and satellite communications as examples detailed by Gilder.

Under current technologies, both pedagogical techniques and hardware delivery systems, students continue to waste time, according to Gilder, because the educational bureaucracy has yet to provide learning environments that truly meet specific ability levels and support real-world learning experiences, even for the very young. There are signs, however, that the restructuring scenarios described by Frick of Indiana University in 1991 still have a chance to become reality.

Some of these signs are indicators of behavior from students themselves. In a fascinating review of tech-savvy student behavior in the twenty-first century, Marc Prensky (2006) makes the case that adult educators have much to learn from how kids are adapting to the new information technologies. While there are many examples of abuse and wasted time, Prensky argues that the reason kids play computer and video games is that they're learning, and learning the information organization, communication and valuing skills so necessary to successful team-work in the Information Age.

Many of today's students are what Prensky terms "digital natives" and the view important skills differently from adults who are mostly "digital immigrants." Through blogs, webcams, and camera phones, natives share differently. Through sites, avatars, and mods, natives create differently. Through reputation systems, natives evaluate differently. Natives also coordinate group communications differently, search for information differently, and through it all, learn differently. Most natives are ready for the emerging Broadband movement and the other changes coming along in the Digital Revolution. The challenge for us immigrants is to observe and learn from the natives as much as possible.

References

Abilock, D. (2001). "Using Technology to Enhance Student Inquiry." In *Technology in Its Place,* edited by J. F. LeBarron and C. Collier, 3–15. Jossey-Bass.

AECT Task Force on Definition and Terminology. (1977). *Educational Technology: Definition and Glossary of Terms.* AECT.

Barron, A. E., et al. (2006). *Technologies for Education: A Practical Guide*. 5th ed. Libraries Unlimited.

Barron, A. E., and G. W. Orwig. (1997). *New Technologies for Education: A Beginner's Guide*. Libraries Unlimited.

Barron, A. E., G. W. Orwig, K. S. Ivers, and N. Lilavois. (2002). *Technologies for Education: A Practical Guide*. 4th ed. Libraries Unlimited.

Callison, D. (1993, Summer). "The Impact of New Technologies on School Library Media Center Facilities and Instruction." *Journal of Youth Services in Libraries* 6 (4): 414–419.

Callison, D., and G. Haycock. (1988, January). "A Methodology for Student Evaluation of Educational Microcomputer Software." *Educational Technology* 28 (1): 25–32.

Eisenberg, M. B., and R. E. Berkowitz. (1990). Information Problem Solving: The big six skills approach to library and information skills. Ablex.

Frick, T. W. (1991). *Restructuring Education through Technology*. Fastback #326. Phi Delta Kappa.

Gilder, G. (2000). *Telecosm: How Infinite Bandwidth Will Revolutionize Our World*. The Free Press.

Haughland, S. W., and J. L. Wright. (1997). *Young Children and Technology*. Allyn & Bacon.

Healy, J. M. (1998). *Failure to Connect: How Computers Affect Our Children's Minds and What We Can Do about It*. Touchstone.

Heinich, R. (1970). *Technology and the Management of Instruction*. Monograph 4. Association for Educational Communications and Technology.

Heinich, R., M. Molenda, J. D. Russell, and S. E. Smaldino. (1996). *Instructional Media and Technologies for Learning*. 5th ed. Merrill.

International Society for Technology in Education. (2000). *National Educational Technology Standards for Students: Connecting Curriculum and Technology*. ISTE. Available at http://www.iste.org.

Johnson, D., and M. Eisenberg. (1999). "Computer Literacy and Information Literacy: A Natural Combination." In *Foundations for Effective School Library Media Programs*, edited by K. Haycock, 140–146. Libraries Unlimited.

Prensky, M. (2006). *Don't Bother Me Mom—I'm Learning*. Paragon House.

Skinner, B. F. (1968). *The Technology of Teaching*. Appleton-Century-Crofts.

Smaldino, S. E., J. D. Russell, R. Heinich, and M. Molinda. (2004). *Instructional Technology and Media for Learning*. 7th edition. Prentice Hall.

Smaldino, S. E., et al. (2005). *Institutional Technology and Media for Learning*. 8th ed. Prentice Hall.

For Further Reading

Ely, D. P. (1992). *Trends in Educational Technology*. ERIC Clearinghouse on Information Resources.

Norton, P., and K. M. Wiburg. (2002). *Teaching with Technology: Designing Opportunities to Learn*. Wadsworth Publishing.

Roblyer, M. D. (2002a). *Integrating Educational Technology into Teaching*. 3d ed. Prentice Hall.

Roblyer, M. D. (2002b). *Starting Out on the Internet: A Learning Journal for Teachers*. 2d ed. Prentice Hall.

Textbook

Daniel Callison

Daniel J. Boorstin, then Librarian of Congress, wrote the following comments in an introduction to The Textbook in American Society, a summary of a conference held at the Library of Congress in 1979. His words remain true today:

> In [our] free society, textbooks are books chosen for us by somebody else . . . by the committee or commission in the state that selects the textbooks. This gives another special significance to the textbook in our civilization because in a free economy, a free society, the textbook is a special test of freedom. Can we provide basic books, foundation books, which present the consensus of a subject, chosen by a government agency . . . ,and yet preserve the freedom to grow and the freedom to dissent, the freedom to be free? (ix-x).

Kenneth Pray of the University of Wisconsin and W. F. Rocheleau of the Illinois Normal Academy wrote in their 1906 series on "Home Study of History" that within "recent years a new element has been made prominent in history courses . . . so prominent that wide-awake and progressive teachers find it necessary to recognize its utility and value. This is the use by teacher and pupil of other books and materials besides the text[book]."

"The up-to-date teacher," concluded Pray and Rocheleau, "looks upon the library as an essential part of the school. That teacher realizes that the lifeblood of the subject flows through books [and other resources], while the text[book] alone can furnish but the dry bones of information."

The Textbook as Instructional Technology

No other instructional technology has had more influence on teaching over the past 100 years than the textbook. An instructional tool that places all students "on the same page at the same time," the textbook, more than blackboards, worksheets, and computers, has led to stepping students through content at a similar pace.

While a great organizer of facts, textbooks too often have become a time-saving device that prevents the use of learning technologies that provide in-depth study and inquiry. Teaching by the text and to the test are activities that stand in the way of exploration and discovery. At best, the textbook is an initial guide, an outline of events, terms, and names. At worst, the textbook indoctrinates a common message without challenge and questioning (Kirk, Matthews, and Kurtts 2001).

Clearly, it has been, and continues to be, the role of the school library media program and collection to move teaching beyond the limits of the textbook and into use of multiple resources for meaningful learning experiences. As such, the school library media center should be the more powerful learning technology, a collection of resources and open learning techniques. The school library media program is the overarching instructional technology, conceptualized as a learning laboratory to give access to both a wide spectrum of resources and a wide variety of teaching approaches.

Often a political instrument, the textbook is the subject of more debate and financing than any other teaching tool. Conservative and liberal groups argue their cases before textbook selection committees annually. More dollars are allotted for textbook funds than for all other instructional resources combined. Textbook adoption in some states drives the content of the curriculum more so than standards for learning.

The textbook can be the great divide between classroom teacher and teacher of Information Inquiry. The textbook can satisfy the instructional isolationist, the teacher who says "there is no time for inquiry, my students must cover all that is in the textbook." Collaboration between classroom teacher and instructional library media specialist can be made more difficult to achieve when only the textbook is the guide for student academic proficiency.

In too many schools, the textbook limits critical thinking and creative output of the learner even though many texts pretend to offer such exercises at conclusions to chapters. Often, collection development in school library media centers follows decisions on textbook adoption rather than leading the decisions for multiple resource collections that are more diverse and more current than any printed textbook can be.

Anthologies of literature often are "watered down" and contain only portions of the full document. Primary sources are edited to support one perspective when the reader who finds the full text discovers that the textbook has been misleading through selective editing. The power of the content accepted for print in textbooks is often so great that outside sources often are questioned as valid because they have been excluded from the text.

For the inquiring mind and for the teacher of Information Inquiry, textbooks may be the single most important instructional tool from which activities in critical thinking should be derived, if for no other reason than to question so-called authority.

Research on Textbooks

Two research reviews provide some insight as to the impact that textbooks have on curriculum, teaching approaches, and student learning. One review was conducted for the Garland Bibliographies series in 1988 by Arthur Woodward, David L. Elliott, and Kathleen Carter Nagel; the other in 1991 by Jeanne S. Chall and Sue S. Conard at Harvard University. Conclusions from these reviews include the following:

- There is an association between the lowering of students' SAT scores and the declining difficulty of their books; a general trend of decreasing difficulty in the most

widely used textbooks over the thirty-year period of 1945 to 1975.

- Teacher's guides have become increasingly prescriptive and leave less and less room for independent teacher decision making; little leeway is given for teachers to change the sequence of topics or to add or delete topics.

- Regardless of length, the point seems not to be so much that knowledge has increased, necessitating longer books, but that textbooks have become national consensus documents designed to sell in as many communities as possible.

- The world as portrayed in textbooks is different in important aspects from that described by the scholar or the "real" world that students experience. Those who have studied textbook content have held up a mirror to the instructional programs of the American schools. What we can see in that mirror is highly selective, sanitized, prepackaged, and often distorted content offered to students in the name of science and social studies and what must seem like endless sequences of isolated skills.

- Often in language arts textbooks, writing opportunities are introduced and mechanics emphasized, but the entire writing process area is left untouched. Neither prewriting, composing, or post-composing are suggested with meaning and substance, nor is the learner's capacity for voice development or self-critical capability developed.

- In basal readers, the acts of writing and open-ended problem solving are missing, and one will search nearly in vain for much attention to the actual act of reading in the midst of the sequence of skills found in most reading texts.

- Most science textbooks fail to reflect the true nature of science. In contrast to the inquiry-based programs developed in the 1960s, the elementary and junior high school textbooks offer mainly cookbook

Key Words for Instruction in Information Inquiry

style recipes in place of bona fide experiments.

Political Agendas and Textbooks

Textbooks have become one of the most common "political footballs" as powerful lobbies for either the "right" or the "left" influence the decisions made at a state-level on which textbooks may or may not be adopted. Longtime educational consultant Diane Ravitch (2004) sees this struggle in terms of censorship and a loss of the basic purpose of textbooks to provide understandable and accurate narrative. Instead, too often, textbooks are accepted or rejected because of the political positioning expected to be reflected in the overall message of the text. Ravitch makes these comparisons:

> Censors on the right aim to restore an idealized vision of the past, an Arcadia of happy family life, in which the family was intact, comprising of a father, a mother, and two or more children, and went to church every Sunday. Father was in charge, and Mother took care of the children. Father worked; Mother shopped and prepared the meals. Everyone sat around the dinner table at night. It was a happy, untroubled setting into which social problems seldom intruded. Pressure groups on the right believe that what children read in school should present this vision of the past to children and that showing it might make it so. They believe strongly in the power of the word, and they believe that children will model their behavior on whatever they read. If they read stories that conflict with their parents' religious values, they might abandon their religion. Critics on the right urge that whatever children read should model appropriate moral behavior.

> Censors on the left believe in an idealized vision of the future, a utopia in which egalitarianism prevails in all social relations. In this vision, there is no dominant group, no dominant father, no dominant race, and no dominant gender. In this world, youth is not an advantage, and disability is not a disadvantage. There is no hierarchy of better or worse; all national and all cultures are of equal accomplishment and value. All individuals and groups share equally in the roles, rewards, and activities of society. In this world to be, everyone has high self-esteem, eats healthful foods, exercises, and enjoys being different. Pressure groups on the left feel as strongly about the power of the word as those on the right. They expect that children will be shaped by what they read and will model their behavior on what they read. They want children to read only descriptions of the world as they think it should be in order to help bring this new world into being. (31)

Lies My Teacher Told Me

In his 1995 award-winning book *Lies My Teacher Told Me: Everything Your American History Textbook Got Wrong,* University of Vermont sociology professor James W. Loewen describes how most textbook editors start their careers in publishing as sales representatives, not as historians. They don't know how to interpret history, but they do know how to read their market. These editors often include whatever is likely to be of concern to textbook selecting stakeholders. Everything gets mentioned, but seldom does anything receive depth and relevance to present-day issues. He quotes Lynn Cheney, former director of the National Endowment of the Humanities, as she decried the results of cramming as many facts as possible into 800 pages, "Textbooks come to seem like glossaries of historical events—compendiums of topics" (280).

Skirting controversy and displaying simplistic solutions to complex issues, Loewen asserts that history textbooks not only are misleading on events, but misleading in how democracy works and does not work:

> The stories that history textbooks tell are predictable; every problem has already been solved or is about to be solved. Textbooks exclude conflict or real suspense. They leave out everything that might reflect badly upon our national character. When they try for drama, they achieve only melodrama, because readers know that everything will turn out fine in the end. 'Despite setbacks, the United States overcame these challenges,' in the words of one textbook. Most authors of history textbooks don't even try for melodrama. Instead, they write in a tone that if

heard aloud might be described as 'mumbling lecturer.' No wonder students lose interest. . . . Textbooks almost never use the present to illuminate the past. . . . The present is not a source of information for writers of history textbooks. . . . Conversely, textbooks seldom use the past to illuminate the present. (13)

The chapters Loewen devotes to events that are misrepresented in typical American history textbooks reads like an open invitation to students to apply standards for information literacy and inquiry in order to dig deeper for truth and relevance.

- The Process of Hero-making

- The True Importance of Christopher Columbus

- Truth about the First Thanksgiving

- "Gone with the Wind:" The Invisibility of Antiracism

- What Textbooks Teach about the Federal Government

Loewen gives detailed descriptions from textbooks and how elaborations are not present to place events within a meaningful context nor described with truthful and yet intriguing narratives to engage student interest. Lack of such, however, should be the stage for establishing projects to critically review textbooks through student inquiry and based on demonstration of the following student proficiencies:

- Compares and contrasts sources related to a topic to determine which are more accurate, relevant, and comprehensive.

- Judges the accuracy, relevance, and completeness of sources and information in relation to a range of topics and information problems.

- Judges and supports judgments of the degree of inaccuracy, bias, or misleading information.

- Judges the quality of decisions in terms of the accuracy and completeness of the information on which they were based.

- Analyzes information from a variety of sources to determine its applicability to a specific information problem or question.

Loewen concludes in his introduction that how textbooks hide real history from students, and seem to consistently, do not much more than duplicate each other in format. Over the past decade, there have been attempts to broaden the personalities covered, increase representation of minorities and women, and even suggest book titles, fiction and nonfiction, that will tell more about the events at hand. Primary documents are being linked more and more to textbooks through compact discs and Web sites, either sold with the text or separately. Such is progress, but Loewen concludes:

Textbooks also keep students in the dark about the nature of history. History is furious debate informed by evidence and reason. Textbooks encourage students to believe that history is facts to be learned. . . . History can be imagined as a pyramid. At its base are the millions of primary sources—the plantation records, city directories, speeches, songs, photographs, newspaper articles, diaries, and letters that document times past. Based on these sources, historians write secondary works. . . . In theory, a few historians, working individually or in teams, then synthesize the secondary literature into tertiary works—textbooks covering all phases of U. S. history. In practice, however, it doesn't happen that way. Instead, history textbooks are clones of each other. (15–16)

Authoritativeness: Primary Sources or Textbooks

The powerful influence that textbook content, text, and illustrations can have on students was evident in a recent project conducted by Frances Jacobson Harris (2002) at the University of Illinois lab school. Her observations of middle grade students who were expected to seek documents and illustrations from primary sources in association with their history text indicate again how the textbook can be more dominate in influencing learning than other artifacts. Unfortunately, third-level summaries of history may make more sense to students than the rich and detailed information found in first-level documents (Trofanenko 2002). Harris reports these findings in her literature review and summary.

There are a number of sound justifications for the use of primary sources in the K–12 setting. One argument is that a dependence on textbooks can compromise student learning. . . . [T]eachers often assign textbook readings without contradicting student assumptions that the textbooks are objective and omniscient conveyers of these events. . . . [Textbook] authors often assume students have more prior knowledge than they actually do. Students' lack of adequate context results in a shallow understanding of historical phenomena.

. . . In studying historical problem-solving methods and skills, [some researchers have] asked high school students and professional historians to look at a range of conflicting written and pictorial sources about a single historical event and to construct the true history. The students gave most credence to the version of history supplied by the textbook, in contrast to the historians who were immediately inclined to examine the credibility of the sources, whether primary or secondary, and gave little attention to the textbook treatment. The historians also relied on two other criteria: corroboration, the act of comparing sources to determine reliability; and contextualization, situating the claims of a document in the particulars of the historical events. Students, on the other hand, viewed the textbook as a primary source offering unbiased factual information. For historians, the question was not if a source was biased, but how its bias influenced the quality of the information.

. . . [T]extbooks appear to speak with a single voice, portraying events from a tidily edited vantage point. A variety of perspectives contribute to any single historical event, which means that there are also multiple possible representations of the event . . . . For able readers, the practice of reading from multiple texts, even those with several challenging features, provides the conditions that can promote historical thinking and more complex understanding of the past.

Trade Books Also Can Be Misleading

Diana C. Rice (2002) from Florida State University has examined the content of many new trade books on the market for support of science education in the elementary grades. She notes the intended advantages in the use of recent trade books, hopefully drawn from a well-weeded collection in the school library media center, to enhance science lessons in the classroom. Advantages of using trade books include the following:

- Trade books, if recent publications, are often more up-to-date than the science textbook.

- Science textbooks can be daunting for many children and multiple trade books allow for different reading levels and interests.

- Science trade books are widely available; have increased dramatically in number, subject, and quality; and often are included as useful additional resources by a growing number of elementary textbook publishers.

- Trade books are, in general, more interesting and less confusing than science textbooks.

- Both fact and science fiction can be useful in supporting the inquiry approach to learning science in the elementary grades as well as in the higher grade levels.

- Trade books, in general, display a more positive presentation of the role for women and minorities in science than found in most science textbooks.

However, argues Rice, it may be common for trade books that contain inaccurate information to be used in a science lesson context and for such information, either read to or read by the student, to influence the student's understanding of a scientific fact, principle, or method. In her examination of reading trade books with inaccurate information to elementary school children, Rice found that even facts that students understood to be correct prior to hearing the reading of the book could be changed. In many cases, students changed their mind from correct to incorrect information upon hearing the incorrect facts read to them from the science trade book. The effect was dramatic enough that she recommends that students be informed clearly when a story is fiction and when a scientific fact is misrepresented in a trade book.

Moreover, the selection process should take into account how accurate the information is that is presented in trade books before they are purchased for the classroom or school library media center collections. Her review of studies pertaining to the impact of text on elementary school students concluded that children do not question what they read when they are given one textbook. The text is held up as embodying the final and whole truth on the subject. Such influence seems to be especially strong in science lessons (Rice, Dudley, and Williams 2001).

Stages for Multiple Resource Reading

Professor Jeanne Chall of the School of Education at Harvard has outlined the stages of reading development that show the progression toward inclusion of multiple resources along with standard reading texts. Chall developed her scale in 1983 and it remains true for the average student today, although notes have been added to include access to electronic information.

- Stage 1 (Grades 1–2). Reading that is primarily associating written words to words in the child's oral vocabulary. Materials are simple text that contains high frequency words and words that are phonetically regular.

- Stage 2 (Grades 2–3). Reading to confirm what is already known. Energy still is concentrated mainly on decoding words and developing fluency in reading connected text. Therefore, the vocabulary is generally within the reader's meaning vocabulary, although not all words need be immediately recognizable.

- Stage 3A (Grades 4–6). Reading from new knowledge, generally from one viewpoint; facts, concepts, how to do things. The reader also is learning to process— how to find information in a paragraph,

chapter, or book. This stage usually does not require special knowledge to understand the text, but subjects studied in school generally are introduced at this stage. Materials include subject-matter textbooks, trade books, reference works, newspapers, magazines, [preselected Web sites], more complex fiction, and nonfiction. Vocabulary goes beyond the elemental and common and is increasingly unfamiliar, i.e., more than that learned from books in school.

- Stage 3B (Grades 7–8). Tasks and characteristics of Stage 3B are similar to those of Stage 3A, but the reader reacts more critically to the text than in Stage 3A [especially if encouraged to do so]. The language of texts becomes more complex in syntax and abstract in vocabulary. [Guided introduction to multiple-text and multimedia resources for greater variety of information should take place. Introduction to search strategies for location of relevant Web sites also is useful.]

- Stage 4 (High School). This stage is characterized by reading from multiple viewpoints. The reader must deal with more than one set of facts, theories, and viewpoints in arriving at a critical synthesis and analysis of the material. A broad range of materials is used [more open and free searching of the Internet is encouraged], including both expository and narrative writing. Topics and language are complex, specialized, literary, etc., including physical and biological sciences, humanities, and high quality and popular literature. Newspapers, [wide use of the Internet based on a selection criteria for quality Web sites and documents], and magazines provide divergent views.

- Stage 5 (College and beyond). The reader constructs knowledge on a high level of abstraction and generality. Past knowledge about the subject and broad general knowledge are needed for full comprehension of the text. The topics and language of the text are the most difficult, abstract, and general. This stage is characterized by wide reading [advanced searches of the Internet] of the most difficult materials [technical reports, plans and policies, legal and medical documents]. (149–150)

Textbook THIEVES

Suzanne Liff Manz (2002), from the Nassau Community College of New York, has summarized a strategy that helps students, elementary through college, skim and extract the key information from standard textbooks. This formula also has useful application to long encyclopedia entries and journal articles. Displayed here as a memory enhancer, the components of THIEVES are followed with useful questions from Manz to stimulate information processing.

T—Title. The title is the entry to a chapter. What do I already know about this topic? How does it relate to preceding chapters? What do I think I will be reading about?

H—Headings. A gateway to the important general subject areas within the chapter. What does the heading let me know I will be reading about? Can I turn this heading into a question that is likely to be answered in the actual content?

I—Introduction. Provides a framework for the chapter. Does the first paragraph introduce the chapter and give an overview of what I will be reading about? Do I know anything about this already?

E—Every first sentence in a paragraph. Preview by reading the first sentence of each paragraph. This may result in eliminating some portions of the text that do not seem to merit further examination.

V—Visuals and vocabulary. Perusing photographs, charts, graphs, maps, or tables provides a segue into reading. Is there narrative in the text to further explain the visuals? How do the captions help me better understand the meaning of the visual? Is there a list of key vocabulary terms and definitions? Are important words in bold type and defined? Do I know what these key words mean?

E—End-of-the-chapter questions. Study questions often will flag important points and concepts found within the text. What information do I learn from the questions? Where are potential answers to the questions located within the text?

S—Summary. Give attention to the conclusion of the chapter.

To this strategy must be added: What questions do I have that the text does not address to my satisfaction? In what manner might I verify opinions, facts, predictions, and conclusions offered by this text? Are there resources for further reading and more elaboration? How may I obtain additional information on some aspects of the text for which I am not clear or am curious?

References

Chall, J. S. (1983). *Stages of Reading Development.* McGraw-Hill.

Chall, J. S., and S. S. Conard. (1991). *Should Textbooks Challenge Students? The Case for Easier or Harder Textbooks.* Teachers College Press.

Harris, F. J. (2002). "There Was a Great Collision in the Stock Market: Middle School Students, Online Primary Sources, and Historical Sense Making." *School Library Media Research* 5. Available at http://www.ala.org/aasl/SLMR/ (accessed December 13, 2002).

Kirk, M., C. E. Matthews, and S. Kurtts. (2001). "The Trouble with Textbooks." *Science Teacher* 68 (9): 42–45.

Loewen, J. W. (1995). *Lies My Teacher Told Me: Everything Your American History Textbook Got Wrong.* Simon & Schuster Touchstone.

Manz, S. L. (2002). "A Strategy for Previewing Textbooks: Teaching Readers to Become THIEVES." *The Reading Teacher* 55 (5): 434–435.

Pray, K., and W. F. Rocheleau. (1906). *Home Study of History.* The Illinois Normal Academy.

Ravitch, D. (2004). *Language Police: How Pressure Groups Restrict What Students Learn.* Knopf.

Rice, D. C. (2002). "Using Trade Books in Teaching Elementary Science: Facts and Fallacies." *The Reading Teacher* 55 (6): 552–565.

Rice, D. C., A. P. Dudley, and C. S. Williams. (2001). "How Do You Choose Science Trade Books?" *Science and Children* 38 (6): 18–22.

Trofanenko, B. (2002). "Images of History in Middle-grade Social Studies Trade Books." *New Advocate* 15 (2): 129–132.

Woodward, A., D. L. Elliott, and K. C. Nagel. (1988). *Textbooks in School and Society.* Garland Publishing.

Time on Task

Daniel Callison

By the time the typical American student graduates from high school, he or she will have spent an average of 703,700 minutes or just over 12,000 hours in a classroom. Common-sense notions and some basic research studies lead to the obvious conclusion that students learn more when given more time to learn and when they spend that time actually engaged in academic tasks.

According to the American Association of School Administrators (1982), a "task" is a goal-oriented set of activities specifically intended to produce a particular learning outcome. Next to people, time is the school's most valuable resource. But it is nonrenewable. Once gone, it is gone. Generally defined for the educational field, "time on task" is that period of time during which a student is actively engaged in a learning activity. Time on task is closely related to other educational terms such as attention, performance, persistence, student behavior, and time management.

A simple conclusion is that time must be efficiently allocated in educational settings, much as time is managed in productive business and industry environments. Application, however, is not always so simple. There are many aspects to timing, integration, association, and level or order of tasks to provide the most effective engaging activities for learning. The product in education is the student who has mastered the process of learning. A wide variety of ability levels, resource support, and adult coaching are just some of the factors that add to the complexities of the business and industry called school.

Time Linked to Learning

Thirty years ago, John B. Carroll (1963) of the University of North Carolina outlined the basic factors that influence the distribution of time for learning. The amount of time needed to learn depends on

- **Aptitude**—not so much what the student is capable of learning, but the amount of time it takes the student to learn a particular fact or concept.

- **Ability**—the student's capacity to understand and incorporate the material based on prior learning.

- **Quality of Instruction**—the effectiveness with which the instruction is presented.

The amount of time actually spent learning depends on

- **Perseverance**—the steadfastness with which students devote themselves to learning the material.

- **Opportunity**—the time the teacher allows for learning and the number of chances the student is given.

Benjamin Bloom (1974), while at the University of Chicago, emphasized that students cannot perform well on a lesson unless they have spent sufficient time mastering the tasks that preceded that lesson. In Bloom's view, quality of instruction depends on four main factors:

- **Instructional Cues**—particular techniques the teacher uses to convey the content to be learned.

- **Reinforcement**—time for the attention and praise the teacher gives a student.

- **Participation**—time for students to become involved in the instruction.

- **Feedback and Correctives**—the information a teacher gives students to let them know if they are responding appropriately to the learning task.

Inherent in Bloom's approach is the relationship between amount of time spent and when time is spent:

- **Timing of Initial Instruction**—through formative testing to determine whether students are ready for the task.

- **Timing of Correctives**—checkpoints in order to determine if actions are needed to get students back on the right track or to intervene with remedial experiences if initial tasks have not been mastered.

- **Timing of Guided Practice**—which should follow the necessary correctives in order to reinforce learning.

- **Timing Student Progress**—so that achievements can be related to the next tasks in the progression or scaffold.

Capabilities of teachers that influence the efficient and effective use of time include the following:

- **Planning**—detailed specifications and guidelines the teacher develops for the classroom.

- **Implementation**—the translation of those plans into classroom strategies and activities.

- **Inducting**—motivating students and increasing their active learning and task involvement.

- **Communication Skills**—the ability to state instructions and expectations clearly.

Timing and Integration of Information Skills

Two factors that tend to be critical in the effectiveness of information skills instruction are:

- **Timing the instruction** to take place at the time-of-need, and

- **Placing the information**—use instruction within a meaningful context of personal interest or school subject assignment.

Several other factors noted above are also critical, but these two, timing and integration, seem to need much attention from those who teach school library media skills. Markel D. Tumlin (1993), from the University of San Diego, has documented some observations of the challenge of introducing new optical discs to the students searching his academic library. These observations have much relevance today to K–12 settings. According to Tumlin, "the skills needed to fully exploit the possibilities of optical products are much more sophisticated than those required to use print sources. Two hour-long class sessions are spent discussing all of the sorts of things that the professional literature on classroom instruction insists are important: Boolean logic, thesauri, database selection, etc. In addition, live demonstrations of actual searches are projected onto a large screen. However, with few exceptions, the students who become the best searchers are those who seek individual assistance after class. Spending some time one-on-one at the workstations helps them develop a better understanding of the systems. The two features of point-of-use [need] instruction most commonly mentioned in the professional literature are that it is useful and that it is time consuming" (217).

Tumlin also reports, "A common criticism of classroom bibliographic instruction is that faculty members schedule them early in the semester, assuming that some students may want to get an 'early start,' however, many students wait to get started on their papers, showing up weeks later having forgotten much of what they heard in the hour that was allotted for them to learn about the library" (218).

Thus, timing is critical in several ways for effective instruction in information access and use, regardless of age level:

- Time is necessary for hands-on practice during, or immediately following, the introduction of a new search method.

- Timing is key for application of method introduced within a meaningful search problem; for example, tied with the assignment that the student currently faces.

- Students are more likely to see relevance of information skills when there is staging of various steps in the information search and use process to coincide with point of need...as close as possible. In addition, successful teachers of information literacy skills don't frontload everything and expect students to retain and apply over an extended research assignment.

- Time for practice, reinforcement, and presentation of new skills is present throughout the duration of the process.

- Time for debriefing is important as it allows students to express and share the success and failures in their search for resources and information.

Creating the point of need for information skills is often associated with the integration of those skills with the content of a specific assignment from the classroom. Collaboration between the classroom teacher and the teacher of library media skills can enhance that integration and lead to precision in the timing of the presentation of specific search skills necessary and the introduction of resources relevant to the topic at hand. Ross Todd (1995) demonstrated how such timing in the integration of information skills with science content led to higher student performance scores at all ability levels, especially higher performance by the most academically advanced student group.

Time for the Task

Perhaps the most frustrating discussion for those experienced in the successful application of information skills and reading practice for learning is the struggle to convince teachers and administrators of the need to allot time for such tasks. Sometimes it seems that student learning is hampered most by schedules that simply move students from one room to another, or from one task to another, without time for concentration and reflection.

Evidence presented by Stephen Krashen (2004) is very convincing in favor of a simple allocation of time each day for everyone in the school (including teachers, administrators, and all staff) to give twenty to thirty minutes to sustained silent reading. The process works at all grade levels. Kept in place for at least a year or two, this time on task can lead to dramatic increases in reading scores and increased demands for more books for reading pleasure from the school library media center.

While some activities, such as school time allotted to reading for pleasure, can be the easiest to manage, they may be the most difficult to initiate. This simple task does not have the movements and actions associated with student engagement and practice educators can normally observe of students in the science lab, at the computer terminal, or in social issues debates. This task is silent, most effective when sustained, and leads to greater gains in learning when followed by engagement for student sharing of thoughts and reflections. There are situations, therefore, when time on task can be pleasurable as well as educational for all.

References

American Association of School Administrators. (1982). *Time on Task.* AASA.

Bloom, B. S. (1974). "Time and Learning." *American Psychologist* 29: 682–688.

Carroll, J. B. (1963). "A Model of School Learning." *Teachers College Record* 64: 723–733.

Krashen, S. (2004). *The Power of Reading.* 2d ed. Libraries Unlimited.

Todd, R. J. (1995). "Integrated Information Skills Instruction: Does It Make a Difference?" *School Library Media Quarterly* 23: 133–138.

Tumlin, M. D. (1993). "Time Management Considerations for Balancing Optical Disc Point-of-Use Instruction with Other Reference Services." *Microcomputers for Information Management* 10 (3): 215–226.

WebQuest

Annette Lamb

In the mid-1990s, educators began exploring ways to make effective use of the vast information resources rapidly emerging on the Internet. Rather than using these new web-based materials for low-level scavenger-hunt types of activities, school library media specialists sought ways to promote higher-order thinking through authentic assignments that emphasized Information Inquiry.

WebQuest Defined

In 1995, Bernie Dodge, Professor of Education from San Diego State University coined the term "WebQuest" to describe a particular type of inquiry-based activity that asks students to use web-based resources and tools to transform what they are learning into meaningful understandings and real-world projects. Most or all of the information used by learners is found on pre-selected Web sites. Rather than spending substantial time using search tools, WebQuests focus on using web-based information to analyze, synthesis, and evaluate information to address high-level questions.

Dodge distinguishes between short-term and long-term WebQuests. The goal of a short-term WebQuest is knowledge acquisition and integration, while in a long-term WebQuest learners analyze and transform knowledge into something that is understandable by others.

Dodge's model is similar to other Information Inquiry models. Critical attributes of a WebQuest include

- an introduction that sets the stage of the activity

- a doable, interesting task

- a set of information resources

- a clear process

- guidance and organizational frameworks

- a conclusion that provides reflection and closure.

Noncritical attributes included group activities, motivational elements, and interdisciplinary approaches.

First used at the university level, library-media specialists like Kathy Schrock, known for her popular *Kathy Schrock's Guide for Educators* (1996) Web site, quickly adapted the WebQuest approach for teaching and learning across grade levels.

Rarely has an educational approach gained so much attention. Many examples across content areas can be found at WebQuest.org (http://webquest.org). More than five million visitors have used the WebQuest page (http://webquest.sdsu.edu) at San Diego State University since 1998.

Multifaceted Approach

WebQuests are a learner-centered approach to teaching, learning, and Information Inquiry drawing on a variety of theories that include the following areas:

- constructivist philosophy
- thinking, understanding, and transformational learning
- authenticity and situated learning environments
- scaffolding
- differentiation
- cooperative learning
- motivation
- motivation, challenge and engaged learning

While working with Bernie Dodge at San Diego State University, Tom March created the first WebQuests for the K–12 environment. His well-known, early WebQuests included *Searching for China, Look Who's Footing the Bill!,* and *Tuskegee Study WebQuest.* March's Web sites BestWebQuests.com and Ozline.com contain resources to assist educators in using and developing web-based materials. He has found that well-designed WebQuests:

- promote dependable instructional practices
- combine research-supported theories
- make effective use of essential Internet resources
- produce open-ended questions
- offer authentic tasks
- motivate students
- allow students to develop expertise in a subject from within a situated learning environment
- offer opportunities for transformative group work.

A growing body of teacher action research, case studies, and experimental research points to the success of WebQuests as a rich instructional approach for promoting Information Inquiry (Hill et al. 2003).

WebQuests in the School Library Media Center

Library media specialists play an important role in the use of WebQuests by making certain that web-based materials are carefully selected to support information needs. In addition, they often collaborate with teachers in promoting student knowledge, skills, and attitudes needed to become effective users of information. For instance, Linda Picceri, a middle school library media specialist, developed a seventh grade oral history WebQuest titled *Historically Speaking* (2001). Students become historians, brainstorm questions, conduct interviews and collect artifacts, and share their findings.

According to Walter Minkel (2000), a former youth services librarian and technology editor for *School Library Journal,* since WebQuests combine traditional resources along with digital information resources, the school library is a logical focal point for WebQuest activities. For example, a middle-grade library became a mock science museum for a WebQuest project.

WebQuest development is time-consuming. Teacher librarians can save time by adapting existing resources. For instance, a dozen or more WebQuests based on the book Hatchet can be found on the Web. Rather than creating one from scratch, teacher librarians can combine elements from a few of the best sources, update Web links, and design additional assessment. WebQuests can also be modified by selecting resources at varied reading levels, creating in additional content, examining different perspectives, or incorporating multimedia elements such as audio or video clips.

Collaborative partnerships are an effective way to design, develop, and manage WebQuests. WebQuests naturally reach across curriculum areas, so library media specialists can often draw on content area, information, technology, and life skills standards when designing these technology-rich learning environments. Carol Truett, professor of Library Science at Appalachian State University, advocates school library media specialists working with language arts teachers. For example, her article "Sherlock Holmes on the Internet: Language Arts Teams Up with the Computing Librarian" (2001) demonstrates this type of collaboration through a WebQuest focusing on mysteries. WebQuests are also used in science and social studies. George Lipscomb (2002), professor of Education at Furman University, points out that students have a difficult time achieving historical empathy. Through a Civil War WebQuest incorporating role-playing and journal writing, eighth-grade students achieved varied degrees of historical empathy.

Literature-based WebQuests incorporate book(s) as a focal point for reading-centered, on-line learning activities. Emphasis may be placed on characters, plot, theme, setting, genre, or authors depending on the particular learning outcome. Teachers often combine WebQuests with the literature circle approach to reading.

WebQuests aren't just for students. For example, Joyce Valenza, a library media specialist in Pennsylvania, developed a WebQuest for media specialists to learn about school library media Web sites (2003).

WebQuests and Information Inquiry

Active, authentic use of information is at the core of the WebQuest philosophy. WebQuests require students to use a variety of authentic reading skills and strategies including skimming, scanning, and interpreting data. Dodge identified three domains to assist in developing web-enhanced, information-rich learning environments: inputs (i.e., articles, resources, experts and other information sources), transformations (i.e., high-level activities such as analysis, synthesis, problem solving and decision making), and outputs (i.e., products such as presentations, reports, and web publishing). He points out that students need scaffolding in each of these domains such as quality resource links, compelling problems, and production templates to assist in building understandings.

Over the past decade, Bernie Dodge has developed a number of tools and approaches to facilitate the development of inquiry-based activities. For example, the *Taxonomy of Information Patterns* (1998) was created to illustrate different ways that information could be visualized. Types of information patterns included cluster, hierarchy, Venn diagram, time line, flowchart, concept map, causal loop diagram, comparison matrix, and inductive tower. Educators can use the *WebQuest Taskonomy* (2002) to design a doable and engaging task that requires students to use information in thoughtful ways.

These tasks include retelling, compilation, mystery, journalistic, design, creative product, consensus building, persuasion, self-knowledge, analytical, judgment, and scientific.

Recently, Dodge introduced templates called *WebQuest Design Patterns* (2004) to streamline WebQuest design. Each design pattern focuses on a unique instructional purpose and can be adapted for different subject areas. For instance, the "time capsule" design pattern directs students to survey a time period and develop judgments about the relative importance of activities and products. Sample topics include an ancient Egyptian, Colonial, or decade time capsule. Other patterns include alternative history, analyzing for bias, ballot, behind the book, beyond the book, collaborative design, commemorative, comparative judgment, compilation, concept clarification, concrete design, exhibit, generic, genre analysis, historical story, in the style of . . . , meeting of the minds, on trial, parallel diaries, persuasive message, policy briefing, recommendation, teaching to learn, simulated diary, travel account, and travel plan.

Rather than writing an essay or making a speech for a teacher, quality WebQuests require students to connect their understanding of information to meaningful situations through original products for authentic audiences. The most effective WebQuest communication products provide students with opportunities to analyze, synthesize, and evaluate information and alternative perspectives.

Increasingly, teacher-librarians are finding students benefit from the development of WebQuests for a particular audience. Once students are shown the WebQuest format, they can easily build their own for others to use. Student WebQuest development can help students and teachers to think differently about Information Inquiry by asking them to design an inquiry project for others.

Library media specialists are under pressure to meet the needs of today's diverse learners. WebQuests provide an engaging, challenging learning environment for Information Inquiry for all ages.

References

Dodge, Bernie. (1995). *Some Thoughts about WebQuests.* Available at http://webquest.sdsu.edu/about_webquests.html (updated May 5, 1995).

Dodge, Bernie. (1998). *A Taxonomy of Information Patterns.* Available at http://projects.edtech.sandi.net/staffdev/tpss98/patterns-taxonomy.html (updated July 18, 1998).

Dodge, Bernie. (2002). *WebQuest Taskonomy: A Taxonomy of Tasks.* Available at http://webquest.sdsu.edu/taskonomy.html.

Dodge, Bernie. (2004). *WebQuest Design Patterns.* Available at http://webquest.sdsu.edu/designpatterns/all.htm.

Hill, J. R., D. Wiley, L. M. Nelson, and H. Han Seungyeon. (2003). "Exploring Research on Internet-based Learning: From Infrastructure to Interactions." In *Handbook of Research on Educational Communications and Technology,* edited by D. H. Jonassen. 2d ed. Association for Educational Communications and Technology.

Lamb, Annette, and Berhane Teclehaimanot. (2005). "A Decade of WebQuests: A Retrospective." In *Educational Media and Technology Yearbook,* Vol. 30, edited by M. Orey, J. McClendon, and R. M. Branch. Libraries Unlimited.

Lipscomb, George. (2002). "Eighth Graders' Impressions of the Civil War: Using Technology in the History Classroom." *Education, Communication & Information* 2 (1): 51.

March, Tom. (December 2003/January 2004). "The Learning Power of WebQuests." *Educational Leadership* 61 (4): 42–47.

Minkel, Walter. (2000). "Solar System WebQuest." *School Library Journal* 46 (11): 34.

Picceri, Linda. (2001). *Historically Speaking.* Available at http://wms.watertown.k12.ma.us/library/oralhistory/index.html.

Schrock, Kathy. (1996). "WebQuests in Our Future: The Teacher's Role in Cyberspace." *Kathy Schrock's Guide for Educators.* Available at http://web.archive.org/web/19970619021119/www.capecod.net/schrockguide/webquest/webquest.htm.

Schrock, Kathy. (2004). "WebQuests in Our Future: The Teacher's Role in Cyberspace." *Kathy Schrock's Guide for Educators.* Rev. ed. Available at http://kathyschrock.net/slideshows/webquests/frame0001.htm.

Teclehaimanot, Berhane, and Annette Lamb. (2004). "Reading, Technology, and Inquiry-Based Learning Through Literature-Rich WebQuests." *Reading Online* 7 (4) (March/April). Available at http://www.readingonline.org/articles/art_index.asp?HREF=teclehaimanot/index.html.

Truett, Carol. (2001). "Sherlock Holmes on the Internet: Language Arts Teams up with the Computing Librarian." *Learning & Leading with Technology* 29 (2) (October): 36–41.

Valenza, Joyce. (2003). *A WebQuest About School Library Web Sites.* Available at http://mciunix.mciu.k12.pa.us/~spjvweb/evallib.html.

Van Leer, Jerilyn. (2003). "Teaching Information and Technology Literacy Through Student-Created WebQuests." *Multimedia Schools* 10 (2) (March/April): 42–45.

Appendix A

Information Inquiry Assessment Rubrics

These are basic templates that can be modified and expanded according to the local learning environment and inquiry activity.

The Information Inquiry Interactions © 2003 Daniel Callison

The Professional as Instructional Media Specialist and Teacher of Inquiry

Basic 0 – 1 – 2 – 3	Progressive 4 – 5 – 6 – 7	Exemplary 8 – 9 – 10
Questioning: Reacts to student questions by locating relevant resources.	Proactive to extend and elaborate on student questions and helps cluster them by relationships of importance to need or task.	Interactive: listening and responding to others, to model and guide through extending and grouping of questions for focused inquiry leading to a meaningful investigation.
Exploration: Reacts to information needs through locally owned resources.	Proactive to extend and elaborate on the search for relevant information in various media in and out of school.	Interactive: learning and sharing with others, to examine closely the merits of resources and evidence discovered.
Assimilation: Reacts to supporting curriculum as designed by others.	Proactive to experiment within the standard curriculum and capitalize on local relevant resources.	Interactive: testing and experimenting, to accept or reject teaching methods and techniques that change the curriculum in order to address diverse student needs.
Inference: Reacts to application of information for learning within established curriculum.	Proactive to enrich the standard curriculum with access to many new and relevant resources.	Interactive: proposing and defending, to establish new curriculum that will best allow for effective use of technologies and resources.
Reflection: Reacts to review and evaluation of routine curriculum led by others.	Proactive to revise routine curriculum to fit needs of local learners.	Interactive: visible and responsive as a respected leader and educator, to provide evidence of successful student and teacher achievements. Promotes curriculum constructed to help students and educators practice effective and ethical use of information

© Daniel Callison, 2006

The Program for Information Inquiry Integrated Across the Curriculum

Basic 0 – 1 – 2 – 3	Progressive 4 – 5 – 6 – 7	Exemplary 8 – 9 – 10
Questioning: Supplements the routine questions raised in the classroom.	Programs are developed as learning units to enrich and extend classroom questions.	Questioning drives the learning and teaching agenda of the entire school.
Exploration: Addresses the extensions of classroom learning as determined by the teacher alone.	Media specialists and teachers collaborate as co-educators to identify learning activities enriched though use of multiple resources and technologies.	Educators and students collaborate to share in the exploration of academic, personal and professional information needs.
Assimilation: Develops and adapts information location and use activities to support classroom needs.	Learning units are designed on authentic learning needs as determined by collaborating educators.	Learning and teaching is student-centered in order to increase assimilation of knowledge and address relevant, authentic needs.
Inference: Derives student achievement based on standard exams and teacher imposed grades without consideration for inquiry achievements.	Student achievement is measured against standards that include specific personal growth, and application of inquiry processes.	Student progress and maturation in inquiry methods are valued and promoted above the basic standard measures of education and training.
Reflection: Programs and activities are adjusted to comply with standards determined by state and national agencies beyond the local schools.	Programs and activities are adjusted to extend inquiry across the curriculum and to enrich standards by making them more authentic and address local needs.	Inquiry is the curriculum and its merits are judged by a community of learners and teachers. Inquiry processes are enriched through collaborative information networks.

The Places for Inquiry, Exploration, Conversation, and Discovery

Basic 0 – 1 – 2 – 3	Progressive 4 – 5 – 6 – 7	Exemplary 8 – 9 – 10
Questioning: Students are encouraged to raise questions in school.	Relevant student questions are captured and displayed in written assignments, posters, bulletin boards, web sites and other school and library media center locations. Space is provided in the school and community to display the processes and products of student and teacher inquiry.	Space and time, in classrooms and media center facilities, are given for student and teacher discussions and debate concerning the most relevant questions for authentic learning matched to the needs and interests of the learners and teachers involved.
Exploration: Students have access to current and relevant resources in school.	Student and teacher access to current and relevant resources extends beyond the school to a community of experts and guided, informed, and yet open access to electronic documents.	The school library media center functions as an information network hub and facilitates links to community agencies, museums, archives, other libraries, human experts, and electronic discussions both local and world-wide.

Basic 0 – 1 – 2 – 3	Progressive 4 – 5 – 6 – 7	Exemplary 8 – 9 – 10
Assimilation: A school library media center is accepted and operated as a core location for relevant resources.	The concept of considering the merits of ideas and information is central to learning in all functional areas of the school with multiple resources and technologies readily available in the classroom as well as the school library.	Students and teachers openly display acceptance or rejection of information resulting from the exploration of resources. Such includes open critical literacy discussion groups, school and public posters and displays, web sites, and audio/video-casts.
Inference: Investments in the school library media center are viewed as investments in quality learning and teaching.	The access and open use of information is accepted as a concept across the school more so than a specific place.	Multiple locations are provided in the school and in the community in which learners may apply, in a constructive manner, information to addressing personal needs, academic and workplace needs, and social action.
Reflection: Revision, renovation and evaluation of the school media center facility and collection is a serious and regular activity in which key stakeholders participate extensively.	Teachers and learners judge the educational environment in terms of quality of information access and support for information examination to select the best information possible.	Information access and use is evaluated in terms of how such leads to improving the common good for the local educational learning environment and local community.

The Processes Accomplished by the Student or Teacher through Information Inquiry

Basic 0 – 1 – 2 – 3	Progressive 4 – 5 – 6 – 7	Exemplary 8 – 9 – 10
Questioning: Raises questions related to academic assignments and content in school texts.	Extends questioning to issues that include personal interests, local issues, and real world problems relevant to the academic curriculum. Student knowledge and ability form the basis for both the foundation and the potential elaboration through inquiry.	Defines questions in terms of proposition, thesis, or plan for change. Develops suitable arguments to be tested with methods that gather evidence from multiple perspectives. Defends merit of new questions regardless of standard academic relevance.
Exploration: Gains an understanding of personal perspective and basic knowledge of the issue through general background reading, viewing and interviews.	Formulates new questions and gains insights from a wide spectrum of information sources that broaden the learner's personal view on the issue. Resources are selected and obtained with mentor supervision and guidance.	Self-directs investigation into resources to address deeper understanding of arguments, claims and evidence. Gain suitable evidence through methods that include analysis of what is read, heard and observed through text, interviews and experiments.

Basic 0 – 1 – 2 – 3	Progressive 4 – 5 – 6 – 7	Exemplary 8 – 9 – 10
Assimilation: Accepts or rejects new information based on reason and fit to initial perspectives on the issue.	With guidance from mentors, strives to accept or reject new information based on logic, merits of evidence, and reasonable context for applying new knowledge.	Derives findings and conclusions that are based on analysis of argument and evidence that seem logical, understandable and of merit, and is able to clearly show changes from previous opinions.
Inference: Define meaning from new information assimilated to previous knowledge or perspective.	Define meaning based on examination and analysis of new information in as unbiased manner possible and with consideration for interpretations offered from mentors and peers.	Can defend new findings, observations, conclusions to various audiences in suitable method that provides clear communication and general understanding if not total acceptance and agreement. Makes clear, logical arguments justified with relevant evidence.
Reflection: Determines remaining information needs and the means to seek the information.	Determines, with input from mentors and peers, if information and evidence gained is adequate, and seeks to extend search and revise investigative methods if necessary.	Understands that one inquiry cycle leads to another and that issues and evidence can evolve over time. Values the investigative work that has given a foundation for future free inquiry on similar or new issues. Learns from success and failures in information access, use and evaluation to improve future inquiry.

The Production and Product of Information Inquiry

Basic 0 – 1 – 2 – 3	Progressive 4 – 5 – 6 – 7	Exemplary 8 – 9 – 10
Questioning: Raises the foundational questions on an issue and organizes them to provide clear communication.	Organizes questions in a manner that communicates issues and related information to a given audience.	Questions are addressed in an organized and clear manner and clearly lead to further questions in need of investigation by other inquirers.
Exploration: Clearly documents the resources (including human experts) explored and interviewed.	Identifies the key or essential resources of the inquiry that provided the most comprehensive coverage, or unique perspective, or most authoritative evidence.	Recommends most likely effective and/or efficient paths to gaining additional information on the subject in the future.
Assimilation: Shows information and evidence that confirms and/or counters initial perspective by using visuals that compare and contrast such findings.	Illustrates examples of new ideas, insights, perspectives gained that were not previously held prior to the inquiry.	Ranks or values the new ideas, insights, perspectives justified with visual, tangible examples of evidence to support arguments.

Basic 0 – 1 – 2 – 3	Progressive 4 – 5 – 6 – 7	Exemplary 8 – 9 – 10
Inference: Lists and illustrates conclusions.	Devises a plan with actions that will implement conclusions and illustrate a vision for that plan.	Implements a plan to bring about the conclusions, findings, or changes derived from the inquiry. Documents the plan and the results in a visual, audio and text record.
Reflection: Considers additional options for more information.	Revises plan and illustrations to best communicate vision to those who share interest and to those who are not aware of the recommendations.	Considers and implements various presentation formats in order to deliver the merits of the plan to different audiences and stakeholders.

The Portfolio of Information Inquiry Products Developed and Documented Over Time

Basic 0 – 1 – 2 3	Progressive 4 – 5 – 6 – 7	Exemplary 8 – 9 – 10
Questioning: Document growth and change in questions of interest over time.	Cluster questions by academic subject and grade level and highlight those of special meaning.	Analyze and synthesize the evolution and maturation of the questions raised over the span of your academic and personal experiences.
Exploration: Document growth and sophistication in abilities to search and locate information to meet changing needs.	Illustrate information search paths taken as a novice compared to more mature methods to seek and acquire needed information.	Analyze the growth and development in methods to obtain information through search, interview, observation, and experimentation and how these may be used to address future information needs in workplace and personal situations.
Assimilation: Document how new information, discussion, story, debate and other interactions with information and perspectives have added to your own feelings, knowledge base and abilities.	Identify specific inquiry experiences at different junctures in your academic experience that have resulted in dramatic changes in your thoughts and/or behavior.	Predict how the inquiry process will impact your future academic, professional and personal experiences.
Inference: List several insights derived from inquiry experiences over time.	Elaborate on several specific inquiry projects, each at a different time in your academic experience, and describe the key insights you gained from each.	Can adequately and convincingly address such questions as: In what manner will the ability to weigh the merits of information and evidence in order to help solve a problem or better inform you on an issue be of value to you in the future?
Reflection: What aspect of the inquiry process has been most valuable to you and what process has been of least value? Briefly tell why for each process.	What resources, what methods, and what mentors and/or peers were most helpful to you in your inquiry experiences? Illustrate specific examples.	What is lifelong learning? Relate your previous inquiry experiences to what you believe will be your likely practice of lifelong learning?

Appendix B
Information Inquiry Elements

Table B.1. Information Search, Use and Inquiry Models Charted for the Five Elements of Information Inquiry

	8 Ws	Big 6	ISP	I-Search	Pathways	Research Cycle	REACTS	Inquiry Process	Alberta Model
Questioning	**Watching** Become more in tune with the world **Wondering** Focus on topic or issue through questioning, finding focus, narrowing topic, and webbing	**Task Definition** What is the problem? What information is needed to solve the problem?—concept mapping and asking questions	**Initiation** Prepare for selection of topic by brainstorming **Topic Selection** Decide on topic through prereading	**Selecting a Topic** Introduce theme, elicit prior knowledge, choose a topic, generate questions	**Appreciation and Enjoyment** **Presearch** Develop an overview—brainstorm, formulate initial questions	**Questioning** Clarify and map out dimensions of essential question	**Recalling** Choose a broad topic and get an overview **Explaining** Narrow the topic from presearch and develop a thesis or purpose	**Connect** Connect to prior knowledge, gain background, establish an idea **Wonder** Develop questions and make predictions	**Planning** Establish topic and topic focus
Exploring	**Webbing** Create search strategy to identify useful information—key words, sources, add to Web	**Information Seeking Strategies** Determine range of sources and prioritize **Locate Sources** Locate sources and information in them. **Information Use** Engage with information	**Prefocus exploration** Investigate to find a focus and deeper understanding **Focus Formulation** Reading and organizing notes for themes	**Designing Search Plan** Different sources (read, watch, ask, do) and sequence to gather **Gathering and Integrating** Follow search plan	**Presearch** Develop an overview and explore relationships **Search** Identify information providers, select resources and tools, seek relevant information	**Planning** Best ways to organize and find information **Gathering** Finding info that is relevant and useful	Is my topic good? Does thesis represent overall concept? **Analyzing** Formulate questions to guide research, plan for research Do questions provide foundation? Is plan workable?	**Investigate** Plan investigation, identify sources, and find information	**Planning** Identify Sources, audience, presentation format, and establish evaluation criteria **Retrieving** Develop retrieval plan, locate and collect resources, and select relevant information
Assimilation	**Wiggling** Use and evaluate information **Weaving** Process information by reviewing results	**Information Use** Extract information What is important?	**Information Collection** Gather information that defines, extends, and supports **Search Closure** Identify need for more information, conclude search	**Gathering and Integrating Information** Sorting, categorizing, reflecting	**Interpretation** Compare/contrast, analyze, classify, filter	**Sorting and Sifting** Set aside data that will contribute to insight **Synthesizing** Looking for patterns and pictures	**Analyzing** Find/analyze/evaluate resources Are source usable/accurate? **Challenging** Evaluate evidence, take notes, compile bibliography Is research complete?	**Investigate** Find, evaluate, and record information **Construct** Organize information to construct relationships	**Retrieving** Select relevant information **Processing** Evaluate, select, and record information
Inference	**Wrapping** Select and develop product **Waving** Communicate with audience	**Synthesis** Organize and present information	Conclude search to prepare for writing from selected and focused notes	**Representing Knowledge** Convey information of product and process Engage in process of creation	**Communication** Apply information to a format and share knowledge	**Evaluating** Do I need more research for new questions before reporting?	**Transforming** Integrating, concluding Conclusions based on research? **Synthesizing** Creating original solutions to problem posed	**Construct** Draw inferences and conclusions and connect to prior knowledge **Express** Select, design, revise, and express conclusions	**Processing** Make connections and inferences **Creating** Organize information into a product and revise/edit product **Sharing** Present findings
Reflection	**Wishing** Assess product and reflect on process	**Evaluation** Judge product and process	Evaluate library search process, determine personal satisfaction		**Evaluation** Process and product			**Reflect** Reflect with others, ask new questions, and set new learning goals	**Evaluating** Evaluate product and inquiry process, transfer learning to new situations

Designed by Katherine Baker, technology teacher, Sycamore Elementary School and graduate student, Indiana University-Indianapolis. Reprinted with permission of Katherine Baker.

Table B.2. Information Inquiry Elements and the Big6 Model (Eisenberg and Berkowitz)

Information Inquiry Element	Big6	Element question	Focus	NETS / Activities
Questioning Raising the information need	Task Definition	Determine exactly what the problem is— What is the problem to be solved?	Provides focus to answering the question, "What is the problem?"	(Basic) Concept mapping and graphic organizers (6.1 NETS) (Advanced) Asking essential questions: (www.joycevalenza.com/questions.html) Ask essential questions to "promote deep and enduring understanding"
		Determine the specific information needs related to the problem— What information is needed in order to solve the problem?		
	Information Seeking Strategies	Determine range of sources— What are all possible sources?	Creates a search plan to answer, "How do I find out?"	Decide which reference sources are likely to provide information, inventory all the computer resources (Basic) Encourage students to use search directories when search engines become frustrating– lii.org, KidsClick9,1/!, Google directory; (Basic to Advanced) Evaluate Web sites (5.3 NETS)
		Prioritize sources— What are the best of all the possibilities?		
Exploring Reading, viewing, listening	Location and Access	Locate sources— Where are these sources?	Sorts the information to answer, "What have I got?"	(Basic) Key word searching that compares the results using several different engines; teach Boolean logic (5.1) (Advanced) Try metasearch engines; explore advanced features of search engines
		Find information— Where is the information within each source?		
	Information Use	Engage with information— What information does this source provide?		(2.2 NETS) (Basic) Determine accuracy, relevance, and comprehensiveness; create bibliographic citations—can use interactive Web tool (Advanced) Identify point of view
Assimilation Accepting, incorporating or rejecting	Information Use	Extract information— What specific information is worth applying to the task?	Select the information to answer, "What is important?"	Extract information using notes, copies, citations; outline major points (2.2 NETS) (Basic) Distinguish among summarizing, paraphrasing and quoting
Inference Application for solution and meaning	Synthesis	Organize information— How does the information from all sources fit together?		Can be as simple as relaying a specific fact; very complex involving several sources, a variety of media or presentation formats, and the effective communication of abstract ideas Create an outline; (3.2, 4.2 NETS) critical thinking (www.criticalthinking.org)
		Present information— How is the information best presented?		
Reflection Adjustment for additional questioning	Evaluation	Judge the product— Was the information problem solved?		Decide whether or not an assignment is finished; judge the product's effectiveness; judge the efficiency of the information problem-solving process: what techniques of note taking worked best, what would you do differently
		Judge the process— What have I learned?		

Table B. 3. Information Inquiry Elements and the Big6 Model (Eisenberg and Berkowitz)

Element	Stage	Purpose	Feelings	Strategies / Actions
Questioning Raising the Information Need	Stage 1—Task Initiation	To prepare for the decision of selecting a topic—recognize a need for information	Apprehension and uncertainty	Strategies: brainstorming, discussing, contemplating possible topics Actions: talking with others, browsing the library, writing out questions
	Stage 2—Topic Selection	To decide on topic for research—identify and select the general area or topic to be investigated	Confusion, anxiety, brief elation after selection, anticipation	Strategies: discussing possible topics, using general sources for overview of possible topics (prereading), read widely Actions: making preliminary search of library, using reference collection to seek background information in the general area of concern, read for overview
Exploring Reading, Viewing, Listening	Stage 3—Prefocus Exploration	To investigate information with the intent of finding a focus and extending personal understanding	Confusion, doubt, uncertainty	Students might be unable to always express precise information needed. Strategies: reading to learn about topic, intentionally seeking possible focuses or point of view, maintain list of key words Actions: locating relevant information, read to learn more about the topic, list facts, ideas, names, and events (look at recalling, summarizing, paraphrasing), making bibliographic citations of useful sources and potential leads
	Stage 4—Focus Formulation	To formulate a focus from the information encountered	Turning point where uncertainty diminishes and confidence increases	Thoughts become more clearly defined as a focused perspective of the topic is formed. Strategies: making a survey of notes, listing possible foci, choosing a particular focus while discarding others, combining several themes to form one focus Actions: reading and organizing notes for themes
Assimilation Accepting, Incorporating, Rejecting	Stage 5—Information collection	To gather information that defines, extends, and supports the focus	Confidence in ability to complete task increases, increased interest	Users have a clearer sense of direction and can specify the need for particular information. Strategies: using key works to search out pertinent information, making comprehensive search of various types of materials(reference, periodicals, nonfiction, etc.), seeking guidance Actions: taking detailed notes with bibliographic citations relevant to focus and research questions
Inference Application for Solution and Meaning	Stage 6—Search Closure/ Preparing to Present	To conclude search for information to prepare for presenting or writing	Sense of relief, satisfaction/ Disappointment	Strategies: returning to library to make summary, identifying need for any additional information, and exhausting resources Actions: rechecking sources for information initially overlooked, confirming information and bibliographic citations, organizing notes, and preparing to present findings
Reflection Adjustment for additional questioning	Stage 7—Assessing the Process	To evaluate the library research process	Sense of accomplishment or sense of disappointment	Strategies: draw a time line, write a summary statement, discuss with teacher Actions: seek evidence of focus, assess use of time, evaluate use of sources, reflect on use of librarian, identify problems and successes, plan research strategy for future assignments

Table B.4. Information Inquiry Elements and Pathways to Knowledge (Pappas and Tepe)

Information Inquiry Element	Pathway	Element	Description
Questioning Raising the Information Need	Appreciation and Enjoyment	Sensing, viewing, listening, reading, curiosity, enjoyment	
	PreSearch— establish a focus	Develop an overview	Brainstorm, formulate initial questions, build background, identify key words, relate to prior knowledge, explore general sources.
Exploring Reading, Viewing, Listening		Explore relationships	Define questions, cluster, outline, webbing, listing, and narrowing and broadening
			Provides searchers with strategies to narrow their focus and develop specific questions or define information need
			Makes a connection between their topic and prior knowledge
		Identify information providers	Home and computer resources, museums, zoos, historical sites, libraries, etc.
	Search— planning and implementing search strategy	Select information resources and tools	Indexes, people, Internet, media, reference resources, etc.
		Seek relevant information	Skim and scan, interview, confirm information and sources, record information, determine relevancy of information, explore and browse widely
Assimilation Accepting, Incorporating, Rejecting	Interpretation— Select and organize information to fit presentation format	Interpret information	Assessing usefulness of information and reflecting to develop personal meaning
			Compare and contrast, integrate concepts, determine patterns and themes, infer meaning, analyze, synthesize, classify, filter, organize, and classify
Inference Application for Solution and Meaning	Communication Construct and present new knowledge	Apply information	Choose appropriate communication format, solve a problem, answer a question, and respect intellectual property
		Share new knowledge	Compose, design, edit, revise, use most effective medium such as video, report, mural, portfolio, and animation
Reflection Adjustment for additional questioning	Evaluation Think about process and product	Evaluate	End product, effective communication, redefining new questions, use of resources, meeting personal information needs Evaluation is ongoing in their nonlinear information process and should occur throughout each stage. Through this continuous evaluation and revision process searchers develop the ability to become independent searchers.

Table B.5. Information Inquiry Elements and Macrorie's I-Search (adapted by Joyce and Tallman)

Inquiry Element	Phase	Teachers	Students
Questioning—Raising the Information Need	Phase 1—Selecting a Topic	**Teachers:** Introduce theme/overarching concepts OR student interest Elicit students' prior knowledge OR create an interest web and "What I knew before I started my I-Search" Help students build background knowledge—skim and scan for information Have students reflect on what they are learning OR choose a topic and reflect "Why I chose this topic" Help them find questions to pursue—"skinny" vs. "fat"	**Students:** Use a graphic organizer to begin formulating questions Send follow up letters to guest speakers to help them process information, generate new questions, and thank the speaker Computer simulations KWL charts
Exploring Reading, Viewing, Listening	Phase 2—Designing a Search Plan	**Teachers:** Guide students to develop a plan by discussing different sources for each of the four ways Introduce students to a process for citing and/or keeping track of materials and resources	**Students:** Develop a search plan that involves gathering information in four ways: reading, watching, asking, and doing—create a brainstorming chart for read, watch, ask, do Describe sequence for gathering information—create a calendar to illustrate what they will be doing during each class period
Assimilation Accepting, Incorporating, Rejecting	Phase 3—Gathering and Integrating Information	**Teachers:** Support students as they delve into content, form conceptualizations and gestalts, and think critically about what they are learning Introduce strategies to help them sort, create semantic maps, make categories, create charts and figures, draft summaries. Help students generate good, fat interview questions	**Students:** Follow search plan, revising as necessary Gather, sort, and integrate information Analyze and synthesize information to make meaning Write in their journals reflecting on the ups and downs of their search process Create Venn diagrams, idea maps, and categorize information
Inference Application for Solution and Meaning	Phase 4—Representing Knowledge	**Teachers:** Explain criteria for evaluation Give examples of possible ways to present information Give students time, a method, and support to produce a product that will represent what they have learned Create a reflection process	**Students:** Convey information about the following: My questions My search process What I have learned What this means to me References Prepare reports and projects through a variety of venues Engage in the process of designing, drafting, revising, editing, and producing or publishing their work

Table B.6. Information Inquiry Elements and the REACTS Process Model (Stripling and Pitts)

Information Inquiry Elements	REACTS Process Model	Steps	Reflection Point
Questioning— Raising the Information Need	**R**ecalling — Fact-finding; reporting on the information	Choose a broad topic / Get an overview of the topic	Calls on students to do preliminary reading and information seeking in anticipation of narrowing the topic, creating a thesis, and writing research questions.
	Explaining — Asking and Searching; posing who, what, when, where questions and finding the answers	Narrow the topic	Reflection Point: Is my topic a good one?
		Develop a thesis or statement of purpose	Reflection Point: Does my thesis statement of purpose represent an effective, overall concept for my research?
		Formulate questions to guide research	Reflection Point: Do the questions provide a foundation for my research?
Exploring Reading, Viewing, Listening	**A**nalyzing — Examining and organizing; posing why and how problems and organizing information to fit the product	Plan for research and production	Reflection Point: Is the research/ production plan workable?
		Find/analyze/evaluate resources	Reflection Point: Are my sources usable and adequate?
Assimilation Accepting, Incorporating, Rejecting	**C**hallenging — Evaluating and deliberating; judging information on the basis of authority, significance, bias, and other factors	Evaluate evidence/take notes/compile bibliography	Reflection Point: Is my research complete?
Inference Application for Solution and Meaning	**T**ransforming — Integrating and concluding; drawing conclusions and creating a personal perspective based on information obtained	Establish conclusions/organize information into an outline	Reflection Point: Are my conclusions based on researched evidence? Does my outline logically organize my conclusions and evidence?
	Synthesizing — Conceptualizing: creating original solutions to problems posed	Create and present final product	Reflection Point: Is my paper/project satisfactory?

Table B.7. Information Inquiry Elements and Research Cycle (McKenzie)

Questioning—Raising the Information Need		Questioning	Clarify and map out the dimensions of the essential question being explored	Brainstorming to form a cluster diagram of all related questions. Subsidiary questions will guide subsequent research efforts. Emphasize research questions that require problem solving or decision making—they are questions that cause students to make up their own minds and fashion their own answers.
Exploring Reading, Viewing, Listening		Planning	Think strategically about the best ways to find and organize pertinent and reliable information	Wise students will ask for help in this stage. If they use cluster diagramming for note taking they can simply attach their findings as notes to the relevant part of the diagram. Goal of planning is to create a storage system that will protect students from accumulating huge mountains of information in hundreds of poorly named files. Organization around key ideas, categories, and questions increases the likelihood that gathering will induce, provoke, and inspire thought.
		Gathering	Proceed to satisfying information sites swiftly and efficiently	Gathering only the information that is relevant and useful. Critically important that the findings are structured as they are gathered. It is also crucial that students only use the Internet when likely to provide the best information—in many cases other sources will prove more efficient and more useful.
Assimilation Accepting, Incorporating, Rejecting		Sorting and Sifting	Move towards more systematic scanning and organizing of data already collected	Much selecting and sorting should occur during the previous stage. This stage is to set aside data that will most likely contribute to insight.
		Synthesizing	Looking for patterns or some kind of picture	Students arrange and rearrange the information until patterns and pictures begin to emerge.
Inference Application for Solution and Meaning		Evaluating	Ask if they need more research before reporting	Timing of reporting and sharing of insights is determined by the quality of the "information harvest" during this stage. Students must usually complete several repetitions of the cycle because they usually don't know what they don't know when they first plan their research
		Reporting		

Table B.8. Information Inquiry Elements and the Ws of Information Exploration and Inquiry (Lamb)

Category	W	Element	Description	Sub-element	Details
Questioning Raising the Information Need	Watching	Exploring	Become more in tune with the world	Exploring/observing	Stop and enjoy—describe how you feel—diagram ideas
				Reading and viewing	Explore different sources including news—read for pleasure
				Writing	Journal writing to explore ideas
				Discussing	Collaboration for ideas/opinions—make a list of topics
				Contemplating	Explore the possibilities of your topics by reflecting on your feelings
	Wondering	Questioning	Focus on a topic, theme, issue, or problem	Finding purpose	What is the problem I need to solve? What is the question I want to ask?
				Questioning	List questions about your topic and possible key words—review questioning techniques
				Connecting prior knowledge	Connect ideas to prior knowledge including attitudes, experience, and knowledge through brainstorming—KWL chart—help identify what you actually need to find out
				Finding focus	Organize ideas (graphic organizer) for a focus
				Narrowing topic	Making it more manageable—view large project in smaller chunks—assign roles in groups—create meaningful questions
				Contemplating	Select and reflect on a topic
Exploring Reading, Viewing, Listening	Webbing	Searching	Create a search strategy for identifying useful information	Plan a search strategy	Analyze questions to determine best approach to information webbing, identify types of information that would be useful, select resource formats
				Identify key ideas	Think about key words and headings to use in search—use who, what, when, where, why, and how
				Use starting points	3–5 resources to get kids started; "pathfinders"—provides background information
				Web information	Add strands to your web of information
	Wiggling	Evaluating	Use and evaluate information resources	Using information resources	Reception scaffolds, skimming and scanning, filtering information
				Evaluating information	Evaluate information for authority, accuracy, currency, etc.
				Communicating/collaborating	Identifies holes in your thinking, can involve an expert, not just peers
Assimilation Accepting, Incorporating, Rejecting	Weaving	Synthesizing	Process information	Processing information	Concept mapping, comparing information, selecting useful information, organizing and clustering key ideas, analyzing
				Reviewing the results	Have questions been addressed? Do you need to evaluate new questions? Are there holes?
				Citing sources	Teach bibliographies, online wizards—understand plagiarism/copyright laws
Inference Application for Solution and Meaning	Wrapping	Creating	Select and develop a product	Choose a product	Product options, start with audience
				Plan a product	Create production scaffolds, storyboards, guidelines
				Develop a product	Technology tutorials
	Waving	Communicating	Communicate with an audience	Identify audience	Who needs to hear, see, or read about your ideas?
				Communicate	How will you share your ideas with your audience?
Reflection Adjustment for additional questioning	Wishing	Assessing	Assess project and reflect on process	Product	Rubrics, teacher and student assessment
				Process	Reflective questions: What would you do next time?

Table B.9. Information Inquiry Elements and the Portfolio of Information Skills (outlined by Callison)

Inquiry Element	Question	Portfolio of Information Skills
Questioning Raising the information need	What do I need to do?	• Analyze the information task • Analyze the audience's information need or demand • Describe a plan of operation • Select important or useful questions and narrow or define the focus or the assignment • Describe possible issues to be investigated
Exploring Reading, viewing, listening	Where could I go?	• Determine the best initial leads to relevant information • Determine possible immediate access to background information (gaining the larger picture) • Consider information sources within and beyond the library
	How do I get the information?	• Identify relevant materials • Sense relationships between information items (supporting or countering each other; one leading to others based on sources cited) • Determine which resources are most likely to be authoritative and reliable • Consider and state the advantages and disadvantages of bias • Consider discovered facts and search for counter facts • Consider opinions and look for counter opinions • Determine extent of need for historical perspective
Assimilation Accepting, incorporating, rejecting	How shall I use the resources?	• Determine if the information is pertinent to the topic • Estimate the adequacy of the information • Test validity of information • Group data in appropriate categories according to appropriate criteria
	Of what should I make a record?	• Extract significant ideas and summarize supporting, illustrative details • Define a systematic method to gather, sort, and retrieve data • Combine critical concepts into a statement of conclusions • Restate major ideas of a complex topic in concise form • Separate a topic into major components according to appropriate criteria • Sequence information and data in order to emphasize specific arguments or issues
Inference Application for solution and meaning	Have I got the information I need?	• Recognize instances in which more than one interpretation of material is valid and necessary • Demonstrate that the information obtained is relevant to the issues of importance if necessary, state a hypothesis or theme, and match evidence to the focused goal of the paper or project • Reflect, edit, revise, and determine if previous information search and analysis steps should be repeated
	How should I present it?	• Place data in tabular form using charts, graphs, or illustrations • Match illustrations and verbal descriptions for best impact • Note relationships between or among data, opinions, or other forms of information • Propose a new plan, create a new system, interpret historical events, and/or predict likely future happenings • Analyze the background and potential for reception of ideas and arguments by the intended audience • Communicate orally and in writing to teachers and peers
Reflection Adjustment for additional questioning	What have I achieved?	• Accept and give constructive criticism • Reflect and revise again, and again if necessary • Describe the most valuable sources of information • Estimate the adequacy of the information acquired and judge the need for additional resources • State future questions or themes for investigation • Seek feedback from a variety of audiences

Table B.10. Information Inquiry Elements and the Inquiry Process (Stripling)

Inquiry Element	Inquiry Process	Skills	Learning Strategies	Teaching Strategies
Questioning — Raising the information need	Connect	Connect to own experiences	Activate prior knowledge	Learning logs, reading/writing workshop, conversations, and K-W-L charts
		Connect to ideas of others		
		Connect to previous knowledge and verify its accuracy		Concept maps
		Gain background and context	Develop an overview of areas of interest	
		Establish an idea through observation and experience		
	Wonder	Develop wonder questions that will lead to new understandings about key ideas	Frame questions using prior knowledge and different levels of thinking including "why" and "how" in addition to asking "what"	Class brainstorming, peer questioning, question stems
			Develop questions that lead to active investigation and decision making, not passive information gathering ("What would happen if . . .")	
		Make predictions and hypotheses	Predict answers to questions and type of information needed	Guide anticipation
Exploring — Reading, viewing, listening	Investigate	Plan investigation and develop search strategies	Consider types of sources, information, and search terms	
		Identify, evaluate, and use multiple sources of information	Use criteria to evaluate all sources, including comprehensiveness, point of view, quality, authoritativeness, and currency	Model use of strategies with read-aloud, inquire-aloud, and guided practice
Assimilation — Accepting, incorporating, rejecting		Find and evaluate information to answer questions	Summarize, interpret, and evaluate main ideas, supporting/conflicting evidence, and point of view; select information to keep or discard	
		Take notes using a variety of formats	Graphic organizers, reading response journals, two-column note taking	
		Formulate new questions or hypothesis		
		Organize information to form relationships among ideas	Organize ideas and extract meaning using graphic organizers	Provide various graphic organizers with different types of comparisons
		Draw inferences justified by collected evidence	Interpret meaning of text by finding patterns and relationships, using the text to support inferences	Questioning: teacher-to-student, student-to-teacher, student-to-student
		Compare and connect evidence to test predictions		
		Recognize points of view, bias, and consider alternatives if necessary		
Inference — Application for Solution and meaning	Construct	Construct clear and appropriate conclusions based on evidence, inferences, and connections	Compare conclusions to hypothesis to generate new understandings	Evidence that supports/evidence that refutes: new explanations
		Connect new understanding to previous knowledge	Compare new ideas to ideas previous held	Record, elaborate, extend
	Express	Select communication format based on topic and audience	Select an organizational pattern for format: comparison, chronology, criticism, and justification of thesis	
		Develop, evaluate, and revise own product based on self-assessment and feedback from others	Use writing process to develop product (prewrite, draft, revise, edit, publish) in any format	Writers' workshop, use of rubrics, peer/teacher conferencing
		Express new ideas or take action to share learning with others		
Reflection — Adjustment for additional questioning	Reflect	Set high standards	Use rubrics and feedback from peers and teacher to assess own work	
		Reflect with others		
		Ask new questions	Reflect on own learning	Reflection log: I used to think/but now I know
		Set new goals for learning through future inquiry		Portfolio reflections

Table B.11. Information Inquiry Elements and the Alberta Inquiry Model (Alberta Learning 2004)

		Inquiry Skills and Strategies	Process Assessment
Questioning Raising the information need	Planning	Establish Topic and Topic Focus	Students create an information pathfinder, step by step plan for gathering resources.
		Identify Information Sources	Students write or talk about their perceived needs for their intended audience.
		Identify Audience and Presentation Format	Students write or talk about their own inquiry process and compare it with the process of others in the class.
Exploring Reading, viewing, listening	Retrieving	Establish Evaluation Criteria	
		Develop Information Retrieval Plan	Students discuss strategies to fill gaps in their information retrieval.
		Locate Resources	Students write or talk about their retrieval strategy and what worked/didn't work.
		Collect Resources	Students write or talk about the sources they found most useful and why.
		Select Relevant Information	
Assimilation Accepting, incorporating, rejecting	Processing	Evaluate Information	Students show and discuss graphic organizers they have created and discuss which have been more appropriate to their inquiry.
		Choose Pertinent Information	Students evaluate Internet sites using a rubric or evaluation checklist.
		Record Information	Students write or talk about which resources were most useful for a deeper understanding of their topic and why.
		Make Connections and Inferences	Students write and talk about why they are creating ideas new to them and how they are linking those ideas to previous knowledge.
			Students write and talk about what new questions, problems, issues, and ideas that have emerged.
Inference Application for solution and meaning	Creating	Organize Information	
		Create Product	
		Think About Audience	
		Revise and Edit	
		Understand Audience	Students write or talk about their reasons for sharing their new knowledge in a particular way.
	Sharing	Present Findings	Students write and talk about the ways they focused on the needs of their particular audience.
		Demonstrate Appropriate Behavior	Students write and talk about what went well with their sharing and what things they need to improve on.
			Students write or talk about the experiences of being in an audience—what were positive/negative and why.
Reflection Adjustment for additional questioning	Evaluating	Evaluate Product	
		Evaluate Inquiry Procedures	
		Transfer Learning to New Situations, Including Beyond School	

Table B.12. Information Inquiry Elements and the model for Student Inquiry in the Research Process (Preddy)

Information Inquiry Elements	Model for Student Inquiry (Preddy)	Description	Skills
Questioning Raising the information need	Orientation — Build a foundation—a common point of reference for the topic. Activate prior knowledge	Brainstorm—what is already known about the general topic. Research (Kuhlthau)—Practice research tasks and skills. Improve basic research skills. Begin to narrow topic focus to personal interests	Skills: Brainstorming, Skimming and Scanning for Information, Categorizing, Basic Questioning, Research Journal/Organizational Tools
	Exploration — Question development—Student takes a leadership role in what will be learned and researched through ownership of question development.	Basic Questioning—begin questioning process. What makes me curious about the topic? What questions do I have? Why did I choose this topic? Burning Questions—narrowing and prioritizing questions	Skills: Reading for Clues, Research Question Help (complex questioning), Burning Questions
	Strategy — Strategic questions—Becoming aware of the information	Critical Questions—What are the most important and critical of the burning questions? Key words—Words related to the final, critical questions. Source Selection—Selecting appropriate resources for each question	Skills: Strategy (questions, key words, sources), Source Types
Exploring Reading, viewing, listening		Source Notes—Taking effective research notes. Reading for Understanding—Analyzing accuracy of information. Reflection—Evaluating the day's experience	Skills: Reading for Understanding, Note Taking, Interview, Primary Sources, Community Resources, Qualitative/Quantitative Data Collection (surveys, questionnaires), Reflection
Assimilation Accepting, incorporating, rejecting	Investigation — Research—Attempting to find answers to strategic questions	Source Usefulness—How to know if this source is useful for my needs. Source—Personal opinion and summarizing	Skills: Source Usefulness, Source Summary, Source Evaluation, Reflection
Inference Application for solution and meaning		Dissemination—Evaluating best way to share what has been learned. Peer Conference—Advice from peer for improving research and product plan. Peer Evaluation—Advice for improving peer's research and product plan	Skills: Product Options, Dissemination, Peer Conference, Peer Evaluation, Reflection
		Organizing Notes—Organizing and evaluating source notes for need and value. Storyboard—Formulating a plan for sharing knowledge. Final Product—Sharing knowledge through product, presentation, and display	Skills: Organizing Notes, Storyboard, Presenting Findings
Reflection Adjustment for additional questioning	Conclusion and Reflection — Organization and presentation of information and reflection of research experience	Annotated Bibliography—Citing, describing and evaluating sources. Peer Evaluation—Evaluating peer's Final Product. Self-Evaluation—What did I learn? What did I do well? What can I do better next time? Student Evaluate Educators/Process—What could the educators do better next time?	Skills: Annotated Bibliography, Evaluation (self, process, peer, educators) Appendix A-16

Designed by Leslie Preddy, library media specialist, Perry Meridian Middle School, Indianapolis.

Appendix C
Key Words in Instruction

Published in School Library Media Activities Monthly 1997–2006
The column will continue on a regular basis after 2006.
Designed for instructional media specialists K–12.

Achievement testing

Several studies have examined the relationship between school library media programs and student achievement. These studies reveal a long history of relatively strong links between school library media programs and higher student achievement in reading and other skills. However, although these findings are encouraging, it should be remembered that they are, at best, based on association, and it should be remembered that strong cause-and-effect evidence remains difficult to establish. (*School Library Media Activities Monthly* 18 no. 2 (October 2001): 39–42)

Analogy

A discussion of the use of the analogy in learning is presented. Analogies are often used by good teachers to make unfamiliar matters understandable to their students. The purpose of analogies is to allow correlated information to be charted from a source known to the learner onto one that is not known. Examples of different types of analogies and the ways in which they can be used are provided. (*School Library Media Activities Monthly* 16 no. 4 (December 1999): 35–37+)

Analysis

The writer discusses the term analysis, which stresses the breakdown of material into its constituent parts and the way those parts may be related. He contrasts analysis and synthesis, defines analysis as an aid to fuller comprehension or as a prelude to and evaluation of material or information, discusses the three basic clusters into which the analysis process can be classified, and considers analysis task questions at several task levels. (*School Library Media Activities Monthly* 15 no. 8 (April 1999): 37–39)

Anchored instruction

Anchored instruction enables children, many of whom may have learning disabilities, to view video and animated adventures on CD-ROM. Teachers use these adventures to organize lessons that assist students in selecting a challenging topic, finding out what it means, and communicating this information to their peers, teachers, and families. Nine steps that must be facilitated by information specialists for anchored instruction are outlined. (*School Library Media Activities Monthly* 13 (March 1997): 30–31)

Assignment

The writer discusses assignments that are designed to engage students in information retrieval and use and research in the library. He describes the characteristics of effective library-based assignments, presents some assignment ideas, and lists questions that focus on the research process. He also discusses the pitfalls of assignments. (*School Library Media Activities Monthly* 17, no. 1 (September 2000): 39–43)

Annual report

Advice for school library media specialists on producing annual reports is presented.(*School Library Media Activities Monthly* 20, no. 3 (November 2003): 40–42, 45)

Audience analysis

The writers discuss audience analysis, which involves the processes of gathering and interpreting information about the recipients of oral, written, or visual communication. They discuss audience analysis in relation to information inquiry and curriculum standards and explore audience analysis in teaching and learning. The writers then examine the importance of authentic audience, audience identification, audience needs assessment, and audience analysis techniques. They also consider the need to adjust style to the audience and discuss authentic assignments and audience. (*School Library Media Activities Monthly* 21, no. 1 (September 2004): 34–39)

Authentic assessment

Authentic assessment is based on the assumption that a much wider spectrum of student performance can be displayed than what is displayed by limited short-answer standardized tests. Techniques include performance assessment, portfolios, and self-assessment. The role of school library media specialists in the development and implementation of authentic assessment is outlined. (*School Library Media Activities Monthly* 14, no. 5 (January 1998): 42–43+)

Authentic learning

The writers explore how teachers of information inquiry can create authentic learning environments. After outlining a number of signs that teachers of information inquiry are reaching levels of learning that can be identified as authentic, the writers discuss authentic achievement, authentic assignments, authentic resources, authentic communications and audiences, authentic assessment, and authentic learning and information inquiry. (*School Library Media Activities Monthly* 21, no. 4 (December 2004): 34–39)

Bias

Information and advice on teaching about bias in resources are provided. Characteristics of confirmation bias, media bias, and belief perseverance are described, and ways of addressing such bias are presented. (*School Library Media Activities Monthly* 21, no. 5 (January 2005): 34–36)

The Brain

Information on some fundamental facts about the human brain and new research results about the growth and development of the brain is provided. Understanding these facts and being aware of these research findings may lead library media specialists to reconsider the best methods of introducing and enhancing information literacy skills. (*School Library Media Activities Monthly* 17, no. 7 (March 2001): 35–38)

Chautauqua: free-inquiry and free-choice learning

An overview of some nontraditional key terms in instruction is provided. This overview focuses on the free-learning model of the Chautauqua Institute, informal learning, questions and inquiry, free-inquiry learning, choice in the library media center, free-choice learning, and the contextual model for learning. (*School Library Media Activities Monthly* 20, no. 1 (September 2003): 33–8)

Cognitive apprenticeship

The cognitive apprenticeship approach to information problem solving and information literacy instruction is discussed. Cognitive apprenticeship gives students the opportunity to observe experts and practice tacit skills and knowledge while receiving expert guidance. (*School Library Media Activities Monthly* 18, no. 3 (November 2001): 37–38, 48)

Collaboration

Collaboration, one of the most frequently used words in the national guidelines for school library media programs, is looked at in a wider context, in order to extend its meaning and application. Reviews of research on cognitive styles and collaboration and schedules and collaboration, some strategies for successful collaboration, and some communication techniques that help teachers of information literacy to identify areas for close collaboration efforts are presented. The difference between collaboration, coordination, and cooperation is also explained. (*School Library Media Activities Monthly* 15, no. 5 (January 1999): 38–40)

(Computer vocabulary) More than activities—hopefully a language of ideas

The writer lists and defines several sets of selected terms that may better help any educator communicate with the digital-savvy student clientele. (*School Library Media Activities Monthly* 22, no. 1 (September 2005): 38–42.

Concept mapping

The writer discusses concept mapping, a heuristic device that has proven to be useful in helping learners to visualize the relationships or connections between and among ideas. (*School Library Media Activities Monthly* 17, no. 10 (June 2001): 30–32)

Constructivism

The writer considers constructivism, a theory about the nature of reality and how people understand the world around them. According to constructivists, people make or construct their own knowledge based on their own experiences. From this perspective, learning potential is considered to be relative to the factors involved in a given learning environment and to those experiences and expectations brought to the situation by both the learner and the teacher. The writer considers constructivist assumptions about learning and the actions that define the constructivist teacher. (*School Library Media Activities Monthly* 18, no. 4 (December 2001): 35–38, 51)

Content literacy

The writer discusses content literacy in reading. He describes content literacy expertise, thematic approaches to content literacy, and a content literacy cross-curriculum sample. (*School Library Media Activities Monthly* 16, no. 3 (November 1999): 38–39+)

Cooperative learning

There is a growing awareness of the merits of cooperative learning in situations where students must deal with multiple resources, address a variety of issues, and present information using a variety of formats. Assignments that demand multiple resources have a tendency to result in richer processes and products from groups of individuals who share a variety of skills than from most students who face such assignments individually. Four approaches to cooperative learning are outlined. (*School Library Media Activities Monthly* 14, no. 3 (November 1997): 39–42

Creative thinking

The writer examines creative thinking. Provides examples of how creative thinking is also part of information literacy and compares creative thinking to critical thinking. (*School Library Media Activities Monthly* 15, no. 4 (December 1998): 41–44+)

Critical thinking

The writer discusses critical thinking in relation to modern instructional programs and information literacy with some comparison to creative thinking. (*School Library Media Activities Monthly* 15, no. 3 (November 1998): 40–42)

Critical literacy

Information on critical literacy is provided. The information relates to critical literacy, discussion and debate about critical literacy, formal debate about critical literacy, and jurisprudential inquiry. (*School Library Media Activities Monthly* 16, no. 9 (May 2000): 34–36)

Currentness

The writer discusses the importance of weeding out-of-date collections to ensure that students have access to current and timely information. He considers some aspects of the currency problem, discusses some of the content that is missing from out-of-date materials, outlines the problem of students' lack of sensitivity to age when selecting materials, and describes useful instructional exercises that can be developed from a few selected science titles that have been weeded from the collection. (*School Library Media Activities Monthly* 15, no. 1 (September 1998): 37–39)

Digital divide

Recent research has revealed that although the digital divide has narrowed in some areas, new gaps are emerging and expanding. Findings from surveys of computer and Internet use by children and adolescents, Internet access in public schools, the generational digital divide, and the growing digital divide between college students and their professors are discussed. (*School Library Media Activities Monthly* 20, no. 6 (February 2004): 37–40, 51)

Experiential learning

Experiential learning can provide dramatic learning opportunities in school library media programs. Two theories of experiential learning, teachers as role models and mentors, the case for experiential learning as the foundation for what library student assistants might accomplish for themselves and others, the student assistant as reviewer and selector, and the importance of tasks that are meaningful to students are discussed. (*School Library Media Activities Monthly* 20, no. 2 (October 2003): 36–39)

Facilitator

Teachers of school library media and information literacy need to know how to facilitate instruction. They must know how to collaborate in planning, intervene and mediate during instructional implementation, and constructively give feedback for the purposes of evaluation. Mediation and intervention actions are discussed. (*School Library Media Activities Monthly* 14 (February 1998): 40–42)

Free inquiry

(Chautauqua: Information, Free-Inquiry and Free-Choice Learning)—An overview of some nontraditional key terms in instruction is provided. This overview focuses on the free-learning model of the Chautauqua Institute, informal learning, questions and inquiry, free-inquiry learning, choice in the library media center, free-choice learning, and the contextual model for learning. (*School Library Media Activities Monthly* 20, no. 1 (September 2003): 33–38)

Gender

The writers review the research on the achievement of girls in comparison to boys. The research indicates that, on average, girls have more exposure to early literacy activities, obtain higher scores on standardized tests, have a more positive attitude toward reading, and spend more time interacting with printed materials. However, these gender-based differences turn out to be minor in comparison to differences found by ethnicity or income. The writers conclude by providing advice to instructional media specialists on motivating all readers, irrespective of gender. (*School Library Media Activities Monthly* 21, no. 10 (June 2005): 33–36)

Grants

Information and advice about grants for school library media professionals is provided. This information and advice relates to grants and how to find them, how to make a basic grant application, features of successful grant applications, how to craft a successful grant proposal, and grant writing resources. (*School Library Media Activities Monthly* 20, no. 9 (May 2004): 36–39)

Illustrations

The writer discusses the value of using illustrations with students to convey information and increase understanding. He discusses visual literacy, offers guidelines for using illustrations, discusses the importance of using visuals to convey information, and describes illustrations that instruct. (*School Library Media Activities Monthly* 16, no. 8 (April 2000): 34–36, 42)

Information fluency

A broad definition of information fluency is provided. Combining current ideas about fluency as they relate to information inquiry, this definition demonstrates how information fluency encompasses a wide range of skills and abilities across several literacy areas. (*School Library Media Activities Monthly* 20, no. 4 (December 2003): 38–39)

Information inquiry

The components of information inquiry are questioning, exploration, assimilation, inference, and reflection. These components link the essential methods that both teachers and learners must practice in order to meet fundamental information and media literacy skills. Information inquiry can result in learners who are fluent in selecting and applying methods to address their information needs when it is integrated with academic content areas across the curriculum and supported by the knowledgeable use of modern information technologies. (*School Library Media Activities Monthly* 18, no. 10 (June 2002): 35–39)

Information and media literacies

The writers examine information literacy and media literacy and demonstrate the potential for dynamic interaction between the two literacies that can lead to a richer application of both approaches and, ultimately, greater student success. (*School Library Media Activities Monthly* 15, no. 2 (October 1998): 25–28+)

Instructional media specialist

The writer offers an insight into the many facets and duties of the instructional media specialist. (*School Library Media Activities Monthly* 18, no. 9 (May 2002): 36–40, 45)

Inquiry

School library media centers exist as learning centers because of inquiry. Inquiry can be viewed as controlled inquiry, guided inquiry, modeled inquiry, or free inquiry. Concepts of inquiry and information literacy relating to past and current emphasis areas, the National Council of Teachers of English 1996 standards that relate directly to the inquiry process, and Edward Victor's elements of inquiry learning for science and education are discussed. (*School Library Media Activities Monthly* 15, no. 6 (February 1999): 38–42)

Integrated instruction

The writer discusses integrated instruction between a librarian and a regular teacher. He focuses on the history of course-related integrated instruction, isolated and individual instruction, why integrated instruction is more powerful than instruction in parallel, independent inquiry, inquiry and the learning academy, immersion, and the challenges to integrated instruction. (*School Library Media Activities Monthly* 17, no. 5 (January 2001): 33–39)

Interview

Interviewing is a skill that teachers can introduce very early in a child's academic experience. Strategies for successful interviewing, whether face-to-face questioning or e-mail and written correspondence, must be practiced and refined. The problems that some students may have conducting interviews are listed, and several techniques for effective interviewing are provided. (*School Library Media Activities Monthly* 15, no. 7 (March 1999): 40–41+)

Knowledge management

The writer discusses knowledge management and the school library media specialist's role in this area. He also discusses electronic learning collaborations, the role of the future instructional media specialist, the areas of global thinking and critical thinking in information literacy, and the implications of global relations and critical thinking for the future development of collections and connections. (*School Library Media Activities Monthly* 16, no. 7 (March 2000): 37–39, 45)

Learning laboratory

Although much has changed during the 40 years since school library media centers were likened to laboratories for research and study, the analogy is still pertinent today, particularly in relation to modern technologies for information search and presentation and learning environments that promote constructivist and open inquiry methods. (*School Library Media Activities Monthly* 17, no. 4 (December 2000): 33–37, 44)

Learning resources

Advice on collection development and resource management is provided. A set of very selective knowledge content areas organized by school levels that illustrates sample target areas for learning resource in-depth collections is presented. (*School Library Media Activities Monthly* 19, no. 9 (May 2003): 33–38)

Lesson plan

Advice is provided on collaborative lesson planning between instructional media specialists and other teachers. (*School Library Media Activities Monthly* 18, no. 1 (September 2001): 35–41)

Literacy

An overview of the meaning and dynamics of literacy is presented. The overview covers the multitude of literacies, emergent literacy, representative types of literacy, and assessment in authentic literacy exercises. (*School Library Media Activities Monthly* 16, no. 6 (February 2000): 36–39)

Literature circles

Advice for school library media specialists on implementing literature circles is provided. The advice relates to aligning literature circles with standards, regarding literature circles as opportunities for collaboration, implementing and facilitating a literature circle for teachers, securing funding for literature circle resources, and using literature circles to promote information literacy, independent learning, and social responsibility. (*School Library Media Activities Monthly* 20, no. 7 (March 2004): 39–43)

Mental models

The writer discusses "mental modeling"—the term used in discussions about students' abilities to visualize or comprehend the demands of the information research process. He describes the behaviorist, cognitivist, and constructivist perspectives; considers the three mental model descriptions—the management, navigation, and organization mental models—that correspond to the three levels of knowledge used to represent domain specific skills required for success in the use of computer programs; and discusses research related to why students make the decisions they make when seeking and using information.(*School Library Media Activities Monthly* 14 (December 1997): 37–39+)

Metacognition

Strategies for developing metacognitive behavior are discussed. They relate to deciding on baseline knowledge, talking about thinking, paired problem solving, keeping a thinking journal, planning and self-regulation, debriefing the thinking process, and self-evaluation. The implications for the timing and structure related to teaching information skills are discussed. (*School Library Media Activities Monthly* 14, no. 7 (March 1998): 43–44)

Models

Information on student-centered and student-created instructional models is provided. This information relates to a student-centered instructional model created by David V. Loertscher and Blanche Woolls, a student-centered authoring cycle model, and two student-centered models created by graduate students. (*School Library Media Activities Monthly* 19, no. 6 (February 2003): 35–37)

A number of models for student composition are described. The models are the Authoring Cycle, the I-Search process, a model for cultural celebration, and the lab report format model.(*School Library Media Activities Monthly* 19, no. 5 (January 2003): 34–36)

Models for expanding student inquiry are discussed. The models are WebQuest, Minnesota's Inquiry Process, Indiana's Student Inquiry Model, constructivist learning models for inquiry, and the Research Cycle. (*School Library Media Activities Monthly* 19, no. 4 (December 2002): 35–38)

A number of instructional models are presented. These models are Gagne's ASSURE model for undertaking instruction that incorporates media, Colburn's learning cycle, Turner's instructional analysis model, Walker and Montgomery's integrated model for teaching library skills, and Kuhlthau's levels of intervention for library skills instruction. (*School Library Media Activities Monthly* 19, no. 3 (November 2002): 36–7)

Several information use models are profiled. The models discussed are the REACT model, the information skills model, the information problem-solving model, the portfolio of information skills model, the pathways to knowledge model, and the literate person model. (*School Library Media Activities Monthly* 19, no. 1 (September [i.e., O] (2002): 36–39, 51)

Models for expanding student inquiry are discussed. Some of these models are based on observation of student and teacher behavior in their search for and use of information, and others are based on the practices of model teachers and how they design and present lessons. Specific learning processes or subtasks that the student experiences as he or she encounters new information and attempts to assimilate it are illustrated by these models, all of which are constructed on the basic components of questioning, exploration, assimilation, inference, and reflection. The Pathfinder model and the Information Search Process are described in detail. (*School Library Media Activities Monthly* 19, no. 1 (September 2002): 34–37)

Motivation

The writer considers motivation, which helps to increase the chances that students will learn what is needed even when they may initially classify the activity as being overly demanding or of no interest. He considers the characteristics of motivation, some legendary teachers' approaches to motivation, motivation in the multigenre research paper, and motivation and information skills instruction. (*School Library Media Activities Monthly* 16, no. 1 (September 1999): 37–39)

Nonfiction

The importance of nonfiction books for children and research on reading related to nonfiction are discussed, and key questions that students must address as they gain practice and become mature users of nonfiction text information are presented. (*School Library Media Activities Monthly* 16, no. 10 (June 2000): 29–32, 35)

Note-taking

Two different note-taking strategies—exploration and collecting information—are beneficial in the student research process. Journals or notebooks are best for the exploration stage, but selected pages can be printed from the Internet or print reference tools and later highlighted to provide a workable pool of preliminary information chunks in a shorter amount of time. Meanwhile, to take notes from media or a live presentation, students must concentrate and develop a system of shorthand. These notes should be transferred into a format that allows the information to be manipulated. Then, students move into a collecting stage where they gather specific information, and the note-taking task becomes focused. (*School Library Media Activities Monthly* 19, no. 7 (March 2003): 33–37, 45)

Online learning and virtual schools

The writers discuss online learning and virtual schools. They note that although the creation of a virtual library can provide access to remote materials that enhance the experience of online learners, it is even more important that students possess the information skills needed to be successful in the virtual learning environment. They then proceed to define online learning and virtual schools; outline the purposes and goals of online education; offer advice on building an online social and learning community, Netiquette, and online orientation; discuss the purposes of Web sites developed and maintained for the school library media center; and examine elements of information literacy. (*School Library Media Activities Monthly* 21, no. 9 (May 2005): 29–35)

Oral history

Advice for school library media specialists on conducting oral history projects is provided. This advice relates to practicing oral history techniques, using questions that drive oral history inquiry, conducting an oral interview, evaluating oral history interviews, and editing oral interviews for presentation. Examples of tried and tested oral history projects are also provided. (*School Library Media Activities Monthly* 20, no. 5 (January 2004): 41–44)

Organizers

The writer discusses organizers—the tools or techniques that help students to identify and classify and to determine possible relationships or connections among ideas, concepts, and issues. He considers David Ausubel's research and ideas concerning advance organizers, the implications to educational structures that derive from Ausubel's work, the use of webbing in organizing ideas and information, and graphic organizers. (*School Library Media Activities Monthly* 16, no. 5 (January 2000): 36–39)

Parent

Information on the role of parents in developing children's literacy and information inquiry skills is provided. This information relates to factors that affect the likelihood of partnerships between school library media specialists and parents, opportunities for parents to influence child development, how parents can help to develop their children's study skills, productive library experiences for parents and children, and how parents can provide a nurturing reading environment for their children, as well as other strategies and techniques for using parents as a key instructional resource. (*School Library Media Activities Monthly* 21, no. 3 (November 2004): 33–38)

Plagiarism

The writer outlines his approach to teaching about plagiarism – library media specialists should encourage what can be done rather than concentrate on what should not be done. Students should be engaged in projects that reward original ideas, thereby discouraging the need to copy or cheat. Moreover, student research should be presented as a chance to explore and share, not just to learn how to follow another set of rules. (*School Library Media Activities Monthly* 22, no. 4 (December 2005): 41–45)

Portfolio

Portfolios can provide a more complete and richer display of a student's abilities to deal with complex problems than letter grades. Educators seeking criteria for student portfolio review should look to the Colorado Information Literacy Rubric, as it provides an invaluable collection of potential evaluation categories. (*School Library Media Activities Monthly* 14 (October 1997): 42–45)

Primary sources

The writers discuss the use of primary sources in the classroom. After outlining reasons for using primary sources, they discuss the rewriting of history for children on the basis of primary sources and critical thinking through history and information literacy. They then consider approaches to teaching with primary sources, levels of story and the interpretation of primary sources, and the issue of when the past becomes history. (*School Library Media Activities Monthly* 20, no. 10 (June 2004): 29–32)

Problem solving

(Schema and problem solving)—The writer explores definitions and issues pertaining to schemas, problem solving, and information problem solving. (*School Library Media Activities Monthly* 14, no. 9 (May 1998): 43–45)

Professional assessment

Information on assessment of school library media specialists' instructional role is provided. The focus is on exemplary teaching and learning goals, the National Board for Professional Teaching Standards, school library impact studies, the National Study of School Evaluation's indicators of quality, library media specialists as agents of learning, and peer assessment. (*School Library Media Activities Monthly* 21, no. 6 (February 2005): 35–37, 41)

Project-based learning

A review of the theory and practice of project-based learning models that move the child to the center of the project as it emerges and as decisions need to be made is provided. Definitions of project-based learning, the 4-H youth development program, problems with project-based learning, positive observations from research, and steps to successful projects are discussed. (*School Library Media Activities Monthly* 22, no. 5 (January 2006): 42–45)

Questioning

The library media center is the best location for students to raise questions. Mastering the formulation of questions in a way that results in organizing the manner in which information is searched, retrieved, and sorted is the main step leading to critical thinking. Although many of the best questions come naturally, the remainder comes from reading, writing, listening, debating, and interacting with each other and with information texts. The actions that take place when students learn and practice effective questions are discussed. (*School Library Media Activities Monthly* 13 (February 1997): 30–32)

Questioning revisited

The writer discusses guided, modeled, and free student questioning that drives the inquiry process. (*School Library Media Activities Monthly* 22, no. 6 (February 2006): 40–43)

Reflection

The writer discusses reflection, which involves considering options and making a judgment. Reflection is important for students who are learning to use information effectively and for teachers who want to evaluate their information literacy instruction. Strategies for encouraging reflection among elementary-level students, techniques designed to help high school students reflect on the research experience, the I-Search process, and strategies for encouraging reflection in teachers are discussed.(*School Library Media Activities Monthly* 16, no. 2 (October 1999): 31–34)

Rubrics

The writer discusses rubrics for use in student performance assessment. He focuses on classification of performance, the advantages and disadvantages of rubrics, assessing process and product with rubrics, types of rubrics, rubrics for information literacy, and a rubric for rubrics. (*School Library Media Activities Monthly* 17, no. 2 (October 2000): 34–36, 42)

Scaffolding

The instructional method of scaffolding, which helps students to climb to a desired educational goal or behavior, is presented. The scaffolding analogy, elaboration theory, other elements of scaffolding, the notion of the Zone of Proximal Development, and inner speech and external speech are discussed.(*School Library Media Activities Monthly* 17, no. 6 (February 2001): 37–39)

Schema and problem-solving

The writer explores definitions and issues pertaining to schemas, problem solving, and information problem solving.(*School Library Media Activities Monthly* 14, no. 9 (May 1998): 43–45)

Scope and sequence

Information on scope and sequence in instruction is provided. This information relates to the advantages and disadvantages of using scope and sequence as an instructional tool and scope and sequence in library skills instruction, levels of learning objectives, technology skills, media literacy skills, and information inquiry skills across disciplines. (*School Library Media Activities Monthly* 18, no. 7 (March 2002): 35–40, 48)

Service learning

The writer discusses service learning. He considers the links between information literacy and social responsibility. He then discusses service learning projects that are supported by school administrators, components of service learning programs, psychosocial stages and service learning, service education and information literacy, and inquiry and community service. (*School Library Media Activities Monthly* 20, no. 8 (April 2004): 39–44)

Sift and sort

(Sift and Sort: The Answers Are in the Questions!)—The writers, an elementary teacher and a library media specialist, share their experiences of teaching young children how to sift through all their factoids to ensure that they begin to understand what information is relevant as opposed to what information is trivial.(*School Library Media Activities Monthly* 21, no. 8 (April 2005): 33–37)

Situated learning

The writer discusses situated learning. He discusses the tools, critical characteristics, criticisms, and some tested methods of situated learning. (*School Library Media Activities Monthly* 15, no. 2 (October 1998): 38–40+)

Social action learning

To teach for understanding of information literacy, educators must offer opportunities for students to put their knowledge to use in new situations. A list of online resources and action suggestions is provided. (*School Library Media Activities Monthly* 22, no. 7 (March 2006): 38–41)

Standards

The evolution of school library standards and information literacy standards is discussed, and some best practices for meeting new standards in specific areas of the curriculum are presented. Elements of the Manzo interactive teaching cycle and the integration of standards and policies are discussed. (*School Library Media Activities Monthly* 15, no. 9 (May 1999): 38–41)

Story

A discussion of the art of storytelling and its success in helping to engage, entertain, and instruct students is provided. (*School Library Media Activities Monthly* 18, no. 5 (January 2002): 39–42)

Strategy: ideas and composition

The writer discusses strategies for ideas and composition that help the maturing, information literate student deal with the complexities inherent in the communication process. The strategies he considers deal with jump-starting the communication process, effectively evaluating information, managing the writing process over time, intervening in order to help the mentor or peer move the writer along when stalled or off-track, helping students extract ideas from text, and starting and concluding a composition. (*School Library Media Activities Monthly* 17, no. 9 (May 2001): 36–41)

Strategy: search and comprehension

The writer discusses strategies for ideas and composition that help the maturing, information literate student deal with the complexities inherent in the communication process. The strategies he considers deal with jump-starting the communication process, effectively evaluating information, managing the writing process over time, intervening in order to help the mentor or peer move the writer along when stalled or off-track, helping students extract ideas from text, and starting and concluding a composition. (*School Library Media Activities Monthly* 17, no. 8 (April 2001): 32–36)

Student information scientist

A two-part article that formed the basis of a presentation delivered by Daniel Callison and Annette Lamb at the 2005 National Conference of the American Association of School Librarians in Pittsburgh, Pennsylvania, is provided. Students can learn valuable practices from the work of adult information scientists. Information on what student information scientists might investigate, ability levels for science and inquiry, and social science and humanity standards for student performance that could also be applied to information science is provided. The writer explores foundations for inquiry skills, modeling of inquiry with early nonfiction, problem identifiers, and the information learning laboratory. (School Library Media Activities Monthly v. 22, no. 2 (October 2005): 39-015-44; v. 22, no. 3 (November 2005): 37–41)

Student journals

The writers discuss the use of student journals in the classroom. After considering assumptions about language and learning used when assigning journals, they discuss the use of journals in the elementary grades and in science and language arts. The writers then discuss journals and the information search and journals and reflection in practice before examining student expression, educator-student communication, the value of journaling, and the use of reflecting and journaling to assess performance. (*School Library Media Activities Monthly* 21, no. 7 (March 2005): 32–35)

Student-talk

The writer believes that more attention should be paid to student talk by library media specialists and other teachers. She discusses students talk as a social curriculum, students' need for frequent opportunities to talk, the increase in vocabularies that results from varied experiences, talking while reading, storytelling, information talking, student talk and collection development, and locations for student talk. (*School Library Media Activities Monthly* 14, no. 10 (June 1998): 38–41)

Synthesis

According to the definition in "Bloom's Taxonomy of Educational Objectives," synthesis is a process of combining elements or parts to constitute a pattern or structure not clearly there or seen before. Although this is the category in the cognitive domain that most clearly provides for creative behavior on the part of the learner, synthesis is not completely free expression because the student is generally expected to work within certain limits. Kinds of synthesis, synthesizing information pieces, summary practice leading to synthesis, and the questions of analysis and synthesis are examined. (*School Library Media Activities Monthly* 15, no. 10 (June 1999): 39–41+)

Taxonomy

The writer considers taxonomy, a key word in instruction. A taxonomy is a systematic classification of what is learned that sorts the type of abilities that an individual acquires or illustrates from learning. A taxonomy can help identify and construct specific learning tasks and objectives, so such classifications can be effective in teaching. A taxonomy displays the range, level, and overall hierarchy of potential learning or demonstrations of student abilities through performance of a task. (*School Library Media Activities Monthly* 17, no. 3 (November 2000): 35–39)

Technology

The writer discusses technology in instruction. He considers the purpose of technology in instruction, where inquiry enters into the design of learning environments compared to instructional technology, questions that teachers and administrators should answer before investing in the next generation of computers, technology foundation standards, the impact of new technologies on school library media centers, instructional technology software, and future trends in technology. (*School Library Media Activities Monthly* 18, no. 6 (February 2002): 36–40)

Textbook

The writer provides an overview of the role of the textbook in the classroom. He considers the influence of the textbook on teaching over the past 100 years; two studies that provide some insight as to the impact that textbooks have on curriculum, teaching approaches, and student learning; James W. Loewen's award-winning book Lies My Teacher Told Me: Everything Your American History Textbook Got Wrong; a study that examined the powerful influence that textbook content, text, and illustrations can have on students; the advantages of using trade books and how they can be misleading; the stages of reading development; and a strategy that helps students to skim and extract key information from standard textbooks. (*School Library Media Activities Monthly* 19, no. 8 (April 2003): 31–35, 40)

Thinking (higher order) skills

An outline of the higher order thinking skills required for information literacy is provided. A sample of the Association of College and Research Librarians' competency standards for higher education, the skills for critical thinking in communication and inquiry released by the Department of Education's Office of Educational Research and Improvement, and authentic tasks for thinking skills are discussed. (*School Library Media Activities Monthly* 18, no. 8 (April 2002): 38–40, 51)

Time on task

The two factors that seem to be the most critical in determining the effectiveness of information skills instruction are discussed. They involve timing the instruction to occur at the time-of-need and placing the information-use instruction within a meaningful context of personal interest or school subject assignment.(*School Library Media Activities Monthly* 14 (April 1998): 32–34)

Virtual schools

The writers discuss online learning and virtual schools. They note that although the creation of a virtual library can provide access to remote materials that enhance the experience of online learners, it is even more important that students possess the information skills needed to be successful in the virtual learning environment. They then proceed to define online learning and virtual schools; outline the purposes and goals of online education; offer advice on building an online social and learning community, Netiquette, and online orientation; discuss the purposes of Web sites developed and maintained for the school library media center; and examine elements of information literacy. (*School Library Media Activities Monthly* 21, no. 9 (May 2005): 29–35)

WebQuests

Library media specialists can use WebQuests to provide an engaging, challenging learning environment for information inquiry for today's diverse learners. WebQuests are inquiry-based activities that challenge students to use Web-based resources and tools to transform what they are learning into meaningful understandings and real-world projects. WebQuests are designed to utilize online information to analyze, synthesize, and evaluate information to address high-level questions. (*School Library Media Activities Monthly* 21, no. 2 (October 2004): 38–40)

Annotations reprinted from Library Literature, with permission granted by H. W. Wilson Company, New York.

Appendix D

Information Literacy Instruction K–16: Selected Bibliographic Resources

Cheryl A. McCarthy, Professor, University of Rhode Island, Graduate School of Library and Information Studies

ACCESS PENNSYLVANIA curriculum guide. (1991). 54p. ED 355 963.

Allen, C., and M. A. Anderson, M. A. (Eds.). (1999). *Skills for life: Information literacy for grades 7–12.* 2d ed. Worthington, OH: Linworth Publishing.

American Association of School Librarians. (1995). Information literacy: A position paper on information problem solving. *Emergency Librarian, 23* (2), 20–23.

American Association of School Librarians. (1999). *A planning guide for* Information Power: *Building partnerships for learning with school library media program assessment rubric for the 21st century.* Chicago: American Library Association.

American Association of School Librarians and Association for Educational Communications and Technology. (1998). *Information literacy standards for student learning.* Chicago: American Library Association.

American Association of School Librarians and Association for Educational Communications and Technology. (1988). *Information power: Guidelines for school library media programs.* Chicago: American Library Association.

American Association of School Librarians and Association for Educational Communications and Technology. (1998). *Information power: Building partnerships for learning.* Chicago: American Library Association.

American Library Association Presidential Committee on Information Literacy. (1989). *Final report.* Chicago: Author. ED 316 074.

Anderson, M. A. (1996). *Teaching information literacy using electronic resources for grades 6–12.* Worthington, OH: Linworth Publishing, Inc.

Anderson, M. A. (1999). Creating the link: Aligning national and state standards. *Book Report, 17* (5), 12–14.

Anderson, M. A. (1999). The media center: *Information Power:* Because student achievement is the bottom line. *Multimedia Schools, 6* (2), 22–23.

Andronik, C. M. (1999). *Information literacy skills grades 7–12.* 3d ed. Worthington, OH: Linworth Publishing.

Arp, L. (1990). Information literacy or bibliographic instruction: Semantics or philosophy? *RQ, 30* (1), 46–49.

Asselin, M. (2000). Research instruction. *Teacher Librarian, 27* (5), 64–65.

Association for College & Research Libraries (ACRL). (n.d.). *Information literacy competency standards for higher education.* Available at www.ala.org/acrl/ilcomstan. html (accessed April 11, 2001).

Association for Teacher-Librarianship in Canada and the Canadian School Library Association. (1998). Students' information literacy needs: Competencies for teacher-librarians in the 21st century. *Teacher Librarian, 26* (2), 22–25.

Australian Library and Information Association. (1994). *Learning for the future: Developing information services in Australian schools.* Australian School Library Association, Goulburn. Carlton, Aust.: Curriculum Corp. ED 377 826.

Barrett, L., et. al. (2003). Information literacy: A crucial role for schools. *Library & Information Update, 2* (5), 42–44.

Barron, D. D. (2001). Thanks for the connections —Now are we information literate? [Web resources on information literacy]. *School Library Media Activities Monthly, 18* (3), 49–51.

Barron, D. D. (2002). The library media specialist, *Information Power,* and social responsibility: Part I (plagiarism). *School Library Media Activities Monthly, 18* (6), 48–51.

Batz, L., and H. Rosenberg. (1999). Creating an information literate school: Information literacy in action. *National Association of Secondary School Principals, NASSP Bulletin, 83* (605), 68–74.

Behrens, S. J. (1994). A conceptual analysis and historical overview of information literacy. *College and Research Libraries, 55* (4), 309–322. EJ 486 800.

Bishop, K., and N. Larimer. (1999). Collaboration: Literacy through collaboration. *Teacher Librarian, 27* (1), 15–20.

Bleakley, A., and J. L. Carrigan. (1995). *Resource-based learning activities: Information literacy for high school students.* Chicago: American Library Association.

Bloom, B. S. (1956). *Taxonomy of educational objectives: The classification of educational goals: Handbook I: Cognitive domain.* New York: McKay.

Branch, J. L. (2003). Nontraditional undergraduates at home, work, and school: An examination of information-seeking behaviors and the impact of information literacy instruction. *Research Strategies, 19* (1), 3–15.

Breivik, P. S. (1998.). *Student learning in the information age.* Phoenix, AZ: Oryx Press.

Breivik, P. S., and E. G. Gee. (1989). *Information literacy.* New York: Macmillan.

Breivik, P. S., V. Hancock, and J. Senn. (1998). *A progress report on information literacy: An update on the American Library Association Presidential Committee on Information Literacy: Final report,* 1–10. Chicago: ALA, Association of Research Librarians.

Breivik, P. S., and J. A. Senn. (1993). Information literacy: Partnerships for power. *Emergency Librarian, 21* (1), 25–28. EJ 469 235.

Breivik, P. S., and J. A. Senn. (1998). *Information literacy: Educating children for the 21st century.* 2d ed. Washington, DC: National Education Association.

Brock, K. (1994). Developing information literacy through the information intermediary process: A model for teacher-librarians and others. *Emergency Librarian, 22* (1), 16–20. EJ 491 450.

Bruce, C. (1997). *The seven faces of information literacy.* Adelaide, Aust.: Auslib Press.

Bucher, K. T. (2000). The importance of information literacy skills in the middle school curriculum. *The Clearing House, 73* (4), 217–220.

Burkhardt, Joanna M., Mary C. MacDonald, and Andree Rathemacher. (2003). *Teaching information literacy: 35 practical standards-based exercises for college students.* Chicago: American Library Association.

Bush, G. (1999). Creating an information literate school: Here and now. *National Association of Secondary School Principals, NASSP Bulletin, 83* (605), 62–67.

California Department of Education. (1994). *Information literacy guidelines.* Denver, CO: Author.

California Media and Library Educators Association. (1994). *From library skills to information literacy: A handbook for the 21st century.* Castle Rock, CO: Hi Willow Research and Publishing.

California Media and Library Educators Association. (1997). *From information skills to information literacy: A handbook for the 21st century.* 2d ed. San Jose, CA: Hi Willow.

Callison, D. (1993). Expanding the evaluation role in the critical-thinking curriculum. *School Library Media Annual (SLMA), 11,* 78–92. EJ 476 208.

Callison, D. (2003). *Key words, concepts, and methods for information age instruction: A guide to teaching information inquiry.* Baltimore, Md.: LMS Associates.

Callison, D., J. H. McGregor, and R. Small (Eds.). (1998) Instructional Intervention for Information Use. *Research papers of the Sixth Treasure Mountain Research Retreat for School Library Media Programs, March 31–April 1, 1997.* San Jose, CA: Hi Willow Research and Publishing.

Carbone, L. (1999). Leadership for a new era: Making the most of technology in our schools. *Schools in the Middle, 9* (4), 26–7.

Colorado Department of Education. (1994). *Model information literacy guidelines.* Denver, CO: Author. ED 373 797.

Colorado State Department of Education. (1996). *Rubrics for the assessment of information literacy.* Denver, CO: Author. ED 401 899.

Cooper, T., and J. Burchfield. (1995). Information literacy for college and university staff. *Research Strategies, 13* (2), 94–106. EJ 507 071.

Craver, K. W. (1997). *Teaching electronic literacy: A concepts-based approach for school library media specialists.* Westport, CT: Greenwood Press.

Davis, H. M. (2002). Information literacy modules as an integral component of a K–12 teacher preparation program: A librarian/faculty partnership. *Journal of Library Administration, 37* (1/2), 207–216.

Donham, Jean. (1999). Collaboration in the media center: Building partnerships for learning. *National Association of Secondary School Principals, NASSP Bulletin, 83* (605), 20–26.

Doyle, C. S. (1994). *Information literacy in an information society: A concept for the information age.* Syracuse, NY: ERIC Clearinghouse on Information and Technology. ED 372 763.

Dreher, M. J. (1995). Sixth-grade researchers: Posing questions, finding information, and writing a report. *Reading Research Report, 40* (Summer 1995). 17pp. ED 384 014.

Dreher, M. J., et al. (1999). Fourth-grade researchers: Helping children develop strategies for finding and using information. In T. Shanahan and F.V. Rodriguez-Brown (Eds.), *48th yearbook of the National Reading Conference,* 311–22. Chicago: National Reading Conference.

Eisenberg, M. B., and R. E. Berkowitz. (1988). *Curriculum initiative: An agenda and strategy for library media programs.* Norwood, NJ: Ablex Publishing Corporation.

Eisenberg, M. B., and R. E. Berkowitz. (1990). *Information problem-solving: The Big6 skills approach to library & information skills instruction.* Norwood, NJ: Ablex Publishing Corporation.

Eisenberg, M. B., and R. E. Berkowitz. (1999). *Teaching information and technology skills: The Big 6 in elementary schools.* Worthington, OH: Linworth Publishing.

Eisenberg, M.B., and R. E. Berkowitz. (2000). *The Big6 collection: The best of the Big6 newsletters.* Worthington, OH: Linworth Publishing.

Eisenberg, M. B., and R. E. Berkowitz. (2004). *The definitive Big6 workshop handbook.* Worthington, OH: Linworth Publishing.

Eisenberg, M. B., and M. K. Brown. (1992). Current themes regarding library and information skills instruction: Research supporting and research lacking. *School Library Media Quarterly, 20* (2), 103–109. EJ 441731.

Eisenberg, M. B., and D. Johnson. (1996). Computer skills for information problem-solving: Learning and teaching technology in context. In *ERIC Digest.* Syracuse, NY: ERIC Clearinghouse on Information & Technology. ED 392 463.

Ewell, P. T. (1997). Organizing for learning: A new imperative. *AAHE Bulletin, 50* (4), 3–6.

Farmer, L. (1999). Making information literacy a schoolwide reform effort. *Book Report, 18* (3), 6–8.

Farmer, L. (2001). Building information literacy through a whole school reform approach. *Knowledge Quest, 29* (2), 20–24.

Fitzgerald, M. A. (1997). Misinformation on the Internet: Applying evaluation skills to on-line information. *Emergency Librarian* (January/February), 9–14.

Fitzgerald, M.A. (2004). Making the leap from high school to college: Three new studies about information literacy skills of first-year college students. *Knowledge Quest, 32* (4), 19–24.

Giguere, M., et al. (1995). Enhancing information literacy skills across the curriculum. In *Literacy: Traditional, cultural, technological: Selected papers from the [23d] annual sonference of the International Association of School Librarianship.* (Pittsburgh, July 17–22, 1994). ED 399 951.

Goodin, M. E. (1991). The transferability of library research skills from high school to college. *School Library Media Quarterly, 20* (1), 33–42. EJ 436 241.

Grassian, Esther S., and Joan R. Kaplowitz. (2001). *Information literacy instruction: Theory and practice.* New York: Neal-Schuman.

Gross, J., and S. Kientz. (1999). Developing information literacy: Collaborating for authentic learning. *Teacher Librarian, 27* (1), 21–25.

Hancock, V. E. (1993). Information literacy for lifelong learning. In *ERIC Digest.* Syracuse, NY: ERIC Clearinghouse on Information Resources. ED 358 870.

Harada, V., and J. Donham. (1998). *Information Power*: Student achievement is the bottom line. *Teacher Librarian, 26* (1), 14–17.

Harada, V. H., and M. Nakamura. (1994). Information searching across the curriculum: Literacy skills for the 90's and beyond. *Catholic Library World, 65* (2), 17–19.

Hardesty, L. (1995). Faculty culture and bibliographic instruction: An exploratory analysis. *Library Trends, 44* (Fall), 339–67.

Haycock, K. (1999). Fostering collaboration, leadership and information literacy: Common behaviors of uncommon principals and faculties. *National Association of Secondary School Principals, NASSP Bulletin, 83* (605), 82–87.

Haycock , K. (1999). Information literacy: Making effective use of resources. *National Association of Secondary School Principals, NASSP Bulletin, 83* (605), 1–15.

Haycock, K. (Ed.). (1999). *Foundations for effective school library media programs.* Englewood, CO.: Libraries Unlimited.

Henri, J., and K. Bonanno (Eds.). (1999). *The information literate school community: Best practice.* Topics in Australian Teacher Librarianship Series. New South Wales: Centre for Information Studies at Charles Stuart University.

Herring, J. E. (1996). *Teaching information literacy skills in schools.* London: Library Association Publishing.

Iannuzzi, P. (1999). We are teaching, but are they learning: Accountability, productivity, and assessment. *Journal of Academic Librarianship, 25*(4), 304–305.

Iannuzzi, P., C. T. Mangrum, and S. S. Strichart. (1999). *Teaching information literacy skills.* Boston: Allyn and Bacon.

Information literacy: A position paper of information problem-solving. (1995). *Emergency Librarian, 23* (2), 20–23.

Information literacy and education for the 21st century: Toward an agenda for action. (1989). A symposium sponsored by the U.S. National Commission on Libraries and Information Science and the American Association of School Librarians, Leesburg, Virginia, April 14–16.

Iowa City Community School District and M. J. Langhorne (Eds.). (1998). *Developing an information literacy program K–12: A how-to-do-it manual and CD-ROM package.* New York: Neal-Schuman.

Johnson, C. M., et. al. (2003). Information literacy in pre-service teacher education: An annotated bibliography. *Behavioral & Social Sciences Librarian, 22* (1), 129–139.

Johnson, D. (1997). *The indispensable librarian-surviving (and thriving) in school media centers.* Worthington, OH: Linworth Publishing.

Johnson, D. (1999). Implementing an information literacy curriculum: One district's story. *National Association of Secondary School Principals, NASSP Bulletin, 83* (605), 53–61.

Johnson, D., and M. Eisenberg. (1996). Computer literacy and information literacy: A natural combination. *Emergency Librarian, 23* (5), 12–16. EJ 526 333.

Jones, C. (2001). Infusing information literacy and technology into your school library media program. *Knowledge Quest, 30* (1), 22–23.

Jones, R. (2005). Information literacy and independent learning. *Library & Information Update, 4* (1/2), 56.

Joseph, M. (1991). The cure for library anxiety—It may not be what you think. *Catholic Library World, 63* (2), 111–14.

Joyce, M. Z., and J. Tallman. (1997). *Making the writing and research connection with the I-search process.* Englewood, CO: Libraries Unlimited.

Kansas Association of School Librarians Research Committee. (1999) Planning and assessing learning across the curriculum. *Knowledge Quest, 28* (1), 10–11, 13–16.

Keenan, N., et al. (1994). *The Montana library and information skills model Curriculum education services.* 106pp. ED 382 216.

Keene, L. (2004). Teaching information literacy skills through censorship and freedom of expression. *School Library Media Activities Monthly, 21* (3), 25–28, 30.

Kendall, J. S., and R. J. Marzano. (1997). *Content knowledge: A compendium of standards and benchmarks for K–12 education.* 2d ed. Denver, CO: Midcontinent Research and Evaluation Laboratory.

Kentucky Department of Education. (1995). *Online II: essentials of a model library media program.* Louisville, KY: Author.

Kester, D. D. (1994). Secondary school library and information skills: Are they transferred from high school to college? *Reference Librarian, 44,* 9–17. EJ 488 269.

Krashen, S. (2004). *The power of reading: Insights from the research.* 2d ed. Westport, CT: Libraries Unlimited.

Kuhlthau, C. C. (1987). Information skills for an information society: A review of research. Syracuse: ERIC Clearinghouse on Information Resources. ED297 740.

Kuhlthau, C. C. (1988). Developing a model of the library search process: Cognitive and affective aspects. *RQ, 28* (2), 232–242.

Kuhlthau, C. C. (1993). Implementing a process approach to information skills: A study identifying indicators of success in library media programs. *School Library Media Quarterly, 22*(1), 11–18. E J473 063.

Kuhlthau, C. C. (2004). *Seeking meaning: A process approach to library and information services.* 2d ed. Westport, CT: Libraries Unlimited.

Kuhlthau, C. C., et al. (1990). Validating a model of the search process: A comparison of academic, public and school library users. *LISR, 12,* 5–31.

Lance, K. C. (2001). *Good schools have school librarians: Oregon school librarians collaborate to improve academic achievement.* Salem: Oregon Educational Media Association.

Lance, K. C. (2001). *Proof of the power: Recent research on the impact of school library media programs on the academic achievement of U.S. public school students.* Syracuse: ERIC Clearinghouse on Information and Technology. ED 1.310/2:456861.

Lance, K. C. (2003). *How school libraries improve outcomes for children: The New Mexico study.* San Jose, CA: Hi Willow Research & Publishing.

Lance, K. C., L. Welborn, and C. Hamilton-Pennell. (1993). *The impact of school library media centers on academic achievement.* Castle Rock, CO: Hi Willow Research and Publishing. ED353989

Lance, K. C., M. J. Rodney, and C. Hamilton-Pennell. (2000). *How school librarians help kids achieve standards: The second Colorado study.* San Jose, CA: Hi Willow Research & Publishing.

Lance, K. C., M. J. Rodney, and C. Hamilton-Pennell. (2000). *Measuring up to standards: The impact of school library programs & information literacy in Pennsylvania schools.* San Jose, CA: Hi Willow Research & Publishing.

Lance, K. C., et al. (2000). *Information empowered: The school librarian as an agent of academic achievement in Alaska schools.* San Jose, CA: Hi Willow Research & Publishing.

Leckie, G. J. (1996). Desperately Seeking Citations: Uncovering Faculty Assumptions About the Undergraduate Research Process. *Journal of Academic Librarianship,* 22(3), 201–8. EJ 526 298.

Lehman, K. (2002). Promoting library advocacy and information literacy from an invisible library [at Thomas Dale High School in Chester, Virginia]. *Teacher Librarian,* 29 (4), 27–30.

Lehman, K., et. al. (2001). Collaborating for Information Literacy. *Knowledge Quest,* 30(1), 24–25.

Lenox, M. F., and M. L. Walker. (1992). Information Literacy: Challenge for the Future. *International Journal of Information and Library Research,* 4(1), 1–18.

Lindsay, E. B. (2004). Distance Teaching: Comparing Two Online Information Literacy Courses. *The Journal of Academic Librarianship,* 30 (6), 482–87.

Loertscher, D., and B. Woolls. (1999). *Information Literacy: A Review of the Research: A Guide For Practitioners and Researchers.* San Jose, CA: Hi Willow Research & Publishing.

Loertscher, D. and B. Woolls. (2002). *Information Literacy: a review of the research; a guide for practitioners and researchers.* 2d ed. San Jose, CA: Hi Willow Research & Publishing.

Logan, D. K. (2000). *Information Skills Toolkit: Collaborative Integrated Instruction for the Middle Grades.* Worthington, OH: Linworth Publishing.

MacDonald, M. C., A. J. Rathemacher, and J. M. Burkhardt. (2000). Challenges in Building an Incremental, Multi-year Information Literacy Plan. *Reference Services Review,* 28(3), 240–47.

Macrorie, Ken. (1988). *The I-Search Paper.* Portsmouth, NH: Heinemann.

Mancall, J. C., Aaron, S. L., & Walker, S. A. (1986). Educating Students to Think: The Role of the Library Media Program—A Concept Paper Written for the National Commission on Libraries and Information Science. *School Library Media Quarterly, Journal of the American Association of School Librarians,* 15(1), 18–27. EJ 344 239.

Marcoux, B. (1999). Developing the National Information Literacy Standards for Student Learning. *National Association of Secondary School Principals, NASSP Bulletin,* 83(605), 13–19.

McCarthy, C. (2003). FLIP It!™: An Information Literacy Framework that Really Works for All Ages! *School Library Media Activities Monthly,* 19(March): 22–23, 30.

McCarthy, C. (1997). A Reality Check: The Challenges of Implementing *Information Power* in School Library Media Programs.

School Library Media Quarterly, 25(4), 205–14.

McElmeel, Sharron L. (1997). *Research Strategies for Moving Beyond Reporting.* Worthington, OH: Linworth Publishing.

McGregor, J. (1999). Teaching the Research Process: Helping Students Become Lifelong Learners. *National Association of Secondary School Principals, NASSP Bulletin,* 83(605), 27–34.

McGregor, J., and D. Strietenbeger. D. (1998). Do Scribes Learn? Copying and Information Use. *School Library Media Quarterly.* Available at www.ala.org/aasl/SLMQ/scribes.html (accessed April 11, 2001).

Mendrinos, R. (1994). *Building Information Literacy Using High Technology: A Guide for Schools and Libraries.* Englewood, CO: Libraries Unlimited. ED 375 820.

Milam, C. (2002). Moving Beyond Technology with Strategic Teaching: Jamie McKenzie'sResearch Cycle. *School Library Media Activities Monthly,* 19(4), 22–23, 34.

Milam, P. (2004). 0;Brain-Friendly Techniques for Teaching Information Literacy Skills. *School Library Media Activities Monthly,* 21(1), 26, 49.

Moyer, S. L., and R. V. Small. Building a Motivational Toolkit for Teaching Information Literacy. *Knowledge Quest,* 29(2), 28–32.

Neuman, Delia. (1999). What Do We Do After the School Has Been Wired?: Providing Intellectual Access to Digital Resources. *National Association of Secondary School Principals, NASSP Bulletin,* 83(605), 35–43.

Nichols, J. (1999). Building Bridges: High School and University Partnerships for Information Literacy. *National Association of Secondary School Principals, NASSP Bulletin,* 83(605), 75–81.

Nichols, J. W. (2001). Sharing a Vision: Information Literacy Partnerships (K–16) [Librarians at Wayne State University Offer Workshops for Local High School Stu-

dents]. *College & Research Libraries News,* 62 (3), 275–77, 285.

Nims, Julia K., et al. (2003). *Integrating Information Literacy into the College Experience: Papers Presented at the Thirtieth LOEX Library Instruction Conference.* Ann Arbor, MI: Pierian Press.

Oberman, C. (1998). The Institute for Information Literacy: Formal Training is a Critical Need. *College and Research Libraries News,* 59(9), 703–5.

Orr, D., et. al. (2001). Information literacy and flexible delivery: are we meeting student needs? [at Central Queensland University]. *Australian Academic & Research Libraries,* 32(3), 192–203.

O'Sullivan, M., and T. Scott. (2000). Teaching Internet Information Literacy: A Critical Evaluation. (Part I). *Multimedia Schools,* 7(2), 40–44.

O'Sullivan, M., and T. Scott. (2000). Teaching Internet Information Literacy: A Collaborative Approach. (Part II). *Multimedia Schools,* 7(3), 34–37.

Pappas, M. L. (1995). Information Skills for Electronic Resources. *School Library Media Activities Monthly,* 11(8), 39–40. EJ 499 875.

Pearle, L. (2002). One Step Beyond: From High School to College [Preparing Students with Research Skills for College and Beyond—Special Issue]. Knowledge Quest, 30(4), 12–44.

Pennell, Victoria (Ed.). (1997). *Information Literacy: An Advocacy Kit for Teacher-Librarians.* Ottawa: Association for Teacher-librarianship in Canada.

Pitts, J., et al. (1995). Mental Models of Information: The 1993–1994 AASL/Highsmith Research Award Study. *School Library Media Quarterly,* 23(3), 177–84. EJ 503 402.

Rader, H. B. (1995). Information Literacy and the Undergraduate Curriculum. *Library Trends,* 44(2), 270–78. EJ 513 796.

Rankin, V. (1999). *The Thoughtful Researcher: Teaching the Research Process to Middle*

School Students. Englewood, CO: Libraries Unlimited.

Reese, J. (2000). Integrating Information Literacy Skills into the Curriculum. *Multimedia Schools* 7(5), 46–47.

Riedling, A. M. (2002). *Learning to Learn: A Guide to Becoming Information Literate.* New York: Neal-Schuman.

Riedling, A.M. (2004). *Information literacy: What Does It Look Like in the School Library Media Center?* Englewood, CO: Libraries Unlimited.

Roth, L. (1999). Educating the Cut-and-Paste Generation. *Library Journal,* 124(18), 42–44.

Salvadore, M. B. (1999). Developing an Information Literacy Program K–12. *School Library Journal,* 45(9), 248–49.

Schrock, K., and M. Frazel. (2000). *Inquiring Educators Want to Know: TeacherQuests for Today's Teachers.* Worthington, OH: Linworth Publishing.

Schroeder, E. E., et. al. (2001). Problem-based Learning: Develop Information Literacy Through Real Problems. *Knowledge Quest,* 30(1), 34–35.

Secretary's Commission on Achieving Necessary Skills (SCANS). (1991). *What Work Requires of Schools: A SCANS Report for America 2000.* Washington, DC: U.S. Department of Education. ED 332 054.

Shannon, D. M. (2002). Kuhlthau's Information Search Process. *School Library Media Activities Monthly,* 19(1), 19–23.

Small, R. V. (2004). *Designing Digital Literacy Programs with Im-Pact: Information Motivation, Purpose, Audience, Content, and Technique.* Englewood, CO: Libraries Unlimited.

Small, R. V., and M. P. Arnone. (2000). *Turning Kids on to Research: The Power of Motivation.* Englewood, CO: Libraries Unlimited.

Snavely, L., and N. Cooper. (1997). The Information Debate. *Journal of Academic Librarianship,* 23, 9–14.

Sonntag, G., and D. M. Ohr. (1996). The Development of a Lower Division, General Education, Course Integrated Information Literacy Program. *College & Research Libraries,* 57(4), 331–38.

Spitzer, K. L., M. Eisenberg, and C. A. Lowe. (1998*). Information Literacy: Essential Skills for the Information Age.* Syracuse, NY: ERIC Clearinghouse on Information and Technology.

Steele, S., and A. Heim. (1997). *Libraries Enhance Student Learning: A Guidebook of Innovative Library Programs for Youth.* Washington, DC: U.S. Department of Education.

Stripling, B. K. (1995). Learning-Centered Libraries: Implications from Research. *School Library Media Quarterly,* 23(3), 163–70.

Stripling, B. K. (1996). Quality in School Library Media Programs: Focus on Learning. *Library Trends,* 14(3), 631–56.

Stripling, B. K. (1999). Expectations for Achievement and Performance: Assessing Student Skills. *National Association of Secondary School Principals, NASSP Bulletin,* 83(605), 44–52.

Stripling, B. K., and J. Pitts. (1988). *Brainstorms and Blueprints: Teaching Library Research as a Thinking Process.* Littleton, CO: Libraries Unlimited.

Texas Education Agency. (1993). *The Library Media Center: A Force for Student Excellence.* 96p p. ED366 345.

Thomas, N. P., and P. K. Montgomery (Eds.). (1999). *Information Literacy and Information Skills Instruction: Applying Research in the School Library Media Center.* Englewood, CO: Libraries Unlimited.

Thompson, H., et. al. (2001). Implementing a Schoolwide Information Literacy Program. *School Library Media Activities Monthly,* 17(6), 24–25, 27.

Todd, R. J. (1995). Integrated Information Skills Instruction: Does It Make a Difference? *School Library Media Quarterly,* 23(2), 133–39.

Todd, R. J. (1999). Transformational Leadership and Transformation Learning: Information Literacy and the World Wide Web. *National Association of Secondary School Principals, NASSP Bulletin,* 83(605), 4–12.

Todd, R. J., et al. (1992). The Power of Information Literacy: Unity of Education and Resources for the 21st Century. Paper presented at the Annual Meeting of the International Association of School Librarianship (Belfast, Northern Ireland, United Kingdom, July 19–24). ED 354 916.

Turner, P., and A. M. Riedling. (2003). *Helping Teachers Teach: A School Library Media Specialist's Role.* 3d ed. Englewood, CO: Libraries Unlimited.

Utah State Office of Education. (1991). *Elementary and Secondary Core Curriculum Standards, Levels K–12: Library Media.* 48pp. ED 371 720.

Walster, D., and L. Welborn. (1996). Writing and Implementing 'Colorado's Information Literacy Guidelines': The Process Examined. *School Library Media Activities Monthly,* 12(6), 25–28, 36. EJ 516 616.

Whelan, D. L. (2003) Why Isn't Information Literacy Catching On? *School Library Journal,* 49(9), 50–53.

Wisconsin Educational Media Association. (1993). *Information Literacy: A Position Paper on Information Problem-Solving.* 6pp. Appleton, WI: Author. ED 376 817.

Witt, S. W., et. al. (2003). Teaching Teachers to Teach: Collaborating with a University Education Department to Teach Skills in Information Literacy Pedagogy. *Behavioral & Social Sciences Librarian,* 22(1), 75–95.

Wolf, S. E. (2004). Making the Grade with Information Literacy. *School Library Journal,* 50(3), LQ6.

Yocum, P., et. al. (2003). Instructor College: Promoting Development of Library Instructors. In *Integrating Information Literacy into the College Experience.* Ann Arbor, MI: Pierian Press.

Yucht, Alice. (1997). *FLIP IT! An Information Skills Strategy for Student Researchers.* Worthington, OH: Linworth Publishers.

Zimmerman, N. P. (2002). Pappas and Tepe's Pathways to Knowledge Model. *School Library Media Activities Monthly,* 19(3), 24–27.

Appendix E

Information Literacy Instruction K–16: Selected Web Resources

Cheryl A. McCarthy, Professor, University of Rhode Island, Graduate School of Library and Information Studies

American Association of School Librarians/ American Library Association & Association for Educational Communications Technology. *Information power: The nine information literacy standards for student learning.* August 25, 2000. www.ala.org/ ala/aasl/aaslproftools/informationpower/ InformationLiteracyStandards_final.pdf (accessed July 21, 2005).

American Association of School Librarians/American Library Association. *Knowledge quest on the Web.* ©2000, 2005. www.ala.org/ala/aasl/aaslpubsandjournals/ kqweb/kqweb.htm (accessed July 21, 2005).

American Association of School Librarians/American Library Association. *School library media research.* 2005. www.ala. org/aaslslmrTemplate.cfm?Section=slmrb (accessed July 21, 2005).

American Library Association. *Community partnerships toolkit.* April 29, 2005. www.ala. org/ala/acrl/acrlpubs/crlnews/backissues20 00/november4/communitypartnerships.ht m (accessed July 21, 2005).

American Library Association. *Library instruction roundtable.* January 10, 2001. www3. baylor.edu/LIRT/ (accessed July 21, 2005).

American Library Association. *Presidential Committee on Information Literacy.* January 10, 1989. www.ala.org/ acrl/nili/ilit1st. html (accessed July 21, 2005).

Association of College and Research Libraries. *Information literacy competency standards for higher education.* April 3, 2001. www.ala.org/acrl/ilcomstan.html (accessed July 21, 2005).

Association of College and Research Libraries. *Information literacy in a nut shell.* 2005. www.ala.org/ala/acrl/acrlissues/acrlinfolit/ infolitoverview/infolitforfac/infolitfaculty. htm (accessed July 21, 2005).

Association of College and Research Libraries. *Information literacy website.* 2005. www.ala.org/ala/acrl/acrlissues/acrlinfolit/ informationliteracy.htm (accessed July 21, 2005).

Association of College and Research Libraries. *Institute for information literacy.* August 3, 2000. www.ala.org/acrl/nili/nilihp.html (accessed July 21, 2005).

Association of College and Research Libraries. *Progress report on information literacy.* July 28, 2000. www.ala.org/acrl/nili/ nili.html (accessed July 21, 2005).

Berger, Pam. *Infosearcher.com.* ©2000. www. infosearcher.com (accessed July 21, 2005).

The Big6. *Big Six kids.* 2005. www.big6. com/kids (accessed July 21, 2005).

The Big6. *Information literacy for the information age.* 2005. www.big6.com (accessed July 21, 2005).

Boston College Libraries. *Need help with research?* 2005. www.bc.edu/libraries/research/ (accessed July 22, 2005)

Brevard Community College. *Brevard information literacy tutorial (BILT).* 2004. www.brevardcc.edu/library/content/bilt/bilthome.htm (accessed July 21, 2005).

Bruce, Christine. *Seven faces of information literacy in higher education.* 1997. http://sky.fit.qut.edu.au/~bruce/inflit/faces/faces1.htm (accessed July 21, 2005).

Bryn Mawr. *Bryn Mawr school library.* April 4, 2005. http://library.brynmawrschool.org/searchpage.htm (accessed July 21, 2005).

California State University, Long Beach, University Library. *Information literacy minimum standards.* February 2, 1998. www.csulb.edu/library/guide/infocomp.html. (July 22, 2005).

California State University System. *CSU information competence project.* February 25, 2001. www.lib.calpoly.edu/infocomp/project/index.html (accessed July 21, 2005).

Central Connecticut State University. *Basic information literacy tutorial.* April 29, 2005. http://mylibrary.ccsu.edu/TILT (accessed July 21, 2005).

Classroom connect. © 2000. http://corporate.classroom.com (accessed July 21, 2005).

Colorado Department of Education. *Colorado information literacy.* December 4, 2000. www.cde.state.co.us/cdelib/slinfolitindex.htm (accessed July 21, 2005).

Colorado Digitization Program. *Evaluating primary and secondary sources of the Depression.* 2003. www.cdpheritage.org/educator/depression.html (accessed July 21, 2005).

Connecticut State Library. *Web junction learning center.* 2004. http://ct.webjunction.org/do/Navigation?category=535 (accessed July 21, 2005).

Curzon, Susan C., Chair, CSU Information Work Group. *Information competence in the CSU.* January 15, 1998. http://library.csun.edu/susan.curzon/infocmp.html (accessed July 22, 2005).

Division of Reference Services, OLIN*Kroch*Uris Libraries, Cornell University Library. *Library research at Cornell: A hypertext guide.* September 9, 1999. www.library.cornell.edu/okuref/research/tutorial.html (accessed July 21, 2005).

Dodge, Bernie. *The WebQuest Page.* November 17, 2000. http://webquest.sdsu.edu/webquest.html (accessed July 21, 2005).

Education World. *International Society for Technology in Education (ISTE), National educational technology standards.* 2000. www.education-world.com/standards/national/technology/index.shtml (accessed July 21, 2005).

Educause. *Educause review.* 2005. www.educause.edu/er/ (accessed July 21, 2005).

Farmer, Lesley, California State University, Long Beach. *Information literacy for K-16 settings.* October 20, 2002. www.csulb.edu/~lfarmer/infolitwebstyle.htm. (accessed July 22, 2005).

Florida International University. *Information literacy at Florida International University home page.* July 19, 2000. www.fiu.edu/~library/ili/ (accessed July 21, 2005).

Florida International University. *Information literacy on the WWW.* February 6, 2001. www.fiu.edu/~library/ili/iliweb.html (accessed July 21, 2005).

Follett Software Company. *Pathways to knowledge.* 2000. www.sparkfactor.com/clients/follett/home.html (accessed July 21, 2005).

Gateway to Education Consortium. *The gateway to educational materials.* ©2000. www.thegateway.org (accessed July 21, 2005).

Grainger, Gail Shea. *Dewey browse.* 2005. www.deweybrowse.org (accessed July 21, 2005).

Grassian, E., and S. E. Clark. *Information literacy sites.* February 1999. C&RL_News. www.ala.org/acrl/resfeb99.html (accessed July 21, 2005).

Groton Public Schools. *Information and tech literacy K-12*. July 1, 2004. www.groton.k12.ct.us/mts/compcurr/lriitcurric.htm (accessed July 21, 2005).

Harvard University. *Education with new technologies: Networked learning community*. 2005. http://learnweb.harvard.edu/ent (accessed July 21, 2005).

Humbolt State University Library. *Online workshop for library skills (OWLS)*. January 14, 2005, http://library.humboldt.edu/owls/ (accessed July 21, 2005).

Illinois Mathematics and Science Academy. *21st century information fluency Project Portal*. March 23, 2005. http://21cif.imsa.edu/ (accessed July 21, 2005).

Information Literacy: Resources for Those Who Teach It. *WEBSITES for library skills & library bibliographic instruction*. January 8, 2003. www.librarysupportstaff.com/teachlib.html#websites (accessed July 21, 2005).

International Association of School Librarians. *Information skills resources on the Internet*. March 13, 2005. www.iasl-slo.org/infoskills.html (accessed July 21, 2005).

International Society for Technology in Education (ISTE). *National educational technology standards project*. April 27, 2001. www.cnets.iste.org (accessed July 21, 2005).

Internet Public Library, University of Michigan. *Teen space: A+ research and writing for high school and college students*. 2005. www.ipl.org/div/teen/aplus/index.html (accessed July 22, 2005).

Internet Scout Project, Computer Sciences Department, University of Wisconsin-Madison. *The scout report*. June 1, 2001. wwwscout.cs.wisc.edu/scout/report (accessed July 21, 2005).

James Madison University. *Go for the gold (tutorial)*. 2005. www.lib.jmu.edu/library/gold/modules.htm (accessed July 21, 2005).

JeffCo Public Schools. *Library services*. 2005. http://jeffcoweb.jeffco.k12.co.us/isu/library/ (accessed July 21, 2005).

Kentucky Virtual Library. *How to do research*. 2005. www.kyvl.org/html/tutorial/research/ (accessed July 21, 2005).

Lincoln Public Schools. *Information literacy*. 2003. http://sites.lps.org/lms/stories/storyReader$11 (accessed July 21, 2005).

ISD. *Information fluency*. August 6, 2003. www.lubbockisd.org/InformationFluency/LessonPlans.htm#3 (accessed July 21, 2005).

LOEX. *LOEX clearinghouse for library instruction*. December 3, 2000. www.emich.edu/public/loex/loex.html (accessed July 21, 2005).

McConnell Library. *Library tutorial*. April 6, 2005. http://lib.radford.edu/tutorial/index.asp (accessed July 21, 2005).

McKenzie, Jamie. Beyond technology to learning and information literacy. *From Now On: The Educational Technology Journal* (May 2001). www.fno.org (accessed July 21, 2005).

McKenzie, Jamie. *The question mark*. 2005. www.questioning.org (accessed July 21, 2005).

Minneapolis Community and Technical College Library. *Information literacy tutorial*. August 14, 2000. www.mctc.mnscu.edu/Library/tutorials/infolit/ (accessed July 21, 2005).

National Forum on Information Literacy. *The National Forum on Information Literacy—overview*. October 4, 2000. www.infolit.org/index.html (accessed July 21, 2005).

National Forum on Information Literacy. *A progress report on information literacy: An update on the American Library Association Presidential Committee on Information Literacy: Final report*. March 1998. www.infolit.org/documents/progress.html (accessed July 21, 2005).

New Mexico State University Library. *The five steps of the research process*. 2005. http://lib.nmsu.edu/instruction/handouts/reserachprocess.htm (accessed July 22, 2005).

New Mexico State University Library. *The good, the bad, and the ugly*. 2005. http://lib. nmsu.edu/instruction/eval.html (accessed July 21, 2005).

North Carolina State University. *Library online basic orientation*. 2003. www.lib.ncsu.edu/ lobo2/ (accessed July 21, 2005).

Oberman, Cerise, Bonnie Gratch Lindauer, and Betsy Wilson. Integrating information literacy in the curriculum: How is your library measuring up? *College and Research Libraries News, 59* (9) (1998), 347–352. www.ala.org/ala/acrl/acrlpubs/crlnews/ backissues1998/may7/integratinginformation. htm (accessed July 21, 2005).

Oberman, Cerise. *The Institute for Information Literacy, CRL news*. 1998. www.ala.org/ ala/acrl/acrlpubs/crlnews/backissues1999/ february4/informationliteracy.htm (accessed July 21, 2005).

Ohio State University Libraries. *net.TUTOR*. 2001. http://gateway.lib.ohio-state.edu/tutor/ (accessed July 21, 2005).

Oregon Educational Media Association. 2003. *Information literacy guidelines: Scientific inquiry*. www.oema.net/infolit/infolit.html (accessed July 21, 2005).

Oregon Educational Media Association. *Oregon school library information systems*. 2004. www.oslis.k12.or.us/ (accessed July 21, 2005).

PENN State University Libraries. *Information literacy and you*. 2002. www.libraries. psu.edu/instruction/infolit/andyou/infoyou. htm (accessed July 21, 2005).

Phillips Academy, Andover. *Oliver Wendell Holmes Library*. 2005. www.andover.edu/ library/home.htm (accessed July 22, 2005).

Prince Edward Island. *Building Information Literacy*. 2005. www.edu.pe.ca/bil/ (accessed July 21, 2005).

Purdue University. *Comprehensive online research education (CORE) tutorial*. 2004. http://gemini.lib.purdue.edu/core/login/ login.cfm (accessed July 21, 2005).

Reed Business Information Publication. *School Library Journal online: For children's, young adult, and school librarians*. ©2001, 2005. www.slj.com (accessed July 21, 2005).

San Francisco State University. *Online advancement of student information skills (OASIS)*. June 10, 2004. http://oasis.sfsu.edu/ (accessed July 21, 2005).

SBC Knowledge Network Ventures. *Nuts & bolts of Big6*. 1996, April 13, 2004. www.kn.pacbell.com/wired/big6/index. html (accessed July 21, 2005).

School-Libraries. *Online resources for school librarians*. June 20, 2002. www.school-libraries. org/resources/literacy.html (accessed July 21, 2005).

Schrock, Kathy. *Kathy Schrock's guide for educators*. June 7, 2001. http://school.discovery. com/schrockguide/ (accessed July 21, 2005).

Shapiro, Jeremy J., and Shelley K. Hughes. Information literacy as a liberal art: Enlightenment proposals for a new curriculum. *Educom Review, 31* (2) (March/April 1996). www.educause.edu/pub/er/review/ reviewArticles/31231.html (accessed July 21, 2005).

Smith, Drew. *Directory of online resources for information literacy*. December 18, 1999. http://bulldogs.tlu.edu/mdibble/doril/ (accessed July 21, 2005).

Social Science Information Gateway. *Information literacy gateway*. April 21, 2005. www.ilit.org (accessed July 21, 2005).

State University of New York. *SUNY information literacy initiative*. October 2, 1997. http://olis.sysadm.suny.edu/sunyconnect2/ ili/Default.htm (accessed July 21, 2005).

Travis, Tiffany, California State University, Long Beach Library. *Best practices for creating effective library assignments*. April 4, 2004. www.csulb.edu/~ttravis/GESI/ infolitpractices.html. (accessed July 22, 2005).

University of Arizona Library. *Information literacy Power Point*. 2005. http://dizzy.library. arizona.edu/conference/LTF%20info%20 lit%20power%20point.ppt (accessed July 21, 2005).

University of Arizona Library. *Information literacy team*. 2005. www.library.arizona.edu/ library/teams/InfoLit2000/plagiarism.shtml (accessed July 21, 2005).

University of Buffalo Library. *Library skills workbook*. January 2005. http://ublib.buffalo. edu/libraries/asl/courses/workbook (accessed July 21, 2005).

University of California-Berkeley. *The teaching library*. July 30, 2004. www.lib.berkeley. edu/TeachingLib/ (accessed July 21, 2005).

University of California L.A. *The information literacy program at UCLA*. September 21, 2004. www.library.ucla.edu/infolit/ (accessed July 21, 2005).

University of California L.A. College Library. *Road to research*. 2004. www.sscnet. ucla.edu/library/ (accessed July 21, 2005).

University of California Santa Cruz. *Information literacy tutorial: Net trail*. 2004. http:// nettrail.ucsc.edu/ (accessed July 21, 2005).

University of Central Florida. *WebLUIS tutorial*. http://reach.ucf.edu:8900/public/libtut/ (accessed July 21, 2005)

University of Louisville. *Information literacy program*. January 22, 2001. www.louisville. edu/infoliteracy/ (accessed July 21, 2005).

University of Maryland. *Information literacy and writing assessment project: Tutorial for developing and evaluating assignments*. 2005. www.umucf.edu/library/tutorials/ information_literacy/toc.html. (July 22, 2005).

University of Minnesota Libraries. *Quick study: Library research guide*. September 1, 1999. http://tutorial.lib.umn.edu/ (accessed July 21, 2005).

University of Nevada, Reno Libraries. *Assessment in library and information literacy instruction*. www2.library.unr.edu/ragains/ assess.html (accessed July 21, 2005).

University of New Hampshire Library. *InfoBoost*. May 2, 2005. www.library.unh. edu/infoboost (accessed July 22, 2005).

University of Rhode Island. *Library skills tutorial*. 2002. www.uri.edu/library/tutorials/ libskills/ (accessed July 21, 2005).

The University of Texas. *Texas information literacy tutorial (TILT)*. 2004. http://tilt.lib. utsystem.edu (accessed July 21, 2005).

University of Washington Libraries. *UWill*. April 18, 2005. www.lib.washington.edu/ uwill/ (accessed July 21, 2005).

University of Washington. *UWired Web*. 2001. www.washington.edu/uwired/ (accessed July 21, 2005).

University of Wisconsin. *Computerized library user education (CLUE)*. January 7, 2005. http://clue.library.wisc.edu/main-menu.html (accessed July 21, 2005).

University of Wisconsin-Madison. *The scout report*. April 27, 2001. http://scout.wisc.edu/ (accessed July 21, 2005).

University of Wisconsin Parkside. *Information literacy tutorial*. October 7, 2004. http:// oldweb.uwp.edu/library/2003/intro/index.htm (accessed July 21, 2005).

Utah State Office of Education. *Library media/information literacy core curriculum for Utah schools*. May 22, 2001. www.usoe.k12.ut.us/curr/library/core.html (accessed July 21, 2005).

Valencia Community College. *Information literacy tutorial*. February 5, 2002. http://faculty. valencia.cc.fl.us/infolit/ (accessed July 21, 2005).

Valenza, J. *Springfield Township high school virtual library*. 2005. http://mciu.org/~spjvweb/index.html (accessed July 22, 2005).

Washington Library Media Association. *Information literacy*. 2004.www.wlma.org/Instruction/ infolit.htm (accessed July 21, 2005).

Western Michigan University. *Searchpath*. 2001–2002. www.wmich.edu/library/ searchpath/ (accessed July 22, 2005).

Wisconsin, Department of Public Instruction. *Wisconsin's model academic standards: Information and technology literacy standards.* September 1, 1998. www.dpi.state.wi.us/dltcl/imt/itls.html (accessed July 21, 2005).

Wisconsin Association of Academic Librarians. *Information literacy ad hoc committee.* February 1, 2001. www.wla.lib.wi.us/waal/infolit/index.html (accessed July 21, 2005).

Xavier University. *XU.tutor* [Electronic version]. 2005. www.xavier.edu/library/xtutot/ index.cfm (accessed July 22, 2005).

Index

About the Authors

Daniel Callison is Director of Library Media Education at Indiana University and serves as professor and executive associate dean for the Indianapolis graduate program on the IUPUI campus. Since 1982 he has taught courses in school library media management, collection development, and reference sources and services. Dr. Callison developed two of the first graduate-level courses in library science for methods in teaching information inquiry and bibliographic instruction for inclusion in master's level education accredited by the American Library Association (ALA). He created Information User Education in 1989 and Information Inquiry for School Teachers in 1991. Dr. Callison is the founding editor for the online refereed journal of the American Association of School Librarians, *School Library Media Research.* In the 1970s, he served as the director of library media services at Topeka High School in Kansas. His high school media production program was the basis for recognition as a national demonstration school library by the National Association of Secondary School Principals. Dr. Callison's current services as faculty and program evaluator have included over twenty of the ALA-accredited programs in library science. Learn more at www.slis.iupui.edu and http://www.slis.indiana.edu/faculty/callison.html. Learn more about online school media certification at http://eduscapes.com/blueribbon/.

Leslie Preddy has been a library media specialist since 1992. She has been a recipient of the Lilly Teacher Creativity Fellowship, American Association of School Librarian's Collaborative School Library Media Award, Indiana Library Federation-Association for Indiana Media Educators Peggy L. Pfeiffer Service Award and is a past General Chair of the Indiana Young Hoosier Book Award Program and past president of the Association for Indiana Media Educators. She has been highlighted in Access learning, Teacher-Librarian, and School Library Journal online. She has published articles for School Library Media Activities Monthly, Knowledge Quest on the Web, and Indiana Principal's Leadership Academy. She is a chapter contributor for *Collaborating to Meet Standards: Teacher/Librarian Partnerships for 7-12* (Linworth 2002). She has been a presenter at state and national conferences in Missouri, Pennsylvania, Florida and Indiana. Learn more at http://pmms.msdpt.k12.in.us/imc/Inquiry/index.htm and http://pmms.msdpt.k12.in.us/imc/preddy.htm .

About the Contributors

Katie Baker is the computer teacher at the Sycamore Elementary School in Indianapolis.

Dr. Larry Johnson has been a classroom teacher, middle/high school library media specialist, university level instructional designer and media services administrator. He is currently adjunct associate professor and teaches online courses for Indiana University at Indianapolis. He is also a web site developer and educational consultant for eduscapes.com.

Dr. Annette Lamb has been a school library media specialist, computer teacher, and professor of education and library science. She is currently teaching online graduate courses for educators and librarians as a professor with the Indiana University School of Library and Information Science at Indianapolis (IUPUI). In addition, she writes, speaks, and conducts professional development workshops on practical approaches to technology integration and information inquiry. Learn more at http://eduscapes.com and at http://eduscapes.com/blueribbon/.

Dr. Cheryl McCarthy is professor of library science at Rhode Island University. She teaches graduate courses in school library media and coordinates field experiences for certification of school media specialists.

Ann Marie Moser is a graduate assistant at the School of Library and Information Science, IUPUI.

Maureen Sanders-Brunner is the head school media specialist at Pike High School in Indianapolis.

Carol L. Tilley. As a candidate for the Ph.D. in Library and Information Science at Indiana University, Carol Tilley coordinates distance education services for the IU School of Library and Information Science at Indianapolis. She teaches several graduate courses online or over interactive television. These courses include Grant Writing, Literature for Children and Young Adults, and Reference Information Sources and Services. She served as a high school library media specialist in Danville, Indiana.